THE OXFORD FRANCIS BACON · XIII

The *Instauratio magna*: Last Writings

EDITED WITH INTRODUCTION, NOTES, COMMENTARIES,
AND FACING-PAGE TRANSLATIONS BY

GRAHAM REES

CLARENDON PRESS · OXFORD

OXFORD

UNIVERSITY PRESS

Great Clarendon Street, Oxford OX2 6DP

Oxford University Press is a department of the University of Oxford.
It furthers the University's objective of excellence in research, scholarship,
and education by publishing worldwide in

Oxford New York

Athens Auckland Bangkok Bogotá Buenos Aires Calcutta
Cape Town Chennai Dar es Salaam Delhi Florence Hong Kong Istanbul
Karachi Kuala Lumpur Madrid Melbourne Mexico City Mumbai
Nairobi Paris São Paulo Singapore Taipei Tokyo Toronto Warsaw

and associated companies in Berlin Ibadan

Oxford is a registered trade mark of Oxford University Press
in the UK and in certain other countries

Published in the United States
by Oxford University Press Inc., New York

British Library Cataloguing in Publication Data

Data available

Library of Congress Cataloging in Publication Data

Data available

ISBN 0–19–818470–0

1 3 5 7 9 10 8 6 4 2

Typeset by Hope Services (Abingdon) Ltd.
Printed in Great Britain
on acid-free paper by
Biddles Ltd.,
Guildford & King's Lynn

THE OXFORD FRANCIS BACON · XIII

General Editors: Graham Rees and Lisa Jardine

Editorial Advisory Board

THIS volume belongs to the new critical edition of the complete works of Francis Bacon (1561–1626). The edition presents the works in broadly chronological order and in accordance with the principles of modern textual scholarship. The works printed below all belong to the colossal six-part *Instauratio magna* and, in particular, to Parts III–V. Three of the pieces edited below—an early version of the *Historia densi & rari*, the 'lost' *Abecedarium nouum naturæ*, and the *Historia & inquisitio de animato & inanimato*—have never been published before. All the texts are presented in the original Latin with facing-page translations.

For
Maria Eve Wakely

PREFACE

THIS volume is one of those for which I have had almost exclusive responsibility. Like other volumes of the edition, it takes its place within a larger chronological plan. However, it should be noted that here the chronological principle has been interpreted flexibly and in the light of Bacon's stated intentions, i.e. this is one of a sequence of volumes (IX–XIII) which contains only the works of the *Instauratio magna*, and excludes ones of the same period which were not written on fulfilment of that ambitious six-part scheme. The ones excluded here will of course appear in other volumes of the edition.

Although ultimate responsibility for this volume lies with me, no printed book (especially one of this complexity) is the work of one individual. In fact the production of this volume has been very much a co-operative enterprise to which many individuals and institutions have contributed. My obligations to libraries, librarians, and funding bodies are enormous. I wish to thank the many librarians who helped me in the work and in my efforts to put together photocopies of exemplars of the main printed copy-text used in the preparation of this volume, the *Opuscula varia posthuma* of 1658. Particular thanks are due to the staff of the university and college libraries of Cambridge, London, and Oxford. I am grateful to Trinity College Cambridge for permission to reproduce photographs of the *Opuscula* title-pages and to the Bibliothèque Nationale de France for permission to reproduce photographs of leaves of certain coll. Dupuy manuscripts.

I have received generous grants from the Aurelius Trust, the Modern Humanities Research Association, the Bibliographical Society, and the Royal Society. I owe debts of gratitude to the British Academy for adopting the Oxford Francis Bacon into its portfolio of research projects and, with the Leverhulme Trust, for awarding me a Senior Research Fellowship; to the Isaac Newton Trust whose quite exceptional generosity will receive its full due in Volume XI of this edition; and to Queen Mary and Westfield College for honouring me with a research professorship.

Colleagues at QMW and, in particular, Lisa Jardine and Paul Hamiliton, have done more than perhaps they know to help this volume to completion. Members of the Editorial Advisory Board of the project have all made major contributions to the work and to the rapid consolidation of our project in the last few years. Here very particular thanks are due to our chairman, Professor J. B. Trapp, whose foresight and experience have helped secure the Oxford Francis Bacon against many of the vicissitudes to which projects of

Preface

this kind are prone. J. B. Trapp, other demands on him notwithstanding, has been in many ways the project's anchor, and this editor in particular has benefited in countless ways from his wise advice and generous support.

For admirable answers to all manner of troublesome questions I am very much indebted to Jonquil Bevan, W. H. Brock, Maureen Cooper, Henri Durel-Leon, Benedino Gemelli, Michael Kiernan, Ronald Latham, Michel-Pierre Lerner, the late D. F. McKenzie, David McKitterick, Randall McLeod, Julian Martin, Peter Morris, Robin Myers, Lidia Procesi, I. A. Shapiro, Michael Treadwell, and Charles Webster. I count myself lucky that scholars of such distinction have been willing to give their time to the discussion of textual and interpretative matters great and small.

Special thanks are due to James Binns, Alan Stewart, Jan Broadway, Constance Blackwell, and Giuliano Ferretti. James has never failed to produce authoritative and detailed comment on all matters relating to Bacon's Latin and the difficulties of translating it. Alan, during his time as MHRA Research Associate to the project, did first-class work on the life of William Rawley and on locations of copies of the *Opuscula*. Jan did splendid work in the Cambridgeshire Record Office on papers relating to Rawley. Constance's knowledge of the republic of letters, her unfailing kindness, and willingness to lend a hand whenever it was needed is deeply appreciated. Giuliano's brilliant archival scholarship has given the Bacon manuscripts in the Bibliothèque Nationale their bizarre history, a history recounted in the Introduction to this volume. In connection with the provenance of the manuscripts, I am indebted to Robin Howells and Jean Braybrook for checking and correcting my translations from early seventeenth-century French, a language in which they are expert and I am not.

Without the support and encouragement of people associated with Oxford University Press this volume would have been much the poorer. Sophie Goldsworthy, Matthew Thomas, Heather Watson, and Frances Whistler have given unstintingly of their patience, knowledge and courtesy—even when taxed to the limit by the excessive demands of this editor.

I come at last to two people who, above all others, have made the completion of this particular volume possible—Marta Fattori and Maria Wakely. Marta has been unfailing in her friendship, wisdom and authority on matters Baconian, and has as ever been the main link between the project and French, Italian, and Swiss scholarship. Maria has been the most precious and abiding influence on my life and work in the years since Oxford Francis Bacon began to take shape. She has worked on all aspects of the analytical-bibliographical foundations of this study; she has done a good portion of the empirical work on Bacon's *Opuscula*—collating exemplars, studying paper and so forth; she has checked notes and commentaries, and read proofs at all stages of the work's progress through the press. She has been my constant adviser, and an inexhaustible source of kindness and strength; indeed, without her help this volume might never have reached publication at all.

G. R.

Queen Mary and Westfield College,
University of London,
Easter, 2000

CONTENTS

Contents

THE COMMENTARIES

APPENDICES

LIST OF PLATES

I, II, III, and IV are reproduced by permission of the Bibliothèque Nationale de France; V and VI by permission of Trinity College Cambridge

LIST OF TABLES

REFERENCES, ABBREVIATIONS, SIGLA, AND SYMBOLS

Volumes of the *Oxford Francis Bacon* are designated by the abbreviation *OFB* followed by a volume number in Roman numerals.

The following abbreviations are used for the titles of Bacon's works, parts of works and plans

AL	*Advancement of learning*
ANN	*Abecedarium nouum naturæ*
CDNR	*Cogitationes de natura rerum*
CDSH	*Cogitationes de scientia humana*
CF	*Calor et frigus*
CS	*Commentarius solutus*
CV	*Cogitata et visa*
DAS	*De augmentis scientiarum*
DFRM	*De fluxu et refluxu maris*
DGI	*Descriptio globi intellectualis*
DO	*Distributio operis*
DPAO	*De principiis atque originibus*
DSV	*De sapientia veterum*
DVM	*De vijs mortis*
HDR	*Historia densi & rari* (Rawley's version)
HDR(M)	*Historia densi & rari* (MS version)
HIDA	*Historia & inquisitio de animato & inanimato*
HNE	*Historia naturalis et experimentalis*
HSA	*Historia soni et auditus*
HSMS	*Historia sulphuris, mercurii et salis*
HV	*Historia ventorum* (published in *HNE*)
HVM	*Historia vitæ et mortis*
IDM	*Inquisitio de magnete*
IL	*Inquisitio legitima de motu*
IM	*Instauratio magna*
NA	*New Atlantis*
NO	*Novum organum*
PA	*Prodromi sive anticipationes philosophiæ secundæ*
PAH	*Parasceve ad historiam naturalem*
PhU	*Phænomena universi*
PID	*Partis instaurationis secundæ delineatio & argumentum*
RPh	*Redargutio philosophiarum*
SI	*Scala intellectus sive filum labyrinthi*
SS	*Sylva sylvarum*
SSWN	*Sylva sylvarum* (working notes)

TC	*Thema cœli*
TDL	*Topica inquisitionis de luce et lumine*
TPM	*Temporis partus masculus*
VT	*Valerius terminus*

The following abbreviations are used for earlier editions of Bacon's works:

BTT	*Baconiana. Or certain genuine remaines of Sr Francis Bacon, Baron of Verulam, and Viscount of St. Albans* . . . , ed. Thomas Tenison, London, 1679
Ess	Sir Francis Bacon, *The essayes or counsels, civill and morall,* ed. Michael Kiernan, Oxford, 1985 (as from 2000, volume XV of *OFB*)
LL	James Spedding, *The letters and life of Francis Bacon,* 7 vols., London, 1861–74
Op	*Opuscula varia posthuma . . . Francisci Baconi . . . nunc primum edita . . . Guilielmi Rawley . . .*, London, 1658
Sc	*Scripta in natvrali et vniversali philosophia. Amstelodami, Apud Ludovicum Elzevirium,* 1653
SEH	*The works of Francis Bacon,* ed. James Spedding, Robert Leslie Ellis, and Douglas Denon Heath, 7 vols., London, 1859–64

In this and all other volumes of this edition, the edited texts will be presented with their copy-text signatures (printed books) or folio numbers (manuscripts) inserted at the appropriate points in the outer margins of edited texts. These signatures or folio numbers are the key to the edition's internal system of reference. They will be used to refer to all Bacon works cited in the apparatus of all volumes. In the case of works not presented in this volume, this method of reference is supplemented by parenthetical references to the corresponding pages in *SEH*. This will make it easier (pending completion of the new edition) for readers to track down references to other Bacon works. As further volumes of the edition are published the need for the rather cumbersome references to *SEH* will diminish. As nearly all the secondary literature on Bacon uses *SEH* as a primary source, Appendix II of this volume provides a list in which the signatures or folio numbers attached to the volume's edited texts are translated into *SEH* references.

Other references:

BJHS	*British journal for the history of science*
BL	British Library
BN	Bibliothèque Nationale de France
Bodl.	Bodleian Library, Oxford
Briquet	C. M. Briquet, *Les filigranes: dictionnaire historique des marques du papier,* 4 vols., repr. New York, 1966
CHRP	*The Cambridge History of Renaissance Philosophy,* ed. Charles B. Schmitt, Quentin Skinner, and Eckhard Kessler, Cambridge University Press: Cambridge, 1988

CHSCP	*The Cambridge History of Seventeenth-Century Philosophy*, ed. Daniel Garber and Michael Ayres, 2 vols., Cambridge University Press: Cambridge, 1998
CSP(Dom)	Calendars of state papers: domestic series
DM	William Gilbert, *De magnete, magneticisqve corporibvs, et de magno magnete tellure; physiologia noua* . . . Londoni excvdebat Petrvs Short anno MDC
DNB	*Dictionary of national biography*
DRN	Bernardino Telesio, *De rerum natura*, ed. Luigi De Franco, vol. I, Casa del Libro: Cosenza, 1965; vol. II, Casa del Libro: Cosenza, 1971; vol. III, La Nuova Italia: Florence, 1976
DSB	*Dictionary of scientific biography*
FBLT	*Francis Bacon's Legacy of Texts*, ed. William A. Sessions, AMS Press: New York, 1990
FBTF	*Francis Bacon: terminologia e fortuna nel XVII secolo*, ed. Marta Fattori, Edizioni dell'Ateneo: Rome, 1984
Gibson	R. W. Gibson, *Francis Bacon: a bibliography of his works and of Baconiana to the year 1750*, Scrivener Press: Oxford, 1950
Gibson(S)	R. W. Gibson, *Francis Bacon: a bibliography of his works and of Baconiana to the year 1750: Supplement*, privately issued: Oxford, 1959
Heawood	E. Heawood, *Watermarks mainly of the 17th and 18th centuries*, Hilversum, 1950
HLQ	*Huntington Library Quarterly*
IELM	P. Beal, *Index of English literary manuscripts 1450–1625*, I, parts 1 and 2, London, 1980 (the Bacon manuscripts are identified alphanumerically: the prefix BcF followed by a number)
LF	*Lessico filosofico dei secoli XVII e XVIII: sezione latina*, ed. Marta Fattori in collaboration with Massimo Bianchi, Rome, 1992–
OED	*Oxford English Dictionary*
OFB	*The Oxford Francis Bacon* [i.e. the volumes of this edition]
Piccard	G. Piccard, *Wasserzeichen*, Verlag W. Kohlhammer: Stuttgart, 1983
STC	*A Short-Title Catalogue of Books printed in England, Scotland, & Ireland and of English Books printed Abroad 1475–1640*, ed. A. W. Pollard and G. R. Redgrave, 2 vols., 2nd edn. revised and enlarged by W. A. Jackson, F. S. Ferguson and Katharine F. Pantzer, London, 1976–86. Vol. III, *Indexes*, compiled by K. Pantzer and P. R. Ridler, London, 1991
Wing	*Short-Title Catalogue of Books printed in England, Scotland, Ireland, Wales, and British America and of English books printed in Other Countries 1641–1700*, ed. Donald Wing, 2nd edn., revised and enlarged, 4 vols., Modern Language Association of America: New York, 1988–98.

In addition:

aof	alternative outer forme
cmt(s)	commentary(ies)
c-t(s)	copy-text(s)
hdm	head margin
inm	inner margin
lc	lower case
nld	normalized
om	omitted or omission
outm	outer margin
para(s)	paragraph(s)
sd	scribal draft
tlm	tail margin
tn(s)	textual note(s)

INTRODUCTION

I

The Texts: Chronology and the *Instauratio magna*

(*a*) The Texts and the *Instauratio magna*

Of the seven Bacon texts presented in this volume three short pieces, derived from manuscripts, have either not been published before or not been published in the form represented below. They are: (i) an early version of the *Historia densi & rari*, (ii) the *Abecedarium nouum naturæ*, and (iii) the *Historia & inquisitio de animato & inanimato*. The manuscript witnesses to these texts were unknown before 1980 and they are to be found in the manuscript collections of the Bibliothèque Nationale de France. The other four texts have all been published before, and they are these: (iv) the later version of the *Historia densi*, (v) the *Inquisitio de magnete*, (vi) *Topica inquisitionis de luce et lumine*, and (vii) the preface to a work that proceeded no further, namely *Prodromi sive anticipationes philosophiæ secundæ*. The copy-texts for these last four are printed editions, namely the *Scripta* published by Isaac Gruter in 1653 and the *Opuscula* published by William Rawley five years later. A full account of the manuscripts and printed books on which our edited texts rest is given below in the third part of the Introduction.[1]

In this volume the texts appear in what I take to be the order in which they were meant to stand in the six-part *Instauratio magna*: i.e. they are presented in the order given above save that the two versions of the *Historia densi* precede the rest. However, it would not be true to say that this sequence exactly coincides with the chronological order of their composition (see Introduction I (*b*) below).[2] The structure of the *Instauratio*, the function of its six parts and the history of its plan are considered in detail elsewhere in *The Oxford Francis Bacon*[3] so here I shall merely outline the plan and indicate how far Bacon managed to carry it out.

Part I was to be a survey of the 'partitions of the sciences', to identify deficiencies in all departments of knowledge and to give precepts or

---

[1] pp. xlix–xci below.

[2] pp. xxv–xxviii below. *OFB* is organized on broadly chronological lines; but the chronological principle is relaxed for *IM* works, which are presented in their *IM* order.

[3] *OFB*, VI, pp. xvii-xix, and in the introductions, notes and *cmts* to vols. IX, X and XI (to be published in due course).

examples to help put the deficiencies right. Part II was to present a comprehensive account of the new way that Bacon had developed for the rebuilding of philosophy. He destined Part III for his new functionally defined natural history, the huge body of data which was meant to be the starting point for the new 'interpretation of nature'. Part IV would demonstrate the precepts of Part II in action; it would present a variety of worked examples which would allow the reader to see from beginning to end how the interpretation of nature would operate in practice. In other words, Part IV would show how the processes of Part II would set to work on materials of the kind presented in Part III to produce the materials that might appear in Part VI, which was to be the repository of the new philosophy. As for Part V, that was to be of a temporary nature; a collection of 'anticipations', i.e. provisional theories and conclusions which Bacon had arrived at by the ordinary use of reason. These, he believed, were worth preserving because they were more likely to be true than the offerings of other philosophers. The anticipations of Part V would be eligible for promotion to Part VI were they able to pass muster when tested against whatever results the implementation of the new way of interpretation might bring.

The works presented in this volume are as it were the last gasp of the *Instauratio*, the furthest points to which Bacon was willing or able to travel on his journey towards the promised land of Part VI, a land which he knew he would never enter. With the *De augmentis scientiarum* (1623) he had fulfilled the requirements of Part I; with the unfinished *Novum organum* (1620) he had completed a smallish portion of Part II; with the *Historia ventorum* (1622) and *Historia vitæ et mortis* (1623) he had completed and published two of the six histories which he had promised to produce to illustrate the requirements of his natural-historical programme. After that, progress was apparently a bit of a struggle. He came close to completing the *Historia densi*, a third of the promised single-subject Latin natural histories but did not give it final form or publish it, and certainly made no further headway with Part III of the *Instauratio*.[4] As for Part IV, Bacon completed nothing more than the introduction, the newly recovered *Abecedarium*. Other items which seem to have been destined for Part IV—*Historia & inquisitio de animato & inanimato*, the *Inquisitio de magnete*, and *Topica inquisitionis de luce et lumine*—look like little more than exploratory studies or sketches

---

[4] The titles of the six natural histories were announced in *HNE* (A4^r (*SEH*, II, p. 11)). A list of the proposed contents of another of these histories, the *Historia grauis & leuis*, survived into the 17th cent. but is now lost, see *OFB*, VI, p. lxxxiv.

for projects which, Bacon knew, were out of his reach. For Part V, he managed to produce nothing more than a preface, the *Prodromi sive anticipationes philosophiæ secundæ*, though he had a very good idea what would be put in that part.[5] So, the *Historia densi* apart, we seem to be concerned with brief forays into territory which Bacon had mapped out but could not occupy.

There can be no doubt that the two versions of the *Historia densi* represent work for Part III. In the *Historia naturalis et experimentalis ad condendam philosophiam* (1622), the preliminaries to which are a prospectus for Part III, Bacon announced titles of six specimen histories he planned for the first six months ('in primos sex menses') of a programme designed to illustrate the requirements of Part III. Among these titles is '*Historia Densi & Rari, nec-non Coitionis, & Expansionis Materiæ per spatia*',[6] which is identical to the full title of the history presented in this edition. And if that were not enough, the organization and structure of the *Historia densi* (at least in the later version) aspires to that laid down for the natural histories in another section of the preliminaries to the *Historia naturalis*, namely the *Norma historiæ præsentis*.[7]

The *Norma historiæ* also bears on the question of the place of the *Abecedarium* in the *Instauratio*. There are certain 'abstract natures'—the schematisms of matter or forms of the first class, simple motions, sums of motions, measures of motions and various other things—written about in an 'Abecedarium Nouum' to be found at the end ('*sub finem huius voluminis*') of the *Historia naturalis*. Now the title *and* outline contents given in the *Norma* exactly match those we find in the Bibliothèque Nationale manuscript,[8] so it seems that the *Abecedarium* belongs to Part III of the *Instauratio*. The *Norma* adds that 'present history' will not only supply the place of Part III but be no mean preparation for Part IV by reason of the titles in the 'Abecedario'. This seems to anchor the *Abecedarium* to Part III and to envisage it as a prelude to Part IV.[9] However, the actual text of the *Abecedarium* tells a rather different story. 'The Abecedarium belongs to Part Four of the *Instauration*, the part which is the ladder or machine of the intellect. Yet this is not the ladder proper, rather it is as a preparative (*parasceue*) to it.' No mention here of Part III at all; the *Abecedarium* belongs to Part IV and is its *parasceue*, and that is that. So why then do the *Historia naturalis et experimentalis* and

---

5   *OFB*, VI, pp. xxxvi–lxix.   6   *HNE*, A4ʳ (*SEH*, II, p. 11).
7   *Ibid.*, C2ʳ–C6ᵛ (*SEH*, II, pp. 17–18). For the structure of *HDR* see pp. xxx–xxxvi below.
8   *Ibid.*, C2ᵛ (*SEH*, II, p. 17), also see pp. 171–225 below.
9   *HNE*, C6ʳ⁻ᵛ (*SEH*, II, p. 18).

Abecedarium disagree? My guess is that Bacon simply changed his mind. When he wrote the *Norma historiæ* he had the *Abecedarium* lined up for Part III and, far from being unable to find the copy when the *Historia naturalis* went to press,[10] he actually pulled it at the last moment because he had begun to think of it more as a preparative to Part IV[11] and less as a special department of natural history. So the *Historia naturalis* was published without the *Abecedarium* and the latter was not published thereafter because, since the task of assembling materials for Part IV could not be accomplished satisfactorily, another opportunity for publication did not arise.[12]

Before leaving the *Abecedarium*, I shall pause to see what it tells us about Part IV for that has a bearing on other pieces published below. It seems that the structure of Part IV would have been very like that of Part III. In the sequence of the *Instauratio* the individual histories were preceded by three items: the *Parasceve ad historiam naturalem*, the *Catalogus historiarum particularium* and the *Norma historiæ*, the last of which describes the procedures adopted in each of the individual histories that were to follow.[13] The sequence of items in Part IV was much the same: Bacon described the *Abecedarium* as a *parasceve*; the bulk of the text is a catalogue of titles; and the work closes with a section entitled *Norma abecedarij* which, like the *Norma historiæ*, sets out the ground rules for the inquiries to come.[14] The *Distributio operis* (the plan of the *Instauratio*) tells us that these inquiries would be actual types ('Typos') and models ('Plasmata') of the new way of producing natural philosophy. Part IV would demonstrate 'the whole process of the mind' and the 'fabric and order of invention' from start to finish in certain subjects both various and remarkable, and would be nothing less than the application of Part II in detail and at large.[15] But this does not tell us quite

---

[10] This is Spedding's conjecture, see *SEH*, II, p. 85 n. 1.

[11] When he wrote Experiment 839 of *SS*, Bacon was still speaking as if *ANN* were actually available to readers, *SS*, 2F2ᵛ (*SEH*, II, p. 615).

[12] See *ANN*, fo. 24ʳ (p. 172, ll. 17–22 below) for Bacon's recurrent complaint about his lack of reliable data.

[13] The first two of these appear at the end of *NO* (a1ʳ–e3ʳ (*SEH*, I, pp. 393–411)); the last appears among the preliminaries of *HNE* (C2ʳ–C6ᵛ (*SEH*, II, pp. 17–18)).

[14] *ANN*, fos. 24ʳ, 24ʳ–36ᵛ, and 36ᵛ–37ᵛ respectively (see below, pp. 172, 174–220, 220–4). Spedding's guess (*SEH*, II, p. 85 n. 1)—based on a short fragment of *ANN* (see below, pp. 214–24) first published by Tenison (*BTT*, F7ʳ–G2ʳ)—that the *Norma abecedarij* should have stood before the *ANN* is surely wrong. He did not know that *ANN* belonged to Part IV of *IM* and forgot that in the parallel case of Part III, the *Norma historiæ* followed *PAH* and the *Catalogus historiarum particularium*.

[15] *DO*, C2ᵛ (*SEH*, I, p. 143): 'vniuersum Mentis processum, atque inueniendi continuatam fabricam & ordinem in certis subiectis, iisque variis & insignibus, tanquàm sub oculos ponant

what a Part IV inquiry would have looked like. To catch a glimpse of that we must turn to the *Norma abecedarij* and other evidence.

According to the *Norma abecedarij*, the inquiries would be selected from those listed in the *Abecedarium*, and each would have begun with a natural history. Indeed, Bacon could not have presented complete worked examples without such an historical foundation. In form the histories would have been very similar to those of Part III, each presenting a comprehensive body of experimental and observational data, in tabular form where appropriate, and enriched with provisional generalizations adduced from the natural-historical materials.[16] The *Norma abecedarij* is explicit about this but not about what was to happen next. However, Bacon evidently meant to adduce 'tables of discovery' from the historical materials and use the tables to produce (among other things) the 'axioms' that he longed to secure. Indeed, in the *Novum organum* he remarked that the strongest means of inspiring hope would be to bring people to particulars digested and arranged in tables of discovery. Such tables do, of course, appear in the *Novum organum* itself: they are an indispensable part of the trial investigation of the form of heat. I refer in particular to the tables of '*Essentiæ & Præsentiæ*', '*Absentiæ in proximo*', and '*Graduum, siue Comparatiuæ*'.[17] Yet such tables, Bacon assures us, belong not just to the second 'but *much more* of the fourth part of my *Instauration*'.[18]

We can now come back to the *Historia & inquisitio*, the *Inquisitio de magnete*, and *Topica inquisitionis de luce*. The first of these seems to have been an introduction to or pilot study for a Part IV inquiry. The text is not just called an *historia* but an *inquisitio*. A plain history would have belonged to Part III, but Part IV inquiries were to have commenced with histories and progressed to *inquisitiones* that would have displayed the whole fabric and order of invention expounded in the *Novum organum*. Indeed, material in the *Historia & inquisitio* is actually set out in tabular form and, brief though it is, the material looks very like an embryonic

. . . Itaque huiusmodi Exemplis Quartam partem nostri Operis attribuimus: quæ reuerà nil aliud est, quam Secundæ Partis applicatio particularis & explicata.'

[16] On the close similarity of *Norma historiæ* and *Norma abecedarij* see *cmts* on *ANN*, fos. 36ᵛ–37ᵛ.

[17] *NO*, V2ᵛ, V3ʳ, Y1ʳ (*SEH*, I, pp. 238, 239, 248).

[18] *NO*, N2ᵛ (*SEH*, I, p. 199): 'Atque licèt longè potentissimum futurum sit remedium ad spem inprimendam, quando homines ad particularia, præsertìm in Tabulis nostris Inueniendi digesta & disposita (quæ partìm ad secundam, sed multò magis ad quartam *Instaurationis* nostræ partem pertinent) adducemus . . .'. The emphasis in the translation is mine. Also see *ibid.*, O2ᵛ (*SEH*, I, p. 204).

form of one of the tables of discovery presented in the *Novum organum* and promised for Part IV. Indeed, Bacon declared that one of the three investigations outlined in the text was 'nihil aliud . . . quam tabula quæ-dam absentiæ ideo recurrendu*m* ad ea quæ sunt in proximo' (fo. 3ᵛ). But although the terminology—'tabula quædam absentiæ', 'in proximo'—is that of the *Novum organum*, the grounds for thinking that the *Historia & inquisitio* belonged to Part IV would be a lot stronger if the title *de animato & inanimato* were actually catalogued in the *Abecedarium*. In fact this title does indeed appear in the *Abecedarium*, where it is singled out as 'Inquisitionem illam nobilem' (fo. 27ᵛ). This is important for, as the *Distributio* insists, all subjects chosen for Part IV are to be most noble among those under inquiry ('inter ea quæ quæruntur, sunt nobilissima').[19]

The grounds for seeing the *Inquisitio de magnete* as a sketch for Part IV are not nearly as strong as those for so placing the *Historia & inqui-sitio*. Spedding regarded it as a loose sheet of notes that properly belonged to Part III,[20] and the piece is not catalogued as a separate title in the *Abecedarium*, although there would have been room for it under various other titles.[21] All the same, the *Inquisitio* is emphatically not among the six natural-historical titles that Bacon promised to tackle from 1622 onwards. Moreover it is, as we shall see, a very late piece—written at a time when one of Bacon's preoccupations was the produc-tion of materials (never more than sketches) for Part IV. However, if the *Inquisitio* (and observe that it is not called an *Historia*) could be seen as notes towards a Part IV inquiry, it is a very primitive contribution that entirely lacks the formal properties that one would expect such an inquiry to possess. In fact only on the very slender evidence of date, title and lack of evidence to the contrary can we associate the piece with Part IV at all.

Like the *Inquisitio de magnete*, the *Topica inquisitionis de luce et lumine* is a very late work and not among the six histories mentioned a moment ago. It is also not a title mentioned in the *Abecedarium*, although the phenomena of light certainly form a major part of the *Abecedarium* inquiry into motion of impression.[22] What really makes the *Topica* a likely candidate for Part IV is its *form*. The piece starts with a set of tables; it begins with a '*Tabula Præsentiæ*', continues with a '*Tabula absentiæ in proximo*', and goes on to a '*Tabula Graduum*'.[23] As we have

[19] *DO*, C2ᵛ (*SEH*, I, p. 143).
[20] *SEH*, II, p. 309.
[21] *ANN*, fo. 30ʳ⁻ᵛ (p. 194, l. 17–p. 196, l. 13 below).
[22] *ANN*, fo. 31ʳ (p. 198, ll. 14–23 below).
[23] *TDL*, X3ʳ–X4ʳ (pp. 244–6 below).

seen in the case of the *Historia & inquisitio de animato*, such tables do not belong to natural histories but to the inquiries of Part IV; indeed, they were to have been the very soul of Part IV.

The last text presented in this volume, the preface to the *Prodromi sive anticipationes philosophiæ secundæ*, seems to belong not to Part IV but to Part V. The case for this is as simple as it is brief. The title is exactly that given to Part V in the *Distributio*; and the description of Part V as provided by the *Distributio* concurs precisely with the one sketched out by the preface.[24] Even the imagery used to indicate the provisional nature of Part V materials is much the same in the *Distributio* as it is in the *Prodromi*. The former tells us that the materials in Part V 'will serve as wayside inns where the mind on its journey to more certain discoveries may rest for a short while'. The latter offers its contents 'as resting places or wayside inns made available to give them [i.e. the pursuers of the true interpretation of nature] comfort and good cheer'.[25]

(*b*) Works and Dates

As for the dates of these pieces, let us first turn to the two versions of the *Historia densi & rari* and to Rawley's chronological list of Bacon's last works.[26] This list helps us date the version of the work subsequently published by Rawley himself, for there is no doubt that the list refers to that version and not to the one offered by the coll. Dupuy manuscript.[27] The *Historia densi* stands immediately after the *Historia ventorum* and *Historia vitæ* but immediately before the lost *Historia grauis & leuis* and *Considerations touching a warre with Spaine* which was written in 1624 and published in 1629.[28] Bacon published the *Historia ventorum* in a volume which also contained preliminaries to Part III as a whole. The general title of this volume was, as we know, *Historia naturalis et experimentalis ad condendam philosophiam*, and it was entered in the Stationers' Register on 20 September 1622 and probably published

---

[24] *DO*, C3ʳ (*SEH*, I, pp. 143–4); cf. *PA*, R2ʳ⁻ᵛ (pp. 260–4 below).

[25] *DO*, C3ʳ (*SEH*, I, p. 144): 'tùm poterunt ista veluti tabernaculorum in viâ positorum vice fungi, vt mens ad certiora contendens in iis paulispèr acquiescat'; cf. *PA*, R2ʳ⁻ᵛ (p. 262, ll. 13–14 below): 'loco diverticulorum, aut tabernaculorum in via præbitorum ad solatium & levamentum esse queant'.

[26] Rawley, *Life*, in *Resuscitatio* (1657), b4ᵛ–c1ʳ (*SEH*, I, pp. 9–10).

[27] *Ibid.*, b4ᵛ where Rawley says that the work is '*not yet Printed*'. In the following year he published the *Historia densi* and the Latin version of his life of Bacon, where he tells us (*Op*, *7ᵛ) that the *Historia densi* is 'jam primum Typis mandata'.

[28] For what became of *HGL* see *OFB*, VI, pp. lxxxiv–lxxxv. For the publication of *Considerations touching a warre with Spaine* see p. lxxix n. 105 below.

before the end of November.[29] The *Historia vitæ* was entered on 18 December 1622, and was published shortly before 10 February 1623 when John Chamberlain noted the recent publication of the *Historia ventorum* and the *Historia vitæ*.[30] In the *Historia naturalis et experimentalis* Bacon gave the titles of the histories planned for the first six months of his ambitious attempt to illustrate the requirements of Part III.[31] He managed to get two out in the period before February 1623, and at that rate of progress the *Historia densi* should have been ready and perhaps published by March of that year. But that did not happen. By that time Bacon may have been more preoccupied with other projects (for instance preparation of the *De augmentis*) than he had expected to be. Whatever the reasons why Bacon failed to carry on with it, the Rawley *Historia densi* was abandoned at some point in 1623 or 1624.

As for the coll. Dupuy version, it cannot have reached its present state before the autumn of 1623[32] and had not yet taken on much of the structure prescribed for natural histories in *Historia naturalis*. Accordingly I am inclined to think that Bacon started work on it when he first conceived the idea of writing illustrations for Part III of the *Instauratio*—early perhaps in 1622 or maybe even in 1621. The Dupuy version must have been written after the *Novum organum* for at one point the former explicitly refers to the latter.[33]

The *Abecedarium* stands on Rawley's list between *The historie of the raigne of King Henry the Seventh* and the *Historia ventorum*. The latter was, as has been seen, published in late 1622. The former, though written between June and October 1621, was not entered in the Stationers' Register until 9 February 1622 even though it was published in March,[34] so it seems that the *Abecedarium* was being written in the spring and summer of 1622. Rawley's evidence is corroborated by the *Historia naturalis*, for we know that Bacon had originally intended to publish the *Abecedarium* at the end of that volume;[35] and so the work must have existed in some form *before* the autumn of 1622.

---

[29] The *Historia ventorum* was probably the recently published Latin work that Bacon alluded to in a letter written to Buckingham on 24 Nov. 1622; see *LL*, VII, p. 395.

[30] *LL*, VII, p. 399.   [31] *HNE*, A4ʳ (*SEH*, II, p. 11).

[32] See pp. lii–liii below.   [33] *HDR(M)*, fo. 21ᵛ, also see p. 30, ll. 20–1 below.

[34] See *The history of the reign of King Henry VII*, ed. Brian Vickers, Cambridge University Press: Cambridge, 1998, p. xii. The brief interval between entry and publication may mean that it was entered when printing was well under way or almost finished. Another instance of late entry was *DAS*, see p. liii n. 18 below.

[35] *HNE*, C2ᵛ (*SEH*, II, p. 17).

Turning now to the four short pieces which stand at the end of the present volume, the first, the *Historia & inquisitio de animato*, does not appear on Rawley's list and is not mentioned in any Rawley preface or Bacon work. But, as I have already suggested, it seems to be closely associated with the *Abecedarium* and was very likely an outline sketch or preface to what was to have been a fully worked example of one of the Part IV inquiries listed in that work. The evidence of this association and the language of the piece may date the *Historia & inquisitio* to about the middle of 1622. In any case, for reasons which we shall come to later,[36] the piece cannot possibly have been written after the autumn of 1623.

The *Inquisitio de magnete* and *Topica inquisitionis de luce* are to be found, together and in that order, on Rawley's list immediately after a string of translations of English works into Latin and a revison of the *De sapientia veterum*, and immediately before the *Sylva sylvarum*. The translations and the *De sapientia* revision (the latter published in 1638), were completed after the 1625 edition of the *Essayes*, an edition entered in the Stationers' Register on 13 March 1625. If due allowance be made for time subsequently spent on the translations and the revision of *De sapientia*, it would be difficult to imagine that the *Inquisitio de magnete* and *Topica inquisitionis* can have been written before the beginning of the third quarter of 1625. As for the *terminus ad quem*, the *Sylva* was Bacon's last work and was published by Rawley in 1626 after Bacon's death (9 April 1626). This dating is consistent with certain manuscript evidence. There exist a couple of notes in Rawley's hand ('Present Experiments touching the Loadstone') which (i) detail work eventually incorporated in the *Inquisitio de magnete*, and (ii) precede notes in the same hand, notes eventually incorporated in the *Sylva*. The earlier parts of the manuscript date to *c.*1623, the later (including the notes on the loadstone) to 1625/6.[37]

The *Prodromi sive anticipationes philosophiæ secundæ* is very difficult to date. Spedding placed it with *Scala intellectus sive filum labyrinthi*, a (superseded?) preface to Part IV. However, I am sure that (i) the *Scala* belongs to the period before 1612,[38] and that (ii) there is no evidence that the *Prodromi* belongs with it. Such slender evidence as we have points in

---

[36] See pp. lii–liii below.

[37] *SSWN*, fo. 29[r–v]; for a transcription of these notes and account of the dating of the manuscript see Graham Rees, 'An unpublished manuscript by Francis Bacon: *Sylva sylvarum* drafts and other working notes', *Annals of science*, **38**, 1981, pp. 377–412.

[38] *SEH*, II, pp. 687–92. *SI* was probably written before *DGI* (1612). In *DGI* and subsequent works Bacon referred to the divisions of *IM* as 'parts'; in earlier references to the plan of *IM* he always spoke of 'books', see *OFB*, VI, p. xvii n. 3.

another direction. In the first place, Bacon uses the imagery of the way-side inn to explain the function of Part V, and this very same imagery occurs in the same context in the *Distributio* (1620).[39] This coincidence may suggest a relatively late date for the *Prodromi*. In the second place, the *Prodromi* begins with words attributed to Solon. Never one to waste a good *bon mot*, Bacon used the same words in the *De augmentis* (1623) but not in any other work. A similar phenomenon occurs in the *Abecedarium* with words attributed to Lysander which crop up again only in the *De augmentis* and the 1624 *Apophthegms*.[40] If the *Prodromi* and *Abecedarium* are parallel cases of short-term fascination with partic-ular sayings, then the *Prodromi* may (although the argument is hardly conclusive) belong to the early 1620s.

(*c*) Summary: Dating and the *Instauratio magna*

Historia densi & rari (**manuscript version**): the text existed in this form in the autumn of 1623, but by then it had probably been superseded in whole or part by the Rawley version and, like the latter, it was designed to illustrate the requirements of Part III of the *Instauratio*. We do not know exactly when Bacon started work on the piece but he began it some time after 1620, and most likely early in 1622.

Historia densi & rari (**Rawley version**): a much expanded version of the item above, it was written as a contribution to Part III of the *Instauratio*. Bacon probably stopped work on it no later than 1624.

Abecedarium nouum naturæ: perhaps at first conceived as a coda to Part III of the *Instauratio*, Bacon came to see it as an introduction to Part IV. It was apparently written in the spring or summer of 1622.

Historia & inquisitio de animato & inanimato: apparently associated with the *Abecedarium*, this piece is probably a sketch for a study destined for Part IV of the *Instauratio*. Its association with the *Abecedarium* may suggest that it was written in 1622; it is certain that it was composed before the autumn of 1623.

Inquisitio de magnete: almost certainly written in the second half of 1625; there is no conclusive evidence as to its place in the *Instauratio*, though it may well be a preliminary sketch for a contribution to Part IV.

Topica inquisitionis de luce et lumine: almost certainly written in the second half of 1625, and quite probably an introduction to a contribu-tion to Part IV.

---

[39] See *PA*, R2ʳ⁻ᵛ (p. 262, ll. 11–16 below).

[40] See *cmt* (p. 337 below) on *PA*, R1ᵛ for Solon's remark. For the parallel instance in *ANN* and *DAS* see *cmt* (p. 305 below) on *ANN*, fo. 24ʳ.

Prodromi sive anticipationes philosophiæ secundæ: undoubtedly a preface to Part V of the *Instauratio*. Evidence which points to 1620–3 as the period of its composition is weak but the only evidence we have.

2

The *Historia densi* and the *Abecedarium*: Contexts and Composition

In this section I leave aside the last four pieces presented in this volume. Their character and philosophical content are given adequate consideration either in the commentaries in this volume, or in the introduction and commentaries to other volumes of this edition. Likewise I leave aside general consideration of Baconian natural history, for that appears, with the edited texts of the *Historia naturalis* and *Historia vitæ*, in Volume XII. Here I examine relatively briefly just two topics: (*a*) the relationships and differences between the two versions of the *Historia densi & rari* and (*b*) the substance of the *Abecedarium* and its place in the structure of Bacon's natural philosophy.

(*a*) Two versions of the *Historia densi & rari*

The manuscript version of the *Historia densi* lacks much of the elaborate system of headings, subheadings and paragraph numbering of the printed version. Nor is the manuscript drafted so as to reproduce in scribal terms the ways in which distinctions between different kinds of passage are given typographical force in the printed version. Then again, the printed version of the *Historia densi* differs in these respects from the two octavo histories (the *Historia ventorum* and *Historia vitæ*) printed by John Haviland in Bacon's lifetime.

The Haviland octavos make use of quite elaborate and consistent typographical distinctions to mark out different kinds of matter. To take the *Historia vitæ* as an example,[1] some materials are set in large italic with a few words in roman (16 lines per page); other are set in a smaller roman with a sprinkling of words in italic (20 lines per page). Cutting across this distinction is another, viz. some materials have their headings set within the box-ruled outer margins; others have headings centred in the text above the passages they identify. The Aditus, Obseruationes majores, Intentiones, list of Operationes, a Commentatio, and Canones mobiles are all set in 16-line italic, with headings centred in the text. However, the Explicationes attached to the Canones are set in 20-line italic with a small admixture of roman. All the Connexiones are also in 16-line italic with a few words in roman, but in every case the heading Connexio is set in the outer margin. Every Mandatum is so headed in

---

[1] The *HV* is less elaborate in these respects than *HVM*.

the outer margin and the substance of each is set in 20-line roman with a few italics, a mix which is also used for every Historia, while the heading of each Historia is centred in the text. Every Monitum is exceptional for, while each is so headed in the margin, its substance is set in 20-line italic with a few words here and there set in roman. More exceptional still are the Topica Particularia (topics of inquiry) which are set in the 20-line predominantly roman mix but with transitions without headings set in 20-line type with italic predominant, and (uniquely) indented from the inner-margin rule and from the inner rule of the outer margin. Where items are numbered, the numbers stand within the box rules of the outer margins.

The printed version of the *Historia densi* never reached the level of consistency and finished perfection achieved in the *Historia vitæ*. It lacks the box rules of the Haviland octavos and so all numbers stand at the beginning of the paragraphs to which they (erratically) refer, and all headings are centred above the passages to which they belong. However, the text is for the most part set either in 28- or 32-line type. Monita, Mandata, and the Historiæ are all set in 32-line type and mainly in roman—except for three anomalous Historiæ at the beginning which are set in type of the same size but mainly in italic. Observationes, Commentationes, Connexiones, and Canones are set in 28-line type and predominantly roman type.[2] In other words, the elaborate typographical style of the *Historia vitæ* is reduced to a simple type-size dichotomy, though the two works do agree as to what should be set in larger and what in smaller type. The Aditus of the *Historia densi* distinguishes itself by matching the Aditus of the *Historia vitæ* in using a larger *and* predominantly italic type,[3] but it differs from the *Historia vitæ* in that its type is far larger than anything found elsewhere in the text. The *Historia densi* is moreover unique in the appearance of a very small italic in, for instance, some section headings and for the first and largest table of results. Lastly, the work has no Topica Particularia (these were either never written or more likely have gone missing),[4] and no Explicationes accompany its Canones—another obvious sign that the text was abandoned before it achieved its final form.

---

[2] Except for one anomalous Connexio (C6ʳ (p. 86, ll. 4–10 below)) which is mainly italic not roman. Also see Appendix I, pp. 341–2 below.

[3] This may be a minute indication that Rawley's manuscript of *HDR* may, like *HDR(M)*, have lacked its Aditus and that Rawley lifted the Aditus from *HNE*. For this issue see p. lxxx below.

[4] *HDR* seems to imply that Topica Particularia underlay the structure of the work in the same way that they do in the *HV* and *HVM*.

As for the manuscript version of the *Historia densi,* different kinds of passage are barely distinguished at all. In the unlikely event that the scribe was working from an exemplar which indicated different kinds of material with script of different sizes or kinds in a manner that was later to be reproduced in type from Rawley's manuscript, there is nothing to show it in the extant copy. Except for a detail or two dealt with below, the script is uniform in size and character throughout, and most likely not because the scribe failed to observe such differences in his exemplar but because the exemplar, a draft of a text still at a relatively early stage of its evolution, probably exhibited none. As for the headings, the heading Monita occurs just once (fo. 8^r), Obseruationes twice (fos. 8^r, 16^r), and none of Bacon's standard headings occurs at all between folios 8^v and 15^v. The headings Mandatum and Commentatio do not appear in the manuscript and, most remarkably of all, Historia is a lexical item which appears nowhere in the text. It is also quite striking that even in the historical sections of the work paragraph numbering, a practice so common in the Rawley version of the text and in the Haviland octavos, is a rare event indeed.

The manuscript *Historia densi* does use the heading Canones mobiles once (fo. 22^v) and in the same place as in the printed version. But this heading is unusual in that, like the other four headings[5] in the second half of the manuscript, it is written slightly but obviously larger than the rest of the text. My suspicion (and it can be no more than that) is that here the scribe was reflecting features of his exemplar, features which (whether the exemplar was Bacon holograph or a copy) were probably authentically Baconian. Why that should happen later in the text rather than earlier I do not know, but I cannot think why the scribe should change his behaviour at these points without his being prompted by cues in his exemplar.

Turning from these formal considerations to the intersection between structure and content, the first point to make is that at 17,660 words the printed *Historia* comes uncannily close (within 0.3%) to being exactly twice the length of the manuscript version at 8,850 words. But even though the manuscript version generally lacks headings, the two versions nevertheless share the same general structure. This is the same as saying that the process whereby the work represented in the manuscript

---

[5] These are (i) Aperturæ metallorum (fo. 15^v), (ii) Obseruatio (fo. 16^r), (iii) De contractionibus, condensationibus, & clausuris corporum (fo. 17^v), and (iv) Optatiua cum proximis (fo. 23^r). The first and third of these do not appear as headings in *HDR* but are subsumed in Connexiones (D7^{r-v} and E6^r).

was converted into the form represented by Rawley's version involved *no* major structural changes. In fact, for the purpose of analysis the work can be divided into two parts, a shorter and a longer. The shorter is centred on three tables of quantitative results, on an exploration of the differences between tangible and pneumatic bodies and on the varieties of pneumatic body. The longer, which ends with a set of canones mobiles and optatiua, proceeds through a succession of inquiries which (i) distinguishes and investigates a series of dilatations (each differentiated by its efficient cause) and (ii) then does the same for a series of contractions, each of which is usually a reciprocal of one of the dilatations. Had Bacon completed and published the work, each of the items in both these series and each of the items in the opening and shorter part of the work would have been anticipated (as required by the *Norma historiæ*) in a series of topics of inquiry which would have stood near the beginning of the work just after the Aditus or preface.

This structure was undisturbed by the process that turned the manuscript text into the Rawley text. The former became the latter as new materials were slotted into an existing framework. The process was almost entirely additive. The added passages—and there are some seventy-two of them[6]—are in general distributed fairly evenly through the text. But while that is true even of the Aditus or preface, the longest single continuous addition (515 words (A1^r–A4^r)), it is also true that the longest continuous additions are appreciably shorter than the longest ones which remain intact from the stage in the work's history represented by the manuscript version. Among the latter, the most extensive is the table with which the manuscript version begins; and since that table, taken over from the incomplete and unpublished *Phænomena universi*, is the basis for much of the whole enterprise, it is not surprising that in Rawley's version it is a focus for much new material.

This new material comprises five distinct passages, three of which are very large by standards of such additions. Together they amount to some 8.5 per cent of the total length of Rawley's version of the text. Of these the longest is the Aditus (515 words (A1^r–A4^r)) which, like others intended for the Latin natural histories, combines dense allusiveness with thematic clarity to produce a kind of mini-essay of the kind that we find in the opening paragraphs of the *Abecedarium*. The other four passages associated with the table follow it. These comprise extra monita (158 words (A6$^{r–v}$)), and expansions to the observationes (113 words

---

[6] Not counting a handful of passages of fewer than ten words each.

(A7^r–A8^r)) and mandata (368 words (A8^{r-v})), as well as reflections on the possibility of making gold (231 words (B1^v–B2^r)), a topic which arises naturally enough from the fact that, if gold could be manufactured at all, it would have to be made from substances rarer than itself. As with the large table so with the two smaller ones which follow it: new explanatory material is incorporated in the text in the form of a monitum, a mandatum and extra observationes (315 words (B3^{r-v}))—all of which are very welcome as the text represented in the manuscript version presents these tables with not one single word of explanation.

Leaving aside these tables of results and the added materials associated with them, it is important to note two related and rather striking phenomena. In the first place, some of the longest passages in the manuscript which recur *unchanged* in the fuller Rawley version contain some of the most explicit *theoretical* material in the text. In the second, some of the longest passages unique to the Rawley version add *experimental* materials mobilized in support of theoretical positions just mentioned. These two points invite closer inspection. When I refer to theoretical materials I mean, in particular, aspects of Bacon's theory of matter, a theory for which the *Historia densi* is an indispensable source. Enough has been said about the theory elsewhere.[7] Here I wish only to point out that Bacon's exploration of the crucial tangible–pneumatic distinction and his most systematic outline of the different types of pneumatic or spirit matter account for one of the longest passages retained intact from the manuscript version (762 words (B4^r–B6^v)). Another passage (328 words (E7^v–E8^v)) compares the effects of fire and age on spirit, and that too is one of the longest passages taken over unaltered in Rawley's version. Also retained intact are the canones mobiles (411 words (G4^v–G6^r)), which, as explicit ventures into the realm of theoretical speculation and provisional conclusions to the entire historical investigation, have, even without the explicationes that were meant to accompany them, a qualitative significance that reaches far beyond the mere numbers of words involved. These three passages account for some 17 per cent of the manuscript text, so the fact of the matter is that the theoretical underpinnings were already in place *before* Bacon undertook revisions which doubled the length of the text, and those same underpinnings remained unchanged *after* the revisions. Conversely, the historical and experimental materials added during revision had no effect whatever even on the wording of the conclusions that supposedly flow from them. Rather

[7] See for instance *OFB*, VI, pp. xxxvi–lxix, and esp. pp. xlii–xlviii and liv–lix.

such materials were added to give credence to positions which had already been staked out.

Among these materials were some of the longest passages unique to the Rawley version. And of these the greatest (in fact the greatest besides the Aditus) is the phial and bladder experiment (384 words (B6^v–B7^r)), a version of which is to be found in the *Phænomena universi*.[8] This experiment was designed to establish, by converting spirits of wine (distilled wine) into pneumatic mattter, the extreme tenuity of pneumatic as compared with tangible matter, and to do so with the object of lethally undermining the Peripatetic decuple theory of the relationship between the four elements and of forcing the reader to digest the philosophical catastrophe that ignorance of pneumatic bodies had wrought.[9]

Further experiments unique to the Rawley version include some on the compression of air and water (128 and 193 words (G1$^{r–v}$, G1^v–G2^r)), experiments which had also first appeared in the *Phænomena universi*— notably the material concerning Drebbel's diving bell and the effects produced by pushing an inverted bowl under water.[10] But there are also some quite new experiments such, for instance, as those to do with the calendar or weather glass—an instrument that seems to have come to Bacon's notice some time after the composition of the *Phænomena* (where it is not mentioned at all) but before the production of the early version of the *Historia densi* (where it is mentioned in passing on three occasions).[11] The instrument is given much more prominence in the Rawley version. Bacon not only expanded one of the passages already in the early version,[12] he also added four new passages (amounting to some 330 words), passages which illuminate directly or indirectly aspects of the pneumatic theory of matter.[13] In fact what Bacon does with the calendar glass could stand as a microcosm of what happened to the experimental content of the work in the process that changed the manuscript version into the text presented by Rawley.

In addition to such experimental work, the Rawley version of the *Historia densi* is shot through with a myriad of small pieces of new observational or empirical material which fill out the bodies of evidence which had already been assembled when the text represented in the manuscript was produced. There is no need to look in detail at these additions here for many will be touched on in the commentary on the

---

[8] *PhU*, Q8$^{r–v}$ (*OFB*, VI, pp. 56–8).   [9] See *cmt* on this passage p. 277 below.
[10] *PhU*, P11^v–P12^v (*OFB*, VI, pp. 40–2).   [11] Fos. 18^v, 20$^{r–v}$, 23^v (pp. 25, 27–8, 34 below).
[12] *HDR*, F2^v, cf. *HDR(M)*, fo. 18^v (p. 138, cf. p. 25 below).
[13] *HDR* C6^v, D6^r, D6^v, F2^v (pp. 88–9, 106–7, 138 below).

edited text. Suffice it to say that the net effect of these small items is much like that of the added experimental material which we have already examined. The effects are simultaneously to strengthen the grounding upon which the pre-existing theoretical materials rest and to make the natural history appear more 'innocent'. By 'innocent' I mean that the work became ostensibly more strictly natural-historical than the manuscript version, a version in which the overtly theoretical matter appears more concentrated in the sense that it constitutes a larger proportion of the text. The strengthening of the theoretical framework was, in other words, accomplished at little cost. The added materials were distributed so evenly that, far from canting the work towards too openly theoretical a stance, they brought it closer to the factual-accumulative norms established in the *Historia ventorum* and *Historia vitæ*—which is no doubt precisely what Bacon intended them to do.

(*b*) The *Abecedarium*: Its Content and the Structure of Baconian Science

The bulk of the *Abecedarium* is given over to a catalogue or synoptic list of natural-philosophical inquiries. The list numbers eighty titles, most of which are accompanied by a paragraph or so indicating the nature and scope of each. The list begins with titles relating to the *exporrectiones* (1–5) and schematisms of matter (6–24). These are followed by titles concerned with simple motions (25–40), sums of motions (41–54), and measures of motions (55–60). The final twenty titles deal with the impressions and perceptions of sense (61–6), the greater masses (67–72), the conditions of beings (73–8), the great schematism, and vicissitudes of things (79–80). The *Abecedarium* takes its name primarily from the subject-matter covered by the first sixty titles, and it is to these that the remarks immediately following are mainly (though not exclusively) addressed. I shall consider the final twenty titles in detail later.

The titles of the *Abecedarium* (especially the first sixty) comprise material central to Bacon's conception of natural history, physics and metaphysics—the three stages of the Baconian scientific pyramid. The base of the pyramid, the base on which all the rest stands, is natural history. Natural history gives rise to a low-level, rule-of-thumb kind of operative knowledge called *experientia literata*. Above natural history stands physics, which yields knowledge of material and efficient causes and can be cashed out in terms of an intermediate form of operative science called mechanics. The highest kind of natural-philosophical knowedge is metaphysics, which investigates formal causes and yields magic, the most powerful form of operative knowledge available to human beings.[14]

The topics of the *Abecedarium* became an increasingly important object of research at all three stages of the scientific pyramid. With regard to metaphysics Bacon wrote in *The advancement* that,

to enquire *the formes* of Sence, of voluntary Motion, of Vegetation, of Colours, of Grauitie and Leuitie, of Densitie, of Tenuitie, of Heate, of Cold, and al other Natures and qualities, which like an *Alphabet* are not many, & of which the essences (vpheld by Matter) of all creatures doe co*n*sist: To enquire I say *the true formes* of these, is that part of METAPHYSICKE, which we now define of.[15]

Later, in the *Descriptio globi intellectualis* (1612) and with regard to natural history (and of a particularly exalted kind of natural history) he remarked:

As for those Virtues which may be reckoned as Cardinal and Catholic in nature,—such as Dense, Rare, Light, Heavy, Hot, Cold, Consistent, Fluid, Similar, Dissimilar, Specific, Organic and the like, together with the motions going to make them, as resistance, connection, coming together, expansion and the rest (the history of which I want absolutely to be compiled and put together, even before I come to the work of the *Intellect*)—I shall deal with the history of these virtues and motions, and the way of putting it together, after I have finished explaining that threefold partition of *Generations, Pretergenerations* and *Arts.* For I have not, of course, included it within that threefold partition of mine, because it is not properly history but a middle term, so to speak, between history and philosophy.[16]

Unfortunately he abandoned the *Descriptio* before the promise could be fulfilled. But he had already written a natural-historical study, the *Phænomena universi,* of the dense/rare polarity, a topic which he returned to with the *Historia densi*; and in the last years of his life he also planned to write natural histories of subjects whose titles appear in the *Abecedarium*—for instance, the *Historia grauis & leuis* and *Historia sulphuris, mercurij, & salis.*

Bacon returned to the natural-historical aspects of these cardinal virtues in the *Distributio operis,* where he declared that Part III of the *Instauratio magna* was not to be concerned merely with the history of bodies for he was under an obligation to produce a separate history of

---

[14] Bacon here appropriates and alters Aristotelian terms: the Baconian causes (material, efficient and formal) are realized in non-Aristotelian ways, and Aristotle's fourth category of cause—the final—had been banished from the domain of natural philosophy by Bacon in *DAS*, Z2ᵛ (*SEH*, I, p. 571).

[15] *AL*, 2G3ᵛ (*OFB*, IV, p. 84, ll. 17–22).   [16] *OFB*, VI, pp. 109–11.

cardinal virtues, i.e. of those original (primis) passions or desires of matter which constitute the primordia of nature (Naturæ primordia), such
as dense and rare, hot and cold, solid and fluid, heavy and light, and the
rest.[17] Recalling this remark in the *Parasceve* (1620), he added the important qualification that until people had become better acquainted with
nature, he would reserve this domain for himself and, to reinforce the
point, he repeated it in the preliminaries to the *Historia naturalis*
(1622).[18]

So much for the importance of the titles of the alphabet for metaphysics and natural history, but what of their place in physics? The material comprehended by the first sixty titles of the *Abecedarium* constitutes,
in effect, a single very large group; it maps out the territory of what the
De augmentis calls abstract physics. The *De augmentis* (1623), written not
long after the *Abecedarium* and in fulfilment of Bacon's plans for Part I
of the *Instauratio*, is a revised, enlarged, Latin version of *The advancement of learning* (1605), and many of the enlargements were incorporated
in the text so as to prepare the way for material that was to appear in later
parts of the *Instauratio*. As he revised *The advancement*, Bacon trans-
formed the discussion of the natural sciences in general and of physics in
particular. To the discussion of physics he made revisions and additions
no doubt specifically designed to prepare the reader for the as yet unpublished *Abecedarium*, which was once, as we know, to have appeared later
in the *Instauratio*. The structure of physics according to the *De augmentis* is displayed in Table 1.

TABLE I. *The Branches of Physics*[19]

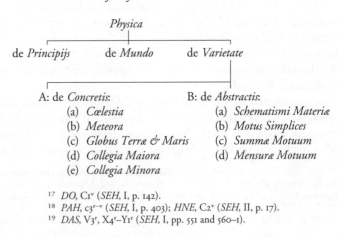

---

[17] *DO*, C1ᵛ (*SEH*, I, p. 142).
[18] *PAH*, c3ʳ⁻ᵛ (*SEH*, I, p. 403); *HNE*, C2ᵛ (*SEH*, II, p. 17).
[19] *DAS*, V3ʳ, X4ʳ–Y1ʳ (*SEH*, I, pp. 551 and 560–1).

Although one of the inquiries catalogued in the *Abecedarium* (the 79th) is concerned with the department of physics called 'de *Mundo*', most of the others are assigned to the department 'de *Varietate*'. According to the *De augmentis*, physics 'de *Varietate*' has two departments: abstract and concrete. The first sixty titles of the *Abecedarium* coincide with the domain of abstract physics. Titles 67–72 cover topics which are assigned by the *De augmentis* to selected aspects of concrete physics (the *Abecedarium* omitting topics corresponding to items A (c) and A (e) of Table 1).

In the *De augmentis* the subject-matter of abstract physics is indicated with a list of most of the first sixty titles of the *Abecedarium*.[20] The *De augmentis* further points out that the difference between concrete and abstract physics is that the former deals with 'creatures', the latter with 'natures'. Adopting Aristotelian terms, Bacon suggested that the former dealt with substances through every variety of their accidents, the latter with accidents through every variety of their substances and, as physics lay between natural history and metaphysics, concrete physics came nearer to natural history, abstract to metaphysics.[21] On this definition much of concrete physics had to do with what Bacon denoted with synonyms like 'substances', 'compound forms' (*formæ copulatæ*)[22] or (in the *Abecedarium*) 'the least general species' (fo. 28ᵛ). Abstract physics is concerned with a more powerful, general study of natures, motions etc. (i.e. 'forms of the first class')[23] inherent in many species. Bacon insists upon this distinction in the *Abecedarium* and it is critical for an understanding of the work. Only the most general natures belong to the Alphabet; these natures, 'the letters of the Alphabet', must not be confused with the 'words and syllables' (fo. 28ᵛ) of the book of nature, i.e. the substances or individual existents in which the simple natures are combined.

The very title of the *Abecedarium* belongs to a range of literacy metaphors which Bacon used throughout his career. According to the *Valerius terminus* (1603), natural philosophers have gone astray by searching for the 'causes and productions of thinges concrete, wᶜʰ are

---

[20] *Ibid.*, X4ʳ–Y1ʳ (*SEH*, I, pp. 560–1). *DAS* omits items corresponding to titles 7, 8, 14, 21, 36, 41, 44, 47, 48, 51, 54 and 56 of *ANN* and removes title 23 of the latter (sensible and non-sensible) from among the schematisms of matter and locates it as part of the 'doctrine concerning man'. The *DAS* list is at its briefest when it comes to the sums of motions (only eight titles compared with the fourteen of *ANN*). These facts strengthen the impression that Bacon may have been trying arbitrarily to inflate the numbers of titles in *ANN*. On this issue see below, pp. xlv–xlvii below.

[21] *DAS*, V3ʳ (*SEH*, I, p. 551).

[22] *NO*, H1ʳ, 2A1ʳ; *DAS*, V3ʳ; Y2ᵛ–Y3ᵛ (*SEH*, I, pp. 172, 257; 551, 565–6).

[23] *DAS*, Y3ᵛ (*SEH*, I, p. 566).

infinite and transitory'; instead they should have sought the causes of abstract natures, 'wch are few and permanent . . . these natures are as the Alphabet or simple le*tt*res, whereof the variety of thinges consisteth'. According to the *Cogitationes de natura rerum* (*c*.1604?), ignorance of the alphabet of nature makes natural philosophers like the illiterates of earlier times who could make out only compound sounds and words and not the elements and letters.[24]

Ignorance of nature's alphabet has resulted in a tragic loss of power over the natural world. In the *Novum organum* Bacon tells us that our knowledge of 'words' i.e. of less general species (infimarum specierum), for instance, man, dog, dove, and of the immediate perceptions of the sense do not materially mislead us even though they are sometimes confused. But such knowledge will not lead to radical transformations of nature.[25] That will only come from knowledge of simple natures well examined and defined, knowledge which will open the way to the noblest axioms and bring whole troops of works after it. Knowledge of these natures may seem useless, but so also the letters of the alphabet in themselves have no use or meaning, but they are the subject-matter for the composition of all discourse.[26] Thus to restore human authority over nature we must, according to the *Historia naturalis*, be humble, become like children and work hard on our ABCs (abecedaria).[27] Here the alphabet image appears with a new edge; it refers to the letters in which the book of nature is written *and* to that childlike humility which, according to the *Abecedarium* and other works, is a condition for fulfilling Bacon's programme; and from humility and knowledge of the letters of the alphabet comes power, *operative* power more certain and secure than any offered by alchemist or magician.[28]

Turning now to the particular letters of the *Abecedarium*, the simple natures and motions comprehended by the first sixty titles or inquiries are among the primary objects of natural philosophy. Although Bacon was prepared to concede that future research might alter the distinctions between them, the natures are, in effect, the elementary contents of nature, the alphabet in which the book of nature is inscribed. The first twenty-four inquiries outlined in the *Abecedarium* are all concerned with the contrasted pairs of simple natures or the cardinal virtues whose

[24] *VT*, p. 51 (*SEH*, III, p. 243); *CDNR*, R10^v (*SEH*, III, p. 22). For further remarks on alphabets and abecedaria see *cmt* (p. 305 below) on *ANN*, p. 172, l. 1 below.
[25] *NO*, E3^v–E4^r (*SEH*, I, p. 159).
[26] *Ibid.*, Q3^r (*SEH*, I, p. 215), also see *AL*, 2G3^r–2H1^r (*OFB*, IV, pp. 81–6).
[27] *HNE*, B5^v (*SEH*, II, p. 15). [28] *AL*, 2H4^r–2I1^r (*OFB*, IV, pp. 89–90).

investigation he had decided to reserve for himself. In connection with these the *Abecedarium* is unique in two ways: nowhere else did Bacon treat them more fully or systematically, and nowhere else did he divide them into two primary groups. In other works (the *De augmentis* for instance) *all* the contrasted pairs are called schematisms of matter (schematismi materiæ),[29] but in the *Abecedarium* this phrase is applied only to the last nineteen of the pairs. The others, the first five, are set up as a separate group under the collective heading 'The Great Determinants of Dimension'.[30]

These are simple natures intimately connected with matter seen in relation to the space it occupies. Dense and rare are the most universal of these, and possibly of all the simple natures; they constitute the calculus that differentiates physical bodies in a most fundamental way, viz. in terms of the quantity of matter that they contain per unit of volume. The primary pair are followed by the heavy–light and hot–cold polarities. Knowledge of heavy and light is the means by which a precise understanding of dense and rare can be obtained; and knowledge of hot and cold is knowledge of the natures primarily responsible for producing changes in density and rarity. In addition to the universality that Bacon ascribes to them, these three pairs have another claim to priority amongst the titles: they are specially important for their peculiar relevance to the inquiries about motions that are to appear later in the text. The two remaining pairs are the volatile–fixed and tangible–pneumatic. Investigation of the former aims at understanding the natures that make some tangible bodies prone to turn into pneumatic and others not, and so is ancillary to tangible–pneumatic distinction, a distinction particularly crucial to the *speculative* philosophy, the philosophy mentioned earlier in connection with the *Historia densi*. The tangible–pneumatic polarity belongs here for obvious reasons. A principal difference of tangible and pneumatic is that of density and rarity. The degrees of dense and rare in tangible bodies are great; so too are the degrees in pneumatic bodies. But these are as nothing compared with the differences *between* the two classes, as the quantitative experiments of the *Phænomena universi* (1611?), *Novum organum* and, above all, the *Historia densi* are intended to show.[31]

From the bulk of matter we move to its schematisms which, in this

---

[29] *DAS*, X4^{r-v} (*SEH*, I, p. 560).   [30] *ANN*, fos. 24^r–25^r (pp. 174–6 below).
[31] See *OFB*, VI, p. 372; *HDR*, B6^v–B7^r (pp. 66–8 below).

context,[32] are contrasted pairs of simple natures and the objects of inquiries 6–24. These are disposed in four groups: (i) inquiries (6–11) into simple natures inhering in tangible bodies both solid and fluid; and (ii) inquiries (12–14) differentiating bodies according to the pneumatics in them. Here Bacon suggests that it would be natural to pass on to the most 'noble' distinction arising from spirits enclosed in terrestrial bodies, that between animate and inanimate. But as the animate nature thrives mainly in exceedingly 'unequal' bodies, Bacon first deals with (iii) inquiries (15–21) concerning inequality; and ends with (iv) inquiries (22–4) comprising animate and inanimate, sensible and non-sensible, and sulphurous and mercurial. Discussion of these groups, groups ultimately differentiated on the basis of the all-important tangible–pneumatic polarity, therefore culminates in some of the most explicitly theoretical or speculative material in the entire work.

The first group begins with the solid–fluid polarity. As we know from other works, this polarity as applied to tangible bodies is itself explicable in terms of the nature of the bodies' pneumatic component. To some degree all other natures are definable in terms of the solid–fluid polarity. The second group of schematisms begins with a formulation of the principle that all tangible bodies at or near the surface of the Earth have spirits imprisoned within them. Bacon then adduces three titles that distinguish tangible bodies by differences in the nature of their enclosed spirits. As this and other texts indicate, these differences have profound consequences for tangible bodies. They determine their qualities and are responsible for many of the changes that take place within them.

As for the third group, the ones concerned with 'inequality', there are no less than seven titles (inquiries 15–21) concerned with this. This testifies to Bacon's preoccupation with prolonging life, a preoccupation expressed in the *Historia vitæ* (in preparation while the *Abecedarium* was being written) and in the speculative treatise *De vijs mortis* abandoned some few years earlier. Accordingly, 'inequality' in its various manifestations is a fitting prelude to the treatment of the animate–inanimate distinction (inquiry 22). Inequality is one of the main reasons why material bodies fall apart. That is especially true of living ones—which are the most unequal of all. There is nothing particularly new about this idea; it is traditional residue in Bacon's idea of physical decay. The idea that inequality was the 'mother of dissolution' had been integral to the treat-

---

[32] For the meanings of 'schematism' see *cmt* (p. 308 below) on *ANN*, fo. 25ʳ, p. 176, ll. 21–3 below.

ments of the topic in the Galenic and Arabo-Latin medical tradition. By
'inequality' Bacon means that which diverges from uniformity of substance or simplicity of internal structure.[33]

As has been said, the most 'unequal' bodies are living ones, and now
Bacon comes to the animate–inanimate polarity (inquiry 22), the fourth
group, and one of the most theory-laden sections of the *Abecedarium*.
Once more his speculative philosophy comes to the surface with the fundamental distinction between material spirits isolated in small pockets
and not 'inflamed', and spirits inflamed and self-continuous, i.e. the distinction between inanimate and animate spirit, a distinction developed
in inquiry 23, into sensible and non-sensible. Sensible beings are animals, non-sensible are plants. The animate spirits of the latter are disposed in branching channels, but the channels carrying the spirits of the
former emanate from a ventricular concentration of animate spirit. This
distinction is another fundamental component of Bacon's speculative
philosophy and is developed extensively in other works. It is therefore
wholly appropriate that he chooses to end the discussion of schematisms
with the sulphur–mercury distinction (inquiry 24), the very hinge on
which the speculative philosophy turns.[34]

Moving now to the next twenty-six inquiries, we pass from simple
natures to simple motions (inquiries 25–40), the sums of motions
(41–54) and measures of motions (55–60). With the simple natures these,
as we have seen, comprise the field of abstract physics and so belong
among the primary objects of the Baconian natural-philosophical enterprise. However, I shall not discuss these inquiries in detail here. In the
first place, notes to the individual inquiries are presented below in the
commentary on the text and, in the second, much of this material will
be looked at again in our edition of the *Novum organum*.

Nevertheless, one or two general remarks would be in order. The simple motions are considered at length in the *Novum organum* and summarily in the *De augmentis*.[35] By default, the *Novum organum* with its
nineteen motions, and the *De augmentis* with its fifteen, throw into
sharp relief Bacon's desire to organize the simple motions of the *Abecedarium* into what may be called a 4^2 structure, i.e. to deal with sixteen
simple motions arranged into four groups of four. The 4^2 arrangement
is perhaps the most obvious expression of a general appetite for fours and

---

[33] See *HVM*, 2E4ᵛ (*SEH*, II, p. 219). On the distinction between similar and dissimilar see
DVM, fo. 18ᵛ (*OFB*, VI, p. 324, l. 32–p. 326, l. 6).
[34] For this distinction see *OFB*, VI, pp. xlii–xlviii and 407.
[35] *NO*, 2O1ʳ–2R2ᵛ (*SEH*, I, pp. 330–46); *DAS*, X4ᵛ–Y1ʳ (*SEH*, I, pp. 560–1).

multiples of four that seems to operate in the text. The appetite is evident, for instance, in the twenty-four titles (one complete run of the Greek alphabet) considered immediately before the simple motions, and those twenty-four together with the sixteen relating to the simple motions carry the running total of inquiries to forty, a number which is itself half the grand total of fourscore.

Moreover the 4^2 simple motions of the *Abecedarium* are presented in the same order as those listed in *De augmentis* save that in the latter one of the headings of the *Abecedarium* (de medijs motuum) does not appear and another two (motus continuationis sui and motus hyles) are presented in reverse order. The motions named and the order of their presentation align the *Abecedarium* much more closely with the *De augmentis* than with the *Novum organum*. Yet when we leave the simple motions for the sums and measures of motions, we find that the *De augmentis* lists only eight sums and five measures. The *Abecedarium* deals with fourteen sums and six measures, which just happen to bring the running total of inquiries up to sixty or threescore. Why Bacon should want to multiply or dissolve distinctions at will in order to reach apparently arbitrary totals is anyone's guess.

The final twenty inquiries of the *Abecedarium* have an *ad hoc* air to them. While they are emphatically not marginal to Bacon's philosophy, they do seem to be make-weights—added in part to drive the total number of inquiries up to eighty, the fourth score. Unlike the first sixty, the final twenty titles do not form a coherent whole. This, and the fact that some lack the explanatory paragraphs which invariably precede each of the first sixty, rather suggests that Bacon decided to go for a final twenty before he knew which they would be.

The final twenty begin with a group concerned with the informations of the senses, i.e. the sense and its objects, and the individual senses. Titles in this group lack explanatory paragraphs. Apart from saying that knowledge of the kind sought in the *Abecedarium* could only originate from information derived from the senses, Bacon was content to list these titles without comment. In this way the *Abecedarium* aligns itself with other texts. Nowhere did Bacon say much about the individual senses and no theory of the workings of each of the external senses emerges from his writings. That is in sharp contrast to his considerable interest in the vital spirit, the material substrate of the senses, a subject which (as he reminds us) has already been set down among the schematisms of matter.

The inquiries concerning the senses are followed by a group concerned with the 'greater masses'—earth, water, air, fire, the heavens and meteors (Bacon uses the word 'meteors' in its traditional sense to comprise 'comets, fiery meteors, winds, rains, storms, and the like').[36] Again, the titles lack the usual explanatory paragraphs. After a few lines indicating the significance of the group for the *Abecedarium*, the titles are simply listed without comment. Nevertheless the titles and the preliminary remarks require some explanation. We know that according to the *De augmentis* the first sixty titles of the *Abecedarium* specify the subject-matter of abstract physics, but the 'greater masses' belong to the domain of concrete physics, the domain concerned with substances through all variety of their accidents. Concrete physics has five departments: the heavens, meteors, the globe of earth and sea, the greater colleges or four 'elements', and the lesser colleges or species. In the *Abecedarium* Bacon invokes the distinction between abstract and concrete and assigns the greater masses to the latter. He thereby transcribes the subject-matter of three of the five branches of concrete physics (the first, second and fourth) into a work supposedly concerned with general and universal natures alone.

Up to a point, this is a tacit admission that the greater masses have been included *ad hoc*. However, Bacon argues that they belong because 'since so many things are brought forth from the earth [and waters], so many pass through the air and are drawn from it, so many are changed and dissolved by fire', the other inquiries would be less clear without them. He also seems to think (in self-contradiction) that the inquiries concerning the heavens and meteors *are* amongst the most general. As for earth, water, air, and fire, Bacon denies that he has included them because they constitute all sublunary things. He had no truck whatever with the Aristotelian element theory and tried to refute it experimentally in the *Historia densi* and denied it repeatedly in other works. According to the *Descriptio* and the *Parasceve*, the four masses are not the beginnings of things but, 'the greater masses of connatural bodies. Now that greatness comes from the texture of their matter being easy, simple, obvious and prepared; whereas species are supplied sparingly by nature because their texture is dissimilar and very often organic', i.e. such things as metals, plants, and animals.[37]

Further evidence that Bacon filled out the final quarter of the

[36] See *DAS*, M3^v (*SEH*, I, p. 501), also see S. K. Henninger Jr., *A handbook of Renaissance meteorology*, Duke University Press: Durham, NC, 1960, pp. 39 f.
[37] *DGI*, D9^r (*OFB*, VI, pp. 108–9); *PAH*, b2^v (*SEH*, I, pp. 397–8).

Abecedarium with odds and ends is supplied by the next group of inquiries (73–8), those relating to the 'Conditions of Beings'. These form a coherent group but not one linked with concrete or abstract physics. They belong, according to Bacon's maps of knowledge, to a province called 'Philosophia prima' which is concerned with two things: (*a*) axioms which belong to several sciences[38] and (*b*) the 'Relative and Adventitious Conditions of Essences' or 'Transcendentals'.[39] The *Abecedarium* is concerned with the latter and they are these: being and non-being, possible and impossible, much and little, durable and fleeting, natural and monstrous, and natural and artificial.

Though incomplete,[40] Bacon justified the inclusion of this list on the ground that these inquiries would, investigated by his methods, give light to the others in the Alphabet. It is not easy to see what exactly he was driving at. The study of adventitious conditions is only a small part of his philosophy but it is a puzzling one. The Latin is ambiguous and the function of the titles obscure. The obscurities arise perhaps from Bacon's tendency to appropriate established terminology for new purposes.[41]

Two reasons are given for including an inquiry into being and non-being: (i) the variety of individuals in nature is infinite but the number of species quite few; (ii) negatives attached to affirmatives are very helpful in informing the mind. The first reason is obscure and seems in fact to be altogether irrelevant for Bacon deals with the question of the relative paucity of species elsewhere, both in the *Abecedarium* and *De augmentis*. In the former he points out that it is impossible for there to be as much of the specific as of the non-specific. In the latter he asks why no one has ever tried to explain that.[42] In neither case is the question raised in connection with being and non-being; it is raised instead in connection with much and little. I think Bacon originally planned to begin the discussion of adventitious conditions with much and little (as he did in

[38] Thus, for instance, *AL*, 2F1ʳ⁻ᵛ (*OFB*, IV, p. 77): 'Is not the rule: *Si inæqualibus æqualia addas, omnia erunt inæqualia.* An Axiome aswell of Iustice, as of the Mathematiques? And is there not a true coincidence betweene commutatiue and distributiue Iustice, and Arithmeticall and Geometricall proportion?'

[39] *DAS*, T2ʳ⁻ᵛ (*SEH*, I, p. 543); cf. *AL*, 2E4ᵛ–2F1ʳ (*OFB*, IV, pp. 76–7).

[40] The longest list appears in *DAS* (2L1ᵛ (*SEH*, I, p. 642)): '*Maius, Minus; Multum, Paucum; Prius, Posterius; Idem, Diuersum; Potentia, Actus; Habitus, Priuatio; Totum, Partes; Agens, Patiens; Motus, Quies; Ens, Non Ens;* & similia.' For other lists see *ibid.*, T2ʳ, V2ʳ (*SEH*, I, pp. 543 and 550).

[41] Lisa Jardine, *Francis Bacon: discovery and the art of discourse*, Cambridge University Press: Cambridge, 1974, pp. 106–7.

[42] *ANN*, fo. 36ʳ (p. 218 below); *DAS*, T2ᵛ (*SEH*, I, p. 543).

the *De augmentis*) but changed his mind, decided to begin with being and non-being but failed to delete the now irrelevant material about species. If a later version of the *Abecedarium* ever turned up, I would be surprised if this undeleted material were still to be found in it.

As for the second reason—that negatives associated with affirmatives help inform the mind—Bacon is probably thinking here of the instances of companionship described in the *Novum organum*. These instances are concrete bodies in which a given simple nature is invariably present or invariably absent. From these universal affirmative or negative propositions may be derived. For example, heat is variable in nearly all bodies but flame is always hot, so the proposition that flame is hot is a universal affirmative. Conversely, a universal negative might state that the nature of solidity can never be predicated on air for, whereas metals can exist in solid and fluid states, air can never renounce its fluidity.[43]

To this Bacon adds that if a universal affirmative or negative is lacking (e.g. a body not susceptible of heat) the lack should be noted 'as a thing that is not (tanquàm Non-Ens)'. Moreover, universal propositions about any concrete body should be accompanied by a record of instances that come closest to what is not; in the case of heat such an instance would be the softest flame, for such an instance would mark out the boundaries of nature 'between being and non-being (inter Ens & Non-Ens)'. These appear to be the grounds for studying being and non-being, for as the *Novum organum* tells us, such inquiries help circumscribe forms, lest those inquiries drift beyond the conditions of matter.[44]

Being and non-being is followed by possible and impossible. The possible is a 'potential' for being; the impossible 'a non-potential' for being. This distinction is elucidated in discussion of the remaining conditions of being. The first is much and little: for example, that species should be more abundant in nature than non-species is impossible and therefore not a potential for being (fo. 36ʳ). This is important to natural philosophy because study of the conditions of essences is a study of extremes of possibility in nature for, just as the softest flames are interesting in connection with being and non-being, so much and little belong with the instances of ultimity of the *Novum organum* which, says Bacon, should be subjoined to the instances of companionship mentioned above. Instances of ultimity indicate the real divisions of nature and the measures of things and how far a nature may act or be acted upon. Among such are the whale (on the one hand) and worms in the skin (on the

---

[43] *NO*, 2F3ʳ⁻ᵛ (*SEH*, I, pp. 287–8).   [44] *Ibid.*, 2F3ᵛ–2F4ʳ (*SEH*, I, p. 288).

other), which represent extremes of size, the study of which might greatly assist investigation of the animate nature, for knowing why that nature subsists only within those limits would be a key to the understanding of it.[45] It is no accident that this very question is raised in the *Historia & inquistitio de animato & inanimato.*[46]

The notion that study of the adventitious conditions is a study of extremes of possibility is borne out by the remaining titles in this group. In connection with durable and fleeting Bacon points out that a leaf cannot last as long as a metal. Here too if one were studying the nature of durability (as Bacon does in the *Historia densi*), it might be useful to discover its extremes. Similarly, with natural and monstrous, and natural and artificial, it might be very useful to determine accurately the borderline between them (fo. 36^r). But having said that, these last two titles are perhaps rather factitious. Nowhere else does Bacon give them as adventitious conditions. Indeed, they seem to have nothing to do with transcendentals at all. Rather, since the two terms of both of these polarities are distinguished by efficient causes, Bacon probably introduced them here at least in part to reinforce his belief in the effective unreality of these distinctions, a belief that is fundamental to his natural-historical programme.[47]

After the adventitious conditions of essences, come the last two titles of the *Abecedarium*, the titles that round up the total to eighty, and which are concerned with the 'great schematism' or fabric of the universe, and the 'great sum' or vicissitudes of things (fo. 36^v). Bacon regarded these as a fitting conclusion to the list, 'the more because several natures which we have presented that seem to be substantive are in reality only relative, according as bodies are located spatially or succeed in time'.

---

[45] *NO*, 2F4^r (*SEH*, I, pp. 288–9). [46] Fo. 3^{r-v} (p. 228 below).

[47] The obliteration of the art/nature distinction is a fundamental aspect of Bacon's philosophy, see *OFB*, VI, pp. 102–4 and 384. The mechanical arts and preternatural phenomena are not different from other natural phenomena, they are merely expressions of nature working in special circumstances.

3
The Texts and their Transmission

(*a*) The Bacon Manuscripts of Monsieur de la Hoguette

Lifted from obscurity by the recent and brilliant archival researches of Giuliano Ferretti,[1] Philippe Fortin de la Hoguette (1585–1668?), the person who brought important Bacon manuscripts to France, was one of the new men who, by a fruitful combination of career and culture, moved from the margins of society to assume new and increasingly important functions in the seventeenth-century French state. Born at Falaise into a recently ennobled family he decided, against his father's wishes, to pursue a military career. He served on the abortive Gambia expedition; later he campaigned in France, Holland and Italy, before finishing up on garrison duties. In 1634, the French expedition to La Coruña in 1639 excepted, he gave up the military life, lived in rural retirement[2] and devoted himself to intellectual pursuits which included the writing of his *Catéchisme royal* (1645) and *Testament* (1648). Inasmuch as these works followed the path marked out by Charron, they played a small but significant part in the formation of the sevententh-century idea of wisdom in France.[3]

Nothing is known of La Hoguette's intellectual life before 1620, the year in which he published his *Remonstrance au roy*. This piece, which belonged to a genre favoured by groups struggling for political influence, was an attack on the king's favourite, Charles d'Albert de Luynes, a man not universally esteemed for his political gifts or his rapid rise from falconer to duke.[4] The small notoriety of the *Remonstrance* brought La Hoguette to the attention of the brothers Dupuy and admittance to their famous *cabinet* with its thousands of books and manuscripts, and

---

[1] *Un 'soldat philosophe': Philippe Fortin de la Hoguette (1585–1668?)*, ECIG: Genoa, 1988; *idem* (ed.), *Fortin de la Hoguette ou le vertige de la politique: lettres aux frères Dupuy et à leur entourage (1623–1661)*, unpub. diss., Université de Lausanne, 1995; *idem* (ed.), Philippe Fortin de la Hoguette, *Lettres aux frères Dupuy et à leur entourage (1623–1662)*, 2 vols., Leo S. Olschki: Florence, 1997 [hereafter La Hoguette, *Lettres*].

[2] *Un 'soldat philosophe'*, pp. 27–42, 126–50, 219–23.

[3] *Ibid.*, pp. 20, 233 ff., 260–6. La Hoguette's *Testament . . . d'un bon père à ses enfans*, Antoine Vitré: Paris, 1648, stood at the 'crocevia nella storia dell'assolutismo francese'; much reprinted in the years of the Regency and Fronde, it went out of fashion in the second half of Louis XIV's reign.

[4] *Un 'soldat philosophe'*, pp. 46–9. This same Luynes, coincidentally, affected the career of another man later connected with the transmission of Bacon manuscripts, viz. William Boswell, see *OFB*, VI, p. lxxii.

access to their vast and influential circle of acquaintance. Contact with the Dupuys was almost certainly a pivotal event in La Hoguette's life: it exposed him to contemporary intellectual culture in its full range and vitality and in particular to the growing French fascination with Francis Bacon's work.

The brothers Dupuy, Pierre (1582–1651) and Jacques (1591–1656), were nephews of the great historian Jacques-Auguste de Thou (1553–1617) and it was under his aegis that the Dupuys were introduced to an extensive network of learned individuals which they were to consolidate and extend in the years to come.[5] Jacques Dupuy devoted most of his life to the *cabinet*, and writing erudite works among which was an index of Latin names in his uncle's celebrated *Jacobi Augusti Thuani historiarum sui temporis* (1604–7).[6] Pierre, apparently the more forceful of the brothers, was a man whose intellect and consuming passion for learning gave him a brilliant career as an advocate in the parlement of Paris, counsellor to the king and confidential adviser to Richelieu. In matters of state business he showed particular skill in legal questions, especially those relating to the rights of the monarchy and, under Richelieu's patronage, he published the two weighty volumes of the *Traités des droits et libertés de l'église gallicane* (Paris, 1639). His *cabinet*, services to the Crown and his vast experience of documentary matters were no doubt factors which persuaded his cousin F.-A. de Thou (1604–42), Maître de la Libraire du Roi, to give Pierre and his brother in 1635 the post of Garde de la Bibliothèque du Roi, in succession to Nicolas Rigault—of whom more later. It was to the royal collection that the Dupuys donated their own (1652) and, through that prudent and generous act, copies of La Hoguette's Bacon manuscripts eventually came to rest in the Bibliothèque Nationale de France.[7]

But we jump ahead. La Hoguette had only just been introduced to the Dupuy circle and was enchanted by the *cabinet* and its habitués. And an impressive bunch they were—among them Denis Petau 'the Catholic Saumaise', Marin Mersenne, Jacques Sirmond the king's confessor, Nicolas-Claude Fabri de Peiresc (admirer of Bacon and soon to become

[5] *Un 'soldat philosophe'*, pp. 63–70.

[6] *Ibid.*, pp. 71–72; La Hoguette, *Lettres*, II, pp. 822–3.

[7] *Un 'soldat philosophe'*, pp. 70–1; La Hoguette, *Lettres*, II, pp. 823–5. For the Dupuy's gift, the nature, various locations and 'dual reality' of the 'royal library' see Roger Chartier, *Forms and meanings: texts, performances, and audiences from codex to computer*, trans. Lydia G. Cochrane *et al.*, University of Pennsylvania Press: Philadelphia, 1995, pp. 26–8 *passim*. Also see Simone Balayé, *La Bibliothèque Nationale des origines à 1800*, Librairie Droz: Geneva, 1988, pp. 64–8.

a friend of La Hoguette's),[8] Elia Diodati, and, later, Guillaume Naudé and La Mothe Le Vayer.[9] This group's contacts were Europe-wide and no less with Britain than elsewhere. To take Peiresc as a single example, in these years he exchanged letters with Barclay and Spelman, and with a number of individuals associated with Bacon, among them John Bill (King's Printer);[10] William Camden the historian;[11] Robert Cotton, the bibliophile; and William Boswell, an eventual custodian of some of Bacon's manuscripts.[12]

Peiresc's contacts with people in Bacon's ambit were allied to a growing enthusiasm in France in the 1620s for the Lord Chancellor's writings, which enthusiasm Peiresc actively promoted. In France Bacon's career had struck a chord, as is evident in the seriousness with which the French political class took his work, and in the associated stream of editions and translations that poured from the French presses.[13] It seems that all aspects of Bacon's work excited interest, and provoked a multiplicity of reactions from a very diverse readership, reactions which ranged from the rabid polemics of Jean-Cécile Frey, to the warm admiration of Séguier, d'Haligre and Richelieu.[14]

Yet it may not have been Peiresc's interest in Bacon that first aroused La Hoguette's. The two may not have been on close terms until the mid-1620s.[15] In a situation where Bacon's name was on many lips and his books in many hands, if any individual could be seen as the begetter of

---

[8] Peiresc was, as we shall see, a Bacon enthusiast and fostered the same enthusiasm in others, among them Cassiano dal Pozzo, an important propagator of Bacon's name in Rome in the first half of the 17th cent.; see Anna Rita Romani, 'Francis Bacon e il carteggio puteano', in *Cassiano dal Pozzo: atti del seminario internazionale di studi*, ed. Francesco Solinas, De Lucca: Rome, 1989, pp. 31–5. In the years 1634–5 dal Pozzo was eager to obtain (often through Peiresc) anything of Bacon's, see Nicolas-Claude Fabri de Peiresc, *Lettres à Cassiano dal Pozzo (1626–1637)*, ed. Jean-François Lhote and Danielle Joyal, Adosa: Clermont-Ferrand, 1989, pp. 159–60, 176, 179, 216.

[9] Balayé, *La Bibliothèque Nationale*, p. 65; *Un 'soldat philosophe'*, pp. 72–7.

[10] For John Bill see *STC*, III, pp. 19–20. Also see the entry in H. G. Aldis, *A dictionary of printers and booksellers in England, Scotland and Ireland, and of foreign printers of English books, 1557–1640*, Bibliographical Society: London, 1910. Bill printed Bacon's works while the latter was at the height of his power. After his fall, Bacon turned to other printers and especially to John Haviland.

[11] For Camden and Bacon see *SEH*, VI, pp. 351–64.

[12] *Un 'soldat philosophe'*, p. 92. For Boswell and Bacon's reputation see *OFB*, VI, pp. lxxii–lxxv; as preserver of Bacon manuscripts, *ibid.*, pp. lxxx–lxxxiii.

[13] See the important pioneering work by M. Le Dœuff, 'Bacon chez les grands au siècle de Louis XIII', *FBTF*, pp. 155–78. Gibson records some thirteen editions of various Bacon works, in Latin or in French translation, published in France between 1619 and 1632.

[14] *Un 'soldat philosophe'*, pp. 107–8 and 161–2.

[15] Ferretti (*ibid.*, pp. 115–16) is rightly cautious about this; an argument from silence—in this case caused by an absence of documentary evidence—leaves a lot to be desired.

La Hoguette's enthusiasm for the Chancellor, that individual was Elia Diodati (1576–1661). An important figure in the cultural organization of Europe in this period, Diodati was born in Geneva to a Protestant family of Italian origins. A great traveller, he became a one-man information exchange who forged links between members of the Dupuy circle and the scholars of Germany, the Low Countries, England and Italy. An acquaintance of Campanella's and a close friend of Galileo's, he was also one of the most important channels between English and French intellectual life. Among other things, he was responsible for the diffusion in France of Sir Philip Sidney's *Arcadia* and of Herbert of Cherbury's *De veritate*. Of more immediate interest is the fact that he tried to have a translation of Bacon's *Sylva sylvarum* prepared—a sign of unusual admiration for Bacon's writings—and much earlier, in 1619 (just before La Hoguette came into the Dupuys' orbit) Diodati, on a visit to England, had actually met the Chancellor himself.[16] In short, he was ideally placed to encourage La Hoguette's Baconianism, and Giuliano Ferretti's view is that Diodati did in fact exert a direct or indirect influence on the Frenchman's special passion.[17]

At all events, in 1622 or thereabouts La Hoguette was a frequent visitor to the Paris salon of Mme des Loges and to the *cabinet* of the brothers Dupuy, and these encounters had a profound effect on his cultural formation. There he got to know of Bacon's plans for the reform of knowledge, plans which so excited him that he decided to visit his hero at the earliest possible moment. Indeed, so strong was his impulse that by September 1623 he was already in London and reporting back to Pierre Dupuy:

After thoroughly reading and rereading the great English chancellor's book, I was overwhelmed by the desire to go and see the man himself and, just as the plan was sudden, so was its execution, only six days having passed between my embarkation at La Rochelle and my arrival here. I have only seen him once as yet, having been here only three days, and that visit was almost entirely taken up in politenesses. I have gathered very little except that he will have the first

---

[16] *Ibid.*, pp. 74–7; for Herbert's associations with Bacon and more particularly Bacon's friends see *OFB*, VI, pp. lxxii–lxxiii. Diodati was not the only man to find that translating the *Sylva sylvarum* was not a job for the faint-hearted. Jacob and Isaac Gruter had a long struggle with the work (*ibid.*, VI, pp. lxxvi–lxxvii and lxxix). For Diodati's failed plans for the *Sylva* see *BTT*, P5ʳ⁻ᵛ.

[17] *Un 'soldat philosophe'*, p. 78: 'direttamente o indirettamente l'amicizia di Diodati sembra inserirsi nel complesso di quelle influenze che rafforzarono il baconianismo di La Hoguette'. Diodati's enthusiasm for Bacon remained until the end of his life; see for instance his correspondence in *BTT*, P3ᵛ–P6ᵛ.

part of his Instauration, which he has had translated from English into Latin, printed in a month's time. I promise you a copy once it is printed to repay you for the loan of your book which I kept in Paris for such a long time.[18]

When La Hoguette left England[19] he carried with him the promised copy of the *De augmentis*; he also carried off certain Bacon manuscripts and a portrait of their author. The *De augmentis* and the portrait he received as gifts from Bacon; the manuscripts he stole from him.

La Hoguette's copy of the *De augmentis*, which came to Peiresc's notice in April 1624,[20] was unselfishly broken up by Pierre Dupuy so that it could be used as printer's copy for the Paris edition which

---

[18] La Hoguette, *Lettres*, I, p. 93: to Pierre Dupuy, London, 26 Sept. 1623, 'Aprés avoir bien leu et releu le livre du Grand chancelier d'Angleterre, il m'a pris envie de le venir voir luy mesme, et comme ce dessein fut prompt, il a esté aussy promptement executé, n'ayant esté que six jours pour venir de la Rochelle où je m'embarquey jusques icy. Je ne l'ay encore veu qu'une fois, n'y ayant que trois jours que je suis arrivé et ceste visite se passa presque toutte en complimentz. J'appriz seulement que dens un mois il feroit mettre sous la presse la premiere partie de son Instauration qu'il a faict traduire d'anglois en latin. Je vous en prometz un exemplaire quand elle sera imprimée pour vous payer l'usure du vostre, que je gardey si long temps à Paris.' This letter also appears in *Lettres inédites de Philippe Fortin de la Hoguette*, ed. Philippe Tamizey de Larroque, N. Textier: La Rochelle, 1888, pp. 30–2. All La Hoguette's letters to Pierre Dupuy are to be found in autograph and in chronological order in BN manuscript coll. Dupuy, no. 715. I have checked Ferretti's transcriptions against the originals. The transcriptions are very accurate though Ferretti silently alters some accidentals, e.g. he occasionally changes case, supplies missing accents, apostrophes, etc. I have retained Ferretti's versions of all quotations. In this particular letter it is not obvious which book La Hoguette had been reading with such assiduity but Ferretti (La Hoguette, *Lettres*, p. 94 n. 1) notes that Benjamin Prioleau, a friend of the Dupuys, recalled many years later (*c.*1665) that Bacon had composed 'un livre intitulé les Essais moraux, à l'imitation de nostre Michel de Montaigne, dont un nommé La Hoguette fut si charmé qu'il en voulut voir l'auteur, bien qu'il se fut retiré au fond de l'isle de Verulamium'. See *Entretiens familiers de feu Monsieur Priolo avec ses enfans touchant la conduite de la vie humaine, et la diversité des evenemens qui en accompagnent le cours, recueillis par M. son fils aisné*, Moulins, Bibliothèque municipale, vol. 28, fo. 280. For Bacon's *Essayes* and coll. Dupuy no. 5 see pp. lxviii–lxx below. For La Hoguette, the *De augmentis* and the preliminaries to its reception in France see pp. liii–liv below and *OFB*, VI, p. lxxiv n. 24. La Hoguette must have misunderstood Bacon in one respect: instead of going to press in October, the *De augmentis* was in fact published then. It was one of the very few works entered in the Stationers' Register after printing. It was entered on 13 Oct.; Bacon sent a presentation copy with a letter dated 22 Oct. to Buckingham; the latter replied on the 27th; see *LL*, VII, pp. 437–8. For late entry in the Register see Maureen Bell, 'Entrance in the Stationers' Register', *The Library*, 6th ser., **16**, no. 1, 1994, pp. 50–4.

[19] It is not clear how long La Hoguette's visit lasted but he cannot have left England before late October (see previous note), and must have reached the Continent before the end of April 1624, see *Un 'soldat philosophe'*, p. 160.

[20] *Lettres de Peiresc aux frères Dupuy*, ed. Philippe Tamizey de Larroque, 7 vols., Imprimerie Nationale: Paris, 1888–98, I, p. 31. It is evident that Peiresc did not know in Jan. 1624 that *DAS* had already been printed, see *OFB*, VI, p. lxxiv n. 24.

appeared in June, as a letter from a grateful Peiresc tells us.[21] As for the portrait which Bacon gave to La Hoguette, we know from Rawley[22] that just such a one had been given to a visitor and we also know that in 1625 La Hoguette had a copy made which he sent to Pierre Dupuy, 'to add to the number of famous men whose [portraits] fill your *cabinet*'. What eventually became of the copy or copies, or of the original, is unknown.[23]

La Hoguette's letter concerning the portrait was his first extant reference to Bacon after his return to France, and it is interesting to note that in the two years since his return neither he nor any of his correspondents mentioned the Bacon manuscripts which La Hoguette had carried off. Ferretti believed that La Hoguette may possibly have concealed their existence from his friends,[24] though his silence may have been because he was away soldiering during the second half of 1624, and so had no time for letters until he took up a garrison appointment at Brouage, not far from La Rochelle, early in 1625.[25] In any case, no more is heard of the

[21] *Lettres de Peiresc*, I, p. 35: Aix, 27 June 1624: 'Je vous remercie trez humblement du livre *De dignitate et augmentis scientiarum*, que j'ai receu avec la vostre du 3 juin, vous m'avez bien obligé et avez obligé tout le public de sacrifier pour sa commodité l'exemplaire que vous en aviez, car ce seroit daumage que les curieux ne peussent voir une si jolie pièce.' Also see Ferretti, *Un 'soldat philosophe'*, pp. 102–4. For this edition and Mersenne's responses to it, see 'Fortin de la Hoguette entre Francis Bacon et Marin Mersenne: critique du syllogisme et théologie: autour de l'édition française de 1624 du *De augmentis scientiarum*', in Marta Fattori, *Linguaggio e filosofia nel seicento*, Olschki: Florence, 2000 (forthcoming).
[22] This '*pictura* sua à capite ad pedes' which Bacon gave to a Frenchman is remembered in Rawley's *Vita*, see *Op*, **5ʳ (cf. *SEH*, I, p. 15).
[23] Ferretti, *Un 'soldat philosophe'*, p. 160. Also see La Hoguette, *Lettres*, I, p. 114, to Pierre Dupuy, from Brouage [south of La Rochelle], 21 Dec. 1625: 'Et pour vous recompenser du port des bagatelles que je vous escris de ce pays, la fortune a faict venir icy un assés bon paintre par qui je fays copier mon Grand chancelier que je vous veux donner pour augmenter le nombre des hommes illustres dont est rempli vostre Cabinet.' This letter also appears in *Lettres inédites*, ed. Philippe Tamizey de Larroque, p. 49. By the end of Jan. 1626 the paint had still not dried; in February it was dispatched but apparently arrived badly damaged. Dupuy had it patched up but in 1635 La Hoguette offered to send a good copy, a copy which reached Dupuy in October of that year (La Hoguette, *Lettres*, I, pp. 120, 124, 126, 134, 374, 375, 377).
[24] *Un 'soldat philosophe'*, p. 160: 'La Hoguette in effetti interrompe ogni discorso su Bacone per quasi due anni, durante i quali, forse, cela agli amici l'esistenza dei manoscritti in suo possesso.'
[25] La Hoguette had been at Breda, where his extraordinary courage attracted attention. In a letter written from London on 2 Oct. 1624, F.-A. de Thou gave Pierre Dupuy this news: 'Je n'ai point veu M. de Verulamio, je crois qu'il est aux champs. Je voudrois que M. de La Hoguette fust ici, [car] nous le verrions ensemble. J'ai veu un Allemand qui m'a dit estre devant Breda lors qu'il se battit, et que tout le monde admiroit son courage, de ce qu'estant estroppié, come vous scaves, du bras droit, il ne laissa de se battre courageusement; il dit qu'il avait ce bras si foible, qu'il estoit contraint de soustenir son espée avec le gauche, qui est une chose fort incommode' (coll. Dupuy no. 703, fo. 196ᵛ). It is worth noting that de Thou had a letter recommending him to the marquis d'Effiat, who was then French ambassador in London and

manuscripts until August 1627 when La Hoguette offered them to the Dupuy *cabinet.* The offer was not accepted. As Peiresc remarked to Pierre Dupuy,

Monsieur de La Hoguette is too kind to people as unworthy as we are. I take good care not to accept offers as honest as his, namely the offer of that sheaf of papers—which he has not had printed—by that great man Verulamius.[26]

What inspired Peiresc's irony is unknown—perhaps La Hoguette's offer had unwelcome strings attached to it or perhaps he appeared a little too condescending when he made it—but La Hoguette dropped the matter and we hear no more of the manuscripts for another two years. Once again La Hoguette was away on active service—this time involved in operations against the English at the Île de Ré and in the siege of La Rochelle[27]—but in the summer of 1629 the manuscripts reapppeared, this time at the centre of a first-class row which agitated La Hoguette and the Dupuy–Peiresc circle for some weeks.[28]

While La Hoguette was staying with Peiresc in July of that year, the latter told his guests of the impending publication of certain posthumous Bacon works. It quickly became apparent to a dumbfounded La Hoguette that these works seemed to be the very ones represented in his manuscripts and that the person planning this disreputable manoeuvre was an acquaintance of his—one Auger Granier de Mauléon (159?–post 1652)—who must either (i) have copied La Hoguette's manuscripts surreptitiously or (ii) copied copies of the same which were by that time available in the Dupuy circle.[29] Granier, a publisher, passionate collector of rare manuscripts and intimate friend of such great figures as La Mothe Le Vayer (1588–1672), arrived in Paris in the early 1620s and

another of Bacon's admirers. De Thou also carried letters from Pierre Dupuy to Turquet de Mayerne and Boswell (see *Un 'soldat philosophe'*, p. 91 n. 208), both of whom had close connections with Bacon. Here we catch sight of part of the network linking Bacon at the end of his life with Continental intellectuals and men of affairs. La Hoguette's first letter from Brouage is dated 10 Feb. 1625. After leaving London he seems to have spent the first half of 1624 in The Hague, see La Hoguette, *Lettres,* I, pp. 95–100.

[26] *Lettres de Peiresc,* I, pp. 319–20, to Pierre Dupuy, Aix, 10 Aug. 1627: 'Monsieur de la Hoguette est trop obligeant à des personnes qui en sont si indignes comme nous. Je n'ay garde d'accepter de si honnestes offres que les siennes, ouy bien un roole des pieces qu'il a non imprimées de ce grand personnage Verulanius.' Also see *Un 'soldat philosophe'*, p. 164.

[27] When the English descended on the Île de Ré, La Hoguette was still based a few miles south at Brouage, so it was quite natural that he was among the first to be involved in the French efforts to dislodge these uninvited guests. He was engaged in operations there and at La Rochelle from July 1627 until Jan. 1629, see *Un 'soldat philosophe'*, pp. 109–14.

[28] *Un 'soldat philosophe'*, pp. 117–18.

[29] *Ibid.,* pp. 122–3; *Lettres de Peiresc,* II, p. 150, to Pierre Dupuy, Aix, 11 Aug. 1629.

quickly became a familiar of the Dupuy *cabinet*. His reputation eventually brought him membership of the fledgeling Académie Française in 1635, from which august body he was expelled in the following year for swindling money out of the Carmelites. For this transgression Granier betook himself as a penitent to the cloister, where he remained for the rest of his days.[30]

La Hoguette's friendship with Granier seems to have begun in the mid-1620s, but was not destined to last. Although La Hoguette had assisted Granier in a number of ways, the latter (with the deplorable want of probity which eventually undid him) failed to repay a debt (1628) he owed to La Hoguette.[31] Worse still, he worked against La Hoguette's attempts (1630–1) to secure a lieutenancy for his nephew in the Sainte-Foy garrison.[32] Relations between the two men never recovered.[33] Granier's behaviour over the lieutenancy may have sprung from resentment actuated by La Hoguette's success in using the good offices of Peiresc and Pierre Dupuy to frustrate Granier's plans for the manuscripts. Early in July 1629 La Hoguette's fury persuaded Peiresc to intervene on his behalf with Pierre Dupuy:

M. de La Hoguette was a bit surprised when I told him that M. Granier was thinking of publishing these writings of Chancellor Bacon, and he told me that he would write to you about it to beg you to put a stop to it, judging that it would be intolerable to prostitute the good name of an author who trusted him and only gave him materials which were rough and not thoroughly worked up. I have advised him that this could partially be put right by a letter to the reader which admitted the theft and the manner in which it took place, but he is not falling for it and I think that you would make him very happy if you prevented this attempt.[34]

But in late July La Hoguette was still furious and was now thinking, as Peiresc reported to Dupuy, of working on the manuscripts—no doubt

[30] La Hoguette, *Lettres*, II, pp. 838–9.

[31] *Ibid.*, I, pp. 211–12: to Pierre Dupuy, Nieul, 17 Apr. 1628.

[32] *Ibid.*, I, pp. 280–1, 281–2, 283, 288–9, letters to Pierre and Jacques Dupuy, from Brouage and Blaye 17 Nov. 1630–11 Nov. 1631.

[33] *Ibid.*, II, pp. 838–9. Also see *Un 'soldat philosophe'*, pp. 122–3 n. 316.

[34] *Lettres de Peiresc*, II, p. 126: to P. Dupuy, Aix, 7 July 1629. 'M^r de La Hoguette fut un peu surpris quand je luy dis que Mr Granier songeoit à donner au public cez escripts du chancellier Baccon, et me dit qu'il vous en escriroit pour vous conjurer de l'empescher, n'estimant pas que cela soit tollerable pour ne prostituer la reputation de l'autheur, qui s'en estoit fié à luy et ne luy avoit baillé que des choses informes et non digérées. Je luy ay remonstré que cela se pouvoit aulcunement reparer par un advertissement au lecteur qui tesmoignast le larrecin en la forme qu'il a esté faict, mais il ne s'en paye pas, et crois que vous luy ferez grand plaisir d'empescher ce coup là.'

with a view to publishing them himself[35]—a plan which he abandoned not long after. A month later and still unappeased, he wrote to Pierre Dupuy to complain about the latter's putative dealings in the matter:

I have not written to you at all since I was at Aix where I forgot—that is how good my memory is—the main thing that made me write. And that was to complain to you about what Monsieur de Peiresc told me, namely that you had gone along with Monsieur de Granier's demands to have the things I stole from the great chancellor printed, things which I wanted to pass on only to the aforesaid Master Peiresc and also to you if that is what you wanted.

It is a piece of work fragmented and disordered which I took from a larger document, and a piece of work which would charge the originator as a thief and whoever had it printed with impertinence. It would not matter if only my reputation were at stake, but so much do I honour the author's that if it is true that the aforementioned Master Granier has pulled this trick on me, I shall never forgive him. I am greatly shocked that this has come about with your assistance. In question is your superabundant goodness, against which I say nothing seeing that I go nowhere without finding that the very mention of your name always brings me some advantage or other.[36]

This letter seems to have had the desired effect. We do not know what influence or pressure Dupuy used to stop it but Granier's scheme sank without trace.

Now the Granier affair had the effect of awakening Peiresc's curiosity about the manuscripts and so he obtained copies of them from La Hoguette or Pierre Dupuy, and in January 1630 wrote to the latter suggesting that he had previously underestimated their importance:

---

[35] *Lettres de Peiresc*, II, pp. 136–7: to P. Dupuy, Aix, 21 July 1629: 'Le pauvre Mr de la Hoguette est en grande colere contre Mr Granier pour les fragments du chancellier Baccon, sur lesquels il vouloit travailler luy mesmes, à ce que j'ay peu comprendre, en ce voyage de la cour, où je l'ay reveu.' La Hoguette still had this plan in mind in early August, see *ibid.*, II, p. 150: to P. Dupuy, Aix, 11 Aug. 1629: 'je descouvris que le dict sieur de la Hoguette avoit quelque dessein d'y travailler à son loisir, s'il en pouvoit trouver la commodité'.

[36] La Hoguette, *Lettres*, I, pp. 253–4: to P. Dupuy, Montauban, 20 Aug. 1629: 'Je ne vous ay point escript depuis Aix où j'oublié le principal subject qui m'obligea de prendre la plume tant j'ay la memoire bonne. C'estoit pour me plaindre de vous de ce que monsieur de Peirest [i.e. Peiresc] m'avoit dict que vous aviés acordé à l'importunitté de monsieur de Granier de faire imprimer le larcin que j'avois faict au Grand chancelier, que je voulois seulement communiquer à mondit sieur de Peirest et à vous si vous en aviés envie.

C'est un ouvrage descousu et sans ordre que j'avois desrobé d'une plus grand pièce qui fera accuser l'autheur de larron et celuy qui le faict imprimer d'impertinence. Patience s'il n'y alloit que de ma reputation, mais j'honore tellement celle de l'autheur, que s'il est vray que mondit sieur de Granier m'ait faict ceste surprise, je ne luy puis jamais pardonner. Je m'estonne fort comme elle s'est faitte par vostre ministere. L'excés de vostre bonté en est cause, contre laquelle je n'ay rien à dire, puisque je ne me trouve en lieu du monde où je ne rencontre quelque faveur en vostre nom.'

I did not reflect on Chancellor Bacon's drafts as I should have done, drafts which deserve attention and greater thanks than I know how to make to M. de La Hoguette and to you for the trouble, begging you to convey my thanks to him when you see him next and to assure him that I am entirely at his service.[37]

But with Granier blocked, and when La Hoguette had convinced others of the importance of the manuscripts, he finally decided not to publish them—as he soon told Pierre Dupuy:

I am reading attentively my manuscripts of my great chancellor, which are a bottomless pit of knowledge. They are very accurate and I shall bring them to Paris with me to communicate them to our friends alone, without having them printed.[38]

In the years after this decision we find but two references to Bacon in La Hoguette's correspondence, one in 1632 asking Pierre Dupuy to send him any new Baconiana that came his way, and another in 1647 referring to Bacon's *Henry VII*.[39] In fact after 1630 the Bacon manuscripts were

[37] *Lettres de Peiresc*, II, p. 217: to P. Dupuy, Boisgency, 17 Jan. 1630: 'Je n'ay pas non plus considéré comme il fault les cahiers du chancelier Baccon, qui meritent de l'attention, et de plus grands remerciements que je n'en sçaurois faire à Mr de la Hoguette et à vous aussy de la peine, vous suppliant de les luy faire de ma part à la première veüe, et l'assurer que je suis tout à luy.' Also see *Un 'soldat philosophe'*, pp. 166–7.

[38] La Hoguette, *Lettres*, I, p. 264: to P. Dupuy, Brouage, 27 Oct. 1630: 'Je lis avec attention mes manuscripts de mon Grand chancelier, qui sont un abisme de science. Ilz sont fort correctz et les emporterey à Paris avec moy pour les communiquer à nos amis seulement, sans les faire imprimer.' Ferretti rightly notes (*ibid.*, p. 265 n. 3) that after 'communiquer' the words 'en faire part' have been crossed out. The word 'abisme' is difficult to render into modern English but is almost certainly an echo of Rabelais, see Paul Céard, 'Encyclopédie et encyclopédisme à la Renaissance', in *L'Encyclopédisme: actes du colloque de Caen 12–16 janvier 1987*, ed. Annie Becq, Éditions Klincksieck: Paris, 1991, pp. 57–67, at p. 57: 'la célèbre lettre du chapitre VIII de *Pantagruel*, et la fameuse phrase qui la conclut: "Somme, que je voye un abisme de science." On est, du reste, d'autant plus fondé à citer cette page que c'est dans *Pantagruel* que se lit pour le premier fois en français le mot d'*encyclopédie*: au terme de la "dispute" où s'affrontent Thaumaste et Panurge, le premier affirme que le second, disciple de Pantagruel, lui a "ouvert le vraye puys et abisme de encyclopédie." ' The Urquhart and Motteux translation gives the first of these instances as, 'In brief, let me see thee an abyss, and bottomless pit of knowledge.' It may be that La Hoguette's decision not to publish may have been to avoid exposing himself as a thief, but such delicacy was rare in his age—consider, for instance, what Isaac Vossius did with Queen Christina's Rudolphine heritage (see S. Åkerman, 'The forms of Queen Christina's academies', in *The shapes of knowledge from the Renaissance to the Enlightenment*, ed. D. R. Kelley and R. H. Popkin (Archives Internationales d'Histoire des Idées 124), Kluwer Academic Publishers: Dordrecht, Boston, and London, 1991, pp. 165–88, at pp. 178–9).

[39] La Hoguette, *Lettres*, I, p. 301: to Pierre Dupuy, Blaye, 4 July 1632: 'Le Grand chancelier me faict bonne compagnie. Si vous aviés de luy quelque chose de nouveau, vous m'obligeriés fort de me l'envoier pour me divertir quelque temps, car mon admiration pour luy s'augmente tousjours.' *Ibid.*, II, p. 539: to Jacques Dupuy, Chamouillac, 17 Mar. 1647: 'Mon Grand

never mentioned again and a 350-year silence descended upon them until Peter Beal announced in 1980 that he had discovered what later turned out to be a copy of La Hoguette's loot in the Bibliothèque Nationale.

(*b*) The Bacon Manuscripts of Messieurs Dupuy

Beal was the first to discover witnesses to the texts that concern us in manuscript BN fonds français no. 4745.[40] His discovery was the prelude to others. I obtained a microfilm of the manuscript in 1982, began work on a transcription and translation and, in March 1984, gave a preliminary account of the manuscript at a colloquium held in Rome.[41] However, in the winter of that year, while staying with friends in Rome, I was introduced by Prof. Marta Fattori to Giuliano Ferretti, who gave me a convincing account of how the Bacon manuscripts had reached the Bibliothèque Nationale and told me that he had discovered a manuscript unrecorded by Beal from which fonds français no. 4745 seemed to have been copied. Ferretti was right.

Fonds français no. 4745 runs to some 218 folios. Drafted throughout in a neat seventeenth-century French hand on paper from a single manufacturer, only the final folio is not uniform with the rest, having presumably been bound with the others at a later date.[42] The volume, a miscellaneous collection, contains almost all the items in coll. Dupuy no. 5,[43] and in the same order. The copyist who prepared fonds français no. 4745 was evidently employed by its original owner Pierre Séguier (1588–1672)—a collector of Bacon texts—to perform a routine scribal chore. The copyist's work is inaccurate and, from a textual-critical point of view, has no authority whatever.[44]

chancelier remarque que Herry [*sic*] septiesme, roy d'Angleterre, commençoit tous ses traittés de paix par ceste preface: Que c'est un bien qui fust annoncé par les anges quand Jesus Christ vint au monde, et dont il fist luy mesme un legat à ses apostres quand il en sortit.'

[40] *IELM*, Bcf 286, BcF 295, BcF 296.

[41] 'Bacon's philosophy: some new sources with special reference to the *Abecedarium novum naturae*', *FBTF*, pp. 223–44.

[42] The piece, an account of the visit of Anne of Austria and the little Louis XIV to the parlement of Paris, is dated 1645 and is drafted in a hand different from the one that appears in the rest of the volume.

[43] Ferretti (*Un 'soldat philosophe'*, p. 170 n. 52) discovered the manuscript in the summer of 1982.

[44] *Ibid.*, p. 170; also see Le Dœuff, 'Bacon chez les grands', p. 163: 'Notons d'ailleurs que c'est aussi de la bibliothèque de Pierre Séguier que proviennent les Manuscrits Fr 17874 et Fr 19092 de la Bibliothèque Nationale, contenant le premier une traduction de deux *Essays* ("de la religion", "de la superstition"), le second des traductions de la préface de l'*Instauratio Magna*, de l'épître dédicatoire au roi Jacques, de la *Distributio Operis*, et du *Novum Organum* (préface,

Coll. Dupuy no. 5 belongs to the massive collection of manuscripts assembled by the Dupuys during the second quarter of the seventeenth century. No. 5 was put together in 1633 by Pierre Dupuy who endorsed it 'Mémoires & discours sur diuerses matieres VI'. It begins with a letter written by Guillaume du Vair to Peiresc.[45] This letter is followed by the group of Bacon pieces and then by a large number of miscellaneous tracts, state papers, letters and legal documents drafted in a variety of hands on paper originating from many different sources. All the items in this volume are mounted on guards. The Bacon group—related to the other papers by nothing more than physical proximity—is as follows:

1. *Historia & inquisitio de animato & inanimato* (fos. 3ʳ–5ᵛ).
2. An untitled early version of the *Historia densi & rari* (fos. 7ʳ–23ᵛ).
3. *Abecedarium nouum naturæ* (fos. 24ʳ–37ᵛ).
4. *Des miracles de nostre sauueur*—a French translation of an English version of the second of Bacon's *Meditationes sacræ* (1597)—(fo. 38ʳ).
5. Italian translations of the essays 'Of Religion' and 'Of Superstition' (fo. 39ʳ⁻ᵛ).
6. French translations of the same two essays (fo. 40ʳ⁻ᵛ).

I begin with the first three items on the list. But first a warning: the facts that these unique manuscripts slumber in the Dupuy collections and that certain manuscripts were stolen from Bacon by La Hoguette do not of course mean that any or all of the former are necessarily the same as or copies of the latter. But I will return to this question later.[46]

However, if these manuscripts were indeed La Hoguette's or copies of them, the manuscript of the *Historia & inquisitio* may be all that it left of La Hoguette's original booty. Ferretti was unable to identify the hand but noted that hands of this type were not unusual among the correspondents of the Dupuy circle.[47] My own view is that the hand could just as well be English and possibly that of a scribe employed by Bacon himself. The letter forms, flow and general appearance are comparable with hands represented in manuscripts prepared for and corrected by

livre I, et début du livre II).' For the two essays mentioned by Le Dœuff see pp. lxvii–lxix below. The hand that drafted fonds français no. 4745 seems to be the same that appears in a copy of a French book inventory in BL Harley 7017 (fos. 353ʳ–59ᵛ). Harley 7017 also contains various Bacon papers, some of them holograph.

[45] Fos. 1ʳ–2ʳ. [46] pp. lxviii–lxx below.

[47] *Un 'soldat philosophe'*, p. 171 n. 58: 'Questo tipo di scrittura è ricorrente nel gruppo dei corrispondenti del *cabinet* Dupuy. È perciò probabile che un'ulteriore indagine possa condurre a identificarne l'autore.' Ferretti has told me (personal communication, 15 Apr. 1989) that the photograph of the first page of *HIDA* in *Un 'soldat philosophe'* (p. 310) has a caption which wrongly identifies the script as Nicolas Rigault's.

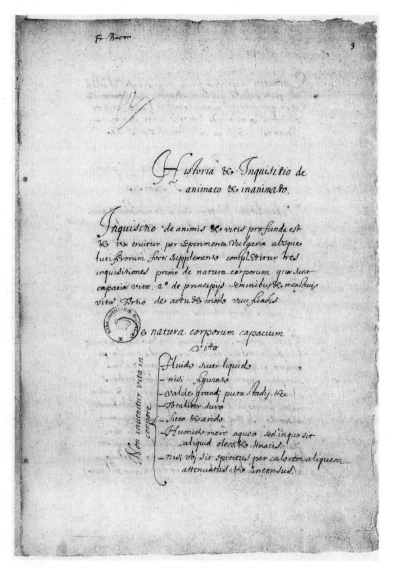

I　*Historia de animato*, BN coll. Dupuy no. 5, fo. 3ʳ
(reduced)—unidentified hand

Bacon,[48] and the manuscript's accidentals are consistent with English origins[49] but, be that as it may, no evidence currently available settles this question.

Examination of the paper sheds no light on the matter. The leaves (fos. 3–6) all measure approximately 308 × 210mm with vertical chain-lines at intervals of 21mm. The watermark is a potmark;[50] I examined this mark in white and ultraviolet light but was unable to make out some of the detail and, unfortunately, the Bibliothèque Nationale no longer offers beta-radiography among its many excellent services. However, it cannot be the case that the text was drafted on what were once two sheets of paper folded in half and quired together. The fact that the potmark appears only on fo. 3, and not on any of the others, means that while it is theoretically possible that folios 3 and 6 may once have been conjugate, no two of fos. 4, 5 and 6 (even though once belonging to sheets from the same pair of moulds) can ever have been conjugate for none bears the potmark.

There can be no doubt about who made the copies of the coll. Dupuy no. 5 *Historia densi* and *Abecedarium*. The individual in question was, as Ferretti has convincingly demonstrated, the young Dupuys' tutor and their predecessor as Garde de la Bibliothèque du Roi, Nicolas Rigault (1577–1654). In his time as Garde de la Bibliothèque, Rigault made his mark by preparing a comprehensive catalogue of its holdings and carrying out other reforms which marked important stages in the library's institutionalization.[51] But Rigault was much more than a first-rate librarian. He was also a lawyer and literary man and was not only a prominent public servant but a translator (Martial and Minucius Felix), historian (he wrote a continuation of de Thou's *Historiarum sui temporis*) and biographer (of Pierre Dupuy). His autograph occurs in other coll. Dupuy manuscripts and it is identical to that which drafted our two Bacon pieces,[52] though there is no mention whatever of the Bacon

---

[48] For instance, *IELM*, BcF 287, BcF 289, BcF 294, BcF 306. For the hand of *HIDA* see Plate I.

[49] The *HIDA* scribe generally used less punctuation (1 : 17 words), fewer diacritical marks (1 : 122 words), fewer capitals (1 : 16 words) and fewer contractions (1 : 82 words) than Bacon or scribes who are known to have worked under his supervision would have done (see *OFB*, VI, pp. 460–6). But orthography and certain forms of contraction (viuifica*tio*nis. Viuifica-*tio*nes, and na*tura*—with the editorial italics represented in each case by a single superscript vertical flourish) are absolutely consistent with the practices of Bacon's scribes.

[50] Similar to Briquet 12570 but slightly wider.

[51] Balayé, *La Bibliothèque Nationale*, pp. 57–60, 62, 102. For Rigault's hand see Plate II.

[52] *Un 'soldat philosophe'*, p. 172 n. 59. For Rigault's handwriting see, for instance, coll. Dupuy no. 835, fos. 40ʳ–43ᵛ.

II *Abecedarium nouum naturæ*, BN coll. Dupuy no. 5, fo. 24ʳ
(reduced)—Rigault's hand

manuscripts in Rigault's extensive correspondence.[53] All the same, it is probable that Rigault made the copies of the Bacon pieces directly from La Hoguette's originals, and made them in the period between October 1630 when, as we have seen, La Hoguette said he was going to bring his loot to Paris, and November 1633 when Rigault left Paris to take up official duties in Alsace.[54]

If all this be true it means that the manuscripts of the *Historia & inquisitio*, the *Abecedarium*, and *Historia densi* are not the copies of the La Hoguette manuscripts acquired by Granier and Peiresc. Ferretti had a good look for these in the Bibliothèque Nationale and in the Peiresc holdings at Aix-en-Provence and Carpentras but failed to find any trace of them. He also searched for the originals brought to France by La Hoguette and any copies that may have been made by the Dupuys themselves. These too, with the possible exception of the *Historia & inquisitio* manuscript, which as I have said may have been one of La Hoguette's originals, have vanished without trace.[55]

Physical examination of the paper used by Rigault indicates that he may not have copied the *Historia densi* and *Abecedarium* at the same time. In fact, as it stands, Rigault's copy may be artefact-creating, i.e. the quality and colour of the paper and the uniformity of Rigault's hand may deceive us into thinking that he copied first the one work and then went on straight away to copy the other. The physical evidence suggests that each piece was copied separately, perhaps on quite different occasions and perhaps (though this is mere guesswork) from two quite different exemplars rather than from a single original. Indeed, we have to bear in mind the possibility that the two copies may only have come together when coll. Dupuy no. 5 was assembled. Papers from two different sources were used for the copy of the *Historia densi*. Folios 7 to 10 measure 308 × 210mm with vertical chain-lines at 21mm intervals, and two of the four leaves bear a distinctive heraldic eagle as a watermark.[56] The remaining thirteen leaves (fos. 11–12) measure on average 338 × 235mm; they have vertical chain-lines at 19mm intervals; and seven leaves bear

[53] *Un 'soldat philosophe'*, p. 173 n. 61. There is no direct evidence that Rigault and La Hoguette knew one another but it is difficult to believe that two individuals so intimately associated with the Dupuy *cabinet* can have failed to meet. It is noteworthy that one of La Hoguette's letters of 1626 is preserved in the Dupuy archive in a copy made by Rigault, see La Hoguette, *Lettres*, I, pp. 140–1.

[54] *Un 'soldat philosophe'*, p. 174.   [55] *Ibid.*, pp. 168–9.

[56] Similar to Briquet no. 216. My thanks to Maria Wakely for making out the shape in the original.

the same watermark—a small 27mm-high bunch of grapes.[57] One cannot be certain that Rigault drafted his copy on leaves which were originally conjugate, but the watermark sequences in the two distinct kinds
of paper used for the task does suggest that he may have worked on
uncut sheets either folded in half and unquired or quired together in
twos or in threes.[58]

The paper used for drafting the *Abecedarium* is quite different. It
emanated from a single pair of moulds. The leaves measure approximately 320 × 210mm and they all have vertical chain-lines set at 24mm
intervals. Seven of the fourteen leaves carry identical watermarks of the
type which Gaudriaut calls a '*cornet sur écu simplifié, couronné*'.[59] As
there are seven leaves with watermarks and seven without, it is reasonable to assume that, although now disjunct, all are halves of seven single
sheets—sheets which were either folded in half and used separately or
quired together in one way or another.[60] In any event it is quite striking
that the two makes of paper on which the *Historia densi* was drafted are
quite different from the single make represented in the *Abecedarium*.
Had the copying of the two works proceeded as a single uninterrupted
task we might expect an overlap, i.e. expect papers appearing in the one
work also to appear in the other. The fact that the papers change with
the works is unlikely to be mere coincidence. More likely is the hypothesis that the two works were copied at different times within the three-
year period during which Rigault could have had access to them.

Rigault's transcriptions of the *Historia densi* and *Abecedarium* must
have differed in detail from the ultimate source of his exemplars; but
since we do not know what his exemplars were—Bacon holograph,

---

[57] This kind of watermark in this and other sizes is, of course, extremely common in papers
of this period.

[58] Of the first kind of paper used in *HDR(M)*, fos. 8 and 10 carry the watermark; 7 and 9
do not. Of the second kind, fos. 11, 14, 15, 17, 20, 21 and 23 have the watermark; 12, 13, 16, 18,
19 and 22 do not. If one assumes that the final leaf was once conjugate with a blank leaf no
longer extant, then the remaining leaves could have been conjugate and unquired or made up
of sheets quired in 2s; leaves of the second kind could have been made up of sheets quired in
2s or 3s; none of the leaves could have belonged to sheets quired in 4s or 5s.

[59] Raymond Gaudriault, *Filigranes et autres caractéristiques des papiers fabriqués en France
aux XVIIᵉ et XVIIIᵉ siècles*, CNRS Éditions: Paris, 1995, items 394 and 395.

[60] Folios 25, 26, 29, 31, 32, 35, and 37 carry the cornet watermark; fols. 24, 27, 28, 30, 33, 34,
and 36 do not. This sequence is consistent with several hypotheses: that the sheets were quired
in two gatherings of three with a single folded sheet at the end, or quired in one quinternion
again with a single folded sheet at the end, or that Rigault took separate sheets from a pile and
folded each individually as his task progressed. The sequence excludes possibilities involving
sheets quired in twos or fours. The sequence is such that it makes the hypothesis that Rigault
was working from a pile of sheets already cut in half rather unlikely.

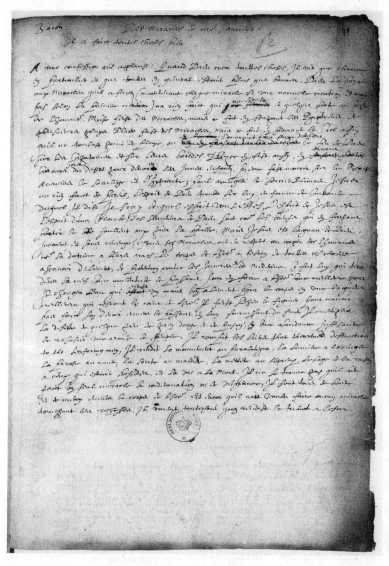

III *Les miracles de nostre sauueur*, BN coll. Dupuy no. 5, fo. 38ʳ
(reduced)—La Hoguette's hand

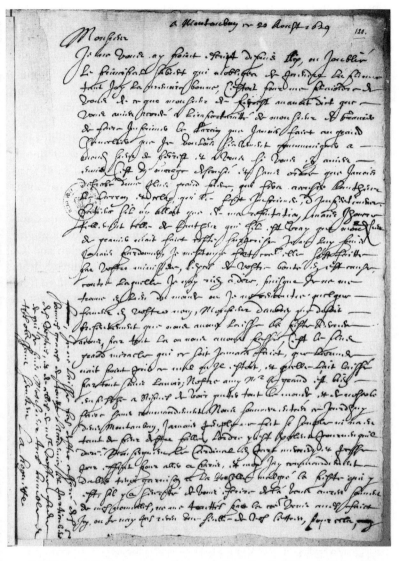

IV BN coll. Dupuy no. 715, fo. 120ʳ (reduced)—La Hoguette's hand

Bacon scribe, or copies of these more or less removed from their originals—it is difficult to judge how faithfully Rigault dealt with them. In the matter of substantives Rigault's versions, in so far as they can be checked against other authoritative witnesses, seem to be reasonably accurate and sometimes coincide exactly with these witnesses for hundreds of words together. Differences between the witnesses and the Rigault versions can more plausibly be attributed to differences in the manuscript traditions that led to them than to inaccuracy on Rigault's part.[61] In the matter of accidentals Rigault's versions are certainly quite different from anything that Bacon or his scribes would have produced. The relative lack of diacritical marks and contractions, and an idiosyncratic distaste for initial capitals in the Rigault drafts make that abundantly clear.[62]

I turn now to the other Bacon items which, in coll. Dupuy no. 5, follow the three already considered, namely *Des miracles de nostre sauueur* and the French and Italian translations of the two 'Of Religion' and 'Of Superstition'. *Des miracles* seems to have been translated directly from the English version that appeared in editions of the *Essayes* printed from 1613 onwards—the scattered English phrases in the text suggest as much—and the hand is undoubtedly La Hoguette's, and he perhaps prepared the text for his own use when he visited England.[63] The paper of this piece (fo. 38) seems to have come from the same batch as that (fo. 39) which carries the Italian translations of the two essays—a fact that seems to suggest that the translations belonged to La Hoguette. However, these two folios cannot have been conjugate,[64] the two essays are not drafted in La Hoguette's hand or, indeed, any hand hitherto identified, and an obvious dittographical lapse on folio 39^r indicates that the translations may be fair copies of another manuscript exemplar no longer extant.[65]

---

[61] The witnesses are of course *HDR* and the *BTT* fragment of *ANN*. For remarks on the relationship between *ANN* and the *BTT* fragment see pp. lxxii–lxxiii below and *tns* to *ANN*, fos. 35^v–37^r, pp. 214–24 below. Differences between *HDR(M)* and *HDR* are recorded in the the *tns* to the former.

[62] This editor has had to supply some 210 initial capitals in *HDR(M)* alone. For the practices of Bacon and his scribes see *OFB*, VI, pp. 460–6. Rigault's use of larger characters for some section headings of *HDR(M)* may echo his exemplar or Bacon's own practice, see p. xxxii above.

[63] *Un 'soldat philosophe'*, pp. 174–5. Any doubts about the identity of the writer of *Des miracles* may be dispelled by comparing a reproduction of a holograph La Hoguette letter (*Un 'soldat philosophe'*, p. 10) with the reproduction of *Des miracles* (Plates III and IV above).

[64] Fols. 38 and 39 measure 334 × 235 and have chain-lines set at 20mm intervals. They cannot have been conjugate because both bear the same watermark, a bunch of grapes which measures some 36 × 18mm.

The French translations of the two essays seem to have a more transparent history. The papers of two leaves that carry them (fos. 40 and 41) and the blank leaf that follows them (fo. 42) all belong to the same batch, a batch different from any others in coll. Dupuy no. 5.[66] They are in Jacques Dupuy's hand and he seems to have translated them in 1624. By April of that year Peiresc was hoping to copy them, and by June the Jacques Dupuy autographs had been sent to him for that purpose. The copies are to be found in the Peiresc papers at Carpentras; they are in the hand of Peiresc's brother Valavez. The originals were returned to Paris.[67]

Why were these two essays translated and why into Italian and French? I think that Jacques Dupuy's French translations are based on the Italian and that the Italian were prepared because in its various forms the published Italian translation (1617–18) of the 1612 *Essayes* omitted 'Of Religion' and 'Of Superstition'—no doubt because they contained matter that might have been offensive to an Italian audience.[68] In addition, the French translation of the 1612 *Essayes*, Baudoin's of 1619, was based not on the original English but on the Italian translation just mentioned and accordingly it also lacked the two essays that appear in the Dupuy

---

[65] On line 21 the first three words of the phrase 'duna colomba farlo scendere' are repeated after the fourth. The repeated words are crossed out and the words 'a la somiglianza' inserted above them.

[66] They measure 330 × 215mm with chain-lines 20mm apart; fo. 41 carries the large B watermark which, according to Gaudriault, belonged to the La Bé family of Troyes whose members manufactured paper from about 1551 to 1647, see *Filigranes et autres caractéristiques*, esp. item 742.

[67] *Un 'soldat philosophe'*, pp. 102–4 and 171. Also see *Lettres de Peiresc*, I, pp. 31–2: Peiresc to P. Dupuy, Aix, 28 Apr. 1624: 'Je vous felicite la jouyssance de ce bel ouvrage du Chancelier d'Angleterre du progrez des sciences et me console au moings mal que je peus en attendant que ceux de Paris se resolvent enfin de le contrefaire comme ils doivent. Et vouldrois bien que vous eussiez desia persuadé quelqu'un pour la traduction de son Henry VII. C'est daumage que ce ne soit plustost le VIII. Combien qu'encores y aura il de quoy remarquer de grandes revolutions dans le VIIIᵉ. Nous attendrons le supplement de ces deux chappittres des Essays moraux.' *Lettres de Peiresc*, I, p. 35: Aix, 27 June 1624: 'J'ay pareillement veu le supplement de ses Essaix moraulx et vous r'envoye vostre autographe aprez vous en avoir rendu mes remerciments.' The Valavez copies are in the Bibliothèque Inguimbertine, Peiresc manuscrit 1789, fos. 44ʳ–46ʳ: 'Supplément de deux chappitres du livre des Essaies Moraux de F. Bacon de Verulamio, chancelier d'Angleterre, traduictz de l'anglois. De la religion, De la superstition.'

[68] For the complicated history of this translation (Gibson, nos. 33–40) see *Ess*, pp. lxxxviii–lxxxix nn. 80–2; Noel Malcolm, *De Dominis (1560–1624): Venetian, Anglican, ecumenist and relapsed heretic*, Strickland & Scott Academic Publications: London, 1984, pp. 47–54. Malcolm sidelines Tobie Matthew, who has traditionally been credited with the translation, and argues that William Cavendish, future second earl of Devonshire, did the work and that de Dominis may have had a role in the translation's revision.

manuscript.[69] Jacques Dupuy and Peiresc evidently did not know of the other French translation of the *Essayes*, namely Gorges' of 1619 which did contain renderings of 'Of Religion' and 'Of Superstition', though these are quite different from the ones prepared by Dupuy.[70]

(*c*) The Manuscript Copy-Texts: Final Considerations

To complete the account of the manuscript copy-texts we still have two jobs to do: (i) we must satisfy ourselves that the texts in coll. Dupuy are one and the same as (or copies of) La Hoguette's booty; for the correspondence of La Hoguette, the Dupuys, or Peiresc *never* actually mentions the titles of any of La Hoguette's Bacon pieces; and (ii) as the Dupuy version of the *Abecedarium* is not the sole witness to the text—a published fragment of the work also exists—we must investigate the relationship between that fragment and the manuscript.

As for (i) we need do little more than bring out points implicit in evidence already presented:

1. The Granier affair shows that, whatever La Hoguette's changeable descriptions of his loot, everyone associated with it recognized sooner or later that the Bacon pieces were substantial and coherent enough to be worth publishing, and that La Hoguette himself thought of publishing the texts. That recognition is perfectly consistent with the character of the coll. Dupuy texts which, though not on the scale of (say) the *Novum organum*, are nevertheless more than rough drafts, lists of notes, or disorganized jottings. They are more like La Hoguette's 'abisme de science' than fragments 'sans ordre'.[71]

[69] For Baudoin's translation (Gibson, nos. 44, 45, 46) see *Un 'soldat philosophe'*, 96 ff.; M. Le Dœuff, 'Bacon chez les grands', pp. 155–78; also see Marta Fattori, 'Fortin de la Hoguette', pp. 13–17; H. F. Kynaston-Snell, *Jean Baudoin et les* Essais *de Bacon en France jusqu'au XVIII*[e] *siècle*, Jouve: Paris, 1939.

[70] Copies of Jacques Dupuy's translations can also be found in BN manuscrit fonds français 17874, fos. 144[r]–145[r]. These copies came from one of the most substantial private libraries assembled in 17th-cent. France, the library of Jean Séguier (1588–1672), chancelier de France, duc de Villemor and one of the new political class whose members were among Bacon's earliest and most influential admirers, see p. lix–lx n. 44 above.

[71] La Hoguette's contrary descriptions of his manuscripts look very much like tactical responses to changing circumstances and an underlying reluctance to publish his acquisitions. His references to 'roole des pieces', 'fragments', 'cahiers', 'un ouvrage descousu et sans ordre' and 'un abisme de science' which was 'fort correctz' (see p. lvii n. 36, p. lviii n. 38 above) are inconsistent, though the last of these descriptions seems to be his most considered verdict. But the bottomless pit was also something 'que j'avois desrobé d'une plus grand pièce' (p. lvii n. 36 above). This larger collection of materials could have comprised much of Bacon's manuscript materials for Parts 3 and 4 of *IM*, and La Hoguette may just have removed and retained the closing 'cahiers' (gatherings or loose papers). Bacon was in the habit of keeping manuscript books bundled up with loose papers relating to them, see *OFB*, VI, p. lxxxiv.

2. Pierre Dupuy compiled the volume containing the Bacon pieces in 1633, i.e. a decade after La Hoguette's visit to England and three years after his decision to bring his manuscripts to Paris but not to have them published. Two of the Latin works in coll. Dupuy no. 5 are copies made by Rigault, who was available to prepare them in the period 1630–3. Rigault had close associations with the Dupuy brothers and links of some sort with La Hoguette.[72] The copyist was in the right place at the right time, and, like La Hoguette, was an intimate of the Dupuys. If Rigault's exemplars of the *Historia densi* and *Abecedarium* did not come directly or indirectly from La Hoguette's hoard, we have to dream up an alternative set of lost exemplars with yet another history, but a history which left no trace in the correspondence of Rigault, the Dupuys or of La Hoguette, who (with his deep admiration for the great Chancellor) would certainly have got to hear of them if they had existed. This alternative is neither plausible nor economical.

3. It would be an astonishing coincidence if texts not brought to France by La Hoguette just happened to end up with a text (the translation of part of an English version of *Meditationes sacræ*) which La Hoguette himself produced and on paper which links it to the Italian translations of 'Of Religion' and 'Of Superstition' on which Jacques Dupuy based his French versions.

4. The Latin works in coll. Dupuy no. 5 existed only in manuscript when La Hoguette visited England; they were all begun not long before his visit and one, the *Historia densi*, was work in progress during it. Had they been published before his visit or written after it, then he would or could not have taken the texts to France.[73] Conversely, if texts in coll. Dupuy were not La Hoguette's, why do they all just happen to be datable to about the time of his trip to England?

In short, while it is an inescapable fact that all these arguments are based on *circumstantial* evidence, the arguments and evidence are such that it would be quite unreasonable to set them aside and admit a genuine possibility that the coll. Dupuy manuscripts were not derived from La Hoguette's.

---

[72] These links are not to be inferred merely from the fact that Rigault and La Hoguette were both habitués of the Dupuy *cabinet*. In La Hoguette's correspondence there exists a letter written in 1626—apparently addressed to Jean de Rechignevoisin de Guron, Governor of Brouage—and copied by Rigault not long afterwards. For this letter and the circumstances of its production see La Hoguette, *Lettres*, I, pp. 140–1.

[73] With one or two exceptions (e.g. *Henry the Seventh*), manuscripts of works published in Bacon's lifetime have not survived, and in any case why would La Hoguette have stolen what he knew to have been published?

(ii) As for the relationship between the coll. Dupuy *Abecedarium* and the printed fragment mentioned a moment ago, the latter was among the Bacon manuscripts inherited from William Rawley by Archbishop Tenison (1636–1715), who published them in 1679. The fragment reproduces some of the materials to be found at the very end of the Dupuy version (fos. 35^r–37^v) and, although it is a very good check on the reliability of the latter, I believe that the fragment is all that remains of an earlier draft of the work than the one represented in the Dupuy version. Where the two texts overlap, they differ in a few very trivial ways, e.g. the Dupuy version has three plurals in places where the fragment has three singulars; in four places the Dupuy version has the verb *nominetur* where the fragment has *numeretur*; and the two versions also display a very few minor differences in wording and word order. However, there is one major difference to be noted. The fragment is 772 words long and corresponds to the last 1,024 words of the Dupuy *Abecedarium* which in all runs to some 7,000 words. In other words, the fragment is 252 words shorter than the corresponding part of the Dupuy text. A good part of this difference can be accounted for in two ways: (i) by supposing that the 38 words with which the Dupuy version begins its account of the massæ majores do not appear in the fragment because those words stood at the very end of the verso of a manuscript leaf that once preceded the first leaf of Tenison's remnant; and (ii) by supposing (at a pinch) that the 130 words (fo. 36^v) missing from the fragment—words which Bacon lavished on items quadruplex H and Θ—made up a leaf of the fragment which went astray before Tenison published it.

But there are other materials which appear in the Dupuy version alone which cannot by any stretch of the imagination be ascribed to physical loss of parts of the Tenison manuscript. These materials bear the marks of Bacon the reviser of his own texts, and point to the typically Baconian process of revision by increment, the process evident in the successive editions of the *Essayes* and, ineffably, in the successive layers of revision that characterize the manuscript of the *De vijs mortis*.[74] In the Dupuy *Abecedarium* the process is more restrained but no less typical. It is best seen in the section that deals with the conditiones entium where, for clarity's sake, Bacon has introduced, into each of four consecutive inquiries (ΓΓΓΓ–ΖΖΖΖ), explanatory formulae which begin 'sed in tali . . .' or 'sed per tale . . .' accompanied by an extra sentence beginning 'Neque enim . . .'. None of this material appears in the Tenison

---

[74] For the revisions of *DVM* see *OFB*, VI, pp. xxxi–xxxv and 467–72.

fragment. In short, the fragment looks like the remnant of a draft superseded by the one represented in the Dupuy version. The latter probably represents the latest extant stage in the evolution of the text;[75] accordingly, coll. Dupuy no. 5 contains the earlier of two extant versions of the *Historia densi* and the later of two versions of the *Abecedarium*.

(*d*) The Printed Copy-Texts and William Rawley

For the remaining texts presented in this volume—the later version of the *Historia densi*, the *Inquisitio de magnete*, the *Topica inquisitionis de luce*, and the piece entitled *Prodromi sive anticipationes philosophiæ secundæ*—I rely on printed copy-texts for which no manuscripts are extant. Of these the first three were published in Rawley's *Opuscula* of 1658, and the last two in Gruter's *Scripta* of 1653. Accordingly, the *Topica inquisitionis* is represented in both collections but, for reasons given later, I have chosen to take the Gruter version as my base-text. Gruter's career as a Bacon scholar, the history of his lost Bacon manuscripts and the printing of the *Scripta* have been dealt with in detail elsewhere.[76] So at this stage I want simply to recall the following points: (i) Gruter's *Scripta* was based on his copy of certain manuscripts which he had inherited from William Boswell; (ii) transmission of Gruter's copy through the press seems to have had no untoward effect upon the texts; (iii) the *Scripta* was produced by two printing shops, the more reliable of which was Lodewijk Elzevier's; (iv) Elzevier printed the duodecimo sheet (signed X) on which the *Topica inquisitionis* appeared;[77] and (v) the Gruter *Prodromi* (R1^r–R3^r) is the sole witness to the text and so is the copy-text for this edition.

As for Rawley, it is seldom appreciated how much of Bacon's life and work are still seen through his eyes. He was the most important disseminator of Bacon's works and propagator of Bacon's reputation in the seventeenth century. Born in 1588 in Norwich (or at any rate in Norfolk), he was evidently a promising student. He was admitted a Bible-Clerk at Corpus Christi or, as it was then known, Bene't College, Cambridge, under the tuition of a Mr Chapman on 22 January 1607, and took both the degrees in Arts before 19 March 1609, when he was elected to a fellowship. On 22 September 1611 he was ordained deacon and soon after

---

[75] Bacon seems often to have prepared more than one copy, and these copies were not necessarily identical. Different copies sometimes ended up in different hands. For instance, Gruter published *TDL* in 1653; Rawley published it from a different manuscript in 1658, see pp. lxxxi–lxxxiii below.

[76] *OFB*, VI, pp. lxx–xcv, but also see below, Appendix I, p. 343.

[77] For sheet X see *OFB*, VI, p. xc. *TDL* runs from X3^r to X8^r in *Sc*.

presented by the Chancellor, Masters and Scholars of the University of Cambridge to the Rectory of Bowthorpe near Norwich, to which he was instituted on 10 December 1612. He kept this sinecure until 1636.[78] The Bowthorpe living was a minor preferment compared with what he acquired several years later, namely the living at Landbeach, just north of Cambridge. This plum was one of the juiciest[79] that Bene't could offer and it fell into his lap not just because he was a former fellow but because the patrons granted Bacon the right to present the new incumbent when the living became vacant in 1616, and Bacon chose Rawley.[80]

I have no idea how Rawley became Bacon's protégé. I note only that both men were alumni of Cambridge and that Rawley had been a younger contemporary of William Boswell's, another man who was later to play a crucial part in the transmission of Bacon's manuscripts. Boswell was a Fellow of Trinity College from 1606 while Rawley was at Bene't in the following year. However, little can be made of either of these facts—not least because Bacon may have known Rawley before he got to know Boswell.[81] In any event, soon after Bacon was made Lord Keeper, Rawley became his domestic chaplain and devoted secretary, a post in which he remained until Bacon's death.[82] A witness to though not a literary executor of Bacon's will, it is not known how Rawley came into

---

[78] Robert Masters, *The History of the College of Corpus Christi and the B. Virgin Mary (Commonly called Bene't) in the University of Cambridge, from its foundation to the present time*, J. Bentham for the author: Cambridge, 1753, pp. 357–8. Francis Blomefield, *An essay towards a topographical history of the County of Norfolk . . .*, Fersfield, 1739, 5 vols., I, p. 637. For the sinecure of Bowthorpe, see *ibid.*, I, pp. 637–40.

[79] Matthew Parker had held it, and it was often held by the Master of Bene't, see J. R. Ravensdale, 'Landbeach in 1549: Ket's rebellion in miniature', *East Anglian Studies*, 1968, pp. 94–116, at pp. 99 and 102. For an indication of the value of the living see William Keatinge Clay, *A history of the parish of Landbeach in the County of Cambridge*, Cambridge Antiquarian Society, Octavo Publications, no. VI, Deighton, Bell & Co: London, 1861, p. 60. Here Clay records details of a three-year lease on some of the assets of the living that Rawley granted to one Thomas Sparrow in 1652.

[80] *A history of the County of Cambridge and the Isle of Ely*, ed. A. P. M. Wright and C. P. Lewis, vol. IX, Oxford University Press for the Institute of Historical Research: Oxford, 1989 (Victoria History of the Counties of England), p. 153. There is some uncertainty about the date; Masters gives 1616, see *History . . . of Corpus Christi*, p. 358.

[81] See *OFB*, VI, pp. lxx–lxxiii.

[82] For Rawley's continued service to Bacon in the years after the latter's fall from office see, for instance, the dedicatory letter to Bacon in Rawley's *A sermon of meekenesse, preached at the Spittle vpon Easter Tuesday*, M. D. C. XXIII, London 1623, A2ʳ⁻ᵛ: 'The timely fruit of your fauour, in my Aduancement vnto that Fortune, by which I subsist: My Attendance vpon your Employments, and Services, at this present: And whatsoever is any way eminent either in my Estate, or Name, I am ready to ascribe it to your Lordship, from whence I haue receiued it.' This sermon was printed by John Haviland whose firm was, in effect, Bacon's main publisher in the last five years of his life; see p. li n. 10 above.

possession of so much of his master's literary estate. The best guess is that his learning and dedicated work as Bacon's amanuensis persuaded the executors to make over most of the literary materials to Rawley in the prescient belief that he would diligently preserve and publish them.[83]

Little is known of Rawley's movements after Bacon's death in 1626. According to William Keatinge Clay, he took up permanent residence in Landbeach in 1630.[84] However, Robert Masters, the eighteenth-century historian of Corpus Christi, tells us that permanent residence began eight years later in 1638.[85] There in 1641 he married Barbara, the daughter of John Wickstead, alderman and mayor of Cambridge. Rawley and his wife had one son William, who later became a Fellow of Bene't. William jr. and Barbara both died (July and August 1666) in the Great Plague and were buried at Landbeach. Rawley himself died a year later and was buried on 20 June 1667 beneath the black marble monument still to be seen in the chancel of his church.[86]

Masters's account can be qualified and supplemented in a number of small ways. Rawley probably lived at Landbeach at least intermittently from 1630 (he signed transcripts of the parish register in 1630, 1633, and 1634–6).[87] He may also have been the Dr Rawley who seems to have been in The Hague in 1633 in the circle of Elizabeth of Bohemia.[88] He retained his living throughout the Interregnum but not without opposition for, in 1644, twelve parishioners got up a petition against him and in 1650 he was accused of being 'no profitable minister'. It seems that in this period and probably for the rest of his life he employed a curate to

---

[83]   For Bacon's will and the obscurities surrounding the passing of Bacon's literary legacy to Boswell and Rawley see *OFB*, VI, pp. lxx–lxxi, lxxiii–lxxiv.

[83]   Clay, *A history of the Parish of Landbeach*, p. 114.

[85]   Masters, *History . . . of Corpus Christi*, pp. 358–9. Masters's dating is probably not as reliable as Clay's; see pp. lxxv–lxxvi below.

[86]   Masters, *History . . . of Corpus Christi*, p. 359. Clay (*A history of the Parish of Landbeach*, p. 69 n. 4) adds that Wickstead was Principal of Bernard's Inn in London and that he died aged 83 and was buried at Landbeach on 5 Jan. 1646–7. The Cottenham Parish Register (Cambridgeshire Record Office P50/1/2) shows that Barbara was also the widow of one Mathew Weld, gent.

[87]   The transcripts are now held in Cambridge University Library. He may also have been the Rawley who in 1635 got the deanery of St Burian in Cornwall, see CSP(Dom) 1637–1638, p. 288, Feb 1637–8, vol. CCCLXXXIII/49: 'Brief notes, principally of various dispensations and presentations to ecclesiastical livings, procured by Archbishop Laud, between March 1634–5 and the present month inc. Dr. Rawleigh, grant of the deanery of St. Borian, alias Burian, Cornwall.'

[88]   CSP(Dom) 1633–1634, p. 58, 15 May 1633, The Hague, vol. CCXXXVIII/76: 'Elizabeth Queen of Bohemia to Bishop Laud. Recommends to him Dr. Rawley, chaplain to King Charles, who has a suit which depends on the Bishop's favour.'

discharge most of his parish duties, and that as late as 1661 he was proctor in convocation for the clergy of the Diocese of Ely.[89]

Although Rawley occupied a choice ecclesiastical snuggery, he never sank into contented provincial torpor. Landbeach was hardly remote either from intellectual life or from the hand of diocesan power for it sat just to the west of the then road between Ely and Cambridge, some twelve miles from the former and four from the latter.[90] In fact Rawley seems never to have lost contact with his alma mater. As we know, his son became a Fellow of Bene't and by September 1663 had become the college's Greek and Rhetoric praelector. Rawley donated copies of the Bacon works to the college as they appeared and in his will left it a number of valuable Greek and Latin works.[91] Nor can it be said that Rawley cut himself off from English and European intellectuals. He corresponded with, among others, Elia Diodati in the early 1630s (that same Diodati who may have inspired La Hoguette's passion for Bacon's works), with John Selden and, in the 1650s, with Isaac Gruter.[92]

As for his work as Bacon's literary assistant, editor and memorialist, nothing directly attributable to Rawley dates from before 1623, the year in which he published a sermon dedicated to his master and contributed a preface to the *De augmentis scientiarum*, a preface describing the gene-

[89] *A History of the County of Cambridge and the Isle of Ely,* p. 153; Clay, *History of the Parish of Landbeach,* p. 95. Clay also tells us (p. 115) that William Jurdan and John Boland were his curates while he was non-resident, and that his curate just before his death was George Thorpe. These details are supported by researches undertaken in the Cambridgeshire Record Office (CamRO) on my behalf by Dr Jan Broadway, who transcribed the Landbeach Churchwardens' Accounts (CamRO P104/1/1). These indicate Laudian innovations in 1639–40 (purchase of perfume and frankincense) but Parliamentarian/anti-Laudian sympathies from 1643 to the Restoration. In those years no payments for washing Rawley's surplice were made and, although one Lawrence was paid 2 shillings for defacing the king's arms in 1650–1, the churchwardens bought mats for communicants to kneel on in 1652–3 which suggests a Puritanism more moderate than that which insisted that communion be taken seated. In 1660–1 the king's arms were set up and in 1661–2 a new surplice was bought. Other documents relating to Landbeach (CamRO P104/1/2, P104/3/1–3, P104/3/4, and P104/R94/8) add little of interest but do confirm details gleaned from other sources.
[90] The modern road (A1309 and A10) runs just to the east of Landbeach. In Rawley's day, the road (now reduced to a track) would have run west of Landbeach via Histon, Rampton and Aldreth, see J. R. Ravensdale, *Liable to floods: village landscape on the edge of the fens AD 450–1850,* Cambridge University Press: Cambridge, 1974, pp. 34–6. Ravensdale (pp. 126–37, 146–50) supplies much information about Landbeach, its very substantial rectory and its connections with Corpus Christi College.
[91] For this information I am indebted to Catherine Hall, Archivist of Corpus Christi College Cambridge (personal communication dated 29 Sept. 1994).
[92] The exchange of letters between Rawley and Diodati, and Gruter's letters to Rawley are preserved in *BTT* (P3ᵛ–R1ʳ).

sis of the text and locating it in the context of the *Instauratio magna*.[93] Immediately after Bacon's death Rawley organized and edited a volume of commemorative verses by, among others, William Boswell and George Herbert.[94] In the same year he edited the work that Bacon had been compiling in the last months of his life, *Sylva sylvarum*, and published it together with the *New Atlantis*, and for both works he supplied letters to the reader—letters which afford invaluable (if sometimes ambiguous) information about what Bacon was up to in these writings.[95]

Three years later he published *Certaine miscellany works*, the first of his collections of Baconiana.[96] In 1638 he published his 'official' translation of the *Historia vitæ* to counter the 'unofficial' one published some months earlier. The former eventually found its way into the 1651 and subsequent editions of the *Sylva* collection, though I cannot say whether Rawley inspired the translation's adoption into what had already become the most popular collection of English natural-philosophical Baconiana.[97] In 1638 Rawley also brought out the *Operum moralium et ciuilium tomus*, a collection which, among other things, contained the first published Latin translations of *Henry VII* and *New Atlantis*, Bacon's last revision of the *De sapientia*, and important but previously published works belonging to the *Instauratio magna*. Some copies even contained reissued sheets of the original 1620 *Novum organum*, sheets which no doubt Rawley himself had assiduously preserved along with his remaining Bacon manuscripts.[98]

[93] See above, p. lxxiv n. 82; *DAS*, ¶2ʳ⁻ᵛ (*SEH*, I, pp. 421–2).

[94] *Memoriæ . . . Francisci, baronis de Verulamio, sacrum*, J. Haviland, 1626 (*STC* 1177; entered in the Stationers' Register 7 May 1626).

[95] *SS*, A1ʳ–A3ʳ; *NA*, a2ʳ⁻ᵛ (*SEH*, II, pp. 335–7; III, p. 127). The volume (*STC* 1168) was entered in the Stationers' Register on 4 July 1626. Rawley tells us that the letter preceding *SS* would have been published in its present form if Bacon had lived. All the same, its contents should, for reasons which will be given in vol. XIV of *OFB*, be treated with caution.

[96] *STC* 1124; entered 2 May 1629; Gibson, no. 191.

[97] The 'unauthorised' translation (Gibson, no. 153) was entered in the Stationers' Register 30 Sept. 1637. Rawley's (Gibson, no. 154) was entered on 5 Jan. 1638. The *SS* is a collection in the sense that the first edition (1626) also contained the *NA*, and later editions progressively accumulated a range of other Baconiana and sub-Baconiana. The addition of the Rawley translation to the 1651 edition (Gibson, no. 176) was but one supplement to the collection. Another Rawleian addition, the English version of his life of Bacon (see p. lxxviii n. 102 below), was added to the 1670 edition of *SS*.

[98] *STC* 1110 (Gibson, no. 197) has the reissued sheets of the 1620 *NO*; most copies of *STC* 1109 (Gibson, no. 196) lack them. Nothing is known of the history of the reissued sheets but it is unlikely that any printer would have kept unsold sheets for long after they had been printed. The probability is that Bacon himself would have bought them up and preserved them, and that they then passed into Rawley's keeping. The *Operum moralium* was entered in the Stationers' Register on 4 Sept. 1638. Rawley's letter to the reader (*Operum moralium*, A3ʳ⁻ᵛ) is not one of his most informative.

After the *Operum moralium*, Rawley published nothing for twenty years, although he still had considerable holdings of unpublished material. The long silence may be explained by his respect for Bacon's wish that some material should stay private, and perhaps by the distractions of the Interregnum and, in particular, threats to Rawley's security of tenure. These considerations were eventually outweighed by others. Rawley was perhaps moved by his correspondence with Gruter to think again about the duties of a custodian of valuable manuscripts. That, coupled with growing exasperation with the quality and authority of other editors' work, seems to have got the better of him.[99] Accordingly, in 1657 he published the *Resuscitatio*,[100] a collection of Bacon's English writings which he published again, with additions, in 1661.[101] The 1657 *Resuscitatio* also contained his English translation of *In fœlicem memoriam Elizabethæ* and the English version of his life of Bacon, a biography published in Latin a year later in the *Opuscula*,[102] a collection which further evidenced his diligence as translator—this time with his Latin version of Bacon's *Confession of faith*. What few manuscripts remained to Rawley after the publication of the *Opuscula* and 1661 *Resuscitatio* were transmitted to Tenison, who published them in his *Baconiana* (1679).[103]

The consequences of Rawley's activities for the reception of Bacon's writings and for the judgements of later editors are inestimable. Bacon scholars still seldom appreciate how much they rely on information and texts derived from Rawley. We need a full and nuanced study of him as memorialist and biographer, editor and translator. But as that study does not exist, I confine myself to just two related issues: how Rawley saw himself as custodian of Bacon's legacy, and how he carried out his editorial functions.

Rawley epitomized himself in the Letter to the Reader to the 1657 *Resuscitatio*. He insisted that he had worked so closely with Bacon, 'that no Man, could pretend a better Interest, or Claim . . . then myself' to ordering Bacon's papers. He had produced a volume containing what 'hath hitherto slept, and been suppressed . . . Not leaving any Thing, to a future Hand, which I found, to be of moment, and communicable to the Publick; Save onely some few *Latine Works*' (which soon appeared in the *Opuscula*). He apologized for publishing what Bacon wanted kept

---

[99] For the transactions with Gruter see *OFB*, VI, pp. lxxviii–lxxix; for Rawley and other editors, translators, and publishers of 'surreptitious' Baconiana see pp. lxxix–lxxx below.

[100] Wing B319 (Gibson, no. 226).   [101] Wing B320 (Gibson, no. 227).

[102] Wing B314 and B315 (Gibson, no. 230 and Gibson(S), no. 230b).

[103] Gibson, nos. 237a and 237b.

private and for republishing some texts already in the public domain, but (he said) 'Surreptitious Copies have been taken; which have since, employed the *Presse*, with sundry Corrupt, and Mangled, *Editions'* and added that justice had to be done now since he was 'Not now in *Vergentibus*, but in *Præcipitantibus Annis*'. It was intolerable that works had been:

obtruded, to the *World*, by unknown Hands; but with such Skars, and Blemishes, upon their Faces; That they could passe, but for *a Spurious*, and *Adulterine Brood*, and not for his *Lordships Legitimate Issue*. And the Publishers, and Printers, of them, deserve to have an *Action*, of *Defamation*, brought against them, by the *State of Learning*, for Disgracing, and Personating, his *Lordships Works*.[104]

This stance was not new. By 1629, with *Certaine miscellany works*, Rawley had begun to see himself as guardian of Bacon's legacy against surreptitious or defective editions and, by 1638, against corrupt translations. In these two cases he acted with the alacrity and determination of a man who wanted to protect Bacon's reputation *and* to establish himself as the arbiter in Baconian textual matters.[105] This is Rawley as Bacon's bulldog and very superior source of textual wisdom. Items in the *Resuscitatio* and *Opuscula* were almost certainly counterblasts against other translators and editors.[106] On the verge of his seventieth year he was still fighting insolent abusers of Bacon's reputation with the same tenacity he had displayed in his early forties.

What then of Rawley as editor? How did this enemy of bad translation and corrupt editing, and champion of the authentic text (i.e. any text produced by Rawley himself) go about his editorial business and, in particular, the business of seeing the *Opuscula* into the public domain? As far as the *Opuscula* is concerned, we have no direct knowledge of the manuscripts on which the collection was based, nor do we know whether the manuscripts Rawley inherited served directly as printer's copy. And even in the cases where works in the *Opuscula* can be

---

[104] *Resuscitatio*, [a2ʳ]–b1ᵛ.

[105] *Certaine miscellany works* contained an edition of *Considerations tovching a warre with Spaine* which was an explicit riposte to the 'unauthorised' 1629 edition (*STC* 1126; Gibson, no. 187) which Rawley denounced as 'corrupt' (A3ʳ–A4ʳ). His 1638 translation of *HVM* was entered in the Stationers' Register just three months after the same had been done for the translation it was meant to supplant (see above, p. lxxvii n. 97).

[106] His English translation of *In fœlicem memoriam Elizabethæ* in the *Resuscitatio* was no doubt a response to the anonymous translation of 1651 (Wing B297; Gibson, no. 220). His edition of *TDL* in *Op* may perhaps have been prompted by Gruter's edition in *Sc* (see pp. lxxxi–lxxxiii below).

compared with other sources of textual authority we seldom have means of deciding whether textual variants are in whole or part a consequence of Rawley's interventions, print shop licence or differences between different manuscripts produced by Bacon himself, i.e. differences of the kind found in the texts of the two versions of the *Abecedarium* where the two cover the same ground.

But granting these difficulties, comparative methods can help us to judge the reliability of texts in the *Opuscula*. To take the *Historia densi* first, we already know that although the coll. Dupuy version is much shorter than the Rawley version, the two contain passages, some of them very long, which coincide pretty well. The very fact of coincidence in two quite distinct manuscript traditions seems to indicate *grosso modo* that even if Rawley's text may sometimes be wrong, it is wrong in, so to speak, an authoritative way. Coincidental sin like coincidental virtue points to the conclusion that Rigault and Rawley stayed faithful to exemplars which transmitted materials which differed little. Almost all the material in the coll. Dupuy version is represented pretty much in the same form in Rawley's. Rigault, Rawley and Rawley's printer seem not to have been responsible for garbling the text flagrantly or at length, though that is not to say of course that in matters of fine detail—in some of the results recorded in the great table of densities for instance[107]— Rawley or the press may not have allowed errors to creep in. This general conclusion is borne out by comparison of the two versions of the Aditus (preface) to the *Historia densi*, viz. the one in the *Opuscula* with the other in the *Historia naturalis*. Both versions are (one word excepted) identical in all substantive matters. They are even identical in error for both omit an obvious *non*.[108] This may mean that Rawley lifted the preface from the *Historia naturalis* (i.e. that like the coll. Dupuy version Rawley's manuscript lacked a preface) but, whatever the case, it suggests that he was perhaps *too* faithful to his exemplars and leaned more towards slavish fidelity than to bold and possibly unwarranted intervention.

The Rawley *Historia densi* can also be compared with Bacon's practice in his other Latin natural histories. We recall that Bacon had the printers set different categories of material in different types—here mainly in italic there in roman, here in larger type there in smaller—and that these differences were represented in these ways (albeit in a reduced form) in the *Opuscula* version of the *Historia densi*, a fact which cannot have

---

[107] For these tables see pp. 2–3 and 40–5 below.   [108] See *tns* p. 38 below.

arisen from independent action by the printers. Whatever else he did Rawley transmitted material which had been marked up to tell the printers how to set the different kinds of material. Whether Rawley himself did the marking or merely transmitted pre-existing and authoritative copy to the press is neither here nor there, for whatever reached the press reflected Bacon's practices. That is also true of the format of the *Opuscula* for, whether by accident or design, the edition is in octavo, the very format of the *Historia ventorum* and *Historia vitæ*—histories published in Bacon's lifetime. Granted that the printer would not have chosen to bring out the *Opuscula* in folio or quarto (nineteen sheets would in either case have made too lean a volume), it may be that the format chosen was at Rawley's urging so that the longest work of the *Opuscula* would have, with the typographical distinctions just noted, some of the formal traits deliberately built into the two octavo histories that John Haviland had produced thirty-five years earlier.

Turning now to the other evidence bearing on Rawley's standing as an editor, i.e. comparison of the Rawley and Gruter versions of the *Topica inquisitionis de luce*, we face a familiar problem—we can seldom be sure whether differences arise from editorial intervention, print shop blunders, or different but equally authentic (though not necessarily equally authoritative) Bacon originals. For a text only about 1,500 words long there are a fair number of differences between our two witnesses:

1. There are four conflicts of word order. These are of no consequence whatever but typical of divergent readings of the sort manufactured by scribal transmission of text.[109]

2. There are fourteen straight grammatical clashes and, on the unsafe assumption that none of these mostly trivial differences was produced by the compositors, there is little to choose between Gruter and Rawley, though the latter comes off just a shade worse. Each has about the same number of 'good' forms (i.e. grammatical habits which are attested by other Bacon texts) as the other and, in cases where emendation of grammar might have been expected of a vigilant seventeenth-century editor, Rawley fails on two counts and Gruter presents the better readings.[110]

3. There are eight straight lexical clashes, i.e. cases in which a word in one version is different from the word in the same place in the other. In

---

[109] See *tns* to p. 244, ll. 11–12, ll. 21–2; p. 252, l. 9; p. 256, l. 10 below. For this cause of scribal disagreement see Peter Beal, *In praise of scribes: manuscripts and their makers in seventeenth-century England*, Clarendon Press: Oxford, 1998, pp. 44–5.

[110] Rawley reads 'elanguentia' where 'elanguentes' would be preferable (see below, *tns* to p. 248, l. 7), and '&' where Gruter offers 'ut' (*tns* to p. 252, l. 12 below).

two cases the reading in Rawley's version is better than Gruter's; in four the reverse is true; and in two the readings are of pretty well equal value.[111]

4. Rawley's text has 8 words not in Gruter's but Gruter's has 24 not in Rawley's. Whereas Rawley's 8 are relatively unimportant, most of Gruter's are not, and more than anything argue for taking Gruter's as our copy-text. Of these 24 words, 11 make an extra sentence of exactly the kind that Bacon might typically have added to the text when revising an earlier draft.[112] Two further words in Gruter seem to indicate one lacuna in Rawley's text; three more seem to indicate another.[113] Another three words in Gruter present the correct version of a remark so lamed in Rawley that the sense is reversed.[114]

5. Also pertinent is a difference in accidentals. In Gruter section headings are accompanied by Roman numerals; in Rawley we find Arabic numerals set into the beginning of the first paragraph of each section. In this respect Gruter's text may be rather more Baconian than Rawley's.[115]

Indeed all the evidence tends to suggest that Gruter's text may be a little more authentic and a slighly later one than Rawley's, and therefore that Gruter's version makes a better copy-text. In this connection it is striking that Rawley *could* have collated his *Topica inquisitionis* with Gruter's; indeed Rawley's interleaved copy of the *Scripta* is now in the British Library.[116] But Gruter's *Topica* seems not to have exerted the slightest discernible influence on Rawley's, and Gruter's work was not even acknowledged in the *Opuscula*. That makes Rawley a bad editor, at least as far as the *Topica* is concerned. Rawley would not of course behave like a modern editor, but certain editorial practices were well known in the seventeenth century—not least those of collating extant witnesses and of recording variants, practices which Rawley observed neither in his edi-

---

[111] 'insolenter'/'violenter' (p. 246, l. 4); 'intensius'/'intentius' (p. 246, l. 24); 'lucis'/'*luminis*' (p. 248, l. 4); 'melius'/'mollius' (p. 248, l. 12); '&'/'aut' (p. 230, l. 5); 'Solis'/'*Lucis*' (p. 250, l. 20); 'commissa'/'commista' (p. 252, l. 20); 'lucis'/'ejus' (p. 254, l. 8).

[112] See p. 256, ll. 1–2 below: 'Lux magis in profundum penetrat, quam sonus, ut in fundo aquarum.'

[113] See p. 254, ll. 20–1 below: 'durationem soni', and p. 246, l. 19 below: 'fere croceæ sunt'.

[114] Gruter's 'in corpore solido & non diaphano' vs. Rawley's 'in corpore *Diaphano*', see *tns* to p. 254, l. 32 below.

[115] Cf. for instance numbering in *NO*, *DAS* and *ANN*.

[116] BL Add. MS 4468; this is not a manuscript but a composite volume. Rawley made it up from leaves of two copies of the *Scripta* with each leaf stuck to a larger leaf of blank paper. On each blank recto a *Scripta* leaf is glued with recto facing up; on each verso another exemplar of the same leaf is glued verso up. The blank leaves were evidently meant to carry notes to the printed text, notes which Rawley never got round to writing.

tion of the *Topica* nor, indeed, anywhere else in the *Opuscula*.[117] He does
not say whether he adopted the Aditus of the *Historia densi* from his
manuscript copy or from the printed version of 1622. He provides us
with almost no machinery, no apparatus, for judging the reliability of his
texts. Bad editors do not always give out bad texts; they may merely fail
to establish them and, since Rawley does not establish his, we have to do
it for him.

This incomplete assessment of Rawley's work differs from that of
Bacon's Victorian editors who, prejudiced in favour of Rawley and
against Gruter, gave particular and unjustified preference to Rawley's
text in the case of the *Topica*. In this their judgement was unsound, and
the textual notes to the edition printed below show Victorian editorial
practices in an interesting if melancholy light.[118] Given what we know
of Gruter we accept his *Topica* as the copy-text for our edition. We also
take his edition of the *Prodromi* as the copy-text for the last of the texts
presented in this volume, which is all we can do for there is no other witness to the text.

(*e*) The *Opuscula* and the Press

To complete the account of the transmission of the texts presented in
this volume two further questions need answers: why did those manuscripts whose texts appeared in the *Opuscula* go to the printer Roger
Daniel, and what did Daniel's firm make of the job?

The *Opuscula* was entered in the Stationers' Register on 6 May 1658
under the hand of Master Lee to Master Redman (John Redmayne or
Redmaine).[119] The edition has two issues differing only in their
imprints: the first names Daniel alone; the second adds that Octavian
Pulleyn financed the edition and gives the latter's address.[120] Of four

[117] As Brian Richardson has shown, effective textual-critical techniques for the study of
non-classical literature had existed since the cinquecento at the very least; see *Print culture in
Renaissance Italy: the editor and the vernacular text, 1470–1600*, Cambridge University Press:
Cambridge, 1994. For a distinguished example of 17th-cent. English practice see Abraham
Whelock's edition of the Anglo-Saxon and Latin texts of Bede (1643). Whelock's work is the
more interesting as it was printed by Roger Daniel, who later printed the *Opuscula*; see David
McKitterick, *A history of Cambridge University Press*, Cambridge University Press: Cambridge,
1992, vol. I, pp. 187–92.

[118] See *tns* to pp. 244–56 below.

[119] See *A transcript of the registers of the worshipful Company of Stationers; from 1640–1708 A.
D.*, ed. G. E. Briscoe Eyre and C. R. Rivington, 3 vols., privately printed for the Roxburghe
Club: London, 1913–14, II, p. 177. Maria Wakely has drawn my attention to the fact that one
Fr. Finch, the first owner of the copy now at King's College Cambridge, dated his copy 4 Mar.
4 i.e. two months before the date in the Stationers' Register.

[120] See Appendix 1, pp. 338–40 below.

men involved in the transaction—Rawley, Daniel, Redmayne and Pulleyn (or Pullen)—the last two need not detain us long. A fairly successful bookseller, once apprenticed to Samuel Man (or Mann) in 1621 and freed in 1629, Pulleyn seems to have started in business with George Thomason in 1636 or thereabouts but to have been on his own from 1645. Elected to the Court of the Stationers' Company in 1653, he served as Under Warden in 1658–9 and 1661, and Upper Warden 1662–3 and 1664–5, and died in 1674.[121] He had a strong interest in publishing learned works—not least in natural philosophy and medicine. Indeed, of the 17 Pulleyn items of the 1650s in Wing's *Catalogue*, some 12 belong to these categories. Apart from the *Opuscula*, among them are anatomical works (requiring expensive cuts) by Glisson, Bartholin and Pecquet, and the first two editions of William Harvey's great embryological work, *Exercitationes de generatione animalivm* (1651), followed in 1653 by its first English translation.[122] In short, Pulleyn was ready to invest in books aimed at specialist markets, but there is no evidence of the size of his share in the *Opuscula* or any other publication, and no reason to think that he played any part in the dealings which led to the transfer of manuscript copy from Rawley to Daniel—not least because his name does not appear on the title-page of the first issue.

As for Redmayne, he may not have been a printer before May 1658, though he had surely begun printing on his own account by 1659. Fifteen books were entered to him in the Stationers' Register in the period from 1649 up to and including 1658; of these most were entered in the period from April 1656. In other words at this stage Redmayne was not printing but financing books or acting as an agent for others. Indeed, my best guess is that the *Opuscula* was entered to him because he was acting for Roger Daniel, who happens to have been his father-in-law. This relationship may be the key fact explaining why the *Opuscula* was printed by but not entered to Daniel himself, although there is no evidence of any financial arrangement between the two men over the book's printing and publication.[123]

---

[121] H. R. Plomer, *A dictionary of the booksellers and printers who were at work in England, Scotland and Ireland from 1641–1667*, Bibliographical Society: London, 1907, pp. 149–50; also see *STC* 4753, 4789, 15496–7, 17553, 20488, 20489, 21537.3, 22058.

[122] Wing B975, B978, B3198, D1515, G853, H1085, H1091, H1091A, H2956, M2667, P1045.

[123] Plomer, *A dictionary*, p. 153; Wing B882, D2552; Eyre and Rivington, I, pp. 332, 403, 436, 460; II, pp. 45, 49, 60, 118, 129, 140, 173, 176. Daniel and Redmayne seem to have shared printing materials, see K. A. Coleridge, 'The printing and publishing of Clement Walker's *History of Independency 1647–1661*', *Bulletin of the Bibliographical Society of Australia and New Zealand*, 8, 1984, pp. 22–61, at p. 31. That Daniel and Redmayne were father- and son-in-law see Stationers' Company Court Book D, fo. 38ᵛ. The late D. F. McKenzie drew my attention to this evidence.

Daniel (*c.*1593–1667) was almost an exact contemporary of Rawley. His career had three phases: the first and last in London, the second in Cambridge. During the first he sold books, but prints may have been his mainstay for, engravings apart, his name appeared on no publication until 1628 when he was named as London bookseller to the Cambridge press. Perhaps fed up with the monopolistic shenanigans of the London book trade, he seems to have been tempted to Cambridge by John and Thomas Buck who from 1625 had held office as University Printers. The leading tempter was the clever and ruthless Thomas (1593?–1670) who, in a series of elaborate agreements, transferred much of the running of the business to Daniel in return for regular income for himself and John.[124]

Thomas Buck and Roger Daniel turned a small business into a substantial one,[125] with Buck more inclined to print books at the instigation of the Stationers' Company, and Daniel the readier (as he claimed) to establish a learned press. However, while both bowed to economic necessity and printed for the schoolbook and almanac market, they produced a varied list which included works of great merit—among them Fuller's *Holy warre* (1639) and *Holy and profane state* (1642), the folio Greek New Testament (1642), Whelock's edition of the Latin and Anglo-Saxon Bede (1643), and Cruso's *Military instructions* (1644). With these, as well as the Bible of 1638 and a number of important books in the smaller formats, Buck and Daniel pursued a policy of 'exceptional scholarly and technical distinction'.[126]

Daniel remained in office until 1650 when the egregious Buck engineered his dismissal. Daniel returned to London, where he quickly reestablished himself: in 1650 he shared in the printing of Edward Leigh's *Critica sacra*; in 1651 he brought out an edition of Photius' letters; and in

[124] See McKitterick, *Cambridge University Press*, I, pp. 169–70. In 1631 Daniel was still Buck's London agent, see W. W. Greg, *A Companion to Arber: being a calendar of documents in Edward Arber's* Transcript of the Registers of the Company of Stationers of London 1554–1640, Clarendon Press: Oxford, 1967, p. 271: 'And lastly concerninge Gerrardes prayers [1631] he [Michael Sparke] saith that the same were printed at Cambridge by Mr Bucke printer of that vniu'sitie, and this ex^t knewe not thereof till they were finished & then one Mr Daniel of London Staiōner agent for the syde Mr Bucke sold the whole impression . . .'. For the background to this see *ibid.*, pp. 82–3.

[125] McKitterick, *Cambridge University Press*, I, pp. 173–4, 265, 270 ff. By the 1640s the University's printing business was no longer a single press with a few cases of type and staffed by just a couple of men whose output amounted to little more than dictionary and a few slimmer volumes per annum. It had ceased to be 'among the least significant manufacturers of books in the country'.

[126] *Ibid.*, I, pp. 173–4, 183, 186–92, 204–6, 384.

1653 the first English edition of the Septuagint. In 1656 he was paid by the Stationers' Company for an edition of Ovid,[127] a work which, like much of his London output, derived in one way or another from his Cambridge years. For, in addition to Bibles, and theological and devotional works,[128] he printed editions of Burgersdijk, Drexel, Heereboord, Stahl and Henry More, and cheap editions of classical texts, as well as the Cambridge-inspired second edition of Barrow's Euclid (1659) and a translation of the same (1660).[129]

Daniel seems to have acquired very high reputation for his editorial skills and passion for accuracy. For instance, in 1657/8 (i.e. just before he printed the *Opuscula*) he attracted an extraordinary encomium from William Dillingham (1617–89), Master of Emmanuel, who praised him in the highest terms for the great works that he had printed in Cambridge and subsequently in London. Of these works the latest was a new edition of Ferrari's *Lexicon geographicum* for which Dillingham wrote a preface commending Daniel for the efficiency with which he had dealt with the mistakes in the text—'At quis Augiæ stabulam expurgabit'.[130]

Now if Dillingham's testimonial reflected contemporary opinion then it was natural that Rawley should commit his Bacon manuscripts to Daniel. Daniel had scholarly habits, printed learned works as well as the bread-and-butter texts, and was still very well known in Cambridge. There is no need to labour the point that Rawley, with his intimate Cambridge connections, no doubt knew both Dillingham and Daniel. Rawley was a Bene't man who enjoyed a Bene't living, and his son became a Fellow of Bene't. It is impossible to believe that Rawley could have been ignorant of the reputation of a man who had been a first-rate University Printer with premises but a stone's throw from that college.[131]

However, Dillingham's assessment of Daniel was not wholly borne out by the *Opuscula*. The texts it contains had rather a bumpy ride through the press. The collational formula for the edition is this:

[127] Stationers' Company Journal Book for Money Disbursed, 10 June 1656.
[128] For instance, Wing B2241, B2249, B2453, B2718, B2731, P995, S781, T790.
[129] McKitterick, *Cambridge University Press*, I, p. 305; Wing B6532, D2169–D2173, E3393, H1353–H1357, M2639, S5165, S5166.
[130] McKitterick, *Cambridge University Press*, I, p. 306.
[131] *Ibid.*, pp. 275–7: in 1632 the press moved from the Angel Inn site to the old Austin Friars buildings just south of Bene't (Corpus Christi). It is noteworthy that the first edition of *Resuscitatio* (1657) edited by Rawley was 'Printed by *Sarah Griffin*, for *William Lee*'. I do not know why the *Opuscula*, published a year later, went to Daniel rather than to the printers of the *Resuscitatio*.

Coll: 8°: *8 (± *1) (*1ᵛ blank) 2*8 3*2 A–K8 (± K5, K6) L–N8 O4 (G7ᵛ
L8ᵛ N7ᵛ blank) [$4 (– *1, O3, O4) signed] 126 leaves present, pp. [*36*]
1–108 *109–110* 111–174 *175–176* 177–204 *205–206* 207–216.

The first thing to notice is that there are two versions of the title-page
and, on that basis, Gibson belatedly identified copies with one title-page
as exemplars of a different edition from copies with the other.[132] In fact,
as the two title-pages are (with several exceptions to be considered later)
the only pages with partly different settings, all copies of the 1658
Opuscula belong to the same edition and, in Bowers's typology, belong
to one of two issues, issues distinguished by title-page. The title-pages
differ in at least four respects: (i) the spacing between lines seven and
eight is reduced in the later version to make room for (ii) a longer
imprint; (iii) in converting the earlier R. Danielis to the later R.
Daniel, the letterspacing of the Daniel component was increased
(from 1.8mm to 2.2mm), leaving the horizontal space taken up by initial
and surname the same in both versions (2.9mm); and (iv) the later version of the date is set in smaller type than the earlier.[133]

How do we know which version is earlier and which later? The answer
is straightforward. The earlier title-*leaf* was cut out and a new one sub-
stituted. Like all leaves of its sheet (and, indeed, all other leaves in the
edition) the cancellandum has vertical chain-lines whereas the cancellans, the later title-leaf, alone has horizonal ones.[134] Yet where the wording of cancellandum and cancellans coincides, the very same pieces of
type were used. This of course eliminates the possibility that the title-
page was reset in its entirety, i.e. after the type-pages of its forme had
been distributed. In other words, the forme to which the cancellandum
belonged was still standing in type when all copies of that sheet had been
wrought off, and when the decision was made to alter the title-page. All
type-pages were removed from the chase and their type was distributed,
except for the type belonging to the title-page. The type-page of the
title-page was then altered, and a number of impressions were made
from the altered type-page alone—with the orientation of the paper

---

[132] Gibson recorded only one edition in his 1950 bibliography (Gibson, no. 230); in the 1959
supplement he recorded the other so-called 'edition' (Gibson(S), no. 230b). The latter has the
cancellans, the former the cancellandum.

[133] For the two versions of the title-page see Appendix I, Plates V and VI. For aesthetic reasons perhaps, there is also a slight reduction of the spacing between lines three and four. It is
strange that Gibson's 'exact' facsimile of the title-page of no. 230 lacks a comma after
'*Verulamio*' on line 8. Gibson(S) (p. 4) states that a comma does appear on the title-page of no.
230b. I know of *no* copy of nos. 230 and 230b without a comma.

[134] Instances of exemplars with the cancellans are noted in Appendix 1.

relative to the type-page now 90° different from that which had obtained for every other leaf in the edition.

So much for the title-page. Let us now turn to other features of the production of the edition. The two leaves of 3* were imposed and printed at the same time and in the same two formes as the four leaves which constitute the final sheet of the edition, sheet O. We know that because some copies of the *Opuscula* actually have a final gathering which has these leaves in the following order: O1, K5, 3*2, O2, O3, 3*1, K6, O4.[135] I shall come back to the significance of K5 and K6 below; for the moment suffice it to say that, on a perfected and unfolded octavo sheet, leaves O1, O2, O3 and O4 sit together in the same half of the sheet (for O was not set up like most other sheets in the edition, i.e. in common octavo format but (as watermark evidence shows) in half-sheet octavo). The other half of the sheet would have had 3*1 and 3*2 sitting side by side with their head margins adjacent to the head margins of K5 and K6. If the binder had done his job properly he would have cut the sheet in half parallel to its shorter sides and folded one half as a four-leaf gathering (signed O). He would then have cut the other half in half again, this time parallel to the longer sides of the original sheet to separate (*a*) the two K leaves from (*b*) the final (and textually independent) gathering (3*2) of the preliminaries.

As for the leaves K5 and K6 printed with O, they constitute a bifolium cancellans meant to replace the first and defective versions of those leaves. For when the first versions of type-pages K5ᵛ and K6ʳ were imposed with the other type-pages of sheet K, a major blunder occurred. What should have been the first line of K5ᵛ ('De *Tinctura* inquirendum; quo modo *Metalla*') turned up instead as the first line of K6ʳ. This made nonsense of the text and, to make matters worse, the mistake seems not to have been noticed until many copies of sheet K had been wrought off and perfected, notwithstanding the fact that the catchword ('De') on all uncancelled versions K5ʳ (outer forme) was *correct*. Apart from being a poor advert for Daniel's correctors, the mistake was expensive. The firm tried to solve the probem in two ways. Someone took a pen and deleted the first line of K6ʳ and the incorrect K5ᵛ catchword (also 'De') and then pasted in a letterpress correction at the head of K5ᵛ.[136] This inelegant solution was not adopted in all copies with corrected leaves. Instead, all

---

[135] For instance, Cambridge University Library (shelfmark LE. 7. 84); Christ's College Cambridge (shelfmark E. 1. 11); and Folger Library (shelfmark B314).

[136] See, for instance, the copy belonging to the Royal Irish Academy (Dublin), shelfmark MR/43/U/25.

four type-pages belonging to K5 and K6 were removed from their original formes. The compositor then set the headline of K5ᵛ higher to make room for the first line of K6ʳ to be transferred to its proper position. He also displaced the final line of K5ᵛ ('*corporis vitrificati* comparati cum *corpore crudo.*') to the top of K6ʳ and changed the K5ᵛ catchword ('*cor-*') to match. After a few other adjustments had been made the four type pages of K5 and K6 were imposed with the type-pages of 3* and O.[137] As the type-pages of K5 and K6 were not for the most part *reset* but corrected and, as most of the original setting was carried over to the formes which contained O, most of K5 and K6 must have been left standing after the other K types had been distributed, or both formes of K was still standing in type when O was being set or imposed. I say *most* of K5 and K6 for there is quite clear evidence that lines 24–31 of K5ʳ were in fact reset. Notice that among the clearest signs of resetting are these: '*Amalgamizatio,*vel' (l. 24) becomes '*Amalgamizatio,* vel'; '*Massam*' (l. 24) becomes '*massam*'; the bendings of certain of the kerns in long s and in f are different (ll. 25–9) in the reset section from those in the first setting; the last two letters of '*Volatilitas*' (l. 30) lose their ligature in resetting; a damaged '&' is replaced (l. 30) with an undamaged one; and '*Conuersio*' is converted (l. 31) to '*Conversio*'.

I am indebted to Randall McLeod for drawing my attention to the evidence of resetting and for the following two suggestions: (i) that the predominantly italic types of these lines were needed to make good a shortage of italic type elsewhere, or (ii) that the lines were distributed after the machining of the outer forme of sheet K. At that point the main error in K—the misplaced first line of K6ʳ—was noticed, and the four type-pages (minus some italic) were then allowed to stand until some time before the O gathering was ready for the press, at which point K5 and K6 were revised and, where necessary, reset before going to press with O.[138]

The decision to print a K5/K6 bifolium cancellans either provided the opportunity for other corrections, or the need for further corrections reinforced the decision to produce the cancellans. Either way, additional corrections were made as illustrated in Table 2.

---

[137] This could lead to mistakes in the placing of the cancellans. In the Carlisle Cathedral copy the sequence of leaves is K1, K2, K3, K4, K6, K5, K7, K8. It could also lead to the K5/K6 cancellans ending up among the preliminaries (see for instance Bodl., shelfmark 8° A 82 Linc.) or being bound at the end of a copy with O (see n. 135 above).

[138] Personal communication dated 7 Apr. 1999. Prof. McLeod was kind enough to collate a photocopy of the Beinecke copy (shelfmark Ih B132 c658) with the copy (shelfmark bac B33 O68 1658a) belonging to the Fisher Library, University of Toronto.

Table 2. *The K5/K6 Bifolium: Further Corrections*

sig.	line no(s)	cancellandum	cancellans
K5ʳ (o)	16	*formas, corpora*	*formas, corpora*
	17–18	fingil-|atim	figil-|atim
K5ᵛ (i)	7 or 8	*Tinctura, Marmoris*	*Tinctura Marmoris*
	14 or 15	*Aeris*	*Æris*
	16 or 17	*corpus,*	*corpus;*
	23 or 24	*Additamentis;* & quo	*Additamentis,* & quo
		tempore;	*tempore,*
	26 or 27	patientur; quo modo fiet;	patientur, quo modo fiet,
K6ʳ (i)	11	Modus *surgendi, bulliendi*	modus *surgendi , bulliendi*
	15	valeat.	valeat:
	19	aperiat,fine radente	aperiat, fine rodente
	30	collineat. Primo,	collineat : Primo,
	31	in *usum* ; ut cum *ferrum*	propter *usum*;ut cum
		igne *molliatur*, facit	*ferrum* igne *molliatur*,facit
K6ᵛ (o)	7	rigidi	validi
	9	*Volatilitatem,*	*Volatilitatem*
	13	poterit;	poterit; [; moved upwards]
	25	*Exufflationis*	*Exſufflationis*

And with these we have dealt with all the major press variants detected. Apart from these a few minor ones should be recorded. They are as follows: (i) 2*4 (catchword)—(il-)li [li]—missing in Christ Church Oxford copy; (ii) B8ʳ (headline) the 'ɪ' of '31' is displaced upwards in some copies; (iii) D4ʳ (l. 27) 'amoveatur' is very slightly displaced to the left in some copies; (iv) E2ʳ (l. 12) in some copies the space between the number 'I' and the large initial 'S' is smaller than in others; (v) F5ʳ (l. 20) in some copies a space after 'Etiam' has ridden up and taken ink; (vi) L1ᵛ (ll. 20–3) and (vii) M2ᵛ (last line) the spacing between words in some copies differs in a number of minute ways from that found in others.

Lastly it will be noted that, besides the problem with the displaced lines on K5ᵛ and K6ʳ, I have found only three press variants which may have required reference to printer's copy ('figil-\|atim' replacing 'fingil-\|atim', '*Æris*' replacing '*Aeris*', and 'propter' replacing 'in'). Sheet K aside, I have found no substantive variants whatever on sheets bearing copy-text for any of the works edited below, and even in the case of K none of the *type-pages* bearing copy-text are among those which exist in variant states.[139]

---

[139]   *IDM* appears on type-pages K7$^\mathrm{v}$–L1$^\mathrm{r}$.

THIS EDITION: PRINCIPLES, CONVENTIONS, AND A NOTE ON THE TRANSLATIONS

(i) Principles and Conventions

Editorial intervention in the texts has been kept to a minimum, but the edited texts are neither literal transcripts nor quasi-facsimiles of the *c-ts*. With regard to printed *c-ts*, ornaments and display initials with their following small capitals have not been recorded or reproduced. Turned letters and wrong-fount letters have been recorded only if bibliographically significant. The running headlines in this edition do not match those of the printed *c-ts*.

The edited texts are accompanied by two banks of textual footnotes (*tns*): the first relates to substantives, the second to accidentals. After the edited texts stand the commentaries (*cmts*). In the main the *cmts* elucidate difficult passages and indicate (especially by quotation) sources, analogues and parallels. In addition they supplement the *tns* and cross-reference passages of the edited texts with passages in other Bacon writings.

Since *c-t* signatures (printed *c-ts*) and folio numbers (manuscript *c-ts*) are the means by which texts in the edition are cross-referenced, superscript vertical bars ($^|$) have been set in the edited text to distinguish each *c-t* page from the next. In the outer margin next to every line of text containing such a bar, the appropriate *c-t* signature or folio number is set in square brackets ([ ]).

Emendation of substantives has been confined to instances where the *c-t* appeared to be deficient or corrupt. Illegible words (in the manuscript *c-ts*) for which no conjecture can be supplied are represented thus: [*illeg.*]. Conjectural reconstructions of illegible words or lacunae are also set in square brackets; arguments (where they are necessary) for reconstructions appear in the *tns* or in the *cmts*. Emendations stand in the established text, and are recorded in the *tns* where the emended word(s) appear as a lemma (or lemmata) preceded by a line number and followed by (1) a closing square bracket ( ]) and then (2) the *c-t* reading and/or editorial remarks. Unemended words requiring editorial comment are lemmatized in the same manner. All editorial remarks in the *tns* are distinguished from the lemma and record of the *c-t* reading by a /.

Where witnesses to the text differ in substantive matters the lemma and square bracket are followed by readings from witnesses other than *c-t* readings followed by its/their signature or folio reference(s); thus for example 'sine igne ullo] sine ullo igne *Op* (L2ᵛ)' means that the *c-t* (in this case the *Scripta* version of the *Topica inquisitionis de luce*) has a reading (retained in the edited text) which differs from the one at L2ᵛ in the *Opuscula* version. However, if the lemma is a reading adopted from a witness to the text other than the *c-t*, the square bracket is followed by a swung dash, the siglum or sigla for the non-*c-t* witness(es) and its/their signature or folio reference(s) followed in turn by a comma and the *c-t* reading; thus 'possit]~ *Op* (L4ʳ), potest' means that non-*c-t* reading (possit) has been adopted into the edited text from the *Opuscula* at L4r and has displaced the *c-t* reading (potest) of the *Scripta*.

Emendation of accidentals: in general, *c-t* accidentals have been preserved. Where accidentals have been emended (generally for the sake of clarity), *c-t* readings have been scrupulously preserved in the *tns* and keyed to the text in the same manner as for substantives. A swung dash to the right of the closing square bracket stands for the lemma; thus, for example, *lemma,*]~; means that the comma following the lemma in the edited text replaces a semicolon in the *c-t*. Where the edited text has punctuation but the *c-t* has none, the ~ is followed by a caret mark (∧); for brackets inserted by the editor, ~ is followed by ∧*lemma*∧.

1. Punctuation: texts have their own regularities or eccentricities which it would be unwise to disturb more than is absolutely necessary. Punctuation has been emended only for clarity or to avoid ambiguity. Emendations are noted in *tns* in the manner indicated in the previous paragraph.

2. *C-t* paragraphing has been retained without exception. Beginnings of paragraphs are indented, outdented or neither in- nor outdented in accordance with *c-t* practice.

3. *C-t* orthography has been retained for the most part. It makes no sense in what aims to be an honest edition to normalize the differing practices of scribes and printers on some arbitrary 'modern' standard. Apparent orthographical errors (typographical in some cases) have been corrected and *c-t* forms noted in the *tns*. Modern practice in the cases of i versus j and u versus v has been (quite properly) ignored. The long s has been silently altered to the modern form. In the edition *c-t* digraphs have been retained.

4. Abbreviations: all *c-t* contractions have been expanded (in italics where the *c-t* has roman, and in roman where the *c-t* has italic). Where

the *c-t* omits a contraction sign (generally a tilde or a horizontal straight line) normally used in the *c-t*, the missing letters have been supplied in italics enclosed in square brackets. Caudate *e* has been represented as an italicized *æ*.

5. Diacriticals: all have been retained or omitted according as the *c-ts* retain or omit them.

6. *C-t* initial capitals and lower-case letters: these have been emended in many cases (especially in the edition of the manuscript version of the *Historia densi*) for clarity's sake. Emendations have been recorded in textual notes thus: *lemma*] lc where editorial capitals have been introduced, and *lemma*] *Lemma* where editorial lower-case initials have displaced *c-t* capitals. Small-caps following display initials have not been recorded or reproduced.

7. Additionally, and in the case of manuscript *c-ts* alone, all deletions have been restored and delimited by angle brackets (⟨. . .⟩). Interlineations have been incorporated in the text and delimited by normal and reverse primes (`. . .´). Underlined matter in the *c-t* has been underlined in the edited text.

It should be noted that Rigault, the scribe who produced two of our manuscript *c-ts*, sometimes used capitals and sometimes lower case for Greek letters and Roman numerals; the edited texts based on Rigault's copies follow his practices. Note too that the *BTT* fragment of the *Abecedarium* is printed in italic but with Greek letters spelt out in roman; in the *tns* I have reversed this and quoted italic in roman and vice versa.

(ii) A Note on the Translations

My general policy with regard to translating Bacon's Latin has been sketched out elsewhere and I shall not repeat it here,[1] except to say that some trouble has been taken with the translation of specialist, semi-technical and technical terms. The effort to reproduce the meanings of these and to alert readers to their character sometimes results in a certain awkwardness which is perhaps unavoidable when modern English is being asked to convey early seventeenth-century distinctions and differences, and when the translator may occasionally have a duty to 'preserve the obscurity of the original' but without being so nervous of it as hardly to dare to translate it at all.[2] Particularly problematic are apparent or par-

---

[1] See *OFB*, VI, pp. cxv–cxvi.
[2] See Jonathan Rée, 'Being foreign is different: can we find equivalents for philosophical terms?', *Times literary supplement*, 6 Sept. 1996, pp. 12–13.

tial synonyms (where I have tried to carry over the *possibility* of difference in the Latin into the English), and certain (sometimes polysemic)
specialist terms for which no modern English word seems to be available
(where I have often chosen to Anglicize the Latin). Thus *schematismus*,
a key term in the *Abecedarium*, has been rendered as *schematism*, and the
Victorian preference for *configuration* has been abandoned not least
because Bacon also used the word *configuratio* but never as a synonym
for *schematismus*. Likewise to translate *lumen* in the present edition of
the *Topica inquisitionis de luce et lumine*, I have simply carried over the
Latin into the English and reserved the word *light* to translate *lux*, with
the object of preserving a distinction with an important philosophical
history. However, where *lumen* is used in a metaphorical sense (as it is in
the *Historia densi*) I have translated it as *light*: no one in their right senses
would dream of talking about *the lumen of induction*.

I have also been careful to translate *virtus* as *virtue*, and *vis* as *power*,
phantasia as *fantasy* and *imaginatio* as *imagination*—once again in an
effort to maintain actual or possible distinctions of meaning in Bacon's
Latin lexis. In the *Historia & inquisitio de animato* I have translated
matrix as *matrix* and not *womb* for it is notable that Bacon never used
the Latin word *uterus* there. I have reserved *womb* for translating *uterus*
(a word which occurs in, for example, the *Novum organum*). Bacon
seems to use *matrix* in a more general sense than *uterus*, meaning any
enclosure (a womb, earth, putrefaction, etc.) which acts like a womb;
uterus is used in other late works in a more restricted sense to refer to the
wombs of oviparous and viviparous creatures.

While distinctions should be maintained in translation, anachro-
nisms should be avoided. In translating the *Inquisitio de magnete* I have
used *loadstone* not *magnet* for *magnes*. But in the case of *aqua fortis* and
aqua regia I have carried the Latin directly into the English version, for
not only was that quite often done in seventeenth-century English but
it would be wrong to translate the terms into the nomenclature of modern chemistry: *nitric acid* may be the same substance as *aqua fortis* but it
is a term belonging to a conceptual framework of which Bacon had no
inkling. However, the plural of *aqua fortis* has not been Englished with
a straight transposition of the Latin. For Bacon *aquæ fortes* was a generic
expression for all *strong waters* and not the specific one indicated by the
singular. The point of translation is to help the reader—even if the help
makes the reader's life more strenuous.

Lastly, I have not translated the manuscript version of the *Historia
densi & rari* (the first text presented in this volume). A translation of the

manuscript version can readily be extracted (if necessary with the help of the tables of page numbers given in Appendix II) from the facing-page translation of the much longer Rawley version of the text (the second work presented below).

HISTORIA DENSI & RARI
(BN coll. Dupuy version)

| [Historia Densi & Rari; necnon
Coitionis & Expansionis
Materiæ per Spatia.]

Tabula expansionis & coitionis materiæ per spatia in tangibilibus
5   (quæ scilicet dotantur pondere) cum supputatione rerum in
corporibus diuersis.

Idem spatium occupa[n]t, seu æque exporriguntur:

Auri puri vncia 1.	siue denarij 20.	gra. 0.	Sanguinis ouillj	den. 1. gr. 5.
10 Argenti viui	den. 19.	gr. 9.	Ligni santallj rubri	den. 1. gr. 5.
Plumbi	den. 12.	gr. 1-d.	Gagatis	den. 1. gr. 5.
Argenti puri	den. 10.	gra. 21.	Cæpe recentis	den. 1. gr. 5.
Plumbi cineritij	den. 10.	gr. 12.	Lactis vaccini	den. 1. gr. 4.
Cupri	den. 9.	gr. 8.	Caphuræ	den. 1. gr. 4.
15 Aurichalci	den. 9.	gr. 5.	Succi mentæ expressi	den. 1. gr. 4.
Chalybis	den. 8.	gr. 10.	Ceruisiæ lupulatæ fortis	den. 1. gr. 3-d.
Aeris communis	den. 8.	gr. 9.	Succi borraginis expressi	den. 1. gr. 3-d.
20				
Ferri	den. 8.	gr. 6.	ligni ebeni	den. 1. gr. 3-d.
Stanni	den. 7.	gr. 22.	pulueris sem. foenic. dulcis	den. 1. gr. 3-d.
magnetis	den. 5.	gr. 12.	Aceti	den. 1. gr. 3-d.
25 lapidis Lydij	den. 3.	gr. 1.	agrestæ ex pomis acerbis	den. 1. gr. 3.
Marmoris	den. 2.	gr. 22-d.	succini lucidi	den. 1. gr. 3.
Silicis	den. 2	gr. 22.	vrinæ	den. 1. gr. 3.
Vitri	den. 2.	gr. 20.	aquæ communis	den. 1. gr. 3. p.m.
30 Christalli	den. 2.	gr. 18.	olei cariophyllorum chymici	den. 1. gr. 3. p.m.
Alabastri	den. 2.	gr. 12.	vini clareti	den. 1. gr. 2-d. qu.

1–3 [Historia . . . Spatia.]] / this title is purely editorial and imported from *HDR*; in *HDR* it
is followed by an aditus (preface) absent from the manuscript   5 rerum] rationum *HDR*
7 occupa[n]t] / cf. *HDR*   10 rubri] *rubei HDR*   13 cineritij] *cinericei, Anglice*
Tynglas HDR   gr. 4.] ~ *d. HDR*   27 gr. 22-d.] ~ *qu. HDR*   28 gr. 22.] ~ *d.*
HDR   29 gr. 20.] ~ *d. HDR*

4 expansionis & coitionis] nouns transposed in *HDR*   5 (quæ] ∧ ~   7 seu] sive
HDR   exporriguntur:] ~ ∧   12 Cæpe] *Cepæ HDR*   15 mentæ] *menthæ HDR*
17 Ceruisiæ] / this and next item transposed in *HDR*   22–3 sem. foenic.] *seminis fœniculi*
HDR   30 Christalli] *Crystalli HDR*

Salis gemmæ	den. 2.	gr. 10.	pulueris sacchari		
			albi	den. 1. gr. 2-d.	
Luti communis	den. 2.	gr. 8-d.	ceræ flauæ	den. 1. gr. 2.	
⟨Nitri⟩ luti albi	den. 2.	gr. 5-d.	radicis chinæ	den. 1. gr. 2.	
Nitri	den. 2.	gr. 5.	carnis pyri brumalis		5
			crudj	den. 1. gr. 2.	
Ossis bouis	den. 2.	gr. 5.	aceti distillati	den. 1. gr. 1.	
Pulueris			aquæ rosaceæ		
margaritarum	den. 2.	gr. 2.	distillatæ	den. 1. gr. 1.	
Sulphuris	den. 2.	gr. 2.	cineris communis	den. 1. gr. 1.	10
Terræ communis	den. 2.	gr. 1-d.	myrrhæ	den. 1. gr. 0.	
Vitrioli albi	den. 1.	gr. 22.	Benjouin	den. 1. gr. 0.	
Eboris	den. 1.	gr. 21-d.	Butyri	den. 1. gr. 0.	
Aluminis	den. 1.	gr. 21.	Adipis	den. 1. gr. 0.	
Olei vitrioli	den. 1.	gr. 21.	olei amygdalini	den. 0. gr. 23-d.	15
Arenæ albæ	den. 1.	gr. 20.	olei maceris viridis		
			expressi	den. 0. gr. 23-d.	
Cretæ	den. 1.	gr. 18.	pulueris herbæ		
			sampsuci	den. 0. gr. 23.	
olei sulphuris	den. 1.	gr. 18.	petrolei	den. 0. gr. 23.	20
Pulueris salis	den. 1.	gr. 10.	pulueris florum		
comm.			rosæ	den. 0. gr. 22.	
Ligni vitæ	den. 1.	gr. 10.	spiritus vini	den. 0. gr. 22.	
Carnis ouillæ	den. 1.	gr. 10.	Ligni quercus	den. 0. gr. 19. d.	
Aquæ fortis	den. 1.	gr. 7.	pulueris ful. com. e		25
			camino	den. 0. gr. 17.	
Cornu bouis	den. 1.	gr. 6.	ligni abietis	den. 0. gr. 15	
Balsami Indi	den. 1.	gr. 6.			
Cerebri vitulini					
crudi	den. 1.	gr. 5. p.m.			30

¹ Modus experimenti circa tabulam suprascriptam.   [fo. 7ᵛ]

Intelligantur pondera quibus vsi summus eius generis & computationis quibus aurifabri vtuntur, vt libra capiat vncias x̄ī̄ī. vncia x̄x̄ denarios, denarius grana x̄x̄īv̄. Delegimus autem corpus auri puri, ad cuius exporrectionis mensuram reliquorum corporum rationes applicaremus; non tantum quia grauissimum; sed quia maxime vnum & sui simile, nihil habens ex volatili. Experimentum fuit tale: vnciam auri puri in 35 figuram aleæ siue cubi efformauimus, dein situlam paruam quadratam ex argento parauimus, quæ cubum illum auri caperet, atque ei exacte

10 gr. 1.] *Gra. d. HDR*   15 amygdalini] ~ *dulcis HDR*   18 gr. 18.] ~ *d. HDR*
22 comm.] *communis HDR*   25 ful. com.] *fuliginis communis HDR*   34 Delegimus]
lc   37 Experimentum] lc   tale:] ~.

3

conueniret, nisi quod situla esset nonnihil altior, ita tamen vt locus intra situlam quo cubus ille auri ascenderat linea conspicua notaretur. Id fecimus liquorum & puluerum gratia, vt cum liquor aliquis intra eandem situlam immittendus esset, non difflueret, sed paulo interius se
5 contineret. Simul autem altera*m* situlam fieri fecimus, quæ cum altera illa pondere & contento prorsus par esset, vt in pari situla corporis contenti tantum ratio appareret. Tum cubos eiusdem magnitudinis siue dimensi fieri fecimus, in omnibus materijs in tabula specificatis quæ sectionem pati possent. Liquoribus vero ex tempore vsi sumus,
10 implendo scilicet situlam, quousque liquor ad locum illum linea signatum ascenderet. Pulueribus eodem modo, sed intelliguntur pulueres maxime & fortiter compressi. Hoc enim maxime ad æquationem pertinet, nec casum recipit. Itaque non alia fuit probatio quam vt vna ex situlis vacua in vna lance, altera cum corpore in altera
15 poneretur lance, & ratio ponderis corporis contenti per se exciperetur. Quanto vero pondus corporis pondere auri est minus, tanto exporrectio corporis est exporrectione auri major. Exempli gratia, cum auri ille cubus det v*n*ciam vnam, myrrhæ vero denarium vnum, liquet exporrectionem myrrhæ ad exporrectionem auri habere rationem vicecuplam; vt vicies
20 plus materiæ sit in auro quam in myrrha in simili spatio, rursus vicies plus sit exporrectionis in myrrha quam in auro in simili exporrectione.

[fo. 8ʳ] ˡ Monita

Melius fieret experimentum in maiori vase quam in minimo. Notandum etiam est quod plurima corpora cuiusdam speciei imprimit majus &
25 minus quoad pondera & spatia. Tum etiam quod tria corporum genera huc retrahi non possunt: primo, ea quæ dimensioni cubicæ satisfacere non possunt, vt folia, flores, pelliculæ, membranæ; Secundo, corpora inæqualiter caua & porosa, vt spongia, suber, vellera; tertio, pneumatica,

2 notaretur] signaretur *HDR*   11 intelliguntur] intelligantur *HDR*   12 maxime] potissimum *HDR*   21 exporrectione] *pondere HDR*   23 Melius . . .] / sentence expanded as a para in *HDR* (see p. 46, ll. 6–11 below)   Notandum . . .] / sentence expanded as a para in *HDR* (see p. 46, ll. 12–19 below)   25 Tum . . .] / sentence expanded as a para in *HDR* (see p. 46, ll. 20–7 below)

2 Id] lc   5 Simul] lc   7 Tum] lc   9 Liquoribus] lc   11 Pulueribus] lc   modo,] ~.   12 Hoc] lc   13 Itaque] lc   15 poneretur lance] *lance* poneretur *HDR*   16 Quanto] lc   17 Exempli] lc   21 sit exporrectionis] exporrectionis sit *HDR*   23 Notandum] lc   25 Tum] lc   26 possunt:] ~.   27 membranæ;] ~.   28 vellera;] ~.

quia pondere non dotantur, vt aer, flamma. Videndum etiam num forte
contractio corporis arctior ex vi vnita nanciscatur majorem rationem
ponderis quam pro quantitate materiæ.

Obseruationes.

In tabula non est ens quod aliud ens in copia materiæ superet vltra   5
proportionem x̄x̄x̄ī̄ī. Tanto enim superat aurum lignum abietis. De
interioribus nihil determinatur; sed cum illa a calore coelesti primo
longius, deinde penitus semota sint, possunt esse corporibus nobis notis
densiora. Opinio de compositione sublunarium ex quatuor elementis
non bene cedit. Aurum in situla illa tabulari est ponderis denariorum   10
x̄x̄. terra co*m*munis den. ī̄ī. paulo plus. aqua den. ī. gr. ī̄ī̄ī. aer & ignis
longe tenuiora, & minus materiata, ponderis vero nullius. At⟨q*ue*⟩ forma
materiam non auget. Videndum igitur, quomodo ex corpore ī̄ī. den. &
corporibus longe tenuioribus educatur per formam in pari dimenso
corpus x̄x̄. den. Duo sunt effugia vnum, quod elementa tenuiora   15
compingant densiora in majorem densitatem quam simplicis elementi;
alterum, quod non intelligant Peripatetici hoc de terra communi, sed de
terra elementari omni ente composito grauiore. At ignis & aer non
condensant, nisi per accidens, vt suo loco dicetur. Terra autem illa quæ
foret auro & omnibus grauior ita sita est, ut vix adsit ad mixtionem.   20

In tabula multa cadunt præter expectationem; veluti quod metalla | [fo. 8ᵛ]
lapidibus tanto grauiora; quod vitrum, corpus scilicet excoctum,
crystallo, corpore glaciato, grauius; quod terra communis tam parum
ponderosa; quod olea distillata vitrioli & sulphuris ad corpus crudorum
tam prope accedant; quod tam parum intersit inter pondus aquæ & vini;   25
quod olea chymica, quæ subtiliora videri possint oleis expressis,
ponderosiora; quod os cornu tanto grauius. &c.

---

1 Videndum . . .] / sentence expanded as a para in *HDR* (see p. 46, ll. 28–33 below)
4 Obseruationes] / before this heading *HDR* (see p. 48, ll. 1–5 below) has an extra para; after
the heading there are three extra sentences (see p. 48, ll. 7–12 below)   5 In tabula non
est] Non invenitur in *Tabula HDR*   7 determinatur] decernimus *HDR*   10 tab-
ulari] cubitali / cf. *HDR*, p. 48, l. 18   20 mixtionem.] / in *HDR* this is followed by an
extra sentence, another observatio, two mandata, and another two observationes (see p. 50,
l. 1–p. 52, l. 10 below)   21 expectationem] opinionem *HDR*   23 glaciato]
conglaciato *HDR*   24 corpus] pondus *HDR*   26–7 quod . . . grauius. &c.] quod
Os sit *Dente* & *Cornu* tanto gravius: & alia similiter haud pauca. *HDR* / in *HDR* this is followed by an extra mandatum (see p. 52, ll. 19–27 below)

1 Videndum] lc   6 Tanto] lc   De] lc   9 Opinio] lc   10 Aurum]   lc
12 At⟨q*ue*⟩] lc   13 Videndum] lc   15 Duo] lc   16 elementi;] ∼.
18 At] lc   19 Terra] lc

Mixtura omnis corporum per tabulam & pondus reuelari & deprehendi
potest. Si enim quæratur quantum aquæ sit admixtum vino, vel
quantum plumbi auro, & sic de reliquis, ponderato composito, &
consule tabulam de pondere simplicium, & mediæ rationes compositi
5 comparatæ ad simplicia dabunt quantum ⟨materiæ⟩ mixturæ.

Tabula exporrectionis materiæ per idem
spatium siue dimensum in corporibus
ijsdem, integris & comminutis.

Mercurius in corpore quantus impleat mensuram tabularem ponderat
10 den. x̄īx̄. gr. īx̄. Sublimatus vero in corpore presso den. īī̄ī. gr. x̄x̄īī.
Plumbum in corpore den. v̄īī̄ī. gr. ⟨v̄īī̄ī⟩ ī. d. In cerusa vero in corpore
presso den. īv̄. gr. v̄īī̄ī. d.
Chalibs in corpore den. v̄īī̄ī. gr. x̄. In puluere præparato, quali ad
medicinas vtuntur, & presso den īī̄ī. gr. īx̄.
15 Crystallum in corpore den. īī̄ī. gr. x̄v̄īī̄ī. In puluere presso den. īī̄ī. gr. x̄x̄.
Santalum rubrum in corpore den. ī. gr. v̄. d. In puluere presso grana
x̄v̄ī. d.
Lignum quercus in corpore gr x̄īx̄. d. In cinere den ī. gr. īī̄ī.

Tabula exporrectionis materiæ per idem
20   spatium siue dimensum, in corporibus
crudis & distillatis.

Sulphur in corpore den. īī̄ī. gra īī̄ī. In oleo chymico den ī. gr. x̄v̄īī̄ī.
Vitriolum in corpore den. ī. gr. x̄x̄īī. In oleo den. ī. gra.x̄x̄ī.
[fo. 9ʳ] ¹ Vinum in corpore den. ī. gr. īī̄ī. d. q. In distillato gr. x̄x̄īī.
25 Acetum in corpore den. ī. gr. īī̄ī. d. In distillato den. ī. gr. īī̄ī.
Hæc de tangibilibus corporibus.
Quantum ad pneumatica, pondere non dotantur, per cuius incubitum
& exporrectionem materiæ in ipsis contentæ iudicium fieri possit.

---

1 Mixtura] / in *HDR* this is preceded by the heading *Vellicationes de Practica* (see p. 52, l. 28
below)   5 mixturæ] / in *HDR* this is followed by an additional sentence, three more
paras and an observatio (see p. 54, l. 2–p. 56. l. 6 below)   10 corpore] *pulvere HDR*
11 v̄īī̄ī] 12 *HDR*   corpore] *pulvere HDR*   16 rubrum] rubeum *HDR*   gr. v̄. d.] d.
om HDR   25 īī̄ī] 3 *HDR*   26 Hæc . . . corporibus.] / instead *HDR* has a monitum, a mandatum and two observationes (see p. 58, l. 1–p. 60, l.11 below)   27 Quantum
. . .] / in *HDR* this sentence is incorporated in the first para of a commentatio; then follows a
para absent from *HDR(M)* (see p. 60, l. 13–p. 62, l. 2)
10 Sublimatus] lc   11 In] lc   13 In] lc   15 In] lc   16 In] lc
18 In] lc   22 In] lc   23 In] lc   24 In] lc   25 In] lc

6

Sunt pneumatica apud nos triplicis naturæ; inchoata, deuincta, pura.
Inchoata sunt fumi omnigeni, atque ex materijs diuersis. Eorum ordo
esse possit, primo volatilium, quæ expirant ex metallis, & nonnullis ex
fossilibus; quæ sunt, prout nomen significat, potius alata quam
pneumatica, quia facile admodum coagulantur vel sublimando, vel   5
cadendo, aut præcipita*n*do. Secundo, vaporum qui expirant ex aqua &
aqueis. Tertio, fumorum (nomine generali retento) qui expirant ex
corporibus siccis. Quarto, halituum, qui expirant ex corporibus oleosis.
Quinto, aurarum quæ expirant ex corporibus mole aqueis, spiritu
inflammabilibus, qualia sunt vina, & liquores exaltati, siue potus fortes.   10
Est & aliud genus fumorum, illi scilicet in quos flamma desinit. Ij vero
non possunt spirare nisi in inflammabilibus, cum flammam
subsequa*n*tur. Hos postfumos, seu fumos secundos appellamus. Itaque
non possunt esse postvapores, quia aquea non inflammantur, sed
postfumi (nomine speciali) posthalitus, postauræ, etiam, vt arbitror,   15
postvolatilia in nonnullis. ⟨at pneumatica deuincta⟩
At pneumatica deuincta ea sunt quæ ipsa solitaria aut soluta non
reperiuntur, sed tantum corporibus tangibilibus inclusa, quos spiritus
etiam vulgo vocant. Participant autem ex aqueo & oleo⟨ginea⟩so, & ex
ijsdem nutriuntur, quæ in pneumaticum versa, constituunt corpus veluti   20
ex aere & flammis, vnde vtriusque mysteria sunt. Accedunt autem
spiritus isti (si ad pneumatica soluta spectes) proxime ad naturam
aurarum, quales ex vino aut sale surgunt. Horum spirituum natura
duplex; alia crudorum, alia viuorum. Crudi insunt omni tangibili; viui
animatis tantum, siue vegetabilibus, siue sensibilibus.   25
At pneumatica pura duo tantum inueniuntur, aër, & flamma, licet illa
quoque magnas diuersitates sortiantur & gradus exporrectionis inæquales.

   ᴵ Tabula pneumaticorum secundum commentationem   [fo. 9ᵛ]
         supradictam, prout ordine ascendunt ad
                 exporrectionem majorem.   30

Volatilia metallorum & fossilium
Postvolatilia ipsorum

3–4 nonnullis ex fossilibus] ex nonnullis Fossilium *HDR* (p. 60, l. 24 below)
10 potus] potius   12 spirare] expirare *HDR*   19 aqueo &] ~ ex *HDR*
21 flammis] *Flamma HDR*

2 Eorum] lc   6 Secundo,] ~ₐ   7 Tertio,] tertioₐ   8 Quarto,] quartoₐ
9 Quinto,] quintoₐ   10 inflammabilibus] inflammatilibus   11 Ij] lc
13 Hos] lc   13 Itaque] lc   19 Participant] lc   21 flammis,] ~.
Accedunt] lc   23 Horum] lc   24 Crudi] lc   tangibili;] ~.   26 At] / no
new para in *HDR*   flamma,] ~.

Vapores
Fumi
Postfumi
Halitus
5 Posthalitus
Auræ
Postauræ
Spiritus crudi deuincti in tangibilibus
Aër
10 Spiritus viui siue incensi deuincti in tangibilibus.
Flamma.
De exporrectionibus horum, tum ad inuicem, tum ad tangibilia collatis, iam videndum. Atque si natura leuis per ascensum sursum posset liquidare raritatem corporum, quemadmodum natura grauis per
15 descensum deorsum liquidat eorum densitatem, res bene posset succedere. Sed multa obsunt. Primo, quod differentiæ motuum in ijs quæ aspectum fugiunt non percipiantur immediate per sensum; deinde, quod non reperiatur in aere & similibus tam fortis appetitus petendi superiora, quam putatur; denique, si aer moueretur sursum, tamen cum
20 continuetur plerumque cum alio aere, motus ille ægre percipi posset. Nam sicut aqua non ponderat super aquam, ita aer non insurgit subter aerem. Itaque alij modi excogitandi sunt.
Atque de exporrectione pneumaticorum ad inuicem, quodque ordo & series raritatis, qualis est in tabula, non leuiter fundata sit, offerunt se
25 quædam probationes non malæ: verum de certis gradibus huiusmodi
[fo. 10ʳ] exporrectionis, & rursus de exporrectione pneumatici comparati ad ¦ tangibile difficilior sane est inquisitio.
Primò igitur fumos omnes, tam secundos quam primos, aëris raritatem non æquare consentaneum est, cum illi perspicui sint, aër
30 minimè, neque ipsi conspicui maneant paulo post cum se aëri miscuerint.
Postfumos præfumis esse tenuiores & rariores satis liquet, cum sint flammæ, corporis tam subtilis, cadauera & solutiones. Experimento quoque manifestissimum est in nocturnis spectaculis intra coenacula,
35 quæ tot lychnis & facibus collucent, etiam post plurimam horarum

24 est] *om HDR*   tabula] ~ *ponitur HDR*   27 sane] *certe HDR*   29 perspicui] *conspicui HDR*

13 Atque] lc   16 Sed] lc   Primo] lc   17 sensum;] ~.   19 putatur;] ~.   22 Itaque] lc   25 malæ:] ~.

8

moram sufficere aërem respirationi, licet tot postfumis in eum receptis. Quod si fuissent illi fumi præfumi (quales sunt ex lychnis & facibus extinctis ⟨)⟩ absque flamma) nemo vel ad longè minorem moram eos sustinere posset.

Spiritus crudos quoscumque in tangibilibus deuinctos etiam aëre 5 densiores iudicamus. Etenim spiritus vegetabilium, aut animalium mortuorum, aut huiusmodi, cum exhalauerint, manifestè retinent quiddam ex crasso, siue tangibili; vt cerni datur in odoribus, qui cum sint fumi parcè exeuntes, nec conferti, vt in fumis conspicuis & vaporibus, tamen si nacti fuerint aliquid tangibile, præsertim ex 10 mollioribus, applicant se ad illud, & planè adhærent, illudque odore inficiunt, vt manifestum sit illos cum crassa natura affinitatem ægre dirimere.

At spiritus viuos aere ipso aliquanto rariores existimamus, tum quia inflammantur nonnihil, tum quia diligenter experti sumus aerem ad 15 minuendum aut subleuandum pondus nihil conferre. Nam vesica inflata non est vacua & compressa leuior, cum sit illa tamen repleta aëre; nec similiter spongia aut vellus lanæ aëre referta illis ipsis vacuis leuiora sunt aëre excluso. At corpus animale viuum & mortuum grauitate manifestè differunt, licet haud tantum quantum putantur. Quare videtur aër 20 pondus non minuere, spiritus autem viuus hoc facere. Atque cum pondus densitates dijudicet, etiam leuatio ponderis raritates dijudicare potest.

Supremo ordine collocatur flamma, tum quia illa manifestissimè | [fo. 10ᵛ] petit superiora tum quia verisimile est rationes pneumaticorum minimè 25 differre a rationibus fomitum suorum; ideoque, quemadmodum oleum est rarius aqua, similiter flammam rariorem esse aere & spiritu. Etiam videtur flamma corpus tenuius, & mollius, & magis cedens quam aër; nam leuissima quæpiam aura commota iuxta flammam lychni eam reddit tremulam.   30

Si aduertas fumum ex cereo recenter extincto exeuntem, & oculis metiaris crassitudinem eius, & rursus intuearis corpus ipsius fumi postea inflammati, videbis expansionem flammæ collatæ ad fumum ampliatam quasi ad duplam.

3 eos] ea / cf. *HDR*, p. 64, l. 29 below   7 manifestè] manifesto *HDR*   10 aliquid] aliquod   15 aerem] *om c-t* supplied by *HDR*   19 manifestè] manifesto *HDR*   23 potest] debet *HDR*   30 tremulam.] / after this *HDR* has an extra two paras (historia) and a monitum (see p. 66, l. 20–p. 68, l. 29 below)

2 Quod] lc   6 Etenim] lc   16 Nam] l.c.   17 aëre;] ∼.   19 At] l.c.
20 Quare] l.c.   21 Atque] l.c.   26 suorum;] ∼.   27 Etiam] lc

Si accipias pauca grana pulueris pyrij, eaque inflammes, magna prorsus fit expansio respectu corporis pulueris. Si vero extincta illa flamma multo amplius adhuc se extendit corpus fumi, id verò non te fallat, ac si corpus tangibile plus expanderetur in fumo quam in flamma.

5 Nam id secus se habet. Sed ratio apparentiæ est, quod corpus flammæ sit corpus integrum, corpus fumi corpus mixtum ex longe majori parte cum aëre. Itaque sicut parum croci multum aquæ colorat, similiter parum fumi in multum aërem se spargit. Nam fumus (vt antea dictum est) non sparsus, minor cernitur corpore flammæ.

10 Si accipias frustulum corticis arantij exterioris, qui aromaticus est, & oleosus, ipsumque subitò comprimas iuxta lychnum, exilit aliquid roris in guttulis; quod tamen constituit corpus flammæ respectu guttularum insigniter amplum.

Commentum illud Peripateticorum de decupla proportione 15 elementorum ad inuicem in raritate, res fictitia est & ad placitum; cum certum sit aerem centuplo, ad minimum, rariorem esse aqua, flammamque oleo. At flammam ipsum aërem decupla minimè superare.

Philosophi & Medici qualitatibus primis tribuunt offertus qui spiritibus solum debentur.

20 A[t]que de exporrectione materiæ in corporibus, secundum consistentias suas diuersas dum quiescunt, hæc inquisita sint.

[fo. 11ʳ] | Ex introceptione siue admissione corporis alieni fit dilatatio, vt videre est in vesica ex follibus per receptionem aëris, in liquoribus de alto fusis & fortiter agitatis, qui cum aëre commiscentur, in ludicris puerorum, & 25 in pulueribus.

Fiunt tumores in ventre animalium & alijs partibus ex flatu & humore aqueo introcepto. Clauso oculorum altero, oculj aperti pupilla dilatatur.

---

1 Si accipias . . .] / in *HDR* this para is headed *Monitum*   2 Si vero] Sed rursus *HDR*
6 mixtum] commistum *HDR*   8 fumus] ~ spissus *HDR*   10 ff. Si accipias . . .]
/ in *HDR* this para is headed Historia   14 ff. Commentum . . .] / in *HDR* this para is
headed *Observatio*   18 ff. Philosophi . . .] / in *HDR* this is revised, enlarged and headed
Monitum (p. 70, l. 25–p. 72, l. 3 below)   20–1 A[t]que . . .] / in *HDR* this is revised,
enlarged and headed *Connexio* and is followed by an extra monitum (see p. 72, l. 4–p. 74, l. 3
below)   22–5 Ex introceptione . . .] / the substance of this para is worked up to become
seven paras in *HDR* (see p. 74, l. 7–p. 76, l. 9 below)   26–8 Fiunt tumores . . .] / the
substance of this para is worked up to become two paras in *HDR*, separated by four extra paras
and followed two extra paras (see p. 76, ll. 10–30 below)

2 Si] lc   5 Nam] lc   Sed] lc   7 Itaque] lc   8 Nam] lc   17 At] lc
27 Clauso] lc

Fiunt dilatationes in corporibus ex spiritu innato absque igne aut calore externo admixto se expandente, vt in ebullitionibus & intumescentia musti & ceruisiæ nouæ.

Semina plantarum, pisorum, fabarum, turgescunt antequam emittent radicem. Arbores quandoque spiritu & succo natiuo tumescentes 5 corticem rumpunt, & emittunt lachrymas. Etiam gemmæ complures videntur esse eruptiones succorum puriorum ex rupibus; cum tam gummi quam gemmæ rupium depræhendantur (ex splendore) esse succi percolati & depurati, adeo vt etiam saxa & lapides videantur ex spiritu innato tumescere. Actus spermatis ad viuificandum, est expansio massæ 10 suæ. Vitriolum erumpendo tanquam germinat, & ferè arborescit. Omnis gleba terræ tumet nitro; etiam lapides quidam in locis humidioribus.

Sudores ex humoribus liquefactis per spiritus dilatatos proueniunt.

Pulsus cordis & arteriarum fit per irrequietam dilatationem 15 spirituum, & receptum eorum per vices.

Motus etiam voluntarius in animalibus, qui expeditur in perfectioribus per neruos, videtur radicem habere in compressione primum, deinde relaxatione spirituum.

In omni carie & putredine tumescere incipiunt spiritus corporis 20 innati, cumque ad exitum properant, soluunt & alterant rei compagem; & si compages rei sit paulo tenacior & viscosior, vt exire non possint, nouas formas moliuntur, vt in vermibus a putredine natis. Sed exordium actionis est a dilatatione spirituum.

¹ Neque spiritus in putredine cohibitus tantum mo⟨l⟩itur animalcula; 25 [fo. 11ᵛ] verum & rudimenta plantarum, vt conspicitur in musco & hirsutie arborum nonnullarum. Exemplum mali citrij.

Similiter rubigines fiunt in metallis, & vitro, & similibus, ex dilatatione spiritus innati, qui tumescit, & vrget partes crassiores, easque ante se agit & extrudit vt exeat. 30

1–3 Fiunt dilatationes . . .] / the substance of this para is worked up as a connexio and the first para of the subsequent historia in *HDR* (see p. 76, l. 32–p. 78, l. 9 below)   4 Semina . . .] / the substance of this para is preceded by two extra paras and is itself worked up as seven separate paras in *HDR* (see p. 78, l. 10–p. 80, l. 2 below)   14 Sudores . . .] / rewritten in *HDR* (see p. 80, ll. 2–4 below)   15 arteriarum] ∼ in Animalibus *HDR* 17 Motus] Quin & ∼ *HDR* / in *HDR* this is followed by nine extra paras (see p. 80, ll. 10–36 below)   20 corporis] caloris   27 Exemplum] / this working note is fully elaborated in *HDR* (see p. 82, ll. 1–7 below)   30 exeat] exeant / cf. *HDR*, p. 82, l. 10 below

5 Arbores] lc   6 Etiam] lc   10 Actus] lc   11 Vitriolum] lc 12 Omnis] lc   23 Sed] lc   27 Exemplum] lc

In agro Herefordiensi fuit terræ motus admodum pusillus & lentus, sed rarus, in quo aliqua iugera terræ per diem integrum paulatim se mouerunt, & in alium locum paulo decliuiorem, se transtulerunt, & ita quieuerunt.

5 In pinnis fidium fit tempore pluuioso vt illæ tumescentes difficilius torqueantur. Similiter pixides ligneæ difficilius extrahuntur ex thecis suis, & ostia lignea difficilius aperiuntur.

Chordæ fidium extentæ paulò rigidius temporibus pluuiosis rumpuntur. Humores in corporibus animalium tempestatibus 10 australibus & pluuiosis depræhenduntur laxari, & tumescere, & fluere, & incumbere magis, & meatus obstruere.

Recepta est opinio, humores & succos, non in animalibus tantum, sed & in plantis, sub plenilunijs magis turgescere & caua implere.

De tumoribus & relaxationibus aëris diligentius videndum, & 15 quatenus in his militent magna ex parte causæ ventorum, cum vapores nec commodè colliguntur in pluuiam, nec dissipantur in aërem limpidum, sed inducunt tumores in corpore aëris.

Atque `hæc´ de dilatationibus corporum per spiritum innatum, siue in maturationibus, siue in rudimentis generationum, siue in excitatione 20 per motum, siue in irritationibus naturalibus, siue in putrefactionibus, siue in relaxationibus.

Transeundum ad aperturas & dilatationes quæ fiunt per ignem & calorem externum actualem.

Aer per calorem dilatatur simpliciter.

[fo. 12ʳ] 25 ⏐ Caro in ventosis attrahitur per motum nexus. Similiter vitrum calefactum ad tertias contenti. Fiat experimentum in fiala ferrea, vt sciatur quousque; vt inde melius de raritate aeris & ætheris ipsius iudicium fieri possit.

Hero describit altaris fabricam, eo artificio, vt superimposito 30 holocausto & incenso, subito aqua descenderet, quæ ignem extingueret. Id non aliam poscebat industriam, quam vt sub altare esset locus

1 In agro] / preceded in *HDR* by additional lines on earthquakes (see p. 82, ll. 11–23 below) and followed by additional instances and mandata (see p. 82, l. 27–p. 84, l. 17 below)   6 thecis] tectis / cf. *HDR*, p. 84, l. 19 below   13 implere.] / after this *HDR* has two extra paras (see p. 84, ll. 27–31 below)   18 Atque . . .] / in *HDR* this and the next para are combined and headed connexio; the resulting para is followed in *HDR* by a section heading, a monitum and the heading *Historia* (see p. 86, ll. 1–19 below)   24 simpliciter.] / *HDR* has an extra sentence here   25–8 Caro . . . possit.] / in *HDR* these working notes are elaborated as two separate paras with a third not present in *HDR(M)* (see p. 86, l. 22–p. 90, l. 7 below)   31 altare] altari

6 Similiter] lc   9 Humores] lc   25 Similiter] lc   26 Fiat] lc fiala] / *sic*   31 Id] lc

concauus & conclusus aëre repletus, qui aer ab igne calefactus, & propterea dilatatus, nullum reperiret exitum nisi in canali ad parietem erecto & curuato, ore super altare inuerso. In canali erecto infusa erat aqua, facto etiam ventre in canali, vt largior copia aquæ reciperetur; ea aqua obice impediebatur ne descenderet, foraminato; qui obex 5 postquam erat versus, dabat locu*m* aeri dilatato, vt aquam eueheret & eijceret.

Sartago fracastorij, papiliones admoti ad ignem aut radios solis, reuiuiscunt, ægroti in deliquijs tam aquis fortibus & calidis intro susceptis, quam calore exteriore, & fricatione, & motu excitantur.   10

Inspiciendæ sunt aperturæ aquæ, olei, spiritus vini, aceti, agrestionis, & vini, per calorem.

Generaliter in liquidis hoc fit, vt pinguia sicut oleum, lac, adeps, & huiusmodi, insurgant & tumeant simul toto corpore. Succi maturi, & magis adhuc immaturi, bullis majoribus; succi effoeti & vapidi, bullis 15 minoribus.

Omnibus liquoribus commune est, vt in parua quantitate citius aperiantur, bulliant, atque consumantur, quam in magna.

Experimentum de aperturis liquorum faciendum est in vasis vitreis, vt motus in corpore melius conspici possint, atque super foculos cum 20 calore æquali, vt differentia verius excipiatur, atque ab igne lento, quia ignis vehemens præcipitat & confundit actiones.

| Sunt verò complura corpora, quæ non sunt liquida, sed consistentia [fo. 12ᵛ] & determinata, attamen per calorem nanciscuntur eam aperturam vt liquescant, siue deueniant liquida, quandiu calor ea vellicet & expandat; 25 qualia sunt cera, adeps, butyrum, pix, resina, gummi, saccharum, mel, & plurima ex metallis, veluti plumbum, aurum, argentum, æs, cuprum; ita tamen vt ad aperturam requira*n*tur non solum gradus caloris longè diuersi, sed & modificationes ignis & flammæ dissimiles. Nam alia metalla colliquantur per ignem simpliciter, vt plumbum; alia per ignem 30 motum & follibus excitatum, vt aurum, argentum; alia non sine admixtione, vt chalybs, qui non nisi admixto sulphure, colliquatur. At ista omnia, si continuetur ignis & urgeat, non solum sortiuntur

2 parietem] ~ Altaris *HDR*   8–10 Sartago . . . excitantur.] / in *HDR* these working notes are elaborated (see p. 88, ll. 25–32 below)   11–12 Inspiciendæ . . . calorem.] / in *HDR* this working note is extensively elaborated (see p. 88, l. 33 p. 90, l. 20 below) 16 minoribus.] / followed by an extra para in *HDR* (p. 90, ll. 25–6 below) 19 Experimentum] preceded by the heading *Monitum* in *HDR*   20 corpore] ~ Liquorum *HDR*   21 atque ab] atque *HDR*   23 Sunt] / preceded by the heading *Historia* in *HDR*   32 sulphure,] ~ aut simile quopiam *HDR*
3 In] lc   4 reciperetur;] ~.   14 Succi] lc   29 Nam] lc   32 At] lc

aperturam colliquationis, sed pertranseunt, & adipiscuntur secundam
aperturam, volatilis, siue pneumatici, siue consumptionis; omnia,
inquam, præter aurum; nam quantum ad argentum viuum, cum natura
sua sit liquidum, incipit illud ab apertura secunda, & facile vertitur in
5 volatile. De auro adhuc dubium est vtrum possit fieri volatile &
pneumaticum, aut etiam potabile, vt loquuntur, hoc est, non dissolubile
quidem (id enim facile est & ⟨tre⟩ tritum per aquas fortes) sed digestibile
aut alterabile per ventriculum humanum. Huius autem rei legitima
videtur probatio; minimè illa, vt vi ignis ascendat aut trudat sursum, sed
10 vt ita attenuetur & subigatur, vt restitui in metallum non possit.
    Inquiratur etiam de vitro & vitrificatis, vtrum per ignem
consumantur, & vertantur in pneumaticum. Habetur enim vitrum pro
corpore fixo & exsucco, & vitrificatio pro morte metallorum. Quæ
[fo. 13ʳ] colliquantur omnia, in via & processu suo ¹ incipiunt ab infimo illo
15 gradu aperturæ, qui est emollitio & inteneratio, antequam colliquantur
& fundantur, vt cera, gummi, metalla colliquabilia, vitrum &c.
    At stannum & ferrum, postquam fuerint perfecta & repurgata nisi
fuerit admixtio, quatenus ad ignem simplicem persistunt, & non
procedunt vltra illum gradum emollitionis, vt reddantur scilicet
20 malleabilia & flexibilia, & exuant fragilitatem suam; minimè autem
pertingunt ad colliquationem siue fusionem.
    Vide[n]tur ferrum & vitrum cum aperiuntur ad illam mollitiem,
dilatari sane in spiritu suo incluso, vnde fit illa subactio partium
tangibilium, vt duritiem & obstinationem suam deponant, neque tamen
25 corpus ipsum integrum localiter dilatari cernitur aut intumescere.
Attamen attentius paulo inquirenti depræhenditur in ipsis inuisibilis
quidam tumor & partium pulsatio, licet cohibeatur ab arcta compage
sua. Nam si accipias vitrum ignitum, & majorem in modum calefactum,
& ponas illud supra tabulam lapideam, aut simile aliquod corpus
30 durum, licet & ipsa tabula seu corpus bene calefactum fuerit, vt frigori
causa imputari non possit, rumpetur prorsus vitrum, duritie lapidis
scilicet tumorem illum occultum vitri repercutiente. Itaque solent in
huiusmodi casu, quando vitrum feruens submouetur ab igne,
substernere ipsi puluerem aliquem aut arenam mollem, quæ suauiter
35 cedens tumorem in partibus vitri non retundat.

2 volatilis] ~ scilicet *HDR*   3 quantum] quatenus *HDR*   cum] ~ in *HDR*
11 Inquiratur] Ignoratur   etiam] ~ ulterius *HDR*   13 exsucco] exsucto
17 stannum & ferrum] *Ferrum & Chalybs HDR*   22 mollitiem] ~ de qua diximus,
HDR   31 rumpetur] rumpitur / cf. *HDR*, p. 94, l. 12 below

3 aurum;] ~,   5 De] lc   8 Huius] lc   12 Habetur] lc
26 Attamen] lc   28 Nam] lc   32 Itaque] l.c.

Etiam pilæ e bombardis emissæ, postquam non solum vehj, sed &
gliscere aut labi omnino desierunt, adeo vt ad aspectum sint prorsus
immobiles, tamen diu post, magnum depræhenduntur habere
tumultum, & pulsationem in minimis, adeo vt si aliquid superponatur,
magnam vim patiatur, neque tam a calore comburente, quam a 5
palpitatione percussiua.

Apertura combustibilium ea est, vt per ignem primo emittant
fumum, dein concipiant flammam, postremo deponant cinerem.

| In corporibus quæ continent humorem ⟨æquæum⟩ aqueum & a [fo. 13ᵛ]
flamma abhorrentem in compage clausa & compacta (qualia sunt folia 10
lauri, & alia non porosa, sales, & similia) ea est apertura per ignem, vt
spiritus in eis contentus aqueus & crudus per calorem dilatatus cum
sonitu emittatur, antequam flamma concipiatur. Si verò in aliquo
corpore (quod rarò fit) in simul fiant eruptio flatus, & conceptio
flammæ, ingens, tumultus excitatur, & potentissima dilatatio, flatu 15
tanquam internis follibus flammam vndequaque exsufflante &
expandente, vt in puluere pyrio.

Duplex est dilatatio, siue apertura, siue attenuatio corporum, in
distillationibus; altera in transitu, cum corpus vertitur in vaporem aut
fumum, qui postea restituitur; altera in corpore restituto, quod semper 20
tenuius est, & magis subtile & expansum, & minus materiatum quam
corpus crudum, ex quo distillatum emanauit. Aqua enim rosacea
(exempli gratia) est [succo] rosarum tenuius, & minus ponderosum.

Distillationes omnes fiunt ex æstu quodam, siue reciprocatione
rarefactionis primò & versionis in pneumaticum, [dein condensationis] 25
& restitutionis in corpus tangibile, remittente se calore & vapore
repercusso.

In distillationibus actiones ⟨distillationis⟩ dilatationis &
condensationis non sunt sinceræ, sed interuenit [actio] illa (quæ maximè
est intentionalis in practica) separationis partium homogenearum, vt 30
succj veri, phlegmatis, aquæ, olej partis tenuioris, partis crassioris.

Distillationes & dilatationes per eas fiunt in clauso, vbi concluduntur
simul corpus distillandum & vapores qui ex eo emittuntur, & aër. Neque

---

2 desierunt] desierint *HDR*   5 neque] ~ id *HDR*   7 Apertura] / before this
HDR has an additional para (see p. 94, ll. 23–5 below)   14 eruptio flatus] eruptio, & flatus / cf. *HDR*, p. 94, l. 33 below   17 pyrio.] / after this *HDR* has five extra paras of history, a connexio, and a section heading (p. 94, l. 35–p. 96, l. 18)   23 [succo]] / cf. *HDR*,
p. 98, l. 3 below   25 [dein condensationis]] / cf. *HDR*, p. 98, ll. 6–7 below
29 [actio]] / cf. *HDR*, p. 98, l. 10 below   30 homogenearum] *heterogenearum HDR*
31 crassioris.] / after this *HDR* has an extra para (p. 98, ll. 13–25)

10 ⟨qualia sunt⟩ ₐqualia (sunt   13 Si] lc   22 Aqua] lc   33 Neque] lc

tamen in stillatorijs & alembicis communibus diligenter arcetur aër
exterior quin per rostrum stillatorij per quod liquor effluit ille subintrare
aliquatenus possit. At in retortis, vbi majore vehementia caloris opus est,
[fo. 14ʳ] non datur aëri exteriori ingressus, sed os receptaculi ori vasis vbi ¹ corpus
5 imponitur per lutationes ita continuatur vt vniuersus processus
rarefactionis & restitutionis intus transigatur. Quod si corpus sit plenum
spiritu vigoroso, vt vitriolum, opus est receptaculo vasto & amplo, vt
vapores liberius ludant, nec vas infringant.

Vtcumque tamen distillationes tanquam intra cellam vndequaque
10 conclusam transigantur; datur tamen spatium vt corporis aliæ partes se
expandere in vapores, aliæ subsidere in fæcibus, vapores rursus se
glomerare & restituere, atque (si heterogenei fuerint) alij ab alijs separari
possint. Quod sequitur igitur pro mandato magno habendum, cum ad
veritatem in imis excutiendam, & ad nouas transformationes aditum
15 præbere possit. Vulcanus enim chymicorum & medicorum licet multa
vtilia genuerit, tamen virtutes veriores caloris minus complexus est, ob
diuortia & separationes partium quæ in operationibus ipsorum semper
interueniunt. Itaque summa rej quam mandamus huc spectat, vt illa
separatio & reciprocatio rarefactionis & condensationis omnino
20 prohibeatur, atque opus caloris intra corpus ipsum atque eius claustra
vertatur in experimentum.

Accipe vas quadratum ferri in figura cubi, habeatque latera bene fortia
& crassa. Impone cubum ligni ad mensuram vasis ad amussim factum,
quique illud prorsus impleat. Superponatur operculum ferri, non minus
25 forte quam latera vasis & lutetur optimè more chymicorum, ita vt sit
clausissimum & ignem tolerare possit. Deinde ponatur vas intra prunas,
atque ita permittatur ad horas aliquas. Post amoueatur operculum, &
vide quid factum sit de ligno.

In simili vase ferreo fiat experimentum de aqua pura qua repleatur ad
30 summum, sed adhibeatur ignis lenior, mora verò sit amplior; quinetiam
[fo. 14ᵛ] amoueatur ab igne certis horis & ¹ refrigescat; dein iteretur operatio
aliquoties. Hoc experimentum de aqua pura delegimus hanc ob causam,

4 sed] si / cf. *HDR*, p. 98, l. 32 below   9 Vtcumque] / in *HDR* this para is preceded by
the heading *Mandata* (see p. 100, l. 4 below)   10 conclusam] clausam *HDR*   12
alij] alia / cf. *HDR*, p. 100, l. 8 below   14 veritatem . . . excutiendam] *Naturam* . . . concutiendam *HDR*   &] & &   21 in experimentum] *om HDR*, which has instead several
additional lines (p. 100, ll. 17–21 below)   23 mensuram] amussim / cf. *HDR*, p. 100, l. 23
below   28 ligno.] / *HDR* concludes this para with several extra lines (see p. 100,
ll. 28–34 below)   30 lenior] leuior

3 At] lc   6 Quod] lc   23 Impone] lc   24 Superponatur] lc   26
Deinde] lc   27 Post] lc   31 refrigescat;] ~.   32 Hoc] lc

quod aqua corpus simplicissimum sit, expers coloris, odoris, saporis, &
aliarum qualitatum. Quamobrem si per calorem temperatum & lenem,
& alternationem calefactionis & refrigerationis, & prohibitionem omnis
euaporationis, spiritus aquæ non emissus, & nihilominus per huiusmodi
calorem sollicitatus & attenuatus, se verterit in partes aquæ crassiores,   5
easque digerere, & in nouum schematismum mutare possit; minus
scilicet simplicem & magis inæqualem, eo vsque vt vel colorem alium
nanciscatur, vel odorem, vel saporem, vel oleositatem quandam, vel
aliam alterationem notabilem, qualis inuenitur in corporibus
compositis, proculdubio res magna confecta foret, & plurima aditum   10
patefaciens. Hæc distillatio clausa nominetur.

Attamen illud addi possit, vt excogitetur etiam aliquis modus per
quem calor operetur, non solum in clauso, sed in tensili: id quod fit in
omni matrice naturali siue vegetabilium siue animalium. Hoc enim
operationem ad multa extendit, quæ per clausuram simplicem effici non   15
possunt. Neque hoc pertinet ad Pygmæum Paracelsi, aut huiusmodi
prodigiosas ineptias, sed ad solida & sana. Verbi gratia, non efficiet
vnquam distillatio clausa vt aqua tota vertatur in oleum, quia oleum &
pinguia majus occupant dimensum quam aqua. At si operatio fiat in
tensili, hoc fortasse fieri possit quæ esset res immensæ vtilitatis, cum   20
omnis alimentatio maximè consistat in pingui.

Bonum esset, & ad multa vtile, vt in distillationibus natura ad
reddendas rationes quandoque compellatur; atque vt ponatur in certo
quantum per distillationem consumptum fuerit, idest, versum in
pneumaticum, & quid maneat siue fixum, siue restitutum in corpore. Id   25
fieri potest, si ante distillationem corpus distillandum | ponderes, etiam   [fo. 15ʳ]
vasa ipsa intra quæ distillatio perficitur. At post distillationem
ponderabis liquorem, ponderabis item fæces, denique ponderabis
iterum vasa. Ex istis enim tribus ponderationibus cognosces quantum
fuerit restitutum, quantum manserit in fæcibus, quantum adhæserit   30

---

11 Hæc . . .nominetur.] / this is much elaborated in *HDR* (see p. 102, ll. 16–20 below)
12 possit,] ∼ ut *Mandati* hujus Appendix *HDR*   modus] ∼ (quod certe difficile non est)
HDR   16 Pygmæum] ⟨p⟩figmentum / cf. *HDR*, p. 102, l. 26 below; the copyist had not
met Paracelsian pygmies and made a mistaken but intelligent guess at a plausible reading
17 Verbi] Exempli *HDR*   23 compellatur] compelleretur *HDR*   ponatur] poneretur
HDR   25 maneat] maneret *HDR*

2 Quamobrem] lc   11 Hæc] lc   13 tensili:] ∼.   14 Hoc] lc
16 Neque] lc   17 Verbi] lc   19 At] lc   25 Id] lc   26 ponderes,] ∼.
27 At] lc   29 Ex] lc

vasibus, atque a decessione ponderis in illis tribus comparati ad corpus integrum, cognosces quantum versum fuerit in pneumaticum.

De caloribus potentialibus consule tabulas medicinales qualitatum secundarum. Ex his poteris excipere ea quæ operantur circa corpus
5 humanum per dilatationem, quæ sunt fere illa quæ sequuntur: confortantia, quæ dilatant spiritus oppressos; abstergentia, quæ roborant virtutem expulsiuam; aperientia, quoad orificia venarum & vasorum; aperientia quoad poros & meatus partium; digerentia; caustica. Hæc præcipuè habent radicem in dilatatione spirituum, & humorum, &
10 succorum, & substantiæ in corpore per spiritus auxiliares, necnon per complexionem tangibilem, quæ insunt in medicinis illis, vel interius vel exterius sumptis.

Possit esse res varij vsus, si operationes secundarum qualitatum medicinalium probentur interdum & exerceantur in corporibus vitæ
15 expertibus. Licet enim dubium non sit plerasque earum nullius prorsus effectus fore; quoniam requiritur spiritus viuus ad eas actuandas ad operationis subtilitatem, aliæ tamen proculdubio super nonnulla corpora inanimata operabuntur. Videmus enim quid possit sal in carnibus, aromata in cadaueribus, coagulum in lacte, fermentum in
20 pane, & huiusmodi. Inseruiet igitur diligentia medicorum circa qualitates secundas ad instruendas complures alias operationes, si animum aduertas cum judicio; id semper supponens, quod virtus fortior requiratur ad operandum super corpus mortuum quam viuum. In corporibus quæ habent arctam compagem, atque naturæ integralis
25 nexibus fortiter deuincta sunt, non exequuntur spiritus opus suum
[fo. 15ᵛ] dilatationis, ¹ nisi prius fiat solutio continui in partibus crassioribus, vel per liquores fortes erodentes & stimulantes tantum, vel per eosdem cum calore.

1–2 corpus integrum] *pondus Corporis* integri *HDR*   2 pneumaticum.] / in *HDR* this is succeeded by a connexio, three paras of historia, a further connexio and a section heading (see p. 104, l. 5–p. 106, l. 1–2 below)   4 Ex] & ex *HDR*   excipere] excerpere *HDR*   8 digerentia] ~ cum maturatione. *Digerentia* cum discussione. *HDR*   9 præcipuè] ~ (sunt & alia) *HDR*   11 complexionem] conceptionem / cf. *HDR*, p. 106, l. 8 below   insunt] inest *HDR*   12 sumptis.] / in *HDR* this is followed by an additional commentatio and a mandatum (see p. 106, l. 18–p. 108, l. 18 below)   14 &] vt / cf. *HDR*, p. 108, l. 9 below   requiritur] ~ plane *HDR*   16 actuandas ad] actuandas, ob *HDR*   23 requiratur] requiritur *HDR*   23 In] / preceded in *HDR* by the heading *Connexio* and several additional lines (see p. 108, ll. 20–3 below)   24 corporibus] ~ enim *HDR*   28 calore.] / following this *HDR* (p. 108, l. 27–p. 110, ll. 1–2 below) adds a sentence and inserts headings to replace Aperturæ metallorum.

4 Ex] lc   5 sequuntur:] ~.   6 oppressos;] ~.   7 expulsiuam;] ~.
8 partium;] ~.   digerentia;] ~,   Hæc] lc   15 Licet] lc   18 Videmus] lc
20 Inseruiet] lc   22 judicio;] ~,   23 In] lc

Aperturæ metallorum.

Accipe pondus auri ad den.1. in paruas bracteolas redacti, quæ etiam manu lacerari possint; accipe etiam pondus 4. den. aquæ regis, & mittantur simul in vitrum. Tum ponatur vitrum super foculum in quo sit ignis prunarum modicus & lenis. Paulo post insurgunt arenulæ 5 quædam, aut grana, quæ deinde post paruam moram se diffundunt, & incorporantur cum aqua, vt aqua efficiatur tanquam electrica, splendida, & veluti croco tincta. Dissolutio autem auri per aquam in quantitatibus prædictis fit tantum ad tertias; neque enim aqua oneratur vlterius; adeo vt si dissoluere cupias totum pondus illud auri den. 1. opus sit effundere 10 portionem in qua solutio facta est, & superinfundere de nouo pondus simile 4. den. aquæ regis, & sic tertiò. Ista dissolutio fit leniter & placidè modico igne absque fumis, & sine calefactione ⟨ven⟩ vitri alia quam per ignem.

Accipe argenti viui in corpore pondus ad placitum, & duplum aquæ 15 fortis; ponito simul in vitro, neque ea ad ignem omnino admoue. Attamen paulo post insurgit intra corpus aquæ instar pulueris tenuissimi, & intra spatium horæ, absque igne, absque fumis, absque tumultu, vertetur corpus commixtum in aquam bene claram.

Accipe plumbum in lamellis ad pondus den. 1. aquæ fortis ad pondus 20 den. 9. Non fit bona incorporatio vt in alijs metallis, sed aqua demittit majorem partem plumbi in calce ad fundum vitri, manente ⟨aqua⟩ aqua perturbata, sed vergente ad diaphanum.

Accipe argentum in lamellis siue bracteolis ad pondus den. 1. aquæ fortis ad pondus den. 4. Pone super foculum in vitro cum igne lento; 25 insurgit argentum in arenis & bullulis intra corpus aquæ, majoribus paulò quam aurum. Deinde incorporantur cum aqua, & vertuntur simul in liquorem tenuem, sed album, & quasi lacteum. Sed postquam paulum ¹ residerit liquor, & refrixerit, eiaculantur (siue hoc [fo. 16ʳ] emanet ex metallo, siue ex aqua, siue ex vtroque) fragmina glacialia 30 intra corpus aquæ. Postquam autem per moram longiorem resederit, penitus clarificat se liquor, & deuenit clarus & crystallinus demissa glacie in fundum. Sustinet aqua operationem qualem in auro, & fit

---

7 efficiatur] ∼, *Aqua HDR*   20 1] 7 / cf. *HDR*, p. 110, l. 22 below   24 argentum . . . ad pondus] *Argenti . . . pondus HDR*   24–5 aquæ fortis ad pondus] *Aqu. fortis pond.* *HDR*   29 paulum] paulisper *HDR*   31–2 resederit, penitus] penitus resederit, *HDR*

3 possint;] ∼,   Tum] lc   5 Paulo] lc   8 Dissolutio] lc   12 Ista] lc 16 fortis;] ∼.   17 Attamen] lc   21 Non] lc   25 Pone] lc   lento;] ∼, 27 Deinde] lc   28 Sed] lc   31 Postquam] lc   33 Sustinet] lc

dissolutio simili fere calore, nec colligit calorem per motum magis quam aurum.

Accipe cuprum in bracteolis ad pondus den. 1. aquæ fortis ad pondus den. 6. Mitte super foculum; insurget cuprum in bullulis siue arenulis
5 majoribus adhuc quam argentum. Paulo post incorporatur cum aqua, & corpus mixtum vertitur in liquorem cæruleum turbidum sed postquam resederit, clarificat se ætheris instar in cæruleum pulchrum & splendidum, demissis in fundum fæcibus instar pulueris, quæ tamen ipsæ per moram im*m*inuuntur, & ascendunt, & incorporantur. At den.
10 illi 6. aquæ fortis soluunt denarium totum cupri, vt sustineat se onerari aqua duplo plus quam in auro & argento. Concipit autem dissolutio cupri calorem manifestum per tumultum interiorem, etiam antequam admoueatur ad ignem.

Accipe ferri in laminis pondus den.1. aquæ fortis pondus den. 9. &
15 cum modico igne surgit ferrum in magnis bullis, non tantum intra corpus aquæ, sed supra, adeo vt ebulliat extra os vitri, atque insuper emittat copiosum & densum fumum croceum, idque cum maximo tumultu & calore vehementissimo, etiam postquam amotum fuerit ab igne, & qualem manus non sustineat.

20   Obseruatio.

Notatu est dignum omnia metalla, licet sint aquis in quibus dissoluuntur insigniter grauiora, in actu primo dissolutionis ascendere in arenulis vel bullis. Atque eo magis hoc notandum est, quod vbi non admouetur ignis, vt in argento viuo, idem faciant.

[fo. 16ᵛ] 25 | Tumultus intra partes corporis inter dissoluendum istam ascensionem causat. Nam in vehementi erosione corpora impelluntur nonnihil motu locali, vt videre est in lapide paruo glareoso, qui positus in aceto forti ad latera patellæ, vt facilius labatur, per vices gliscit vt pisciculus. At quæ sine impetu isto miscentur, nisi quassata non

6 mixtum] commistum *HDR*   liquorem] colorem / cf. *HDR*, p. 112, l. 9 below   11 aqua]
aquæ   13 ignem.] / after this *HDR* has an extra para (see p. 112, ll. 17–20 below)
14 laminis] ~ ad   fortis] ~ ad   15 cum modico igne] sine igne *HDR*   18–19
etiam . . . igne,] *om HDR*   19 sustineat.] / followed in *HDR* (see p. 112, l. 30–p. 114,
l. 13 below) by a monitum and mandata absent from *HDR(M)*   21 Notatu . . .] / *HDR*
has a revised version of this para (see p. 112, ll. 15–19 below)   25 Tumultus . . .] this para
headed *Commentatio* in *HDR*   29 pisciculus.] / after this *HDR* has an extra sentence
(see p. 114, ll. 25–7 below)   miscentur,] ~ (ut arbitror) *HDR*

4 Mitte] lc   foculum;] ~,   5 Paulo] lc   9 At] lc   11 Concipit] lc
23 Atque] lc   26 Nam] lc   29 At] lc

ascendunt, velut saccharum in fundo aquæ non dulcificat in summo, nec crocus colorat, nisi moueantur & agitentur.

Fiunt etiam dilatationes per amplexum & occursum corporis amici. Saccharum, & gummi nonnulla, vt tragacanthum, in liquoribus infusa soluuntur. Papyrus, seta, lana, & huiusmodi porosa, liquoribus immersa 5 aut alias humectata, ita se aperiunt, vt deueniant magis mollia, lacerabilia, & quasi putria.

Cogitandum de inueniendis menstruis substantiarum specialium; videntur enim posse esse liquores & pulpæ, tantæ cum corporibus determinatis sympathiæ, vt illis admotis partes suas facile laxent, easque 10 libenter imbibant; seque per hoc in succis intenerent & renouent. Hoc enim pertinet ad vnum ex magnalibus naturæ, nempe vt rerum humores maximè radicales refocillari, & nutritio ab his extra fieri possit, vt in carnibus, ossibus, membranis, lignis, &c.

Transeundum est ad dilatationes per assimilationem & versionem; 15 quando scilicet corpus imperans & magis actiuum subigit corpus accommodum, & obsequiosum, & magis passiuum, ita vt illud in se plane vertat, seque ex eo multiplicet & renouet. Quod si corpus assimilans sit tenuius & rarius quam corpus assimilatum, manifestum est assimilationem fieri non posse absque dilatatione. 20

Aër, maximè cum commotus est, vt in ventis, lambit humiditatem terræ, eamque deprædatur & in se vertit.

Processus desiccationis in lignis, herbis, & huiusmodi tangibilibus non admodum duris & obstinatis, fit per deprædationem aëris, qui spiritum in corpore euocat, & exsugit, & in se transubstantiat. Itaque ¹ 25 [fo. 17ʳ] tardè hoc fit in oleosis & pinguibus, quia spiritus & humidum ipsorum non est tam consubstantiale aeri. Multi tumores in corporibus animalium discutiuntur absque suppuratione aut sanie, per insensibilem

2 moueantur & agitentur] / singular verbs in *HDR*, followed by a connexio not in *HDR(M)*   5 soluuntur.] / *HDR* adds clauses here (see p. 116, ll. 12–13 below)   7 putria.] / after this *HDR* has an extra para (see p. 116, ll. 17–21 below)   8 Cogitandum] / para headed *Mandatum* in *HDR*   substantiarum specialium] substantialium specierum / cf. *HDR*, p. 116, l. 23 below)   10 laxent] laxant / cf. *HDR*, p. 116, l. 25 below   11 succis] ~ suis *HDR*   13 his] *om HDR*   14 &c.] / here *HDR* adds a sentence and the heading *Connexio* (see p. 116, l. 29–p. 118, l. 2 below)   15 est] *om HDR*   20 dilatatione.] / after this *HDR* has a section heading   21 Aër,] ~ & *HDR*   ventis] decoctis / cf. *HDR*, p. 118, l. 12 below   24 &] aut *HDR*   27 est tam consubstantiale] / plurals in *HDR*   aeri.] / followed by an extra para in *HDR* (see p. 118, ll. 19–27 below)   28 insensibilem] insensilem *HDR* / Rigault may have normalized Bacon's Telesian form (*q.v. OFB*, VI, p. 176, *tns*)

4 Saccharum] lc   tragacanthum] tragrachantum   5 Papyrus] lc   8 specialium;] ~,   11 Hoc] lc   18 Quod] lc   25 Itaque] lc   27 Multi] lc

21

transpirationem versa⟨i⟩ planè in pneumaticum & euolante⟨s⟩. In omni alimentato, cum pars alimentata tenuior est alimento (vt spiritus atque sanguis floridus per arterias in animalibus leuiores sunt quam cibus & potus) necesse est vt alimentatio inducat dilatationem.

5 Omnium pernicissima dilatatio, est dilatatio oleosorum in flammam.

Et est alia dilatatio, quæ fit ⟨ab⟩ non ab appetitu aliquo in corpore ipso quod dilatatur, sed per violentiam corporum externorum, quæ cum suis motibus præualeant, necessitatem imponunt corpori alicui vt dilatetur et distrahatur.

10 Bacula lignea, & similia, flexionem nonnullam patiuntur, sed per vim. Illa autem vis distrahit partes exteriores ligni in loco vbi arcuatur, & comprimit interiores. Quod si vis illa paulo remittatur, restituit se baculum & resilit. Sed si diutius in ea positura detineatur, figitur in ea, nec resilit amplius.

15 Similis est ratio horologiorum, (eorum scilicet quæ mouentur per torturam laminarum) in quibus videre est continuum & graduatum nixum laminarum ad se restituendum.

Pannus & similia filacea extenduntur majorem in modum, & resiliunt citius dimissa; non resiliunt longius detenta.

20 Caro quæ surgit in ventosis non est tumor, sed violenta extensio carnis integralis per attractionem.

Qualem rarefactionem toleret aer, (pro modo scilicet violentiæ) tali experimento exprimere possis. Accipe ouum vitreum, in quo sit foramen minutum; exuge aërem anhelitu quantum potes; deinde affatim obtura foramen digito, & merge ouum in aquam ita obturatum. Post tolle digitum, & videbis ouum attrahere aquam cum sibilo.

Sunt & dilatationes per deaceruationem, quæ fiunt in positura partium, non in substantia corporis. Siquidem corpus manet in eadem densitate substantiæ, sed figuram nanciscitur ampliorem in superficie 30 minorem in profunditate.

1 versa⟨i⟩ . . . euolante⟨s⟩] versi . . . evolantes *HDR* / Rigault's attack on the grammar is unwarranted   In omni] / in *HDR* this is preceded by an additional para (see p. 120, ll. 1–4 below) 3 floridus] *om HDR*   leuiores] leuiora   5 Omnium . . . flammam.] / in *HDR* this is expanded and followed by two additional paras (see p. 120, ll. 8–23 below)   6–9 Et est . . . distrahatur.] / in *HDR* this is preceded by the heading *Connexio* and expanded; then come section headings (see p. 120, l. 24–p. 122, l. 4 below)   20 tumor] tenuior 23 exprimere] elicere *HDR*   24 quantum] quam   26 aquam] / here *HDR* extends the para, then adds an extra para, and a commentatio (see p. 122, l. 21–p. 124, l. 24 below)   27–30 Sunt . . . profunditate.] / in *HDR* this is preceded by the heading *Connexio* and expanded; then come section headings (see p. 124, l. 25–p. 126, l. 5 below)

1 In] lc   11 Illa] lc   12 Quod] lc   13 Sed] lc   23 Accipe] lc 24 minutum;] ~.   potes;] ~.   25 Post] lc   28 Siquidem] lc

¹ Aurum per malleationem in immensum dilatatur, vt in auro foliato; [fo. 17ᵛ]
item per distractionem, vt in argenteis filis inauratis. Inauratio enim fit
in massa antequam distrahatur.

Argentum etiam fit foliatum, licet non ad tam exquisitam tenuitatem
quam aurum　　　　　　　　　　　　　　　　　　　　　　　　　5
Reliqua quoque metalla per malleationem dilatantur in bracteolas &
lamellas tenues. Gutta atramenti in calamo dilatatur ad exarationem
multarum literarum; quod & fit per penicillum in pigmentis & vernice.
Crocus in parua quantitate magnam inficit quantitatam aquæ.

De contractionibus, condensationibus,　　10
& clausuris corporum.

Actioni dilatationis per introceptionem corporis alieni; reciproca est
actio contractionis per emissionem aut expressionem corporis alieni;
quocirca instantijs de dilatationibus, opponendæ sunt eædem instantiæ
postquam dilatationes resederint.　　　　　　　　　　　　　　15
Metalla omnia per ignem soluuntur & restituuntur. Reperiuntur
tamen modi mortificationum metallorum; vt in argento viuo, si
fundatur cum therebentina, saliua hominis, aut butyro, nunquam
postea restituitur.
De mortificatione omnium metallorum inquirendum. Magna enim 20
debet esse antipathia eorum quæ prohibent ne ea coëant; cumque omnis
restitutio ipsorum fit genus quoddam condensationis, pertinebit scilicet
cognitio priuationis ad cognitionem formæ.
Spiritus emittitur vel ex agitatione sua propria, vel sollicitatus ab aere
ambiente, vel prouocatus & irritatus ab igne siue calore.　　　　25
Idem faciunt (quoad attenuationem & emissionem spiritus, &
actiones quæ ex ea sequuntur) ignis siue calor, & tempus siue ætas.
Verum ætas per se solummodo est curriculum aut mensura motus. Igitur
cum de ætate loquimur, intelligimus de virtute & operatione composita
ex agitatione spiritus innati, & aere ambiente, atque radijs coelestium. ¹ 30 [fo. 18ʳ]

7 tenues.] / in *HDR* this is followed by an extra para (see p. 126, ll. 12–13 below)　　8 ver-
nice] vernitie　　10 De contractionibus] / in *HDR* this title and the para following are
expanded and embodied in two paras of a connexio, a section heading and a third para (p. 126,
l. 17, p. 128, l. 5 below)　　16–23 Metalla . . . formæ.] / much expanded in *HDR* (p. 128,
l. 6–p. 130, l. 6 below)　　24–5 Spiritus . . . calore.] / in *HDR* this stands at the end
of a para headed *Connexio*, a para itself preceded by a mandatum (p. 130, ll. 1–16 below)
26 ff. Idem . . .] / in *HDR* this is headed *Commentatio*.

1 foliato;] ~　　2 Inauratio] lc　　7 Gutta] lc　　12 alieni;] ~,　　16 Reperiuntur]
lc　　20 Magna] lc　　21 coëant;] ~.　　28 Verum] lc　　Igitur] lc

Sed illud interest, quod ignis & calor vehemens dilatet corpora
confertim, & fortiter, & visibiliter; ætas autem instar caloris lenissimi,
paulatim & leniter & occultè. Fumi enim & vapores scilicet spissi sunt
& conspicui, perspirationes verò neutiquam, vt manifestum est in
5 odoribus. Attamen magis subtilis & exquisita est ea corporum ⟨ea
corporum⟩ attenuatio & rarefactio quæ fit per ætatem, quam quæ fit per
ignem. Nam ignis præcipitans actionem, pneumaticum quod in corpore
est rapide euolare facit; humidum quoque quod præparatum est, in
pneumaticum subinde vertit, vnde partes tangibiles sedulo se interim &
10 gnauiter constipant, & non parum spiritus, tanquam manu injecta;
morantur & detinent. At ætas pneumaticum iam factum ad
euolationem non vrget subitò; vnde fit vt illud diutius manens in
corpore; quidquid in tenue digeri possit sensim & seriatim præparet;
parum ex pneumatico iam facto placide & successiue interim euolante,
15 adeo vt anticipet ferè, & tanquam fallat constipationem partium
tangibilium. Quamobrem in dissolutione per ætatem, sub finem negotij
parum admodum tangibilis figitur, & manet; etiam puluis ille putris, qui
per longos annorum circuitus manet tanquam consumptionis reliquiæ,
qualis in sepulchris & monumentis vetustis nonnunquam inuenitur, res
20 quasi nihili [est], & omni incineratione quæ fit per ignem minutior &
magis destituta. Nam cineres etiam succum habent, qui possit elici &
verti in sales, huiusmodi puluis minime. Verum quod ad inquisitionem
præsentem pertinet, & cuius causa hæc dicta sunt, certum est spiritum,
quandiu detinetur in corpore, partes tangibiles colliquare, intenerare,
25 conficere, subruere; verum ab eius emissione partes tangibiles continuo
se contrahere & constipare.

   In senectute cutes animalium corrugantur, membra arescunt; pira,
poma diu seruata rugas colligunt, nuclei contrahuntur in nuces, casei
fiunt rugosi, ligna tractu temporis contrahuntur in arctum, vt
30 disiungantur & hient; globi lusorij etiam.
[fo. 18ᵛ]   ¹ Nemo nugetur, aiens istam contractionem in desiccationibus nihil
aliud esse quam absumptionem humidi. Nam si id tantum ageretur vt

---

3 occultè] occulto *HDR*   9 vertit,] ~ atque tale factum emittit: *HDR*
17 etiam] Etenim *HDR*   20 [est]] / cf. *HDR*, p. 132, l. 15 below   21 destituta]
destitutus *HDR* / the *c-t* adj. presumably agrees with res; the *HDR* adj. with puluis
27–30 In senectute . . . etiam.] / expanded in *HDR* and preceded by a section heading (p. 132,
ll. 23–32 below)   31 ff. Nemo . . .] / preceded by an extra para and headed *Monitum* in
HDR (p. 134, ll. 1–3 below)

1 Sed] lc   3 Fumi] lc   5 Attamen] lc   7 Nam] lc   11 At] lc
16 Quamobrem] lc   17 manet;] ~ₐ   21 Nam] lc   27 arescunt;] ~,
30 hient;] ~ₐ   32 Nam] lc

24

humidum in spiritum versum euolaret, deberent corpora manere in priore exporrectione & dimenso suo, & solummodo caua fieri, vt pumices aut suber, non autem localiter contrahj & minui dimenso suo.

Quandiu spiritus in corpore detinetur, si per ignem aut calorem excitatus & dilatatus fuerit, tamdiu agitat se molitur exitum, partes 5 tangibiles emollit, intenerat, colliquat. Atque hoc est proprium opus spiritus, qui digerit & subigit partes. Sed postquam spiritus sibi exitum inuenerit, & emissus fuerit, tum præualet opus partium, quæ a spiritu vexatæ conspirant & se stringunt, tam ex desiderio nexus, & mutui contactus, quam ex odio motus & vexationis. Atque inde sequitur 10 coarctatio, induratio, obstinatio. Est in processu contractionis partium ab igne finis & vltimitas. Nam si minor sit copia materiæ per violentam deprædationem ignis quam vt cohærere possint, tum demum se deserunt, & incinerantur, & calcinantur.

Actioni dilatationis per calorem actualem externum, reciproca est 15 actio contractionis per frigus actuale externum. Atque hæc condensatio est omnium maximè propria & genuina. Maxime potens etiam foret, nisi quod non habemus hic apud nos in superficie terræ frigus aliquod intensum. Frigus autem & caloris ⟨intensio⟩ remissio (nam vtrumque hoc loco coniungere visum est) alia simpliciter manente natura sua 20 condensat, alia rarefacta, sed imperfectè, restituit, alia per condensationem planè vertit & transformat de natura in naturam.

Aer in vitro calendari percipit gradus tam frigidi quam calidi.

Stellæ tempore hyemali noctibus valde serenis & gelidis apparent grandiores quam noctibus æstiuis serenis. Quod fit præcipuè ex 25 vniuersali condensatione aëris, qui tum vergit magis ⎮ ad naturam aquæ. [fo. 19ʳ] Nam sub aqua omnia apparent longe grandiora.

Rores matutini sunt proculdubio vapores, qui in aerem purum non erant plene dissipati & versi, sed hærebant imperfectè mixti, donec per frigora noctis, præsertim in regione media quam vocant aëris, fuerint 30 repercussi, & in aquam condensati.

---

3 suo.] / followed by ten paras of historia and then by the heading *Observationes* in *HDR* (p. 134, l. 10–p. 136, l. 4 below)   4 Quandiu] ~ (ut paulo ante innuimus) *HDR* 13 cohærere] cohibere / cf. *HDR*, p. 136, l. 16 below   14 incinerantur] incinerant 15–22 Actioni . . . naturam.] / begins with an extra sentence in *HDR* and ends in one (p. 136, l. 30 below)   23 Aer . . . calidi.] / preceded by a section heading in *HDR* and followed by additional material, including two mandata (p. 138, ll. 1–20 below)   29 plene] plane / cf. *HDR*, p. 138, l. 26 below

6 Atque] lc   7 Sed] lc   10 Atque] lc   11 Est] lc   16 Atque] lc 17 Maxime] lc   19 Frigus] lc   25 Quod] lc   27 Nam] lc

Condensatio pluuiæ, & niuis, & grandinis, fit similiter per frigus mediæ regionis, quod vapores coagulat magis vt plurimum in alto, quam rores. Occurrunt verò dubitationes duæ: altera, vtrum guttæ ipsorum congelentur & condensentur in ipso casu, an fuerint illæ prius collectæ
5 & congregatæ in moles majores aquarum, in aëre propter distantiam a terra pensiles, quæ postea per violentiam aliquam conquassatæ frangunt se & ⟨[*illeg.*]⟩ comminuunt in guttas, vt in nonnullis cataractis, quæ tam subitò & confertim descendunt, vt videantur quasi ex vasibus fusæ & dejectæ; altera, vtrum non solum vapores, qui olim fuerant humores &
10 aquæ, & solummodo restituuntur, sed etiam pars magna aëris puri & perfecti, per frigus in illis regionibus vehemens & intensum non fuerit coagulata, & mutata planè, & versa in pluuiam.

In distillationibus humores primo vertuntur in vapores: illj per remotionem ab igne destituti, per latera stillatorij contrusi, &
15 nonnunquam per frigidam ab extra infusam accelerati, restituunt se in aquas & liquores. Imago prorsus familiaris rorum & pluuiæ.

Argentum viuum præcipuè, nec non metallica alia, cum volatilia facta fuerint, properant tamen ad se restituendum, & occursu alicuius solidi & materiati magnopere gaudent. Itaque facile hærent, facile decidunt,
20 adeo vt quandoque sit necesse vapores ipsorum igne persequi, & de igne in ignem transmittere, factis tanquam scalis receptaculorum ignis ad nonnullam distantiam inter se circa vas, ne vapor, postquam per
[fo. 19ᵛ] ascensionem paulò fuerit ⌐ remotior ab igne, citius quam expedit se restituat.
25 Quæ ab igne colliquata fuerint, post remissionem caloris densantur & consistunt vt prius, vt metalla, cera, adeps, gummi &c.

Vellus laneum super terram diutius iacens colligit pondus, quod fieri non posset, nisi aliquod pneumaticum densaretur in ponderosum.

Solebant antiquitus nautæ velleribus lanæ, tanquam tapetibus aut
30 aulæis, vestire latera nauium noctu, ita vt non tangerent aquam, & inde mane exprimere aquam dulcem ad vsum nauigantium.

Experimentum lanæ in puteum demissæ, qua nocte vna pondus suum duplò augebat, licet aquam non attingeret. Parietes & vitra fenestrarum sudore videntur sub regelationibus, aut tempestatibus australibus.

---

3 duæ:] ∼ circa quas diligens fieri debet Inquisitio *HDR*   4 illæ] illo   7 cataractis] ∼ *Indiæ Occidentalis HDR*   9 dejectæ] desertæ / cf. *HDR*, p. 140, l. 6 below
12 pluuiam] ∼ & reliqua de quo paulo post inquiremus *HDR*   30 tangerent] attingerent *HDR*   32–5 Experimentum . . . australibus.] / in *HDR* (see p. 140, l. 30–p. 142, l. 7 below) this is elaborated as three separate paras

3 Occurrunt] lc   duæ:] ∼.   9 dejectæ;] ∼.   16 Imago] lc   19
Itaque] lc   27 pondus,] ∼.   33 Parietes] lc

Anhelitus, super corpora polita vertitur in quiddam roscidum, quod postea instar nubeculæ dissipatur.

Lintea in ædibus colligunt humiditatem. Pulueres in repositorijs talem colligunt humiditatem, vt quasi glebefiant.

Nebulæ sunt condensationes aëris, imperfectè commixtæ ex longè 5 majore parte aëris & parum aquei vaporis, & fiunt hyeme quidem sub mutatione tempestatis a gelu ad regelationem, aut contra, æstate verò & vere ex expansione roris.

Fiat experimentum per interpositionem panni lintei aut lanei, vtrum exudationes marmorum & similium in tempestatibus australibus & 10 pluuiosis sint meræ condensationes aeris a duritie & læuore lapidum repercussi, instar anhelitus in speculo, an participent nonnihil ex succo & pneumatico intrinseco lapidis.

Quod ipse aer vertatur in aquam in regionibus supernis omnino necessariò concluditur ex conseruatione rerum. Nam certissimum est 15 humores maris & terræ verti in aërem purum, postquam vaporum naturam te[*m*]pore, consortio & rarefactione plenaria penitus exuerint. Itaque si non esset reciprocatio, vt aër vicissim quandoque verteretur in aquam quemadmodum aqua vertitur in aerem, non sufficerent ¹ plane [fo. 20ʳ] vapores qui remanent nouelli & imperfectè mixti ad pluuias & imbres, 20 & redintegrationes specierem, sed secutæ forent siccitates intollerabiles, & conflagratio, & venti impetuosi, & tumores aëris ex aëre perpetuò multiplicato.

Gelu, aqua, liquores, oleum, adeps, terra, & vestes, indurescunt.

Spiritus vini non gelascit, nec, vt opinior, aquæ fortes, & argentum 25 viuum.

Omnia dura redduntur per frigus magis friabilia. Patet in ossibus animalium.

Condensantur aquæ in lapides splendentes, siue crystallinos, vt videre est in aliquibus cauernis. Vtrum verò materia ipsorum sit prorsus aquea, 30 an succus natiuus lapidis, ambigitur; præsertim cum gemmæ & cristalla

---

1–2 Anhelitus . . . dissipatur.] / expanded in *HDR* (p. 142, ll. 8–11 below)   3–4 Lintea . . . glebefiant.] / expanded as two separate paras in *HDR* (see p. 142, ll. 12–15 below) 5 Nebulæ] / preceded by an extra para in *HDR* (see p. 142, ll. 16–18 below)   9–13 Fiat . . . lapidis.] / expanded as two paras in *HDR* (see p. 142, ll. 24–32 below)   14 Quod . . .] / headed *Commentatio* in *HDR*   17 te[*m*]pore] / the unemended *c-t* reading would do just as well, but cf. *HDR*, p. 144, l. 5   24–8 Gelu . . . animalium.] / these notes are much expanded as part of an historia in *HDR* (p. 144, ll. 14–31 below)   29–2 Condensantur . . . pendeant.] / this para revised and expanded in *HDR* (p. 146, ll. 1–9 below)

3 Pulueres] lc   15 Nam] lc   17 plenaria] ~.   18 Itaque] lc   27 Patet] lc

in rupibus apertis exsurgant sæpe, & excrescant in sursum, non decidant aut pendeant.

Sunt quædam aquæ quæ lignum, & paleas, & huiusmodi, condensant in materiam lapideam, adeo vt pars ligni adhuc integra quæ fuerit sub 5 aqua fiat saxea, quæ emineat maneat lignea, quod etiam vidi.

Inquirendum an aquæ metallicæ habeant naturam insaxentem in quale corpus densetur flamma. Spiritus vini.

Sequitur actio quæ opponitur dilatationi per calorem potentialem, scilicet contractio per frigus potentiale.

10 Quamobrem consulendæ sunt tabulæ medicinales qualitatum secundarum ad inquisitionem de frigore potentiali, in quibus excerpi debent potissimum astrictio, opilatio, inspissatio, stupefactio.

Opium, hyosciamus, cicuta, solanum, mandragora, & huiusmodi narcotica, spiritus animalium manifestò densant, in se vertunt, 15 suffocant, & motu priuant. Vtrum verò super corpora mortua aliquid possint, fiat experimentum macerando carnes in succis ipsorum, ad experiendum si succedat denigratio & gangræna; vel macerando semina & nucleos, ad experiendum vtrum morbificent ita vt non crescant; vel [fo. 20ᵛ] liniendo summitatem vitri calendaris per | interius succis ipsorum ad 20 experiendum vtrum aliqualiter contrahant aërem.

Apud Indias occidentales reperiuntur, etiam per deserta arenosa & valde arida, cannæ magnæ quæ super singulas iuncturas siue genicula bonam copiam præbent aquæ dulcis, magno commodo itinerantium.

Referunt esse in quadam insula ex Terceris aut ex Canarijs arborem 25 quæ perpetuo stillet, imo quæ nubeculam quandam roscidam semper habeat impendentem. Digna autem res cognitu esset, vtrum inueniatur in vegetabili aliquo potentiale frigus quod denset aerem in aquam.

Vix inuenitur corpus in quo emineat tantum potentiale frigus, quantum in nitro. Nam vt aromata, & alia, licet ad tactum minime, 30 tamen ad palatum aut linguam habent calorem perceptibilem; ita etiam nitrum ad linguam vel palatum habet frigus perceptibile magis quam semperuiuum, aut aliqua herba ex maximè frigidis. Itaque videtur

---

3 Sunt] / preceded by an extra para in *HDR* (p. 146, ll. 10–14 below)   6–7 Inquirendum . . . vini.] / revised in *HDR* (p. 146, ll. 19–26 below)   8–9 Sequitur . . . potentiale.] / before this *HDR* adds much new material culminating in a connexio of which this sentence is the last (see p. 146, l. 27–p. 148, l. 18 below)   10 Quamobrem . . .] / this sentence is expanded in *HDR* and preceded by a section heading (see p. 148, ll. 19–24 below) 15 Vtrum] vt / cf. *HDR*, p. 148, l. 27   19 liniendo] linendo *HDR* 27 aquam.] / *HDR* adds an extra sentence and another para (see p. 150, ll. 8–14 below) 32 semperuiuum] semperuiua

15 Vtrum] lc   26 Digna] lc   29 Nam] lc   32 Itaque] lc

subjectum accommodum ad experiendum virtutem potentiale frigidi.
In nitro sic fiat experimentum.

Accipe minutam vesicam ex pellicula quantum fieri potest tenui.
Infla, & liga, & merge eam intra nitrum per aliquot dies, & exime, &
nota si vesica aliqualiter flaccescat, quod si facit, scias frigus nitri aërem   5
contraxisse. Idem fiet citius fortasse per folia vmbilici veneris.

Acetum in vnguentum rosarum infusum, illud reddit magis
induratum & solidum.

Actioni dilatationis per amplexum opponitur actio contractionis per
fugam & antiperistasim. Quemadmodum enim corpora versus grata &   10
amica se laxant vndequaque, atque eunt in occursum; ita cum incidunt in
odiosa & inimica, fugiunt vndequaque, & se contrudunt & constringunt.

Calor ignis per antiperistasim videtur nonnihil densari, & fieri ᴵ   [fo. 21ʳ]
acrior, vt sub gelu.

Contra in regionibus torridis videtur densari frigus per antiperistasim,   15
adeo vt si quis se accipiat ex campo aperto & radijs solaribus sub
arborem patulam, statim cohorreat.

Meritò dubitari possit vtrum opium & narcotica stupefaciant a
potentiali frigido, vel a fuga spirituum. Nam vt opium partes habere
calidas, ex fortitudine odoris, ex amaritudine, & prouocatione sudoris,   20
& alijs signis constat; verum cum emittat vaporem inimicum &
horribilem spiritibus, fugat illos vndequaque; vnde se coagulant, &
suffocantur.

Actioni dilatationis quæ fit per assimilationem & versionem ⟨tenuis
densius⟩ in tenuis, opponitur actio contractionis, quæ fit per   25
assimilationem & versionem in densius. Intelligimus autem quandò hoc
fit, non fieri per frigidum vel actuale vel potentiale, sed per imperium
corporis magis actiui, quod se multiplicat ex corpore magis passiuo.
Assimilatio autem ad densum est minus potens quam assimilatio ad
rarum quia corpora densa magis sunt ignaua & inertia ad opus   30
assimilationis, quam tenuia.

---

1 subjectum] secretum / cf. *HDR*, p. 150, l. 20   2 In . . . experimentum] / *HDR*
has a different sentence here followed by the heading *Mandatum* (see p. 150, ll. 20–2 below)
4 aliquot] aliquos *HDR*   6 Idem . . . veneris.] / *HDR* has a different sentence here followed by the heading *Historia* (see p. 150, ll. 26–9 below)   7–8 Acetum . . . solidum.] /
revised in *HDR* and followed by the heading *Connexio* (see p. 150, l. 30–p. 152, l. 1 below)   35
12 constringunt.] / followed by heading in *HDR*   16–17 accipiat . . . sub arborem pat-
ulam] recipiat . . . sub arbore patula *HDR*   18 Meritò] / preceded in *HDR* by an extra
para (see p. 152, ll. 14–18 below)   24 Actioni . . .] / preceded in *HDR* by the heading
Connexio   29 est] magis rara ~ & *HDR*   potens] ~ multo *HDR*

4 Infla] lc   6 Idem] lc   10 Quemadmodum] lc   26 Intelligimus] lc
29 Assimilatio] lc

29

Lutum inter lapides paruos densatur in materiam lapideam.

Omnia dura & solida aliquid ex liquoribus, & in fundo maximè & per latera adhærentibus condensant.

Dentes densant ea quæ ex manducatione cibi & humoribus oris
5 adhærent in squammas, quæ purgari & abscindi possunt, verum æquè duras ac ipsum os dentium.

Quæcumque alimenta vertuntur in corpus alimentatum magis durum quam corpus ipsius alimenti (sicut cibus & potus in animalibus vertuntur in ossa, caluariam, cornua) in assimilando densantur.

10 Actioni dilatationis per violentiam externam, siue appetitu aut contra appetitum corporis dilatati opponitur actio contractionis per violentiam similiter externam, cum corpora ponuntur in necessitate absque illis quæ in ipsa agunt cedendi & se comprimendi.

[fo. 21ᵛ] ˡ Aer per violentiam siue compressionem externam aliquam
15 condensationem facile patitur, majorem verò non tolerat, vt in violento impetu ventorum & terræ motibus, liquet. Patet hoc etiam per catinum ligneum immersum in aqua perpendiculariter, cuius ora tamen madefacta apparebit. Patet instrumento vrinatorum.

At quantum ipsum condensationis quod libenter tolleraturus sit aër,
20 cognoscere & supputare possis per modum de quo fit mentio lib. ī̄. in organo nouo, vbi & loquimur de quanto condensationis aquæ.

At omnis motus quem vocant violentus, veluti pilarum ex tormentis, sagittarum, spiculorum, machinarum, & aliorum infinitorum, expeditur per compressionem præternaturalem corporum, & nixum
25 ipsorum ad se restituendum; quod cum commode ad tempus facere non possint, loco mouentur. Nam solida, præsertim dura, vlteriorem compressionem ægrè admodum tolerant.

Quo corpora sunt rariora, eo ab initio se contrahunt facilius; quod si vltra terminos suos compressa fuerint, eo se vindicant potentius, vt in
30 flamma & aëre clauso manifestatur.

1 Lutum] / preceded in *HDR* by Supra notavimus   2 Omnia] / preceded in *HDR* by an extra para (see p. 154, l. 7 below)   4 Dentes] / this and preceding para transposed in *HDR* (see p. 154, ll. 7–10 below)   8 durum] densum *HDR*   9 assimilando] ~ (ut manifestum est,) *HDR*   densantur] *condensantur HDR*   10 Actioni . . .] / preceded by heading *Connexio* in *HDR*   aut] sive *HDR*   13 ipsa] ipsum / see *tn* to *HDR*, p. 154, l. 21 below   14 Aer . . .] / preceded in *HDR* by a section heading 16–18 Patet hoc . . . vrinatorum.] / these working notes are elaborated in *HDR* (p. 154, l. 27–p. 156, l. 11 below)   19–21 At . . . aquæ.] / these working notes are elaborated in *HDR* (p. 156, ll. 12–33 below); the reference is to *NO*, 2N1ʳ (*SEH*, I, p. 324)   27 tolerant.] / after this *HDR* adds two sentences (p. 158, ll. 3–5 below)
16 Patet] lc   18 Patet] lc   26 Nam] lc   28 facilius;] ~.

Flamma simpliciter compressa, licet sine flatu, vt in puluere pyrio, tamen magis furit, vt ⟨in⟩ conspici datur in fornacibus & reuerberatorijs, vbi flamma impeditur, arctatur, repercutitur, sinuat.

Dilatationi per deaceruationem non opponitur actio reciproca, quia corpora deaceruata non coaceruantur rursus nisi per conflationem, vt in   5
restitutione metallorum.

Efficientia dilatationis corporum quæ ex inquisitione priore [in lucem] prodeunt, sunt nouem. Ī. Introceptio siue admissio corporis alieni. ĪĪ. Expansio naturalis siue præternaturalis ⟨corporis⟩ spiritus innati. ĪĪĪ Ignis siue calor actualis externus, aut etiam remissio frigoris.   10
ĪV̄. Calor externus potentialis, siue spiritus auxiliares. V̄. Liberatio spiritu*m* a vinculis partium. V̄Ī. Assimilatio ex imperio corporis rarioris magis actiui. V̄ĪĪ. Amplexus siue itus in occursum corporis amici. V̄ĪĪĪ. Distractio ¹ a violentia externa. ĪX̄. Dilatatio siue applanatio partium.   [fo. 22ʳ]

Efficientia verò contractionis corporum sunt octo. Ī. Exclusio aut   15
depositio corporis introcepti. ĪĪ. Angustatio siue constrictio partium post spiritum emissum. ĪĪĪ. Frigus externum actuale, aut etiam remissio caloris. ĪV̄. Frigus externum potentiale. V̄. Fuga & antiperistasis. V̄Ī. Assimilatio ex imperio corporis densioris magis actiui. V̄ĪĪ. Compressio per violentiam externam. V̄ĪĪĪ. Oneratio, si modò aliqua sit.   20

Actiones dilatationis per spiritum innatum, & per liberationem spirituum, & per deaceruationem, atque rursus actiones contractionis per constrictionem, sunt actiones sine reciproco. Reliquæ actiones sunt reciprocæ.

Dilatationes per introceptionem & per deaceruationem sunt   25
pseudodilatationes, sicut contractiones per exclusionem sunt pseudocondensationes; sunt enim locales, non substantiales.

Expansio per ignem siue calorem sine separatione, est omnium simplicissima. Ea fit in pneumatico puro, sicut aere, vbi nihil exhalat, nihil residet, sed mera fit dilatatio, eaque ad ampliationem spatij siue   30

---

4 Dilatationi] / preceded by heading *Monitum* in *HDR*   deaceruationem] aceruationem
6 metallorum] ∼, de qua supra. *HDR* / *HDR* then adds a commentatio and a mandatum and
the heading *Observationes* (p. 158, l. 16–p. 160, l. 1 below)   7–8 [in lucem]] / cf. *HDR*,
p. 160, ll. 2–3   14 Dilatatio] *Deacervatio HDR*   16 introcepti] intercepti
constrictio] *Contractio HDR*   26 sicut] ∼ & *HDR*

8 Introceptio] lc   9 Expansio] lc   10 Ignis] lc   11 Calor] lc
Liberatio] lc   12 Assimilatio] lc   13 Amplexus] lc   14 Distractio] lc
15 Exclusio] lc   16 Angustatio] lc   17 Frigus] lc   18 Frigus]
lc   Fuga] lc   19 Assimilatio] lc   Compressio] lc   20 Oneratio] lc
23 Reliquæ] lc   27 pseudocondensationes;] ∼.   29 Ea] lc

exporrectionis insignem. Proxima huic dilat`at´ioni est expansio quæ fit
in colliquatione metallorum, aut in emollitione ferri, & ceræ, &
similium, ad tempus, antequam aliquid fiat volatile, & emittatur. Verum
hæc dilatatio occulta est, & fit intra claustra corporis integralis, nec
5 visibiliter exporrectionem mutat aut ampliat. At simul ac incipit in
corpore aliquo quippiam euolare, tum actiones fiunt complicatæ, partim
rarefacientes, partim contrahentes, adeo vt contrariæ illæ actiones ignis,
quæ vulgo notantur: *Limus vt hic durescit, & hæc vt cera liquescit Vno
eodemque igni*, in hoc fundantur, quod in altera spiritus emittitur, in
10 altera detinetur.

   Condensatio quæ fit per ignem, licet non sit pseudodensatio (est enim
substantialis) tamen est condensatio secundum partes, quam secundum
[fo. 22ᵛ] totum. Nam contrahuntur certè partes crassiores; | ita tamen vt corpus
integrum reddatur magis cauum & porosum & minus ponderosum.

15   Canones mobiles.

   Summa materiæ in vniuerso eadem manet, neque fit transitio a nihilo
ad nihilum.

   Ex summa in aliquibus corporibus est plus, in aliquibus minus, sub
eodem spatio.
20 Copia & paucitas materiæ constituunt notiones densi & rari rectè
acceptas. Est terminus siue non vltra densi & rari, sed non in ente aliquo
nobis noto.

   Non est vacuum in natura, nec congregatum, nec intermixtum.

   Inter terminos densi & rari est plica materiæ, per quam se complicat
25 & replicat absque vacuo.

   Differentiæ densi & rari in tangibilibus nobis notis parum excedunt
rationes x̄x̄x̄ī̄ī. partium.

   Differentia a rarissimo tangibili ad densissimum pneumaticum habet
rationem centuplam, & amplius.

---

1 insignem.] / here *HDR* adds a sentence (see p. 160, l. 28–p. 162, l. 1 below) dilat`at´ioni]
~ (quatenus ad simplicitatem) *HDR*   2 colliquatione] colliquatura / the *c-t* form is
probably Rigault's incorrect reading; Bacon preferred colliquatio, cf. *HDR*, p. 162, l. 2 below
5 incipit] incipiat *HDR*   9 fundantur] fundentur *HDR*   12 condensatio] ~
potius *HDR*   16 transitio] transactio *HDR* / transacto also appears in the same context
in the aditus to *HDR* (see p. 36. l. 23 below)   a] aut ~ *HDR*   17 ad] aut ~ *HDR*
1 Proxima] lc   3 Verum] lc   5 At] lc   7 contrahentes,] ~.
8 notantur:] ~.   8–9 *Limus vt hic durescit, & hæc vt cera liquescit Vno eodemque igni*] /
editorial italics; this Virgil quotation is set as verse in *HDR* (p. 162, ll. 10–11 below)
13 Nam] lc   21 Est] lc

32

Flamma est aëre rarior, vt & oleum aquis.

Flamma non est aër rarefactus, vt nec oleum est aqua rarefacta, sed sunt plane corpora hæterogenea, & non nimis amica.

Spiritus vegetabilium & animalium, sunt auræ compositæ ex pneumatico aëreo & flammeo, quemadmodum & succi eorum ex aqueo 5 & oleoso.

Omne tangibile apud nos habet pneumaticum, siue spiritum copulatum & inclusum.

Spiritus, quales sunt vegetabilium & animalium, non inueniuntur apud nos soluti, sed in tangibili deuincti & conclusi.   10

Densum & rarum sunt opificia calidi & frigidi; rarum calidi.

Calor super pneumatica operatur per expansionem simplicem.

Calor in tangibili exercet duplicem operationem, semper dilatando ┤ [fo. 23^r] pneumaticum, sed crassum interdum contrahendo, interdum laxando.

Norma autem huius rej talis est. spiritus emissus corpus co*n*trahit & 15 indurat; detentus intenerat & colliquat.

Colliquatio incipit a pneumatico in corpore expandendo; aliæ dissolutiones a crasso liberando operationem pneumatici.

Post calorem & frigus, potentissima sunt ad rarefactionem & condensationem corporum consensus & fuga.   20

Restitutio a violentia & dilatat & condensat in aduersum violentiæ.

Assimilatio & condensat & dilatat, prout est assimilans assimilato rarius aut densius.

Quo corpora sunt rariora, eò majorem sustinent ⟨n⟩ `et´ dilatationem & contractionem per externam violentiam ad certos terminos.   25

Si tensura aut pressura in corpore raro transgrediatur terminos sustinentiæ, tum corpora rariora potentius se vindicant in libertatem quam densiora, quia magis sunt actiua.

Potentissima omnium expansio, est expansio aëris & flammæ conjunctim. Imperfectæ sunt dilatationes & contractiones vbi facilis & 30 procliuis est restitutio.

Densum & rarum magnum habent consensum cum graui & leui.

Parcè suppeditatur homini facultas ad condensationem, ob defectum potentiæ frigidi.

Ætas est instar ignis lambentis, & exequitur opera caloris, sed 35 accuratius.

---

1 aquis] *Aqua HDR*   3 nimis] minus   11 opificia] propria ∼ *HDR*   18
dissolutiones] operationes / cf. *HDR*, p. 164, l. 23   22 condensat & dilatat] / verbs
transposed in *HDR*
3 hæterogenea] / *sic*   30 Imperfectæ] lc

Ætas deducit corpora, vel ad putrefactionem, vel ad arefactionem.

Optatiua cum proximis.

Versio aëris in aquam. Prox. fontes in cauis montium. Exsudatio
lapidum. Roratio anhelitus. Vellus super latera nauium. Augmentum
5 ponderis in metallis. Prox. versio ferri in cuprum. qu. incrementum
[fo. 23ᵛ] plumbi in cellis. qu. versio argenti viui in aurum. qu. Insaxatio terræ, |
& materiarum ex vegetabilibus aut animalibus. Prox. aqua insaxans.
Lapis compositus ex lapidibus paruis incrustatis. Stillicidia crystallina in
speluncis. Calculi in renibus & vesica & cyste fellis. Squammæ ⟨dens⟩
10 dentium. Varij vsus motus dilatantis & contrahentis in aëre per calorem.
Prox. vitrum calendare. Altare Heronis. Organum musicum
splendentibus radijs solis. Impostura de imitatione fluxus & refluxus
maris & amnium.

4 nauium] ~ qu. *Meteora Aquea*, &c. *HDR*   8 compositus] constans / cf. *HDR*,
p. 166, l. 20   13 amnium.] / after this *HDR* has three additional paras (see p. 166,
l. 28–p. 168, l. 3 below)

3 Prox.] lc   Exsudatio] lc   4 Roratio] lc   Vellus] lc   Augmentum] lc
5 Prox.] lc   6 Insaxatio] lc   7 Prox.] lc   8 Lapis] lc   Stillicidia] lc
9 Calculi] lc   Squammæ] lc   10 Varij] lc   11 Prox.] lc   Altare] lc
Organum] lc   12 Impostura] lc

HISTORIA DENSI & RARI
(Rawley's version)

| Historia Densi & Rari; nec-
non Coitionis & Expansionis
Materiæ per Spatia.

Aditus.

5 *Nil mirum, si Natura Philosophiæ & Scientiis debetrix sit, cum ad*
reddendas rationes nunquam adhuc sit interpellata. Neque enim de
Quanto Materiæ, & Quomodo *illud per Corpora sit distributum,*
[A1ᵛ] *(in aliis copiose, in aliis parce), instituta est Inquisitio dili|gens &*
dispensatoria, secundum veros, aut proximos veris calculos. Illud recte
10 receptum est, Nil deperdi, aut addi Summæ Vniversali; etiam
tractatus est à nonnullis ille locus, Quomodo Corpora laxari possint &
contrahi, absque Vacuo intermisto, secundum plus & minus. Densi
autem & Rari *naturas, alius ad copiam & paucitatem Materiæ*
retulit; alius hoc ipsum elusit; plerique, Auctorem suum secuti, rem
15 *totam per frigidam illam distinctionem Actus & Potentiæ discutiunt,*
& componunt. Etiam qui illa Materiæ rationibus attribuunt, (quæ
[A2ʳ] *vera est sententia), neque Materiam* | *primam Quanto plane*
spoliatam, licet ad alias Formas æquam volunt, tamen in hoc ipso
Inquisitionem terminant, ulterius nihil quærunt, neque quid inde
20 *sequatur perspiciunt; remque quæ ad infinita spectat, & Naturalis*
Philosophiæ veluti Basis est, aut non attingunt, aut non urgent.

Primo igitur, quod bene positum est, non movendum: Non scilicet
fieri in aliqua Transmutatione Corporum transactionem aut à
Nihilo, aut ad Nihilum; sed Opera esse ejusdem Omnipotentiæ, creare
25 *ex Nihilo, & redigere in Nihilum; ex cursu Naturæ vero hoc*
[A2ᵛ] *nunquam fieri. Itaque* | *Summa Materiæ totalis semper constat; nil*
additur, nil minuitur. At istam summam inter Corpora per portiones

---

1–3 nec-non . . . Spatia] / *om HNE* (R4ʳ). The whole title and the preface following it *om* in
HDR(M) (see p. 2 above)
4 ff. Aditus . . .] / *SEH* (II, pp. 243–4) does not use large type (as *c-t*) for the Aditus
8 *parce*),] ~,) 10 *Vniversali*;] ~: 14 *Auctorem*] / nld in *SEH* (II, p. 243) as
authorem 17 *sententia*),] ~,) 26–7 nil additur] *Nil additur* 27 *minuitur*.] ~:

History of Dense and Rare; or of
the Coition and Expansion
of Matter in Space

Preface

It is no wonder that nature be in debt to philosophy and the sciences when she has never yet been summonsed to render her account. For no careful audit, by precise or near-precise calculation, of the quantity of matter and how it is distributed through bodies (in some abundantly, in others sparsely), has yet [1] been set in motion. It has rightly been received that nothing is subtracted or added to the universal sum, and some have dealt with the topic of how bodies can be relaxed or contracted more or less without an interspersed vacuum. But as to the natures of Dense and Rare, someone has assigned them to abundance and scarcity of matter; someone else has ridiculed this idea, but most follow their author and dismiss the whole matter and put it to rest with that frigid distinction between act and power. Those too who attribute these things to the proportions of matter (which is the right view) and deny that the first matter [1] is quite devoid of quantity though impartially disposed to other forms, give over their investigations there and take the question no further and do not look into what follows from it; and they do not touch or press on with the matter, a matter which bears on a multitude of things and is as the foundation of natural philosophy.

Thus in the first place what has been well established should not be dislodged: namely that in any transmutation of bodies no transaction can come of nothing or be reduced to nothing; but it is the work of the same Omnipotence to create something from nothing and to reduce it to nothing, things which never happen in the course of nature. Therefore [1] the whole sum of matter always stays the same; nothing is

dividi, nemini dubium esse possit. Neque enim quisquam
subtilitatibus abstractis tam dementatus esse queat, ut existimet
tantum Materiæ inesse Dolio Aquæ, quantum decem Doliis Aquæ,
neque similiter Dolio Aeris, quantum decem Doliis Aeris. At in
5 corpore eodem non dubitatur, quin copia Materiæ multiplicetur pro
mensura Corporis; in corporibus diversis, ambigitur. Quod si
demonstretur, unum Dolium Aquæ in Aerem versum, decem dare
[A3^r] Dolia Aeris; (istam $^|$ enim computationem propter Opinionem
receptam sumimus, licet centupla verior sit), bene habet: etenim jam
10 non amplius sunt diversa Corpora, Aqua & Aer, sed idem Corpus
Aeris in decem Doliis. At unum Dolium Aeris, (ut modo concessum
est) decima tantum pars est decem Doliorum.
    Itaque resisti jam non potest, quin in uno Dolio Aquæ decuplo plus
sit Materiæ, quam in uno Dolio Aeris. Itaque, si quis asserat Dolium
15 Aquæ totum in Dolium Aeris unicum verti posse, idem prorsus est ac
si asserat aliquid posse redigi ad nihilum. Etenim una Decima Aquæ
[A3^v] ad hoc suffi$^|$ciet, reliquæ novem partes necesse est ut annihilentur.
Contra, si quis asserat Dolium Aeris in Dolium Aquæ verti posse,
idem est acsi asserat aliquid posse creari ex nihilo. Etenim Dolium
20 Aeris, [non] nisi ad decimam partem Dolii Aquæ attinget, reliquæ
novem partes necesse est ut fiant ex nihilo. Illud interim plane
confitemur, de rationibus, & calculis, & quota parte Quanti Materiæ,
quæ diversis Corporibus subest, & qua industria & sagacitate de illis
informatio vera capi possit, arduam Inquisitionem esse; quam tamen
25 ingens & latissime fusa utilitas compenset. Nam & Densitates
[A4^r] & Ra$^|$ritates Corporum nosse, & multo magis Condensationes &
Rarefactiones procurare & efficere, maxime interest &
Contemplativæ & Practicæ. Cum igitur sit res (si qua alia) plane
fundamentalis & catholica, accincti debemus ad eam accedere;
30 quandoquidem omnis Philosophia, absque ea, penitus discincta &
dissoluta sit.

---

20 [*non*] / this emendation suggested in *SEH* (II, p. 244 n. 1); *c-t* agrees with *HNE* (R7^v)
6 *Corporis*;] ∼: 9 *sit)*,] ∼,) 13 *Itaque*] / no new para in *HNE* (R7^r). *SEH*
follows *HNE* in the Latin (II, p. 244) but *c-t* in translation (V, p. 340) 15 *est*] ∼,
19 *acsi*] / *nld* in *SEH* (II, p. 244) as ac si

added and nothing taken away. But it cannot be doubted that this sum is divided among bodies in various portions. For no one can be so crazed by abstract subtleties as to imagine that there can be as much matter in one barrel of water as in ten, or likewise that one of air contains as much as ten. But no one doubts that in a given body the abundance of matter varies in proportion to size, though whether the same be true of different bodies is problematic. But if one could demonstrate that one barrel of water turned into air yields ten barrels of air (for though [1] *a hundred would be nearer the mark, I have adopted this figure to take account of received wisdom), I would not argue with it, for they are now no longer different bodies, water and air, but the same body of air in ten barrels. Alternatively, one barrel of air (as has just been conceded) is only one tenth of ten barrels. Therefore it is now impossible to deny that there is ten times more matter in one barrel of water than in one of air. Thus if someone claims that a whole barrel of water could be one barrel of air that would be exactly the same as claiming that something could be reduced to nothing. For a tenth of the water would be enough* [1] *for the purpose, necessarily leaving the other nine parts to be annihilated. On the other hand, if someone claims that a barrel or air could be turned into a barrel of water, that would be like saying that something could be created from nothing. For the barrel of air would only amount to one tenth of the barrel of water, necessarily leaving the other nine parts to be made out of nothing. Meanwhile I freely confess that to determine the proportions and calculations and what amount of the quantum of matter exists in various bodies and by what industry and skill true information about these matters can be acquired, makes for a difficult inquiry which nevertheless repays the effort with its hugely important and widespread utility. For to know the* Densities *and* [1] Rarities *of bodies, and much more to get hold of and bring about their* Condensations *and* Rarefactions *is something of the greatest importance for contemplation and practice. Seeing therefore that this matter is (of all others) clearly fundamental and catholic, we must gird ourselves up to tackle it; since without it all philosophy is thoroughly undisciplined and lax.*

| Tabula Coitionis & Expansionis Materiæ per Spatia in
Tangibilibus (quæ, scilicet, dotantur pondere),
cum Supputatione rationum in
Corporibus diversis.

5 [*Historia.*]

Idem spatium occupant, sive æque exporriguntur:

Auri puri	*Vncia vna sive Den.* 20.	*Gra.* 0
Argenti vivi	*Den.* 19.	*Gra.* 9
Plumbi	*Den.* 12.	*Gra.* 1.*d.*
10 *Argenti puri*	*Den.* 10.	*Gra.* 21
Plumbi cinericei, Anglice Tynglas	*Den.* 10.	*Gra.* 12
Cupri	*Den.* 9.	*Gra.* 8
Aurichalci	*Den.* 9.	*Gra.* 5
Chalybis	*Den.* 8.	*Gra.* 10
15 *Æris communis*	*Den.* 8.	*Gra.* 9
Ferri	*Den.* 8.	*Gra.* 6
Stanni	*Den.* 7.	*Gra.* 22
Magnetis	*Den.* 5.	*Gra.* 12
Lapidis Lydii	*Den.* 3.	*Gra.* 1
20 *Marmoris*	*Den.* 2.	*Gra.* 22. *d.qu.*
Silicis	*Den.* 2.	*Gra.* 22. *d.*
Vitri	*Den.* 2.	*Gra.* 20. *d.*
Crystalli	*Den.* 2.	*Gra.* 18
Alabastri	*Den.* 2.	*Gra.* 12
25 *Salis gemmæ*	*Den.* 2.	*Gra.* 10
Luti communis	*Den.* 2.	*Gra.* 8. *d.*
Luti albi	*Den.* 2.	*Gra.* 5. *d.*
Nitri	*Den.* 2.	*Gra.* 5
Ossis bovis	*Den.* 2.	*Gra.* 5
30 *Pulveris margaritarum*	*Den.* 2.	*Gra.* 2
Sulphuris	*Den.* 2.	*Gra.* 2
Terræ communis	*Den.* 2.	*Gra.* 1. *d.*
Vitrioli albi	*Den.* 1.	*Gra.* 22.

1 ff. Tabula . . .] / for differences between this table those in *HDR(M)* and *PhU* see *OFB*, VI,
p. 336   5 [*Historia.*] / in *SEH* (II, p. 245) this emendation stands before the previous
heading   11 *cinericei*] cineritij *HDR(M)* (fo. 7ʳ), *cinerei PhU* (*OFB*, VI, p. 14)

1–4 Tabula . . .] / set in small roman type in *c-t*; also cf. *HDR(M)*, pp. 2–3 above
2 pondere),] ~,)   6 Idem spatium . . .] / set in small roman type in *c-t*   exporriguntur:] ~,   9 *d.*] / this and all others in *SEH nld* as ½ (II, pp. 245–6)   20
d.qu.] / this and all others in *SEH nld* as ¾ (II, pp. 245–6)

[1] A Table of the Coition and Expansion of Matter in relation to Space in Tangible Bodies (i.e. bodies which have weight), with a Computation of the proportions in different Bodies

[*History*]

The following occupy the same space, or are of equal bulk:

Pure gold	*One Ounce or* 20 *Dwt.*	0 *Gr.*
Quicksilver	19 *Dwt.*	9 *Gr.*
Lead	12 *Dwt.*	1½ *Gr.*
Pure Silver	10 *Dwt.*	21 *Gr.*
Tin Glass	10 *Dwt.*	12 *Gr.*
Copper	9 *Dwt.*	8 *Gr.*
Yellow Brass	9 *Dwt.*	5 *Gr.*
Steel	8 *Dwt.*	10 *Gr.*
Common Brass	8 *Dwt.*	9 *Gr.*
Iron	8 *Dwt.*	6 *Gr.*
Tin	7 *Dwt.*	22 *Gr.*
Loadstone	5 *Dwt.*	12 *Gr.*
Touchstone	3 *Dwt.*	1 *Gr.*
Marble	2 *Dwt.*	22¾ *Gr.*
Flint	2 *Dwt.*	22½ *Gr.*
Glass	2 *Dwt.*	20½ *Gr.*
Crystal	2 *Dwt.*	18 *Gr.*
Alabaster	2 *Dwt.*	12 *Gr.*
Rock-Salt	2 *Dwt.*	10 *Gr.*
Common Clay	2 *Dwt.*	8½ *Gr.*
White Clay	2 *Dwt.*	5½ *Gr.*
Nitre	2 *Dwt.*	5 *Gr.*
Ox Bone	2 *Dwt.*	5 *Gr.*
Pearl Powder	2 *Dwt.*	2 *Gr.*
Sulphur	2 *Dwt.*	2 *Gr.*
Common Earth	2 *Dwt.*	1½ *Gr.*
White Vitriol	1 *Dwt.*	22 *Gr.*

	Eboris	*Den.* 1.	*Gra.* 21. *d.*
	Aluminis	*Den.* 1.	*Gra.* 21
	Olei vitrioli	*Den.* 1.	*Gra.* 21
	Arenæ albæ	*Den.* 1.	*Gra.* 20
[A5ʳ] 5	¹*Cretæ*	*Den.* 1.	*Gra.* 18. *d.*
	Olei sulphuris	*Den.* 1.	*Gra.* 18
	Pulveris salis communis	*Den.* 1.	*Gra.* 10
	Ligni vitæ	*Den.* 1.	*Gra.* 10
	Carnis ovillæ	*Den.* 1.	*Gra.* 10
10	*Aquæ fortis*	*Den.* 1.	*Gra.* 7
	Cornu bovis	*Den.* 1.	*Gra.* 6
	Balsami Indi	*Den.* 1.	*Gra.* 6
	Cerebri vitulini crudi	*Den.* 1.	*Gra.*5. *paulo minus.*
	Sanguinis ovilli	*Den.* 1.	*Gra.* 5
15	*Ligni santali rubei*	*Den.* 1.	*Gra.* 5
	Gagatis	*Den.* 1.	*Gra.* 5
	Cepæ recentis	*Den.* 1.	*Gra.* 5
	Lactis vaccini	*Den.* 1.	*Gra.* 4. *d.*
	Caphuræ	*Den.* 1.	*Gra.* 4
20	*Succi menthæ expressi*	*Den.* 1.	*Gra.* 4
	Succi boraginis expressi	*Den.* 1.	*Gra.* 3. *d.*
	Cervisiæ lupulatæ fortis	*Den.* 1.	*Gra.* 3. *d.*
	Ligni ebeni	*Den.* 1.	*Gra.* 3. *d.*
	Pulveris seminis fœniculi dulcis	*Den.* 1.	*Gra.* 3. *d.*
25	*Aceti*	*Den.* 1.	*Gra.* 3. *d.*
	Agrestæ, ex pomis acerbis	*Den.* 1.	*Gra.* 3
	Succini lucidi	*Den.* 1.	*Gra.* 3.
	Vrinæ	*Den.* 1.	*Gra.* 3.
	Aquæ communis	*Den.* 1.	*Gra.* 3. *paulo minus*
30	*Olei caryophyllorum Chymici*	*Den.* 1.	*Gra.* 3. *paulo minus*
	Vini clareti	*Den.* 1.	*Gra.* 2. *d.qu.*
	Pulveris sacchari albi	*Den.* 1.	*Gra.* 2. *d.*
	Ceræ flavæ	*Den.* 1.	*Gra.* 2
	Radicis Chinæ	*Den.* 1.	*Gra.* 2
35	*Carnis pyri brumalis crudi*	*Den.* 1.	*Gra.* 2
	Aceti distillati	*Den.* 1.	*Gra.* 1
	Aquæ rosaceæ distillatæ	*Den.* 1.	*Gra.* 1
	Cineris communis	*Den.* 1.	*Gra. d.*
	Myrrhæ	*Den.* 1.	*Gra.* 0
40	*Benjovin*	*Den.* 1.	*Gra.* 0
	Butyri	*Den.* 1.	*Gra.* 0
	Adipis	*Den.* 1.	*Gra.* 0
	Olei amygdalini dulcis	*Den.* 0.	*Gra.* 23. *d.*

Ivory	1 *Dwt.*	21½ *Gr.*
Alum	1 *Dwt.*	21 *Gr.*
Oil of Vitriol	1 *Dwt.*	21 *Gr.*
White Sand	1 *Dwt.*	20 *Gr.*
ˈChalk	1 *Dwt.*	18½ *Gr.*
Oil of Sulphur	1 *Dwt.*	18 *Gr.*
Powder of Common Salt	1 *Dwt.*	10 *Gr.*
Lignum Vitæ	1 *Dwt.*	10 *Gr.*
Mutton	1 *Dwt.*	10 *Gr.*
Aqua Fortis	1 *Dwt.*	7 *Gr.*
Ox Horn	1 *Dwt.*	6 *Gr.*
Indian Balsam	1 *Dwt.*	6 *Gr.*
Raw Calves' Brains	1 *Dwt.*	and just under 5 *Gr.*
Sheep's Blood	1 *Dwt.*	5 *Gr.*
Red Sandalwood	1 *Dwt.*	5 *Gr.*
Jet	1 *Dwt.*	5 *Gr.*
Fresh Onion	1 *Dwt.*	5 *Gr.*
Cow's Milk	1 *Dwt.*	4½ *Gr.*
Camphor	1 *Dwt.*	4 *Gr.*
Pressed Mint Juice	1 *Dwt.*	4 *Gr.*
Pressed Borage Juice	1 *Dwt.*	3½ *Gr.*
Strong Hoppy Beer	1 *Dwt*	3½ *Gr.*
Ebony Wood	1 *Dwt.*	3½ *Gr.*
Sweet Fennel Seed Powdered	1 *Dwt.*	3½ *Gr.*
Vinegar	1 *Dwt.*	3½ *Gr.*
Verjuice of Unripe Apples	1 *Dwt.*	3 *Gr.*
Clear Souse	1 *Dwt.*	3 *Gr.*
Urine	1 *Dwt.*	3 *Gr.*
Common Water	1 *Dwt.*	and just under 3 *Gr.*
Chemical Oil of Cloves	1 *Dwt.*	and just under 3 *Gr.*
Claret	1 *Dwt.*	2¾ *Gr.*
White Sugar Powder	1 *Dwt.*	2½ *Gr.*
Yellow Wax	1 *Dwt.*	2 *Gr.*
China Root	1 *Dwt.*	2 *Gr.*
Flesh of Raw Winter Pear	1 *Dwt.*	2 *Gr.*
Distilled Vinegar	1 *Dwt.*	1 *Gr.*
Distilled Rose-Water	1 *Dwt.*	1 *Gr.*
Common Ashes	1 *Dwt.*	0½ *Gr.*
Myrrh	1 *Dwt.*	0 *Gr.*
Benzoin	1 *Dwt.*	0 *Gr.*
Butter	1 *Dwt.*	0 *Gr.*
Lard	1 *Dwt.*	0 *Gr.*
Oil of Sweet Almond	0 *Dwt.*	23½ *Gr.*

	Olei maceris viridis expressi	*Den.* o.	*Gra.* 23. *d.*
[A5ᵛ]	¹*Pulveris herbæ sampsuci*	*Den.* o.	*Gra.* 23
	Petrolei	*Den.* o.	*Gra.* 23
	Pulveris florum rosæ	*Den.* o.	*Gra.* 22
5	*Spiritus vini*	*Den.* o.	*Gra.* 22
	Ligni quercus	*Den.* o.	*Gra.* 19. *d.*
	Pulveris fuliginis communis è camino	*Den.* o.	*Gra.* 17
	Ligni abietis	*Den.* o.	*Gra.* 15

10 ### *Modus experimenti circa Tabulam suprascriptam.*

Intelligantur *Pondera*, quibus usi summus, ejus generis & computationis, quibus *Aurifabri* utuntur; ut *Libra* capiat *Vncias* 12; *Vncia* 20 *Denarios*; *Denarius Grana* 24. Delegimus autem corpus *Auri puri*, ad cujus exporrectionis mensuram reliquorum Corporum Rationes 15 applicaremus; non tantum quia gravissimum, sed quia maxime unum, & sui simile, nihil habens ex *Volatili*. *Experimentum* fuit tale: Vnciam *Auri puri* in figuram Aleæ, sive Cubi, efformavimus; dein *Situlam* parvam, quadratam, ex *Argento* paravimus, quæ Cubum illum *Auri* caperet, atque ei exacte conveniret; nisi quod *Situla* esset nonnihil altior; 20 ita tamen ut locus intra *Situlam*, quo Cubus ille *Auri* ascenderat, *Linea* conspicua signaretur. Id fecimus *Liquorum* & *Pulverum* gratia; ut cum *liquor* aliquis intra eandem *Situlam* immittendus esset, non difflueret, sed paulo interius se contineret. Simul autem aliam *Situlam* fieri fecimus, quæ cum altera illa, pondere & contento, prorsus par esset; ut [A6ʳ] 25 in pari *Situla*, Corporis contenti tantum ¹ ratio appareret. Tum *Cubos* ejusdem magnitudinis, sive dimensi, fieri fecimus, in omnibus *materiis* in *Tabula* specificatis quæ sectionem pati possent; *Liquoribus* vero ex tempore usi sumus, implendo scilicet situlam, quousque *Liquor* ad locum illum *Linea* signatum ascenderet. *Pulveribus* eodem modo. Sed 30 intelligantur Pulveres maxime & fortiter compressi. Hoc enim potissimum ad æquationem pertinet, nec casum recipit. Itaque, non alia fuit *Probatio*, quam ut una ex *situlis* vacua in una *lance*, altera cum corpore in altera *lance* poneretur; & ratio ponderis corporis, contenti per se exciperetur. Quanto vero *pondus Corporis pondere Auri* est minus, 35 tanto *exporrectio corporis* est *exporrectione Auri* major. Exempli gratia, cum *Auri* ille Cubus det *Vnciam* unam, *Myrrhæ* vero *Denarium* unum;

---

10 *Modus experimenti . . .*] / this heading inset at start of para to which it belongs in *SEH* (II, p. 246), also cf. *HDR(M)*, p. 3 above   13 20] ~.   17 efformavimus;] ~:

Pressed Oil of Green Mace	0 Dwt.	23½ Gr.
The Herb Marjoram Powdered	0 Dwt.	23 Gr.
Petroleum	0 Dwt.	23 Gr.
Rose-Flowers Powdered	0 Dwt.	22 Gr.
Spirit of Wine	0 Dwt.	22 Gr.
Oak Wood	0 Dwt.	19½ Gr.
Ordinary Chimney Soot Powdered	0 Dwt.	17 Gr.
Fir Wood	0 Dwt.	15. Gr.

*The Way in which the experiment used for the above Table
was conducted*

Let it be understood that the weights I have used belong to the system
employed by the goldsmiths, so that a pound has 12 ounces, an ounce 20
pennyweights, and a pennyweight 24 grains. Now I chose a body of pure
gold as the standard of bulk to which I would relate the weights of the
other bodies because it was not only the heaviest but also the most uniform and homogeneous substance, and having nothing volatile about it.
The experiment was as follows. I fashioned an ounce of pure gold into
the shape of a die or cube; then I prepared a small cubical vessel of silver
which would hold the gold body and fit round it snugly, save only that
the vessel would be a bit taller and such that the height inside the vessel
to which the cube of gold reached could be marked by a distinct line. I
did this for the sake of liquids and powders, so that when any liquid was
poured into the vessel, it would not overflow but be kept inside a little.
Now at the same time I had a second vessel made which was of just the
same weight and capacity as the first one, so that only the value for the
body ¹ held in the matching one would be furnished. Then I had cubes
made of the same size or dimension for all the materials specified in the
Table as were capable of being cut into shape; but I used liquids without
further ado, i.e. by filling the vessel to the point where the liquid came
up to the line marked; and I did the same with powders, i.e. with powders compressed as much as it is possible for them to be. For this goes a
long way to equalizing their distribution and reduces the chance of error.
So I carried out the trial in exactly this manner: one of the vessels was
placed empty with the ounce of gold in one scale, the other vessel with
the body in it in the other scale, and the difference of weight of the body
was taken down. Now by how much the weight of the body is less than
that of gold, by that much is the bulk of the body greater than that of
gold. For example, since the gold cube weighs one ounce and the cube

liquet, *exporrectionem Myrrhæ* ad *exporrectionem Auri* habere rationem vicecuplam; ut vicies plus *Materiæ* sit in *Auro* quam in *Myrrha*, in simili spatio; rursus, vicies plus exporrectionis sit in *Myrrha* quam in *Auro*, in simili *pondere.*

5 *Monita.*

1. Parvitas vasis quo usi sumus, & forma etiam, (licet *ad Cubos* illos recipiendos habilis & apta), ad rationes exquisitas verificandas minus propria fuit. Nam nec minutias infra *Grani* quadrantem facile excipere licebat; & quadrata illa superficies in parvo, nec sensibili ascensu, sive
[A6ᵛ] 10 altitudine, notabilem *ponderis* differentiam tra'here potuit, contra quam fit in vasis in acutum surgentibus.

2. Minime dubium est, etiam complura *Corpora* quæ in *Tabula* ponuntur, intra suam speciem magis & minus recipere, quoad *pondera* & *spatia*; nam & *Vina*, & *Ligna* ejusdem speciei, & nonnulla è reliquis,
15 sunt certe alia aliis graviora. Itaque quoad *calculationem* exquisitam, casum quendam ista res recipit: neque ea individua, in quæ Experimentum nostrum incidit, naturam speciei exacte referre, neque cum aliorum Experimentis, fortasse, omnino in minimis consentire possunt.

20 3. In *Tabulam* superiorem conjecimus ea *Corpora* quæ Spatium, sive Mensuram, commode implere, Corpore integro, & tanquam similari, possent; quæque etiam *Pondus* habeant, ex cujus rationibus de Materiæ coacervatione judicium fecimus. Itaque tria genera *Corporum* huc retrahi non poterant: primo, ea quæ dimensioni cubicæ satisfacere non
25 poterant; ut *Folia, Flores, Pelliculæ, Membranæ*: secundo, *corpora* inæqualiter cava, & porosa; ut *Spongia, Suber, Vellera*: tertio, *pneumatica,* quia pondere non dotantur; ut *Aer, Flamma.*

4. Videndum, num forte *contractio Corporis* arctior ex vi unita nanciscatur majorem *rationem Ponderis,* quam pro *quantitate Materiæ.*
30 Id utrum fiat necne, ex Historia propria Ponderis inquiratur. Quod si fiat, fallit certe *Supputatio:* & quo *Corpora* sunt tenuiora, eo paulo plus
[A7ʳ] habent *materiæ* in simili *exporrectione,* quam pro ' calculo *Ponderis,* & *Mensuræ* quæ ex eo pendet.

5 *Monita.*] / cf. *HDR(M)*, p. 4, l. 22–p. 5, l. 3 above   9 &] nec / cf. *PhU*, P2ʳ (*OFB*, VI, p. 22, l. 4). I am indebted to Benedino Gemelli for drawing my attention to this
2 vicecuplam;] ~:   7 apta),] ~,)   10 potuit,] ~:   18 omnino] ~, minimis] ~,   22 habeant,] ~;

of myrrh one pennyweight, it is evident that the bulk of the myrrh compared with the bulk of the body of gold is as twenty to one; so that in the same space there are twenty times more matter in gold than in myrrh, or contrariwise that myrrh has twenty times the bulk of the same weight of gold.

Advice

1. The smallness of the vessel that I used as well as its shape (even though handy and convenient for receiving the cubes) was less suitable for determining precise values. For one could not easily measure minute differences below a quarter of a grain, and that square surface could, with a small or imperceptible increase in height, bring about a big ' difference in weight, which is not what happens in conical vessels.

2. There is also no doubt that many bodies set down in the Table vary within their own species as regards their weights and the spaces they fill. For both wines and woods of the same species, and some of the other substances are certainly some heavier than others. Therefore as regards precise calculation, a certain degree of chance enters into the matter; and, what is more, the individual samples with which my experiment deals may neither represent exactly the nature of their species nor happen altogether to agree with the experiments of others in their smallest details.

3. I included in the above Table bodies which could conveniently fill the space or measure with the body whole and as it were uniform, and which also have weight, from whose proportions I made an estimate of their concentration of matter. Thus three kinds of bodies could not be considered here. First, those which could not be made into the shape of a cube, such as leaves, flowers, pellicles and membranes; secondly, bodies unevenly hollow and porous, such as sponges, cork and wool; and thirdly, pneumatic substances, like air and flame, because they are weightless.

4. See whether the closer contraction of a body resulting from concentrated force perhaps acquires a greater amount of weight than its quantity of matter would warrant; and whether this be the case or not is inquired of the particular history of weight. But if it be the case, the computation certainly breaks down; and the more tenuous the bodies are, a little more matter do they have in the same bulk than would appear from ' a reckoning of their weight and volume.

Hanc *Tabulam* multis abhinc annis confeci, atque (ut memini), bona usus diligentia. Verum possit, proculdubio, *Tabula* multo exactior componi; videlicet, tum ex pluribus, tum ampliore quapiam Mensura: Id quod ad exactas rationes plurimum facit; & omnino paranda est, cum
5 *res* sit ex *Fundamentalibus.*

Observationes.

1. Licet, atque adeo juvat, animo prospicere, quam finita & comprehensibilis sit *Natura Rerum* in *Tangibilibus. Tabula* enim *Naturam* claudit, tanquam in pugno. Nemo itaque expatietur,
10 nemo fingat aut somniet. Non invenitur in *Tabula* Ens, quod aliud Ens in copia *materiæ* superet, ultra proportionem tricesimam duplam: tanto enim superat *Aurum Lignum Abietis.* De *Interioribus* autem *Terræ* nihil decernimus, cum nec sensui nec experimento subjiciantur. Illa, cum à *calore cœlestium* primo
15 longius, deinde penitus semota sint, possint esse *Corporibus* nobis notis densiora.

2. Opinio de *compositione Sublunarium* ex quatuor *Elementis,*
[A7^v] non bene cedit. *Aurum* enim in *situla* illa tabulari est ponderis |
Den. 20; *Terra communis* Den. 2, paulo plus; *Aqua* Den. 1, gran.
20 3; *Aer,* [&] *Ignis,* longe tenuiora, & minus *materiata, ponderis* vero nullius. At *Forma Materiam* non auget. Videndum igitur, quomodo ex *Corpore* 2 Den. & *Corporibus* longe tenuioribus, educatur, per *Formam,* in pari dimenso, *Corpus* 20 Den. Duo sunt Effugia: unum, quod *Elementa* tenuiora compingant densiora in
25 majorem densitatem, quam simplicis *Elementi*; alterum, quod non intelligant *Peripatetici* hoc de *Terra communi,* sed de *Terra elementari,* omni Ente composito graviore. At *Ignis* & *Aer* non condensant, nisi per accidens, ut suo loco dicetur. *Terra* autem illa, quæ foret *Auro* & omnibus gravior, ita sita est, ut vix adsit ad

6 *Observationes*] / cf. *HDR(M)*, p. 5, l. 4–p. 6, l. 5 above   19–20 gran. 3] gran. 33 / emended thus with appropriate note in *SEH* (II, p. 248) although the Table (p. 42, l. 29 above) has *Gra.* 3. *paulo minus*   20 *Ignis*] / *SEH* (II, p. 248) misreads as ignes   24 densiora] / *SEH* (*loc. cit.*) misreads as densiorem
1 memini),] ~,)   15 penitus] ~,   19 1,] ~.   20 *materiata,*] ~;   22 2] ~.   23 20] ~.

I compiled this table many years ago, and (as I recall) took a great deal of trouble over it. But I do not doubt that a much more accurate one could be put together, namely one with more observations made on a more generous scale, which is something that contributes greatly to exact calculation; and this should emphatically be done, for it is fundamental to the whole business.

Observations

1. It does the mind a power of good to see how finite and comprehensible is the nature of things in tangible bodies. For the table gets to grips with nature as if in a wrestling match. Let no one therefore go astray or go in for fictions or dreams. In the Table we find no being that exceeds any other in quantity of matter by a proportion of more than 32 to 1: for by so much does gold exceed fir wood. But of the entrails of the Earth we can decide nothing since they are subject neither to sense nor experiment. These, since they are at both further off and in that case quite removed from the heat of the heavenly bodies, could be denser than any bodies known to us.

2. The opinion that sublunary things are made up of the four elements does not come well out of this. For the gold in the vessel weighed in at ¹ 20 pennyweight; common earth at little more than 2; water at 1 dwt. and three grains; air [and] fire, much more tenuous and less materiate, weigh nothing at all. But form does not increase matter. So work out how it is possible by means of form to derive from a body weighing 2 dwt. and from other much more tenuous ones, a body weighing 20 dwt. in the same dimension. There are two ways out of this: the one that the more tenuous elements compress the denser ones into a greater density than the element would have had by itself; the other that the Peripatetics are not talking about common earth but of an elementary earth which is denser than every composite being. But fire and air do not condense things except by accident, as I shall explain in the proper place. On the other hand, that earth which should be heavier than gold and all things else is so situated that

mistionem. Melius igitur foret, ut plane nugari desinant, & cesset *Dictatura.*

3. Diligenter notanda est *Series* sive *Scala Coacervationis Materiæ*; & quomodo ascendat à *Coacervatione* majore ad
5 minorem: idque interdum per gradus, interdum per saltum. Siquidem utilis est hæc *Contemplatio*, & ad *Iudicium*, & ad *Practicam. Coagmentatio Metallica* & *subterranea* maxima est; ita ut ex 32 illis partibus, occupet 12. Tantum enim distat *Aurum* à
[A8^r] *Stanno.* In illo $^|$ descensu ab *Auro* & *Argento* vivo magnus saltus ad
10 *Plumbum.* A *Plumbo* ad *Stannum* gradatio. Rursus magnus saltus à *Metallis* ad *Lapides*: nisi quod se interponat *Magnes*; qui inde convincitur esse *Lapis metallicus.* A *Lapidibus* vero ad reliqua, usque ad levissimum, continui & pusilli gradus.

Mandata.

15 1. Cvm *Fons Densitatis* videatur esse in *profundo Terræ*, adeo ut versus Superficiem ejus *Corpora* eximie extenuentur, illud notatu dignum est, quod *Aurum* (quod est ex *Metallis* gravissimum), nihilominus reperiatur quandoque in Arenulis et Ramentis Fluviorum; etiam fere purum. Itaque inquirendum diligenter de situ ejusmodi locorum; utrum non
20 sint ad pedes *montium*, quorum fundi & radices æquiparari possint *Mineris* profundissimis, & *Aurum* inde eluatur; aut quid tandem sit quod pariat tantam *Condensationem* versus *summitates Terræ.*

2. De *Mineris* in genere quærendum, quæ ex iis soleant esse depressiores, & quæ propius ad superficiem Terræ; & quali situ
25 Regionum, & in qua Gleba nascantur; & quomodo se habeant ad Aquas; & maxime, in quibus *Cubilibus* decumbant et jaceant; & quomodo circundentur, aut misceantur Lapide, aut aliquo alio Fossili: Denique, omnes Circumstantiæ examinandæ, ut per istas explorari
[A8^v] possit, qua ratione Succi & Spiri$^|$tus Terræ in *Condensationem* istam
30 *Metallicam* (quæ reliquas longe superat) coeant, aut compingantur.

Observationes.

4. Dvbium minime est, quin & in *Vegetabilibus*, atque etiam in *Partibus Animalium*, se ostendant *Corpora* complura *Ligno Abietis*

it is hardly available for mixture. So it would be better if they stopped splitting hairs and that the dictatorship should cease.

3. The series or scale of the concentration of matter should be carefully noted, and how it goes from a greater to a lesser concentration and does so sometimes by steps and sometimes by leaps. For this study serves equally for judgement and for practice. The closeness of mass is greatest in metallic and subterranean things, such that of those 32 parts they take up 12; for gold and tin differ by that much. Descending [1] the scale from gold and quicksilver, there is a big jump down to lead; from lead to tin there is a gradual decline. Again, there is a big jump from metals to stones, except that loadstone stands in between which shows then that it is a metallic stone. But from stones to the rest down to the lightest, the descent is gentle and continuous.

Directions

1. Since the source of density seems to lie in the depths of the Earth, such that towards its surface bodies thin out remarkably, it is worth noting nevertheless that gold (which is the heaviest metal) is sometimes found in the sands and alluvia of rivers and that practically pure. Diligent inquiry should therefore be made into the location of such places to see if they do not lie at the bottom of mountains, the foundations and roots of which are on a level with the deepest lodes, and the gold washed away from there; or what it is after all that gives rise to such condensation towards the Earth's surface.

2. Investigate lodes in general, to see which of them are usually deeper, and which nearer to the surface of the Earth; and in what geographical situation and soils they arise and how they lie in relation to the waters, but above all in what beds they lie and rest, and how they are surrounded and mixed with stone or any other kind of fossil material. In fine, all circumstances should be examined so that by these means we can find out how the juices and spirits [1] of the earth combine or are put together in this metallic condensation (which far surpasses the others).

Observations

4. There is no doubt but that in vegetables as well as in the parts of animals one can find many bodies a lot lighter than fir wood.

longe leviora. Nam & *Lanugines* nonnullarum *plantarum, Alæ Muscarum,* & *spolia Serpentum;* atque artificialia quoque diversa, ut *Lineus pannus extinctus* (quali utimur ad fomites flammarum), & *folia Rosarum,* quæ supersunt à distillatione, & hujusmodi,
5 superant levitate (ut putamus) ligna levissima.

5. Cohibenda & corrigenda est illa cogitatio, in quam *Intellectus humanus* propendet, nempe, *Dura* esse maxime *Densa.* Nam *Argentum vivum* fluit, *Aurum* molle est, & *Plumbum.* Illa vero durissimis *Metallis* (*Ferro* & *Ære*) sunt *densiora* & graviora;
10 Lapidibus vero adhuc multo magis.

6. In *Tabula* multa cadunt præter opinionem: Veluti, quod *Metalla Lapidibus* tanto graviora; quod *Vitrum* (corpus scilicet
[B1ʳ] excoctum) *Crystallo* (corpore conglaciato) ¹ gravius; quod Terra communis tam parum ponderosa; quod Olea distillata *Vitrioli* &
15 *Sulphuris,* ad pondus crudorum tam prope accedant; quod tam parum intersit inter *pondus Aquæ* & *Vini;* quod *Olea Chymica* (quæ subtiliora videri possint) Oleis expressis ponderosiora; quod *Os* sit *Dente* & *Cornu* tanto gravius: & alia similiter haud pauca.

Mandatum.

20 3. Natura *Densi* & *Rari,* licet cæteras naturas fere percurrat, neque secundum earum Normas regatur, videtur solummodo magnum habere consensum cum *Gravi* & *Levi.* At suspicamur etiam, eam posse habere consensum cum Tarda & Celeri exceptione & depositione *Calidi* & *Frigidi.* Fiat igitur *Experimentum,* si Rarius corpus non admittat, &
25 amittat, Calorem aut Frigus celerius, *Densius* vero tardius. Idque probetur in Auro, Plumbo, Ferro, Lapide, Ligno, &c. Fiat autem in simili *gradu Caloris,* simili *Quanto,* & *Figura corporis.*

Vellicationes de Practica.

1. Mistura omnis *Corporum* per *Tabulam* & *Pondera* revelari &
30 deprehendi potest. Si enim quæratur quantum *Aquæ* sit admistum *Vino,*
[B1ᵛ] vel quantum *Plumbi Auro,* & sic de reliquis; ponde¹rato *Compositum,* &

---

14 Olea distillata] Olea *Aqua* distillata / the inexplicable *Aqua* is retained in *SEH* (II, p. 250) but does not appear in *HDR(M)* (p. 5, l. 24 above)
3 *extinctus*] ~, flammarum),] ~)ₐ 9 *Ære*)] ~,)

For the down of some plants, flies' wings and snake skins as well as various artificial things, charred linen rags (such as we use for starting fires), rose petals left over from distillation, and things of that kind, are (I believe) lighter than the lightest woods.

5. We must restrain and put right that thought to which the Human Intellect is partial, namely that hard bodies are especially dense. For quicksilver is fluid, and gold and lead are soft. But these are denser and heavier than the hardest metals (iron and brass), and much more so than stones.

6. Many things in the table are other than one might suppose: for instance that metals are so much heavier than stones; that glass (namely a smelted body) is heavier than crystal (a solidified body); ᴵ that common earth is so light; that distilled oils of vitriol and sulphur differ so little in weight from their raw materials; that water and wine differ so little in weight; that chemical oils (which appear to be subtler) are heavier than oils produced by pressing; that bone is so much heavier than tooth or horn; and not a few other things of the kind.

Direction

3. The nature of dense and rare, although it runs through practically all the other natures, is not run by their rules but seems only to have close consent with heavy and light. But I also think it can have consent with quick and slow taking up and putting off of hot and cold. So do an experiment to see whether a rare body does not take in or give out heat and cold more rapidly than a dense one. And try this with gold, lead, iron, stone, wood, etc., and do it with the same degree of heat, and a body of the same size and shape.

Incentives to Practice

1. All mixture of bodies can be laid bare and discovered by means of the table and weights. For if you want to know how much water is mixed with the wine, or lead with the gold, and so on for the rest, then, once you have weighed ᴵ the composite body, look up the table for the weights

consule *Tabulam* de *pondere simplicium,* & mediæ rationes *Compositi,* comparatæ ad *Simplicia,* dabunt Quantum misturæ. Arbitror hoc esse *Εΰρηκα* illud *Archimedis,* sed utcumque ita Res est.

2. Confectio *Auri,* aut transmutatio *metallorum* in illud, omnino
5 pro suspecta habenda est. *Aurum* enim omnium *Corporum* ponderosissimum, & densissimum. Igitur, ut aliud quippiam vertatur in *Aurum,* prorsus *Condensatione* opus est. *Condensatio* autem (præsertim in *Corporibus* valde materiatis, qualia sunt *Metalla*), apud nos Homines, in superficie Terræ degentes, vix superinducitur: Pleræque enim Ignis
10 Densationes *pseudodensationes* sunt, si totum respicias (ut postea videbimus); hoc est, *Corpora* in partibus aliquibus suis condensant, Totum minime.

3. Verum versio *Argenti vivi* aut *Plumbi* in *Argentum,* (cum *Argentum* sit illis rarius), habenda est pro sperabili; cum tantum Fixationem, & alia
15 quædam innuat, non Densationem.

4. Attamen si *Argentum vivum,* aut *Plumbum,* aut aliud *Metallum,* verti posset in *Aurum* quatenus ad cæteras *Auri* proprietates, dempto *pondere,* ut, scilicet, fierent magis quam sunt fixa, magis malleabilia, magis sequacia, magis durabilia, & minus exposita Rubigini, magis
20 splendida, etiam flava, & hujusmodi; esset proculdubio Res utilis & lucrativa, licet *pondus Auri* non explerent.

[B2ʳ]   ¹*Observatio.*

7. Neque *Auro* est ponderosius quicquam; neque ipsum *Aurum purum* per artem, (quatenus adhuc innotuit), redditur sese
25 ponderosius. Plumbum *tamen notatum est & mole & pondere*

---

14 habenda] habendum / silently emended thus in *SEH* (II, p. 251); cf. *NO,* 2H4ʳ (*SEH,* I, p. 300): habenda est illa Causa pro suspectâ   25–6 (over) Plumbum *tamen . . . plenius.*] / in *c-t* this is a separate para, numbered 1, not set in large type but mainly in italic (for a similar anomaly see B6ᵛ–B7ʳ, p. 66, l. 21–p. 68, l. 17 below) and preceded by the heading Historia. The passage, with its italic, may suggest that the convention used in the printer's copy to mark up passages to be set in larger type had been misread as an instruction to set in italic (see *cmt,* p. 274 below). In *SEH* (II, p. 251) the heading is placed after the passage, and the passage is presented as a second unnumbered para of the observatio. Had *SEH* followed Bacon's normal practice the para should have been renumbered 8 but was not since that would have involved renumbering the next observatio (see p. 58, l. 20 below). I have avoided this problem by moving the heading to p. 56, l. 10 and making a single (larger-type) para of the observatio. In the printer's copy headings may have been marginalia and so could have misled the printer as to their proper location

1 *simplicium,*] ~;   3 *Εΰρηκα*] / no cap. or diacriticals over the υ in *SEH* (II, p. 250)
8 *Metalla*),] ~,)   10 respicias] ~;   11 videbimus);] ~)ₐ   14 rarius,]
~,)   18 *pondere,*] ~;   20 splendida] spendida   24 innotuit),] ~,)

of the simple bodies, and the average values of the composite compared with the simple bodies will give you the proportions of the mixture. I imagine that this is Archimedes' *eureka*, but in any event this is how the matter stands.

2. The making of gold or transmutation of metals into it should be regarded as something altogether doubtful. For of all bodies gold is the heaviest and densest; so for anything to be turned into gold there has to be condensation. But condensation (especially in very materiate bodies, such as metals are) can scarcely be superinduced by us humans, living as we do on the Earth's surface. For most densations by fire are (as we shall see later) pseudo-densations if you are thinking of the whole body, i.e. they condense bodies in certain of their parts, but not in the whole.

3. But the turning of quicksilver or lead into silver (as silver is rarer than them) should be regarded as something to be hoped for, since it only implies fixation and certain other things but not densation.

4. Yet, if quicksilver, or lead, or other metal could be turned into gold in every respect other than weight, i.e. if they became more fixed, malleable, flowing, and more durable and less subject to rust, more shiny, yellow, and so on, that would undoubtedly be a useful and lucrative matter, even if they did not take on the weight of gold.

ᴵ *Observation*

7. There is nothing heavier than gold; and so far no way has been found to make gold itself heavier by art. Yet it has been noted that lead increases in both mass and weight, especially if it is stored in

augeri, præsertim si condatur in Cellis subterraneis, ubi res situm facile colligunt. Id quod maxime deprehensum est in Statuis Lapideis, *quarum pedes plumbeis vinculis erant alligati; quæ vincula inventa sunt intumuisse, ut portiones illorum ex* Lapidibus 5 *penderent, quasi verrucæ. Vtrum vero hoc fuerit auctio* Plumbi, *an pullulatio* Vitrioli, *inquiratur plenius.*

[B2ᵛ]
¹*Tabula Exporrectionis Materiæ* per idem
spatium sive Dimensum, in *Corporibus*
iisdem integris & comminutis.

10   Historia.

Mercurius *in corpore,* *quantus impleat* Mensuram Tabularem, *ponderat*	{	*Den.* 19. *Gra.* 9	}	Sublimatus *vero in pulvere presso*	} *Den.* 3. *Gra.* 22.

15 Plumbum *in corpore*   *Den.* 12.   { *In* Cerussa *vero in* } *Den.* 4. *Gra.* 8. *d.*
                  Gra. 1. *d.*   { pulvere *presso.* }

Chalybs *in corpore*   *Den.* 8.   *In* pulvere *præ-parato,*
                 Gra. 10.   *(quali ad* medicinas   *Den.* 2.
                         utuntur,) & presso   *Gra.* 9.

20 Crystallum *in corpore Den.* 2, *Gra.* 18.   *In* pulvere *Presso Den.* 2, *Gra.* 20.
Santalum rubeum *in corpore Den.* 1, *Gra.* 5.   *In* pulvere *presso Gra.* 16. *d.*
Lignum Quercus *in corpore Gra.* 19. *d.*   *In* cinere *Den.* 1, *Gra.* 2.

Tabula Exporrectionis Materiæ per idem spatium
sive Dimensum, in *Corporibus* crudis
25   & distillatis.

Sulphur *in corpore Den.* 2, *Gra.* 2.   *In* oleo chymico *Den.* 1, *Gra.* 18.
Vitriolum *in corpore Den.* 1, *Gra.* 22.   *In* oleo *Den.* 1, *Gra.* 21.
Vinum *in corpore Den.* 1, *Gra.* 2. *d.qu.*   *In* distillato *Gra.* 22.
Acetum *in corpore Den.* 1, Gra. 3. *d.*   *In* distillato *Den.* 1, *Gra.* 1.

10 Historia.] / moved, in effect, from its *c-t* position (see *tn* to B2ʳ above)
20 Crystallum] Crystallus / emended thus (with note to that effect) in *SEH* (II, p. 252)
1 *augeri,*] ~;   20 2,] ~.   2,] ~.   21 1,] ~.   22 1,] ~.   26 1,]
~.   27 1,] ~.   1,] ~.   28 1,] ~.   29 1,] ~.   1,] ~.

underground cellars, where things easily gather rust. This has been
detected most of all in stone statues whose feet were secured with
leaden links, links which were found to have become swollen so
that portions of them hung like warts from the stone. But inquire
more fully whether this was the lead growing or a sprouting of
vitriol.

¹ *A Table of the Bulk of Matter* in the same
space or Dimension, in the same *Bodies*
whole and finely divided

History

Mercury undivided, such as may fill the measure used in the table, weighs	{ 19 Dwt. 9 Gr.	{ But Sublimed as a compressed powder	} 3 Dwt. 22 Gr.

Solid Lead	12 Dwt. 1½ Gr.	{ But in compressed white lead powder.	} 4. Dwt. 8½ Gr.

Solid Steel	8. Dwt. 10 Gr.	{ In a powder prepared as for medicines, and compressed.	} Dwt. 2. 9 Gr.

Solid Crystal, 2 Dwt. 18 Gr.   In a compressed powder 2. Dwt. 20 Gr.
Solid Red Sandalwood, 1 Dwt. Gr. 5.   In a compressed powder, 16½ Gr.
Solid Oak, 19½ Gr.   In ashes, 1 Dwt. Gr. 2.

A Table of the Bulk of Matter in the same space
or Dimension, in *Bodies* crude
and distilled

Solid Sulphur, 2. Dwt. 2. Gr. 2.   In a chemical oil, 1. Dwt. 18. Gr.
Vitriol in a body, 1 Dwt. 22 Gr.   In oil, 1 Dwt. 21 Gr.
Wine in a body, 1 Dwt. 2¾ Gr.   In a distillate 22 Gr.
Vinegar in a body, 1 Dwt. 3½ Gr.   In a distillate 1 Dwt. 1 Gr.

¹*Monitum.*

6. *Modus* versionis *Corporis* in pulverem, ad Apertionem sive Expansionem Corporis multum facit. Alia enim est ratio *pulveris* qui fit per simplicem *Contusionem,* sive *Limaturam;* alia ejus qui per
5 *Sublimationem,* ut in *Mercurio;* alia ejus qui per *Aquas Fortes,* & *Erosionem,* (vertendo ea tanquam in *Rubiginem*), ut in *Croco Martis,* & nonnihil in *Chalybe* præparato; alia ejus qui per *Exustionem,* ut *Cinis, Calx.* Itaque ista æquiparari nullo modo debent.

Mandatum.

10 4. Indigentissimæ sunt illæ duæ *Tabulæ* priores. Ea demum foret *Tabula* exacta *Corporum* cum suis *Aperturis,* quæ *Corporum* singulorum *integrorum pondera* primo, dein *Pulverum* suorum *crudorum,* dein *Cinerum, Calcium,* & *Rubiginum* suarum, dein *Malagmatum* suorum, dein *Vitrificationum* suarum (in iis quæ *vitrificantur*), dein
15 *Distillationum* suarum (subtracto pondere *Aquæ,* in qua dissolvuntur) nec-non aliarum eorundem Corporum alterationum, *Pondera* exhiberet: ut hoc modo de *Corporum Aperturis,* & arctissimis naturæ integralis *Nexibus,* judicium fieri posset.

¹*Observationes.*

20 8. *Pvlveres* non sunt proprie *Corporum Aperturæ,* quia augmentum spatii fit non ex dilatatione *Corporis,* sed ex interpositione *Aeris.* Attamen per hoc optime capitur æstimatio de *Corporum* unione interiore, aut porositate. Nam quo *Corpora* sunt magis unita, eo major intercedit differentia inter *Pulverem* suum & *Corpus*
25 *integrum.* Igitur Ratio *Argenti vivi crudi* ad *sublimatum* in pulvere

---

1 *Monitum*] *Monita* / emended thus in *SEH* (II, p. 252), which notes that this heading, as part of a new article of inquiry should have been numbered 1; in fact, in *HV* and *HVM* single monita are not numbered at all; in *HDR(M)* this monitum, the following mandatum and observationes are *om* (see p. 6 above)   9 *Mandatum*] / the para following should not have been numbered, see previous *tn*   13 *Malagmatum*] / this word occurs four times in *HDR* but in two forms: malagm– (here and at E6ᵛ (p. 128, l. 7 below), and amalgm– (D4ʳ and G6ᵛ (p. 100, l. 31 and p. 166, l. 30 below))   19 *Observationes*] / the two paras following should, in accordance with the practice of *HV* and *HVM,* have been numbered 1 and 2; the numbering should not have followed on from the previous observatio (B2ʳ); these observationes do not appear in *HDR(M)* (see p. 7 above)

6 *Rubiginem*),] ~,)   14 suarum] ~,   *vitrificantur*)] ~ ∧

¹*Advice*

6. The manner of turning a body into a powder makes a great deal of difference to its opening or expansion. For the result obtained from a powder produced by simple contusion or filing is one thing; the result from the one made by sublimation, as in mercury, another; from the one made by strong waters and eating away (by turning bodies as into rust), as in Crocus Martis and to a certain extent in prepared steel, another; from the one made by burning, as ashes and lime, another. Therefore these are not to be regarded as comparable.

Direction

4. The two tables above are pretty meagre. The only precise table of bodies and their openings would be one which displayed the weight of the individual bodies whole first, then of their crude powders, next of their ashes, limes and rusts; next of their amalgamations, then of their vitrifications (in those bodies capable of vitrification), then of their distillations (once the weight of the water they are dissolved in was taken away), and of all other alterations of the same bodies; so that in this manner a judgement might be formed of the openings of bodies and very close-knit connections of the nature in its whole state.

¹*Observations*

8. Powders are not strictly speaking openings of bodies, because the increase in volume comes about not from dilatation of the body but from air getting in. Yet an excellent estimate can be made from this of the internal compactness or porosity of bodies. For the more compact the bodies are, the greater is the difference that obtains between their powder and the body whole. So crude quicksilver is five times and more heavier than its sublimate. For

est quintupla, & amplius. Rationes *Chalybis* & *Plumbi* non ascendunt ad quadruplam. At in *Corporibus* levioribus & porosis laxior quandoque est positura partium in *integris* quam in *Pulveribus pressis*; ut in ligno Quercus, gravior est *cinis* quam
5 *Corpus* ipsum: Etiam in *pulveribus* ipsis, quo corpus est gravius, eo pressus *pulvis* minus habet dimensum ad non pressum. Nam in levioribus, pulverum partes ita se sustentare possunt, (utpote qui Aerem intermistum minus premant, & secent), ut Pulvis non pressus triplicem impleat mensuram ad pulverem pressum.
10   9. *Distillata* plerunque attenuantur, & pondere decrescunt; sed hoc facit *Vinum* duplo plus quam *Acetum.*

[B4ʳ]   ¹*Commentatio.*

1. Atque *Tangibilia* per *Familias* jam censa sunt, tanquam *Divites* & *Inopes.* Restat altera Classis, videlicet *Pneumaticorum.* Ea vero
15 pondere non dotantur, per cujus incubitum, de *exporrectione Materiæ* in ipsis contentæ judicium fieri possit. Opus est igitur alio quopiam interprete. At primum, species *Pneumaticorum* proponendæ sunt; deinde *Comparatio* facienda.
    Quemadmodum in *Tangibilibus interiora Terræ*, ita in
20 *Pneumaticis Ætherea* ad tempus seponimus.
    Sunt *Pneumatica* apud nos triplicis naturæ; *Inchoata, Devincta, Pura. Inchoata* sunt *Fumi omnigeni*, atque ex *Materiis* diversis. Eorum Ordo esse possit; Primo, *Volatilium*, quæ expirant ex *Metallis*, & ex nonnullis Fossilium; quæ sunt (prout nomen
25 significat) potius *Alata* quam *Pneumatica*; quia facile admodum coagulantur vel *sublimando*, vel *cadendo*, aut *præcipitando.* Secundo, *Vaporum*; qui expirant ex *Aqua* & *Aqueis.* Tertio, Fumorum (nomine generali retento), qui expirant ex *Corporibus* siccis. Quarto, *Halituum* qui expirant ex *Corporibus oleosis.*
[B4ᵛ] 30 Quin¹to, *Aurarum*; quæ expirant ex *corporibus* mole aqueis, spiritu

---

12 ff. *Commentatio*] / *SEH* (II, p. 253 n. 1) plausibly suggests that the first para below would have been a connexio if *HDR* had been finished (the discussion moving on from tangible to pneumatic bodies). I believe that the heading *Commentatio* would have been placed after this para and that the commentatio ends just before the table on B5ʳ (see p. 62, l. 20 below). The substance of this commentatio also appears in *HDR(M)* (see p. 6, l. 27–p. 7, l. 27 above)
8 secent),] ~,)   28 Fumorum] ~;   retento),] ~,)   29 *Halituum*] ~;

steel and lead the proportions do not quite reach to four to one. But in lighter and porous bodies, there is sometimes a looser arrangement of the parts in their whole than in their compressed powders, as in oak the ashes are heavier than the body itself. Even in the powders themselves the heavier the body the smaller the space filled by the compressed as compared with the uncompressed powder. For in lighter bodies the parts of powders (as they squeeze and cut up the intermixed air less) can support themselves in such a way that an uncompressed powder may take up three times more room than a compressed.

9. Distilled substances generally get thinner and lose weight; but wine does this twice as much as vinegar.

ᴵ *Speculation*

1. I have thus taken a census of tangible bodies family by family as if in terms of their wealth and poverty. That leaves a different class to be dealt with, namely that of pneumatic bodies. But these are not endowed with weight, which would serve to let us make an estimate of the bulk of matter contained within them. So we need another kind of interpreter. But first of all the species of pneumatic bodies must be set down; and then we must compare them together.

Just as I held over discussion of the insides of the Earth when I discussed tangible bodies, so I do the same with ethereal bodies when I discuss things pneumatic.

The pneumatics here with us have a threefold nature: inchoate, attached and pure. The inchoate are fumes of all kinds, made from diverse kinds of matter. These may be ranked as follows: first, volatile bodies which exhale from metals and some fossils, and which (as their name indicates) are fleeting rather than pneumatic bodies, because they are very easily coagulated either by sublimating, or by falling or precipitating; second, vapours which exhale from water and watery bodies; and third, fumes (keeping the general name for the particular sense) which exhale from dry bodies; fourth, exhalations from oily bodies; fifth, ᴵ breaths given

inflammabilibus; qualia sunt *Vina*, & *Liquores exaltati*, sive *potus fortes*.

Est & aliud genus *Fumorum*; illi scilicet in quos *Flamma* desinit. Ii vero non possunt expirare, nisi ex *inflammabilibus*, cum
5 *Flammam* subsequantur. Hos *Post-fumos*, seu *Fumos secundos*, appellamus. Itaque non possunt esse *Post-vapores*, quia *Aquea* non inflammantur; sed *Post-fumi* (nomine speciali), *Post-halitus*, *Post-auræ*; etiam, ut arbitror, *Post-volatilia*, in nonnullis.

At *Pneumatica Devincta* ea sunt, quæ ipsa solitaria aut soluta
10 non reperiuntur, sed tantum *Corporibus tangibilibus* inclusa; quos *Spiritus* etiam vulgo vocant. Participant autem & ex *aqueo*, & ex *oleoso*, & ex iisdem nutriuntur; quæ in *Pneumaticum* versa, constituunt *Corpus* veluti ex *Aere* & *Flamma*; unde utriusque *Mysteria* sunt. Accedunt autem *Spiritus* isti (si ad *Pneumatica*
15 soluta spectes) proxime ad naturam *Aurarum*, quales ex *vino* aut *sale* surgunt. Horum *Spirituum* natura duplex; alia *Crudorum*, alia *Vivorum*. *Crudi* insunt omni *tangibili*; *Vivi animatis* tantum, sive
[B5r] *vegetabilibus*, sive *sensibilibus*. At *Pneumatica Pura* duo tantum ǀ inveniuntur, *Aer* & *Flamma*; licet illa quoque magnas diversitates
20 sortiantur, & *Gradus exporrectionis* inæquales.

Tabula *Pneumaticorum*, secundum *Commentationem* supra dictam, prout ordine ascendunt ad *Exporrectionem* majorem.

Volatilia Metallorum & Fossilium.
Post-volatilia ipsorum.
25 Vapores.
Fumi.
Post-fumi.
Halitus.
Post-halitus.
30 Auræ.
Post-auræ.
Spiritus crudi devincti in Tangibilibus.
Aer.

21 Tabula] / here the larger type of the commentatio gives way to the smaller; nevertheless I am inclined to think that p. 63, l. 21–p. 66, l. 19 should be regarded as a continuation or amplification of the commentatio and not as, for example, an historia
7 *Post-fumi*] ∼,   speciali),] ∼,)

off by bodies of watery mass and inflammable spirit, such as are wines and strong distilled liquors or strong drinks.

Now there is another kind of fumes, namely those in which flame ends. But these can only be given out by inflammable bodies, since they follow on from flame. These I call *after-fumes*, or *secondary fumes*. There cannot therefore be *after-vapours* because watery bodies cannot catch fire. But there can be *after-fumes* (using the term in the special sense), *after-exhalations, after-breaths*, and also, as I believe, in some bodies, *after-volatiles*.

But attached pneumatics are those which are not found on their own or free but only enclosed in tangible bodies and which they commonly call spirits. They also partake of watery and oily substances and are nourished by them, and these substances when turned into pneumatic matter constitute a body made up as it were of air and flame, whence they embody the secret natures of both. Now these spirits (if you are thinking of free pneumatics) come very close to the nature of breaths of the kind that arise from wine or salts. These spirits have a double nature: some are crude and others living. The crude are found in all tangible bodies, the living only in animate bodies, be they vegetable or sensible. But we come across only two ¹ pneumatic bodies: air and flame, although these also exist in great variety and unequal degrees of bulk.

Table of Pneumatic Bodies arranged, according to the above Speculation, in ascending order of Bulk

Volatiles of metals and fossils.
After-volatiles of the same.
Vapours.
Fumes
After-fumes.
Exhalations.
After-exhalations.
Breaths.
After-breaths.
Crude spirits attached to tangible bodies.
Air.

Spiritus vivi, sive incensi, devincti in Tangibilibus.

Flamma.

De *Exporrectionibus* horum, tum ad invicem tum ad *Tangibilia* collatis, jam videndum. Atque si *Natura levis*, per Ascensum sursum,
5 posset liquidare *Raritatem Corporum*, quemadmodum *Natura gravis*, per Descensum deorsum, liquidat eorum *Densitatem*, Res bene posset succedere. Sed multa obsunt. Primo, quod *Differentiæ Motuum* in iis quæ aspectum fugiunt non percipiantur immediate per *sensum*; deinde,
[B5^v] quod non reperiatur ¹ in *Aere*, & similibus, tam fortis Appetitus petendi
10 superiora, quam putatur; Denique, si *Aer* moveretur sursum, tamen cum continuetur plerumque cum alio Aere, *Motus* ille ægre percipi posset. Nam sicut *Aqua* non ponderat super *Aquam*; ita *Aer* non insurgit subter *Aerem*. Itaque alii Modi excogitandi sunt.

Atque de *Exporrectione Pneumaticorum* ad invicem, quodque *Ordo* &
15 *series Raritatis*, qualis in *Tabula* ponitur, non leviter fundata sit, offerunt se quædam *probationes* non malæ: verum, de certis gradibus hujusmodi *Exporrectionis*, & rursus de *Exporrectione Pneumatici comparati* ad *Tangibile*, difficilior certe est inquisitio.

Primo igitur *Fumos* omnes, tam secundos quam primos, *Aeris*
20 Raritatem non æquare consentaneum est; cum illi conspicui sint, *Aer* minime; neque ipsi conspicui maneant paulo post, cum se *Aeri* miscuerint.

Post-fumos Præ-fumis esse tenuiores & rariores, satis liquet; cum sint *Flammæ* (*corporis* tam subtilis), Cadavera, & Solutiones. Experimento
25 quoque manifestissimum est, in nocturnis spectaculis, intra Cœnacula quæ tot Lychnis & Facibus collucent, etiam post plurium horarum moram, sufficere *Aerem* Respirationi, licet tot *Post-fumis* in eum receptis. Quod si fuissent illi *fumi Præ-fumi*, (quales sunt ex *Lychnis* & *Facibus* extinctis, absque *Flamma*) nemo, vel ad longe minorem moram, eos
30 sustinere posset.

Spiritus crudos quoscunque in *Tangibilibus* devinctos, etiam *Aere*
[B6^r] densiores judicamus. Etenim ¹ *spiritus Vegetabilium*, aut *Animalium mortuorum*, aut hujusmodi, cum exhalaverint, manifesto retinent quiddam ex crasso, sive *Tangibili*; ut cerni datur in *Odoribus*, qui cum
35 sint *Fumi* parce exeuntes, nec conferti, ut in *Fumis* conspicuis & *Vaporibus*, tamen, si nacti fuerint aliquid *Tangibile*, præsertim ex mollioribus, applicant se ad illud, & plane adhærent, illudque Odore

---

8 *sensum*,] ~:   10 putatur;] ~:   24 subtilis),] ~,)   34 *Tangibili*;]
~:   *Odoribus*,] ~;

Living or inflamed spirits attached to tangible bodies.
Flame.

Now we must examine the bulk of these pneumatics compared both with each other and with tangible bodies. And if by upward motion the nature of light could make the rarity of bodies unmistakable in the same way as the nature of heavy by downward motion makes their density obvious, this business might turn out well. But many things stand in the way of it. In the first place, the differences of motions in them, motions which escape our sight, are not directly perceived by the sense; in the second place, we do not find ' in air and the like as strong an appetite for seeking higher bodies as people suppose; and thirdly, if air went upwards yet, as it mostly stayed in touch with other air, that motion could barely be perceived. For as water does not bear down on water, so air does not rise up from under air. We must therefore think up other ways of proceeding.

Now certain fairly reliable proofs are available concerning the bulk of pneumatics compared with each other, and that the order and series of rarity as set out in the table is soundly based. But of the exact degrees of bulk and again of the bulk of pneumatic compared with tangible, the inquiry is certainly trickier.

First then it is reasonable to suppose that all fumes, both primary and secondary, do not attain to the rarity of air, since they are visible but air is not; and they themselves do not stay visible long once they have mixed in with air.

It is fairly clear that after-fumes are thinner and rarer than fore-fumes, since they are the corpses and solutions of flame (which itself is a body subtle enough). For experiment makes it abundantly clear that in night entertainments in rooms illuminated by so many lamps and torches, even after many hours have passed, the air is still breathable, even though it has taken up so many after-fumes. But if these had been fore-fumes (which come without flame from lamps and torches which have been put out), no one could put up with them even for a much shorter period of time.

All crude spirits attached to tangible bodies are also denser than air in my view. For 'the spirits of vegetables or dead animals, or things of that kind, once they have exhaled, evidently retain something of the gross or tangible body—as can be seen in odours which, as they are fumes going out sparingly and not as a body like visible fumes and vapours, yet if they come across anything tangible, especially of the softer kind, they attach themselves to it and plainly stick to it and infect it with their odour, so

inficiunt; ut manifestum sit, illos cum crassa natura affinitatem ægre dirimere.

At *Spiritus vivos Aere* ipso aliquanto *rariores* existimamus: tum quia inflammantur nonnihil; tum quia diligenter experti sumus, *Aerem* ad
5 minuendum aut sublevandum pondus nihil conferre. Nam *vesica inflata* non est vacua & compressa levior, cum sit illa tamen repleta *Aere*; nec similiter *spongia*, aut *vellus Lanæ*, *Aere* referta, illis ipsis vacuis leviora sunt, *Aere* excluso. At *Corpus Animale vivum* & *mortuum Gravitate* manifesto differunt; licet haud tantum quantum putantur. Quare
10 videtur *Aer* pondus non minuere; *spiritus* autem vivus hoc facere. Atque cum *pondus Densitates* dijudicet, etiam *Levatio ponderis Raritates* dijudicare debet.

Supremo Ordine collocatur *Flamma*: tum quia illa manifestissime petit superiora; tum quia verisimile est, rationes *Pneumaticorum* minime
15 differe à rationibus *Fomitum* suorum; ideoque, quemadmodum *Oleum* est rarius *Aqua*, similiter Flammam rariorem esse *Aere* & *Spiritu*. Etiam videtur Flamma *Corpus tenuius*, & *mollius*, & magis *cedens*, quam *Aer*.
[B6ᵛ] Nam levissima quæpiam | *Aura*, commota juxta *flammam* lychni, eam reddit tremulam.

20   Historia.

2. *Qvantam vero* Expansionem *assequatur* Pneumaticum *collatum ad* Tangibile, *licet sit res ardua inventu, tamen curam de ejus inquisitione non abjecimus. Certissima autem visa est nobis fore probatio, si Corpus aliquod* Tangibile (*Exporrectione ejus prius capta & mensurata*), *verti posset plane*
25 *in* Pneumaticum, *& deinde* Pneumatici *illius* Exporrectio *itidem notaretur; ut pensitatis utriusque rationibus, de* multiplicatione dimensi *evidens Demonstratio fieri posset.*

3. *Accepimus igitur* Phialam vitream *parvam, quæ unciam fortasse unam capere posset. In eam* spiritus Vini, (*quia ex* Liquoribus *proxime accedebat*
30 *ad* Pneumaticum, *cum esset levissimus*), *unciam dimidiam infudimus. Deinde* Vesicam *accepimus admodum grandem, utpote quæ octo* Pintas

---

20 ff. Historia.] | here follow two paras, *om* in *HDR(M)*, mainly (and anomalously) in italic; two further such paras, each headed Historia occur below on B7ᵛ. In *SEH* (II, p. 258) these two further headings are omitted and these paras are numbered successively 1–4. Although *SEH* is probably correct (if one follows the practice of *HVM*), I have not interfered with *c-t* numbering or headings

24 *mensurata*),] ~,)   30 *levissimus*),] ~,)

that it is clear that they can scarcely shake off their affinity with the gross nature.

But I believe that living spirits are somewhat rarer than air itself, both because they are somewhat inflamed and because I have taken pains to find out that air has no capacity for increasing or reducing weight. For an inflated bladder when it is filled with air is no lighter than one empty and flattened out; and the same is the case with a sponge or fleece which are no lighter full of air than when they are empty and the air shut out. But a living animal body clearly differs in weight from a dead one, but not by as much as people think. Therefore it seems that air does not diminish weight but that living spirit does. And what is more just as weight determines densities, so lessening of weight should determine rarities.

Last in order comes flame, both because it quite obviously seeks higher things, and because it is likely that pneumatic bodies vary from each other in the same way that their nurseries do; and for that reason, just as oil is rarer than water, so flame is rarer than air and spirit. It seems moreover that flame is thinner, softer, and more yielding than air. For the slightest ¹ ruffled breath of air brought near the flame of a lamp makes the flame flicker.

History

2. But as for the degree of pneumatic matter's expansion compared with that of tangible, though it be a difficult thing to find out, I have still not abandoned any care in its investigation. Now it seemed to me the most certain test would be that if any tangible body (its bulk having been taken and measured beforehand) could be altogether turned into a pneumatic one, after which the bulk of the pneumatic would likewise be noted down, so that the multiplication of dimension that had taken place could be clearly demonstrated by comparing the values before and after.

3. So I took a small glass phial capable of holding about an ounce. Into this I poured about half an ounce of spirit of wine (because as the lightest of liquids it came closest to the pneumatic state). Then I took a very large bladder, which as might be imagined was capable of holding eight wine pints (or a gallon as our people call it). Now the bladder was not

vinarias (Galonium *scilicet, ut nostrates appellant*) *capere posset.* Vesica
autem erat non vetus, & propterea non sicca & renitens, sed recens & mollis.
Ex illa vesica Aerem *omnem, quoad fieri potuit, expressimus; ut latera ejus*
essent quasi contigua & cohærentia. Vesicam *insuper per exterius* Oleo
5 *parum oblevimus, & molliter fricavimus; ut porositas vesicæ* Oleo
obturaretur, atque etiam, ut inde fieret magis cedens & tensibilis. Hanc circa
os Phialæ (*ore scilicet* Phialæ *intra os* Vesicæ *recepto*), *applicuimus; eamque*
filo cerato arcte ligavimus. Tum demum Phialam *supra prunas ardentes in*
[B7ʳ] *Foculo col·locavimus. Non ita multo post ascendebat* Aura Spiritus vini *in*
10 vesicam, *eamque paulatim undequaque fortiter admodum inflavit. Quo*
facto, continuo vitrum ab igne removimus; & in summitate vesicæ foramen
acu fecimus; ut Aura *potius expiraret, quam relaberetur in guttas. Deinde,*
vesicam *à* Phiala *sustulimus, & per lances, quantum de illa semiuncia*
spiritus vini *diminutum fuisset, & in* Auram *versum, probavimus. Erat*
15 *autem deperditum non plus* (*pondere*) *denariis sex. Adeo ut sex illi denarii*
in Corpore spiritus vini, *qui quadragesimam partem* Pintæ (*ut memini*),
non implebant, in Auram *versi, spatium octo* Pintarum *adæquarent.*

Monitum.

Memini etiam *vesicam* ab igne remotam paulum flaccescere incepisse; ut
20 non obstante tam insigni *Expansione,* non videretur tamen *Aura* versa
fuisse in *Pneumaticum* purum & fixum, cum ad se restituendam
inclinaret. Attamen fallere possit hoc Experimentum, si ex eo
conjiciamus, *Aerem communem* esse adhuc hujusmodi *Aura* rariorem;
quoniam arbitramur *spiritum vini* in *Pneumaticum* versum (licet minime
25 purum) tamen propter calorem, superare *raritatem Aeris frigidi;* cum &
ipse *Aer* per calorem, majorem in modum dilatetur, & *exporrectionem*
Aeris frigidi haud paulum superet. Itaque arbitramur, si Experimentum
fiat in *Aqua,* multo minorem futuram Expansionem; licet *Corpus Aquæ*
plus Materiæ contineat quam *spiritus Vini.*

[B7ᵛ] 30 ·Historia.

Si advertas Fumum *ex Cereo recenter extincto exeuntem, & oculis metiaris*
crassitudinem ejus, & rursus, intuearis corpus ipsius Fumi *postea*

30 Historia.] / *om* in *SEH* (II, p. 258); see *tns* to B6ᵛ above
2 *vetus,*] ~;   7 *recepto*),] ~,)   16 *memini*),] ~,)   24 versum] ~,
25 purum) tamen] purum, tamen)

old and so not dry and stiff but fresh and soft. As far as possible I squeezed all the air out of it so that the sides were as good as contiguous and stuck together. In addition I smeared the bladder on the outside with a little oil and gently rubbed it in so as to block the bladder's pores with the oil and make it softer and more yielding as well. I fixed the bladder round the phial's mouth (i.e. put its mouth inside the bladder's) and tied it tightly with waxed twine. Then I placed the phial [1] over hot coals in a brazier. Not long after that the breath of the spirit of wine rose up into the bladder and gradually blew it up quite strongly all round. When that had happened I took the glass from the fire forthwith and punctured the top of the bladder with a needle to let the breath out rather than let it revert to drops. Then I took the bladder from the phial, and with the scales I showed how much of that half ounce of spirit of wine had been lost and turned into a breath. Now by weight the loss amounted to not more than six pennyweights, so that the six pennyweights spirit of wine, which in a body did not (as I recall) fill a fortieth of a pint, filled a space amounting to eight pints when turned into breath.

Advice

I recall too that when I removed the bladder from the fire it began to go down a bit so that, never mind the striking expansion, the breath still seemed not to have been turned into a pure and stable pneumatic body, as it was still disposed to change itself back again. Yet the experiment can lead us astray if we infer from it that common air is even rarer than this kind of breath; for I judge that spirit of wine turned pneumatic (albeit impure) is still rarer than cold air because of its heat, since the air itself is greatly dilated by heat and far surpasses the bulk of cold air. I judge then that if the experiment were conducted with water the expansion would be much less, though the body of water contains more matter than spirit of wine.

[1]History

If you pay attention to the fume coming from a wax candle just put out, and gauge its thickness by eye, and again if you inspect the body of that

inflammati; videbis expansionem Flammæ, collatæ ad Fumum, *ampliatam quasi ad duplam.*

Monitum.

Si accipias pauca grana *Pulveris pyrii,* eaque inflammes, magna prorsus
5 fit *Expansio* respectu corporis *pulveris.* Sed rursus, extincta illa *Flamma,*
multo amplius adhuc se extendit *corpus Fumi.* Id vero non te fallat, ac si
Corpus Tangibile plus expanderetur in Fumo, quam in *Flamma*; nam id
secus se habet. Sed ratio apparentiæ est, quod *corpus Flammæ* sit corpus
integrum, corpus Fumi *corpus* commistum, ex longe majore parte, cum
10 *Aere.* Itaque, sicut parum *Croci* multum *Aquæ* colorat; similiter parum
Fumi in multum *Aerem* se spargit. Nam Fumus spissus, (ut antea dictum
est), non sparsus, minor cernitur corpore Flammæ.

Historia.

Si *accipias frustulum corticis* Arantii *exterioris, (qui aromaticus est, &*
15 *oleosus), ipsumque subito comprimas juxta Lychnum, exilit aliquid Roris in
guttulis; quod tamen constituit corpus* Flammæ *(respectu guttularum)
insigniter amplum.*

[B8ʳ] ## ¹*Observatio.*

Commentum illud *Peripateticorum,* de decupla proportione
20 *Elementorum* ad invicem in Raritate, res fictitia est, & ad
placitum; cum certum sit, *Aerem* centuplo (ad minimum)
rariorem esse *Aqua, Flammamque Oleo*; at *Flammam* ipsum *Aerem*
decupla minime superare.

Monitum.

25 Non est, cur ista *Inquisitio* & *Commentatio* circa *Pneumatica* videatur
cuipiam nimis subtilis aut curiosa. Certum enim est, omissionem &
inobservantiam circa illa obstupefecisse *Philosophiam* & *Medicinam,*
easque tanquam syderasse; ut fuerint ad veram causarum

13 Historia.] / *om* in *SEH* (II, p. 258); see *tn* to B6ᵛ above
12 est),] ~,)   15 *oleosus),*] ~,)

70

same fume when it is set alight, you will see that the expansion of the flame is about double that of the fume.

Advice

If you take a few grains of gunpowder and set fire to them, a great expansion takes place relative to the powder. But again, once the flame is out, the body of the fume is still more extended. But do not let this fool you into thinking that the tangible body expands more in fume than flame, for the opposite is true. But the cause of the appearance is that the body of flame is an integral one, whereas the body of fume is a body mixed together to a very great extent with air. So just as a little saffron colours a great deal of water, so a small amount of fume disperses itself through a great deal of air. For (as I have said before) fume thick and undispersed appears slighter than the body of flame.

History

If you take a piece of orange peel (which is aromatic and oily) and suddenly squeeze it next to a candle, a kind of dew spurts out in droplets, and yet (compared with the droplets) this creates a very considerable body of flame.

¹Observation

The fabrication of the Peripatetics concerning the decuple proportion that the elements bear to each other in rarity is an arbitrary fiction, seeing that it is certain that air is at least a hundred times rarer than water, and flame than oil but that flame itself is not ten times rarer than air.

Advice

No one should think that this inquiry and speculation about pneumatic bodies is too subtle or overscrupulous. For it is certain that neglect and lack of attention to them has made philosophy and medicine as stupid as any star-struck imbecile, so that when it came to the true investiga-

investigationem attonitæ, & quasi inutiles, *Qualitatibus* tribuendo, quæ *spiritibus* debentur: ut in *Titulo* proprio, de *Pneumatico* ipso, fusius apparebit.

Connexio.

5 Atque de *Exporrectione Materiæ* in *Corporibus* secundum consistentias suas diversas, dum quiescunt, hæc inquisita sint. De [B8ᵛ] *Appetitu* autem & *Motu Corporum,* unde ¹ *tumescunt, residunt, rarefiunt, condensantur,* dilatantur, contrahuntur, majorem, minorem locum occupant, accuratius, si fieri possit, 10 inquirendum; quia fructuosior est *Inquisitio,* Naturam simul & relevans, & regens. Attamen carptim facienda est *Inquisitio ista,* & cursim. Iste enim *Titulus,* de *Denso* & *Raro,* tam generalis est, ut si plenarie deductus foret, multa ex sequentibus *Titulis* anticipaturus esset, quod fieri non oportet.

15 ### Monitum.

Non difficile nobis foret, *Historiam,* quam jam subjungemus, sparsam, in ordinem meliorem (quam qua usi sumus) redigere, *Instantias* quæ inter se affines sunt simul collocando. Id consulto evitavimus, duplici ratione moti. Primo, quod multæ ex *Instantiis* ancipitis naturæ sint, & 20 ad plura spectent. Itaque *Ordo accuratus* in ejusmodi rebus aut iterat, aut fallit. Deinde, (id quod præcipue in causa fuit, cur à *Methodo* aliqua exacta abhorreremus) hoc quod agimus, omnium Industriæ ad Imitationem patere volumus. Quod si *Methodo* aliqua *artificiali* & *illustri* collectio ista *Instantiarum* connexa fuisset, desperassent 25 proculdubio complures, se ejusmodi *Inquisitionem* facere potuisse. Quare & *Exemplo* & *Monito* cavemus, ut quisque in *Instantiis* [Crʳ] comparandis & proponendis suo Iudicio, suæ Memoʲriæ, suæ Copiæ inserviat. Satis sit si de Scripto, & non memoriter, (id enim in tantis instantiarum fluctibus ludicrum quiddam esset) semper procedat 30 *Inventio*; ut veræ *Inductionis* lumine postea absolvi possit. Atque illud perpetuo memoria tenendum, nos in hoc Opere, *Stipem* tantummodo & *Tributum* à sensu ad ærarium scientiarum exigere; neque *Exempla,* ad illustranda *Axiomata,* sed *Experimenta,* ad ea constituenda, proponere.

17 sumus)] ~,)

tion of causes they have stood by dumbfounded and almost useless, and have attributed to qualities what they should have ascribed to spirits— as will appear at greater length in the specific title concerned with pneumatic matter itself.

Connection

So much then for the inquiry into the bulk of matter in bodies according to their different consistencies while they are at rest. But now we must look even more acutely if possible into the appetite and motion of bodies which cause them ¹ to swell, or subside, to become dense or rare, or fill a greater or smaller space; for this inquiry, at once revealing and ruling nature, is more profitable. Nevertheless this inquiry must be made selectively and in passing. For this title of Dense and Rare is so general that if it were given full-scale treatment, it would anticpate many of the titles to follow, which would not be a good thing.

Advice

It would not be difficult for me to make the scattered history which I shall now subjoin more systematic than it is by putting instances which are alike all together. But two things have persuaded me not to do that. In the first place, many of the instances are of an uncertain nature and point in many directions; and accurate order thus leads in things like this either to repetition or error. In the second place (and this is what is really at stake in my distaste for any exact method), I wish to leave what I am about open to industry of everyone to copy. But if this collection of instances had been given the coherence of any artificial or perspicuous method, many would no doubt have given up hope of being able to conduct an inquiry of the same kind. Both by example and advice I therefore stipulate that everyone look to his own judgement, memory ¹ and store in producing and setting down instances. Let it be enough that invention always proceed by writing and not by memory (for it would be absurd to use the latter when faced with such floods of instances) so that afterwards it can be brought to perfection by the light of true induction. Indeed, it should always be borne in mind that in this work I only exact a small fee or tribute from sense to the treasury of the sciences, and do not propose examples to throw light on axioms, but experiments to

Neque tamen dispositionem *Instantiarum* prorsus negligemus, neque discincti hoc aggrediemur; sed ita Instantias collocabimus, ut sibi invicem lucem præbeant nonnullam.

Dilatationes per introceptionem simplicem, sive admissionem corporis
5 *novi.*

Historia sparsa.

1. Ex *introceptione Corporis* alieni, nil mirum si sequatur *Dilatatio Corporis* alicujus; quandoquidem hoc sit plane Augmentum sive Additio, non *Rarefactio* vera. Attamen cum *Corpus* quod introcipitur
10 fuerit *Pneumaticum*, (veluti *Aer*, aut *Spiritus*) aut etiam cum *Corpus introceptum* (licet fuerit Tangibile), tamen sensim illabatur, & se insinuet; vulgo habetur magis pro Tumore quodam, quam Accessione.

2. *Vesica*, aut alia tensilia, (ut Folles) inflantur *Aere* integro, atque extenduntur; adeo ut indurentur, & ictum, jactum, pati possint: Etiam
[C1ᵛ] 15 | Bulla *Aquæ* est instar *Vesicæ*, nisi quod est tam fragilis.

3. Liquores de vase in vas de alto fusi, aut Cochlearibus & spatulis, aut ventis, fortiter agitati, committuntur & commiscentur cum *Aere*; unde se attollunt in *Spumam*. Illi paulo post residunt, & minorem locum occupant, Aere (fractis *Spumæ Bullulis*) exeunte.
20 4. Extruunt pueri, ex *Aqua* saponi admista (unde fit paulo tenacior) Turres bullatas; adeo ut parum admodum *Aquæ* (*Aere* introcepto) magnum locum occupet.

5. At non invenitur quod *Flamma*, per inflationem Follium aut agitationem aliam exteriorem, cum *Aere* misceatur, & spumescat, in eum
25 modum, ut possit constitui *Corpus commistum* ex *Flamma* & *Aere*, instar *spumæ* quæ commista est ex *Aere* & *Liquore*.

6. At contra, certum est, per *Mistionem* interiorem in *Corpore* antequam inflammetur, fieri posse *Corpus commistum* ex *Aere* & *Flamma*. Nam *Pulvis pyrius* habet partes non-*inflammabiles* ex *Nitro*,

---

4 *Dilatationes . . .*] / this heading is set in very small italics in *c-t* and is one of a number of such in *HDR*. All of these would probably have been listed in order among the particular topics if such topics were extant. On the model of *HVM*, I have followed these headings with the heading [*Historia.*] save that here an existing one (*Historia sparsa*) already stands before para 1. In *c-t* the small italic title precedes para 2; I have brought it back to a point just before *Historia sparsa*. *SEH* (II, p. 260 n. 1) sets the small italic headings in roman capitals, and in this case suggests that the heading should change places with *Historia sparsa* and para 1 be regarded as a monitum

11 Tangibile), tamen] Tangibile, tamen)   20 admista] ~,

establish them. All the same, I shall not altogether neglect arrangement in setting out the instances, nor deal with the matter without discipline, but will put them together in such a way that they shed mutual light on each other.

Dilatations by simple introception or letting in of a new body

Scattered History

1. It is not surprising if the dilatation of any body follows when another body is taken into it; for this is evidently an increase or addition and not true rarefaction. Yet when the body taken in is pneumatic (as air or spirit) or even when the body taken in happens to be a tangible one, if it slips in gradually and insinuates itself, it is commonly taken for a swelling rather than something extra.

2. A bladder or other tensile bodies (such as bellows) are blown up and extended by plain air to such a degree that they are hardened and can put up with being struck or thrown around. A ¹ bubble of water is also like a bladder, except that it is so very fragile.

3. Liquors poured from above from one container into another, or vigorously whipped up with spoons and ladles, or by winds, are joined and mixed up with air, whence they raise themselves into froth. Not long afterwards they sink back again and take up less room, the air leaving when the little bubbles of froth burst.

4. Children build bubble towers from water with soap added (which makes the water more tenacious) such that when the air is taken in a very little water takes up a lot of room.

5. But we do not find that flame, by the bellows' blast or other agitation from outside, gets mixed with air or that it froths up in such a way as to constitute a body made up of flame and air, like the froth which is made up of air and liquor.

6. On the other hand, it is certain that a body made of air and flame can come about through an inward mixture in a body before it is set on fire. For gunpowder has non-inflammable parts derived from the nitre and inflammable ones derived in the main from sulphur, as a result of

alias *inflammabiles*, præcipue ex *Sulphure*; unde etiam magis albicat & pallescit quam cæteræ *Flammæ* (licet *Flamma* ipsa *Sulphuris* vergat ad cæruleum), adeo ut possit illa Flamma recte comparari *Spumæ* potentissimæ, ex *Flamma* & *Aere* coagmentatæ, sive *Vento* cuidam igneo.

5   7. Quemadmodum autem *Spuma* est corpus compositum ex *Aere* & *Liquore*; ita etiam Pulveres omnes sunt compositi ex Aere & *Minutiis*
[C2ʳ] *Corporis pulverizati*; ut non aliter differant à *spumis*, quam ¦ *Contiguum* differt à *Continuo*: nam magna moles ipsorum consistit ex Aere, qui partes *Corporis* sublevat; ut ex Tabula secunda & tertia liquet.

10   8. Fiunt *Tumores* in ventre Animalium, & aliis partibus, ex *flatu*, & *humore aqueo* introcepto, & admisso; ut in *Hydrope*, *Tympanite*, & similibus.

        9. Est genus *Columbarum*, quod capite intra collum recepto, *inflatur*, & *tumet*.

15   10. *Respiratio* per *pulmones* (Follium instar) *Aerem* attrahit, & reddit; dilatante se, per vices, *pulmone*, & residente.

        11. *Fœmellæ prægnantes* tument Mammillas, lacteo scilicet Humore turgentes.

        12. *Glans virgæ* in Masculis, cum arrigitur in venerem, multum
20 dilatatur mole.

        13. Inspice in *Speculum*, & nota latitudinem utriusque *oculi Pupillæ*; dein claude alterum *oculum*; & videbis *pupillam* oculi aperti manifeste dilatatam, *Spiritibus* qui utrique oculo inserviebant in unum confluentibus.

25   14. *Rima Globorum lusoriorum*, & similiter *Lignorum* aliorum, à siccitate contractæ, per immissionem, & moram nonnullam in Aqua, & imbibitionem ipsius *Aquæ*, implentur, & consolidantur.

        15. Est genus quoddam Fungi, qui excrescit ex arbore, quem vocant *Auriculam Iudæi*, qui immissus in *Aquam* magnopere intumescit: quod
30 non facit *Spongia*, aut *Lana*.

[C2ᵛ]   ¦ *Connexio.*

Atque de *Introceptionibus* Corporis alieni, (quæ sunt *pseudo-Rarefaciones*) hæc inquisita sint. Transeundum ad *Dilatationes* & *Tumores* quæ fiunt in *Corporibus* ex *Spiritu innato* (sive illi sunt
35 naturales, (ut loquuntur) sive præternaturales), absque igne, aut

2 *Flammæ*] ~,   3 cæruleum),] ~:)   34 *innato*] ~,   35 loquuntur)]
~,)   præternaturales),] ~,)

which its flame grows whiter and paler than other flames (though the flame itself of sulphur has a bluish tinge) to such an extent that this flame can truly be likened to a very strong froth composed of flame and air or to a kind of fiery wind.

7. Now in the same way as froth is a body made up of air and liquor, so also are all powders made up of air and smallest parts of the pulverized body, so that they differ from froth only [1] as a contiguous body differs from a continuous; for the great mass of them consists of air which raises up the parts of the body, as is apparent in the second and third tables.

8. Tumours arise in the belly and in other parts of animals from the absorption or taking in of wind or a watery humour, as in dropsy, tympanites, and the like.

9. There is a race of pigeons which, when the head is drawn back into the neck, is inflated and swollen up.

10. Respiration by means of lungs (like bellows) draws in and expels the air, the lung alternately dilating and deflating.

11. The breasts of pregnant women swell up, distending of course with the milky humour.

12. In sexually excited males the glans of the penis gets very much bigger when it is erect.

13. Look in a mirror and note the size of the pupils in each eye, then close one eye and you will see that the pupil of the open one is noticeably enlarged by the flowing together of the spirits which used to supply both.

14. Cracks in bowls for the sport of that name, and likewise in other wooden objects shrunken by dryness, close up and become solid again by being put in water and left there for a while, and by drinking in that same water.

15. There is a certain kind of fungus called Jew's Ear which grows out of trees, which when put in water swell up exceedingly; which sponge and wool do not.

[1] *Connection*

So much then for introceptions of one body by another (which are pseudo-rarefactions). Now we must go on to the dilatations and swellings which arise in bodies from the innate spirit (whether these be natural, as they say, or preternatural) without fire or any calore manifesto externo: licet in his quoque sequatur quandoque Accessio sive *Introceptio Humoris,* præter ipsam *Dilatationem* simplicem.

Dilatationes per Spiritum innatum se expandentem.

5   [*Historia.*]

16. *Mustum,* aut *Cervisia* nova, & similia, in doliis reposita, intumescunt, & insurgunt admodum; adeo ut nisi detur spiraculum, dolia infringant; sin detur, se attollant, & exundent cum spuma, & quasi ebulliant.

10   17. *Liquores spirituosi* arctius conclusi (ut in utribus fortiter obturatis) magno impetu sæpe erumpunt, & opercula sua quandoque ejiciunt tanquam è Tormento.

18. Audivi, *Mustum* nuper *calcatum,* & quasi *fervens,* in *vitro* crasso & forti repositum (ore *vitri* bene lutato & clauso, ut *Mustum* nec erumpere
15 nec perfringere posset) non reperiente exitum *spiritu,* se per continuas
[C3ʳ] Circulationes & vexatioⁱnes vertisse plane in *Tartarum;* ut nihil restaret in *vitro,* præter *Auram* & *Fæces:* Verum de hoc mihi parum constat.

19. *Semina plantarum,* ut *Pisorum, Fabarum,* & ejusmodi, turgescunt nonnihil, antequam emittant *Radicem* aut *Caulem.*

20   20. *Arbores* quandoque *spiritu* & *Succo nativo* tumescentes *Corticem* rumpunt, & emittunt *Gummi* & *lacrymas.*

21. Etiam *Gemmæ* complures videntur esse *Eruptiones Succorum puriorum* ex *Rupibus;* cum tam *Gummi* quam *Gemmæ Rupium* deprehendantur (ex splendore) esse *Succi* percolati & depurati; adeo ut
25 etiam *saxa* & *lapides* videantur ex Spiritu innato tumescere.

22. Neque dubium est, quin in *Spermate Animalium,* primus actus ad vivificandum sit quædam *Expansio Massæ.*

23. *Vitriolum* erumpendo tanquam *germinat,* & fere *arborescit.*

24. Lapides tempore & Senio (præsertim in locis humidioribus)
30 emittunt *salem,* qui est ex natura *Nitri.*

25. Omnis *Gleba terræ* tumet *Nitro:* itaque si terra quævis sit cooperta & accumulata, ita ut *succum* ejus non exhauriatur per *Solem* & *Aerem,* nec se consumat in emittendo *vegetabili;* colligit *Nitrum,* ut internum *Tumorem.* Ideo in aliquibus *Europæ* partibus struunt *Mineras artificiales*

---

5 [*Historia.*]] / see *tn* to C1ʳ (above). The para numbers following this heading should start with 1
10 conclusi] ~,   14 repositum] ~,

obvious external heat; though in these cases also there sometimes follows an addition or introception of humour besides the simple dilatation itself.

Dilatations caused by the innate Spirit expanding itself

[*History*]

16. New wine or beer and the like, stored in barrels, swell and bubble up extremely, such that unless they have a vent, they will burst the barrel; but if they do have one they rise and gush up with froth, and practically boil.

17. Spirituous liquors strictly pent up (as in bottles tightly sealed) often burst with considerable force and pop their corks as if from a gun.

18. I have heard that new wine, recently pressed and practically seething, laid up in a strong and thick glass bottle (with the mouth of the glass well sealed and closed up so that the wine could neither burst out nor break through) has, when the spirit has found no way out, quite turned itself into tartar by uninterrupted circulations and vexations, ¹ so that nothing was left in the glass besides breath and dregs. But I do not take this for an established fact.

19. Seeds of plants, as of peas, beans, and the like, swell somewhat before they put out root or stalk.

20. Trees, swelling with spirit and natural juice, sometimes burst their bark and shed gums and tears.

21. Many gems also seem to be discharges of purer juices from rocks, as both gums and gems from rocks can be identified by their brilliance as strained and purified juices, such that even boulders and stones seem to swell with an innate spirit.

22. There is no doubt but that in animal sperm the first step towards vivification is a certain expansion of the mass.

23. Vitriol in bursting out sprouts so to speak, and practically grows into a tree.

24. With time and age stones (especially in damper places) give out a salt which is nitrous in nature.

25. All soil swells with nitre; if therefore any earth be covered or piled up so that its juice is not drawn off by the Sun or air and does not consume itself in putting forth vegetable matter, it gathers nitre as an inner swelling. So in some parts of Europe they establish artificial nitre mines

Nitri, accumulata terra, in domibus ad hoc paratis, prohibito aditu Solis.

[C3ᵛ]   26. *Sudores* in Animalibus, per motum dilatatis ¹ *spiritibus,* atque *Humoribus* veluti liquefactis, proveniunt.

5   27. *Pulsus Cordis* & *Arteriarum* in Animalibus fit per irrequietam *dilatationem Spirituum,* & receptum ipsorum, per vices.

28. Quin & *Motus voluntarius* in Animalibus, qui expeditur (in perfectioribus) per nervos, videtur radicem habere in *Compressione* primum, deinde *Relaxatione, Spirituum.*

10   29. In omni *Contusione Membri* alicujus in Animalibus, sequitur *Tumor.* Idem evenit in plerisque *Doloribus.*

30. *Aculei Vesparum* & *Apum* majorem inducunt *Tumorem,* quam pro inflictu: Id multo magis faciunt *punctiones Serpentum.*

31. Etiam *Vrtica, Bryonia,* & alia nonnulla, levant *Cutem,* & *vesicas* in 15 illa causant.

32. Habetur pro evidenti signo *veneni,* (præsertim ejus generis quod operatur ex *qualitate maligna,* non per *Erosionem*), si Facies aut Corpus intumescat.

33. In *vesicationibus Colli* aut alterius alicujus partis, quæ adhibentur 20 ad *Curationes Morborum,* assurgit *Humor aqueus,* sive *Ichor,* qui postea, cute scissa aut puncta, effluit.

34. Omnes pustulæ ex causa interna, & hujusmodi efflorescentiæ & Apostemata, inducunt tumores apparentes, & sublevant cutem.

35. *Iracundia* subito effervescens (in nonnullis) inflat buccas; similiter 25 & Fastus.

36. *Ranæ* & *Bufones* tument; & complura Animalia per ferociam [C4ʳ] erigunt *cristas,* & *pilos,* & plu¹*mas*: quod fit ex *Contractione Cutis* per *Tumorem spirituum.*

37. *Galli,* quos *Indicos,* alii *Turcicos,* vocant, irati, magnopere tument, 30 & pennas tanquam jubas erigunt. *Aves* cum dormitant, dilatato *spiritu,* per receptum caloris ad interiora, nonnihil tument.

38. In omni *Carie* & *Putredine* tumescere incipiunt Spiritus *Corporis* innati; cumque ad exitum properant, solvunt & alterant *rei compagem*; &, si *compages rei* sit paulo tenacior & viscosior, ut exire non possint, 35 novas *Formas* moliuntur, ut in *Vermibus* è putredine natis; sed *exordium* actionis est à *Dilatatione spirituum.*

39. Neque *spiritus* in *Putredine* cohibitus tantum molitur *Animalcula,* verum & *rudimenta Plantarum*: ut conspicitur in *Musco,* & hirsutie

17 *Erosionem*),] ~ ,)   24 buccas;] ~:   35 natis;] ~:

by piling up earth in houses readied for the purpose, and by keeping off the Sun.

26. Animals break into a sweat when the spirits are ¹ dilated by motion, and the humours are as it were dissolved.

27. The pulse of heart and arteries in animals is caused by the spirits' alternate and tireless dilatation and recovery.

28. Likewise voluntary motion in animals, which (in the higher ones) is accomplished by the nerves, seems to originate first in the compression and then in the relaxation of the spirits.

29. If any animal bump a part of its body it gets a swelling. The same happens in most pains.

30. Wasp and bee stings produce a larger swelling than the wound would lead you to expect. That happens a great deal more with snake bites.

31. Nettles, bryony and some other things also raise the skin and blister it.

32. If the face or body swell up, that is taken as a clear symptom of poison (especially of the kind that works by a malign quality and not by eating you away).

33. When blisters are raised on the neck or any other part by way of treating illnesses, a watery humour or ichor comes up which afterwards, when the skin has been scratched or pricked, drains away.

34. All pustules arising from an internal cause, and suchlike efflorescences and abscesses induce perceptible swellings, and lift up the skin.

35. Rage boiling up suddenly (in some people) puffs the cheeks up, as likewise does pride.

36. Frogs and toads swell up and many animals raise their combs, hair and ¹ feathers in anger; and this happens when the skin is contracted by the swelling of the spirits.

37. Angry Indian or Turkey-cocks as they call them swell up a lot, and raise their hackles like a mane. Sleeping birds, their spirit dilated by the withdrawal of heat into their innards, swell up a bit.

38. In all rot and putrefaction the innate spirits of the body begin to swell; and when they hurry to escape, they dissolve and alter the structure of the thing; and, if the structure of the thing be a little more tenacious or viscous so that they cannot escape, they get new forms going, as in worms born of putrefaction. But the beginning of the action springs from dilatation of the spirits.

39. Spirit confined in putrefaction not only gets animalculæ going but also rudiments of plants, as we see in moss and the shaggy growths of

Arborum nonnullarum. Memini me expertum esse, casu quodam, non de industria, quod cum æstivo tempore *Malum Citrium*, ex parte sectum, in Conclavi reliquissem, post duos menses inveni in parte secta *putredinem* quandam germinantem; adeo ut in *capillis* quibusdam
5 exurgeret ad altitudinem pollicis ad minus, atque in summitate *capillorum* singulorum ascivisset Caput quoddam, instar capitis *pusilli clavi*; plane incipiens imitari *plantam*.

40. Similiter, *Rubigines* fiunt in *Metallis*, & *vitro*, & similibus, ex *Dilatatione Spiritus innati*, qui tumescit, & urget partes crassiores,
10 easque ante se agit, & extrudit, ut exeat.

[C4^v]   41. Utrum *Terra* in superficie tumescat, præ'sertim ubi *glebæ* sunt spongiosæ & cavæ, inquirendum. Certe inveniuntur quandoque in ejusmodi *Glebis Arbores* instar *Malorum Navium*, quæ sub terra, nonnullos pedes in altum, jacent demersæ & sepultæ: ut verisimile sit,
15 *Arbores* illas per Tempestates fuisse olim dejectas; postea vero, attollente se paulatim Terra, coopertas fuisse & sepultas.

42. At subito & manifeste intumescit Terra in T*erræ-motibus*; unde sæpenumero erumpunt scaturigines *Aquarum*, vortices, & *globi Flammarum, Venti* vehementes et peregrini, atque ejiciuntur *Saxa,*
20 *Cineres.*

43. Neque tamen *Terræ-motus* omnes prorsus subito fiunt; nam evenit nonnunquam, ut Terra contremuerit per plures dies: & nostro tempore, apud nos, in *Agro Herefordiensi*, fuit *Terræ-motus*, admodum pusillus & lentus, sed rarus; in quo aliqua jugera *terræ*, per diem integrum, paulatim
25 se moverunt, & in alium locum, paulo decliviorem, nec multo distantem, se transtulerunt, & ita quieverunt.

44. Utrum *moles Aquarum* in *Maribus* aliquando tumescant, inquirendum. Nam in ipsis *Fluxibus Maris*, necesse est ut illi fiant vel ex *Motu progressivo*; vel ex *Sublatione Aquarum* in sursum, per virtutem, &
30 consensum aliquem magneticum; vel denique, per *Tumorem*, sive *Relaxationem* aliquam in ipsis *Aquis*. Atque postremus iste *modus* (si modo talis aliquis sit, inter causas *Fluxus* alicujus) pertinet ad *inquisitionem* præsentem.

[C5^r]   45. *Aqua* in *Fontibus* & *Puteis* nonnullis tu'mescit, & residit; adeo ut
35 æstus quosdam videatur pati.

46. Etiam erumpunt quandoque in quibusdam locis *Scaturigines Aquarum*, absque aliquo *Terræ-motu*, intra aliquos annos, ex causis incertis. Fitque ista *Eruptio* plerumque in magnis *Siccitatibus*.

---

5 pollicis] ~,   6 ascivisset] / *nld* as adscivisset in *SEH* (II, p. 264)

some trees. I recall that one summer I left a cut lemon by accident rather than design in a closed room and that after a couple of months I found a certain putrefaction growing on the cut such that it had pushed itself up in certain hairs at least an inch high, and at the top of each particular hair had a kind of head, like the head of a small wart, plainly starting to imitate a plant.

40. Likewise rusts arise in metals and glass, and the like from the dilatation of the innate spirit which, in order to escape, swells and urges on the grosser parts and drives them before it and ejects them.

41. It should be inquired whether the surface of the ground swells up, especially ¹ where the soils are spongy and full of holes. Certainly in soils of this kind we sometimes find trees like the masts of ships, lying sunk and buried a few feet in the ground; and it seems likely that these trees were blown over once upon a time but were afterwards covered up and buried as the earth gradually rose up over them.

42. But in earthquakes the earth swells up suddenly and manifestly, whence on many occasions springs of water burst out, and whirlwinds, fireballs, and severe, outlandish winds; not to mention the stones and ashes that are cast out.

43. All the same, not all earthquakes happen altogether suddenly, for it sometimes happens that the earth shakes for some days, and in my time in Herefordshire here in England there was an earthquake small, slow and intermittent, in which for a whole day some acres of land gradually shifted themselves, and transferred to another spot not far off and a little further down where it settled.

44. Inquire whether the mass of the waters in the seas sometimes swells. For in the tides themselves it is necessary that they are caused in them either by a progressive motion or by the waters rising through some magnetic virtue or consent, or lastly some swelling or relaxation in the waters themselves. And this last means (if it turn out that this be among the causes of any tide) is relevant to the present inquiry.

45. Water in some wells and fountains swells ¹ and sinks down again, to such an extent that it appears to be undergoing certain tidal motions.

46. In certain places springs of water too sometimes burst out without any earthquake, at intervals of some years and from causes unknown. And this outbreak mostly happens during severe droughts.

47. Etiam notatum est, intumescere quandoque Maria, absque *Fluxu*, aut *Vento* aliquo exteriore; idque fere *Tempestatem* aliquam magnam præcedere.

Mandata.

5 Non foret indignum *Experimento*, ut probetur, utrum fiat interdum aliqua Relaxatio in corpore *Aquæ*, etiam in minore *Quanto*. Atqui si exponatur *Aqua* Soli vel Aeri, fiet potius *Consumptio*. Itaque *Experimentum* faciendum in vitro clauso. Accipe itaque *vitrum*, quod habeat ventrem amplum, collum vero longum & angustum, atque
10 infundatur Aqua, donec venter, & pars inferior colli impleatur. Fiat autem hoc per tempestatem *Aeris* Borealem & siccam; atque ita permittatur, donec succedat *Tempestas* Australis & pluviosa; & vide, si Aqua insurgat aliqualiter in collo *vitri*. Etiam de *Tumoribus Aquæ* in *Puteis* facienda est diligentior *Inquisitio*; utrum fiant magis noctu quam
15 interdiu, & quali *Tempestate* anni.

¹*Historia.*

1. In *Pinnis fidium ligneis* fit, tempore pluvioso, ut illæ tumescentes difficilius torqueantur. Similiter *pyxidesligneæ* difficilius extrahuntur ex thecis suis, & *ostia lignea* difficilius aperiuntur.
20   2. *Chordæ Fidium* extentæ paulo rigidius temporibus pluviosis rumpuntur.
  3. *Humores* in *corporibus* Animalium, *tempestatibus Australibus* & pluviosis, deprehenduntur laxari & tumescere, & fluere, & incumbere magis, & meatus obstruere.
25   4. Recepta est opinio, *Humores* & *Succos*, non in *Animalibus* tantum, sed & in *Plantis*, sub *Pleniluniis* magis turgescere, & cava implere.
  5. *Sales* in locis humidis se solvunt, aperiunt, & dilatant: Id quod faciunt (aliqua ex parte) *Saccharum* & *Condita* quæ, nisi reponantur in *cameris* ubi aliquando accenditur Ignis, Situm colligunt.
30   6. Etiam omnia quæ per *Ignem cocta*, & majorem in modum *contracta* sunt, tractu temporis nonnihil laxantur.
  7. De *Tumoribus* & *Relaxationibus Aeris*, diligentius videndum; & quatenus in his militent (magna ex parte) causæ ventorum; cum vapores

16 *Historia.*] / deliberately *om* in *SEH* (II, p. 265) which (probably rightly) alters the number-ing of subsequent paras to follow on from that preceding the mandata
7 *Consumptio.*] ~:   28 *Condita*] ~;

47. It has also been noted that the seas sometimes swell without a tide or any external wind; and this generally comes before any big storm.

Directions

It would be worth while to test by experiment whether there is sometimes any relaxation in the body of water, even in a small quantity. But if the water be exposed to the sun or air, it is rather consumption that takes place. So do this experiment in a closed glass, taking one with a large belly but a long and narrow neck, and pour in the water till it fills the belly and the bottom of the neck. But do this in dry weather with a north wind, leaving it till the weather turns wet with southerly winds, and see if the water rise at all in the neck of the glass. A more careful inquiry should also be made concerning swellings of water in wells to see whether they take place more at night than by day and in what season of the year.

¹*History*

1. In wet weather the wooden pegs of stringed instruments swell and so become harder to twist. Likewise wooden drawers become harder to pull from their chests, and wooden doors harder to open.

2. In wet weather the strings of musical instruments break when stretched a little more tightly.

3. In wet weather with southerly winds we observe that the humours in animal bodies loosen, swell and flow, as well as burden and block the passages more.

4. Received opinion has it that at full moon the humours and juices not just in animals but also in plants swell and fill up the hollows more.

5. Salts in damp places dissolve, open and dilate themselves; and the same thing happens (to some degree) in sugar and preserves which, unless they are stored in a room where a fire is sometimes lighted, gather mould.

6. Likewise all things which have been baked by fire and a great deal contracted are somewhat relaxed by the passage of time.

7. All swellings and relaxations of air should be looked into more carefully, and how far the causes of winds (to any significant degree) are

nec colliguntur commode in *pluviam,* nec dissipantur in *Aerem lympidum,* sed inducunt tumores in *corpore Aeris.*

[C6^r]   ¹*Connexio.*

Atque de *Dilatationibus Corporum* per *spiritum innatum,* sive in
5 *Maturationibus,* sive in *rudimentis Generationum,* sive in
Excitatione per *motum,* sive in *Irritationibus naturalibus* aut *præter-
naturalibus,* sive in *Putrefactionibus,* sive in *Relaxationibus,* hæc
pauca ex cumulo *Naturæ* inquisita sunto. Transeundum jam ad
Aperturas & Dilatationes quæ fiunt per *Ignem,* & *Calorem*
10 *externum* actualem.

*Dilatationes & Aperturæ Corporum quæ fiunt per ignem, & calorem
actualem, simplicem, externum.*

Monitum.

Aperturæ Corporum per Calorem sive Ignem (de quibus jam
15 inquiremus) proprie spectant ad *Titulos* de *Calido* & *Frigido,* & de *Motu
Hyles,* & de *Separationibus* & *Alterationibus.* Attamen carpendum &
prægustandum est aliquid ex ipsis in præsenti *Titulo;* cum absque aliqua
notitia ipsorum, non possit inquiri recte de *Denso* & *Raro.*

Historia.

20 1. *Aer* per calorem dilatatur simpliciter. Neque enim separatur quippiam,
aut emittitur, ut in *Tangibilibus;* sed simpliciter fit *Expansio.*
[C6^v]   ¹2. In *Ventosis,* Vitro, & Aere intra ipsum contento, calcefactis, &
Ventosis Carni applicatis, quando paulo post *Aer,* qui per calorem
dilatatus fuerit, remittente calore, se recipiat paulatim & contrahat;
25 attrahitur per *motum nexus* Caro. Quod si *Ventosas* fortius attrahere
cupias, accipe *Spongiam* frigida madefactam, & pone eam super ventrem
Ventosæ; ut per *Refrigerationem* amplius contracto *Aere, ventosa* fortius
attrahat.
     3. Accipe *vitrum,* & calefacias illud; mitte illud post in *Aquam:*
30 attrahet *Aquam,* pro minimo, ad tertias contenti; unde liquet, *Aerem* à

---

11 *Dilatationes*] / see *tn* to C1^r (p. 74 above). I have transposed this and the next title which
are silently transposed thus in *SEH* (II, p. 266)
29 illud;] ~:

involved in these, since vapours are neither gathered readily into rain nor dissipated into clear air, but they induce swellings in the body of the air.

[|]*Connection*

Now concerning the dilatations of bodies by the innate spirit—either in maturations, or the rudiments of generations, or excitation by motion, or natural or preternatural irritations, or putrefactions, or relaxations—let these few things plucked from the heap of nature be inquired. We must now pass on to the openings and dilatations which arise from fire or actual external heat.

Dilatations and Openings of Bodies which arise from fire and actual, simple and external heat

Advice

The openings of bodies by heat or fire (which I shall now look into) properly belong to the titles of Hot and Cold, of Motion of *Hyle*, and of Separations and Alterations. Nevertheless a snatched foretaste of some of these things must be given in this title since without some acquaintance with them the topic of dense and rare cannot be rightly investigated.

History

1. Air is just dilated by heat. For nothing is separated or discharged as in tangible bodies, but it is only expansion that takes place.

[|]2. In cupping glasses, once the glass with the air inside is heated and applied to the flesh, the air, which has been dilated by the heat, and the heat abating, soon after reverts gradually to its former state and contracts, and then the flesh is drawn up by motion of connection. But if you want the cupping glasses to draw more strongly, take a sponge moistened in cold water and place it on the belly of the glass so that when the air is more fully contracted by refrigeration, it draws more strongly.

3. Take a glass and heat it; then put it in water and it will draw up the water to fill at least a third of itself, from which it is evident that the air

Calore rarefactum fuisse pariter ad tertias contenti. Sed hoc parum est. Nam cum *Vitrum*, quo usi sumus, tenue esset, majorem calefactionem, absque periculo rupturæ, non facile patiebatur. Quod si fuisset *Phiala ferrea* aut *ænea*, & majorem in modum calefacta, arbitror *Aerem* posse
5 dilatari ad duplum, aut triplum: quod *experimento* dignissimum est, etiam ad quousque; ut inde melius de *Raritate Aeris* superne, atque adeo *Ætheris* ipsius, judicium facere possimus.

4. In *Vitro* quod appellamus *Calendare*, (quod *tempestatum*, quatenus ad calorem & frigus, tam accurate demonstret varietates & gradus)
10 evidentissime patet, quam parva *accessio caloris* expandat *Aerem* notabiliter; adeo ut *Manus Vitro* superposita, *Radii* aliqui *Solis*, ipse *Anhelitus astantium* operetur; quin & ipsius Aeris externi inclinationes ad Calorem & Frigus, (tactui ipsi imperceptibiles), Aerem nihilominus in vitro sensim, & perpetuo, dilatent, & contrahant.

[C7ʳ] 15 ⁱ5. *Hero* describit *Altaris* fabricam, eo artificio, ut superimposito *Holocausto*, & incenso, subito *Aqua* descenderet, quæ *Ignem* extingueret. Id non aliam poscebat industriam, quam ut sub *Altare* esset locus concavus & conclusus, *Aere* repletus; qui *Aer* ab Igne calefactus, & propterea dilatatus, nullum reperiret exitum, nisi in *Canali* ad parietem
20 Altaris erecto & curvato, ore super Altare inverso. In *Canali* erecto infusa erat Aqua; (facto etiam ventre in *Canali*, ut largior copia *Aquæ* reciperetur) ea Aqua obice impediebatur, ne descenderet, foraminato; qui obex postquam erat versus, dabat locum *Aeri* dilatato, ut *Aquam* eveheret & ejiceret.

25 6. Inventum fuit *Fracastorii* ad excitandos *Apoplecticos*, ut poneretur *Sartago* fervens circa caput, ad nonnullam distantiam; unde *Spiritus* in cellis *Cerebri* suffocati & congelati, & ab *Humoribus* obsessi, dilatarentur, excitarentur, & vivificarentur.

7. Etiam *Papiliones*, quæ hyeme jacent emortuæ, admotæ ad *Ignem*,
30 aut *Radios Solis*, Motum & Vitam recipiunt. *Ægroti* quoque in *deliquiis*, tam *Aquis fortibus* & *calidis* intro sumptis, quam *Calore exteriore*, & *Fricationibus*, & *Motu*, excitantur.

8. *Apertura Aquæ* talis est. Sub primo *Calore* emittit *vaporem* paucum & rarum. Neque intra corpus alia conspicitur Mutatio. Continuato
35 *Calore*, corpore integro non insurgit, nec etiam *Bullis minutis* in modum *spumæ*; sed per *Bullas majores* & rariores ascendit, & in copiosum
[C7ᵛ] *vaporem* ⁱ se solvit. Ille *vapor*, si non impediatur, aut repercutiatur, *Aeri* se immiscet; primo conspicuus, dein insensibilis, & se deperdens.

---

5 dignissimum est,] ∼;   13 imperceptibiles),] ∼,)   22 reciperetur)] ∼:)

was correspondingly rarefied by that third. But this does not go far enough. For since the glass I used was thin it could not easily take more heating without risk of breakage. But if the phial were of iron or bronze and heated strongly, I judge that the air could be dilated to two or three times its volume; and this would be well worth an experiment, as also would the question how far the rarefaction could be taken, so that we can be in a better position to form a judgement about the rarity of the air higher up as well as of the ether itself.

4. In what we call a calendar glass (which, as far as heat and cold are concerned, demonstrates the varieties and degrees of the weather so nicely) it is perfectly clear how a small increase in heat can visibly expand the air, such that a hand put on it, a few of the Sun's rays, or the very breath of onlookers make it work; indeed, the imperceptible inclinations of the outside air itself towards hot and cold likewise dilate and contract the air in the glass gradually and unceasingly.

⎮5. Hero describes the construction of an altar, so contrived that when the offering was laid on it and set alight, water suddenly fell down and put the fire out. This required no other contrivance than that there would be a hollow and enclosed place full of air beneath the altar, air which, when heated and so dilated by the fire, could find no way out except through a pipe going up the wall of the altar and which was then curved round with the pipe's mouth hanging down from above. Water was put in the pipe going up (the pipe having a belly to hold a greater quantity of water); the water was prevented from going downwards by a stopcock which, when it was opened, let in the dilated air to force up the water and eject it.

6. Fracastoro found out that a remedy for apoplectic fits was to place a hot pan about the head at a distance, whence the suffocated and congealed spirits in the cells of the brain, obstructed by the humours, were dilated, stimulated and vivified.

7. Butterflies moreover, which drop down dead in winter, get life and motion back again when they are put by the fire or in the Sun's rays. Also sick people who pass out are brought round both by drinks hot and strong taken internally and by external heat and frictions.

8. The opening up of water is as follows: when first heated it gives off a slight and rarefied vapour. No other change is observed within its body. With further heating it does not rise up as a whole nor even boil up in smaller bubbles in the manner of froth but it rises in larger bubbles, and resolves itself ⎮ into an abundant vapour. This vapour, if it is not hindered or forced back, mingles with the air, and is at first visible but then disappears and is lost to sight.

9. *Apertura Olei* talis est. A primo *calore* ascendunt Guttulæ quædam, aut Granula, per corpus *Olei* sparsa; idque cum crepitatione quadam. Interim, nec Bullæ in superficie ludunt, (ut in Aqua) nec corpus integrum tumet, nec quicquam fere Halitus evolat. At post moram
5 nonnullam, tum demum *corpus* integrum insurgit, & dilatatur *Expansione* notabili, tanquam ad duplum; & copiosissimus & spissus admodum evolat *Halitus.* Is *Halitus,* si Flammam interea non conceperit, miscet se tandem cum *Aere,* quemadmodum & *vapor Aquæ.* Majorem autem calorem desiderat, ad hoc ut bulliat, *Oleum,* quam
10 *Aqua*; & tardius multo bullire incipit.

10. *Apertura spiritus vini* ea est, ut *Aquam* potius referat, quam *Oleum.* Nam ebullit, magnis utique *Bullis,* absque *Spuma,* aut totius corporis *elevatione*; longe autem minore *Calore,* & multo celerius expanditur, & evolat, quam *Aqua.* Utriusque vero *Naturæ* particeps, (tam *aqueæ,*
15 scilicet, quam *oleosæ*) & facile se immiscet *Aeri,* & cito concipit *Flammam.*

11. *Acetum* & Agresta & Vinum in hoc differunt, in processu suæ *Aperturæ*: quod *Acetum* insurgat in minoribus *Bullis,* & magis circa *Latera vasis*; *Agresta* & *Vinum* in majoribus Bullis, & magis in *Medio*
20 *vasis.*

12. Generaliter in *Liquidis* hoc fit, ut pinguia, sicut *Oleum, Lac, Adeps,*
[C8ʳ] & hujusmodi, insurgant ¹ & tumeant simul toto corpore; *Succi maturi* (& magis adhuc *immaturi*) *Bullis* majoribus; *Succi effœti* & *vapidi, Bullis* minoribus.

25 13. Omnibus *Liquoribus* commune est, etiam *Oleo* ipsi, ut antequam bulliant, paucas & raras semibullas circa Latera vasis jaciant.

14. Omnibus *Liquoribus* commune est, ut in parva quantitate citius aperiantur, bulliant, atque consumantur, quam in magna.

Monitum.

30 *Experimentum* de *Aperturis Liquorum* faciendum est in vasis vitreis, ut Motus in Corpore Liquorum melius conspici possint; atque super Foculos, cum *Calore æquali,* ut differentia verius excipiatur; atque *Igne* lento; quia *Ignis* vehemens præcipitat & confundit actiones.

9. The opening up of oil is as follows: when first heated certain droplets or grains diffused through the body of the oil rise up with a kind of crackling noise. Meanwhile no bubbles play on the surface (as they do in water), nor does the whole body swell up *en masse*, and almost no exhalation escapes. But after a while then indeed the whole body rises up and dilates with a remarkable expansion to about twice its size; and an extremely abundant and thick exhalation escapes. This exhalation, if it does not catch fire in the meantime, mixes in the end with the air, as does water vapour. But oil needs more heat than water to boil and it starts boiling much more slowly.

10. The opening of spirit of wine is such that it may be likened to water rather than oil. For it boils with especially large bubbles without froth or even the rising of its whole body; however, it expands and escapes with much less heat and much more quickly than water. But, sharing as it does in both natures (i.e. of the watery as well as the oily) it both easily mixes in with air and readily catches fire.

11. Vinegar differs from verjuice and wine in the process of opening up in this respect: that vinegar rises up in smaller bubbles and more around the sides of the container, verjuice and wine in larger ones more towards the middle of the container.

12. It generally happens in liquids that greasy bodies, like oil, milk, fat and so forth rise up and ¹ swell as a body and at once; ripe juices (and unripe ones still more) with larger bubbles; exhausted and vapid juices in smaller.

13. It is common to all liquors, oil itself included, to throw up a few rare half-bubbles around the sides of the vessel before they start boiling.

14. It is common to all liquors to open up, boil, and be consumed more quickly in small than in large quantities.

Advice

You should do the experiment of opening up liquors in glass vessels, so that the motions in the body of the liquors can be seen better; and do it on braziers with an equable heat so that the difference can be grasped more accurately; and with a slow fire, because a fierce one forestalls and confounds the actions.

Historia.

1. Sunt vero complura *Corpora* quæ non sunt liquida, sed consistentia & determinata, attamen per *Calorem* nanciscuntur eam *Aperturam*, ut liquescant, sive deveniant *liquida*, quamdiu *Calor* ea vellicet &
5 expandat; qualia sunt *Cera, Adeps, Butyrum, Pix, Resina, Gummi, Saccharum, Mel*; & plurima ex *Metallis*, veluti *Plumbum, Aurum, Argentum, Æs, Cuprum.* Ita tamen ut ad *Aperturam* requirantur non solum *Gradus Caloris* longe diversi, sed & *Modificationes Ignis* &
[C8ᵛ] *Flammæ* dissimiles. Nam alia *Metalla* colliquantur per *Ignem* simpli|citer,
10 ut *Plumbum*; alia, per Ignem motum, & Follibus excitatum, ut *Aurum* & *Argentum*; alia, non sine admistione, ut *Chalybs*, qui non, nisi admisto *Sulphure*, aut simile quopiam, colliquatur.

2. At ista omnia, si continuetur Ignis, & urgeat, non solum sortiuntur *Aperturam Colliquationis*, sed pertranseunt, & adipiscuntur secundam
15 Aperturam; (*volatilis* scilicet, sive *Pneumatici*, sive *Consumptionis*), omnia, inquam, præter *Aurum*: Nam quatenus ad *Argentum vivum*, cum in natura sua sit liquidum, incipit illud ab *Apertura* secunda, & facile vertitur in *volatile*. De *Auro* adhuc dubium est, utrum possit fieri *volatile*, aut *pneumaticum*, (aut etiam *Potabile*, ut loquuntur), hoc est, non
20 dissolubile quidem, (id enim facile est, & tritum, per *Aquas fortes*), sed *digestibile*, aut *alterabile* per *ventriculum humanum*. Hujus autem Rei legitima videtur Probatio: minime illa, ut vi ignis ascendat, aut trudatur sursum; sed ut ita attenuetur & subigatur, ut restitui in *Metallum* non possit.

25 3. Inquiratur etiam ulterius, de *Vitro* & *vitrificatis*, utrum per ignem consumantur, & vertantur in *Pneumaticum*. Habetur enim *Vitrum* pro *corpore fixo*, & *exucco*; & *vitrificatio* pro *Morte Metallorum*.

4. Quæ colliquantur omnia, in via & processu suo incipiunt ab infimo illo Gradu *Aperturæ*, qui est *Emollitio* & *Inteneratio*, antequam
30 colliquantur & fundantur; ut *Cera, Gummi, Metalla colliquabilia, vitrum*, & similia.

[D1ʳ] 5. At *Ferrum* & *Chalybs*, postquam fuerint per|fecta & repurgata, (nisi fuerit Admistio) quatenus ad Ignem simplicem, persistunt, & non procedunt ultra illum gradum *Emollitionis*, ut reddantur (scilicet)

1 *Historia*.] / this *om* in *SEH* (II, p. 269), where numbering of the subsequent paras follows on from that of paras preceding the monitum   28 colliquantur] colliquentur / cf. *HDR(M)* p. 14, l. 14 above; *SEH* (II, p. 270) follows *c-t*
15 *Consumptionis*),] ~;)   19 loquuntur),] ~;)   20 *fortes*),] ~,)

92

History

1. There are certainly lots of bodies which are not liquid but consistent and determinate yet get opened up by heat to the extent that they melt or become liquid as long as the heat prompts or expands them. Of this kind are wax, fat, butter, pitch, resin, gums, sugar, honey and most metals, as lead, gold, silver, brass and copper. Yet for their opening up these need not just very different degrees of heat but dissimilar modifications of fire and flame. For some metals are melted by mere ¹ fire, as lead; others by fire moved and excited by bellows, as gold and silver; others not without some admixture, as steel, which only melts if sulphur or something of the sort be added.

2. But all these bodies, if the fire is kept up and spurred on, not only attain the opening up of colliquation but pass through that and achieve a second opening up (i.e. they reach the volatile state, or that of the pneumatic, or of consumption), all (I say) except gold. For as far as quicksilver is concerned, since it is by nature liquid, it starts off with the second opening up and it is easily made volatile. It is still a matter of doubt whether gold can be made volatile or pneumatic (or indeed *potable* as they say), i.e. not soluble (for with strong waters that is easy and familiar) but digestible or alterable by the human stomach. A fair test of this seems to be not that it ascend or be driven upwards by the fire's force, but that it be so attenuated and tamed that it cannot be made into a metal again.

3. Also inquire further of glass and glassy bodies, to see whether they are consumed by fire and turn into a pneumatic body. For glass is taken for a fixed body lacking juice, and vitrification for the death of metals.

4. All bodies that melt set off on their way and process at the lowest level of opening up, which is being made soft and workable, before they are melted and spread out, as wax, gums, metals capable of melting, glass and the like.

5. But iron and steel, once they have been brought to perfection ¹ and refined (so long as nothing has been added) do not, if exposed to simple fire, stay as they are and do not get beyond the stage of softness, i.e. they

malleabilia & *flexibilia*, & exuant *Fragilitatem* suam; minime autem pertingunt ad *Colliquationem*, sive *Fusionem*.

6. Videntur *Ferrum* & *Vitrum*, cum aperiuntur ad illam Mollitiem de qua diximus, dilatari sane in *spiritu* suo *incluso*; unde fit illa *Subactio*
5 *partium tangibilium*, ut *Duritiem* & *Obstinationem* suam deponant: neque tamen Corpus ipsum integrum localiter dilatari aut intumescere cernitur. Attamen attentius paulo inquirenti, deprehenditur plane in ipsis invisibilis quidam *Tumor*, & *partium Pulsatio*; licet cohibeatur ab arcta compage sua. Nam si accipias vitrum ignitum, & majorem in
10 modum calefactum, & ponas illud supra *Tabulam lapideam*, aut simile aliquod *Corpus durum*; (licet & ipsa *Tabula* illa, seu corpus bene calefactum fuerit, ut Frigori causa imputari non possit) rumpetur prorsus *vitrum*, duritie *Lapidis* scilicet *Tumorem* illum occultum *vitri* repercutiente. Itaque solent in hujusmodi casu, quando *vitrum fervens*
15 summovetur ab igne, substernere ipsi *Pulverem* aliquem, aut *Arenam* mollem, quæ suaviter cedens, *Tumorem* in partibus *vitri* non retundat.

7. Etiam *Pilæ* è *Bombardis* emissæ, postquam non solum vehi, sed & gliscere aut labi omnino desierint, adeo ut ad aspectum sint prorsus immobiles, tamen diu post magnum deprehenduntur habere
[D1ᵛ] 20 Tumultum, & pulsationem in miniˡmis; adeo ut, si aliquid superponatur, magnam vim patiatur: neque id tam à *Calore comburente*, quam à *palpitatione percussiva*.

8. *Bacula lignea recentia*, sub cineribus calidis detenta & versata, induunt *mollitudinem*, ut melius *flectantur* ad arbitrium. Experire quid
25 fiat in *Baculis* antiquioribus, & in *Cannis*.

9. Apertura Combustibilium ea est, ut per ignem primo emittant *Fumum*, dein concipiant *Flammam*, postremo deponant *Cinerem*.

10. In *Corporibus* quæ continent *Humorem aqueum*, & à Flamma abhorrentem, in Compage clausa & compacta (qualia sunt Folia Lauri,
30 & alia non porosa, Sales, & similia) ea est Apertura per ignem, ut spiritus in iis contentus, (aqueus, & crudus), per calorem dilatatus, cum sonitu emittatur, antequam Flamma concipiatur. Si vero in aliquo *Corpore* (quod raro fit) insimul fiant & *Eruptio flatus* & *Conceptio flammæ*, ingens *Tumultus* excitatur, & potentissima *Dilatatio*; *Flatu*, tanquam internis
35 Follibus, Flammam undiquaque exufflante & expandente, ut in *pulvere pyrio*.

11. *Panis* in *Furno* nonnihil tumescit; licet fiat minoris ponderis quam ante: Etiam in summo *panis* quandoque colligitur tanquam Bulla, aut

29 compacta] ~,   31 crudus),] ~,)   32 concipiatur.] ~:

94

become malleable and flexible, and cease to be brittle, but do not get as far as melting or fusion.

6. When they have opened up to the point of the softness I have spoken of, iron and glass seem at any rate to be dilated in respect of their enclosed spirit, whence originates the working up of the tangible parts, so that they cast off their hardness and stubbornness; and yet we do not see that the whole body itself dilates or swells up locally. All the same, if we look into the matter a little more closely, we distinctly detect in them a certain invisible swelling or pulsation of the parts, although this is held back by their close compaction. For if you take a very hot glass and put it on a stone table or some such other hard body (the table or hard body having been well heated so that cold cannot be taken for the cause), the glass will in fact break because of the hardness of the table resisting this occult swelling of the glass. So it is usual in cases of this kind that when they take the hot glass off the fire, they put some powder or soft sand under it which, giving way nicely, does not resist the swelling in the parts of the glass.

7. Likewise cannon shot, once they have been fired and when they have completely stopped not only being carried along but also growing in violence or tumbling down, such that to all appearances they are totally motionless, we find that for a long time after they have a commotion or pulsation in their smallest ¹ parts to such an extent that if anything is put on top of them it will experience a great shock; and that comes not so much from the burning heat as from the percussive throbbing.

8. New wooden staves, held and turned over beneath hot ashes, get soft so that they can be bent more as one might wish. Find out if this happens in older staves and canes.

9. The opening up of combustible bodies is as follows: that at first by fire they give off a fume, then they generate flame, and finally deposit ash.

10. In close, compact bodies containing a watery humour that shuns flame (as are laurel leaves, other non-porous bodies, salts and so on) the process of opening up goes like this: the crude and watery spirit contained in them dilated by fire, is given off noisily before flame is generated. But if in any body (and this seldom occurs) the outbreak of wind and generation of flame happen simultaneously, a great commotion is stirred up and a mighty dilatation, with the wind, like bellows within, blowing out and expanding the flame on all sides, as in gunpowder.

11. Bread in the oven swells a certain amount, though this makes it lighter than before. Sometimes too at the top of the loaf a bubble or

vesica crustæ; ut cavum quiddam aere impletum maneat inter pelliculam illam crustæ, (quæ exscindi solet) & massam panis.

12. Etiam *Carnes assatæ* nonnihil tument, præsertim si maneat *Epidermis*, ut in *porcellis.*

5 13. At *fructus assati* quandoque exiliunt, ut *Castaneæ*; quandoque
[D2ʳ] effringunt corticem, & emit¹tunt pulpam, ut *Poma*: quod si ab Igne magis torrefiant, asciscunt crustam carbonariam, ut cavum sit quiddam (ut in Pane) inter crustam & Carnem Fructus; quod & fit in *Ovis.*

14. Si vero *Calor* sit lenis & cæcus, nec detur spiraculum facile ad
10 emittendum *vaporem*, ut fit in pyris sub cinere assatis, & multo magis in iis quæ reponuntur in ollis, atque deinde sub cinere sepeliuntur, atque similiter in Carnibus suffocatis, vel intra crustas panis, vel inter patinas; tum *Tumor* ille & *dilatatio* per *calorem* repellitur, & in se vertitur, atque tanquam in *Distillatione* restituitur, & reddit *Corpora* magis humectata,
15 & tanquam mersa in succis suis.

15. At in *Aridis*, si *Flamma* fuerit suffocata, nec facilem reperiat exitum, rarefiunt *Corpora*, & redduntur cava & porosa, ut in *Carbonibus* è ligno, & *Pumicibus* quæ ejiciuntur ex *montibus flammantibus.*

Connexio.

20 Transeundum jam esset ad *Dilatationes* & *Aperturas Corporum* quæ fiunt per *Calorem* in *Distillationibus*; in quibus magis accurate datur cernere hujusmodi *Aperturas*, quam in *Coctionibus* & *Vstionibus.* Verum cum in illis immorari haud parum oporteat, cumque proprie pertineat *Inquisitio* ipsarum ad *Titulos* de *Calido*
[D2ᵛ] 25 & *Frigido*, & ¹ de *Motu Hyles*, & de *Separationibus*; exiguum quiddam est quod proponi debet in hoc *Titulo.*

Dilatationes per calorem externum in distillationibus.

[Monita.]

1. Duplex est *Dilatatio*, sive *Apertura*, sive *Attenuatio Corporum*,
30 in *Distillationibus.* Altera in transitu, cum *Corpus* vertitur in Vaporem aut Fumum, (qui postea restituitur); altera in *Corpore*

27 *Dilatationes*] / see *tn* to C1ʳ (p. 74 above)   28 [*Monita.*]] / the paras following seem to be monita rather than an historia and certainly nothing that should be set in the anomalously large type used here
31 restituitur);] ~;)

blister gathers, so that a certain hollow filled with air if left between the skin of the crust (which is usually cut off) and the rest of the loaf.

12. Meats roasted also swell to a degree, especially if the skin is kept on, as in sucking-pigs.

13. But fruits roasted sometimes jump up, as chestnuts do; sometimes they burst their rinds and give ˡ out their pulp, like apples; but if they are further scorched they assume a crust of charcoal, so that there is a certain hollow (as in bread) between the crust and the meat of the fruit; and the same thing happens in eggs.

14. But if the heat be gentle and hidden, and no ready outlet is available for vapour to escape—as happens in pears roasted beneath ashes and much more in things put in pots and then buried in ashes, and likewise in meats cooked *en croûtes* or in pans—then the swelling and dilatation caused by the heat is kept down and turned back on itself and, as in distillation, it is reconstituted, and it makes the bodies more moist and as it were steeped in their own juices.

15. But in dry bodies, if the flame is stifled and finds no easy way out, the bodies are rarefied and made hollow and porous, as in charcoal and the pumice-stones thrown out from the mountains that erupt with flame.

Connection

Now we must move on to the dilatations and openings up of bodies which come about by heat in distillations, in which we can see these openings up more precisely than in cooking and burning. But as these things deserve to be meditated upon for a good while, and as the inquiry into them properly belongs to the titles of Hot and Cold, ˡ Motion of Hyle, and Separation, there is no need to say much about it in this one.

Dilatations by external heat in distillations

[*Advice*]

1. Whether it be an opening up or an attenuation, the dilatation of bodies in distillations is of a double nature: the one in the passing over, when the body is turned into a vapour or fume (which is afterwards turned back again); the other in the body

restituto, quod semper tenuius est, & magis subtile & expansum, & minus materiatum quam *Corpus* crudum, ex quo distillatum emanavit. *Aqua* enim *Rosacea* (exempli gratia) est *succo Rosarum* tenuius, & minus ponderosum.

5   2. *Distillationes* omnes fiunt ex *Æstu* quodam sive *Reciprocatione Rarefactionis* primo, & versionis in *pneumaticum*; dein *Condensationis*, & *Restitutionis* in *Corpus tangibile*, remittente se Calore, & Vapore repercusso.

3. In *Distillationibus*, actiones *Dilatationis* & *Condensationis* 10 non sunt sinceræ; sed intervenit actio illa (quæ maxime est intentionalis in Practica) *separationis Partium heterogenearum*; ut *succi veri, phlegmatis; Aquæ, Olei; partis tenuioris, partis crassioris.*

[D3ʳ] |4. In *Distillationibus* optime inquiritur & decernitur de *gradibus* & *diversitatibus Calorum*; ut *Carbonum, Furni calefacti,* 15 *Balnei, Cinerum, Arenæ calidæ, Fimi, Solis, Ignis quiescentis, Ignis follibus excitati, Ignis conclusi & reverberati, Caloris ascendentis, Caloris descendentis,* & hujusmodi: Quæ omnia ad *Aperturas Corporum,* & præcipue ad complicatas actiones *dilatandi* & *contrahendi* (de quibus postea dicemus) insigniter faciunt. Neque 20 tamen ullo modo videntur *calores* illi Imitatores *caloris Solis* & *Cælestium*; cum nec satis lenes sint & temperati, nec satis lenti & continuati, nec satis refracti & modificati per corpora media, nec satis inæqualiter accedentes & recedentes. De quibus omnibus, sub *Titulo Calidi* & *Frigidi,* & *Titulis* aliis ad hoc propriis, 25 diligenter inquiremus.

5. Distillationes & Dilatationes per eas fiunt in clauso, ubi concluduntur simul *corpus distillandum,* & *vapores* qui ex eo emittuntur, & *Aer.* Neque tamen in *stillatoriis* & *Alembicis* communibus diligenter arcetur *Aer* exterior; quin per Rostrum 30 *Stillatorii,* per quod *liquor* effluit, ille subintrare aliquatenus possit. At in *retortis,* ubi majore vehementia *caloris* opus est, non [D3ᵛ] datur *Aeri* ex|teriori ingressus; sed Os Receptaculi Ori vasis (ubi corpus imponitur) per *Lutationes* ita continuatur, ut universus processus Rarefactionis & Restitutionis intus transigatur. Quod si

---

12 *phlegmatis*;] ~,   *Olei*;] ~, / in this and the preceding item the punctuation in *c-t* (followed in *SEH* (II, p. 272)) is misleading: the clause is not a plain six-item list but three axiological antitheses   19 dicemus)] ~,)

turned back, which is often thinner, more subtle and expanded and less materiate than the crude body from which the distillate emanated. For instance rose water is a thinner, lighter body than the juice of roses.

2. All distillations work by a certain tidal motion or reciprocation, of rarefaction to begin with and turning into a pneumatic body, and then of condensation, and turning back into a tangible body once the heat has eased off and the vapour been driven back.

3. In distillations, the actions of dilatation and condensation are not simple, for (and this is very much to the purpose in practical applications) the action of separation of heterogeneous parts intervenes—as of pure juice from phlegm, water from oil, the thinner parts from the grosser.

⌐4. In distillations it is very important to look into and determine the degrees and varieties of heat, as of coals, a hot oven, a bath, ashes, hot sand, dung, the Sun, fire undisturbed, fire stimulated by bellows, fire shut in and reverberated, heat rising, heat sinking and the like. For all of these things contribute enormously to the openings up of bodies, and especially to the interwoven actions of dilating and contracting (which I shall speak of later). Yet these heats do not seem in any way to ape that of the Sun and the heavenly bodies, since they are neither gentle and temperate enough, nor sufficiently slow and continued, nor refracted enough and modified by bodies intervening, nor sufficiently variable in their approaches and retreats. And we shall look carefully into all these matters under the title of Hot and Cold, and other titles suitable to them.

5. Distillations and through them dilatations take place in closed vessels where the body to be distilled, the vapours given out by it and the air are all shut up together. Yet in ordinary stills and alembics the outside air is not carefully kept out but it can get in to some degree via the beak of the still which lets the liquor get out. But in retorts, where we need heat of greater intensity, the outside air is given ⌐ no way in, but the mouth of the receptacle is joined so snugly by luting to the mouth of the vessel (where the body is put) that the whole process of rarefaction and restitution

corpus sit plenum *spiritu vigoroso,* (ut *vitriolum*), opus est *Receptaculo* vasto & amplo, ut *vapores* liberius ludant, nec vas infringant.

Mandata.

5 1. Utcunque tamen *Distillationes* tanquam intra cellam undiquaque clausam transigantur; datur tamen spatium, ut corporis aliæ partes se expandere in *Vapores,* aliæ subsidere in *Fæcibus, Vapores* rursus se glomerare & restituere, atque (si heterogenei fuerint) alii ab aliis se *separare* possint. Quod sequitur igitur, pro *Mandato magno* habendum,
10 cum ad *Naturam* in imis concutiendam, & ad novas *Transformationes* aditum præbere possit. *Vulcanus* enim *Chymicorum* & *Medicorum,* (licet multa utilia genuerit), tamen virtutes veriores *caloris* fortassis minus complexus est, ob Divortia & Separationes partium, quæ in operationibus ipsorum semper interveniunt. Itaque *summa Rei* quam
15 mandamus huc spectat; ut illa *separatio* & *Reciprocatio Rarefactionis* & *Condensationis* omnino prohibeatur, atque opus Caloris intra corpus ipsum atque ejus claustra vertatur: hoc enim fortasse Proteum Materiæ
[D4^r] per Manicas constrictum tenebit, & se versiones suas experiͥri & expedire compellet. De hoc complura nobis in mentem veniunt, & alia
20 reperiri possunt. Proponemus Exemplum unum aut alterum ex facillimis, ad hoc tantum, ut percipi possit quid velimus.

2. Accipe *Vas quadratum Ferri,* in *Figura Cubi,* habeatque *Latera* bene fortia & crassa. Impone *Cubum ligni* ad Mensuram *vasis* ad amussim factum, quique illud prorsus impleat. Superponatur *Operculum Ferri*
25 non minus forte quam Latera Vasis; & lutetur optime, more Chymicorum, ita ut clausissimum, & *Ignem* tolerare possit. Deinde ponatur *Vas intra prunas,* atque ita permittatur ad *horas aliquas.* Post amoveatur *Operculum;* & vide quid factum sit de *Ligno.* Nobis quidem videtur, (cum prohibita plane fuerint *Inflammatio* & *Fumus,* quo minus
30 *pneumaticum* & *humidum ligni* emitti potuerint), alterum ex his eventurum; vel ut *Corpus ligni* vertatur in *quoddam Amalgma;* vel ut solvatur in *Aerem,* sive *pneumaticum* purum, simul cum *Fæcibus,* (magis crassis quam sunt cineres) in Fundo, & *Incrustatione* nonnulla in *Lateribus vasis.*

---

1 *vitriolum*),] ~,)   12 genuerit), tamen] genuerit, tamen) / cf. *tn* to G1^v–G2^r (p. 156 below)   30 potuerint),] ~,)

is carried on inside. But if the body is full of a vigorous spirit (like vitriol) we need a hugely capacious receptacle so that the vapours can have freer play and not break the vessel.

Directions

1. Nevertheless no matter how we carry out distillations as in a cell enclosed on all sides, there is still enough room for some parts of the body to expand into vapours, for others to sink down in dregs and again for the vapours to concentrate and turn back again, and (if they be heterogeneous) for some to separate themselves from the others. So the following direction can be regarded as one of great significance since it can open the door to stirring nature to its depths and to new transformations. For the Vulcan of the chemists and physicians (though it has produced many useful things) has nevertheless failed to embrace the truer virtues of heat, because of the divorces and separations of parts which always intervene in their operations. Therefore the nub of the direction comes down to this: that the separation and reciprocation of rarefaction and condensation be completely prohibited and the work of heat be applied within the body and its confines; for perhaps this will keep the Proteus of matter in handcuffs and force it to act ¹ the contortionist and get free that way. In this connection many instances come into my mind and yet more can be discovered. But I shall give just one or two of the easiest examples, and only for the sake of making clear what I mean.

2. Take a square container of iron, in the form of a cube with strong, thick sides. Put a wooden cube in it, a cube made to the precise measure and which completely fills it. Put an iron lid on top no less strong than the sides of the container, and seal it up as well as you can in the manner of the chemists, so that it is as tight as a drum and can withstand the fire. Then put the container among the coals and leave it there for some hours. Next remove the lid and see what has happened to the wood. Now since flame and fume were completely suppressed and for that reason no pneumatic or moist part of the wood could have been given off, it seems to me that one of these two things must have happened: either that the body of the wood will change into a sort of amalgam, or that it would dissolve into air or a pure pneumatic body, together with dregs (thicker than ashes) at the bottom of the vessel and some encrustation around the sides.

3. In simili *Vase* ferreo fiat *Experimentum* de *Aqua pura*; qua repleatur ad summum. Sed adhibeatur Ignis lenior; Mora vero sit amplior. Quinetiam amoveatur ab igne certis horis, & refrigescat; dein iteretur *Operatio* aliquoties. Hoc *Experimentum* de *Aqua* pura delegimus hanc ob 5 causam; quod *Aqua* corpus simplicissimum sit, expers Coloris, Odoris, Saporis, & aliarum Qualitatum. Quamobrem, si per *calorem* [D4ᵛ] temperatum & leǀnem, & alternationem *Calefactionis* & *Refrigerationis*, & prohibitionem omnis *Evaporationis, spiritus Aquæ* non emissus, & nihilominus per hujusmodi Calorem sollicitatus & attenuatus, se 10 verterit in partes Aquæ crassiores, easque ita digerere, & in novum schematismum mutare possit, (minus scilicet simplicem, & magis inæqualem), eo usque, ut vel colorem alium nanciscatur, vel odorem, vel saporem, vel Oleositatem quandam, vel aliam *Alterationem* notabilem, (qualis invenitur in *Corporibus compositis*), procul-dubio res magna 15 confecta foret, & ad plurima aditum patefaciens.

4. Circa Distillationem clausam, (ita enim eam appellare licet, ubi non datur spatium ad Evaporationem), quivis multa alia poterit comminisci. Pro certo enim habemus, *Calorem analogum*, operantem in *corpus* absque *separatione* aut *consumptione partium*, mirabiles 20 Metaschematismos effingere & producere posse.

5. Attamen illud addi possit, ut *Mandati* hujus Appendix; ut excogitetur etiam aliquis modus, (quod certe difficile non est), per quem *Calor* operetur non solum in *Clauso*, sed in *Tensili*: id quod fit in omni *Matrice naturali*, sive *vegetabilium*, sive *Animalium*. Hoc enim 25 operationem ad multa extendit, quæ per *clausuram simplicem* effici non possunt. Neque hoc pertinet ad *Pygmæum Paracelsi*, aut hujusmodi prodigiosas ineptias; sed ad solida & sana. Exempli gratia, non efficiet unquam Distillatio clausa, ut *Aqua* tota vertatur in *Oleum*: quia *Oleum*, [D5ʳ] & *pinguia*, majus occupant dimensum ǀ quam *Aqua*. At si *Operatio* fiat 30 in *Tensili*, hoc fortasse fieri possit: Quæ esset res immensæ utilitatis, cum omnis *Alimentatio* maxime consistat in *pingui*.

6. Bonum esset, & ad multa utile, ut in *Distillationibus, Natura* ad rationes reddendas quandoque compelleretur; atque ut poneretur in certo, quantum per *Distillationem* consumptum fuerit, id est, versum in 35 *pneumaticum*; & quid maneret, sive fixum, sive restitutum in *Corpore*. Id fieri potest, si ante *Distillationem* corpus *distillandum* ponderes, & vasa ipsa intra quæ *Distillatio* perficitur. At post *Distillationem* ponderabis *Liquorem*; ponderabis item *Fæces*; denique ponderabis iterum *vasa*. Ex

---

2 lenior;] ~:   12 inæqualem),] ~,)   14 *compositis*),] ~;)
17 Evaporationem),] ~,)   22 non est),] ~,)   27 gratia, non] gratia; Non

3. In an iron container of the same kind do the experiment with pure water up to the brim. But let the fire be gentler and the time longer; remove it from the fire at certain hours and cool it down, and then repeat the operation several times. Now I have chosen the experiment of pure water for this reason: that water is the simplest of bodies, lacking colour, smell, taste, and other qualities. And therefore, if the spirit of the water, ׀ subjected to a temperate and gentle heat, to alternation of heating and cooling, and to suppression of all evaporation, were not given off but were provoked and attenuated by heat of this sort to turn itself on the grosser parts of the water and could so dispose and change them into a new schematism (namely, one less simple and more unequal) until it either took on some colour, smell, taste, a kind of oiliness, or some other remarkable alteration (of the sort one finds in composite bodies), then no doubt an extraordinary thing would be accomplished, opening the way to many others.

4. Concerning closed distillation (for that is what I may be permitted to call it when no room is given for evaporation), any one will be able to think up many other trials. For I am convinced that suitable heat acting on a body without separation or consumption of the parts is capable of fashioning and producing marvellous metaschematisms.

5. But let me add as an appendix to this instruction that some means should also be thought up (and this certainly is not difficult) by which heat may work not just in a closed but in a tensile container, for this is what happens in all natural matrices be they vegetable or animal. For this stretches the operation to many things which simple enclosure cannot do. But this has to do not with Paracelsus' pygmies or any such prodigious nonsense but with things sensible and solid. For instance, no closed distillation will completely change water into oil, because oil and fat take up more room ׀ than water. But if the operation were performed in a tensible container, perhaps it could be done; and that would be something of enormous utility seeing that all alimentation is in the main based on fat.

6. It would be good and useful in lots of ways if, as in distillations, nature were sometimes forced to submit her accounts, and if it were established for certain how much was used up in distillation, i.e. was changed into a pneumatic body, and what remained, either fixed or changed back again in the body. This can be done if you weigh the body and the still before you start. But afterwards you will weigh the liquor, and also the dregs, and then the vessels again. For from these three

istis enim tribus *ponderationibus,* cognosces quantum fuerit *restitutum,* quantum manserit in *Fæcibus,* quantum *adhæserit vasibus,* atque à decessione ponderis in illis tribus, comparati ad *pondus Corporis* integri, cognosces quantum versum fuerit in *pneumaticum.*

5 *Connexio.*

Transeundum à *Dilatationibus* & *Rarefactionibus* quæ fiunt per *Calorem actualem,* ad Dilatationes & Relaxationes quæ fiunt per *Remissionem Frigoris* vehementis & intensi; quæ ipsa Remissio censeri debet pro calore comparato.

[D5ᵛ] 10 ¹*Dilatationes & Relaxationes corporum per remissionem frigoris.*

[*Historia.*]

1. Quæ per *Frigus vehemens* concreverunt, neque tamen eo usque, ut per moram *Frigoris* in *Densatione* sua fixa sint, ea absque *Calore manifesto,* & per *Remissionem* tantum *Frigoris,* se aperiunt & restituunt; ut fit in 15 *Glacie, Grandine, Nive.* Sed hoc faciunt per *calorem* manifestum admotum multo celerius.

2. Verum *Delicatoria,* quorum vigor consistit in *spiritu nativo subtili,* ut *Poma, Pyra,* Granata, & similia, si semel fuerint congelata, *suffocato spiritu,* non recipiunt postea pristinum vigorem.

20 3. At *Vinum* & *Cervisia* per gelu ad gustum languescunt, nec vigent; attamen, succedentibus Regelationibus, & *Tempestatibus Australibus,* reviviscunt & relaxantur, & quasi denuo fervescunt.

Connexio.

Transeundum à *Dilatationibus* quæ fiunt per *Calorem externum* 25 *actualem,* atque etiam per *Remissionem Frigoris,* (quæ, ut jam diximus, est *Calor comparatus*) ad *Dilatationes Corporum* quæ fiunt per *Calores potentiales,* sive *spiritus auxiliares* alterius Corporis applicati & admoti.

---

11 [*Historia.*]] / in *c-t* this stands before the previous heading; see *tn* to C1ʳ (p. 74 above)

weighings you will know how much has been restored, how much has stayed behind as dregs and how much has stuck to the vessels; and from the shortfall in the weight of these three compared with the weight of the whole body, you will know how much has turned into a pneumatic body.

Connection

We must now pass from Dilatations and Rarefactions caused by actual heat to Dilatations & Relaxations caused by the remission of bitter and intense cold, which remission should itself be taken for relative heat.

¹*Dilatations and Relaxations of bodies by remission of cold*

[*History*]

1. Things caused to set by bitter cold, yet not so much that they have become fixed in their densation by the persistence of the cold, open themselves up and return to their original condition merely by the remission of cold and without manifest heat, as happens in ice, hail and snow. But they do this much more quickly when they are exposed to manifest heat.

2. But more delicate things—as apples, pears, pomegranates and the like—whose vigour consists in a subtle native spirit, do not afterwards recover their former vigour once they have been frozen, as the spirit has been stifled.

3. But in the cold wine and beer lose their taste and activity yet, in the following thaw and south winds, they come back to life, relax and practically start fermenting again.

Connection

We must now go on from dilatations caused by actual external heat and also by remission of cold (which, as I have already said, is a relative heat) to dilatations of bodies caused by potential heats or the auxiliary spirits of another body applied and brought near.

[D6ʳ]   ¹*Dilatationes corporum quæ fiunt per calorem potentialem,*
        sive per spiritus auxiliares alterius corporis.

[*Historia.*]

De *Caloribus potentialibus*, consule *Tabulas Medicinales Qualitatum*
5 *secundarum*; & ex his poteris excerpere ea quæ operantur super *corpus*
humanum per *Dilatationem*: Quæ sunt fere illa quæ sequuntur.
    Confortantia, quæ dilatant spiritus oppressos.
    Abstergentia, quæ roborant virtutem expulsivam.
    Aperientia quoad orificia venarum & vasorum.
10   *Aperientia* quoad poros & meatus partium.
    Digerentia cum maturatione.
    Digerentia cum discussione.
    Caustica.
    Hæc præcipue (sunt & alia) habent Radicem in *Dilatatione spirituum*,
15 & *Humorum*, & *Succorum*, & *Substantiæ*, in corpore, per *spiritus*
auxiliares; necnon per *complexionem tangibilem*, quæ inest Medicinis
illis, vel interius vel exterius sumptis.

Commentatio.

Patet in *vitro Calendari*, quam exquisito sensu, sive perceptione,
20 præditus sit *Aer communis* Calidi & Frigidi; utpote, quæ tam
[D6ᵛ] subtiles ejus differentias & Gradus statim di¦judicare possit. Nec
dubito, quin perceptio Spiritus Animalibus vivis versus calorem &
frigus sit adhuc longe acutior: nisi quod *Aer* sit *pneumaticum*
purum & sincerum, & nihil habeat *Tangibilis* admisti; at
25 *spirituum* perceptio retundatur & hebetetur *Corpore tangibili* in
quo sunt devincti. Attamen, non obstante hoc Impedimento,
videntur adhuc *spiritus vivorum* potiores ipso Aere, quoad hanc
perceptionem. Neque enim hactenus nobis constat, quod *Calor*
potentialis (de quo jam loquimur) *Aerem* possit dilatare; cum
30 certum sit, quod hoc faciat super *spiritus* in *Animalium membris*
contentos; ut in Qualitatibus (quas diximus) secundis
Medicinarum liquet. Sed de hoc inquiratur paulo accuratius, ex
Mandato proxime sequente.

3 [*Historia.*]] / see *tn* to C1ʳ (p. 74 above)
14 alia)] ~,)

[|]Dilatations of bodies caused by potential heat,
or the auxiliary spirits of another body

[*Historia*]

On potential heats consult the tables listing the secondary qualities of medicines, and pick out from these the ones which work on the human body by dilatation, practically all of which are given below.

Cordials, which dilate oppressed spirits.

Abstergents, which strengthen the expulsive virtue.

Aperients in respect of the mouths of the veins and vessels.

Aperients in respect of the pores and passages of the parts.

Digestives with maturation.

Digestives with dispersal.

Caustics.

These in particular (and there are others) are rooted in the dilatation of the spirits, humours, juices and substance in the body by auxiliary spirits as well as by the tangible complexion present in these medicines, be they taken internally or externally.

Speculation

It is evident from the calendar glass what a fine sense or perception of hot and cold ordinary air is endowed with, as it can at once pick up such subtle differences and [|] degrees of them. Nor can it be doubted that the spirit in living animals has a far sharper perception of heat and cold, save that air is a pure and clear pneumatic body with no admixture of tangible matter, while the perception of the spirits is blunted and numbed by the tangible body in which they are trapped. However, this obstacle notwithstanding, and as far as this perception is concerned, the spirits of living things seem to be more effective than the air itself. For so far it is not apparent to me that potential heat (which I am speaking of now) can dilate the air, while it is certain that it can do that to the spirits contained in the members of animals, as is evident (as I have said) in the secondary qualities of medicines. But look into this a little more precisely on the lines of the direction given immediately below.

Mandata.

1. Accipe duo *Vitra Calendaria* ejusdem magnitudinis. Impone in altero *Aquam*, in altero *spiritum vini*, fortem & acrem; atque ita calefiant *vitra*, ut *Aqua* & *spiritus vini* ad parem altitudinem ascendant. Colloca ea
5 simul, & dimitte per spatium aliquod; & nota, si *Aqua* deveniat altior quam *spiritus vini*. Nam si hoc fit, palam est calorem spiritus vini potentialem *Aerem* dilatasse, ita ut spiritum vini depresserit.

[D7ʳ] ¹2. Possit esse res varii usus, si *Operationes secundarum qualitatum medicinalium* probentur interdum, & exerceantur in *corporibus* vitæ
10 expertibus. Licet enim dubium non sit, plerasque earum nullius prorsus effectus fore, quoniam requiritur plane *spiritus vivus* ad eas actuandas, ob *Operationis subtilitatem*: aliæ tamen procul-dubio super nonnulla *Corpora Inanimata* operabuntur. Videmus enim quid possit *sal* in *Carnibus*, *Aromata* in *Cadaveribus*, *Coagulum* in *Lacte*, *Fermentum* in
15 *Pane*, & hujusmodi. Inserviet igitur diligentia *Medicorum* circa *qualitates secundas*, ad instruendas complures alias *Operationes*, si animum advertas cum judicio: id semper supponens, quod virtus fortior requiritur ad operandum super *corpus mortuum*, quam *vivum*.

Connexio.

20 Transeundum ad *Dilatationes corporum* quæ fiunt per *Liberationem spirituum*, refractis nimirum ergastulis partium crassiorum, quæ illos arcte detinuerant, ut se dilatare non possent. In *Corporibus* enim quæ habent arctam compagem, atque naturæ integralis nexibus fortiter devincta sunt, non exequuntur *spiritus*
25 opus suum *Dilatationis*, nisi fiat prius *Solutio Continui* in *partibus crassioribus*; vel per *Liquores fortes* erodentes, & stimulantes
[D7ᵛ] tantum, vel per eosdem cum *Caˡlore*. Atque hoc cernitur in *Aperturis*, & *Dissolutionibus Metallorum*, de quibus nunc (ut in reliquis) pauca proponemus.

---

6 palam est] ~,

Directions

1. Take two calendar glasses of the same size. Put water in the one and spirit of wine strong and sharp in the other, and so heat the glasses that the water and spirit climb to the same height. Put them together and leave them for a while and see if the water stands higher than the spirit of wine. For if that is what happens it is obvious that the potential heat of the spirit of wine has dilated the air so as to push down the spirit of wine.

ˡ2. It could be useful in various ways if the operations of the secondary qualities of medicines were in the meantime tried out on and administered to lifeless bodies. For although it is certain that most of them would have no effect whatever—because a living spirit is obviously needed to trigger them by reason of the subtlety of their operation—others will nevertheless work upon some inanimate bodies. For we see what salt can do in meats, spices in corpses, rennet in milk, yeast in bread, and so on. Thus if you consider it judiciously, the physicians' diligence in the matter of secondary qualities will serve for planning many other operations, always bearing in mind that a stronger virtue is needed for working on a dead body than on a living.

Connection

We must pass on to dilatations of bodies caused by liberation of the spirits when they evidently break out of the jails of the grosser parts which had kept them in close confinement and so stopped them dilating. For in bodies with a tight structure and strongly bound together by the ties of the integral nature, the spirits do not perform their work of dilatation, unless solution of continuity in the grosser parts be brought about first, either by corrosive and pricking strong liquors by themselves, or by the same together with ˡ heat. And we see this in the openings up and dissolutions of metals, about which I shall now (as in the rest) set down a few details.

Dilatationes corporum per liberationem spirituum suorum.

[*Historia.*]

1. Accipe pondus *Auri puri* ad Denarium 1 in parvas bracteolas redacti, quæ etiam manu lacerari possint.

5   2. Accipe etiam pondus 4 Den. *Aquæ Regis;* & mittantur simul in *vitrum.* Tum ponatur *vitrum* super Foculum, in quo sit ignis prunarum modicus & lenis. Paulo post insurgunt Arenulæ quædam, aut Grana; quæ deinde, post parvam moram, se diffundunt, & incorporantur cum *Aqua;* ut *Aqua* efficiatur, *Aqua* tanquam *Electrica, splendida,* & veluti
10   *Croco tincta. Dissolutio* autem *Auri* per *Aquam* in quantitatibus prædictis fit tantum ad tertias. Neque enim *Aqua* oneratur ulterius; adeo ut, si dissolvere cupis totum pondus illud *Auri* Den. 1. opus sit effundere portionem in qua solutio facta est, & super infundere de novo pondus simile 4. Den. *Aquæ Regis,* & sic tertio. Ista Dissolutio fit leniter &
15   placide modico Igne, absque Fumis, & sine *calefactione vitri,* alia quam per Ignem.

3. Accipe *Argenti vivi* in corpore pondus ad placitum, duplum *Aquæ Fortis:* ponito simul in vitro, neque ea ad ignem omnino admove.
[D8ʳ] Atta⌐men paulo post insurget intra corpus Aquæ instar pulveris
20   tenuissimi, & intra spatium horæ, absque igne, absque fumis, absque tumultu, vertetur corpus commistum in aquam bene claram.

4. Accipe *Plumbum* in *lamellis* ad pond. Den. 1. *Aquæ fortis* ad pond. Den. 9. Non fit bona Incorporatio, ut in aliis *Metallis;* sed *Aqua* demittit majorem partem *Plumbi* in calce ad *Fundum Vitri,* manente aqua
25   perturbata, sed vergente ad diaphanum.

5. Accipe *Argenti* in lamellis, sive bracteolis, pondus Den. 1. *Aqu. fortis* pond. Den. 4. pone super Foculum, in Vitro, cum igne lento. Insurgit *Argentum* in arenis, aut bullulis, intra corpus Aquæ, majoribus paulo quam *Aurum;* deinde incorpora[n]tur cum Aqua, & vertuntur simul in
30   Liquorem tenuem, sed album, & quasi lacteum. Sed postquam paulisper residerit liquor, & refrixerit, ejaculantur (sive hoc emanet ex *Metallo,* sive

---

1 *Dilatationes*] / *SEH* (II, p. 278) has LATATIONES   2 [*Historia.*]] / in *c-t* this stands before the previous heading; see *tn* to C1ʳ (p. 74 above)   5 *Regis*] / in connection with the acid Bacon prefers the genitive of rex to the adjectival form regia   31 residerit] / *c-t* agrees with *HDR(M)* (fo. 16ʳ) but is silently *nld* in *SEH* (II, p. 278) perhaps to comply with the form resederit which occurs on p. 112, ll. 2 and 10 below. I have let the *c-t* forms stand: Bacon was probably not meaning to distinguish between resido and resideo but using (proper) alternative future perfects of resido

3 Denarium 1] ~.   5 4] ~.

Dilatations of bodies by the liberation of their spirits

[*History*]

1. Take a pennyweight of pure gold in small leaves which can also be torn by hand.

2. Also take four pennyweights of aqua regia and put them in a glass with the gold. Then put the glass on a moderate and gentle coal fire. Soon afterwards certain specks or grains rise up which soon diffuse themselves and are incorporated with the water so that the water is made as if it were amber, bright, and as if dyed with saffron. But only a third of the gold is dissolved by the water in the quantities mentioned. For the water will not be loaded up with any more, so that if you want to dissolve the lot you must pour away the portion in which the solution was made and pour in a fresh four pennyweights of aqua regia, and then do the same again a third time. This dissolution takes place slowly and gently with a moderate fire, without fumes or heating of the glass, apart from that provided by the fire.

3. Take quicksilver in a body of whatever weight, and twice the amount of aqua fortis, put them in a glass together but nowhere near a fire. [1] All the same in a short while the body of the water will rise up like a very fine powder and, in an hour's time the mixed body will, without fire, fumes or commotion, turn into an agreeably clear water.

4. Take a pennyweight of lead in strips and nine pennyweights of aqua fortis. The incorporation is not as good as in other metals, but the water deposits the greater part of the lead as a lime at the bottom of the glass, leaving the water troubled but tending to transparency.

5. Take a pennyweight of silver in strips or leaves and four pennyweights of aqua fortis and put them in a glass on a brazier with a slow fire. The silver rises within the body of the water in specks or little bubbles a bit bigger than the ones you get with gold; then they are incorporated with the water and both together are turned into a thin liquor but white and almost milky. But, after the liquor has settled and cooled down for a little while, icy splinters (coming either from the metal, the

ex *Aqua*, sive ex utroque) Fragmina glacialia intra corpus *Aquæ*;
postquam autem per moram longiorem penitus resederit, clarificat se
liquor, & devenit clarus & crystallinus, demissa glacie in Fundum.
Sustinet *Aqua* onerationem, qualem in *Auro*, & fit dissolutio simili fere
5 calore, nec colligit calorem per motum magis quam *Aurum*.
    6. Accipe *Cuprum* in bracteolis ad pon. Den. 1. *Aq. Fortis* ad pond.
Den. 6. Mitte super Foculum. Insurget *Cuprum* in bullulis, sive arenulis,
[D8ᵛ] majoribus adhuc quam *Argentum*. Paulo post incorⁱporatur cum *Aqua*,
& corpus commistum vertitur in Liquorem cæruleum, turbidum; sed
10 postquam resederit, clarificat se *Ætheris* instar, in cæruleum, pulchrum,
& splendidum, demissis in fundum fæcibus instar pulveris, quæ tamen
ipsæ per moram imminuuntur, & ascendunt, & incorporantur. At Den.
illi 6 *Aq. Fort.* solvunt Den. totum *Cupri*, ut sustineat se onerari Aqua
duplo plus quam in *Auro* & *Argento*. Concipit autem dissolutio *Cupri*
15 calorem manifestum, per tumultum interiorem, etiam antequam
admoveatur ad ignem.
    7. Accipe *Stannum* in bracteolis, ad pond. Den. 1. *Aquæ fort.* ad pond.
Den. 3. & vertitur totum *Metallum* in Corpus simile *Flori lactis*, aut
coagulo; nec facile se clarificat; & concipit sine igne calorem
20 manifestum.
    8. Accipe *Ferri* in laminis pond. Den.1. *Aquæ Fortis* pond. Den. 9; &
sine igne surgit *Ferrum* in magnis bullis, non tantum intra corpus *Aquæ*,
sed supra, adeo ut ebulliat extra os vitri, atque insuper emittat copiosum
& densum Fumum croceum; idque cum maximo tumultu, & calore
25 vehementissimo, & qualem manus non sustineat.

Monitum.

Dubium non est, quin vires variæ *Aquarum Fortium* diversorum
generum, & Modi *Ignis*, sive *Caloris*, qui adhibetur, istas *Aperturas* etiam
variare possint.

[E1ʳ] 30   ⁱ*Mandata.*

Qualis sit ista *Dilatatio Metallorum* per *Aperturas*, videndum: utrum sit
instar *Dilatationis Auri foliati*, quæ est *Pseudo-Rarefactio*, (ut mox
dicemus), quia corpus *dilatatur* potius *Loco* quam *substantia*, qualis
itidem est *Dilatatio pulverum*; an revera Corpus ipsum *Metallorum*

---

1 *Aquæ*,] ~:   33 dicemus),] ~,)

water, or both) are thrown up within the body of the water; but after a longer interval when it has settled completely, the liquor clarifies itself and becomes clear and crystalline, the ice having been sent to the bottom. The load the water will bear is the same as for gold, and the dissolution takes place with about the same heat, and it does not gather heat by motion any more than gold does.

6. Take one pennyweight of copper leaf and six of aqua fortis. Put them on a brazier. The copper will rise in small bubbles or specks, yet still bigger than those of silver. Shortly afterwards it is incor|porated with the water and the mixed body turns into a liquor blue and opaque, but once it has settled down it clarifies itself into something bright, blue and beautiful like the ether, the dregs being deposited like a powder at the bottom; and yet these very dregs get smaller with time and rise up and are incorporated. Thus those six pennyweights of aqua fortis dissolve the pennyweight of copper completely, so that the water can bear to be laden with twice as much as is the case with gold and silver. But the dissolution of copper generates evident heat by internal commotion even before it is moved to the fire.

7. Take one pennyweight of tin leaf and three pennyweights of aqua fortis, and the whole amount of the metal is turned into a body resembling cream or rennet; it does not easily clarify itself and generates manifest heat without the presence of fire.

8. Take a pennyweight of iron sheeting and nine pennyweights of aqua fortis and, in the absence of fire, the iron rises up in large bubbles, not just within the body of the water but above, to the extent that it foams up out of the mouth of the glass and gives off abundant and dense yellow fumes; and it does that with an extremely violent commotion and with heat so very fierce that you cannot touch it.

Advice

No doubt the different powers of various kinds of strong waters, and of the type of fire or heat which is brought to bear, can also cause these openings up to vary.

| Directions

Look into the nature of the dilatation of metals by opening up, and see whether it is like the dilatation of gold leaf which, because the body dilates rather in the room it occupies than in substance, is, like the

dilatetur in *substantia*. Hoc hujusmodi experimento probari potest.
Pondera *Argentum vivum*; excipe etiam modulum ejus in situla: pondera
similiter *Aquam fortem*, & excipe modulum ejus in altera situla: deinde,
dissolve & incorpora ea, modo supradicto: postea, pondera
5 incorporatum, & immitte illud etiam in duas illas situlas, & nota, si
pondus & mensura *Compositi*, ad pondus & mensuram *Simplicium* juste
respondeat. Delegimus autem *Argentum vivum* ad experimentum, quia
minor est suspicio alicujus consumptionis, cum fiat *Dissolutio* sine igne.

Videndum (obiter) utrum Dissolutio *Argenti vivi* lapides
10 ponderosissimos, aut fortasse stannum, sustineat, ut innatent. Etenim ex
rationibus Ponderum hoc colligi potest. Neque hoc pertinet ad
Miraculum & Imposturam, sed ad investigandam naturam *Misturarum*,
ut suo Titulo apparebit.

Observatio.

15 Notatu etiam dignum est, (licet non sit præsentis *inquisitionis*),
[E1ᵛ] omnia *Metalla*, ¹ licet sint *Aquis* in quibus dissolvuntur insigniter
graviora, tamen, in actu primo *Dissolutionis*, ascendere in Arenulis
vel Bullis. Atque eo magis hoc notandum est, quod ubi non
admovetur *Ignis*, ut in *Argento vivo*, idem faciant.

20 ## *Commentatio.*

Tumultus intra partes corporis inter dissolvendum, istam
Ascensionem causat. Nam in vehementi Erosione Corpora
impelluntur nonnihil motu locali; ut videre est in lapide parvo
glareoso, qui positus in Aceto forti, ad latera patellæ, (ut facilius
25 labatur) per vices gliscit, ut *Pisciculus*. Est & genus Lapidis, aut
Fossilis, quod immissum in Acetum irrequiete se agitat, & huc
illuc currit. At quæ sine impetu isto miscentur, (ut arbitror) nisi
quassata, non ascendunt: velut *saccharum* in fundo aquæ non
dulcificat in summo; nec *Crocus* colorat, nisi moveatur & agitetur.

15 *inquisitionis*),] ~,)

dilatation of powders, a pseudo-rarefaction (as I shall explain in a moment), or whether in reality the very body of the metals is dilated in substance. This can be tested by an experiment of this kind: weigh quicksilver and get its measure in a vessel; do the same with aqua fortis and get its measure in another vessel; then dissolve and incorporate them in the way mentioned above; afterwards weigh the incorporated body and put it in the two vessels as well, and note whether the weight and measure of the composite body corresponds fully to the weight and measure of the simple bodies. Now I have chosen to experiment with quicksilver for, since its dissolution takes place without fire, the risk of any consumption is slighter.

See, incidentally, whether a dissolution of quicksilver supports very heavy stones or perhaps tin, so that they float. For this may be gathered from their relative weights. And this has nothing to do with marvel or imposture but with the investigation of mixtures, as will appear under its own title.

Observation

It is also worth noting (though not in the present inquiry) that all metals, [1] though they be a lot heavier than the waters in which they are dissolved, nevertheless ascend in specks or bubbles in the first stage of dissolution. And this should be noted the more because the same thing happens in the absence of fire, as in quicksilver.

Speculation

The commotion within the parts of the body causes this frothing up when it is being dissolved. For when they are being violently eaten away, bodies are to a certain extent driven by local motion, as we see in pea gravel which, when it is put to the side of the vessel in strong vinegar (so that it can slide more easily), moves back and forth like a little fish. Again, here is a type of stone or fossil that restlessly agitates itself when put in vinegar and scuttles about hither and thither. There are things which mix without this rushing about and ascend (as I think) only if they are shaken, as sugar at the bottom of the water does not sweeten the water at the top; and saffron does not colour it without being moved and shaken.

Connexio.

Transeundum ad aliud genus *Dilatationum*, quod etiam communi
[E2ʳ] vocabulo ¹ *Dissolutionum* (in aliquibus) nuncupatur. Fit autem ubi
Corpora versus alia corpora amica ruunt in amplexum; & si datur
5 copia, aperiunt se, ut illa introcipiant. Neque fit hæc *Apertura*
tumultuose, aut per penetrationem corporis ingredientis, (ut in
Aquis Fortibus), sed placide, & per Relaxationem Corporis
recipientis.

Dilatationes per amplexum & occursum corporis amici.

10 *Historia.*

1. *Saccharum*, & *Gummi* nonnulla, ut *Tragacanthum*, in *liquoribus*
infusa, solvuntur; laxant enim libenter (instar spongiarum) partes suas,
ad recipiendum *Liquorem*.
2. *Papyrus, Seta, Lana,* & hujusmodi porosa, *Liquoribus* immersa, aut
15 alias humectata, ita se aperiunt, ut deveniant magis mollia, lacerabilia, &
quasi putria.
3. *Gaudia subita*, ut ob nuntium bonum, aspectus ejus quod fuit in
desiderio, & similia, licet non corpus amplectantur, sed phantasiam
aliquam, nihilominus *spiritus Animalium* insigniter *dilatant*; idque
20 interdum cum periculo repentini *Deliquii*, aut *Mortis*. Simile facit
Imaginatio in Venereis.

[E2ᵛ] ¹*Mandatum.*

Cogitandum de inveniendis *Menstruis* substantiarum specialium:
videntur enim posse esse *Liquores* & Pulpæ, tantæ cum corporibus
25 determinatis sympathiæ, ut illis admotis, partes suas facile laxent, easque
libenter imbibant; seque per hoc in succis suis intenerent & renovent.
Hoc enim pertinet ad unum ex *Magnalibus Naturæ*: nempe, ut rerum
Humores maxime radicales refocillari, & *Nutritio ab extra* fieri possint, ut
in *Carnibus, Ossibus, Membranis, Lignis*, &c. Etiam in iis quæ operantur
30 per *Divulsionem* & *Penetrationem*, est *Sympathia*, sive *Conformitas*: *Aqua*

---

10 *Historia.*] / in *c-t* this stands before the previous heading; see *tn* to C1ʳ (p. 74
above)   17 aspectus] aspectum / emended thus in *SEH* (II, p. 281) with note to that
effect
7 *Fortibus*),] ~;)

Connection

We must pass on to another class of dilatations which, in common parlance, are also referred to in some cases as | dissolutions. Now this happens where bodies rush to embrace other friendly bodies and, if given the means, open up to take them inside themselves. This opening up does not take place with commotion or with the entering body penetrating it (as in strong waters), but calmly and with the receiving body relaxing.

Dilatations by the embrace and contact of a friendly body

History

1. Sugar and some gums (like tragacanth), infused in liquors, dissolve; for (like sponges) they willingly slacken their parts to take the liquor in.

2. Paper, animal hair, wool and suchlike porous bodies so open themselves up when immersed in liquors, or otherwise moistened, that they become softer, more easily torn and practically rotten.

3. Sudden joys, as you have with good news, on seeing something you have been longing for, and so forth, although they embrace not the body but only the fantasy, dilate the spirits of animals strikingly, and they sometimes do it enough to risk sudden fainting fits or death. The imagination does the same in sexual love.

| *Direction*

Give thought to discovering the menstruums of special substances; for it seems possible that these can be liquors or pulps which have such sympathy with determinate bodies that when the latter come near, they readily slacken their parts and drink them in with pleasure, and by this means make their juices tender and new. For this bears on one of the magnalia of nature, namely that the most radical humours of things can be rekindled and nourished from the outside, as for example in flesh, bones, membranes, timber, etc. There is sympathy or conformity even

fortis siquidem non solvit *Aurum*, ut nec *Aqua Regia* communis *Argentum*.

Connexio.

Transeundum ad *Dilatationes* per *Assimilationem* aut *Versionem*;
5 quando scilicet Corpus imperans & magis activum subigit corpus accommodum & obsequiosum, & magis passivum, ita ut illud in se plane vertat, seque ex eo multiplicet & renovet. Quod si *Corpus assimilans* sit tenuius & rarius quam *Corpus assimilatum*, manifestum est, *Assimilationem* fieri non posse absque *Dilatatione*.

[E3ʳ] 10 ¹*Dilatationes quæ fiunt per assimilationem, sive versionem in tenuius.*

Historia.

1. Aer, & maxime cum commotus est (ut in *Ventis*) lambit Humiditatem *Terræ*, eamque deprædatur, & in se vertit.

2. Processus *Desiccationis* in Lignis, *Herbis*, & hujusmodi tangibilibus,
15 non admodum duris aut obstinatis, fit per *Deprædationem Aeris*, qui spiritum in corpore evocat & exugit, & in se transubstantiat: Itaque tarde hoc fit in *oleosis* & *pinguibus*, quia *Spiritus* & *Humidum* ipsorum non sunt tam consubstantialia Aeri.

3. *Spiritus* in *Tangibilibus* (qualia diximus) deprædantur partes ipsas
20 crassiores Corporis in quo includuntur. Nam *spiritus* qui proximi sunt *Aeri*, ipsi *Aeri* obediunt, & exeunt cito; at qui in magis profundo corporis siti sunt, illi partes interiores adjacentes deprædantur, & novum inde *spiritum* gignunt, & secum copulant, ut una tandem exeant: unde fit in istis Corporibus, per ætatem & moram, *Diminutio Ponderis*; quod
25 fieri non posset, nisi pars aliqua non *pneumatica* in *pneumaticum* sensim verteretur. Nam spiritus jam factus in corpore non ponderat, sed levat pondus potius.

4. Multi *Tumores* in *Corporibus Animalium* discutiuntur absque suppuratione aut sanie, per insensilem *Transpirationem*, versi plane in
30 *pneumaticum*, & evolantes.

---

11 *Historia.*] / in *c-t* this stands before the previous heading; see *tn* to C1ʳ (p. 74 above)   21 in magis] / possibly a scribal or compositor's transposition; Bacon preferred magis in

12 commotus est] ~,

in things which operate by divulsion and penetration, for aqua fortis
does not dissolve gold, nor common aqua regia silver.

Connection

We must pass on to dilatations by assimilation or version, i.e.
when a dominant and more active body subdues a suitably
obsequious and more passive one, such that it quite changes it into
itself and multiplies and renews itself by it. But if the assimilating
body be thinner and rarer than the body assimilated, it is obvious
that assimilation can only take place with dilatation.

¹*Dilatations caused by assimilation or version into a thinner body*

History

1. Air, especially when it is stirred up (as in winds), sucks up the earth's
moisture, preys upon it and turns it into itself.

2. The process of desiccation in wood, plants and suchlike tangible
bodies which are not extremely hard and stubborn, comes about by pre-
dation of the air, which calls out the spirit in the body, sucks it up and
turns it into its own substance. Accordingly this happens slowly in oily
and fat bodies because their spirit and moisture are not so like the substance of the air.

3. The spirits in tangible bodies (such as I spoke of) prey on the actual
grosser parts of the body enclosing them. For the spirits adjacent to the
air obey the air itself and make a quick exit; but those spirits located
deeper within the body prey on the interior parts next to them and
thence generate new spirit which they combine with so that in the end
they depart together: and this brings about the weight loss in these bodies with age and time. And that could not happen unless some non-
pneumatic part were insensibly turned into pneumatic matter. For the
spirit already made in the body rather reduces its weight than adds to it.

4. Many swellings in the bodies of animals are dispersed without suppuration or purulence by gradual transpiration, the swellings having
been altogether turned into pneumatic matter and escaping.

[E3ᵛ]　¹5. *Esculenta flatuosa* gignunt Ventositates, succis suis versis in *Flatum*, & exeunt per Ructus & Crepitus; etiam partes internas extendunt, & torquent: Quod faciunt etiam Alimenta proba & laudata, quandoque, ob debilitatem *Functionum*.

5　　6. In omni *alimentato*, cum pars alimentata tenuior est *Alimento*, (ut *spiritus* atque *sanguis* per Arterias in Animalibus leviores sunt quam *Cibus* & *Potus*) necesse est ut *Alimentatio* inducat *Dilatationem*.

　　7. Omnium *Aperturarum, Dilatationum* & *Expansionum* maxima, quatenus ad analogiam inter corpus ante *Dilatationem* & post, 10　omniumque pernicissima, & quæ minima mora & brevissimo actu transigitur, est *Dilatatio oleosorum* & *inflammabilium* in *Flammam*; quod fit quasi affatim, & sine gradibus. Estque (quoad *Flammam* successivam) plane ex genere *Assimilationum*; multiplicante se *Flamma* super Fomitem suum.

15　　8. At quod potentissimum in hoc genere est, non ad velocitatem primæ *Inflammationis*, (nam *Pulvis pyrius* non tam cito inflammatur quam *Sulphur*, aut *Caphura*, aut Naphtha), sed ad successionem *Flammæ* semel conceptæ, & ad superandum ea quæ resistunt, est commistio illa expansionum in *Aerem* simul & in *Flammam* (de qua supra diximus) 20　quæ invenitur in *pulvere pyrio*, (ut liquet in *Bombardis* & *Cuniculis*).

　　9. Notant autem *Chymistæ*, etiam *Argenti Vivi* expansionem per ignem esse admodum violentam; quin & *Aurum* vexatum, & occlusum, [E4ʳ]　¹ quandoque potenter erumpere, cum periculo operantium.

Connexio.

25　Transeundum ad eas *Dilatationes*, vel *Distractiones* & *Divulsiones*, quæ fiunt, non ab Appetitu aliquo in corpore ipso quod dilatatur, sed per violentiam *Corporum externorum*, quæ, cum suis motibus prævaleant, necessitatem imponunt Corpori alicui ut *dilatetur* & *distrahatur*. Atque ista *Inquisitio* pertinet ad *Titulum* de *Motu* 30　*Libertatis*; sed, (ut in reliquis) aliquid de hoc, sed parce, & paucis, jam inquiremus. Iste autem *Motus* est plerunque geminus. Primo, Motus *Distractionis* à vi externa; deinde, *Motus Contractionis* vel *Restitutionis* à motu Corporis proprio: qui posterior *Motus* licet ad

17 Naphtha),]　~,)　　19 *Flammam*]　~,　　20 *Cuniculis*).]　~.)

ᴵ5. When their juices have been turned into wind, flatulent foods beget ventosities which escape by belch and fart; they also stretch and rack the innards, as tried and tested diets sometimes do too because of the weakness of the bodily functions.

6. In everything nourished alimentation necessarily induces dilatation, when the part nourished is more tenuous than the nourishment (as, for instance, arterial spirit and blood in animals are lighter than food and drink).

7. Of all openings up, dilatations and expansions, the greatest, as far as the resemblance between the body before and after dilatation is concerned, and the most rapid of all and the one which takes place with the least delay and by the shortest route, is the dilatation of oily and inflammable bodies into flame; for it happens pretty well at once and not by stages. Now this (in the case of successive flame) is obviously a species of assimilation, the flame multiplying itself over its fuel.

8. But the most powerful thing of this class—and not for the speed with which it catches fire (for gunpowder does not burst into flame as quickly as sulphur, camphor or naphtha) but for the succession of flame once generated, and for how it bears down what gets in its way—is the combined and simultaneous effect of expansions into air and flame (spoken of above) which we find in gunpowder (as we see in artillery and mines).

9. On the other hand, the chemists observe that the expansion of quicksilver by fire is also extremely violent; why even gold vexed and shut in ᴵ sometimes bursts out with fury, endangering the people working with it.

Connection

We must pass on to those dilatations or disruptions and divulsions caused not by some appetite in the body dilated itself, but by the violence of bodies outside which, since their motions have the upper hand, force the other body to dilate and be disrupted. Now this inquiry belongs under the title of Motion of Liberty but (as with other topics) I shall now look into it somewhat, though sparingly and in brief. This motion is generally of two kinds: first, motion of disruption by an outside force; and secondly motion of contraction or restitution by the proper motion of the body; and this second motion, although it bears on condensations, is

Condensationes spectet, tamen ita conjunctus est cum priore, ut hic commodius tractari debeat.

Dilatationes sive distractiones à violentia externa.

[*Historia.*]

5 1. *Bacula Lignea*, & similia, Flexionem nonnullam patiuntur, sed per vim; illa autem vis distrahit partes exteriores *Ligni* in loco ubi arcuatur, & comprimit partes interiores: Quod si vis illa paulo post remittatur, [E4^v] restituit se *Bacu¹lum* & resilit; sed si diutius in ea positura detineatur, figitur in ea, nec resilit amplius.

10   2. Similis est ratio *Horologiorum*, (eorum scilicet quæ moventur per torturam *Laminarum*), in quibus videre est continuum & graduatum nixum *Laminarum* ad se restituendum.

   3. *Pannus*, & similia Filacea, extenduntur majorem in modum, & resiliunt citius dimissa; non resiliunt longius detenta.

15   4. *Caro*, quæ surgit in *Ventosis*, non est *Tumor*, sed violenta Extensio *Carnis integralis* per Attractionem.

   5. Qualem *Rarefactionem* toleret *Aer* (pro modo scilicet violentiæ) tali *Experimento* elicere possis. Accipe *ovum vitreum*, in quo sit Foramen minutum; exuge *Aerem* anhelitu quantum potes; deinde affatim obtura 20 *Foramen* digito, & merge *ovum* in aquam ita obturatum. Post tolle digitum, & videbis *ovum* attrahere *aquam*, tantum scilicet, quantum exuctum fuerit *Aeris*; ut *Aer* qui remansit possit recuperare exporrectionem suam veterem, à qua fuerat vi distractus, & extensus. Memini autem intrasse Aquam, quasi ad decimam partem contenti *Ovi*. 25 Etiam memini me reliquisse *Ovum* (post exuctionem) cera obturatum per diem integrum, ut experirer, si per moram illam (quæ certe nimis brevis erat ad Experimentum justum) *Aer dilatus* figi posset, nec curaret de Restitutione, ut fit in *Baculis* & *pannis*. Sed cum tolleretur Cera, *Aqua* intrabat ut prius: etiam si *Ovum* appositum fuisset ad aurem, *Aer* novus 30 intrarat cum sibilo.

[E5^r]   ¹6. At qualem *Rarefactionem Aqua* sustineat, possit forte hoc modo deprehendi. Accipe *Folles*: attrahe *Aquam*, quantum impleat *Cavum Follium*; neque tamen eleva Folles ad summum, sed quasi ad dimidium: Deinde obstrue Folles, & nihilominus eleva eos paulatim; & videbis,

---

4 [*Historia.*]] / see *tn* to C1^r (p. 74 above)   17 toleret] tolleret

11 *Laminarum*),] ~,)   17 *Aer*] ~,   19 minutum;] ~:   27 justum)] ~,)

nevertheless so linked with the first that it is more convenient to deal with it here.

Dilatations or disruptions by violence from outside

[*History*]

1. Wooden staves and the like put up with some degree of bending, but only by force. Now this force pulls asunder the outer parts of the wood where the bending takes place and compresses the parts inside. But if that force is slackened off a bit later, the stave restores ¹ itself and springs back, but if it is kept in that position longer, it stays that way and does not spring back any more.

2. The same goes for clocks (at least those driven by coiled springs) in which you see the springs' continued and steady straining to unwind themselves.

3. You can stretch cloth and similar textiles a very great deal, and they spring back when you let them go; but held longer they do not spring back.

4. There is no swelling when flesh rises in cupping glasses, but a violent extension of the whole flesh by attraction.

5. With the following experiment you can establish what rarefaction air will put up with (according to the degree of violence applied). Take a glass egg with a little hole in it; suck out as much of the air as you can, then immediately stop the hole with your finger and with it so stopped put the egg under water. Then take your finger away and you will see the egg draw in the same amount of water as there was air sucked out, so that the air left behind can regain the old bulk from which it had been distracted and extended by force. Now I recall that the water that got in filled about a tenth of the egg's volume. I also recall that after I sucked it out I left the egg sealed up with wax for a whole day (which was certainly too short a time for a reliable experiment) to establish whether the delay could fix the dilated air so that it would not bother restoring itself, which is what happens with staves and cloth. But when I removed the wax, the water got in as before; but if the egg were put to the ear instead, fresh air would have entered with a hiss.

⌐6. But you can perhaps detect what rarefaction water will stand in the following way. Take a pair of bellows and suck in as much water as the space inside will hold; yet do not open the bellows fully but about halfway. Then block up the bellows and still open them up gradually,

quatenus ista aqua recepta se dilatari patiatur. Aut etiam per *Fistulam*, aut *Syringam*, attrahe nonnilhil *Aquæ*; deinde Foramen obtura, & Embolum adhuc paulatim attrahe.

Commentatio.

5 Suspicor etiam fieri *Distractionem spiritus Aquæ* in *Conglaciatione*; sed subtilis est hujus rei ratio. Primo, pro certo poni possit, in omni *Excoctione*, (puta *Luti*, cum fiunt Lateres & Tegulæ, Crustæ panis, & similium), multum ex *pneumatico* corporis exhalare, & evolare, (ut paulo post monstrabimus), atque inde necessario
10 sequi, ut Partes crassiores per *Motum Nexus* magna ex parte (nam est & alius *Motus*, de quo nunc sermo non est) se contrahant. Nam sublato *spiritu*, nec alio *Corpore* facile subintrante, *ne detur vacuum*, (ut loquuntur), in locum illum quem occupabant *spiritus* succedunt *partes*; unde fit illa *Durities* & *Contractio.* Eadem
[E5ᵛ] 15 prorsus ratione, sed modo contrario, videtur ¹ necessario sequi, ut *spiritus* in *Conglaciatione* distrahantur. Etenim *partes crassiores* per *Frigus* contrahuntur; itaque relinquitur aliquod *spatium* (intra *claustra Corporis*) occupandum: unde sequitur, si aliud *corpus* non succedat, ut *spiritus præ-inexistens* per *Motum Nexus* distrahatur
20 tantum, quantum *partes crassiores* contrahantur. Sane id conspicitur in *Glacie,* quod corpus interius reddatur rimosum, crustulatum, & parum tumescat; quodque ipsa *Glacies,* non obstante insigni partium *contractione,* sit (in toto) levior quam ipsa *Aqua*: Idque *Dilatationi Pneumatici* merito attribui possit.

25 ## Connexio.

Transeundum ad *Dilatationes* per *Deacervationem*; quando, scilicet, quod erat cumulatum & acervatum, fit applanatum. Istæ autem *Dilatationes* pro *pseudo-Dilatationibus* habendæ sunt; *Dilatatio* enim fit in *positura* partium, non in *substantia* corporis.

---

8 similium),] ~,)   9 monstrabimus),] ~;)   11 non est)] ~,)
13 loquuntur),] ~,)

and you will see how far the water taken in lets itself be dilated. Alternatively draw up some water with a tube or syringe, then block the hole and go on gradually drawing out the piston.

Speculation

I suspect as well that distraction of the spirit of water happens in freezing but the reason for this is a subtle one. In the first place we can take it as a certainty that in all thorough baking (as of clay in the production of bricks and tiles, and of crusty bread and the like) a lot of the body's pneumatic matter exhales and escapes (as I shall show in a moment) and it necessarily follows from this that the grosser parts contract themselves and do so by Motion of Connection in the main (for there is another motion involved which I am not speaking of at the moment). For the spirit being carried off and no other body easily getting in, the room once taken up by the spirits is taken over by the parts, in order (as the saying is) to prevent a vacuum, and it is from this that the hardness and contraction arise. For the very same reason but in the opposite way it seems ¹ to follow of necessity that the spirits are distracted in freezing. For cold makes the grosser parts contract; some room is therefore left behind (within the body's confines) ready to be taken up, and it follows from this that if no other body occupies it, the pre-existing spirit is distracted by Motion of Connection by as much as the grosser parts are contracted. We certainly see that in ice the body becomes fissured inside, and crusted, and it swells up a little, and that the very ice, the remarkable contraction of the parts notwithstanding, is (as a whole) lighter than the water itself. And this can with good cause be attributed to the dilatation of the pneumatic matter.

Connection

We must go on now to dilatations by spreading, i.e. when what was heaped and piled up gets flattened out. But these dilatations should be taken for pseudo-dilatations, for the dilatation takes place in the disposition of the parts and not in the substance of the

Siquidem Corpus manet in eadem Densitate substantiæ; sed Figuram nanciscitur ampliorem in superficie, minorem in profunditate.

[E6ʳ] ¹*Dilatationes per Deacervationem.*

5 [*Historia.*]

1. *Avrum per Malleationem* in immensum dilatatur, ut in *Auro foliato*; item per *Distractionem*, ut in argenteis filis inauratis; *Inauratio* enim fit in Massa antequam distrahatur.

2. *Argentum* etiam fit foliatum, licet non ad tam exquisitam
10 tenuitatem quam *Aurum*. Reliqua quoque *Metalla* per Malleationem dilatantur in bracteolas & lamellas tenues.

3. *Cera*, & hujusmodi, premuntur, & finguntur in oblinimenta tenuia.

4. *Gutta Atramenti* in *calamo dilatatur* ad exarationem multarum
15 literarum; quod & fit per *penicillum* in pigmentis, & vernice.

5. *Crocus* in parva quantitate magnam inficit quantitatem Aquæ.

Connexio.

Atque de *Dilatationibus* & *Rarefactionibus*, & *Aperturis Corporum*, hæc inquisita sunto. Superest jam ut de contrariis Actionibus
20 simili diligentia inquiramus, id est, de *Contractionibus*, & *Condensationibus*, & *Clausuris* corporum. Quam partem visum est seorsum tractare, eo magis, quod non omnes actiones ex hac parte sint reciprocæ; sed nonnullæ earum propriæ, & per se
[E6ᵛ] expli¹candæ. Etiam, quamvis contraria ratione consentiant; tamen
25 in *Experimentis* valde diversis investigantur, & se conspicienda præbent.

Actioni Dilatationis per Introceptionem corporis alieni reciproca est *actio Contractionis* per Emissionem aut Expressionem corporis alieni: Itaque de eo primo est inquirendum.

5 [*Historia.*]] / see *tn* to C1ʳ (p. 74 above)
15 literarum;] ~:

body. At any rate the body keeps the same density of substance but its surface gets greater and its depth decreases.

ᴵ*Dilatations by Spreading*

[*History*]

1. Gold is dilated enormously by hammering, as in gold leaf; the same thing happens with drawing out as in silver gilt threads; for the gilding takes place before the mass is drawn out.

2. Silver can also be made into leaf though not to the exquisite thinness of gold. By hammering the other metals can also be dilated into leaves and thin plates.

3. Wax and the like are pressed out and moulded into thin coatings.

4. A drop of ink in a quill can be dilated enough to write many letters, and the same thing happens in paints and varnish applied with a brush.

5. A small quantity of saffron can colour a large quantity of water.

Connection

So much then for the dilatations, rarefactions and openings up of bodies. It now remains for us to investigate with similar care the contrary actions i.e. the contractions, condensations, and closings up of bodies. I have decided to deal with this part by itself, and the more so because not all the actions belonging to it have reciprocal actions, and some of them need to be explained by themselves and in their own right. ᴵ For however much their contraries coincide with them, yet we investigate and expose them to view by very different experiments.

The action of dilatation by introception of a foreign body is the reciprocal of the action of contraction by the giving off or squeezing out of a foreign body. We should therefore look into this first.

Contractiones per emissionem aut depositionem corporis introcepti.

[*Historia.*]

1. Consule *Instantias* de *Dilatationibus* per *Introceptionem,* & oppone illis easdem *Instantias* postquam *Dilatationes* resederint: In his intelligimus, 5 ubi datur residere.

    2. *Metalla* pura & perfecta, licet variis modis vexentur & alterentur, ut in *Sublimationibus, Præcipitationibus, Malagmatibus, Dissolutionibus, Calcinationibus,* & hujusmodi; tamen (natura *metallica* cum aliis corporibus non bene conveniente) per Ignem & conflationem 10 plerunque restituuntur, & vertuntur in corpus quale prius. Est autem *Condensatio* ista minus vera, quia videtur esse nihil aliud quam Emissio & *Exclusio Aeris* qui se miscuerat, aut Aquarum in quibus dissoluta erant, ad hoc, ut partes genuinæ corporis metalli rursus coire possint. Neque tamen dubium est, quin corpus longe minus spatium occupet [E7ʳ] 15 quam prius, sed minime videtur densari substantia. Atque hæcˡ *potestas Clavium,* quæ *aperit* & *claudit,* viget maxime in *Metallis.* Etiam *Metalla* impura, & *Marcasitæ,* atque *Mineræ Metallorum,* eodem modo (per ignem congregatis partibus homogeneis, & emissa & exclusa Scoria, & purgamentis) depurantur. Etenim omne *Metallum* purum densius est & 20 ponderosius impuro.

    3. Ad magis arctam autem *Condensationem Metallorum* facit, si *Metalla* sæpius fusa, sæpius in aquis extincta sint; unde magis obstinata fiunt, & indurescunt. Utrum vero pondere ipso augeantur, pro ratione dimensi, hactenus non constat. De eo fiat *Experimentum.* Atque ista 25 Induratio magis adhuc potenter fit per crebras *Solutiones* & *Restitutiones,* quam per *Fusiones* & *Extinctiones.* Inquirendum etiam est, in quali genere, aut mixtura *Aquarum,* indurescant magis.

    4. Reperiuntur tamen *Modi Mortificationum metallorum,* id est, *prohibitionum,* ne cum soluta & aperta fuerint, restituantur. Id maxime 30 cernitur in *Argento vivo;* quod, si strenue tundatur, & inter tundendum injiciatur parum *Terebinthinæ,* aut *salivæ Hominis,* aut Butyri, mortificatur *Argentum vivum,* & nanciscitur aversationem & fastidium ad se restituendum.

---

2 [*Historia.*]] / see *tn* to C1ʳ (p. 74 above)
9 conveniente)] ~,)

Contractions by the giving off or deposition of a body taken in

[*History*]

1. Consult the instances of dilatations by introception and set against them same instances after the dilatations have subsided; here I have in mind those cases where subsidence can take place.

2. Metals pure and perfect—although they may be vexed and altered as in sublimations, precipitations, amalgamations, dissolutions, calcinations and the like—are still (the metallic nature not agreeing very well with other bodies) generally restored by fire and melting down, and turn into a body of the kind they were before. But this condensation is not a real one for it seems to be nothing other than the giving off or shutting out of the air blended with them, or of the waters they were dissolved in, with the effect that the true parts of the metal's body can come together again. Yet there can be no doubt but that the body takes up much less room than before, but at the same time its substance does not seem to have become any denser. Now this ¹ power of the keys, which binds and loosens, flourishes exceedingly in metals. Indeed, impure metals, marcasites and metal ores are purified in the same way (fire bringing together the homogeneous parts, and giving off and excluding the dross and slag). For every pure metal is denser and heavier than an impure one.

3. Now greater condensation in metals can be encouraged if they are often fused and often quenched in waters, for thereby they become more stubborn and grow harder. But whether they put on weight relative to their size has not been established hitherto. Do an experiment on this. And this hardening is made all the greater by frequent solutions and reductions than by fusions and quenchings. We should also inquire what kinds and mixtures of waters produce more hardness.

4. Yet ways have been found to mortify metals, i.e. ways of stopping them being restored when they have been dissolved and opened up. You can see this best in quicksilver which if it is vigorously beaten, and turpentine, human saliva or butter is put in during the beating, the quicksilver is mortified and develops a distaste and dislike for restoring itself.

Mandatum.

Diligenter inquirendum de *Mortificationibus,* hoc est, de Impedimentis *Restitutionum* omnium *Metallorum.* Magna enim debet esse *Antipathia* eorum quæ prohibent ne ea coeant. Cum¦que omnis *Restitutio* ipsorum sit genus quoddam *Condensationis,* pertinebit scilicet cognitio *Privationis* ad cognitionem *Formæ.*

Connexio.

Dilatationibus per *spiritum* innatum se expandentem, non opponitur proprie Actio aliqua reciproca; cum *contractio* res aliena sit à *spiritu,* qui non contrahitur, nisi cum aut suffocatur, aut patiatur, aut colligit se (Arietis instar) ut fortius se dilatet. Attamen commode hoc loco substituemus Actionem illam quæ est propria partium crassiorum, sed per accidens imputari debet *spiritui innato*; ea est, ubi per Evolationem, sive Emissionem *spiritus,* contrahuntur & indurantur partes. *Spiritus* autem emittitur vel ex agitatione sua propria, vel sollicitatus ab Aere ambiente, vel provocatus & irritatus ab Igne, seu Calore.

Commentatio.

Idem faciunt quoad *Attenuationem* & *Emissionem spiritus,* & *actiones* quæ ex ea sequuntur, *Ignis* sive Calor, & *Tempus* sive Ætas. Verum *Ætas* per se *Curriculum* est solummodo, aut *Mensura Motus.* Igitur cum de *Ætate* loquimur, intelligimus de virtute & operatione composita ex agitatione *spiri¦tus innati,* & *Aere ambiente,* atque *Radiis cælestium.* Sed illud interest, quod Ignis, & *calor vehemens,* dilatet corpora confertim, & fortiter, & visibiliter; *Ætas* autem, instar *Caloris* lenissimi, paulatim, & leniter, & occulto: *Fumi* enim & *vapores* scilicet spissi sunt & conspicui, *Perspirationes* vero neutiquam; ut manifestum est in *Odoribus.* Attamen magis subtilis & exquisita est ea corporum *Attenuatio* & *Rarefactio* quæ fit per *Ætatem,* quam quæ fit per *Ignem.* Nam *Ignis*

7 *Connexio*] *Historia* / *SEH* (II, p. 287 n. 1) proposes this emendation. I have gone further and altered *c-t* by deleting the numeral 1 from the beginning of the para and setting the para in the larger type

Direction

Look carefully into mortifications, i.e. obstacles to the restoration of all metals. For the antipathy of the obstacles which stops the metals coalescing again must be great. And ¹since all restoration of metals is a certain kind of condensation, knowledge of its privation will naturally have a bearing on knowledge of the form.

Connection

Strictly speaking there is no action to set against dilatations caused by expansion of innate spirit, since contraction is foreign to the spirit which only contracts when it is stifled, is made to do so, or when it gathers itself up (like a ram) to dilate with more vigour. Yet this is a convenient point at which to deal with that action which is proper to the grosser parts but which should be ascribed to the innate spirit *per accidens*, and that is where the parts are contracted and hardened by escape or emission of the spirit. Now the spirit is given off as a result either of its own agitation, or because it has been coaxed by the surrounding air, or provoked and irritated by fire or heat.

Speculation

As far as attenuation and emission of spirit and the actions which follow from them are concerned, fire or heat and time or age produce the same results. But age in itself is but the course or measure of motion. So when I speak of age I mean the combined virtue and operation of the innate spirit's ¹ agitation, of the surrounding air and of the rays of the heavenly bodies. But there is a difference to be noted here, that fire and fierce heat dilate bodies as a whole and both vigorously and visibly, while age, like the gentlest of heats, works slowly, gradually and secretly. For Fumes and vapours are obviously thick and conspicuous, but perspirations are not, as is clear in the case of odours. Yet that attenuation and rarefaction of bodies that occurs by age is more subtle and fine than that brought about by fire. For fire, driving

præcipitans actionem, *pneumaticum* quod in Corpore est rapide evolare facit; Humidum quoq*ue*, quod præparatum est in *pneumaticum* subinde vertit, atque tale factum emittit: unde partes Tangibiles sedulo se interim & gnaviter constipant, & non
5 parum *spiritus* (tanquam manu injecta) morantur & detinent. At *Ætas pneumaticum* jam factum ad *Evolationem* non urget subito; unde fit ut illud diutius manens in Corpore, quicquid in tenue digeri possit sensim & seriatim præparet, parum ex *pneumatico* jam facto placide & successive interim evolante; adeo ut anticipet
10 fere, & tanquam fallat, *constipationem partium tangibilium.* Quamobrem in *Dissolutione* per *Ætatem*, sub finem negotii,
[E8ᵛ] parum admodum tangibilis figitur & manet. Etenim | pulvis ille putris, qui per longos annorum circuitus manet, tanquam consumptionis reliquiæ, (qualis in Sepulchris & Monumentis
15 vetustis nonnunquam invenitur), res quasi nihili est, & omni *Incineratione* quæ fit per ignem minutior, & magis destitutus. Nam *cineres* etiam succum habent, qui possit elici, & verti in *Sales*: hujusmodi Pulvis minime. Verum quod ad *Inquisitionem* præsentem pertinet, & cujus causa hæc dicta sunt, certum est
20 *spiritum*, quandiu detinetur in corpore, partes tangibiles colliquare, intenerare, conficere, subruere; verum ab ejus Emissione partes tangibiles continuo se contrahere & constipare.

Contractiones per angustationem partium crassiorum post spiritum emissum.

25 *Historia.*

1. In senectute *Cutes Animalium* corrugantur, & Membra arescunt.

2. *Pyra* & *poma* diu servata rugas colligunt; *Nuces* autem ita contrahuntur, ut non impleant Testam.

3. *Casei veteres* in cortice exteriore efficiuntur rugosi. Ligna in
30 Trabibus, Postibus, & palis, tractu temporis (præsertim si ponantur viridia) contrahuntur in arctum, ut disjungantur & hient. Simile fit in *Globis Lusoriis.*

25 *Historia.*] / in *c-t* this stands before the previous heading; see *tn* to C1ʳ (p. 74 above)
15 invenitur),] ~,)

the action headlong, causes the body's pneumatic part to escape in a hurry; and it also promptly turns the moisture which is ready for it into pneumatic matter and when that has been done, gives it off; whence in the meantime the tangible parts zealously and industriously crowd in on themselves and (as if by grabbing hold of them) keep back and detain an appreciable amount of spirit. But age does not drive the pneumatic matter already made to get away fast; whence it happens that, staying behind longer in the body, it gradually and bit by bit makes ready whatever can be worked up into a tenuous substance, a little of the pneumatic matter already made escaping meanwhile in a calm and orderly way, to such an extent that it practically forestalls and almost avoids the crowding in of the tangible parts. And this is the reason why in dissolution by age so very little tangible stuff remains stable or gets left behind at the end of the process. For ¹ that corrupt dust which remains time out of mind as a relic of consumption (such as we sometimes find in ancient tombs and monuments) is something that verges on nothing, and slighter and more empty than any incineration produced by fire. For even ashes have a juice which can be extracted and turned into salts, but powder of the former kind has nothing of the sort. But as far as the current inquiry is concerned, and the reason I have said these things, is that it is certain that the spirit while it is detained in the body melts, softens, works up and undermines the tangible parts, but that after it has been given off the tangible parts immediately contract and crowd themselves together.

Contractions by congestion of the grosser parts once the spirit has been given off

History

1. In old age the skins of animals wrinkle and the members dry out.

2. Pears and apples stored for a long time shrivel up; and nuts so contract that they do not fill their shells.

3. Old cheeses get wrinkled rinds. Wooden beams, posts and stakes (especially if they are set up unseasoned) contract with the passage of time so that they come apart and leave gaps. The same thing happens with bowling balls.

[F1ʳ]   ⌐4. *Terra* in magnis *siccitatibus divellitur*, & in superficie sua plena rimarum efficitur; etiam quandoque *Rimæ* tam in profundum penetrant, ut ad *Eruptionem Aquarum* causam præbeant.

Monitum.

5 Nemo nugetur, aiens, istam *Contractionem* in *Desiccationibus* nihil aliud esse quam *absumptionem Humidi*. Nam si id tantum ageretur, ut *Humidum* in *spiritum* versum evolaret, deberent corpora manere in priore exporrectione & dimenso suo, & solummodo cava fieri, ut *Pumices*, aut *Suber*; non autem localiter contrahi, & minui dimenso suo.

10   ## Historia.

1. *Lutum* per Fornaces cogitur in *Lateres* & *Tegulas*: at si instet calor vehemens, ut in medio Fornacis, vertitur etiam nonnulla pars *Luti* & funditur in *vitrum*.

2. *Ligna*, si suffocetur *Flamma*, vertuntur in *Carbones*; materiam 15 scilicet magis spongiosam & levem quam *Ligna* cruda.

3. *Metalla* pleraque sepulta in *crucibulis* inter prunas ardentes, & multo magis per *fornaces* reverberatorias, vertuntur in materiam friabilem, & calcinantur.

4. Complura *Fossilia* & *Metalla*, & ex *Vegetabilibus* nonnulla, 20 *vitrificantur* per ignes fortes.

[F1ᵛ]   ⌐5. Omnia quæ *assantur*, si *Ignem* plus æquo tolerent, incarbonantur, & recipiunt se in angustius dimensum.

6. *Papyrus, Membrana, Lintea, pelles*, & similia, per ignem non solum corrugantur in partibus, sed etiam se complicant & convolvunt, & 25 tanquam rotulantur in toto.

7. *Lintea* à flamma primo concepta, paulo post suffocata, vertuntur in substantias raras, quæ vix inflammantur, sed facile ignescunt; quibus utimur ad Fomites Flammarum.

8. *Pinguia*, ut *Cera, Butyrum, Lardum, Oleum*, & similia, per ignem 30 deveniunt frixa & fæculenta, & tanquam fuliginosa.

9. *Ova* contrahuntur ab *Igne*, & quatenus ad *Albumen* ipsorum, colorem mutant à claro in candidum.

---

10 *Historia*.] / *om* plausibly in *SEH* (II, p. 289) with note to that effect. *SEH* carries on the number sequence from before the monitum
2 efficitur;] ∼:   27 raras,] ∼;   32 candidum.] ∼:

|4. During long droughts the earth is torn apart, and its surface becomes a mass of cracks; and the cracks sometimes even go down so far that they cause an eruption of waters.

Advice

I hope no one be so frivolous as to say that this contraction in droughts is nothing other than an exhaustion of water. For if it were the escape of moisture turned into spirit that alone did the trick, then bodies should keep their original bulk and dimensions and only become hollow like pumice or cork but not contract locally and get smaller.

History

1. Furnaces make clay gather into bricks and tiles; but if the heat be fierce, as in the midst of the furnace, a certain amount of the clay is also turned and melted down into glass.

2. Wood, if the flame be stifled, turns into charcoal, i.e. into a material more spongy and light than plain wood.

3. Most metals consigned to crucibles amid hot coals, and much more to reverberatory furnaces, are turned into friable matter and undergo calcination.

4. Many fossils and metals, and some vegetable bodies, are vitrified by strong fires.

|5. If it be overdone, everything that is roasted is turned to charcoal and takes up less room.

6. Fire makes paper, vellum, linen, hides and the like not only buckle in their parts but also makes them curl, writhe and as it were scroll up in their entirety.

7. Linen first set on fire and put out soon after is turned into rare substances which catch fire reluctantly but easily smoulder; and this is what we use for tinder.

8. Fat substances, like wax, butter, lard, oil and so on are made arid, cloudy and what one might call sooty by fire.

9. Fire makes eggs contract and, as far as their whites are concerned, changes them from transparent to milky white.

10. Quin etiam si *Ovum* testa exutum injiciatur in *spiritum* vini *bonum* & *fortem,* elixatur, & fit candidum; similiter & *offa panis* injecta in ipsum devenit quasi tosta.

Observationes.

5 1. Quamdiu (ut paulo ante innuimus) *spiritus* in corpore detinetur, si per ignem aut calorem excitatus & dilatatus fuerit, tamdiu agitat se; molitur exitum, partes tangibiles emollit, intenerat, colliquat; atque hoc est proprium opus *spiritus,* qui digerit & subigit partes. Sed postquam *spiritus* sibi exitum
10 invenerit, & emissus fuerit, tum prævalet opus partium, quæ à
[F2ʳ] *spiritu* vexatæ conspiꞌrant, & se stringunt; tam ex desiderio *Nexus,* & mutui *contactus,* quam ex odio *Motus* & *vexationis.* Atque inde sequitur *Coarctatio, Induratio, Obstinatio.*

2. Est in processu *Contractionis* partium ab Igne, Finis &
15 ultimitas: Nam si minor sit copia *Materiæ,* per violentam *Deprædationem* Ignis, quam ut cohærere possint; tum demum se deserunt, & incinerantur, & calcinantur.

Connexio.

Atque de *Contractionibus* quæ fiunt ab *Emissione spiritus* è
20 corporibus, sive is emittatur per ætatem, sive per ignem, sive per calorem potentialem, hæc inquisita sunto. *Actioni* vero *Dilatationis* per *calorem actualem externum,* reciproca est *Actio Contractionis* per Frigus *actuale externum.* Atque hæc *Condensatio* est omnium maxime propria & genuina; Maxime potens etiam
25 foret, nisi quod non habemus hic apud nos, in Superficie Terræ, *Frigus* aliquod intensum. *Frigus* autem & *Caloris remissio* (nam utrumque hoc loco conjungere visum est) alia simpliciter, manente natura sua, condensat; alia rarefacta, (sed imperfecte) restituit; alia per *condensationem* plane vertit & transformat de
[F2ᵛ] 30 *natura* in *naturam.* De ꞌ his omnibus jam pauca sunt proponenda.

---

4 ff. *Observationes.*] /in *c-t* these are set (wrongly) in small type
8 colliquat;] ~: 26 *remissio*] ~,

10. Why even if a shelled egg be thrown into good strong spirit of wine it is poached and goes white; and in the same way a hunk of bread thrown into the spirit almost becomes toast.

Observations

1. As I said a little while ago, as long as the spirit is kept in the body, and if it be excited or dilated by fire or heat, for so long does it bestir itself, try to get out, soften, make tender and melt the tangible parts; and that is the proper work of the spirit which is to loosen and undermine the parts. But after the spirit has found a way out for itself and has been given off, then the work of the parts gets the upper hand, parts which, vexed by the spirit, conspire ˡ and draw themselves in tight—as much from a desire for connection and mutual contact as from hatred of motion and vexation. And it is from this that constriction, hardening and stubbornness come.

2. In the process of contraction of the parts by fire there is an end and last extreme. For if by the violent depredations of fire the amount of matter be brought to the point where the parts cannot hang together, then they part company, and are incinerated and calcined.

Connection

And so much for contractions caused by emission of spirit from bodies, be it given off through age, or fire or potential heat. Now the reciprocal of the action of dilatation by actual external heat is the action of contraction by actual external cold. And this condensation is the most proper and genuine of all; it would also be the most powerful if only we had here on the Earth's surface any intense cold available to us. But cold and a remission of heat (for I have thought fit to put them together here) condense some things in an uncomplicated way, leaving their nature unchanged; some others they restore (though imperfectly) that have been rarefied; and some others again they completely change by condensation and transform one nature into another. On ˡ all these questions I must now say a few words.

Contractiones corporum per frigus actuale externum.

Historia.

1. Aer in *vitro Calendari* percipit Gradus tam Frigidi quam Calidi. Atque temporibus nivalibus, super caput *vitri* quasi pileum ex *Nive* posuimus; 5 qui, licet aer ipse illo tempore fuisset hyemalis & asper, tamen frigus in tantum auxit, ut Aqua per paucos gradus, Aere contracto, insurgeret.

2. Superius posuimus, *Aerem* in *viro* ad tertias per calorem dilatatum fuisse, atque tantundem, remittente calore, se contraxisse.

Mandata.

10 1. *Experimento* plane dignum est, ut probetur, utrum *Aer* per calorem *dilatatus*, figi in eadem *Exporrectione* possit, ut se restituere & contrahere non laboret. Itaque accipe *vitrum Calendare* robustum, idemque vehementer calfacito; deinde os bene obturato, ne *Aer* se contrahere possit, & per aliquot dies obturatum dimittito. Deinde in *Aquam* ita 15 obturatum mergito, & postquam in *Aqua* fuerit, aperito, & videto quantum Aquæ trahat, atque utrum sit ad eam proportionem quam alias tracturum fuisset si *vitrum* statim in aquam fuisset missum.

[2.] Etiam obiter nota (etsi ad *Titulum* de *Calido* & *Frigido* potius [F3ʳ] pertineat) utrum *Aer* ita fortiter | *dilatatus*, & per vim *detentus*, retineat 20 *calorem* suum multo diutius quam si os *vitri* apertum fuisset.

1. *Stellæ* tempore hyemali, noctibus valde serenis & gelidis, apparent grandiores quam noctibus æstivis serenis: Quod fit præcipue ex universali *Condensatione Aeris*, qui tum vergit magis ad naturam *Aquæ*. Nam sub *Aqua* omnia apparent longe grandiora.

25 2. *Rores matutini* sunt, procul-dubio, *vapores*, qui in Aerem purum non erant plene dissipati & versi, sed hærebant imperfecte misti, donec per *Frigora noctis*, præsertim in Regione media quam vocant Aeris, fuerint repercussi, & in *Aquam* condensati.

3. Condensatio *Pluviæ*, & *Nivis*, & *Grandinis*, fit similiter per Frigus 30 mediæ regionis, quod Vapores coagulat magis (ut plurimum) in alto, quam *Rores*. Occurrunt vero *Dubitationes* duæ, circa quas diligens fieri debet Inquisitio. Altera, utrum Guttæ ipsorum congelentur &

---

2 *Historia.*] / in *c-t* this stands after the next pair of mandata   18 [2.]] / silently emended thus, but without brackets, in *SEH* (II, p. 291)   26 plene] / *HDR(M)* (p. 25, l. 29 above) has plane

14 possit,] ∼;   dimittito.] ∼:   15 mergito,] ∼;

Contractions of bodies by actual, external cold

History

1. Air in a calendar glass perceives degrees of cold as well as of heat. In snowy weather I put a kind of cap of snow on the head of the glass which, although the air at the time was wintry and wild, yet it so increased the cold that, the air having contracted, the water rose by a few degrees.

2. As I said above, the air in the glass was dilated by one third by heat, and with the heat's remission contracted by the same amount.

Directions

1. It would be well worth while showing by experiment whether air dilated by heat could be fixed in that same bulk so that it would not make efforts to restore or contract itself. So take a stout calendar glass and heat it strongly; then stop its mouth up well so that the air cannot contract again, and leave it stopped up for some days. Then put it still stopped up in water, and once it is in the water open it up and see how much water it draws in, and whether it draw in as much as it would have done if the glass had been put in the water straight away.

[2.] Also observe in passing (though this really belongs to the title of Hot and Cold) whether air so strongly ^{1} dilated and kept in by force, holds on to its heat much longer than it would if the mouth of the glass were open.

1. In winter weather and on extremely clear and frosty nights, the stars appear larger than on clear summer nights. The main cause of this is the universal condensation of the air which then tends more towards the nature of water; for under water everything seems a great deal larger.

2. Morning dews are undoubtedly vapours which have not been completely dissipated and turned into pure air but which hang imperfectly mixed until the cold of the night, especially in what they call the middle regions of the air, drives them down and condenses them into water.

3. The cold of the middle region causes the condensation of rain, snow and hail in the same way for it coagulates vapours higher up (for the most part) than dews. But here we meet two problems which ought to be looked into with care. The first is whether their drops are congealed and condensed as they fall, or first collected and gathered together

condensentur in ipso casu; an fuerint illæ primo collectæ & congregatæ in moles majores Aquarum, in Aere (propter distantiam à Terra) pensiles, quæ postea, per violentiam aliquam conquassatæ, frangunt se, & comminuunt in Guttas; ut in nonnullis Cataractis *Indiæ Occidentalis*, quæ tam subito & confertim descendunt, ut videantur quasi ex vasibus fusæ & dejectæ. Altera, utrum non solum *vapores* (qui olim fuerant

[F3ᵛ] *Humores*, & Aquæ, & | solummodo restituuntur), sed etiam pars magna *Aeris puri* & perfecti, per Frigus (in illis Regionibus vehemens & intensum) non fuerit coagulata, & mutata plane, & versa in pluviam, & reliqua de quo paulo post inquiremus.

4. In *Distillationibus*, Humores primo vertuntur in *vapores*, illi, per remotionem ab igne destituti, per latera *stillatorii* contrusi, & nonnunquam per *Frigidam* ab extra infusam accelerati, restituunt se in *Aquas* & *Liquores*. Imago prorsus familiaris *Rorum*, & Pluviæ.

5. *Argentum vivum* præcipue, nec non *Metallica* alia, cum *volatilia* facta fuerint, properant tamen ad se restituendum, & occursu alicujus *solidi* & *materiati* magnopere gaudent. Itaque facile hærent, facile decidunt; adeo ut quandoque sit necesse *vapores* ipsorum igne persequi, & de igne in ignem transmittere, factis tanquam scalis Receptaculorum ignis, ad nonnullam distantiam inter se, circa vas; ne vapor, postquam per ascensionem paulo fuerit remotior ab igne, citius quam expedit se restituat.

6. Quæ ab *Igne* colliquata fuerint, post *remisionem caloris* densantur & consistunt, ut prius; ut *Metalla, Cera, Adeps, Gummi*, &c.

7. *Vellus laneum* super terram diutius jacens, colligit *pondus*; quod fieri non posset, nisi aliquid *pneumaticum* densaretur in *ponderosum*.

8. Solebant antiquitus *Nautæ, velleribus lanæ*, tanquam *Tapetibus* aut *Aulæis*, vestire latera *Navium* noctu, ita ut non attingerent *Aquam*; atque inde mane exprimere aquam dulcem, ad usum navigantium.

[F4ʳ] |9. Etiam expertus sum de industria, quod alligando quatuor uncias *lanæ* ad *Funem*, qui demittebatur ad Puteum 28 orgyarum, ita tamen ut aquam per sex orgyas non attingeret, ex mora unius noctis crevisset pondus *lanæ* ad quinque uncias & drachmam unam; & hæsissent per exterius *lanæ* plane guttæ aquæ, ut ex iis tanquam lavare aut madefacere manus quis possit. Idque iterum atque iterum expertus sum, variante quantitate ponderis, sed semper multum aucta.

---

6 fuerant] / *SEH* (II, p. 291) reads fuerunt although the grammar of c–t is perfectly respectable
26 aliquid] aliquod / silently emended thus in *SEH* (II, p. 292)
7 restituuntur),] ~ₐ,   31 28] ~.

into greater masses of water which hang in the air (because of their distance from the Earth), and are afterwards shaken by some violence and
break up and disperse themselves into drops, as in some downpours in
the West Indies which come down so suddenly and heavily that you
would think they had been tipped and flung down out of buckets. The
second is whether not only vapours (which were once humours and
waters, and ¹ are just now restored) but also a good part of pure and perfect air be not coagulated, quite changed and turned into rain and the
rest by cold (fierce and intense in those regions)—a matter which I shall
look into shortly.

4. In Distillations, Humours are turned into vapours first; and these,
let down by the removal of the fire, crammed together by the sides of the
still, and sometimes hurried along by cold infused from outside, turn
themselves back into waters and liquors again; this is a well-known imitation of dews and rains.

5. Quicksilver in particular and some other metallic bodies, once they
have been made volatile, still rush to restore themselves, and are highly
delighted when they meet up with anything solid and materiate. So they
easily stick and settle, to such an extent that it is sometimes necessary to
harry them with fire and send them from one fire to the next, making as
it were a kind of ladder of fire holders at regular intervals about the vessel in case the vapour, getting further away from the fire by ascension,
restore itself more rapidly than is desirable.

6. Things which have been melted by fire become dense and consistent as before once the heat has slackened off as, for example, metals,
wax, fat, gums and so on do.

7. A woollen fleece lying on the ground for a long while gains weight,
which could not happen unless something pneumatic had condensed
into something with weight.

8. The sailors of antiquity used to dress the sides of the ship at night
with fleeces, like rugs or hangings, but not so they touched the water;
and later they could wring out fresh water for the mariners' profit.

¹ 9. I have also carefully made the following trial. By tying four ounces
of wool to a rope which I let down into a well to a depth of 28 fathoms,
yet which still failed by six fathoms to touch the water, I found that in
the course of one night the weight of the wool increased to five ounces
and one dram; and that evident drops of water clung to the outside of
the wool, so that one could as it were wash or moisten one's hands. Now
I tried this time and time again and, although the weight varied, it
always increased mightily.

10. *Lapides,* ut *Marmora,* & *Silices,* atque etiam *Trabes ligneæ* (præsertim pictæ, & *oblitæ* oleo) manifesto madefiunt sub Regelationibus, aut tempestatibus Australibus; ut tanquam exudare videantur, & Guttæ inde detergi possint.

5   11. In *Gelu madido* (quod Anglice *Rynes* vocant), fit Irroratio in ædibus super *vitra Fenestrarum*; idque magis interius versus cubiculum, quam exterius ad Aerem apertum.

12. *Anhelitus,* qui est *Aer* primo attractus, ac deinde intra cavum Pulmonum brevi mora parum humefactus, super specula aut corpora 10 polita (qualia sunt *Gemmæ, laminæ Ensium,* & similia) vertitur in quiddam roscidum, quod paulo post instar *Nubeculæ* dissipatur.

13. *Lintea,* etiam in ædibus (ubi ignis non accenditur) colligunt *Humiditatem,* ita ut Foco appropinquata fument.

14. *Pulveres* omnes in Repositoriis conclusi colligunt humiditatem, ut 15 hæreant, & quasi glebefiant.

[F4ᵛ] ¹15. Existimatur Origio *Fontium,* & *Aquarum dulcium,* quæ ex terra scaturiunt, fieri ex Aere concluso in cavis terræ (præsertim montium) coagulato & condensato.

16. *Nebulæ* sunt *Condensationes* Aeris imperfecte commistæ ex longe 20 majore parte *Aeris* & parum *Aquei vaporis*: & fiunt, *hyeme* quidem, sub mutatione tempestatis à Gelu ad Regelationem, aut è contra; *Æstate vero* & *Vere,* ex expansione *Roris.*

Mandata.

1. Quia versio *Aeris* in *Aquam* utilissima res esset, idcirco omnes 25 Instantiæ quæ ad hoc innuunt diligenter pensitandæ: atque inter alia, in certo ponendum, utrum *Exudationes Marmorum,* & similium, in tempestatibus Australibus & pluviosis, sint meræ *condensationes Aeris* à duritie & lævore Lapidum repercussi, instar *Anhelitus* in *Speculo*; an participent nonnihil ex *succo* & *pneumatico* intrinseco *lapidis.*

30   2. Probatio fieri possit per *pannum lineum,* aut *lanum,* supra *Lapidem* positam. Nam si tunc quoque exudat *Lapis,* participat Exudatio ex causa interiore.

---

19 imperfecte] imperfectæ, / cf. *HDR(M)* (p. 27, l. 5 above); also see *HDR,* p. 138, l. 26 (imperfecte misti) and p. 144, l. 9 (imperfecte misti)   23 *Mandata*] *Mandatum* 5 vocant),] ~,)

10. Stones, like marble and flint, as well as wooden beams (especially those painted or coated with oil) evidently grow damp during thaws and in south winds, so that they seem to sweat as it were, and thence drops of moisture can be wiped off.

11. In damp frosts (which they call *Rynes* in English) a dewiness besprinkles the glass of windows in buildings; and this happens more on the side facing into the room than on the side facing the open air.

12. Breath, which is air first taken in and slightly moistened by its short stay in the lung cavity, turns, on mirrors and polished bodies (as gems, sheet metal, sword blades and the like), into a certain dewy substance which is dissipated soon afterwards like a little cloud.

13. In unheated houses linen too gathers moisture, so that it steams when it is put near the fire.

14. All powders shut up in cupboards gather moisture so that they stick together and practically grow lumpy.

15. People believe that fountains and sweet waters gushing from the earth originate from air enclosed in the hollows of the earth (and especially of mountains) which has coagulated and condensed.

16. Mists are condensations of air, made from an imperfect mixture of a very large amount of air and a very small one of water vapour, and in winter they happen when the weather turns from freezing to thaws or the other way round; but in summer and spring by expansion of dew.

Directions

1. As conversion of air into water would be a very useful thing, all instances which bear on it should be carefully considered; and among other things, we should establish for sure whether the exudations of marble and the like in south winds and wet weather are mere condensations of air repelled by the hard and polished surface of the stones, like breath on a mirror, or whether they partake in some measure of the juice and inner pneumatic matter of the stone.

2. You could test this by putting a linen cloth or wool on the stone. For if the stone exudes even then, the exudation partakes of an internal cause.

Commentatio.

Quod ipse *Aer* vertatur in *Aquam* in *Regionibus supernis,* omnino
[F5^r] necessario concluditur ex conservatione rerum. Nam certissimum
est, *Humores Maris* & *Terræ* verti in *Aerem* purum, postquam
5 vaporum naturam, tempore, & consortio, & rarefactione
plenaria, penitus exuerint. Itaque si non esset *Reciprocatio,* ut *Aer*
vicissim quandoque verteretur in *Aquam,* quemadmodum *Aqua*
vertitur in *Aerem,* non sufficerent plane *vapores,* qui remanent
novelli & imperfecte misti, ad Pluvias, & Imbres, &
10 reintegrationes specierum, sed secutæ forent *siccitates*
intolerabiles, & *conflagratio,* & *venti impetuosi,* & *Tumores Aeris,*
ex Aere perpetuo multiplicato.

Historia.

1. In *Conglaciatione Aquæ,* moles corporis integri non decrescit, sed
15 intumescit potius. Fit tamen manifesta Densatio in partibus; adeo ut
conspiciantur *Rimæ* & *Divulsiones* intra corpus *Glaciei.* Etiam
quandoque (si aer subintret) cernuntur sensim *Capillitia,* & *Fila,* &
Flosculi. Glacies autem innatat *Aquæ;* ut manifestum sit, non fieri
Densationem integralem.
20   2. *Vinum* tardius congelascit quam Aqua; *spiritus vini* non omnino.
    3. *Aquæ Fortes* & *Argentum vivum* (arbitror) non gelascunt.
    4. *Oleum* & *Adeps* gelascunt & densantur, sed non ad indurationem.
[F5^v]   ¹*Gelu* Terram facit concrescere, eamque reddit siccam & duram.
    5. *Poeta* ait de *Regionis hyperboreis,*

25   *Æraque dissiliunt vulgo, vestesque rigescunt.*

    6. Id quod faciunt *Tabulæ ligneæ,* præsertim in juncturis *glutinatis.*
    7. Etiam *Clavi,* per contractionem *Frigoris,* decidunt (ut referunt) è
parietibus.
    8. *Ossa Animalium* per *gelu* deveniunt magis crispa; adeo ut Fractura
30 ipsorum per hujusmodi tempora & facilius fiat, & ægrius curetur.
Denique, omnia dura redduntur per Frigus magis fragilia.

---

13 *Historia.*] / *om* plausibly in *SEH* (II, p. 294) with note to that effect. *SEH* carries on the
number sequence from before the previous mandata (p. 142, l. 22 above)   23 *Gelu . . .*]
/ also unnumbered in *c-t*

Speculation

That the very air is turned into water in the upper regions, is the inescapable ¹ conclusion to be drawn from the conservation of things. For it is absolutely certain that the humours of earth and sea are turned into pure air after they have completely put aside, by time, association and plenary rarefaction, the nature of vapours. Thus if there were no reciprocation, i.e. that air did not sometimes turn into water for a change in the same way that water is turned into air, there would obviously not be enough recent and imperfectly mixed vapours left for rains and showers, and renewal of species, but instead there would be unbearable droughts, conflagrations, gale-force winds and swellings of the air, caused by the incessant multiplication of air.

History

1. When water freezes the mass of the whole body does not decrease but rather swells up. Yet there is a manifest densation in the parts, to such an extent that you can see cracks and splitting within the body of the ice. Sometimes too (if air gets in) hair-line and thread-like cracks, and flower-like forms can be seen. But ice floats on water, so it is obvious that no densation of the whole takes place.

2. Wine freezes more slowly than water, spirit of wine not at all.

3. Strong waters and quicksilver do not (I believe) freeze.

4. Oil and fat freeze and become dense, but not to the point of hardness.

¹Frost makes the earth stiff and renders it dry and hard.

5. The poet says of the northern regions that:

Bronze vessels regularly crack and clothes become stiff.

6. The same thing happens in wooden tables, especially along glued joints.

7. They also say that nails contracted by the cold fall out of walls.

8. The bones of animals become more brittle in frosty weather to the extent that at such times they break more easily and mend with more difficulty. In short all hard things are made more fragile by cold.

9. *Condensantur* manifesto *Aquæ* aut *succi* in *lapides splendentes*, sive crystallinos; ut videre est in cavernis subterraneis intra rupes, ubi cernuntur stillæ multiformes (instar stillarum congelaciatarum) sed fixæ & saxeæ, pensiles, quæ in ipso decasu (lento scilicet & tardo) congelatæ

5 fuerunt. Utrum vero Materia ipsarum sit prorsus *Aqua*, an *succus nativus lapidis* (saltem *commistus*) in dubio est; præsertim cum gemmæ & crystalla in Rupibus apertis exurgant sæpe & excrescant (quod non potest imputari Aquæ adhærenti) in sursum, & non decidant aut pendeant.

10 10. *Lutum* manifesto condensatur in *Lapides*; ut videre est in aliquibus *Lapidibus* magnis compositis ex parvis *Calculis*, qui materia lapidea satis polita, & æque dura ac ipsi *Calculi*, in interstitiis *Calculorum* conglutinantur. Sed videtur hæc *Condensatio* fieri non solum ex Frigore Terræ, sed per *Assimilationem*, de qua paulo post.

[F6ʳ] 15 ¹11. Sunt quædam *Aquæ* quæ *Lignum*, etiam *paleas*, (ut aiunt) & hujusmodi, *condensant* in *Materiam lapideam*; adeo ut pars ligni, adhuc integri, quæ fuerit sub *Aqua* sit saxea, quæ emineat maneat Lignea, quod etiam vidi. De eo diligentius inquirendum, cum multum lucis præbere possit ad *Operativam Condensationis*.

20 ## *Mandatum.*

Probabile est *Aquas Metallicas*, ob densitatem quam contraxerint à *Metallis*, posse habere *Naturam insaxantem.* Fiat Probatio per stipulam, Folia crassiora, Lignum, & similia. Sed arbitror, deligendas esse *Aquas Metallicas*, quæ fiunt per *Ablutionem*, aut crebram *Extinctionem*, potius

25 quam per *Dissolutionem*; ne forte *Aquæ illæ fortes* & *corrosivæ* impediant *condensationem.*

Historia.

12. In *China* habent *Mineras Porcellanæ artificiales*, defodiendo (nonnullas Orgyas subter terram) Massam quandam Cæmenti, ad hoc

30 præparati & proprii; quæ post quadraginta aut circiter annos sepulta, vertitur in *Porcellanam*; ita ut transmittant homines hujusmodi *Mineras* de hærede in hæredem.

---

27 *Historia.*] / *om* plausibly in *SEH* (II, p. 295) with note to that effect. *SEH* carries on the number sequence from before the mandatum (p. 146, l. 19 above)

2 rupes,] ∼;   6 *lapidis*] ∼,

9. Waters or juices are evidently condensed into brilliant or crystalline stones, as we see in underground caves within the rocks where drops of many shapes (like icicles) but fixed and stony are found hanging which, in their slow and long-drawn-out fall, have become congealed. But whether their matter be plain water or the native juice of the stone (or at least a mixture of the two) is an open question, especially as gems and crystals often arise and grow up out of bare rocks (which cannot be ascribed to water clinging to them) and do not fall or hang down.

10. Clay evidently condenses into stones, as we see in certain large stones made up of little pebbles which are held together by stony matter (well polished and quite as hard as the pebbles themselves) in the gaps between them. But this condensation seems to be caused not just by the cold of the earth but by assimilation—of which more in a moment.

ᶦ11. There are certain waters which condense wood, straws and (so they say) things of that kind into a stony material, to the extent that the part of the wood, still whole, which was underwater is stony, and the rest above the surface stays woody; and I have seen this with my own eyes. Look into this more carefully since it will shed a great deal of light on the operative aspects of condensation.

Direction

It is likely that metallic waters, by reason of the density that they have picked up from the metals, can have a petrifying nature. Let this be tested with straws, thicker leaves, wood and the like. But it is my belief that the metallic waters chosen should be those produced by washing or frequent quenching rather than dissolution, just in case the strong and corrosive waters get in the way of condensation.

History

12. In China they have artificial mines for porcelain, made by burying some fathoms underground a certain mass of cement made ready and fit for the purpose, a mass which after forty years or so turns into porcelain, such that people hand down these mines from generation to generation.

13. Accepi rem fidei probatæ, de *Ovo*, quod diu jacuerat in fundo
Aquæ, quæ circuibat ædes; quod inventum versum erat manifesto in
[F6ᵛ] *Lapidem*, manentibus coloribus & distinctionibus *vi¹telli, albuminis,
testæ*: sed Testa erat fracta hic, illic, & splendescebat in crustulis.
5   14. Audivi sæpius de versione *Albuminis Ovi* in Materiam *lapideam*;
sed nec veritatem rei, nec modum novi.
     15. *Flamma*, procul-dubio, cum extinguitur, vertitur in aliquid;
videlicet in *post-fumum*, qui & ipse vertitur in *Fuliginem*. De *Flammis*
vero *spiritus vini*, & hujusmodi *Aurarum*, diligentior facienda est
10   *Inquisitio*, in quale corpus densentur, & qualis sit *post-aura* ipsarum.
Neque enim apparet Fuliginosum aliquod, ut in *Flammis* ex *oleosis*.

Connexio.

Atque de *Contractionibus* corporum per *Frigus actuale*, sive hoc
fiat in *Aere*, sive in *Aquis*, & *liquoribus*, sive in *Flamma*; ac rursus
15   sive illa sit *Contractio simplex*, sive *Restitutio*, sive *Coagulatio*, &
versio, hæc inquisita sint. Sequitur *Actio* quæ opponitur
Dilatationi per *Calorem potentialem*, scilicet *Contractio* per *Frigus
potentiale*.

Contractiones corporum per frigus potentiale.

20   [*Historia.*]

1. Quemadmodum consulendæ sunt *Tabulæ Medicinales* Qualitatum
secundarum ad Inquisitionem *de calore potentiali*, similiter consulendæ
[F7ʳ] sunt ad *Inquisitionem* de *Frigore potentiali*: in qui¹bus excerpi debent
potissimum *Astrictio, Repercussio, Oppilatio, Inspissatio, Stupefactio*.
25   2. *Opium, Hyoscyamus, Cicuta, Solanum, Mandragora*, & hujusmodi
Narcotica, spiritus Animalium manifesto densant, in se vertunt,
suffocant, & motu privant. Utrum vero super corpora mortua aliquid
possint, fiat *Experimentum* macerando carnes in *succis* ipsorum (ad
experiendum si succedat Denigratio, & Gangræna) vel *macerando*
30   *semina* & *nucleos* (ad experiendum utrum *mortificent* ipsa, ut non
crescant) vel linendo summitatem *vitri Calendaris* per interius, succis
ipsorum (ad experiendum utrum aliqualiter contrahant *Aerem*).

---

20 [*Historia.*]] / see *tn* to Cɪʳ (p. 74 above)
32 *Aerem*).] ~.)

13. I have heard it claimed as a proven fact that an egg which had lain for a long time at the bottom of a moat was found evidently to have turned into stone, with the colours and distinctions of [1] the yolk, white and shell still remaining, save that the shell was broken here and there and it glittered with little encrustations.

14. I have often heard of egg whites being turned into stony matter but I do not know if it is true or how it happens.

15. Flame without question turns into something else when it is put out, i.e. into an after-fume which is itself turned into soot. But we should inquire more carefully concerning the flame of spirit of wine and breaths of that sort to find out what kind of body they are condensed into, and what their after-breaths are like. For they do not appear to be anything sooty as they are in flames from oily bodies.

Connection

So much then for contractions of bodies by actual cold, whether it happen in air or in waters and liquors, or in flame; and again whether it be simple contraction, or restitution, or coagulation and conversion. Now follows the action which is opposed to dilatation by potential heat, i.e. contraction by potential cold.

Contractions of bodies by potential cold

[History]

1. Just as we should consult tables listing the secondary qualities of medicines for the inquiry into potential heat, so we should do the same for the inquiry into potential cold. In these tables [1] astringency, repercussion, stopping up, thickening, and stupefaction ought to be picked out especially.

2. Opium, henbane, hemlock, nightshade, mandrake and suchlike narcotics evidently condense the spirits of animals, turn them back on themselves, stifle them and deprive them of motion. But to see whether they have any effect on dead bodies do the experiment of steeping the flesh in their own juices (to see if blackness or gangrene supervene), or of steeping seeds and nuts (to see if they mortify and so not grow), or of smearing the top of a calendar glass on the inside with their juices (to see whether they contract the air in any way).

3. Apud *Indias Occidentales* reperiuntur, etiam per Deserta arenosa & valde arida, *Cannæ* magnæ, quæ super singulas juncturas, sive genicula, bonam copiam præbent *Aquæ dulcis*, magno commodo itinerantium.

4. Referunt esse in quadam *Insula*, aut ex *Terceris*, aut ex *Canariis*, 5 *Arborem* quæ perpetuo stillet; imo quæ *Nubeculam* quandam roscidam semper habeat impendentem. Digna autem res cognitu esset, utrum inveniatur in *vegetabili* aliquo *potentiale Frigus*, quod denset *Aerem* in *aquam*. Itaque de hoc diligenter inquiratur. Sed magis existimo, has esse *Cannas geniculatas*, de quibus diximus.

10 5. Inveniuntur super *Folia* nonnullarum *Arborum* (veluti *Quercus*) quæ unita sunt, nec humorem sugunt, aut condunt, præcipue *Mense*

[F7ᵛ] *Maij* apud nos, *Rores dulces*, instar *Mannæ*, & quasi mel¦liti: utrum vero sit vis aliqua in foliis coagulans, an tantum illa *Rores* commode excipiant & custodiant, non constat.

15 6. Vix invenitur corpus, in quo emineat tantum *potentiale Frigus* quantum in *Nitro*. Nam ut *Aromata*, & alia (licet ad tactum minime) tamen ad *Linguam* aut *Palatum* habent Calorem perceptibilem; ita etiam *Nitrum*, ad *linguam* vel *palatum* habet *Frigus perceptibile*, magis quam *Sempervivum*, aut aliqua *Herba* ex maxime *Frigidis*. Itaque videtur
20 subjectum accommodum ad experiendum virtutem *potentialis Frigidi* in *Nitro*. Poterit autem esse *Mandatum* tale.

Mandatum.

Accipe minutam *vesicam* ex *pellicula*, quantum fieri potest, tenui. Infla, & liga; & merge eam intra *Nitrum* per aliquos dies, & exime; & nota si
25 *vesica* aliqualiter flaccescat: quod si facit, scias Frigus *Nitri* Aerem contraxisse. Fiat idem *Experimentum* mergendo *vesicam* intra *Argentum vivum*. Sed debet suspendi *vesica* per filum, ut mergi possit, & minus opprimi.

Historia.

30 7. Accipe *unguentum Rosarum*, aut hujusmodi; infunde *Aceti* nonnihil; tantum abest ut *Liquor Aceti* reddat *Vnguentum* magis liquidum, ut contra illud reddat magis induratum & solidum.

---

29 *Historia.*] / silently *om* in *SEH* (II, p. 297)
5 imo] / the modern dictionary lemma is immo   16 & alia] ~,   24 nota]
~,   31 nonnihil;] ~:

3. In the West Indies they find, even in sandy and very dry deserts, great canes which on every joint or knot offer a good supply of fresh water, to the great benefit of travellers.

4. They say that on an island either in the Azores or the Canaries, there is a tree which constantly sheds drops, and more precisely that it always has a dewy mist hanging over it. Now it would be worth knowing whether potential cold can be found in any vegetable body which can condense air into water. Let this therefore be looked into carefully. But I am more inclined to think that these are only the canes with knots I mentioned earlier.

5. Here in England, particularly in the month of May, we find that on the leaves of some trees (like the oak) which have a firm texture and do not suck up or store moisture, there are sweet dews, like manna, and almost as ¹ sweet as honey; but whether there is any coagulating power in the leaves or whether it is only that they readily take up and preserve the dews is unknown.

6. We scarcely find any body in which potential cold is as obvious as it is in nitre. For as aromatic and other bodies have a heat detectable by the tongue or palate (though not at all to the touch) so nitre has a cold which is so detectable and greater than that of the house-leek or any of the coldest plants. Nitre therefore seems to be an appropriate subject for testing out the virtue of potential cold. And this might be a direction for doing that:

Direction

Take a small bladder of the thinnest skin you can find. Blow it up and tie it off, and bury it in nitre for some days; and then take it out and see if the bladder has gone down at all; and if it has you will know that the cold of the nitre has contracted the air. Do the same experiment by submerging the bladder in quicksilver. But to keep it submerged without pressing down on it you must keep the bladder in position with a thread.

History

7. Take an ointment of roses or the like and pour some vinegar on to it. The liquor of the vinegar is so far from rendering the ointment more liquid that it makes it harder and more solid.

[F8ʳ]   ¹ *Connexio.*

Actioni Dilatationis per *Amplexum* opponitur [actio] *Contractionis*
per *Fugam* & *Antiperistasin.* Quemadmodum enim *Corpora* versus
grata & amica se laxant undiquaque, atque eunt in occursum; ita
5 cum incidunt in odiosa & inimica, fugiunt undiquaque, & se
contrudunt & constringunt.

Contractiones corporum per fugam & Antiperistasin.

[*Historia.*]

1. *Calor Ignis* per *Antiperistasin* videtur nonnihil densari, & fieri acrior,
10 ut sub Gelu.

2. Contra, in *Regionibus torridis,* videtur densari Frigus per
Antiperistasim; adeo ut, si quis se recipiat ex campo aperto & Radiis
solaribus sub arbore patula, statim cohorreat.

3. Attribuitur, nec prorsus male, ista operatio *Contractionis* per
15 *Antiperistasim mediæ regioni Aeris,* ubi colligit se & unit *natura frigidi,*
fugiens Radios solis directos sparsos à *Cœlo,* & reflexos resilientes à *Terra;*
unde fiunt magnæ *Condensationes* in illis partibus *Pluviarum, Nivis,
Grandinis,* & aliorum.

4. Merito dubitari possit, utrum *Opium* & *Narcotica* stupefaciant à
20 *potentiali Frigido,* vel à *fuga spirituum.* Nam videtur *Opium* partes habere
[F8ᵛ] calidas ex fortitudine Odoris, ex Amaritudine, & ¹ provocatione sudoris,
& aliis signis. Verum cum emittat vaporem inimicum & horribilem
spiritibus, fugat illos undiquaque; unde se coagulant, & suffocantur.

Connexio.

25 *Actioni Dilatationis,* quæ fit per *Assimilationem* & *Versionem* in
tenuius, opponitur *actio Contractionis,* quæ fit per *Assimilationem*
& *versionem* in *densius.* Intelligimus autem, quando hoc fit non
[fieri] per *Frigidum,* vel *actuale* vel *potentiale,* sed per imperium
corporis magis activi, quod se multiplicat ex corpore magis
30 passivo. *Assimilatio* autem ad *Densum* magis rara est, & minus

2 [actio]] / emended thus in *SEH* (II, p. 297)   8 [*Historia.*]] / see *tn* to Cıʳ (p. 74
above)   28 [fieri] / cf. *HDR(M),* p. 29, l. 27 above
12 *Antiperistasim* / *nld* as antiperistasin in *SEH* (II, p. 297) here and in the next para

ᴵ *Connection*

Set against the action of dilatation by embrace is [the action] of contraction by flight and antiperistasis. For just as bodies lay themselves open all round to attractive and friendly things and go to meet them, so when they happen on things hateful and hostile they fly from them all round and pull back and withdraw into themselves.

Contractions of bodies by flight and Antiperistasis

[*History*]

1. The heat of fire seems to be condensed and made sharper to a certain extent by antiperistasis, as in frost for instance.

2. On the other hand in torrid climes cold seems to be condensed by antiperistasis, such that people who get out of the open and the Sun's rays and under a shady tree immediately start shivering.

3. They are not entirely wrong to ascribe this operation of contraction to the middle region of the air where the nature of cold gathers and concentrates itself, escaping from the direct rays of the Sun scattered from the heavens and the indirect ones rebounding from the Earth, as a result of which great condensations of rain, snow, hail and other things happen in those parts.

4. It can well be questioned whether opium and narcotics induce stupefaction by potential cold or by flight of the spirits. For by its strong smell, bitterness and ᴵ power to make one sweat, and other signs, it seems that opium has hot parts. But on the other hand, since it gives off a vapour harmful and horrible to the spirits, it puts them to flight on all sides, whence they coagulate and get stifled.

Connection

Opposed to the action of dilatation caused by assimilation or version into a thinner body is the action of contraction which is caused by assimilation or version into a denser one. Now I mean when this is caused it is caused not by a cold body, be it actual or potential, but by the dominion of a more active body which multiplies itself at the expense of a more passive. But assimilation

potens multo, quam *Assimilatio* ad *Rarum*; quia *Corpora densa* magis sunt ignava & inertia ad opus *Assimilationis* quam *tenuia*.

Contractiones corporum per assimilationem, sive versionem in densius.

[*Historia.*]

5 1. Supra notavimus, *Lutum* inter lapides parvos densari in materiam lapideam.

2. *Latera Doliorum* densant *Fæces* vini in *Tartarum*.

3. *Dentes* densant ea quæ ex manducatione Cibi & humoribus oris adhærent in squamas, quæ purgari & abscindi possint; verum æque 10 duras ac ipsum os Dentium.

[G1^r] |4. Omnia *Dura* & *solida* aliquid ex Liquoribus & in fundo (maxime) & per latera adhærentibus *condensant*.

5. Quæcunque *Alimenta* vertuntur in *Corpus alimentatum* magis densum quam corpus ipsius alimenti (sicut *cibus* & *potus* in *Animalibus* 15 vertuntur in *ossa, calvariam,* & *cornua*) in *assimilando* (ut manifestum est) *condensantur*.

Connexio.

Actioni Dilatationis per violentiam externam, sive ex appetitu sive contra appetitum *Corporis Dilatati*, opponitur *Actio Contractionis* 20 *per violentiam* similiter externam; cum corpora ponuntur in necessitate, ab illis quæ in ipsa agunt, cedendi, & se comprimendi.

Contractiones corporum quæ fiunt per violentiam externam.

[*Historia.*]

1. A*er* per violentiam sive compressionem externam aliquam 25 *Condensationem* facile patitur; majorem vero non tolerat: ut in violento *impetu ventorum,* & *Terræ-motibus,* liquet.

2. Accipe *catinum ligneum,* inverte concavum ejus, & dimitte in aquam perpendiculariter, & facito illum descendere, impellens manu. Portabit secum *Aerem* usque in fundum *vasis,* nec recipiet *Aquam*

4 [*Historia.*]] / see *tn* to C1^r (p. 74 above)   21 ipsa] ipsum / *HDR(M)* (fo. 21^r) makes the same apparent error; *SEH* (II, p. 299) follows *c-t*   23 [*Historia.*]] / see *tn* to C1^r (p. 74 above)

to a dense body is more unusual and much less powerful than assimilation to a rare one because dense bodies have less zest and energy for the work of assimilation than rare ones.

Contractions of bodies caused by assimilation or version into something denser

[History]

1. I have noted above that clay between small stones is condensed into stony matter.

2. The sides of barrels condense the dregs of wine into tartar.

3. Teeth condense things, which stick to them from the chewing of food and the humours of the mouth, into scales which can be cleaned off or broken away but are just as hard as the bone of the teeth itself.

⊦4. All hard and solid bodies condense somewhat of the liquors that stick to them both at the bottom (where they stick most) and at the sides.

5. Whatever nourishment is changed into a body nourished denser than the body of the nourishment itself (as food and drink are turned into bone, skull and horn) is condensed (as is obvious) by assimilation.

Connection

Opposed to the action of dilatation by external violence, either for or against the appetite of the body dilated, is the action of contraction by violence likewise external when bodies are forced by the things acting on them to give way and compress themselves.

Contractions of bodies caused by external violence

[History]

1. Air easily puts up with some condensation by violence or external compression; but it does not put up with much, as we see in the violent shock of winds and earthquakes.

2. Take a wooden bowl, turn it upside down and, keeping it level, push it under water with your hand. It will carry air down with it to the very bottom of the vessel, and it will not take in any air except for a

[G1ᵛ] interius, nisi parum infra summa la⎮bra; Id ex colore Ligni madefacti apparebit. Tanta autem fuerat *Condensatio* aut *compressio Aeris*, non amplior. Hoc ipsum insigniter apparebat, invento Instrumento ad usum operariorum sub *Aqua*. Illud tale erat; Deprimebatur *Dolium* magnum
5 & concavum aere impletum. Illud stabat supra tres pedes *metallicos*, crassos, ut mergi posset. Pedes erant breviores statura *Hominis*. *Vrinatores*, cum *Respiratione* iis opus esset, flectebant se, & inserebant capita ipsorum in dolium, & respirabant: & hoc repetebant, & opus continuabant ad moram nonnullam; quousque scilicet *Aer*, qui per
10 insertionem capitis semper in quantitate nonnulla è dolio exibat, ad minimum diminutus esset.

3. At *Quantum ipsum Condensationis*, quod libenter toleraturus sit *Aer*, cognoscere & supputare possis hoc modo; Accipe plevem *Aquæ* plenam, mitte in eam *Globulum* ex *metallo*, aut Lapidem, qui resideat in
15 Fundo. Super impone catinum, vel impellens manu, vel ex metallo ita fabricatum, ut fundum sponte petat. Si Globulus fuerit talis magnitudinis, ut *Aer condensationem* (qualis ad Globulum intra *catinum* recipiendum sufficiat) libenter pati possit, condensabit se *Aer* placide, & nullus erit alius Motus: sin majoris fuerit magnitudinis quam *Aer* bene
20 ferre possit, resistet aer, & levabit latus aliquod ipsius catini, & exibit in bullis.

4. Etiam ex *Compressione vesicæ* videbis quousque comprimi possit sine ruptura; aut etiam ex Follibus levatis, & denuo (obturatis prius
[G2ʳ] fora⎮minibus) compressis. De *Condensatione Aquæ* tale à nobis factum est
25 *Experimentum*: *Globum* fieri fecimus *plumbeum*, cum lateribus bene crassis, & *foramine* in summo non magno. *Globum Aqua* replevimus, & Foramen *Metallo* (ut meminimus) optime solidavimus. Tum *Globum* illum, tanquam ad duos polos contrarios, primo malleis, deinde per Pressiorum robustum, fortiter compressimus. Cum autem ea *Applanatio*
30 multum sustulisset ex capacitate Globi, adeo ut ad octavam quasi diminuta fuisset, tamdiu & non amplius sustinuit se *Aqua* condensari. Sed ulterius vexata & compressa non tolerabat, sed exibat Aqua ex multis partibus *solidi Metalli*, ad modum parvi Imbris.

5. At omnis *Motus*, quem vocant, *violentus*, veluti *Pilarum* è *Tormentis*,
35 *Sagittarum, Spiculorum, Machinarum*, & aliorum infinitorum, expeditur per *Compressionem præternaturalem Corporum*, & Nixum

23–4 (obturatis prius fora⎮minibus) compressis.] obturatis (prius fora⎮minibus compressis.) / *SEH* (II, p. 299) adopts the absurd *c-t* parentheses and so offers an absurd translation (*ibid.*, III, p. 395)

1 la⎮bra;] ~: 6 posset.] ~: 14 plenam,] ~: 25 *Experimentum*:] ~;

little inside the rim ¹ as will appear from the colouring of the moistened wood. Now the condensation or compression of the air was so much and no more. This very same thing was strikingly shown in the invention of a device for the use of people working under water. It was like this: a large, empty barrel full of air was submerged. It stood on three thick metal legs to make it sink and these were shorter than a man's height. The divers, when they needed to take a breath, ducked down and put their heads inside the barrel and drew breath; they kept on doing this and got on with their job for some time until the air was practically exhausted by the small amounts lost every time someone put his head in.

3. But you can get to know and ascertain the amount of condensation that air will readily put up with in this way: take a basin full of water and put a little metal or stone ball in it which will stop at the bottom. Over this put a bowl made of metal so it will sink by itself or one which you have to push down by hand. If the ball is of such a size that the air can willingly endure condensation (sufficient to let the ball into the bowl) then the air will condense without any fuss, and there will be no other motion; but if the ball be bigger than the air can well bear, the air will resist and lift up a side of the bowl and escape in bubbles.

4. You will also see from the compression of a bladder how far it can be squeezed without bursting, or also from bellows opened up and then (once the holes ¹ have been blocked up) shut down again. On the condensation of water, this was the experiment I performed: I had a lead globe made with good thick sides and a small hole at the top. I filled the globe with water and (as I recall) had the hole perfectly soldered up with metal. Then, as if from the opposite poles, I compressed it hard, first with hammers and then with a powerful press. Now when this flattening had cut the capacity of the globe by about an eighth, so far and no further would the water let itself be condensed. And it would no longer suffer vexation and compression, but the water in many places came out through the solid metal like a slight drizzle.

5. But all motion which they call violent, as of shot from guns, arrows, spears, machines and a host of other things, works by preternatural compression of bodies and their struggle to restore themselves which, when

ipsorum ad se restituendum; quod cum commode ad tempus facere non possint, loco moventur. Nam *solida*, præsertim dura, ulteriorem *compressionem* ægre admodum tolerant. Verum hujusce rei Inquisitionem ad *Titulum* de *Motu libertatis* rejicimus. Etenim, ut sæpius diximus, 5 *Titulus* præsens de *Denso* & *Raro* spicas tantum legit, non demetit.

6. Quo *Corpora* sunt *rariora*, eo ab initio se contrahunt facilius; quod si ultra terminos suos compressa fuerint, eo se vindicant potentius; ut in *Flamma* & *Aere clauso* manifestatur.

[G2ᵛ]   7. *Flamma* simpliciter compressa (licet sine | flatu, ut in *pulvere pyrio*) 10 tamen magis furit, ut conspici datur in *Fornacibus reverberatoriis*, ubi *Flamma* impeditur, arctatur, repercutitur, sinuat.

Monitum.

Dilatationi per *Deacervationem* non opponitur *Actio Reciproca*: quia corpora deacervata non coacervantur rursus, nisi per *Conflationem*; ut in 15 *Restitutione Metallorum*, de qua supra.

Commentatio.

Est & aliud Genus fortasse *Contractionis corporum*, non ex Reciprocis, sed positivum, & per se. Arbitramur enim, in *Dissolutione corporum* quæ fit in *liquoribus*, ut in dissolutione 20 *Metallorum*, etiam *Gummi*, *sacchari*, & similium, recipi corpus aliquatenus intra *Liquorem*; neque tamen *Liquorem* pro rata parte *Corporis* recepti dilatari, aut exporrigi. Quod si fit, sequitur ut sit *Condensatio*, cum idem spatium contineat plus corporis. Certe in *Dissolutione Metallorum*, si *Aqua* semel exceperit onus suum, non 25 dissolvit amplius, nec operatur. Hanc autem *condensationem* (si talis quæpiam sit) contractionem corporum per *onerationem* appellare possumus.

[G3ʳ] |*Mandatum.*

1. Imitte *Aquam* in *Cineres* pressos ad sumum; & nota diligenter, 30 quantum decrescat de *Exporrectione Cinerum* postquam receperint Aquam, ab ea quam habuerunt prius intermisto Aere.

29 1.] / silently *om* in *SEH* (II, p. 301)
6 facilius;] ~:

they cannot achieve that promptly, they move somewhere else. For solid bodies, especially the hard ones, will scarcely stand much further compression. But I leave the inquiry into this matter to the title on Motion of Liberty. For, as I have often said, the present title, on dense and rare, only gleans the ears, it does not bring in the entire harvest.

6. The rarer the bodies are the more easily they contract from the outset; but if they are compressed beyond their limits, the more effectively do they get their own back, as we plainly see in flame and enclosed air.

7. Flame simply compressed (though without ^{1} a blast, as in gunpowder) still rages more, as we can see in reverberatory furnaces where the flame is held back, restricted, reflected and bent.

Advice

There is no reciprocal action opposed to dilatation by spreading; because bodies spread out do not get gathered up again save by melting down, as in the restoration of metals mentioned above.

Speculation

There is perhaps another kind of contraction of bodies which is not one of the reciprocal actions but one which exists positively and in its own right. For I judge that in the dissolution of bodies which takes place in liquors, as in the dissolution of metals and also of gums, sugar and the like, the body is to some degree taken into the liquor yet the liquor is not dilated or increased in bulk to the amount of the body taken in. But if this does happen, it follows that condensation takes place since the same space now contains more body. Certainly in the dissolution of metals, if the water has once taken on its full load, it dissolves no more and stops working. Now this condensation (if any such thing exists) I may call contraction of bodies by loading.

^{1}Direction

1. Pour water on ashes pressed down as hard as possible, and carefully note how far the bulk of the ashes diminishes when they have taken on the water; compared with the bulk they had before when they were mixed with air.

Observationes.

Efficientia *Dilatationis Corporum* quæ ex *Inquisitione* priore in lucem prodeunt, sunt 9. 1. *Introceptio* sive *Admissio* Corporis alieni. 2. *Expansio* naturalis, sive præternaturalis, *Spiritus* innati. 3.
5 *Ignis,* sive *Calor* externus actualis; aut etiam *remissio Frigoris.* 4. *Calor* externus potentialis, sive *spiritus Auxiliares.* 5. *Liberatio* spirituum à vinculis partium. 6. *Assimilatio* ex imperio Corporis rarioris magis activi. 7. *Amplexus,* sive itio in occursum, Corporis Amici. 8. *Distractio* à violentia externa. 9. *Deacervatio,* sive
10 *Applanatio* partium.

Efficientia vero *Contractionis Corporum* sunt 8. 1. *Exclusio* aut *Depositio* Corporis introcepti. 2. *Angustatio* sive *Contractio* partium post spiritum emissum. 3. *Frigus* externum actuale; aut
[G3ᵛ] etiam *Remissio Caloris.* 4. *Frigus* ¹ externum potentiale. 5. *Fuga* &
15 *Antiperistasis.* 6. *Assimilatio* ex imperio corporis densioris magis activi. 7. *Compressio* per violentiam externam. 8. *Oneratio,* si modo aliqua sit.

Actiones *Dilatationis* per *spiritum innatum,* & per *Liberationem spirituum,* & per *Deacervationem;* atque rursus, actiones
20 *Contractionis* per *Constrictionem,* sunt Actiones sine reciproco. Reliquæ Actiones sunt reciprocæ.

Dilatationes per *Introceptionem* & per *Deacervationem* sunt pseudo-dilatationes; sicut & *contractiones* per exclusionem sunt pseudo-condensationes: sunt enim locales, non substantiales.

25 *Expansio* per *Ignem* sive *Calorem* sine separatione est omnium simplicissima: Ea fit in *Pneumatico puro,* sicut *Aere;* ubi nihil exhalat, nihil residet, sed mera fit *Dilatatio,* eaque ad *Ampliationem* spatii sive *Exporrectionis* insignem. Utrum simile quippiam fiat in *Flamma,* videlicet, utrum Flamma post
30 *Expansionem* primæ *Accensionis* (quæ est magna) jam facta Flamma (ubi magnus est ambientium ardor) se adhuc magis expandat, difficile cognitu est, propter celerem & momentaneam extinctionem Flammæ: verum de hoc in Titulo de Flamma

Observations

The efficients of bodily dilatation which have come to light in the preceding inquiry are nine altogether. 1. The introception or admittance of a foreign body. 2. Natural or preternatural expansion of the innate spirit. 3. Fire or actual external heat or, indeed, remission of cold. 4. External potential heat or auxiliary spirits. 5. The freeing of the spirits from the bonds of the parts. 6. Assimilation resulting from the dominion of a rarer and more active body. 7. Embracing or going out to meet a friendly body. 8. Disruption by violence from outside. 9. Spreading or flattening out of the parts.

But the efficients of contraction of bodies are eight in all. 1. Exclusion or deposition of a body taken inside. 2. Congestion or contraction of the parts after the spirit has been given off. 3. Actual external cold or, indeed, remission of heat. 5. External ¹ potential cold. 5. Flight and antiperistatis. 6. Assimilation resulting from the dominion of a denser and more active body. 7. Compression by external violence. 8. Loading, if any such thing exists.

The actions of dilatation by the innate spirit, by liberation of the spirits and by spreading and, on the other hand, the actions of contraction by constriction are actions without a reciprocal. The other actions are reciprocal.

Dilatations by the introception of bodies and by spreading out are pseudo-dilatations; just as contractions by exclusion are pseudo-condensations: for they take place not in substance but by local motion.

Expansion by fire or heat without separation is the simplest of all. This happens in a pure pneumatic body such as air where nothing exhales, nothing settles down but only mere dilatation takes place and that with a remarkable ampliation of space or bulk. Whether something of the sort happens in flame, i.e. whether flame after the initial expansion when it is first lighted (which is great) having now been made into flame (where the surrounding bodies are in a state of agitation) expands itself still further, is difficult to know on account of the rapid and momentary extinction of flame; but we shall look into this matter

[G4ʳ] inquiremus. Proxima | huic *Dilatationi* (quatenus ad simplicitatem) est *Expansio*, quæ fit in *Colliquatione Metallorum*, aut in *Emollitione Ferri* & *Ceræ*, & similium, ad tempus, antequam aliquid fiat volatile, & emittatur. Verum hæc *Dilatatio*
5 occulta est, & fit intra claustra *Corporis integralis*, nec visibiliter Exporrectionem mutat aut ampliat. At simul ac incipiat in corpore aliquo quippiam evolare, tum Actiones fiunt complicatæ, partim *rarefacientes*, partim *contrahentes*: adeo ut Contrariæ illæ Actiones *Ignis*, quæ vulgo notantur,

10   *Limus ut hic durescit, & hæc ut cera liquescit,*
               Vno eodemque igni,

in hoc fundentur, quod in altera *spiritus* emittitur, in altera detinetur.

   Condensatio quæ fit per *Ignem*, licet non sit pseudo-densatio
15 (est enim substantialis) tamen est *Condensatio* potius secundum Partes quam secundum Totum. Nam contrahuntur certe partes crassiores; ita tamen, ut corpus integrum reddatur magis cavum & porosum, & minus ponderosum.

[G4ᵛ] | *Canones Mobiles.*

20 1. Summa *Materiæ* in *Vniverso* eadem manet; neque fit transactio, aut à *Nihilo*, aut ad *Nihilum*.

   2. Ex summa in aliquibus *Corporibus* est plus, in aliquibus minus, sub eodem spatio.

   3. *Copia* & *Paucitas Materiæ* constituunt notiones *Densi* & *Rari*,
25 recte acceptas.

   4. Est *Terminus*, sive *Non Vltra*, *Densi* & *Rari*, sed non in *Ente* aliquo nobis noto.

   5. Non est *Vacuum* in *Natura*, nec congregatum, nec intermistum.

30 6. Inter *Terminos Densi* & *Rari* est *Plica Materiæ*, per quam se complicat & replicat absque *vacuo*.

   7. *Differentiæ Densi* & *Rari* in *Tangibilibus* nobis notis parum excedunt rationes 32 partium.

35

in the title on Flame. As far as simplicity is concerned, next [1] to this dilatation stands the expansion that takes place in the melting of metals or in the softening of iron and wax and the like in the time before anything becomes volatile and is given off. But this dilatation is hidden and takes place in the confines of the body as a whole, and does not visibly change or increase its bulk. But as soon as anything in the body starts escaping, then the actions become complicated, partly rarefying, partly contracting, such that those contrary actions of fire commonly observed—

As by one and the same fire this clay grows hard,
That wax grows soft,

—rest on this: that in the one the spirit is given off, in the other it is kept in.

The condensation wrought by fire, although it is not a pseudo-condensation (for it is substantial) is still rather a condensation of the parts than of the whole. For certainly the grosser parts are contracted but yet in such a way that the body as a whole is rendered more hollow and porous and less heavy.

[1]*Provisional Rules*

1. The sum of matter in the universe stays the same, and there is no transaction which either comes from nothing or gets reduced to it.

2. Of this sum there is, in bodies occupying the same space, more in some than in others.

3. Abundance and scarcity of matter constitute the notions of dense and rare rightly understood.

4. There is a boundary or *non ultra* of dense and rare, but not in any entity known to us.

5. No vacuum exists in nature, either collected or interspersed.

6. Between the boundaries of dense and rare there exists a fold of matter by which it can curl up and unwind itself without a vacuum.

7. The differences of dense and rare in tangible bodies known to us do not fall much outside the range of 32 parts to 1.

8. *Differentia* à *rarissimo Tangibili* ad *densissimum Pneumaticum* habet rationem centuplam & amplius.

9. *Flamma* est *Aere* rarior, ut & *Oleum Aqua.*

[G5ʳ]   ⌐10. *Flamma* non est *Aer* rarefactus, ut nec *Oleum* est *Aqua*
5 rarefacta; sed sunt plane *corpora heterogenea*, & non nimis amica.

11. *Spiritus Vegetabilium*, & *Animalium*, sunt Auræ compositæ ex *Pneumatico Aereo* & *Flammeo*; quemadmodum & *succi* eorum ex *aqueo* & *oleoso.*

12. Omne *Tangibile* apud nos habet *Pneumaticum*, sive *spiritum,*
10 copulatum & inclusum.

13. *Spiritus*, quales sunt *Vegetabilium* & *Animalium*, non inveniuntur apud nos soluti, sed in *Tangibili* devincti & conclusi.

14. *Densum* & *Rarum* sunt propria opificia *Calidi* & *Frigidi*; *Densum Frigidi, Rarum Calidi.*

15   15. *Calor* super *Pneumatica* operatur per *Expansionem* simplicem.

16. Calor in Tangibili exercet duplicem operationem; semper dilatando *pneumaticum*, sed *crassum* interdum contrahendo, interdum laxando.

20   17. *Norma* autem ejus Rei talis est: *Spiritus emissus* corpus contrahit & indurat, *detentus* intenerat & colliquat.

18. *Colliquatio* incipit à *pneumatico* in corpore expandendo, aliæ Dissolutiones à *Crasso*, liberando operationem *pneumatici.*

[G5ᵛ]   ⌐19. Post *Calorem* & Frigus, potentissima sunt ad *Rarefactionem*
25 & *Condensationem* corporum *Consensus* & *Fuga.*

20. *Restitutio* à *violentia* & *dilatat* & *condensat*, in adversum *violentiæ.*

21. *Assimilatio* & *dilatat* & *condensat*, prout est *assimilans assimilato Rarius* aut *Densius.*

30   22. Quo *Corpora* sunt *Rariora*, eo majorem sustinent & *Dilatationem* & *Contractionem* per externam *violentiam*, ad certos Terminos.

23. Si *Tensura* aut *Pressura* in *Corpore Raro* transgrediatur Terminos sustinentiæ, tum *Corpora Rariora* potentius se vindicant
35 in Libertatem quam *Densiora*, quia sunt magis *activa.*

24. Potentissima omnium *Expansio* est *Expansio Aeris* & *Flammæ* conjunctim.

8. The difference between the rarest tangible body and the densest pneumatic one is as 100 to 1 and more.

9. Flame is rarer than air, just as oil is rarer than water.

ᴵ10. Flame is not air rarefied, just as oil is not water rarefied; but they are clearly heterogeneous bodies and not altogether friendly.

11. The spirits of vegetables and animals are breaths made up of an airy pneumatic body and a flamy one, in the same way as their juices are made up of a watery and an oily.

12. Every tangible body here with us has a pneumatic body or spirit associated with and shut up in it.

13. Here with us we do not find spirits of the kind in vegetables and animals in a free state but only attached and confined in a tangible body.

14. Dense and rare are the proper works of hot and cold; dense of cold, and rare of hot.

15. Heat works on pneumatic matter by simple expansion.

16. Heat has a twofold operation in tangible matter: it always dilates the pneumatic part, but sometimes contracts and sometimes relaxes the gross.

17. The rule governing this matter is this: spirit given off contracts and hardens a body, kept in it softens and melts it.

18. Melting begins with the expansion of the pneumatic matter in the body; other dissolutions start with the gross matter freeing the operations of the pneumatic.

ᴵ19. After heat and cold the most powerful agents of rarefaction and condensation are the consent and flight of bodies.

20. Recovery from violence both dilates and condenses in opposition to the violence.

21. Assimilation dilates and condenses according as the body assimilating is rarer or denser than the body assimilated.

22. The rarer the bodies the more they put up with dilatation and contraction by external violence within certain limits.

23. If tension or pressure in a rare body go beyond the limits it can stand, then, because rarer bodies are more active, they free themselves from oppression more effectively than dense ones.

24. The most powerful expansion of all is that of air and flame working together.

25. Imperfectæ sunt *Dilatationes* & *Contractiones* ubi facilis & proclivis est *Restitutio.*

26. *Densum* & *Rarum* magnum habent consensum cum *Gravi* & *Levi.*

27. Parce suppeditatur *Homini* Facultas ad *Condensationem,* ob defectum *potentis Frigidi.*

[G6ʳ] 28. *Ætas* est instar *Ignis lambentis,* & ¹ exequitur opera *Caloris,* sed accuratius.

29. *Ætas* deducit *Corpora* vel ad *Putrefactionem,* vel ad *Arefactionem.*

Optativa cum Proximis.

1. Versio Aeris in Aquam.
   Prox. *Fontes* in cavis Montium. *Exudatio* Lapidum. *Roratio* Anhelitus. *Vellus* super latera navium, qu. *Meteora Aquea,* &c.

2. Augmentum Ponderis in Metallis.
   Prox. *Versio* Ferri in Cuprum, qu. *Incrementum* Plumbi in cellis, qu. *Versio* Argenti vivi in Aurum, qu.

3. Insaxatio Terræ, & Materiarum, ex Vegetabilibus aut Animalibus.
   Prox. *Aqua* insaxans. *Lapis* compositus ex lapidibus parvis incrustatis. *Stillicidia crystallina* in speluncis, *Calculis* in Renibus, & vesica, & Cyste fellis. *Squamæ* dentium.

4. *Varii usus* Motus dilatantis & contrahentis in Aere per Calorem.
   Prox. *Vitrum* Calendare. *Altare Heronis. Organum musicum* splendentibus radiis solis. Impostura de *Imitatione Fluxus* & *Refluxus Maris,* & Amnium.

[G6ᵛ] 5. *Inteneratio Membrorum* in Animaliᵢbus per Calorem proportionatum, & spiritum detentum.
   Prox. Emollitio *Ferri.* Emollitio *Ceræ.* Omnia *Amalagmata.* Pertinet ad Instaurationem Iuventutis. Nam omnis *Humectatio,* præter eam quæ fit ex *spiritu* nativo detento, videtur esse *Pseudo-inteneratio,* & parum juvat; ut in proprio *Titulo* videbimus.

25. Those dilatations and contractions which are ready and prone to recovery are imperfect.

26. Dense and rare have a consensual relationship with heavy and light.

27. Humans are poorly supplied with means of condensation for they lack cold powerful enough.

28. Age is like a licking flame and ᴵ does the work of flame, only more meticulously.

29. Age carries bodies either to putrefaction or arefaction.

Desiderata with their Closest Approximations

1. Turning of Air into Water.

APPROX. Springs in the hollows of mountains. Exudation from stones. Moisture from breath. Fleece on the sides of ships. Query watery meteors etc.

2. Increase of the weight in metals.

APPROX. Turning iron into copper. Query increase of lead in cellars. Query turning quicksilver into gold.

3. Turning to stone earth and of vegetable or animal matter.

APPROX. Water that turns to stone. Stone made up of little stones crusted together. Crystal icicles in caves. Stones in the kidneys and bladder, and in the gall-bladder. Scales on the teeth.

4. Different uses for the dilating and contracting motion caused by heat in air.

APPROX. The calendar glass. Hero's altar. Musical instrument worked by the shining rays of the Sun. The imposture of the imitation of the ebb and flow of the sea and great rivers.

5. Softening of the members in animals ᴵ by proportionate heat and keeping in of the spirit.

APPROX. The softening of iron. The softening of wax. All amalgams. This has relevance for the restoration of youth. For all humectation, except that caused by keeping in the native spirit, seems to be a pseudo-softening and does not help much, as we shall see in the proper title.

Monitum.

Parce proponimus sub isto Titulo *Optativa* & *Vellicationes* de *Praxi*: quia cum sit tam generalis & late patens, magis idoneus est ad informandum Iudicium, quam ad instruendam Praxin.

Advice

Under this title I set down few desiderata and incentives to practice, for the business is so general and extensive that it is more suitable for informing the judgement than giving directions for practice.

ABECEDARIUM NOUUM NATURÆ

ᴵ Abecedarium nouum naturæ.

Occurrit mihi interdum dictum non insulsum vnius e Græcia, qui cum quidam ex opido non magno magnum quiddam perorasset, respondit; *Amice, verba tua ciuitatem desiderant.* Equidem verissime obijci mihi
5 posse existimo, quod verba mea, (quoad opus Instaurationis) ætatem siue sæculum desiderent, quia in huius ætatis genio spem magnam non habeo. Neque tamen per hoc ingenijs huiusce ætatis aliquid detractum intelligo, aut volo; sed quia vt ait ex politicis nescio quis, *quædam statim placent, quædam tractu temporis inualescunt.* Quamobrem posteritati
10 inseruio, nec quidquam aut nomini meo, aut gustui aliorum defero; sed satis gnarus cuiusmodi ea sint quæ affero, opus in æuum spargo. Igitur Abecedarium hoc exaraui, & edidi, rem parum solemnem & nihil de pompa⟨e⟩, sed imitationem quandam tanquam puerilem, attamen omnino consentaneam eius instituto, quæ tendat in regnum hominis,
15 quod consistit in scientijs, quemadmodum in regnum coelorum nisi sub persona infantis ingressus non datur.

Pertinet autem Abecedarium ad Instaurationis partem quartam, quæ est scala siue machina intellectus. Neque tamen est vera scala, sed quasi parasceue ad eam; omnino enim non suppetit mihi instantiarum &
20 experimentorum copia ad veram scalam. Vtilius autem iudicaui opus vrgere & promouere in multis, quam perficere in paucis, ne sim id quod sacerdotibus quispiam objicit ex patribus.

3 opido] / *sic* 4 *Amice* . . . *desiderant*] / editorial italics 7 Neque] lc 8–9 *quædam . . . inualescunt*] / editorial italics 9 Quamobrem] lc 11 Igitur] lc 18 Neque] lc 19 eam;] ~. 20 Vtilius] lc

' A New Abecedarium of Nature

From time to time I am put in mind of the *bon mot* of the man from Greece who, when somebody had finished a great speech on behalf of a rather small town, replied, *My friend, your words lack only a city big enough to match.* As for me, I am pretty sure that, because I have little faith in the genius of our times, my own words (as far as the work of instauration is concerned) could be accused of lacking an age or era to match them. Nevertheless, in saying this I do not have the slightest intention of disparaging the talents of the present age in any way; rather I say it because, as one or other of the political writers has remarked, *Certain things give satisfaction immediately, certain others bear fruit with the passage of time.* That is why I am devoted to posterity and put forward nothing for the sake of my name or taste of others, but, knowing well enough the nature of the things that I impart, I deal out work for ages to come. Accordingly I have written and published this Abecedarium, a work with little formality and quite without ostentation; rather it is like some child's copybook exercise but at least one wholly fit for what it teaches, for it carries us forward into the kingdom of man which, in relation to the sciences, is like the Kingdom of Heaven: none enters it except in the likeness of a little child.

The Abecedarium belongs to Part Four of the *Instauration*, the part which is the ladder or machine of the intellect. Yet this is not the ladder proper, rather it is as a preparative to it. Indeed, the supply of instances and experiments available to me is wholly insufficient for the actual ladder. However, in case I come in for the criticism that someone levelled against the priests in consequence of their fathers, I have judged it more useful to urge and advance the work in many things than to perfect it in a few.

Ordo Abecedarij.

Exporrectiones magnæ.

Cum omnis omnium corporum diuersitas referatur vere, vel ad copiam
& paucitatem materiæ in ijsdem contentæ (id quod in rationes illas
5 densi & rari, si recte accipiantur, incidit), vel ad partium aut
disparitatem inter se, aut posituram & collocationem; cumque omnis
motus corporum & partium ipsorum sit vel sphæricus, idest
vndequaque corpus aut contrahens aut expandens, vel orbicularis siue
rotans, vel in linea recta, vel etiam ex his tribus compositus &
[fo. 24ᵛ] 10 complicatus, manifestissimum est ¹ inquisitionem de exporrectione
materiæ per spatia, quæ fit ex eiusdem copia & inopia, & de motu
coitionis & dilatationis, qui est sphæricus, esse omnium in natura
[maxime] simplicem & vniuersalem. Igitur prima Inquisitio de Raro &
Denso esto, & Alpha numeretur.
15 Explicatio Alpha, siue de Denso & Raro.

Cum natura grauis & leuis, & motus, quem vocant, ad centrum terræ &
ad ambitum coelj, summum habeat cum denso & raro consensum,
præsertim cum de densis ex ratione ponderum præcipue iudicium
faciamus, & hæc res ad seriem motuum proprie pertineat, visum istam
20 Inquisitionem de graui & leui anticipare, & eam proximam a raro &
denso ponere. Ea Inquisitio Beta numeretur.
Explicatio Beta, siue de Graui & Leui.

Cum densum & rarum, licet ex alijs causis & motibus quandoque
conficiantur, sint tamen frigoris & caloris opificia, licet & hæc res
25 quoque ad seriem motuum pertineat, visum est hanc Inquisitionem
anticipare, præsertim cum ad operatiuam partem scientiarum tantum
conducat. Tertia sit Inquisitio, & Gamma numeretur.
Explicatio Gamma, siue de calido & frigido.

2 Exporrectiones] Exporrectrices / Rigault seems to have misread Exporrectiones, reading
-ion- as -ric-. To accept the *c-t* reading would be to accept an apparent nonce formation. For
further remarks on this see *cmts* on p. 307 below   13 [maxime]] / cf. e.g. *OFB*, VI,
p. 128, ll. 32, 34; p. 208, l. 2; p. 322, ll. 7–8
1–2 Ordo . . . magnæ.] lc / in *c-t* this is all on the same line with no stop after Abecedarij and
no cap. for Exporrectiones   5 incidit),] ~)   13 Igitur] lc   21 Ea]
lc   22 Leui.] ~   27 Tertia] lc

The Order of the Abecedarium

The great Determinants of Bulk

All diversity of all bodies may be properly attributed either to the abundance or scarcity of matter contained within them (and that is what matters in the relations between dense and rare rightly understood), or to the parts' disparity among themselves or their arrangement and collocation. Moreover, all the motion of bodies and their parts is either spherical (i.e. the body contracting or expanding at all points), or circular and rotating, or rectilinear, or made up and compounded of these three. Now since all this be so, it is perfectly clear ¹ that the inquiry about bulk of matter in space, which bulk arises from the abundance and scarcity of that very matter, and about the spherical motion of coition and dilatation, is of all things in nature [the most] fundamental and universal. Therefore let the first inquiry be concerned with dense and rare and let it be counted as Alpha.

  Explanation Alpha, or that concerning dense and rare.

Since the nature of heavy and light and the motion which they call *motion towards the centre of the Earth and towards the heights of the heavens* has very close consent with dense and rare (especially as we form a judgement on dense substances mainly by calculating their weights) and since this subject is peculiarly relevant to the list of motions, it seemed right to put this inquiry about heavy and light before the rest and place it nearest to dense and rare. Let this inquiry be counted as Beta.

  Explanation Beta, or that concerning heavy and light.

Since dense and rare, though sometimes brought about by other causes and motions, are still products of heat and cold, and though this matter too is relevant to the list of motions, it seemed right that this inquiry come before them, especially as it contributes so much to the operative part of the sciences. Let it be the third inquiry and counted as Gamma.

  Explanation Gamma, or that concerning hot and cold.

At termini magni, & tanquam duo regna densi & rari, sunt Tangibile &
Pneumaticum. Etsi enim sunt certe plurimi gradus densitatis in
tangibilibus, & tenuitatis in pneumaticis, tamen eminet prorsus &
maxime insignis est differentia ipsius tangibilis & pneumatici inter sese;
5 eo magis quod sit complurium naturarum constitutio. Nam omne
tangibile est visibile, dotatum pondere, resistit obstinatius, & alia id
genus. At pneumaticum inuisibile est, nisi sit lucidum, pondus omnino
exuit, facile cadit sub initijs, & similia. Ideo consentaneum est vt de istis
duabus magnis familijs corporum, tangibilis & pneumatici, quarum
10 sectam & nationem tot virtutes sequuntur, iam Inquisitionem
instituamus. Cum sit ordine quarta, Delta numeretur.

[fo. 25ʳ]   ¹ Explicatio Delta, siue de Tangibili & Pneumatico.

Rursus quia inueniuntur corpora quæ habent naturam potentialem ad
pneumaticum, idest, in vaporem & spiritum solui & verti possunt per
15 ignem, aut alijs modis; inueniuntur itidem alia quæ hoc omnino
respuunt, aut ægre admodum patiuntur; igitur subiungenda est
Inquisitio de volatili & fixo. Ea quinta est, & Epsilon nominatur.

Explicatio Epsilon, siue de volatili & fixo.

Atque istæ quinque Inquisitiones versantur circa exporrectionem
20 materiæ, eiusque copiam aut paucitatem.

Transeundum est iam a quanto materiæ ad schematismos, & quasi telas
eius; neque tamen ipsas particulares & accuratas (illæ enim ad
Abecedarium non pertinent) sed magis catholicas & communes.

Prima igitur & latissime patens schematismorum differentia est talis.
25 Sunt quædam corpora quæ se determinant, & plane consistunt; partes
autem suas vt locatæ sunt sustinent & tuentur. Itaque integralitatem
quandam suscipiunt, adeo vt & in figuras efformari & effingi possint.
Sunt alia quæ labuntur & fluunt, & partes suas statim confundunt &
vniunt, nec se determinant aut effingi patiuntur. Est itaque in ipsis
30 primordijs schematismorum materiæ ponenda Inquisitio de
Determinato, siue consistenti, & fluido, siue liquido. Videntur autem
primo intuitu naturæ hæ tantum habere locum in tangibili; neque enim
inuenitur pneumaticum figuratum. Verumtamen de hoc amplius

5 Nam] lc   7 At] lc   8 Ideo] lc   11 Cum] lc   17 Ea] lc
25 consistunt;] ~,   26 Itaque] lc   28 Sunt] lc   29 Est] lc
31 Videntur] lc   33 Verumtamen] lc

Now the great boundaries and, as it were, two kingdoms of dense and rare are the tangible and pneumatic. For though there are certainly many degrees of density in tangible bodies and tenuity in pneumatic, it is nevertheless the very difference between tangible and pneumatic that is truly conspicuous and really remarkable—the more so because it is constitutive of a good number of natures. For every tangible body is visible, has weight, resists more stubbornly, and other things of that kind. But pneumatic matter is invisible (unless it be bright), absolutely weightless, gives way easily right from the start, and so forth. That is why it is now appropriate to set up an inquiry concerning those two great families of bodies, the tangible and pneumatic, the two sects or nations with which so many other virtues take sides. Since this is fourth in order, let it be counted as Delta.

ᴵ Explanation Delta, or that concerning tangible and pneumatic.

On top of that, because we find bodies which have a nature capable of assuming the pneumatic state (i.e. they can be dissolved and turned into vapour and spirit by fire or in other ways), and because we also find others which have nothing whatever to do with this or scarcely put up with it at all, an inquiry concerning volatile and fixed should therefore be subjoined. This is the fifth and is designated Epsilon.

Explanation Epsilon, or that concerning volatile and fixed.

And these five inquiries are concerned with the bulk of matter and its abundance or scarcity.

But now we must pass on from the quantity of matter to its schematisms and, as it were, networks—but not, however, to the particular or precise (for these do not belong to the Abecedarium) but to the more catholic and common ones.

Accordingly the first and most widespread distinction between schematisms is as follows: there are certain bodies which keep their shape and stay firm; moreover, they support and maintain their parts in set positions. They thus assume a certain structural integrity such that they can be fashioned and formed into shapes. There are other bodies which run and flow away, and immediately blend and bring their parts together, and do not keep their shape or allow themselves to be moulded. Thus, in relation to the very primordia of the schematisms of matter, an inquiry should be set up concerned with stable or consistent and fluid or liquid. However, at first blush, the former natures seem to be located only in tangible matter, for we do not come across pneumatic matter

inquirendum. Sexta itaque Inquisitio de Determinato & fluido esto; ea
Zeta nominetur.

Schematismus Zeta, siue de Determinato & fluido.

Subiungenda est Inquisitio de potentiali ad fluorem; videlicet de eo
5 quod in fluidum verti possit, quale est colliquabile per ignem, &
dissolubile per aquam & alios modos, & contra de eo quod non liquescit
aut soluitur in fluorem. Intelligimus autem hoc de fluore tangibili; quod
enim volatile est erga fluorem pneumaticum, id colliquabile aut
[fo. 25ᵛ] dissolubile est erga | fluorem tangibilem. Septima igitur Inquisitio de
10 Colliquabili atque Dissolubili, & non Colliquabili nec Dissolubili esto;
ea Eta nominetur.

Schematismus Eta, siue de Colliquabili & Dissolubili, & Non.

Inueniuntur corpora quæ sunt mediæ cuiusdam naturæ inter
determinatum & fluidum, vt nec libere fluant, nec constanter
15 determinentur, sed sequacia sint, & tanquam fluida ligata, adeo vt in fila
quædam se continuari patiantur. Ea viscosa aut glutinosa appellare
solemus. Octaua igitur Inquisitio de Glutinoso fluido & consistente
puris esto, & Theta nominetur.

Schematismus Theta, siue de Glutinoso fluido & consistente puris.

20 Rursus inueniuntur corpora, quæ cum sint plane determinata pura,
neque etiam colliquabilia, aut dissolubilia, secundum totum tamen
multum habent intra se fluoris, in tantum vt ille ab illis exprimi aut elici
non difficile possit; alia contra, in quibus determinati partes sunt longe
potiores, vt pote cum sint nullo modo succulenta, sed a fluoribus quasi
25 destituta. Atque hoc sensu (nam notiones illæ elementares de
qualitatibus primis humidi & sicci toties decantatæ sunt vagæ & parum
vtiles) instituenda est Inquisitio de Humido & Sicco vt speciebus
determinati. Nona sit, & Iota nominetur.

Schematismus Iota, siue de Humido & Sicco.

1 Sexta] lc   esto;] ~.   7 Intelligimus] lc   tangibili;] ~.   10 esto;]
~.   16 Ea] lc   23 possit;] ~.   25 Atque] lc   28 Nona] lc

that has any definite shape. All the same, this question should be examined more fully. Thus let the sixth inquiry be concerned with stable and fluid; let it be designated Zeta.

Schematism Zeta, or that concerning stable and fluid.

An inquiry should be subjoined about the capacity for fluidity, namely about that which can be turned into a fluid (such as a thing capable of being liquefied by fire and dissolved both by water and other means) and, on the other hand, about that which does not liquefy or dissolve into a fluid. Now what I am getting at here is *tangible* fluid; for what is volatile produces a pneumatic fluid, while that which is capable of being melted or dissolved generates ¹ a tangible fluid. Therefore let the seventh inquiry be about liquefiable and soluble and not liquefiable or soluble; let this be designated Eta.

Schematism Eta, or that concerning liquefiable and soluble, and not.

We find bodies which are of a particular nature halfway between solid and liquid so that they neither flow freely nor retain their forms permanently, but are sticky and, so to speak, fluids which bond in such a way that they let themselves be drawn out in certain threads. These are usually called viscous or glutinous substances. Therefore let the eighth inquiry be concerning the glutinous which is fluid and made up of pure substances; and let it be designated Theta.

Schematism Theta, or that concerning glutinous which is fluid and made up of pure substances.

Again, we find bodies which, though they are clearly stable bodies pure and simple and not even capable of being liquefied or dissolved as a whole, nevertheless contain within themselves a lot of liquid—so much that it can be forced or coaxed from them without difficulty; on the other hand, there are other bodies in which the parts of the stable body are far stronger, since, as one might expect, these bodies are not at all juicy but almost devoid of fluids. Now in this sense (for the much–trumpeted element theories concerning the primary qualities of moist and dry are vague and virtually useless) an inquiry should be established concerned with moist and dry as species of stable matter. Let this be the ninth inquiry and designated Iota.

Schematism Iota, or that concerning moist and dry.

Atque naturæ colliquabilis aut dissolubilis, glutinosi [&] humidi ad rationes fluorum proprie spectant, cum sint fluores, aut potentiales, aut ex potiore parte. Igitur ordine sequi debent naturæ quæ in determinatis potissimum vigent, licet habeant etiam in fluoribus tam tangibilibus
5 quam pneumaticis locum, sed obscurum. Prima earum est Durum & Molle, quæ ex resistentia & cessione iudicantur. Inueniuntur enim corpora, quæ fortem habent resistentiam aut motum plagæ, idest, non facile cedunt, & summouentur, & in se vertuntur; alia contra facile
[fo. 26ʳ] pelluntur, & ¹ obediunt, & se recipiunt. Decima sit & Kappa nominetur.
10   Schematismus Kappa, siue de Duro & mollj.

Altera natura est fragile & Lentum, siue Tenax & Tensibile, quæ ex separatione obstinata atque subita, aut lenta & gradatim facta iudicantur. Inueniuntur enim corpora tanquam peremptoria & refractaria, quæ aut in sua consistentia prorsus manere & persistere, aut
15 omnino abrumpi volunt; alia quæ non tam facile se deserunt, sed se extendi & flari antequam penitus separentur patiuntur. Neque hæ naturæ prorsus sequuntur rationes duri & mollis; quare visum est de illis per se inquirere. Vndecima sit, & Lambda nominetur.
        Schematismus Lambda, siue de Fragili & Tensili.

20 Cum vero certissimum sit apud nos (nam de interioribus terræ non constat) nullum inueniri corpus tangibile in quo pneumaticum non sit ⟨admi⟩ permixtum & inclusum, cumque naturæ illæ de quibus proxime locuti sumus diuidant corpora secundum rationes fluorum tangibilium, aut partium corporum determinatorum, minime autem secundum
25 naturam pneumatici cum illis conclusis, consentaneum est vt adducamus alias diuisiones corporum ex rationibus pneumatici in illis contenti, ex quo plurimæ virtutes & operationes emanant, quæ vulgo qualitatibus attribuuntur, ac si nihil plane esset in substantia nisi quod caderit sub aspectum. Prima itaque Inquisitio secundum pneumaticum
30 talis est: inueniuntur corpora quæ multum habent ex pneumatico aduentitio, non innato, quod moli corporis se inseruit, aere scilicet communi, aut huiusmodi quopiam, minime autem spiritu corporis intrinseco; alia vero quæ intra claustra sua parum alieni recipiunt, præter

---

1 dissolubilis, glutinosi [&] humidi] dissolubilis glutinosi humidi / emendations seemingly demanded by the three preceding titles

1 dissolubilis,] ~ₐ   3 Igitur] lc   6 Inueniuntur] lc   13 Inueniuntur] lc   16 Neque] lc   17 mollis;] ~.   18 inquirere] Inquirere   20 nos] ~.   25 conclusis,] ~ₐ   30 est:] ~.

Now the natures of liquefiable or soluble, glutinous [and] moist properly refer to the behaviour of fluids, since fluids are either potential or
more fully realized. Thus natures which flourish principally in stable
bodies ought to come next on the list, though these natures also find a
place (but an obscure one) in tangible as well as pneumatic fluids. The
first of these is hard and soft, which are judged by resistance and yielding. For we find bodies which put up strong resistance or exhibit motion
of percussion, i.e. they give way, and get driven back and turned in on
themselves with difficulty; on the other hand, we find other bodies
which get driven back, give way ¹ and recover themselves easily. Let this
be the tenth inquiry and that designated Kappa.

    Schematism Kappa, or that concerning hard and soft.

A second nature is fragile and pliant or tenacious and elastic, which are
assessed by stubborn and abrupt fracture or by slow separation made
gradually. For we find, as it were, self-willed and intractable bodies
which want either to stay and continue in their consistency to the bitter
end or want to be utterly broken up; we find other bodies which are not
so brittle but allow themselves to be stretched and expanded before they
are pulled apart altogether. These natures do not quite follow the behaviour of hard and soft, so it is appropriate to investigate them separately.
Let this be the eleventh inquiry and that designated Lambda.

    Schematism Lambda, or that concerning fragile and tensile.

Now since it is quite certain that on the surface of the Earth (for its
entrails are unknown to us) we find no tangible body in which pneumatic matter is not intermixed and enclosed, and since the natures
which we spoke of just now differentiate bodies according to the behaviour of tangible fluids or of the parts of stable bodies but not according
to the nature of the pneumatic matter enclosed in them, it is appropriate to adduce further distinctions between bodies, distinctions made in
accordance with the behaviour of the pneumatic matter they contain.
For from this proceed most virtues and operations commonly ascribed
(as if the visible apects of a substance were the end of the matter) to qualities. Accordingly the first inquiry framed in terms of pneumatic matter
is as follows: we find bodies containing much foreign, adventitious
pneumatic matter which has crept into the mass of the body, originating
no doubt from the common air or something of that kind, but not at all
from the intrinsic spirit of the body. But we find other bodies which, in

tangibiles suas partes & spiritum suum proprium. Itaque duodecima Inquisitio de Poroso, siue cauo, & de Vnito sive clauso esto; ea Mi nominetur.

Schematismus Mi, siue de Poroso & Vnito.

[fo. 26ᵛ] 5   ¹ Rursus accidit corporibus, etiam illis quæ satis vnita sunt, & parum habent pneumatici aduentitij, vt alia ex ijs nihilominus spiritu natiuo & proprio repleta sint, & turgeant, & sint tanquam bullitiosa; alia copia spiritus destituantur, sintque quoad spiritum ieiuna & euanida, vt pote in quibus partes tangibiles longe dominentur. Itaque plane constituenda

10   est diuisio corporum ex copia & paucitate [spiritus] sui proprij in ijsdem contenti, & facienda Inquisitio decimatertia quæ Ni nominetur.

Schematismus Ni, [siue] de Spirituoso & Ieiuno.

Rursus inueniuntur corpora quæ prædita sunt spiritu acri, forti, potenti, & vigenti, qualia sunt sales, vitriolum, argentum viuum, & nonnulla ex

15   vegetabilibus, nec minus ex animalibus; alia vero ⟨sunt⟩ nacta sunt spiritu*m* lenem, segnem, debilem, & ⟨facill⟩ facile succumbentem. Sumenda igitur est diuisio corporum ex virtute & efficacia spirituum non minus quam ex copia, & adiungenda Inquisitio de Acri & Leni, & cum sit decimaquarta Xi nominetur.

20   Schematismus Xi, siue de Acri & Leni.

Atque videtur hic locus esse vt pergamus ad nobilem illam corporum differentiam, nimirum Animati & Inanimati. Et si enim natura animati trahat secum varia ornamenta; vt corpus organicum, figuram, & co*m*plures motus; tamen differentia animati maxime radicalis consistit

25   in natura spiritus contenti. Verum quoniam natura animata semper viget in corpore admodum inæquali, vt inquisitio de inæqualitate corporum in partibus suis lucem, & tanquam faciem præbeat ad inquisitionem de inanimato, præponendæ videntur eæ ⟨quæ [*illeg.*]⟩ Inquisitiones quæ esse possunt de inæqualitate corporum in partibus

30   suis, & tum demum deueniendum ad inquisitionem de animato, vt vltimo gradu tam exaltationis spiritus, quam multiplicis inæqualitatis.

---

10 [spiritus]] / this is evidently missing here   12 [siue]] / supplied on model of other such titles   27 faciem] facem   28 [*illeg.*]] / one word   29 Inquisitiones] Inquisitione   31 quam] / stands in *c-t* at end of line and recurs dittographically at the start of next

2 esto;] ~.   4 Vnito.] ~ᴧ   9 Itaque] lc   12 Ni,] ~ᴧ
17 Sumenda] lc   24 motus;] ~,

addition to their tangible parts and their proper spirit, admit little else within their walls. Thus let the twelfth inquiry be concerned with porous or hollow and compact or closed. Let this be designated Mu.

Schematism Mu, or that concerning porous and compact.

ⁱ Again, it happens in bodies, even those tolerably compact and which contain precious little adventitious pneumatic matter, that some of them are none the less abundantly provided with their own native spirit, and they swell and are, as it were, effervescent; but others lack this abundance and are, as far as spirit is concerned, insipid and feeble inasmuch as they are ones in which the tangible parts are very much in control. Thus a distinction between bodies should be set up according to the abundance and scarcity of the proper [spirit] contained in them; and a thirteenth inquiry should be made which may be designated Nu.

Schematism Nu, [or] that concerning spirituous and insipid.

Again, we find bodies (such as salts, vitriol, quicksilver, some vegetables no less than animals) furnished with a sharp, strong, powerful, and flourishing spirit. But other bodies have been endowed with a gentle, sluggish, weak spirit which easily gives in. So a distinction between bodies should be derived from the virtue and power of their spirits no less than from their abundance; and an inquiry should be added concerning sharp and gentle, and since it is the fourteenth, let it be designated Xi.

Schematism Xi, or that concerning sharp and gentle.

Now this seems to be the moment for proceeding to that truly noble distinction between animate and inanimate. For although the animate nature brings with it various trappings (as an organic body, shape, and a great many motions), the most fundamental distinction belonging to animate being still consists in the nature of the enclosed spirit. But yet, because the animate nature always flourishes in an exceedingly unequal body, those inquiries which have to do with the inequality of bodies in respect of their parts should stand first so that they may give light and, as it were, form to the inquiry about inanimate; and then indeed we should come to the inquiry about animate, as the final stage not only of the spirit's exaltation but also of manifold inequality.

Prima itaque diuisio sumpta ex corporis inæqualitate intra partes suas talis est: inueniuntur corpora tam inæqualiter & imperfecte coagmentata, vt ⟨subst⟩ subsistant in transitu tantum, nec durare, aut ad
[fo. 27ʳ] tempus paulo ¹ longius se sustinere possint. Itaque decimaquinta
5 Inquisitio sit, & Omicron nominetur.
     Schematismus Omicron, siue de absoluto & imperfecto mixto.

Cum vero inueniantur corpora quæ fere ex homogeneis constant, & sint simplicioris mixturæ, alia vero quæ manifeste sunt composita, & habent in partibus suis plura heterogenea, adeo vt etiam heterogenea illa
10 separari possint, eaque ipsa in aliquibus corporibus discrepantia tantum sint, in aliquibus vero tanquam opposita & contraria, consentaneum est vt fiat iam Inquisitio de simplici & composito eo quo diximus sensu. Ea sit decimasexta, & Pi nominetur.
     Schematis. Pi, siue de simplici & composito.

15 Rursus inueniuntur corpora quæ habent inæqualitatem magis texturæ quam mixturæ, adeo vt habeant in partibus suis fibras apparentes, & venilas, & huiusmodi; alia vero quæ obtinent posituram partium magis simplicem, & ex æquo perfusam. Itaque decimaseptima Inquisitio sit, & Ro nominetur.
20   Schematis. Ro, siue de fibroso & venoso, & simplicis posituræ.

Atque paulo altius penetrandum in naturam rerum. Cum enim in corporibus compositis nonnulla ⟨inueniatur⟩ inueniatur, præter heterogeneam illam in mixtura, aut fibrositatem in textura partium suarum, alia profunda & occulta dissimilaritas, licet ad aspectum
25 corpora illa appareant similaria, nec experimento alio fere quam per sympathias accurata dissimilaritas eorum eruatur, aut perducatur ad actum; qualis inuenitur præcipue in radicibus plantarum, & seminibus, & in spermate animalium; alia vero corpora, quamuis sint composita, & ex heterogeneis conflata, tamen tantam & tam variam dissimilaritatem
30 minime assequuntur visum est hanc inquisitionem ab illa de simplici & composito segregare, & propriam inde Inquisitionem constituere. Ea sit xviii.ᵃ & Sigma nominetur.
     Schemat. Sigma, siue de similari & dissimilari interiori.

---

2 est:] ~.   4 Itaque] lc   12 Ea] lc   18 Itaque] lc   20 venoso,]
~ˇ   21 rerum.] ~ˇ Cum] lc   22 ⟨inueniatur⟩] / deleted because
blotted   30 assequuntur] ~;   31 Ea] lc   32 nominetur.] ~ˇ

Thus the first distinction derived from inequality within the parts of a body is as follows: we find bodies so unequally and imperfectly compounded that they last but fleetingly and cannot persist or sustain themselves [1] for any length of time. Thus let this be the fifteenth inquiry and designated Omicron.

Schematism Omicron, or that concerning perfectly and imperfectly mixed.

Now since we find bodies which are for the most part made up of homogeneous substances and are of a simpler mixture, and others which are manifestly compounded and whose parts contain very many heterogeneous substances, such that these substances can still be separated, and that these are merely different in some bodies, but as opposites and contraries in others, it is appropriate that an inquiry now be made concerned with simple and compounded in the sense just outlined. Let this be the sixteenth inquiry and designated Pi.

Schematism Pi, or that concerning simple and compound.

Again, we find bodies whose inequality lies more in texture than mixture such that they have evident fibres and little veins, and things of that kind in their parts, whereas we find others which have a more simple and evenly distributed arrangement of parts. So let this inquiry be the seventeenth inquiry and designated Rho.

Schematism Rho, or that concerning fibrous and venous, and of simple arrangement.

But we must dig a little more deeply into nature. For since, besides heterogeneity of mixture or fibrosity of texture in the parts of composite bodies, we find some other profound and hidden dissimilarity of the kind found especially in plant roots and both in seeds and animal sperm, though these bodies look similar, and their precise dissimilarity is not brought out or drawn into act by practically any other experiment than by sympathies; and since again we find other bodies, although they are compounded and made up of heterogeneous substances, which fail nevertheless to equal such great and diverse dissimilarity at all, it is appropriate to separate this inquiry from the one about simple and compound and then establish it as an inquiry in its own right. Let this be the 18th and designated Sigma.

Schematism Sigma, or that concerning the internally similar and dissimilar.

[fo. 27ᵛ] ¹ Sequitur Inquisitio de similari & dissimilari exteriore vel de integrali & non integrali. Integrale autem dicitur, cum virtutes & functiones corporis alicuius præcipue consistunt in conspiratione partium suarum, eo ordine positarum vt altera alteram excipiat & iuuet, & non in
5 partibus diuersis & confusis, qualia sunt animata, & machinæ, & organa mechanica, & huiusmodi. Ea Inquisitio sit x̄īx̄.ᵃ & Tau nominetur.
    Schematismus Tau, siue de integrali, & non.

Huic subiungatur Inquisitio de specificato & non specificato. Specificatum autem est, collatio materiæ ex ordine vniuersi, quæ
10 constituit speciem propriam. Neque vero hæc sub priori inquisitione de integrali continetur. Sunt enim integralia quæ non sunt specificata; vt plurima ex artificialibus. Sunt & specificata quæ non sunt integralia; vt metalla & gemmæ. Itaque seorsim fieri debet ista Inquisitio ordine x̄x̄.ᵃ Vpsilon nominetur.
15   Schematis. Vpsilon, siue de specificato, & non.

Cum vero inueniantur corpora quæ sunt rudimenta & inchoationes specierum, atque alia quæ partus existunt specierum commixti & biformes, præter species ipsas perfectas; visum est etiam huic Inquisitioni, quæ ad naturæ sinus occultos perscrutandos & excutiendos
20 admodum est vtilis, non deesse. Ea sit x̄x̄ī.ᵃ & Φ nominetur.
    Schematismus Φ, siue de participijs & interspeciebus, & specificato perfecto.

Cum vero ventum est ad Inquisitionem illam nobilem, quam ante in hunc locum rejecimus, de animato & inanimato. Certissimum enim est
25 omne tangibile hic apud nos habere in se conclusum, ex concoctione & rarefactione facta per solem & coelestia, pneumaticum quiddam. Itaque reperiuntur pneumatica, quæ nihil habent tangibilis, at non reperitur tangibile, quod nihil habeat pneumatici. Pneumaticum vero istud Democrito vacui partes plerumque sustinebat, & in philosophia recepta
30 operationes eius qualitatibus fere deputantur. Iste vero spiritus (hoc enim vocabulo pneumaticum illud commodius appellabimus) in rebus
[fo. 28ʳ] inanimatis a tangibili siue crasso ¹ in ordinem redactus est, &

---

16 Cum] / Rigault first wrote Iam then changed the I to a C
2 Integrale] lc   6 Ea] lc   10 Neque] lc   11 Sunt] lc   12 Sunt] lc   13 Itaque] lc   20 Ea] lc   24 Certissimum] lc   30 Iste] lc

¹ There follows an inquiry about externally similar and dissimilar or about integral and non-integral. Now we speak of *integral* when the virtues and functions of any body subsist not in parts unlike and disordered but chiefly in mutual co-operation, the parts being set up in such a way that one sustains and assists another: animate beings and machines and mechanical devices and the like are of this nature. Let this inquiry be the 19th and designated Tau.

Schematism Tau, or that concerning integral and non-integral.

Let an inquiry concerned with specific and non-specific be annexed to this. Now a specific body is an assemblage of matter according to the order of the universe, an assemblage which constitutes a species in its own right. But this inquiry is not covered by the previous one about integral; for not only are there integral bodies which are not specific, as are many things of artificial origin, but there are also specific bodies which are not integral, as gems and metals. Thus this inquiry ought, in its own right, to be made the 20th in order. Let it be designated Upsilon.

Schematism Upsilon, or that concerning specific and non-specific.

But since we find bodies that are rudiments and commencements of species, and, in addition to the perfect species themselves, others which are births of mixed species and are biform, it would be a good idea to have this inquiry available, which is extremely useful for looking into and searching nature's secret hiding-places. Let this be the 21st inquiry and designated Φ.

Schematism Φ, or that concerning hybrids and interspecifics, and the true specific.

As we have now come for sure to that noble inquiry concerning animate and inanimate (which we previously put off until now), it cannot be denied that every tangible body amongst us has a certain pneumatic component enclosed in it which is attributable to the concocting and rarefying influence of the Sun and heavenly bodies. Accordingly we find pneumatic substances which have no trace of tangible matter, but no tangible body devoid of pneumatic matter. In fact, that pneumatic stuff was what frequently played the roles ascribed to the void in Democritus' philosophy, and in the received philosophy its operations are generally assigned to qualities. Indeed, this spirit (for that is a better name for pneumatic matter) is, in inanimate things, reduced to order and everywhere fenced in, beseiged and made discontinuous ¹ by tangible or gross vndequaque septus & obsessus, & a continuatione sui abscissus, neque etiam aliquam incensionem adeptus est. At in omni animato spiritus ille & sibi prorsus continuatur, & ramosus euadit, & nonnihil ⟨[*illeg.*]⟩ incensus est; vnde plurimæ aliæ naturæ, & motus, & functiones quæ animatis insunt pendent, vt paulo ante diximus. Ea Inquisitio sit x̄x̄ɪɪ.ᵃ & Chi nominetur.

Schematis. Chi, siue de animato & inanimato.

Atque hoc genus de quo diximus spiritus, nempe sibi continuati, ramosi, & nonnihil incensi, tam vegetabili naturæ, quam animali siue sensibili commune est. At natura spiritus animalium habet hoc insuper, vt & majorem in modum incensus sit, & continuatus per ampliores meatus, &, quod caput rei est, habet in corpore quasdam sedes siue cellas, in quibus per se congregatus est, vbi veluti cathedra siue vniuersitas spiritus residet, ad quam rami spiritus referuntur. Ea Inquisitio sit x̄x̄ɪɪɪ.ᵃ & Psi nominetur.

Schematismus Psi, siue de sensibili & non sensibili.

Superest natura, digna certe qua Inquisitiones de consistentijs corporum claudamus. Videri autem possit debuisse collocari post densum & rarum, & exporrectiones materiæ, atque ante schematismos, cum sit schematismorum intimus & maxime substantialis; sed melius visum est illam perspicuitatis gratia retro post illas collocare, quia tam schematismos quam exporrectiones istas percurrit. Habet enim locum in raro & denso, in tangibili & pneumatico, in determinatis & fluoribus, in spiritibus, in specificatis, etiam, vt arbitramur, in æthere & vbique. Ad eam explicandam vtemur vocabulis chimistarum. Etenim si vtamur verbis scholasticis, ea etiam ad sensum scholasticum restringentur. Statuunt Chymistæ tria principia, Sulphur, Mercurium, & Salem. Atque quatenus ad Salem, si intelligant cinerem & fæces terreas, pertinet ad Inquisitionem de volatili & fixo; si naturam salis absque parabola, illa aut in ¹ inquisitione de acri locum habebit, aut sub duobus illis alteris principijs Sulphuris & Mercurij comprehendetur. Omne enim sal habet intra se alias partes inflammabiles, alias flammam exhorrentes. Verum altera illa duo principia reuera sunt naturæ primordiales, & penitissimi

3 nonnihil] non nisi / cf. *DVM*, fo. 30ᵛ (*OFB*, VI, p. 356, l. 31)   8 ramosi] ramosiue / the –ve suffix is not Bacon's style and is in any case redundant

2 At] lc   5 Ea] lc   10 At] lc   14 Ea] lc   18 Videri] lc
22 Habet] lc   24 Ad] lc   25 Etenim] lc   27 Atque] lc   28 fixo;]
~.   31 Omne] lc

matter, and, what is more, it has not acquired any inflammation. But in every animate being the spirit is certainly self-continuous, and both becomes branching and is somewhat inflamed; and it is on this that many other natures and motions and functions which are present in animate beings depend, as we said a little earlier. Let this be the 22nd inquiry and designated Chi.

Schematism Chi, or that concerning animate and inanimate.

Now the kind of spirit which we have described, namely the self-continuous, branching, and somewhat inflamed, is as common to the vegetable nature as to the animal or sensible. But the animal spirit's nature has these extra features: it is inflamed to a greater degree as well as continued via larger passages, and, above all, it has certain seats or cells in the body where it gets together in itself, and where as it were its cathedral or university is located, to which the spirit's branches feed back. Let this inquiry be the 23rd and designated Psi.

Schematism Psi, or that concerning sensible and non-sensible.

There remains a really worthy nature with which we may conclude the inquiries concerning the consistencies of bodies. However, it may seem that this should have been placed after dense and rare and the titles about the bulk of matter, but before the schematisms since it is the most profound and substantial of the latter. But, for the sake of clarity, it is more appropriate to place it at the end after the schematisms because it runs through them as well as through matters relating to bulk. For it finds a place in dense and rare, tangible and pneumatic, in things stable and fluid, in spirits, in specific bodies, and also, I believe, in the ether and everywhere else. I shall make use of the chemists' terminology for explaining this for, were we to use scholastic terms, we would only be stuck with scholastic meanings. The chemists postulate three principles: sulphur, mercury, and salt. And, as for salt, if they mean ash and earthy dregs, it belongs to the inquiry concerning volatile and fixed; but if they mean it in its literal meaning, the nature of salt ¹ shall either find a place in the inquiry about sharp, or be put in with those two principles, the sulphurous and mercurial. For all salt has within it some inflammable parts and some which shrink from flame. But the other two principles are the truly primordial categories of nature and the deepest materiæ schematismi. Has autem naturas vocabulis varijs, oleosi & aquei, pinguis & crudi, inflammabilis & non inflammabilis, flammei & aerei, stellaris & ætherei puri, denique sulphuris & mercurij (quæ delegimus) insignire possumus. Eaque inquisitio sit $\overline{\text{xxiv}}$.ᵃ & Omega 5 nominetur.

Schemat. Omega, siue de sulphureo & mercurialj.

Atque Inquisitiones de exporrectionibus & schematismis materiæ, siue de formis primæ classis (nam ita quoque non male appellare illas licet) iam absoluimus. Transeamus deinceps ab illis ad motus & appetitus 10 rerum simplices. Intelligantur & in his & in illis pertinere ad Abecedarium catholica tantum. Itaque nec in spirituum differentijs ad spiritum humanum inquisitionem produximus, nec in specificati inquisitione de singulis metallis, plantis, aut animalibus inquirere destinamus, vt nec de texturis minutioribus, malleabilis, scissilis, 15 lacerabilis, & huiusmodi, nisi cursim tantum, & obiter. Abecedarium enim non deducit rem ad infimas species. Atque eumdem modum etiam in motibus & reliquis tenebimus; neque enim sunt confundendæ literæ alphabeti cum sillabis & verbis.

Motus Simplices.

20 Quantum Naturæ, siue summa materiæ vniuersalis neque accessionem recipit, neque diminutionem. Inest siquidem omni portioni materiæ, vel minimæ, vis & resistentia, qua se contra vniuersos rerum exercitus tueri possit, nec annihilari se patiatur, cum & subsistat & spatium nonnullum occupet. Neque refert qualem formam adepta sit illa portio, nec vbi 25 collocetur. Vis enim ista, tum in omni materia, tum vbique locorum, [fo. 29ʳ] siue in summitatibus cæli, siue intra viscera terræ, tenet. | Eam vim motum antitypiæ appellamus, atque de eo $\overline{\text{xxv}}$.ᵃ inquisitio esto, quæ duplex αα nominetur.

Motus simplex αα, siue de motu antitypiæ.

30

Corpora mutuo nexu & contactu se inuicem fouent. Plena autem & absoluta diuulsio corporis (etiam ex parte aliqua eius) ab alio corpore, est quasi gradus ad annihilationem, quæ non datur. Igitur corpus

---

1 Has] lc   4 Eaque] lc   9 Transeamus] lc   10 Intelligantur] lc   11 Itaque] lc   16 Atque] lc   21 Inest] lc   24 Neque] lc   25 Vis] lc   26 Eam] lc   vim] ∼,   30 Plena] lc   32 Igitur] lc

schematisms of matter. We can, however, denote these natures by a variety of names: of oily and watery, fat and crude, inflammable and non-inflammable, flamy and airy, stellar and pure ethereal, and finally, by the terms which we have chosen, sulphur and mercury. And let this be the 24th inquiry and let it be designated Omega.

Schematism Omega, or that concerning sulphurous and mercurial.

We have now finished the inquiries about the bulk and schematisms of matter or (for so also may one truly call them) forms of the first class. From these let us pass on next to the simple motions and appetites of things. In the case both of these and of the natures discussed already, only the most universal are taken to belong to the Abecedarium. Therefore in the case of differences of spirits we did not extend the inquiry to the human spirit, and in the case of the inquiry about specific we did not choose to inquire about individual metals, plants or animals—as not, for example, about the slighter textures of malleable, scissile, tearable, and the like, except cursorily and in passing. For the Abecedarium does not descend to the least general species; and we shall stick firmly to the same limits in connection with motions and so forth, for the letters of the alphabet should not be confused with the syllables and words.

The Simple Motions

The quantum of nature or universal sum of matter admits neither increase nor decrease; for a force and resistance inheres in every particle of matter, be it ever so small, with which it can defend itself against entire armies of things, and will not let itself be annihilated since it both stands firm and takes up some space. It makes no difference what sort of form the particle may have acquired nor where it happens to be situated; for this force rules not only in all matter but in all places, whether in the heights of the heavens or the bowels of the Earth. ¹ We call this force *motion of resistance*; and let the 25th inquiry, which may be designated αα, be concerned with this.

Simple motion αα, or that concerning motion of resistance.

Bodies support each other by mutual connection and contact. However, complete and absolute severing of one body (at any point) from another is like a step towards the impossible, namely annihilation. Thus a body

cuiuscumque generis, & vbiuis collocatum, si quid aliud forsan experiatur vt ipsum loco moueat, alterutrum facit, vt aut corpus aliud post se trahat, aut ipsum non obediat, nec moueatur. Illum motum, aut inhibitionem motus, motum nexus appellamus. De eo inquisitionem
5 $\overline{\text{xxvi}}$.ᵃᵐ conficimus. Ea duplex ββ nominetur.

Motus simplex ββ, siue de motu nexus.

Corpora naturalia suam exporrectionem siue dimensum libenter tuentur, & præternaturalem siue pressuram siue tensuram fugiunt. Alia tamen alijs longe cedunt benignius aut obstinatius pro modo texturæ
10 suæ; quinetiam postquam vim subierint, si detur copia, se in libertatem vindicant & restituunt. Hunc itaque motum, motum libertatis appellamus. Videtur enim libertatis quidam amor, qui se constringi aut trahi ægre patiatur. Duplex autem est motus iste; alius a pressura, alius a tensura; atque vterque eorum geminus, quatenus corpora cedunt, &
15 quatenus se restituunt. Quoniam autem iste motus constituit eum qui vulgo violentus vocatur, atque ad innumera pertinet, ideo diligens admodum, & bene particularis facienda est de eo inquisitio. Ea $\overline{\text{xxvii}}$.ᵃ est, & γγ nominatur.

Motus simplex γγ, siue de motu libertatis.

20 Etiam illibenter ferunt corpora separationem partium suarum, & solutionem continuitatis suæ: alia tamen ægrius, vt determinata; alia [fo. 29ᵛ] facilius, vt fluida; quæ tamen & ipsa appetitum se | continuandi haud obscurum produnt; præsertim si tentetur comminutio eorum in particulas valde exiguas. Igitur de motu continuationis sui, tanquam
25 motu nexus speciali, constituitur inquisitio $\overline{\text{xxviii}}$.ᵃ Ea duplex δδ nominatur.

Motus simplex δδ, siue de motu continuationis sui.

Itaque muniuntur ⟨corpora⟩ naturâ corpora ad conseruationem ipsorum motibus quatuor prædictis, tanquam armis defensiuis, quibus se
30 tueantur ab annihilatione, a vacuo, a tortura, & a separatione. Transeundum iam est ad motus per quos corpora videntur appetere meliorationem conditionis suæ, & ferri in potius quiddam, vt magis gaudeant.

---

3 Illum] lc   4 De] lc   5 Ea] lc   6 nexus.] ~ₐ   8 Alia] lc
10 suæ;] ~. copia,] ~ₐ   11 Hunc] lc   12 Videtur] lc   13 Duplex]
lc   15 Quoniam] lc   17 Ea] lc   21 suæ:] ~.   22 fluida;] ~.
24 Igitur] lc   25 Ea] lc

of any kind whatsoever and wheresoever situated, if some other happens to try and move it locally, causes one of the two of them either to carry off the other before it or avoid giving ground or getting moved itself. We call that motion or inhibition of motion *motion of connection*. We adduce a 26th inquiry about this. Let it be designated ββ.

Simple motion ββ, or that concerning motion of connection.

Natural bodies readily defend their bulk or dimension, and fly from preternatural compression or stretching. Nevertheless, according to the nature of their textures, some bodies give way with a great deal more readiness or reluctance than others; once, moreover, they have given in to a force, they deliver and restore themselves to liberty if an opportunity presents itself. We therefore call this motion *motion of liberty*. For there seems to be a certain love of liberty which will hardly suffer itself to be constrained or diverted. However, this motion is of two sorts, one away from compression, the other from stretching; and both motions are a pair as far as bodies give way and as far as they restore themselves. But since this motion constitutes the one commonly called *violent*, and is also relevant to countless things, an extremely careful and very particular inquiry about it should therefore be undertaken. This is the 27th inquiry and is designated γγ.

Simple motion γγ, or that concerning motion of liberty.

Bodies also put up with separation of their parts and disruption of their continuity unwillingly, some however with more difficulty (like stable bodies), others more easily (like fluids); and these very bodies nevertheless betray a marked propensity [1] for self-continuity, especially if one tries to break them up into exceedingly small particles. Thus let a 28th inquiry be set up concerning motion of continuity as a special form of motion of connection. This is designated δδ.

Simple motion δδ, or that concerning motion of continuity.

Thus, for self-preservation bodies are defended by nature by the four motions just mentioned, as by defensive weapons with which to guard themselves against annihilation, a vacuum, torment, and separation. Now we must move on to the motions by which bodies seem to strive for an improvement of their condition, and to be brought to a better state and so be happier.

Primo itaque certum est corpora, si debitis modis immutentur, mutare sphæram, hoc est se contrahere in minorem, vel expandere in ampliorem sphæram; idque libenter & cupide, non grauatim & ægre; adeo vt paulo post noua forma delectata restitui non curent, sed illa noua
5 exporrectione gaudeant. Quoniam vero hoc pertinet ad densum & rarum, ad copiam scilicet & paucitatem materiæ (quæ naturæ, vt diximus, maxime sunt primordiales) idcirco hunc motum nomine ab ipsa materia sumpto insigniuimus, & motum hyles appellauimus. Eius autem inquisitionem anticipauimus in inquisitione de calido & frigido,
10 & obiter in inquisitione de denso & raro hanc ipsam attigimus. Nihilominus quoniam ista condensatio & rarefactio constans sit & sine relapsu, licet proprie sint opificia caloris & frigoris, minime tamen ab illis solis dispensantur, sed etiam ab alijs causis, consentaneum est vt inquisitio etiam de hoc motu seorsum co*n*stituatur. Ea x̄x̄ix̄.ᵃ cum sit
15 duplex ϵϵ nominatur.

Motus simplex ϵϵ, siue de motu hyles.

Corpora appetunt coniungi cum globis, seu massis majoribus connaturalium suorum, prout disponuntur in vniuerso, & si ab ijs seiuncta fuerint in tali forte distantia, in qua perceptio fieri possit (quæ
[fo. 30ᵛ] 20 distantia, | Orbis virtutis, non male vocatur) feruntur recte ad illas massas, modo nihil obsit, vt exules repatriari gaudent. Hinc oritur motus grauis & leuis, qui naturalis dicitur. Videtur autem hic motus etiam nonnullum habere consensum cum motu hyles; in motu enim hyles, mouentur corpora introrsum aut extrorsum, quoad sphæram suam; in
25 hoc autem motu similiter introrsum aut extrorsum, quoad sphæram vniuersi. Verum de hoc parum adhuc liquet: hinc motum de quo agimus, motum congregationis maioris appellamus, necnon motum magneticum magnum. Eius vero inquisitionem, quoad graue & leue, supra anticipauimus. Quatenus vero ad alia, veluti vim lunæ, quæ aquas
30 oceani putatur attollere & humida omnia refocillare, vel vim solis ad ligandum Mercurium ad certum distans, & similia, pertinent etiam ad hunc motum magneticum magnum. Quare & illa inquisitio de graui & leui quantum opus fuerit hic retractari possit, & de reliquis magneticis magnis facienda est inquisitio principalis. Ea cum sit x̄x̄x̄.ᵃ duplex ζζ
35 nominatur.

Motus simplex ζζ, siue de motu congregationis majoris.

8 Eius] lc   11 Nihilominus] lc   14 Ea] lc   21 Hinc] lc   23 hyles;]
∼.   26 liquet:] ∼.   28 Eius] lc   29 Quatenus] lc
31 Mercurium] lc   32 Quare] lc   34 Ea] lc

In the first place then it is certain that bodies change their sphere if they be altered by due means; that is, they contract into a smaller sphere or expand into a larger (and that readily and eagerly, and not unwillingly and with difficulty), to the extent that a little afterwards, delighted by the new form, they do not trouble to return to their former state but enjoy their new bulk. Now since this is relevant to dense and rare, namely to the abundance and scarcity of matter (natures which are, as we have said, especially primordial), we have therefore marked out this motion with a name derived from matter itself and called it *motion of hyle.* However, we anticipated the investigation of this topic in the inquiry about hot and cold, and touched on this very thing in passing in the inquiry concerning dense and rare. Yet, since that condensation and rarefaction are constant and unfailing, and they are, even if properly the works of heat and cold, still not at all controlled by them alone but by other causes too, it is certainly proper that an inquiry concerning this motion be prepared separately. As it is the 29th, it is designated ϵϵ.

Simple motion ϵϵ, or that concerning motion of hyle.

Bodies long to be united with the spheres or greater masses of their con-naturals, according as they are situated in the universe; and if they happen to have been set apart from those masses within the distance that perception reaches to (a distance aptly called ¹ the orb of virtue), they are carried straight to those masses and, provided nothing gets in their way, like exiles they rejoice to be going home again. Hence springs the motion of heavy and light which is called *natural.* But this motion also seems to have some consent with motion of hyle; for in the latter case bodies are moved inwards or outwards with respect to their own sphere, yet in this motion they are moved in like manner inwards or outwards with respect to the sphere of the universe. But so far I have not made my meaning sufficiently plain: hence I call the motion which we are discussing *motion of the major congregation* and also the *great magnetic motion.* Now we anticipated the inquiry into this topic above with respect to heavy and light. But in respect of other things, like the Moon's power, which is supposed to raise up the waters of the ocean and revive all moist bodies, or the Sun's to hold Mercury to a fixed distance, and the like, these are also related to this great magnetic motion. And therefore the inquiry concerning heavy and light can, as far as is necessary, be brought up again here, and the remaining great magnetic motions should be made the meat of the inquiry. This, as it is the 30th, is designated ζζ.

Simple motion ζζ, or that concerning motion of the major

At particulares & proprias corporum amicitias & lites, siue sympathias & antipathias, diligenter & sollicite inquirere oportet, cum & tantas secum ferant ⟨[*illeg.*]⟩ vtilitates, & innumeris fabulis & ingenij co*m*mentis infoelicibus scateant. Interim verissimum est corpora alia
5 quædam corpora allicere, & hoc agere vt secum illa vniantur, quædam autem summouere a se & pellere. Atque has operationes exercent corpora & erga adiacentia & vicina, & intra partes proprias. Eum motum, motum congregationis minoris appellamus. Huius vero motus species etiam magis particulares notatas habemus apud nos, sed magis vt
10 visum est, ne quid forte prætereamus quod adhuc satis explicite non inuenimus, inquisitionem de re constituere generalem. Ea est x̄x̄x̄ı.ᵃ & duplex HꜢ nominatur.

Motus simplex HH, siue de motu co*n*gregationis minoris.

[fo. 30ᵛ] ¹ Videtur autem inesse aliquibus corporibus appetitus quidam, non tam
15 coitionibus aut exclusionis, quam disponendi se ad quemdam situm, ordinem, & posituram eis magis gratam & conformem. Ille vero appetitus certe vel ex primis originibus, vel ex diuturna consuetudine & positura ortum habet. Eum motum, motum disponentem, siue motum situs appellamus, atque inquisitio de eo est ordine x̄x̄x̄ı̄ı.ᵃ & duplex θθ
20 nominatur.

Motus simplex θθ, siue de motu disponente.

Neque vero dotauit corpora natura solummodo appetitu & nixu se conseruandi, aut etiam conditiones suas euehendi & meliorandi, verum etiam se multiplicandi, & formam suam propagandi, & alijs corporibus
25 quæ ad hoc sunt apta & susceptibilia imponendi. Ad ea igitur desideria & motus iam transeundum est.

Inuenitur in corporibus desiderium alia corpora plane occupandi, & de veteri esse suo desinendi, eaque in se vertendi, & quantum suum inde augendi. Neque hoc intelligimus de generationibus plantarum aut
30 animalium, quæ res composita est, & magnam seriem motuum complectitur sed de generatione simplici, atque corporum similarium non integralium, qualis conspicitur in inflammatione, & alimentatione,

---

28 veteri] venti / I owe this reading to Prof. Lidia Procesi
4 Interim] lc   6 Atque] lc   7 Eum] lc   8 Huius] lc   9 nos,] ~.
11 Ea] lc   16 Ille] lc   18 Eum] lc   25 Ad] lc   29 Neque] lc

congregation.

We must, moreover, investigate the individual and particular friendships and quarrels or sympathies and antipathies of bodies with diligence and care, seeing that they bring with them such a number of useful things, as well as swarm with the countless fables and sorry fictions of misplaced ingenuity. At the same time, it is an undeniable fact that bodies do entice certain other bodies (and do this so that they may be united with them) but, on the other hand, keep and drive certain others away from them. Moreover, they bring these operations into play both with regard to adjacent and neighbouring bodies as well as within their own parts. We call this motion *motion of the minor congregation.* Now we have species and even very definite particular instances of this motion amongst us, but it is more to the point to set up a general inquiry about the matter, for fear of accidentally neglecting what has not yet been found out with sufficient clarity. This is the 31st and is designated HH.

Simple motion HH, or motion of the minor congregation.

ᴵ Now in some bodies there seems to be a certain appetite not so much of coition or exclusion as of disposing themselves in a certain situation, condition, and position more pleasant and agreeable to them. Now this appetite certainly springs either from their earliest beginnings or from habit and position long maintained. We call this motion *motion of disposition*, or *motion of situation.* Thus an inquiry concerned with this is 32nd in order and is designated θθ.

Simple motion θθ, or that concerning motion of disposition.

Now nature has not only endowed bodies with an appetite or impulse for preserving themselves or even for raising or bettering their condition, but also for multiplying themselves and propagating their form, and for imposing themselves upon other bodies which are adapted and susceptible to this. Accordingly we must now go on to these desires and motions.

One finds a desire in bodies for wholly ingrossing others, for giving up their former state, and turning those others into themselves and thereby increasing their quantity. But I do not have the generation of plants or animals (which is a composite thing and encompasses a great series of motions) in mind here, but I mean the simple generation of non-integral bodies of uniform constitution—as is seen in burning and alimentation, and the like. We call this [motion] *motion of assimilation*,

& huiusmodi. Hunc [motum] motum assimilationis appellamus, de quo instituetur inquisitio x̄x̄x̄i̅i̅i̅.ᵃ quæ duplex II nominabitur.

Motus simplex II, siue de motu assimilationis.

Neque vero assimilant corpora tantum in corpore aut concreto, veluti
5 cum flamma generat flammam, caro carnem, verum etiam in natura simplici siue virtute, vt cum calidum generat calidum, magnes (qui & ipse [non] vertitur) induit ferrum verticitate. Hanc autem vim diffusiuam siue transitiuam motum excitationis appellamus, quia non tam subigit corpora (id quod facit assimilatio) quam insinuare se videtur,
[fo. 31ʳ] 10 ˡ & excitare in corpore altero naturam, ad quam habebat illud ante no*m*ullam prædispositionem, sed latentem & torpentem. De hoc motu inquisitio x̄x̄x̄i̅v̅.ᵃ instituatur, quæ duplex KK nominetur.

Motus simplex KK, siue de motu excitationis.

At in motu assimilationis, atque etiam excitationis, remoto primo
15 assimilante aut excitante, manet omnino quod assimilatum est & excitatum, vt sit quædam successio; at inueniuntur naturæ & virtutes quæ assimilant certe, & excitant, seque multiplicant & diffundunt, ita tamen vt prorsus pendere videantur ex primo mouente, adeo vt sublato eo aut cessante, secundariæ illæ naturæ assimilatæ & excitatæ statim
20 deficiant & pereant; quales sunt radiationes lucis, & dilatationes sonorum. Eum motum, motum impressionis appellamus, de quo inquisitionem x̄x̄x̄v̅.ᵃᵐ conficimus, quæ duplex ΛΛ numeratur.

Motus simplex ΛΛ, siue de motu impressionis.

Admoniti autem contemplatione motus huius, de quo iam diximus,
25 impressionis, necnon aliorum motuum quæ operantur ad distans absq*ue* communicatione ⟨materiæ⟩ substantiæ, veluti magneticorum, egregij prorsus vsus rem fore iudicamus si etiam de medijs motuum, quoru*m* in motibus ad distans partes sunt eximiæ, inquisitionem propriam constituamus. Ea ordine x̄x̄x̄v̅i̅.ᵃ duplex MM nominatur.
30 MM, siue de medijs motuum.

---

1 [motum]] / emended on model of other such phrases in *ANN* 7 [non]] / cf. *NO*,
2Q1ᵛ (*SEH*, I, p. 341): Similiter Magnes induit Ferrum nouâ partium dispositione, & Motu
Conformi; ipse autem nihil ex Virtute perdit. 20 dilatationes] dilationes
1 Hunc] lc 7 Hanc] lc 11 De] lc 19 cessante,] ~ₐ 21 Eum]
lc 22 numeratur.] ~ₐ 29 Ea] lc

198

concerning which a 33rd inquiry shall be set up, which shall be designated II.

Simple motion II, or that concerning motion of assimilation.

Bodies do not just assimilate in a body or concrete state as, for instance, when flame generates flame, or flesh flesh, but also in the case of a simple nature or virtue, as when heat begets heat, and a loadstone (which is [not] itself changed) bestows verticity on iron. Now we call this diffusive or transitive force *motion of excitation* because it does not so much subdue bodies (which is what assimilation does) as appears to insinuate itself ˡ into the other body and excite within it a nature to which it previously had some inclination, but one hidden and dormant. Let a 34th inquiry be established concerning this motion, an inquiry which may be designated KK.

Simple motion KK, or that concerning motion of excitation.

Now in motion of assimilation and of excitation as well, once the primary cause of assimilation or excitation has been withdrawn, that which has been assimilated or excited in general remains, so that there is a measure of succession; but we find natures and virtues which without doubt assimilate and excite, and both multiply and diffuse themselves, but nevertheless in such a way that they seem to depend entirely on the primary motive cause, such that if this be taken away or cease acting, the secondary natures assimilated and excited immediately fail and come to an end; light rays and diffusion of sounds are of this sort. We call this motion *motion of impression*, concerning which we adduce a 35th inquiry which is counted as ΛΛ.

Simple motion ΛΛ, or that concerning motion of impression.

However, prompted by consideration of this motion of impression which we have just mentioned, as well as of the other motions which act at a distance without communication of substance as, for instance, the magnetic ones, we judge that it would be a very useful thing if we also set up on its own an inquiry referring to the media of motions, media whose roles in motions acting at a distance are extraordinary. This is the 36th in order and designated MM.

MM, or that concerning the media of motions.

Atque de corporum appetitu & contentione, vel ad conseruandam naturam suam, vel ad euehendam siue meliorandam, vel [ad] propagandam, has inquisitiones ordina[ui]mus. Est & aliud genus appetitus, quo videntur corpora velle frui, & exercere naturam suam, cum nec sint posita in aliqua necessitate se conseruandi, nec laborent desiderio se vel exaltandi vel multiplicandi. Atque primo, cum corpora haud pauca sint tanquam societates quædam aut ciuitates, in quibus aliqua natura prædominatur & excellit, certum est eam ¦ quæ excellit naturam exercere in reliquis veluti imperium quoddam, adeo vt domet & disponat illas prout conducat, non ad effectus suos proprios, sed ad bene esse imperantis, quæ interim plane se fruitur, & perpetuo exercet vim & potestatem suam. Hunc motum, motum regium appellamus, atque de eo inquisitionem $\overline{\mathrm{xxxvii}}$.ᵃᵐ conficimus, quæ duplex NN nominatur.

         Motus simplex NN, siue de motu regio.

Corpora vero quæ ita foeliciter composita & collocata sunt, vt nec sibi nec alijs molesta sint aut negotium facessant, sed sint prorsus seipsis contenta, ideoque ab omni mutationis desiderio sint libera, nihil scilicet habent quod agant, nisi vt natura sua fruantur. Horum nimirum duplex est genus: alterum eorum quæ motu gaudent, alterum eorum quæ amant quietem, & motum exhorrent. Quare sequitur inquisitio de rotatione spontanea, qualis est coelestium. Is enim motus sine termino est, neque itinerarius videtur vt quiescat, sed se exercet libenter & perpetuo. Ea $\overline{\mathrm{xxxviii}}$.ᵃ sit, & duplex ΞΞ nominetur.

         Motus simplex ΞΞ, siue de rotatione spontanea.

Huic subiungitur inquisitio de motu cui motus nomen vix comperit, per quem corpora ad quietem inclinant, & motum illibenter suscipiunt atque adspirant ad immobile. Hunc motum siue appetitum, motum decubitus appellamus, de quo inquisitionem $\overline{\mathrm{xxxix}}$.ᵃᵐ conficimus, quæ duplex OO nominatur.

         Motus simplex OO, siue de motu decubitus.

---

2 [ad]] / Bacon's style almost demands this emendation cf., for instance, *PAH*, c3ʳ (*SEH*, I, p. 402); *DAS*, N4ʳ, Y4ᵛ, 2C1ᵛ (*SEH*, I, pp. 508, 568, 589)   3 ordina[ui]mus] ordinamus / a perfect seems to be required here cf. p. 190, l. 9, p. 196, l. 22 above

3 Est] lc   6 Atque] lc   12 Hunc] lc   19 Horum] lc   20 genus:] ~.   21 Quare] lc   22 Is] lc   24 Ea] lc   28 Hunc] lc

Now these inquiries we [have] set out concerning the appetite and striving of bodies either to preserve their nature or raise or improve it, or to propagate it. But there is another class of appetite whereby bodies seem to wish to enjoy and to exercise their nature, seeing that they are neither placed under any necessity to preserve themselves nor suffer from the desire to raise or multiply themselves. Thus, in the first place, since most bodies are like certain communities or cities in which some nature has the upper hand and is pre-eminent, it is true ¹ that the pre-eminent nature exerts, as it were, a degree of authority over the others, to the extent that it tames and arranges them as is profitable not to their own operations but to the good of the governing nature which, for the time being, enjoys itself and constantly exerts its power and authority. We call this motion *royal motion*, concerning which we adduce the 37th inquiry which is designated NN.

Simple motion NN, or that concerning royal motion.

But bodies which are so favourably compounded and placed that they cause annoyance and trouble neither to themselves nor others but are perfectly satisfied in themselves and so are free of all desire for change, evidently have nothing to do except enjoy their own nature. In fact these bodies are of two sorts: ones which rejoice in motion, and others which love quiet and shrink from motion. Hence there follows an inquiry concerning spontaneous rotation, such as is the motion of the heavens. For this motion is endless, and does not seem to be journeying to a resting place, but to exercise itself willingly and forever. Let this be the 38th inquiry and designated ΞΞ.

Simple motion ΞΞ, or that concerning spontaneous rotation.

To this we subjoin an inquiry about a motion for which the name of motion barely serves, a motion by which bodies tend to keep still, support motion grudgingly and aspire to immobility. We call this motion or propensity *motion of repose*, concerning which we adduce a 39th inquiry which is designated double OO.

Simple motion OO, or that concerning motion of repose.

Inter hos duos motus rotationis perpetuæ & decubitus se offert motus tanquam medius, videlicet corporum quæ ita locantur inter commoda & incommoda, vt nec statu suo contenta sint, & tamen si ab eo recedere experiantur, incidant in ea quæ rursus fugiant; vnde perpetuo agitantur, & tentant, & irrequiete se habent. Eum motum, ¹ motum trepidationis vel palpitationis appellamus, de quo inquisitionem x̄x̄x̄x̄ conficimus, quæ duplex ΠΠ nominatur.

[fo. 32ʳ] 5

Motus simplex ΠΠ, siue de motu trepidationis.

Atque motus simplices corporum sunt tales. Ii autem coniuncti, complicati, continuati, alternati, frenati, repetiti, omnes actiones corporum & materiati constituunt, pro diuersitate exporrectionum & schematismorum materiæ ex quibus emanant.

10

Transeundum itaque nunc est motus compositos & pronectos, & quasi pensa sint, summas motuum, quæ scilicet ex simplicium motuum aggregatione & dispensatione proueniant. Etiam motus quosque appellamus; nimirum cum post complures motus simplices producatur res ad summam quandam, idest ad affectum siue mutationem notabilem. Atque hic Peripatetici auspicantur, parum aut nihil de corpore naturæ stringentes.

15

Summæ Motuum.

20

Primo igitur inquiramus de disordinatione partium in corporibus, cum absque aliquo addito aut detracto fiat mutatio in corpore, soluta tantum compage eius, aut varie disposita. De qua x̄x̄x̄x̄ī.ᵃ inquisitio conficitur, quæ duplex PP nominatur.

Summa PP, siue de disordinatione partium.

25

Separatio corporum, tam integralium, quam partium in corpore similari, magnos producit effectus, cum partes magis homogeneæ separatæ aliquando liberentur ab impedimentis, aliquando exaltentur a virtute respectu compositi. Rursus si forte virtus sit ita complicata, vt in composito præcipue consistat, in partibus minime, tum contra partes illæ simplices exuunt virtutes compositi, & redduntur tanquam magis

30

---

5 Eum] lc 8 trepidationis.] ∼ ∧ 15 Etiam] lc 18 Atque] lc 20
Motuum] lc 23 De] lc

Between those two motions of perpetual rotation and repose, there
occurs what might be called an intermediate motion, namely a motion
of bodies which are so placed between convenient and inconvenient circumstances that they are not satisfied with their situation and yet, if they
try to retreat from it, they fall into a state which again they shun. For this
reason they are constantly agitated, and they struggle and act restlessly.
We call this motion ¹ *motion of trepidation* or *palpitation*, concerning
which we adduce a 40th inquiry which is designated IIII.

Simple motion IIII, or that concerning motion of trepidation.

Such, then, are the simple motions of bodies. But these, connected
together, complicated, continued, alternated, curbed, and repeated constitute all actions of bodies and of material substance, according to the
variety of bulk and schematisms of matter from which they originate.
So now we must move on to motions compounded and interwoven and
like threads spun together, to the sums of motions which may evidently
arise from the aggregation and control of the simple motions. Yet we call
all of these motions too, and no wonder seeing that after many simple
motions the matter is brought to a particular conclusion, i.e. to a
remarkable state or alteration. But here the Peripatetics make a beginning, getting a feeble grip on the body of nature or no grip at all.

The Sums of Motions

Therefore let us first inquire about the disarrangement of parts in bodies, since change may occur in a body without anything having been
added or subtracted, when only its structure has been loosened or
arranged differently. We adduce a 41st inquiry about this, which is designated PP.

Sum PP, or that concerning the disarrangement of parts.

Separation, whether of integral bodies or of the parts in bodies of uniform constitution, gives rise to great effects since the more homogeneous
of the separated parts are sometimes freed from constraints, and at other
times raised from the virtue exerted by the compound. On the other
hand, if the virtue happens to be so intricate that it resides chiefly in
the compound and not at all in the parts, then the simple parts divest
themselves of the virtues of the compound and are rendered, as it were,

adiaphoræ. Ideo de separatione constituatur inquisitio x̄x̄x̄x̄ii.ᵃ quæ
duplex ΣΣ nominetur.

Summa ΣΣ, siue de separatione.

[fo. 32ᵛ] ⌐At compositio & mixtura corporum ad innumera pertinet, & est magis
5 in parte hominis. Atque corpora ipsa ingredientium in compositum vel
mixtum, & quantitates ipsorum satis se, præsertim in artificialibus,
manifestant & sunt tanquam in medio positæ. Quatenus autem natura
ferat istam incorporationem, & quomodo corpora quæ miscentur se
mutuo insinuent, & applicent, & vniant, & collocentur (id quod ad
10 præparandi & conficiendi modos pertinet, atque ex motuum
simplicium aggregatione & serie pendet & erui debet) res est magis
abstrusa & abscondita. Mixtionem autem quatuor elementorum scholæ
permittimus, cum sit phantasticum quiddam & verbula. Loquimur
autem de mixturis magis secundum sensum. x̄x̄x̄x̄iii.ᵃ igitur inquisitio
15 constituatur de summa compositionis & mixturæ. Ea duplex TT
nominetur.

Summa TT, siue de compositione & mixtura.

A disordinatione, separatione, & mixtura corporum procedendo,
videtur locus vt de generatione inquiramus. Attamen præponenda
20 videtur inquisitio de putrefactione, quæ est rudimentum generationis,
siue superinductio formæ nouæ, & est summa diuersorum motuum
simplicium, qui partim ad dissolutionem naturæ veteris, partim ad
tentamenta quædam naturæ nouæ pertinent. Sit hæc x̄x̄x̄x̄iiii.ᵃ
inquisitio, quæ duplex YY nominetur.
25 Summa YY, siue de putrefactione.

Iam vero sequitur summa motuum quæ pertinet ad generationem
corporum. Atque ne in inquisitione confundantur capita, traducto
vocabulo generationis ad sensum nostrum, intelligimus generationem
esse propagationem ex semine, aut e menstruo, siue collatione materiæ
30 quæ sit instar seminis, a quibus per seriem motuum simplicium sensim
[fo. 33ʳ] producatur corpus specificatum. Itaque x̄x̄x̄x̄v.ᵃ ⌐ inquisitio de
generatione esto. Ea duplex ΦΦ nominetur.
Summa ΦΦ, siue de generatione.

1 Ideo] lc   5 Atque] lc   7 Quatenus] lc   12 Mixtionem] lc
13 Loquimur] lc   15 Ea] lc   19 Attamen] lc   23 Sit] lc
27 Atque] lc   28 nostrum,] ~ˬ   31 Itaque] lc   32 Ea] lc

more neutral. Let us therefore set up a 42nd inquiry concerned with separation, and that designated ΣΣ.

Sum ΣΣ, or that concerning separation.

ᴵ But the compounding and mixture of bodies bear on countless things, and are more completely at man's command. Now the bodies themselves and the amounts of them entering into a compound or mixture display themselves tolerably well in artificial things particularly and are placed as if out in the open. Yet how far nature will bear this incorporation and how the bodies which are mixed together may reciprocally insinuate themselves, join, unite and put themselves together (which is what counts for means of preparation and production, and what is also uncertain and must be derived from an aggregation and series of simple motions), that is a matter more abstruse and hidden. However, we pass over the scholastic four–element mixtion theory as it is a thing extravagant and garrulous. We prefer to speak of mixtures more according to sense. Thus let a 43rd inquiry be established, one concerning the sum of compounding and mixture. Let this be designated TT.

Sum TT, or that concerning compounding and mixture.

Advancing from disarrangement, separation, and mixture of bodies, this seems to be the place to inquire about generation. However, it does seem that priority should be given to the inquiry concerned with putrefaction. Putrefaction is a rudiment of generation, or the superinduction of a new form, and sum of various simple motions which belong in part to the dissolution of an old nature, and in part to certain tentative efforts of a new. Let this be the 44th inquiry which may be designated YY.

Sum YY, or that concerning putrefaction.

Now, however, comes the sum of motions which relates to the generation of bodies; and, lest the headings in the inquiry be confused, when the term *generation* is converted to our use, we mean that generation is propagation from seed, or from a menstruum or gathering of matter which may be equivalent to seed, things from which a specific body is gradually formed by a series of simple motions. Thus let the 45th ᴵ inquiry be about generation. Let it be designated ΦΦ.

Sum ΦΦ, or that concerning generation.

Huic summæ generationis opponitur summa illa corruptionis &
interitus, qua destruitur forma specificati. Atque iste effectus, licet
plerumque transigatur per motus simplices longe pauciores, & magis
subtiles, & magis accuratos quam summa genera*ti*onis, nihilominus
5 omnino collocandus est inter summas. Loquimur item de tali
corruptione seu mortificatione quæ non destituitur, vt quandoque fit in
metallis. Hæc igitur summa in $\overline{\text{xxxxvi}}$.ᵃᵐ inquisitionem incidit, &
duplex XX nominatur.

Summa XX, siue de corruptione.

10 Inter terminos generationis & corruptionis interiacet duratio rei. Itaque
de conseruatione corporum quæ durationem rei prolongat, & interitum,
aut etiam gradus & declinationes versus interitum arcet, inquisitio sequi
debet. Neque argutijs opus est, quod minime scilicet oporteat reponere
conseruationes corporum inter summas mutationum, cum sint potius
15 mutationum priuationes. Etenim simile quiddam fecimus collocando
appetitum ad quietem inter motus [simplices]. Neque enim reperitur
aliqua conseruatio quæ seruet res simpliciter immutatas, sed quæ motus
& mutationes in deterius alijs motibus & mutationibus salutaribus
impediat, retundat, & æquilibret. Itaque de conseruatione constituatur
20 inquisitio $\overline{\text{xxxxvii}}$.ᵃ Ea duplex ΨΨ nominetur.

Summa ΨΨ, siue de conseruatione.

Quoniam vero præcipue conseruantur corpora per alimentatione*m* quæ
deprædationes corporis a spiritu vitali, necnon aere circumfuso factas
reparat, visum est instituere inquisitionem de summa alimentationis.
25 Neque vero existimet quispiam hanc inquisitionem sub illa de
[fo. 33ᵛ] assimilatione contineri, nam licet verum sit vltimam | actionem
alimentationis esse ipsam assimilationem, tamen memoria tenendu*m* est
assimilationem esse motum simplicem, alimentationem vero summa*m*,
quæ per præparationes, digestiones, attractiones, separationes, &
30 huiusmodi desinat tandem in assimilationem. Itaque de alimentatione
inquisitio $\overline{\text{xxxxviii}}$.ᵃ esto, quæ duplex ωω nominetur.

Summa ωω, siue de alimentatione.

---

4 subtiles] subitos / surely the copyist's error; cf. *NO*, L4ᵛ (*SEH*, I, p. 191): Res enim . . . subtilis est certè & accurata, confectio horologiorum; also cf. *NO*, T3ᵛ (*SEH*, I, p. 234):
Schematismus res est longè subtilior, & accuratior   16 [simplices]] / an obvious lacuna

2 Atque] lc   5 Loquimur] lc   7 Hæc] lc   10 Itaque] lc
13 Neque] lc   15 Etenim] lc   16 Neque] lc   19 Itaque] lc
20 Ea] lc   25 Neque] lc   30 Itaque] lc   31 esto,] ∼.

Set against the sum of generation is that of corruption and destruction, the sum by which the form of a specific body is overthrown. Now this effect, although it is often accomplished by simple motions much slighter and both more subtle and exact than the sum of generation, should nevertheless be expressly placed among the sums. We also speak of such corruption or mortification which does not destroy the form, as sometimes happens in metals. So this sum thus falls within the 46th inquiry and may be designated XX.

> Sum XX, or that concerning corruption.

Bounded by generation and corruption is the duration of a thing. Therefore an inquiry ought to follow concerning the conservation of bodies, which prolongs a thing's duration and holds off its destruction, or at any rate the steps and processes leading to destruction. And it is no use arguing that, as conservations of bodies are privations rather than sums of changes, it is quite wrong to place them amongst the sums; for we did something similar in placing the appetite for rest among the [simple] motions. For nowhere do we come across conservation that can keep things unaltered in a straightforward way, but we do find one that can retard, blunt, and balance motions and changes for the worse with other motions and changes of a wholesome kind. Thus let a 47th inquiry be established, one concerned with conservation. Let this be designated $\Psi\Psi$.

> Sum $\Psi\Psi$, or that concerning conservation.

Now seeing that bodies are chiefly conserved by alimentation, which repairs the ravages inflicted on the body by the vital spirit as well as the ambient air, an inquiry should be set up about the sum of alimentation. But let no one run away with the idea that this inquiry is comprised by the one about assimilation; for although it is true that the final ¹ act of alimentation is assimilation itself, we should nevertheless remember that assimilation is a simple motion, but that alimentation is a sum which, by preparations, digestions, attractions, separations and the like, eventually ends up in assimilation. Thus let the 48th inquiry be about alimentation, an inquiry which may be designated $\omega\omega$.

> Sum $\omega\omega$, or that concerning alimentation.

Sequitur summa augmentationis, cum corpora absque appositione aut adjectione corporis plane eiusdem, sed introcepto aut admisso corpore diuerso per alimentationem, vel accretionem, vel vtrumque, augentur mole & quanto suo. De ea sit inquisitio $\overline{\text{xxxxix}}$.ᵃ quæ triplex A
5   nominetur.

Summa AAA, siue de augmentatione.

Subiungitur summa ad eam de augmentatione relatiua, cum corpora absque manifesta & exteriore detractione aut sublatione alicuius partis corporis sui decrescunt inter claustra sua, & consumuntur. De ea
10 inquisitio $\overline{\text{L}}$.ᵃ esto, quæ triplex B nominetur.

Summa BBB, siue de diminutione.

Visum est autem hoc loco non omittere inquisitionem de summa nobili prorsus & rara, nempe versionis, siue metamorphoseos corporum, effectu profecto in natura potissimo, vt pote per quod hominis potestas
15 (in quantum conceditur) exaltatur maxime. Id fit cum corpora nec ex seminalibus principijs, nec ex alimentorum prædispositionibus, sed per metaschematismorum vias profundas & potentes de specificato in specificatum, vel saltem de corpore perfecto in perfectum transeunt, transplantantur, & vertuntur. De ea summa instituimus inquisitionem
20 $\overline{\text{LI}}$.ᵃᵐ quæ triplex Γ nominatur.

Summa ΓΓΓ, siue de metamorphosi.

[fo. 34ᵛ] | Iam vero deuenit inquisitio, licet saltu maximo (neque enim res cognatas disiungere licebit) a summa mutationis maxima ad summam ex interioribus minimorum, idest alterationem simplicem, quæ commune
25 possit esse diuersorium omnium mutationum, quæ nec sub motibus simplicibus, nec sub summis motuum quos iam ante recensuimus comprehenduntur. De ea inquisitio $\overline{\text{LII}}$.ᵃ esto, quæ triplex Δ nominetur.

Summa ΔΔΔ, siue de alteratione.

Superest summa plane extranea & forinseca, & nihil ad schematismos
30 corporis pertinens. Ea est latio localis cum corpora locum & ʿnilʾ aliud mutant. Enimuero recte accipiendum est vocabulum illud lationis localis. Neque enim dubium est quin pleraque, tam ex motibus simplicibus quam ex summis, sint plane lationes locales per minima siue

---

23 licebit] licebat / cf. *NO*, O3ᵛ (*SEH*, I, p. 205)

| 4 De] lc | 9 De] lc | 15 Id] lc | 19 De] lc | 28 De] lc |
| 30 Ea] lc | 31 Enimuero] lc | 32 Neque] lc | | |

The sum of growth comes next, seeing that bodies may be increased in their mass and quantity without apposition or annexation of an identical body, but by a different body absorbed or admitted by alimentation or accretion or both. Let the 49th inquiry which may be designated triple A be about this.

Sum AAA, or that concerning growth.

We subjoin a sum relative to that concerning growth since bodies grow smaller and are wasted away within their own bounds without obvious, external withdrawal or removal of any of the body's own parts. Let the 50th inquiry, designated triple B, be about this.

Sum BBB, or that concerning diminution.

However, it would not seem proper at this point to leave out an inquiry about a really noble and rare sum, namely that of the transformation or metamorphosis of bodies, a most powerful effect in nature and one by which human power is (as far as it is allowed) raised to the highest degree. This occurs most of all when bodies are changed, transplanted, and altered from one species to another, or at least from one perfect body to another, by reason neither of seminal principles nor predispositions of foods but by the profound and powerful means of metaschematisms. Concerning this we have set up a 51st inquiry which is designated triple Γ.

Sum ΓΓΓ, or that concerning metamorphosis.

¹ As it would not do to separate related topics, the inquiry now moves on, albeit with a mighty leap, from the greatest sum of change to the sum arising from the depths of the *minima*, i.e. to simple alteration which can be the common lodging-house for all changes not comprised by the simple motions or sums of motions already reviewed above. Let the 52nd inquiry, which may be designated triple Δ, be concerned with this.

Sum ΔΔΔ, or that concerning alteration.

There remains a sum which is wholly extrinsic and external, and nothing to do with a body's schematisms. This is local motion, when bodies change position and `nothing' else. But this expression *local motion* must be taken in its proper sense. For no one doubts that most of the simple motions no less than the sums are just local motions *per minima* or through particles; and these motions cannot take place or be

per particulas; neque aliter fieri aut expediri possunt. Sed loquimur de motu locali manifesto corporis integri per spatium notabile, non occulto intra claustra corporis ipsius. De ea inquisitio $\overline{\text{LIII}}$.ᵃ conficitur, quæ triplex E nominatur.

5   Summa EEE, siue de latione.

Quoniam vero omnis latio localis, siue vehat integra, siue obrepat per particulas, mouetur aut in lineis sphæricis, aut in circularibus, aut in rectis, aut in obliquis & compositis (id quod ad naturas & rationes motuum magni est momenti) visum est inquisitionem separatim
10 constituere de lineis lationis. Ea $\overline{\text{LIV}}$.ᵃ esto, quæ triplex Z nominetur.
                Summa ZZZ, siue de lineis lationis.

Postquam vero iam de motibus simplicibus, atque etiam de motibus compositis, siue de summis motuum inquisitiones enumeratæ sunt, videndum ne vagæ sint illæ inquisitiones, & parum certæ, atque
15 intellectui quidem quodammodo satisfacientes, sed operi minime respondentes. Quamobrem accedendum propius ad mathematica, siue mensuras & scalas motuum, sine quibus bene numeratis, & pensitatis,
[fo. 34ᵛ] & limitatis, doctrina motuum fluctuat, nec constanti tramite ¹ traducitur ad practicam. Quocirca primo inquiremus de mensura quanti, & de
20 virtute vnionis siue cumulationis, quia conducat illa & faciat ad motus & operationes inde manentes. De mensura quanti igitur fiat inquisitio $\overline{\text{LV}}$.ᵃ quæ triplex H nominetur.
          Mensura motus HHH, siue de mensura quanti.

Quoniam vero quantitas corporum varie colligatur & deuincitur, &
25 virtus quanti ipsius, si vinculum fuerit arctum, communicatur magis, si laxum, minus; igitur non perficitur inquisitio de mensura quanti absque inquisitione de mensura vinculi. De ea inquisitio $\overline{\text{LVI}}$.ᵃ esto, quæ triplex Θ nominetur.
         Mensura motus ΘΘΘ, siue de mensura vinculi.

30

Procedendo inquiremus de mensura spatij, siue de orbe virtutis, hoc est, ad quæ spatia corporum vires perferantur, cessant, intendantur, & remittantur, siue fiat operatio tantum ad tactum, siue ad distantiam

---

1 Sed] lc   3 De] lc   5 latione.] ~ₐ   10 Ea] lc   16 Quamobrem] lc
19 Quocirca] lc   21 manentes.] ~ₐ   De] lc   25 magis,] ~ₐ   27 De] lc

produced in any other way. But we are speaking here of the manifest local motion of whole bodies over a distinct distance, and not of the motion hidden within the confines of the body itself. We adduce a 53rd inquiry about this which is designated triple E.

Sum EEE, or that concerning local motion.

But since all local motion, be it transporting whole bodies or stealing through the particles, is conveyed on spherical or circular paths, or on straight or oblique and compound ones (which is an issue of great moment for the natures and modes of motions), it seems proper to establish a separate inquiry about the paths of motion. Let this be the 54th which may be designated triple Z.

Sum ZZZ, or that concerning the paths of motion.

But now when the inquiries concerned with simple motions as well as the compound motions or sums of motions have been reckoned up, we must be careful that they are not diffuse, lacking in rigour, and in a manner intellectually satisfying but useless in practice. This is why we must get closer to the mathematics or measures and scales of motions, without which, well counted and weighed and defined, the doctrine of motions may falter and not be reliably translated ¹ into practice. For this reason we shall first inquire concerning the measure of quantity and virtue of concentration or accumulation, because that promotes and contributes to the operations and motions remaining thereafter. Thus let the 55th inquiry be about measure of quantity, an inquiry which may be designated triple H.

Measure of motion HHH, or that concerning measure of quantity.

But seeing that the quantity of bodies is bound or overcome in various ways, and the virtue of the quantity itself is communicated more if the bonds be tight, and less if slack, the inquiry about the measure of quantity is therefore incomplete without an inquiry about the measure of bonding. Let the 56th inquiry which is designated triple Θ be about this.

Measure of motion ΘΘΘ, or that concerning the measure of bonding.

Moving on, we shall inquire about measure of distance or the orb of virtue; this is the distance which the powers of bodies may travel to, stop at, build up to and die down from—whether the operation occur by minorem, [siue ad majorem,] siue non excitetur bene in spatijs intimis, siue languat in vltimis, & huiusmodi. Nam de potestate mediorum antea per se inquisiuimus. Mensura igitur spatij $\overline{LVII}$.ᵃ inquisitio instituatur, quæ triplex I nominetur.

5   Mensura motus III, siue de mensura spatij.

Sequitur inquisitio de mensura temporis, videlicet quanto spatio temporis motus sua faciant curricula, quique sint citatiores & anteuertant, qui tardiores & subsequantur, atque quibus interuallis fiant motuum inceptiones, cessationes, restitutiones siue periodi, &
10 huiusmodi. De ea fiat inquisitio $\overline{LVIII}$.ᵃ quæ triplex K nominetur.
     Mensura motus KKK, siue de mensura temporis.

Sequitur inquisitio de mensura fortitudinis, quantum scilicet possint & polleant motus, & quæ vincere possint, & quibus contra effectibus
[fo. 35ʳ] impares sint, quique ex ijs in concursu & conflictu ¹ prædominentur &
15 reliquos doment & frænent, qui vero succumbant & lateant, atque in qualibus subiectis motus singuli præcipue vigeant, in quibus rursus langueant, & similia. Itaque de mensura fortitudinis conficitur inquisitio $\overline{LIX}$.ᵃ quæ triplex Λ nominatur.
     Mensura motus ΛΛΛ, siue de mensura fortitudinis.

20 Quoniam vero fortitudo motuum & virtutis in corporibus quandoque intenditur & confortatur, quandoque remittitur & debilitatur, ratione corporum ambientium & circumfusorum, quæ interdum sunt cognata, interdum contraria, ideo non perficitur inquisitio de mensura fortitudinis absque inquisitione de mensura peristaseos. Ea $\overline{LX}$.ᵃ esto, &
25 triplex M nominetur.
     [Mensura] MMM, siue de mensura peristaseos.

Atque inquisitiones de motibus cum eorum summis & mensuris iam pertransiuimus. Cum vero iudicium, tam de schematismis materiæ

---

1 [siue ad majorem,]] / the *c-t* contrast between ad tactum, siue ad distantiam minorem makes no sense; also cf. *NO*, 2M4ʳ (*SEH*, I, p. 322): Inueniuntur etiam quidam Motus & Virtutes contrariæ illis quæ operantur per Tactum, & non ad Distans; quæ operantur scilicèt ad Distans, & non ad Tactum; Et rursùs, quæ operantur remissiùs ad Distantiam minorem, & fortiùs ad distantiam maiorem.   4 triplex] duplex   22 circumfusorum] circumcessorum / cf. *DVM*, fo. 5ʳ (*OFB*, VI, p. 282): Crassiorum postremo loco de differentijs ambientium aut Circunfusorum dicendum est.   26 [Mensura] / this supplied on the model of other such titles

2 Nam] lc   3 Mensura] lc   10 De] lc   17 Itaque] lc   24 Ea] lc   28 Cum] lc

contact alone, or at a [greater or] lesser distance, whether it be not excited well over the shortest distances, or slacken off over the longest, and the like. Then again we have examined the power of media in themselves earlier on. Thus let a 57th inquiry be established concerning the measure of distance, which inquiry is designated triple I.

    Measure of motion III, or that concerning measure of distance.

Next comes an inquiry about measure of time; namely, how great a stretch of time motions take to run their courses; and which are quicker and act first, which slower and come along after, and the intervals in which the beginnings, ends, returns or periods and so on of motions happen. Let the 58th inquiry which is designated triple K be about this.

    Measure of motion KKK, or that concerning measure of time.

There follows an inquiry concerning measure of strength, namely how far motions carry power and weight, and which things they may vanquish; and to which effects they may, on the contrary, be unequal; and which of them may, in colliding and clashing, [^1] get the upper hand and control and curb the rest, and which again succumb and lie low; and also in what sorts of subjects individual motions flourish especially, and in which, on the contrary, they are enfeebled, and the like. Thus a 59th inquiry, which is designated triple Λ, is adduced concerning measure of strength.

    Measure of motion ΛΛΛ, or that concerning the measure of
strength.

But seeing that strength of motions and virtue in bodies is sometimes intensified and strengthened, and at other times diminished and weakened by reason of the ambient bodies crowded round, bodies which are sometimes cognate, sometimes contrary, the inquiry about measure of strength is accordingly incomplete without an inquiry about the measure of surrounding circumstances. Let this be the 60th and designated triple M.

    [Measure] MMM, or that concerning the measure of surrounding
circumstances.

Now indeed have we gone right through the inquiries about motions with their sums and measures. But since judgement about the schematisms of

quam de motibus, fiat per informationem sensus, facta perceptione, vel
per impressionem simplicem, vel per comparationem, vel per
experimenta deductoria (neque enim alia patet in natura ianua) videtur
omnino inquisitio de impressionibus & perceptionibus sensus esse ex
5 catholicis, & pertinere ad Abecedarium. Quamobrem sequuntur
inquisitiones, primo de sensu & obiectis sensus in genere, deinde de
singulis sensibus atque eorum obiectis. Nam de ipsa natura susceptibili
sensus iam ante inter schematismos materiæ inquisitio designata est.

Inquisitio $\overline{LXI}$.ᵃ Informatio sensus NNN, siue de sensu & obiectis
10 sensus.

Inquisitio $\overline{LXII}$.ᵃ Informatio ΞΞΞ, siue de visu & visibili.

Inquisitio $\overline{LXIII}$.ᵃ Inform. OOO, siue de auditu & sono.

Inquisitio $\overline{LXIV}$.ᵃ Infor. ΠΠΠ, siue de olfactu & odore.

Inquisitio $\overline{LXV}$.ᵃ Informatio PPP, siue de gustu & sapore.

15 Inquisitio $\overline{LXVI}$.ᵃ [Informatio] ΣΣΣ, siue de tactu & tangibilj.

[fo. 35ᵛ] | Massæ majores.

Pertinent quoque ad Abecedarium inquisitiones de massis majoribus in
concreto (cum reliquæ omnes inquisitiones sint in abstracto) terra, aqua,
aëre, flamma & ignitis; ⟨[*illeg.*]⟩ non quod ex illis sublunaria sunt
20 composita (quæ res fictitia est) sed quod cum tam multa producantur a
terra [& aquis], tam multa pertranseant in aërem, & ab eo excipiantur,
tam multa mutentur & soluantur ab igne, minus perspicuæ forent
inquisitiones cæteræ, nisi natura massarum istarum, quæ toties
occurrunt, bene cognita & explorata. His adiungimus inquisitiones de
25 coelestibus & meteoris, cum & ipsæ sint massæ majores, & ex catholicis.

11 ΞΞΞ] XXX   15 [Informatio]] / cf. titles immediately above this one
16 Massæ majores.] *om BTT* (F7ʳ)   17–20 Pertinent . . . sed quod] / *om BTT*
(F7ʳ)   19 sublunaria] sublimata / cf. *OFB*, VI, p. 108, l. 10, p. 254, l. 29   21 [&
aquis]] / *c-t om*, imported from *BTT* (F7ʳ)   in aërem] in *om BTT* (F7ʳ)   24 explo-
rata] explicatâ *BTT* (F7ʳ)   25 meteoris] Meteoricis *BTT* (F7ʳ)

5 Quamobrem] lc   7 Nam] lc   13 odore.] ~ ∧   24 His] lc
25 meteoris,] ~.

matter as well as about motions depends on the information of the sense once perception has taken place, either by simple impression or by comparison or by reductive experiments (for no other means of access lies open in nature), the inquiry concerning the impressions and perceptions of sense seems to be altogether amongst the most catholic, and to belong to the Abecedarium. For this reason there follow inquiries first about the sense and objects of sense in general, and then about the particular senses and their objects. Then again the inquiry concerning the very nature susceptible of sense has already been outlined among the schematisms of matter.

The 61st inquiry: Information of the sense NNN, or that concerning sense and the objects of sense.

The 62nd inquiry: Information ΞΞΞ, or that concerning vision and the visible.

The 63rd inquiry: Information OOO, or that concerning hearing and sound.

The 64th inquiry: Information ΠΠΠ, or that concerning the sense of smell and odour.

The 65th inquiry: Information PPP, or that concerning the sense of taste and flavour.

The 66th inquiry: Information ΣΣΣ, or that concerning touch and the tangible.

ᴵ The greater Masses

While all the other inquiries are in the abstract, inquiries about the greater masses in the concrete sense—earth, water air, flame and burning matter—also belong to the Abecedarium, not because sublunary bodies are composed from them (which is a fabrication) but, since so many things are brought forth from the earth [and waters], so many pass through the air and are drawn from it, and so many are changed and dissolved by fire, the other inquiries would be less clear unless the nature of those masses which crop up so often were not well understood and examined. To these we add inquiries concerning the heavens and meteors since these too are greater masses and among the most catholic.

Inquisitio $\overline{\text{LXVII}}$.ᵃ mas. major. TTT, siue de terra.

Inquisitio $\overline{\text{LXVIII}}$.ᵃ mass. major. YYY, siue de aqua.

Inquisitio $\overline{\text{LXIX}}$.ᵃ mass. major. ΦΦΦ, siue de aëre.

Inquisitio $\overline{\text{LXX}}$.ᵃ mass. major. XXX, siue de igne.

5 Inquisitio $\overline{\text{LXXI}}$.ᵃ mass. major. ΨΨΨ, siue de cælestibus.

Inquisitio $\overline{\text{LXXII}}$.ᵃ mass. major. ΩΩΩ, siue de meteoris.

Conditiones Entium.

Supersunt ad inquirendum in Abecedario conditiones entium, quæ videntur esse tanquam transcendentia, & parum stringunt de corpore
10 naturæ, tamen eo quo vtimur inquirendi modo haud parum afferent illustrationis ad reliqua. Primo igitur cum optime obseruatum fuerit a Democrito naturam rerum esse copia materiæ & indiuiduorum varietate amplam, atque, vt ille vult, infinitam, coitionibus tamen & speciebus in tantum finitam, vt etiam angusta & tanquam paupercula
15 videri possit (quandoquidem tam paruæ inueniantur species quæ sint aut esse possint, vt exercitum millenarium vix conficiant) cumque negatiua affirmatiuis subiuncta ad informationem intellectus plurimum valeant, constituenda est inquisitio de Ente [& non Ente]. Ea ordine est $\overline{\text{LXXIII}}$. & quadruplex A nominatur.
20   Cond. ent. AAAA, siue de ente & non ente.

[fo. 36ʳ]   ¹ At possibile & impossibile, nihil aliud sunt quam potentiale ad ens, & non potentiale ad ens. De ijs inquisitio $\overline{\text{LXXIV}}$ᵃ conficiatur, quæ quadruplex B nominetur.
     Cond. ent. BBBB, siue de possibilj & impossibilj.

1–6 Inquisitio $\overline{\text{LXVII}}$.ᵃ ... meteoris.] / in *BTT* (F7ᵛ) the abbreviation mass. maj. is taken back to the beginning of each item, the numerals are written in words and the Greek letters written thus: Triplex *Tau* etc.   6 meteoris] Meteoricis *BTT* (F7ᵛ)   13 tamen] verò *BTT* (F8ʳ)   18 [& non Ente]] / imported from *BTT* (F8ʳ)   19 nominatur] numeratur *BTT* (F8ʳ)   20 AAAA] Quadruplex *Alpha BTT* (F8ʳ)   21 At] Ad *BTT* (F8ʳ) / silently and correctly emended in *SEH* (II, p. 86)   sunt] est *BTT* (F8ʳ)   21–2 & non] aut non *BTT* (F8ᵛ)   22 ijs] eo *BTT* (F8ᵛ)
5 cælestibus.] ∼ᴧ   6 $\overline{\text{LXXII}}$.] ∼ᴧ   7 Entium] lc   11 Primo] lc   18 Ea] lc   22 De] lc

The 67th inquiry: greater mass TTT, or that concerning earth.

The 68th inquiry: greater mass YYY, or that concerning water.

The 69th inquiry: greater mass ΦΦΦ, or that concerning air.

The 70th inquiry: greater mass XXX, or that concerning fire.

The 71st inquiry: greater mass ΨΨΨ, or that concerning the heavens.

The 72nd inquiry: greater mass ΩΩΩ, or that concerning meteors.

The Conditions of Beings

It remains for us to inquire in the Abecedarium into the conditions of beings which seem to be like transcendentals and to have little contact with the body of nature, but which will nevertheless, by the means of inquiry which I use, bring not a little light to the rest. In the first place then, since Democritus has well observed that the nature of things is abundant and (as he has it) infinite in quantity of matter and variety of individuals, yet only finite in coitions and species—so that it even seems scanty and, as it were, impoverished (inasmuch as we find so few species that exist or could exist that they hardly muster an army of a thousand)—and as negatives subjoined to affirmatives have great force for the information of the intellect, an inquiry should be set up concerned with being [and non-being]. This is the 73rd in order and may be designated quadruple A.

Condition of beings AAAA, or that concerning being and
non-being.

ᴵ But possible and impossible are nothing other than the potential for being or the absence of potential for being. Concerning these let the 74th inquiry be adduced which may be designated quadruple B.

Condition of beings BBBB, or that concerning possible and
impossible.

Sequuntur potentialia ad ens verum sub certis conditionibus, sine quibus habentur illa de genere impossibilium.

Multum, paucum, rarum, consuetum, sunt potentialia ad ens, sed in tali quanto. Neque enim possibile est in natura vt ta*n*tum sit specificati
5 quantum non specificati. De ijs inquisitio $\overline{\text{LXXV}}$.ᵃ esto, quæ quadruplex Γ nominetur.

   Condit. ent. ΓΓΓΓ, siue de multo & pauco.

Durabile & transitorium, æternum & momentaneum, sunt potentialia ad ens, sed in tali mora, siue duratione. Neque enim possibile est vt
10 folium ab arbore diuulsum talis sit durationis, qualis metallum. De illis $\overline{\text{LXX}}$ $\overline{\text{VI}}$.ᵃ inquisitio esto, quæ quadruplex Δ nominetur.

   Condit. ent. ΔΔΔΔ, siue de durabilj & transitorio.

Naturale & monstrosum sunt potentialia ad ens, sed per tale efficiens, videlicet per cursum naturæ ordinarium aut per aberrationes eius.
15 Neque enim possibile est ⟨[*illeg.*]⟩ vt monstra sint frequentia. De ijs inquisitio $\overline{\text{LXXVII}}$.ᵃ esto, quæ quadruplex E nominetur.

   Cond. ent. EEEE, siue de naturalj & monstroso.

Naturale etiam opponitur artificiali. Hæc sunt potentialia ad ens, sed per tale efficiens, videlicet per naturam ipsam, aut per manum hominis.
20 Non enim possibile est vt pleraque artificialium existant nisi per manum hominis. De ijs inquisitio $\overline{\text{LXXVIII}}$.ᵃ conficiatur, quæ quadruplex Z nominetur.

   Cond. ent. ZZZZ, siue de naturali & artificialj.

1–2 Sequuntur . . . impossibilium.] *om BTT* (F8ᵛ)   3 Multum] Etiam ~ *BTT* (F8ᵛ)   3–5 sed in tali . . . specificati.] in Quanto. *BTT* (F8ᵛ)   6 Γ nominetur] *Gamma* numeretur *BTT* (F8ᵛ)   9–10 sed in tali . . . qualis metallum] in Duratione *BTT* (F8ᵛ)   11 nominetur] numeratur *BTT* (F8ᵛ)   13 monstrosum] monstruosum / *BTT* (F8ᵛ) has Monstrosum (Bacon's preferred form)   13–14 sed . . . videlicet] *om BTT* (F8ᵛ)   14 ordinarium] *om BTT* (F8ᵛ)   aberrationes] deviationes *BTT* (F8ᵛ–G1ʳ)   15 Neque . . . frequentia.] *om BTT* (G1ʳ)   16 nominetur] numeratur *BTT* (G1ʳ)   17 monstroso] monstruoso / *BTT* (G1ʳ) has monstroso (Bacon's preferred form)   18–22 Naturale . . . nominetur] Naturale & Artificiale sunt potentialia ad Ens, sine Homine, & per Hominem. De iis Inquisitio septuagesima octava conficitur, quæ quadruplex zeta numeretur *BTT* (G1ʳ)

4 Neque] lc   5 De] lc   9 Neque] lc   10 De] lc   15 Neque] lc   De] lc   18 Hæc] lc   20 Non] lc   21 De] lc

There follow potentialities for being but under fixed conditions, without which they are held to belong to the category of things impossible.

Much, little, rare, common are potentialities for being but with reference to a particular quantity. For in nature it is not possible for as much to be made specific as non-specific. Let the 75th inquiry be about these, an inquiry which may be designated Γ.
    Condition of beings ΓΓΓΓ, or that concerning much and little.

Durable and fleeting, eternal and momentary are potentialities for being but with reference to a particular lapse of time or duration. For it is impossible for a leaf torn from a tree to last as long as a metal. Let the 76th inquiry be about these, an inquiry which may be designated quadruple Δ.
    Condition of beings ΔΔΔΔ, or that concerning durable and
                fleeting.

Natural and monstrous are potentialities for being but by a particular efficient, namely by the ordinary course of nature or by its aberrations. For it is impossible for monsters to be common. Let the 77th inquiry be about these, an inquiry which may be designated quadruple E.
    Condition of beings EEEE, or that concerning natural and
                monstrous.

Natural is also set against artificial; these are potentialities for being but by a particular efficient, namely by nature itself or by the hand of man. For it is impossible for very many artificial bodies to exist except by human intervention. Concerning these the 78th inquiry may be adduced which may be designated quadruple Z.
    Condition of beings ZZZZ, or that concerning natural and
                artificial.

[fo. 36ᵛ] ¹ Supersunt inquisitiones duæ, quibus visum est Abecedarium claudere & consummare: altera de schematismo magno, siue de integralitate & configuratione vniuersi; altera de summa magna, siue de vniuersitate rerum, atque tempestatibus majoribus. Hæ vero duæ inquisitiones si
5 ad particularia deducantur, tantum absunt vt sint litteræ, vt potius sint naturæ textus & sermo. Verum in genere acceptæ pertinent ad Abecedarium; eo magis quod nonnullæ naturæ quas posuimus quæ videntur substantiuæ, sunt reuera tantum relatiuæ, prout corpora sita sunt loco, aut succedunt tempore. Itaque de integralitate muɴdi
10 LXXIX.ª inquisitio constituitur quæ quadruplex H nominatur.
   Schematismus magnus quadruplex H, siue de integralitate mundj.

At inquisitio LXXX.ª de vicissitudine rerum aut tempestatibus majoribus esto. Ea quadruplex Θ, nominetur.
   Summa magna quadruplex Θ, siue de vicissitudine rerum.

15 Atque ab his elementis conficitur Abecedarium. At in explicatione ipsorum exempla non adjunximus, quia ipsæ inquisitiones coɴtinent totas acies exemplorum. Tituli secundum quos ordo Abecedarij est dispositus nullo modo eam auctoritatem habento, vt pro veris & fixis rerum diuisionibus recipiantur. Hoc enim esset profiteri scire nos quæ
20 inquirimus. Nam nemo res vere dispertit, qui non naturaɱ ipsarum penitus cognouit. Satis sit si ad ordinem inquirendi (id quod nunc agitur) commode se habeant.

Norma abecedarij.

Abecedarium hoc modo conficimus, & regimus. Historiæ &
25 experimenta omnino primas partes tenent. Ea, si enumerationem & seriem rerum particularium exhibeant, in tabulas conficiuntur, aliter sparsim excipiuntur.

1–16 Supersunt . . . ipsorum] *om BTT* (Gɪʳ)   3 vniuersitate] vniuersalitate   16 exempla] ~ in explicatione ordinis Abecedarij *BTT* (Gɪʳ)   24 Historiæ] Historia *BTT* (Gɪᵛ)   27 sparsim] / in an almost identical passage *HNE* has *seorsùm* (C4ʳ (*SEH*, II, p. 17))

2 consummare:] ~.   3 vniuersi;] ~.   4 Hæ] lc   6 Verum] lc
9 Itaque] lc   13 Ea] lc   15 At] lc   17 Tituli] lc / new paragraph in *BTT* (Gɪʳ)   19 Hoc] lc   20 Nam] lc   21 Satis] lc   24 Historiæ] lc   25 Ea] lc

ᴵ There remain two inquiries with which it would be right to close and round off the Abecedarium, the one concerning the great schematism or wholeness and configuration of the universe; the other about the great sum or the universality and greater periods of things. But these two inquiries, if they be drawn to particulars, are so far from being letters that they are rather the text and discourse of nature; but taken in a general sense, they belong to the Abecedarium, the more because several natures which we have presented that seem to be substantive are in reality only relative, according as bodies are located spatially or succeed in time. Thus a 79th inquiry is set up concerning the wholeness of the world, an inquiry designated quadruple H.

The great schematism, quadruple H, or that concerning the wholeness of the world.

But let the 80th inquiry be about the vicissitudes of things or the greater periods; let this be designated quadruple Θ.

The great sum, quadruple Θ, or that concerning the vicissitudes of things.

And so the Abecedarium is made up of these elements; but we have not added examples in explaining them because the inquiries themselves contain whole troops of examples. The titles by which the order of the Abecedarium has been laid out should by no means be accorded the authority of true and fixed divisions of things. For this would be to claim that we know the things we are inquiring into. For no one who has not thoroughly investigated their nature apportions things truly. Let it be sufficient if that which we now speak of is convenient for the course of inquiring.

The Rule of the abecedarium

I construct and organize the Abecedarium in this manner: the first parts are entirely given over to the histories and experiments. These, if they display an enumeration or sequence of particular things, are written up in tabular form; otherwise they are noted down piecemeal.

[fo. 37ʳ] ᴵ Cum vero historia & experimenta sæpissime nos deserant, præsertim lucifera illa, & instantiæ crucis, per quas de veris rerum causis intellectui constare possit, mandata damus de experimentis nouis; hæc sint tanquam historia designata. Quid enim aliud nobis primo viam
5 ingredientibus relinquitur?

Modum experimenti alicuius subtilioris explicamus, ne error subsit, atque vt alios ad meliores modos excogitandos excitemus.

Etiam monita & cautiones de rerum fallacijs & inueniendi erroribus quæ nobis occurrunt, aspergimus. Obseruationes nostras super
10 historiam & experimenta subteximus, vt interpretatio naturæ magis sit in procinctu.

Etiam commentationes & scrutinia de quæstione aut indagatione aliqua particulari proponimus.

Etiam canones, sed tantum mobiles, & axiomata inchoata qualia nobis
15 inquirentibus, non pronunciantibus, se offerunt, constituimus. Vtiles enim sunt, si non prorsus veri.

Denique tentamenta quædam interpretationis quandoque molimur, licet prorsus humi repentia, & vero interpretationis nomine nullo modo, vt arbitramur, decoranda. Quid enim nobis supercilio opus est, aut
20 impostura, cum toties profiteamur nec nobis historiam & experimenta, qualibus opus est, suppetere, nec absque his interpretationem naturæ perfici posse; ideoque nobis satis esse si initijs rerum non desimus.

Perspicuitatis autem & ordinis gratia, aditus quosdam ad inquisitiones instar præfationum, substernimus.

25 Item connexiones & vincula, ne inquisitiones sint magis abruptæ, interponimus. Ad vsum vero, vellicationes quasdam de practica suggerimus.

Etiam optatiua eorum quæ adhuc non habentur, vna cum proximis suis, ad erigendam humanam industriam proponimus.

[fo. 37ᵛ] 30 ᴵ Neque sumus nescij inquisitiones inter se aliquando complicari, ita vt nonnulla ex inquisitis in titulos diuersos incidant. Sed modum eum adhibebimus, vt & repetitionem fastidia, & rejectionum molestias, quantum fieri possit, vitemus; postponentes tamen hoc ipsum, quando necesse fuerit perspicuitati docendi in argumento tam obscuro.

6 alicuius] *om BTT* (G1ᵛ)   12–13 Etiam commentationes . . . proponimus.] *om BTT*
(G1ᵛ)   15–16 Vtiles . . . veri] Utiles . . . veræ *BTT* (G1ᵛ) / emended as utilia . . . vera in
SEH (II, p. 88)   18 repentia] *BTT* (G1ᵛ), repentis   26 vellicationes] vellicationis
BTT (G2ʳ) / silently corrected in *SEH* (II, p. 88)

3 nouis;] ~.   4 Quid] lc   9 Obseruationes] lc   15 Vtiles] lc
19 Quid] lc   25 Item] / no new paragraph in *BTT* (G2ʳ)   26 Ad] lc / new paragraph in *BTT* (G2ʳ)   31 Sed] lc

ⁱ But since I very often lack history and experiments, especially the experiments of light and crucial instances which can inform the mind about the true causes of things, I give directions for new experiments; these may be as a history in embryo. For what other alternative is left to me who is just setting out on the road?

I explain the ways of performing any subtler experiment in case it is flawed, and also so as to prompt others to work out better ways.

I also intersperse the advice and cautions which suggest themselves to me about the fallacies of things and for detecting errors. I append my observations on the history and experiments to make the interpretation of nature readier.

I also put forward speculations and researches on any particular question or investigation.

I also establish rules (though only provisional ones) and imperfect axioms such as crop up in the course of inquiry, and not with the intention of laying down the law. For they are useful if not altogether true.

In the end I sometimes make certain attempts at interpretation, though extremely humble ones and (in my opinion) quite unworthy to be honoured by the true name of interpretation. For what need do I have of arrogance or deceit when I so often freely confess that history and experiments of the kinds needed are not available to me, and that the interpretation of nature cannot be accomplished without them? And that is the reason why it is enough for me to play a part in getting things started.

But for the sake of clarity and order I submit some few introductions to the inquiries by way of prefaces.

In addition, I interpose connections and links to stop the inquiries being too abrupt. For the sake of use I do indeed supply some incentives to practice.

To stimulate human industry I also set out desiderata for things unavailable hitherto, together with their closest approximations.

ⁱ I know very well that the inquiries are sometimes so mixed up with one another that among the things investigated some fall under various titles. But I shall as far as possible take measures to avoid the nuisance of repetitions and the irksomeness of rejections; yet, when it is necessary, I shall treat this problem as something far less important than giving clear instruction in an argument of such obscurity.

Hæc est Abecedarij norma & regula. Deus vniuersi conditor, conseruator, & instaurator, opus hoc, & in ascensione ad gloriam suam, & in descensione ad bonum humanum, pro sua erga homines beneuolentia & misericordia protegat & regat, per filium suum vnicum nobiscum Deum.

This then is the rule and basic principle of the Abecedarium. May God, the Founder, Preserver, and Renewer of the universe, for his goodwill and compassion to man protect and guide this work, both in its ascent to His glory, and in its descent to the good of man, through His only Son, God with us.

HISTORIA & INQUISITIO DE ANIMATO & INANIMATO

¹ Historia & Inquisitio de animato & inanimato.

Inquisitio de animis & vitis profunda est & vix eruitur per Experimenta Vulgaria absque luciferorum forte supplemento. Complectitur tres inquisitiones: primo de natura corporum quæ sunt capacia vitæ; 2° de
5 principijs seminibus & menstruis vitæ; tertio de actu & modo viuificatio*n*is.

De natura corporum capacium vitæ.

10 Non inuenitur vita
in corpore

15

$$\left\{ \begin{array}{l} \text{fluido siue liquido} \\ \text{nisi figurato} \\ \text{valde grandj puta stadij \&c.} \\ \text{Totaliter duro} \\ \text{sicco \& arido} \\ \text{Humido merè aqueo, sed in quo sit aliquid} \\ \text{oleosi \& tenacis} \\ \text{Nisj vbj sit spiritus per calorem aliquem} \\ \text{attenuatus \& incensus.} \end{array} \right.$$

¹Quoniam autem hæc prima inquisitio nihil aliud est quam tabula quædam absentiæ ideo recurrendu*m* ad ea quæ sunt in proximo, veluti limax est inter viuentia ex maximè liquidis, ostrea ex minime figuratis,
20 Balena ex Grandissimis &c.

De Principiis Vitæ & primo de menstruis sparsis.

Videndum diligentissimè de menstruis sparsis & de viuificatis absque semine aut analogo seminis; ibj enim se produnt principia vitæ quæ in viuificatis ex semine magis occultantur.
25 Dubium non est quin terra emittat ex sese varias plantas absque semine aut analogo seminis ex glomerationibus succorum intra terram.
Fuerit prorsus, quatenus ad Vegetabilia, experime*ntum* luciferum valde bonum nisi quod sit multæ patientiæ, si quis effoderet terram in campo

3 supplemento.] ~ ^ Complectitur] lc 4 inquisitiones:] ~ ^ vitæ;] ~.
5 vitæ;] ~. tertio] Tertio 7 vitæ.] ~ ^ 10–11 Non . . . corpore] / this is
written at 90° to a long curly bracket embracing the list 18 proximo,] ~ ^ 19
liquidis,] ~: figuratis,] ~. 23 seminis;] ~ ^ 27 prorsus,] ~;
Vegetabilia,] ~ ^ 28 patientiæ,] ~ ^

| History and Inquiry concerning animate and inanimate

The inquiry into souls and lives lies deep and is unlikely to be unearthed by common experiments without a powerful underpinning of experiments of light. It comprises three inquiries: in the first place of the nature of bodies which are able to support life; in the second, of the principles, seeds and menstrua of life; and in the third, of the act and mode of vivification.

Of the nature of bodies able to support life

Life is not found in a body
$$\begin{cases} \text{fluid or liquid} \\ \text{unless it has a definite shape} \\ \text{extremely large as, for instance, of length etc.} \\ \text{completely hard} \\ \text{dry and arid} \\ \text{made of plain watery moisture without something oily and tenacious in it} \\ \text{unless a spirit rarefied and inflamed by some degree of heat is present.} \end{cases}$$

| In view of the fact that this first inquiry is nothing other than what might be called a table of absence, we must therefore fall back on instances of proximity as, for example, the slug is among the most liquid of living things, the oyster among those with the least definite shape, the whale among the largest, etc.

On the Principles of Life and, in the first place, on scattered menstrua

Observe with the utmost care scattered menstrua and things vivified without seed or an equivalent of seed; for in these circumstances the principles of life, which are less apparent in things vivified from seed, reveal themselves.

There is no doubt but that the earth puts forth from itself plants many and various without seed or the equivalent of seed from aggregations of juices within the earth.

As for vegetable bodies, it would certainly be an extremely good experiment of light, save that it would take a lot of patience, if someone were

altius sumptam, quam quo semina aut fibræ radicis alicuius plantæ penetrare potuerint atq*ue* ex eadem massa partes in diuersas ollas apertas dis-
tribueret, miscendo in vna olla terram cum portione conueniente Cretæ;
in alia, cum arena; in alia cum glarea, in alia cum limo ex fundo stagnj,
5 in alia cu*m* fimo equino, in alia cum fimo bubalino, in alia cum fimo
columbino, [in alia cum fimo] ouino, [in alia cum] cinere, [in alia] cum
[fo. 4ʳ] fuligine ᴵ & videndum qualem herbam singulæ terræ edant expositis
scilicet ollis ad solem & imbrem.

Videndum est etiam de visco qui licet non sit ex menstruo sparso in
10 terra, tamen prouenit ex menstruo sparso in arbore aliena absque
proprio aliquo semine.

Videndum etiam de diuersis generibus muscj quæ prodeunt aut ex solo
aut ex muris aut ex corticibus arborum, quæ omnia rudimenta sunt
herbarum & proueniunt absque semine.

15 A menstruis sparsis in Vegetabilibus transeundu*m* est ad menstrua sparsa
in animalibus vbj infinita est copia ⟨menstruo?⟩ experimentorum at
incredibilis negligentia obseruationum. Loquimur de animalibus
generatis ex putredine cuiusvis generis, ex quibus cernj possit qua figura
& ex quo genere materia potissimum prodeat; at licet quatenus in
20 exactas effigies & colores incomprehensibilis sit naturæ lusus, tamen per
species proprietas materiæ fortasse perspicj possit cum huiusmodj
animalcula alias omnino pedibus vacent, alias sint multiplices, alias
hirsuta, ⟨aliùs⟩, alias glabra, alias subsultantia, aliàs alata, alias testacea,
aliàs aculeata &c. Obseruatio autem, eò (vt videtur) penetrare possit vt
25 ad placitum & artificialiter huiusmodj animalia generarj possint, cum
nobis fere nihil innotescat nisi efformatio apium & fortasse vermiculorum
[fo. 4ᵛ] ᴵ (vt Batauj solent) ex caseo, & motus pilorum ex cauda equina
proiectorum in aquam limosam & huiusmodj paucula.

Inter cætera animalcula præcipuè videndum de ijs quæ generantur in
30 alto in aëre, qualia sunt nonnulla ex ranis, culicibus, locustis & alia.

---

6 [in alia cum fimo] . . . [in alia cum] . . . [in alia]] / such extensive restoration is seldom justified but seems necessary here. The *c-t* is virtually meaningless here, so I suspect scribal
lacunae resulting from eyeskip brought on by mechanical repetition of parallelisms
15 transeundu*m* est] transeundu*m* &   18 cuiusvis] cuius vis

3 miscendo in] miscendo In   3–4 Cretæ; in] Cretæ; In   6 ouino,] ∼ˎ
9 sparso in] sparso In   10 terra,] ∼ˎ   13 arborum,] ∼ˎ   16 experi-
mentorum] ∼.   17 Loquimur] lc   18 generis,] ∼ˎ   19 prodeat;]
∼ˎ   20 lusus,] ∼ˎ   23 subsultantia,] ∼ˎ   24 (vt videtur)] / scribe seems
to have added the brackets afterwards   25 possint,] ∼ˎ   27 Batauj] lc
caseo,] ∼ˎ   30 alto] ∼,   aëre,] ∼ˎ   ranis,] ∼ˎ   culicibus,] ∼ˎ

to dig up in a field earth thoroughly prepared, which thereby the seeds
or root fibres of whatever plant could penetrate, and if he were to dis-
tribute parts of the same mass into different open pots by mixing the
earth with a suitable portion of chalk in one pot, with sand in another,
with gravel in another, with mud from the bottom of a pond in another,
with horse dung in another, with ox dung in another, with pigeon drop-
pings in another, [with] sheep [dung in another], [with] ash [in
another], with soot [in another] ¹ and see what sort of vegetation particular earths give out once of course the pots have been put out in the sun
and rain.

Observe mistletoe which, although it does not originate from a menstruum scattered in the ground, nevertheless issues without any seed of
its own from a menstruum scattered in a different tree.

Also observe the various kinds of moss which sprout either from soil or
walls or tree bark, and which are all rudiments of herbaceous plants and
come up without seed.

From scattered menstrua in vegetables we must proceed to scattered
menstrua in animals where the supply ⟨in menstrua?⟩ of experiments is
limitless but the carelessness of observations beyond belief. I am speaking of animals generated from putrefaction of whatever kind, animals
which let us make out with what shape and from what origin their matter mainly derives. But although a sport of nature is incomprehensible as
far as finished likeness and colours are concerned, yet the particular quality of their matter can probably be ascertained through these appearances, since animalcules of this kind are sometimes quite without feet,
sometimes they have lots; sometimes they are hairy, ⟨another⟩ at others
bald; sometimes leaping, at others winged; sometimes furnished with
shells, at others with prickles etc. Now observation may be able to reach
(as it seems) so far that animals of this kind can be generated at pleasure
and artificially, seeing that practically nothing is familiar to us except the
formation of bees and perhaps of worms generated ¹ (as the Dutch ones
usually are) from cheese, and the motion of horsehair worms cast into
muddy water from a horse's tail, and little creatures of that kind.

Among other animalcules, take particular note of those which are engen-
dered high up in the air—as are some of the frogs, gnats, locusts, and
other things.

De spermatibus & seminibus.

In Vegetabilibus sunt plura analoga seminis nam præter fructus & grana vitam concipiunt radices, surculj, vimina &c. At videndum de partibus plantarum quæ vitam non concipiunt, vt folia, flores, caules, &
5 speciatim videndum in incisionibus & inoculationibus quæ partes & quomodo positæ sint vitales, quæ non.

Videndum ad quod tempus partes Vitales virtutem viuificantem continent; nam semina nonnulla etiam ad biennium durant fertilia, post hæc radices aliquandiu durant; ad breue autem tempus ⟨viu?⟩ vimina &
10 ad breuissimum surculj & gemmæ; etiam longius & durius durant huiusmodj vitalia pro na*tura* plantæ.

Videndum si vitalia ista aliam patiantur ad Viuificandum matricem quam terram & truncum arborum in quibus inseruntur: velutj si
[fo. 5ʳ] semina ⟨&⟩ aut nuces mittantur in truncos ¹ arborum, vt vimina solent,
15 aut si mittantur semina coepæ in capita cœparum, aut fabæ aut pisa in radices aliquas bulbosas, idque tam intra terram quam extra.

Quod ad spermata animalium, non habent aliquod analogum, nec tolerant momentum durationis cum inijciantur cum calore & motu.

Videndum autem qualia `sint´ spermata piscium, auium, quadrupedum,
20 & si quæ femellæ concipiant absq*ue* spermate masculorum.

Videndum si spermata patiantur ad Viuifica*n*dum aliam matricem quam propriam femellarum, quod non videtur fierj nisj in animalibus ambiguæ speciej vt in mulis & in monstris. Nam pygmeus Paracelsi non est parabola sed delirium.

25 ## Actus & Processus viuificandj

Spectandæ attentè sunt Viuifica*tio*n*es* & incrementa animalium ex putredine natorum cu*m* facillime oculis subiiciantur.

Videndum in pisis aut fabis aut alijs in terram emissis & quotidie extractis quale sit ⟨diariu*m*⟩ diarium naturæ in nutritione & Viuificatione.
[fo. 5ᵛ] 30 ¹Videndum similiter in ouis qualis sit diurnus ⟨p⟩ processus vsque ad exclusionem auis.

---

3 radices,]~ₐ surculj,] ~ₐ   4 concipiunt,] ~ₐ folia,] ~ₐ flores,] ~ₐ caules,]
~ₐ   5 inoculationibus] in oculationibus   6 vitales,] ~ₐ   8 continent;
~ₐ   9 durant;] ~ₐ   10 gemmæ;] ~ₐ   14 arborum,] ~ₐ solent,] ~ₐ
15 coepæ .   .   . cœparum] / *sic*   cœparum,] ~ₐ   16 bulbosas,] ~ₐ
17 animalium,] ~ₐ   19 spermata] ~, piscium,] ~ₐ   22 femellarum,] ~ₐ
videtur] Videtur   23 monstris.] ~ₐ   Nam] lc

Of sperm and seed

In vegetables there are many equivalents of seed; for, besides fruits and grains, roots, scions, switches etc. conceive life. But we must take note of the parts of plants which do not conceive life—as for example leaves, flowers and stalks; and in particular we must note in graftings and inoculations which parts may be the vital ones and which not, and how these are disposed.

Note how long the vital parts retain the vivifying virtue; for some seeds stay fertile even for two years; roots last for some considerable time after the former; switches for a short time however, and slips and buds for the shortest; also note that the durability and hardiness of vital parts of this kind vary with the nature of the plant.

Note whether these vital parts put up with another matrix for vivifying besides the ground or tree trunk into which they are implanted: for example, if seeds or nuts be put in tree ¹ trunks (as switches are), or onion seeds be placed in the heads of onions, or beans or peas in any bulbous roots whatever, and that both in the ground as well as out of it.

As for animal sperm, it does not have any equivalent and once it is infused with life and motion, lasts no time at all.

Take note of what kind the sperm of fish, birds, quadrupeds may be, and whether any females conceive without male sperm.

Note whether sperm for vivifying puts up with a matrix other than that of females of its own species, a thing that does not appear to happen except in hybrid animals, as in mules and monsters. Again, Paracelsus' pygmy is not metaphor but madness.

The Act and Process of vivifying

Vivifications and growths of animals generated from putrefaction should be examined closely since they open themselves to inspection very readily.

In peas, beans and other plants put into the ground and taken up again daily, note the successive entries in nature's diary in respect of nutrition and vivification.

¹ We should likewise observe in eggs what daily developments may take place right up to the hatching of the bird.

Videndum similiter in abortiuis & Cæsaribus animalium qualia sint rudimenta motus & figura in viuificationibus.

Videndum de exclusione ouorum non solum per incubitum sed & per alios calores.

5 Videndum de Clausuris matricum ad Viuificandu*m* quoniam & semina Vegetabilium requirunt clausuram vt sepeliantur in terra vel exponantur aerj.

Videndum ad Viuificandum requirj quatuor: spiritus inclusus; calor spiritu⟨u⟩m attenuans & dilatans; materia lenta & ⟨sequax⟩; & matrix
10 clausa cum tempore conueniente. Spiritus enim, rej præinexistens, a calore paululum incenditur; inde se dilatat atque exitu*m* molitur &, occurrens materiæ glutinosæ & tenacj, cohibetur, ne exhalet, & agit ante se materiam facilem & sequacem eamque pro motu suo efformat. At quùm hoc non subito fiat, opus est clausura in matrice conueniente ad
15 inimica prohibenda & alimentum suppeditandum.

---

9 ⟨<u>sequax</u>⟩;] / with the underlining the scribe undid the deletion after he changed his mind about a correction (*inm*) which he then erased   15 inimica] minima / *c-t* makes no obvious sense; perhaps the scribe misread indistinct minims here

2 viuificationibus.] ~ₐ   8 quatuor:] ~ₐ   9 ⟨<u>sequax</u>⟩;] ~:   10 Spiritus] lc
11 incenditur;] ~ₐ inde] Inde   11 molitur &,] ~ₐ   12 tenacj,] ~ₐ
13 se] ~, efformat.] ~ₐ At] lc   14 fiat,] ~ₐ

We should likewise observe in abortions and caesarean sections of animals what the rudiments of motion and shape may be in vivifications.

We should observe the hatching of eggs not only by incubation but also by other heats.

We should observe the enclosures of matrices for vivifying, seeing that the seeds of vegetable bodies call for enclosure according as they are buried in the ground or exposed to the air.

We should note that four things are needed for vivifying: an enclosed spirit, heat attenuating and dilating the spirit, soft and ⟨sticky⟩ matter, and a matrix closed up for the right length of time. For the pre-existent spirit of the thing is inflamed a little by heat; then dilates itself and strives for an outlet and, meeting sticky and clinging matter, it is kept in to stop it exhaling, and drives the compliant and sticky matter before it, and shapes it according to its own motion. But as this cannot come about suddenly, enclosure in a suitable matrix is necessary to keep harmful influences at bay and supply nourishment.

INQUISITIO DE MAGNETE

Inquisitio de *Magnete.*

Magnes trahit pulverem *Chalybis præparati,* quali utuntur ad Medicinam, etiam *chalybem calcinatum* in tenuissimum pulverem nigrum, æque fortiter, ac limaturam ferri crudam: *Crocum* autem *Martis,* qui est rubigo ferri artificiosa, hebetius & debilius. Si vero ferrum
5 dissolvatur in Aqua forti, & guttæ aliquæ dissolutionis ponantur super vitrum planum, non extrahit *Magnes* Ferrum, nec trahit *Aquam* ipsam *ferratam.*

Magnes Scobem suum trahit, quemadmodum limaturam Ferri; parvaque admodum *Magnetis* frustula, alterum alterum trahit, ut
10 pensilia fiant, & Capillata, quemadmodum Acus.

Pone *Magnetem* in tali distantia à Ferro, ut non trahat: Interpone *pileum Ferri,* servata distantia, & trahet; virtute *Magnetis* per Ferrum melius diffusa, quam per Medium Aeris solius.

Magnes immissus intra Aquam fortem, ibique per plures horas
15 manens, virtute non minuitur.
Magnes Fricatione contra pannum (ut utimur in *Electro*) aut contra alium *Magnetem,* aut calefactus ad ignem, virtute non augetur.

Magnes alius alio est longe virtuosior: Quinetiam *virtutem* suam, pro modo ejus, Ferro tactum transmittit; *Virtutem,* inquam, non solum
20 *verticitatis,* sed etiam *attractionis simplicis.* Nam si accipias *Magnetem* fortiorem, eoque ferrum (puta cultellum) tangas; deinde magnete debiliore similiter alium cultellum, videbis cultellum *fortiore magnete* tactum, majus trahere pondus ferri, quam qui debiliore tactus est.

Magnes ad æque distans ferrum trahit per Aerem, Aquam, Vinum,
25 Oleum.

Magnete, aut pulvere ejus, in Aqua Forti immerso, nihil omnino dissolvitur, sicut in *Ferro* fit; licet *Magnes* videatur esse corpus *ferro* consubstantiale.

Pulvis Magnetis ferrum intactum non trahit, nec tactum etiam:
30 Attamen ipse *pulvis* à Ferro tacto trahitur, & adhæret: ab intacto autem minime: Adeo ut *pulvis Magnetis* videatur passivam Virtutem aliquo modo retinere, activam autem non omnino.

Acus super planum posita, quæ *Magnete* non trahitur propter pondus;
eadem super imposita fundo Vitri elevato, ut utrinque propendeat,

---

3 Medicinam,] ~;   8 Ferri;] ~:   19 transmittit;] ~.

[|] *An Inquiry concerning the Loadstone*

The loadstone attracts powder of prepared steel of the kind used in medicine, and also steel calcined to a very fine black powder just as strongly
as raw iron filings; but it attracts crocus martis, which is an artificial rust
of iron, more dully and weakly. But if iron be dissolved in aqua fortis and
some drops of the solution are put on a flat piece of glass, the loadstone
does not extract the iron, or attract the iron solution itself.

The loadstone attracts its own dust in the same way as it does iron filings; and extremely small pieces of a loadstone will attract each other so
that they hang down hair-like in the same way that needles do.

Place a loadstone far enough away from the iron so that it does not
attract it. Keeping the distance the same, put an iron cap between them,
and it will attract it; the virtue of the loadstone being better diffused
through iron than through the medium of the air alone.

A loadstone put in aqua fortis and left there for some hours does not
have its virtue reduced.

¹A loadstone rubbed against a cloth (as we do with amber) or another
loadstone, or heated by fire, does not have its virtue increased.

One loadstone has much greater virtue than another. What is more,
once it has been touched with iron, it transmits its virtue in proportion
to its capacity; and by that I mean not just the virtue of verticity but also
that of plain attraction. For if you take a stronger loadstone and touch
iron with it (a knife for example), and then touch another knife with a
weaker loadstone, you will see that the knife touched by the stronger
loadstone will attract a greater weight of iron than the one touched by
the weaker.

A loadstone attracts at an equal distance through air, water, wine, and
oil.

When a loadstone or its powder has been immersed in aqua fortis, it
is not dissolved at all in the way that iron is, even though loadstone
appears to be a body consubstantial with iron.

Loadstone powder does not attract iron whether it be touched or
untouched. But the powder is itself attracted by touched iron and sticks
to it, but is not attracted by untouched iron, so that loadstone powder
seems to keep a passive virtue in some fashion, but an active one not at all.

A needle which, when it is placed on a flat surface, is not attracted by
a loadstone because of its weight, will be attracted when it is [|] placed on

trahetur; Quod eo magis relatu dignum puto, quia hujusmodi quiddam fortasse occasionem dedit frivolæ illi Narrationi, Quod Adamas *Magnetis* virtutem impediat. Pone enim *Acum* super Adamantem parvum, in Tabulam Sectum, Magnete præsente ad distans majus quam

5 in quo trahere posset, tamen trepidabit: Illa autem Trepidatio, non prohibitio Motus est, sed Motus ipse.

Magnes Ferrum tactum longe vivacius trahit, quam intactum: Adeo ut Ferrum, quod intactum in data distantia non trahit, id in triplici distantia tactum trahat.

10 Nihil extrahitur Ferri aut metallicæ materiæ ex *Magnete* per ignem, & nota Separationis.

Magnes non solvitur in *Aqua Regis* plus quam in *Aqua Forti.*

Magnes in Crucibulo positus, citra tamen quam ut flammam immittat, minuitur multum pondere, & immensum Virtute, ut vix

15 Ferrum attrahat.

Magnes ægre liquefit, sed tamen Figuram nonnihil immutat, & rubescit, ut Ferrum.

Magnes combustus integer, virtutem passivam, ut se applicet alteri

[L₁ʳ] *Magneti,* re¹tinet; activam ad ferrum trahendum fere perdit.

20 *Magnes* in Crucibulo combustus emitit Fumum, vix tamen visibilem, qui laminam æris superimpositam nonnihil albicare facit: ut solent etiam *Metalla.*

Magnes in comburendo penetrat per Crucibulum, idque tam extra, quam intra fracto, quod à splendore splendescere facit.

25 Consentiunt omnes, *Magnetem,* si comburatur, ita ut Flammam quandam luridam & sulphuream jaciat, prorsus fieri virtute evanidum; eamque nunquam postea recuperare; licet refrigeretur in positura Australi, & Septentrionali: Id quod lateribus virtutem indit, & in Magnetibus non prorsus combustis vires renovat.

30 Experimentum factum est, de Ferro *Magnete* tacto, ac etiam de *Magnete* ipso, collocatis super *fastigium Templi* D. *Pauli, Londini,* quod est ex altissimis *Templis Europæ*; annon minuerentur virtute attractiva, propter distantiam à terra? sed nihil prorsus variatum est.

the bottom of a glass upturned so that the needle hangs over on both sides—a thing which is all the more worthy of note because something of this sort perhaps gave rise to the frivolous tale that adamant restricts the loadstone's virtue. For put a needle on a small square piece of adamant, with a loadstone close by but not close enough for it to be able to attract it, and the needle will still tremble; and that trembling is not a hindering of the motion but the motion itself.

Loadstone attracts touched iron much more vigorously than untouched, to such an extent that where it fails to attract untouched iron in a given distance, it succeeds with touched three times further off.

No iron or metallic material is extracted from loadstone by fire or any known way of separation.

Loadstone is not dissolved in aqua regia any more than it is in aqua fortis.

Loadstone put in a crucible, yet not heated to the point where it gives off flame, loses a great deal of weight and an immense amount of virtue so that it scarcely attracts iron.

Loadstone can scarcely be melted but it nevertheless changes shape a bit and, like iron, glows red.

A loadstone burnt whole keeps [1] its passive virtue, so that it can attach itself to another loadstone; but it as good as loses the active power of attracting iron.

A loadstone burnt in a crucible gives off a fume which, though almost invisible, makes a brass sheet placed above it turn rather white; as other metals are also made to do.

A loadstone in burning penetrates through the crucible, and does that too whether the crucible be cracked on the inside or the outside, which makes it shine brightly.

Everyone agrees that a loadstone, if it is burnt to such an extent that it casts off a lurid and sulphureous flame, becomes completely enfeebled and never thereafter recovers its virtue, even though it be cooled in a north–south orientation—a practice which endows bricks with virtue and renews the power of loadstones not entirely burnt.

An experiment has been performed with iron touched with a loadstone, and also with the loadstone itself, which were set on the highest point of St Paul's Cathedral in London—one of the tallest cathedrals in Europe—to see whether their attractive virtue grew less with distance from the ground; but it did not make any difference at all.

TOPICA INQVISITIONIS DE LVCE ET LVMINE

ᴵ TOPICA INQVISITIONIS
De
LVCE ET LVMINE.

I. *Tabula præsentiæ.*

5 Videndum primò, quæ sint ea, cujuscunque generis, quæ progignunt
lucem: ut stellæ, meteora ignita, flamma, ligna, metalla & alia ignita,
saccharum inter scalpendum & frangendum, Cicendula, rores aquæ
salsæ percussæ & sparsæ, oculi quorundam animalium, ligna nonnulla
putria, magna vis nivis. Aër fortasse ipse tenuem possit habere lucem,
10 animalium visui, quæ noctu cernunt, conformem; ferrum & stannum,
cum in aquam fortem immittuntur resolvenda, ebulliunt & sine igne
[X3ᵛ] ullo acrem caloᴵrem concipiunt; utrum vero lucem aliquam edant,
inquiratur. Oleum lampadum magnis frigoribus scintillat; nocte suda
circa equum sudantem conspicitur nonnunquam lux quædam tenuis;
15 circa capillos quorundam hominum accidit, sed raro, lux etiam tenuis,
tanquam flammula lambens, ut factum est Lucio Martio in Hispania;
ventrale cujusdam fœminæ nuper inventum est, quod micaret, sed inter
fricandum; erat autem tinctum in viridi, atque tincturam illam
ingreditur alumen, & crepabat nonnihil cum micabat. Vtrum alumen
20 inter scalpendum aut frangendum micet, inquiratur; sed fortiore, ut
puto, indiget fractione, quia magis contumax est, quam saccharum;
Similiter tibialia nonnulla, inter exuendum nituerunt, sive ex sudore,
sive ex tinctura aluminis. *Alia.*

---

4 I. *Tabula*] / the roman numerals preceding this and the other subtitles appear in *Op* as
arabic numerals placed at the beginning of the paragraph immediately following the subtitle.
This very un-Baconian practice was not adopted in *SEH*   7 inter scalpendum]
interscalpendum   12 edant] edunt *Op* (L2ᵛ)   16 est Lucio] est in *Lucio Op* (L2ᵛ)
/ *SEH* (II, p. 317) silently follows *Sc*   17 micaret, sed] micaret, minime immotum, sed
Op (L2ᵛ) / *SEH* silently follows *Op* in the Latin (II, p. 317) but not in the translation (V, p. 409)
18 tinctum] intinctum *Op* (L2ᵛ) / *SEH* (II, p. 317) silently follows *Op*; cf. *NO*, Xɪʳ (*SEH*, I,
p. 242): 'sales, quibus gremiale tinctum erat'   21–2 indiget . . . tibialia] indiget
fractione, quam *Saccharum*, quia magis contumax est. *Tibialia Op* (L3ʳ) / *SEH* (II, p. 317)
silently follows *Op*

6 alia ignita,] ~:   9 nivis. Aër] nivis, aër   11–12 sine igne ullo] sine ullo igne
Op (L2ᵛ) / *SEH* (II, p. 317) follows *Op* and does not record the reading in *Sc*   12 concipiunt;] ~ᴧ   13 inquiratur. Oleum] inquiratur, oleum   scintillat;] ~,   16
lambens,] ~;   18 fricandum;] ~,   21 contumax est,] ~ ᴧ

ᴵ TOPICS OF INQUIRY
Concerning
LIGHT AND LUMEN

I. *Table of presence*

Note first which are the bodies of every kind whatever that produce light, like stars, fiery meteors, flame, wood, metals and other fiery bodies, sugar when it is being scraped and broken, the firefly, sea spray dashed and scattered, the eyes of certain animals, some kinds of rotten wood, a great mass of snow. Perhaps the very air may hold a soft light adapted to the eyes of animals with night vision; iron and tin when put in aqua fortis to be dissolved boil up and, without any fire, get very ᴵ hot, but look and see whether they give off any light. Lamp oil shimmers in very cold weather; on a clear night a certain weak light is sometimes seen round a sweating horse; a weak light like a lambent little flame also plays, but infrequently, round some people's hair, as happened to Lucius Marcius in Spain; recently a certain woman's stomacher was found to glitter, but only when it was rubbed; now this had been dyed with a green containing alum, and it crackled a bit when it glittered. See whether alum glitters when it is being scraped or broken, though I imagine that it would take more breaking than sugar because it is more stubborn. Likewise some stockings have sparkled when being taken off, either because of sweat or alum dye. *Other examples.*

II. *Tabula absentiæ in proximo.*

Videndum etiam quæ sint ea, quæ nullam lucem edant, quæ tamen cum iis quæ edant, magnam habent similitudinem. Aqua bulliens non edit lucem; aër licet violenter fervefactus non edit lucem; Specula & [X4ʳ] 5 Diamantes, quæ lucem tam ⸌ insigniter reflectunt, nullam edunt lucem originalem. *Alia.*

Videndum est etiam accurate in hoc genere instantiarum de Instantiis migrantibus, ubi scilicet adest & abest lux quasi transiens. Carbo ignitus lucet, sed fortiter compressus statim lucem deponit; Humor ille 10 Crystallinus Cicendulæ, morte vermis, etiam fractus & in partes divisus, lucem ad parvum tempus retinet, sed quæ paulo post evanescat. *Alia.*

III. *Tabula graduum.*

Videndum quæ lux sit magis intensa & vibrans, quæ minus: flamma lignorum fortem edit lucem; flamma spiritus Vini debiliorem; flamma 15 carbonum penitus accensorum, fuscam admodum & vix visibilem. *Alia.*

IV. *Colores Lucis.*

Videndum est de coloribus lucis, quales sint, quales non. Stellæ aliæ candidæ sunt, aliæ splendidæ, aliæ rubeæ, aliæ plumbeæ; flammæ ordinariæ fere croceæ sunt, & inter eas coruscationes cœlitus, & flammæ [X4ᵛ] 20 pulveris pyrii maxime albicant; flamma sulphuris cœrulea ⸌est & pulchra. In aliquibus autem Corporibus sunt purpureæ flammæ; non inveniuntur flammæ virides: quæ maxime ad viriditatem inclinat, est lux Cicendulæ. Nec inveniuntur coccineæ flammæ; ferrum ignitum rubicundum est, & paulo intensius ignitum, quasi candescit. *Alia.*

---

4 violenter] ~ *Op*, insolenter *Sc* (L3ʳ) / *SEH* (II, p. 318) silently follows *Op*; cf. e.g. *NO*, P1ʳ (*SEH*, I, p. 207): 'De vento autem igneo, tàm subitò & violentèr se expandente . . .' 17 quales non. Stellæ] quales non. Stellarum *Op* (L3ᵛ) / *SEH* (II, p. 318) silently follows *Op* but cf. *NO*, Y3ᵛ (*SEH*, I, p. 250): 'Ex traditione Astronomorum ponuntur stellæ aliæ magis, aliæ minùs Calidæ'　　　19 fere croceæ sunt] *om* in *Op* (L3ᵛ) / *SEH* (II, p. 318) notes *om* in *Op* and follows *Sc*　　　22 est lux] lux *om Sc*, est *lux Op* (L3ᵛ) / *SEH* (II, p. 318) silently follows *Op*　　　24 intensius] intentius *Op* (L3ᵛ) / *SEH* (II, p. 318) silently follows *Sc*

2 lucem edant,] ~ₐ　　　17 quales non. Stellæ] quales non stellæ　　　23 flammæ;] ~:

II. *Table of absence in proximity*

Next note which are the bodies that give off no light but yet have a close resemblance to those that do. Boiling water does not give off light; air, though violently heated, does not give off light; mirrors and diamonds, which reflect $^|$ light so strikingly, give off none that originates with them. Other examples.

Migratory instances should also be noted in detail in instances of this kind, i.e. where light is present and absent, inasmuch as it comes and goes. A burning coal gives light but, strongly compressed, immediately stops doing so; when the worm is dead, the crystalline humour of the firefly, when broken and split up into parts, keeps its light for a short while but the light fades away soon after. *Other examples.*

III. *Table of degrees*

Note which light is more intense and vibrant and which less: flame from wood gives off strong light; flame from spirit of wine a weaker one; flame from coal thoroughly alight a dim and almost invisible one. *Other examples.*

IV. *Colours of light*

It should be noted in relation to the colours of light what kinds exist and what do not. Some stars are white, others bright, some reddish, others leaden; ordinary flames are pretty well yellow, and among them celestial coruscations and the flames of gunpowder tend to come nearest to white; the flame of sulphur is a $^|$ fine blue. In certain bodies the flames are purple; but green flames are not to be found; the one that tends most towards green is the light of the firefly. Nor are scarlet flames to be found; hot iron is ruddy and when heated a bit more strongly, almost white. *Other examples.*

V. *Reflexiones Lucis.*

Videndum quæ corpora lucem reflectunt, ut specula, aquæ, metalla polita, Luna, gemmæ; omnia liquida & superficie valde æquata & lævi splendent nonnihil: splendor autem est gradus quidam pusillus lucis.

5 Videndum attente, utrum lux corporis lucidi, ab alio corpore lucido, reflecti possit, ut si sumatur ferrum ignitum & opponatur radiis Solis. Nam reflexiones Lucis omnino superreflectuntur (elanguentes tamen paulatim) de speculo in speculum. *Alia.*

VI. *Multiplicationes Lucis.*

10 Videndum de multiplicatione Lucis ut per specula perspectiva & similia, quibus acui potest lux & in longinquum projici aut etiam reddi, [X5^r] ad distinguendas res visibiles subtilius & melius, ut videre ¹ est apud pictores, qui phialam aqua plenam ad candelam adhibent.

Videndum etiam, num omnia in majore quanto, lucem non 15 reflectant. Lux enim (ut credi possit), aut pertransit, aut reflectitur: qua de causa Luna, etiamsi [non] fuerit corpus opacum, tamen ob magnitudinem, lucem reflectere possit.

Videndum etiam, utrum aggregatio corporum lucidorum lucem multiplicet. Atque de æqualiter lucidis dubitandum non est. Utrum vero 20 lux, quæ majore luce plane obruitur, ut videri per se non possit, adjiciat tamen aliquid lucis, inquiratur. Etiam splendida quæque nonnihil lucis contribuunt, magis enim lucidum erit cubiculum serico quam lana ornatum. Multiplicatur etiam lux per refractionem, nam gemmæ angulis

---

4 lucis] *luminis Op* (L3^v) / *SEH* (*loc. cit*) silently follows *Op*; the lux–lumen distinction is philosophically very important (see *cmt*, pp. 333–4 below); that *Sc* may be correct is suggested by *NO*, 2H4^v (*SEH*, I, p. 300): 'quòd Luna radios Solis reflectat; neque videtur fieri Reflexio Lucis nisi à Solidis'   7 elanguentes] *elanguentia Op* / *SEH* (*loc. cit*) notes the reading in *Op* but not that it is following *Sc*   9 *Multiplicationes*] ~ *Op* (L3^v), *Multiplicatio Sc* / *SEH* (II, p. 319) follows *Op* but does not note the *Sc* form; given that most of these subheadings are plural, the plural seems appropriate here   11 longinquum] ~ *Op* (L4^r), longinquam *Sc* / *SEH* (*loc. cit.*) follows *Op* but does not note form in *Sc*   12 melius] ~ *Op* (L4^r), mollius *Sc* / *SEH* (*loc. cit*) follows *Op* but also notes form in *Sc*   15 possit] ~ *Op* (L4^r), potest *Sc* / *SEH* (II, p. 319) follows *Op* but does not note form in *Sc*; cf. *DAS*, 3D3^v (*SEH*, I, p. 752): 'Vix credi possit, vitam quantum perturbet, *inutilis Curiositas*, circa illas res, quae nostrâ intersunt'   16 [non]] / *SEH* (V, p. 41 n. 1) suggested that Bacon 'meant to write *non*'; I am sure that he did, see *OFB*, VI, pp. 400–1   20 plane] penitus *Op* (L4^r) / plane adopted in *SEH*, which fails to note *Op* reading (*loc. cit.*)   22 erit] ~ *Op* (L4^r), fuerit *Sc* / fuerit not adopted or noted in *SEH* (*loc. cit.*)

3 lævi] / *nld* in *SEH* (II, p. 318) as levi   15 possit,] ~$_\wedge$,   19 multiplicet.] ~, *Sc*, ~? *Op* (L4^r)   19 non est.] ~:   Utrum] lc   21 lucis,] ~$_\wedge$

V. *Reflections of light*

Note which bodies reflect light, as mirrors, waters, burnished metals, the Moon, gemstones; all liquids and everthing with a very smooth and polished surface shine somewhat: and shininess is a kind of very low-level light.

Note carefully whether the light of one lucid body can be reflected from another, as for example if one could take a red-hot iron and set it over against the rays of the Sun. For reflections of light get reflected again from mirror to mirror (though they gradually get weaker). *Other examples.*

VI. *Multiplications of light*

Take note of the multiplication of light, as by perspective glasses and the like with which the light can be brought to a point and projected into the distance or rendered more subtle and better for making out visible bodies—as we see [1] with painters who position a flask full of water in front of a candle.

Note too whether all bodies on a large scale do not reflect light. For light (as can be believed) either goes straight through or gets reflected; and it may be because of its size that the Moon, though it is [not] an opaque body, can nevertheless reflect light.

Note too whether aggregation of lucid bodies multiplies light. In the case of bodies equally lucid this should not be doubted. But inquire whether a light, so far overwhelmed by a stronger one that it cannot be seen at all, does not still add some light. All kinds of bright bodies give some light, for a room will be more lucid when hung with silk rather than with woollen fabrics. Light is also multiplied by refraction, for

intercisæ, & vitrum fractum magis splendent quam si plana fuerint. *Alia.*

VII. *Modi obruendi lucem.*

Videndum de modis obruendi lucem, veluti per exsuperantiam
5 majoris lucis, mediorum crassitudines & opacitates: radii solis certe in
flammam foci immissi flammam veluti fumum quendam albiorem
apparere faciunt. *Alia.*

[X5ᵛ]   ᴵVIII. *Operationes sive effectus lucis.*

Videndum de operationibus sive effectibus lucis, quæ paucæ sunt, ut
10 videtur, & ad corpora præsertim solida, alteranda parum possunt. Lux
enim præ omnibus se generat, alias qualitates parce. Lux certe aërem
nonnihil attenuat, spiritibus animalium grata est, eosque exhilarat,
colorum omnium & visibilium radios submortuos excitat, omnis enim
color lucis imago fracta est. *Alia.*

15   IX. *Mora Lucis.*

Videndum est de mora lucis, quæ (ut videtur) momentanea est.
Neque enim lux, si per multas horas in Cubiculo duraverit, magis illud
illuminat, quam per momentum aliquod; cum in calore & aliis contra
fiat. Etenim & prior calor manet, & novus superadditur. Attamen
20 crepuscula nonnihil à reliquiis Solis provenire, ab aliquibus putantur.

X. *Viæ & processus Lucis.*

Videndum attente de viis & processibus Lucis. Lux circumfunditur;
utrum vero una ascendat paululum, an æqualiter deorsum & sursum
[X6ʳ] circumfundatur, inquiratur. Lux ipsa lucem undique cirᴵca se parit; ut

---

5 &] aut *Op* (L4ʳ) / *Op* not followed or noted in *SEH* (II, p. 319)   9 quæ paucæ] qui
pauci *Op* (L4ᵛ) / *SEH* (II, p. 319) silently follows *Op*; for Bacon a relative pronoun referring to
two nouns, one feminine and one masculine, did not have to be masculine, cf. *NO*, 2F4ᵛ (*SEH*,
I, p. 289): 'At *Instantiæ Fœderis* ostendunt operationes & effectus, quæ deputantur alicui ex illis
Heterogeneis vt propria, competere etiam alijs ex Heterogeneis'   16 (ut videtur)] *om* in
Op (L4ᵛ) / *SEH* (II, p. 319) silently follows *Op*   20 Solis] *Lucis Op* (L4ᵛ) / *SEH* (II, p.
320) follows *Op* but notes the *Sc* form; that *Sc* may be correct see *NO*, 2H4ᵛ (*SEH*, I, p. 300):
'Certè Causa Crepusculi inter alias, est Reflexio radiorum Solis à superiore parte Aëris'
11 Lux] / new paragraph in *Op* (L4ᵛ) and *SEH* (II, p. 319)

gems cut and glass broken shine more brightly than if they were not. *Other examples.*

VII. *Means of overpowering light*

Take note of means of overpowering light as, for instance, by another light too strong for it, or by the grossness and opacity of its media; the Sun's rays when they are directed on the flame of a fire certainly make it look like a kind of white smoke. *Other examples.*

ᴵVIII. *Operations or effects of light*

Take note of the operations or effects of light which are few (apparently) and have little capacity for altering bodies, especially solid ones. For light above all generates itself, but generates other qualities sparingly. It certainly attenuates air a bit; it is pleasing to the spirits of animals and cheers them up; it perks up the dying rays of all colours and visible objects, for all colour is a fragmented image of light. *Other examples.*

IX. *The Lasting of Light*

Take note of the lasting of light which (as it appears) is short-lived. For light shining for a long time in a room does not illuminate it any more than if the light had only been there for an instant, though the opposite is true of heat and other things, where the earlier heat persists and further heat adds to it. Nevertheless some people believe that twilights issue in some measure from leftovers of sunlight.

X. *The Passages and processes of Light*

Note carefully the passages and processes of light. Light spreads out all around, but inquire whether it goes upwards a little at the same time, or whether it spreads out evenly up and down. Light itself generates light
ᴵ all round it so that when a screen is put in front of it the body of the

cum corpus lucis, umbraculo scilicet interposito, non cernatur. Lux ipsa tamen omnia circum illuminat, præter ea quæ sub umbram umbraculi cadunt; quæ tamen ipsa nonnihil Lucis accipiunt à Luce circumjecta; nam multo melius aliquid intra umbram umbraculi situm cerni potest,

5 quam si nulla omnino adesset Lux. Itaque corpus visibile corporis alicujus lucidi, & ipsa Lux, res discrepantes esse videntur. Lux, corpora fibrosa & inæqualis posituræ non penetrat, sed tamen à soliditate [&] duritia corporis non impeditur, ut fit in vitro & similibus. Itaque recta linea & pori non transversi, hæc tantum videntur lucem perferre.

10 Delatio Lucis fit optime per aërem; qui quo purior fuerit, eo melius lucem transmittit. Vtrum lux per corpus aëris vehatur, inquiratur. Sonos certe videmus à ventis vehi, ut longius secundo vento quam adverso audiri possint. Vtrum vero simile aliquid fiat in Luce, inquiratur. *Alia.*

XI. *Diaphaneitas Lucidorum.*

15 Videndum est etiam de diaphaneitate Lucidorum. Filum Candelæ
[X6ᵛ] intra flammam cernitur; at per majores flammas ¹ objecta ad visum non perveniunt. At contra, omnis Diaphaneitas, ex corpore aliquo ignito perit, ut in vitro videre est, quod ignitum, non amplius manet diaphanum. Corpus aëris diaphanum est, item aquæ; at illa duo

20 diaphana commista, in nive aut spuma, non amplius diaphana sunt, sed acquirunt lucem quandam originalem.

XII. *Cognationes & hostilitates Lucis.*

Videndum de Cognationibus atque etiam hostilitatibus lucis. Cognationem maxime habet lux cum tribus rebus (quatenus ad

25 generationem lucis): calore, tenuitate & motu. Videndum igitur de conjugiis & divortiis eorum, erga lucem, atque eorundem conjugiorum & divortiorum gradibus. Flamma spiritus vini, aut ignis fatui, longe

---

2 præter ea] ~ *Op* (L4ᵛ), præterea *Sc* / *SEH* (II, p. 320) silently follows *Op*   4 umbra-
culi] *om* in *Op* (L4ᵛ) / *SEH* (II, p. 320) silently adopts reading in *Sc*   7–8 soliditate [&]
duritia] soliditate duritiæ *Sc*, *Op* (L5ʳ)   9 transversi . . . perferre] transversi, videntur
Lucem tantum perferre *Op* (L5ʳ) / *SEH* (*loc. cit.*) silently follows *Op*   12 vehi, ut] vehi;
& *Op* (*loc. cit.*) / *SEH* (*loc. cit.*) notes the discrepancy and follows *Sc*   17 ex corpore] ~
Op (L5ʳ), ex *om* in *Sc* / *SEH* (II, p. 320) silently follows *Op*   20 commista] ~ *Op* (L5ʳ),
commissa *Sc* / *SEH* (II, p. 320) silently follows *Op*; also cf. *DAS*, Y3ᵛ–4ʳ (*SEH*, I, p.
566)   26 eorum] ~ *Op* (L5ᵛ), earum *Sc* / *SEH* (II, p. 321) silently follows *Op*
1 cernatur.] ~,   10 Delatio] / new paragraph in *Op* (L5ʳ)   15 est etiam] etiam
est *Op* (*loc. cit.*) / *SEH* (II, p. 320) silently follows *Sc*   25 lucis):] ~ₐ:

light cannot be seen. Nevertheless that very light lights up everything around it except for the things which lie in the screen's shadow, and even these things are to some degree illuminated by the surrounding light; for something situated within the shadow of the screen can be seen much better than if there were absolutely no light present at all. Thus the visible body of any lucid body and the light itself seem to be quite different things. Light does not penetrate fibrous bodies with an uneven arrangement of parts, but it is still not stopped by the solidity [and] hardness of bodies, as we see in glass and the like. Thus a straight line and pores not transverse alone seem to transmit light. The carrying of light takes place best through the air, and the purer it is the better it transmits light. Inquire whether light is carried by the body of the air. Certainly we see that sounds are borne along by winds so that they can be heard further away when the wind is with and not against them. But inquire whether something of the same kind happens in the case of light. *Other examples.*

XI. *Transparency of Lucid Bodies*

We must also take note of the transparency of lucid bodies. The wick of a candle can be seen within the flame, but through greater flames ¹ objects cannot be made out. On the contrary, all transparency disappears from any body made fiery, as we see with glass which when it is made fiery it stays transparent no longer. The body of air is transparent and so too of water; but those two bodies mixed together in snow or froth are no longer transparent but acquire a certain original light.

XII. *Light's Kinsfolk and adversaries*

Take note of light's kinsfolk and also of its adversaries. As far as its generation is concerned light has kinship with three things in the main: heat, tenuity and motion. Note therefore their marriages and divorces in relation to light, and the stages of their marriages and divorces. The flame of spirit of wine, or the ignis fatuus has a much gentler heat but much

ferro ignito, calore lenior est, verum lumine fortior. Cicendulæ & rores aquæ salsæ, & multa ex illis quæ enumeravimus, lucem jaciunt, calida ad tactum non sunt. Etiam metalla ignita tenuia non sunt, at calore tamen ardente prædita. At contra aër est inter tenuissima corpora, sed luce [X7ʳ] 5 vacat, rursus idem aër, atque etiam venti, | motu rapidi sunt, lucem tamen non præbent. At contra, metalla ignita motum suum hebetem non exuunt, lucem nihilominus vibrant.

In cognationibus autem lucis, quæ non ad generationem lucis, sed ad processum tantum spectant, nihil tam Conjunctum est quam sonus.
10 Itaque de eorum sympathiis & dissidiis accurate videndum. In his conveniunt lux & sonus in ambitum circumfunduntur. Lux & sonus per longissima spatia feruntur sed lux pernicius, ut in tormentis videmus, ubi lux citius cernitur, quam auditur sonus, cum tamen flamma pone sequatur. Lux & sonus subtilissimas distinctiones patiuntur, ut in verbis
15 articulatis soni, in omnibus visibilium imaginibus lux. Lux & sonus nihil fere producunt aut generant, præterquam in sensibus & spiritibus Animalium. Lux & Sonus facile generantur & brevi evanescunt. Nam non est quod quis putet sonum illum, qui ad tempus aliquod, à Campana aut chorda percussa, durat, à prima percussione fieri, nam si campana vel
20 chorda tangatur, sonus statim perit. Vnde manifestum est, durationem [X7ᵛ] soni per succes|sionem creari. Lux à majore luce, sicut sonus à majore sono, obruitur. Et cætera. Differunt autem, quod lux (ut diximus) sono velocior sit. Lux majora spatia vincat quam sonus. Lux utrum in corpore aëris deferatur, quemadmodum sonus, incertum sit. Lux in linea recta
25 tantum, sonus in linea obliqua & undiquaque, feratur. Etenim cum quid in umbra umbraculi cernitur, non est quod quis putet, quod lux ipsa penetret umbraculum, sed aërem tantum circumfusum illuminat, qui etiam aërem pone umbraculum, vicinitate nonnihil illustrat. At sonus ab uno latere parietis redditus, ex altera parte parietis auditur, non multum
30 debilitatus. Etiam sonus intra septa Corporum solidorum auditur, licet exilior factus, ut fit in sonis infra lapides hæmatites, aut in corporibus percussis, infra aquam. At lux in corpore solido & non diaphano,

---

8 generationem lucis] *generationem* ejus *Op* (L5ᵛ) / *SEH* (II, p. 321) silently follows *Op*
20 tangatur] tangatur & sistatur *Op* (L5ᵛ) / *SEH* (II, p. 321) silently follows *Op*   20–1
durationem soni] *om* in *Op* (L6ʳ) / *SEH* (II, p. 321) notes the difference and follows *Sc*
23 vincat] vincit *Op* (L6ʳ) / *SEH* (II, p. 321) silently follows *Sc*   30 auditur] audiatur
Op (L6ʳ) / *SEH* (II, p. 321) silently follows *Sc*   31–2 aut in corporibus percussis, infra] ∼
Op (L6ʳ), aut corpora percussa intra *Sc* / *SEH* (II, p. 321) silently follows *Op*   32 corpore
. . . non diaphano] corpore *Diaphano Op* (L6ʳ) / *SEH* (II, p. 322) notes the difference and follows *Sc*
22 Differunt] / new paragraph in *Op* (L6ʳ)

stronger illuminating power than fiery iron. Fireflies, sea spray and many
of the other things which I have listed give off light but are not hot to
the touch. Fiery metals are also not tenuous bodies but are fiercely hot.
On the other hand, air is one of the most tenuous bodies but is devoid
of light; then again, that same air and the wind too ¹ move very fast but
still give no light. By contrast fiery metals do not give up their sluggish
motion, yet they still flicker with light.

Now among the kinships of light which relate not to its generation
but only to its process, nothing is so closely allied to it than sound. So
the sympathies and dissents of the two of them must be noted in detail.
Light and sound agree in the following ways. They spread outwards in
all directions. Light and sound travel long distances but light more
quickly as we see with artillery where we see the flash sooner than we
hear the bang, yet with the flame taking up the rear. Light and sound
experience the most subtle distinctions, as for instance in the spoken
word in the case of sound, and all visible images in the case of light.
Light and sound produce or generate practically nothing apart from in
the senses and spirits of animals. Light and sound are easily generated
and quickly die away. For no one should imagine that the sound which
lasts for a while after the striking of the bell or the string is caused by the
initial stroke for if you lay a finger on the bell or string, the sound ceases
immediately. And it is evident from this that the lasting of sound is produced by succession. ¹ One light is overpowered by a greater one, just as
one sound is by a louder. Etcetera. On the other hand, the two differ in
that light is (as I have said) swifter than sound. Light carries further than
sound. It is uncertain whether light, like sound, is carried in the body of
the air. Light only moves in a straight line, sound obliquely and all
around. For when anything can be seen in the shadow of a screen, no
one should suppose that light penetrates the screen but only that it illu-
minates the surrounding air, air which in turn brightens up the neighbouring air behind the screen a bit. But sound made on one side of a wall
can be heard not much fainter on the other. Sound can also be heard
within the confines of solid bodies though it becomes weaker, as happens in the case of sounds in bloodstones and of bodies struck under
water. But you cannot see light at all in a solid body which is not

undique obstructo, omnino non cernitur. Lux magis in profundum penetrat, quam sonus, ut in fundo aquarum. Omnis sonus generatur in motu, & Elisione corporum manifesta; Lux non item.

[X8ʳ]   At hostilitates lucis (nisi quis privaᶦtiones pro hostilitatibus habere
5 velit) non occurrunt; verum, quod maxime credibile est, torpor corporum, in partibus suis, maxime est luci inimicus. Nam fere nihil lucet, quod non aut propria natura insigniter mobile est, aut excitatum vel calore vel motu, vel spiritu vitali. *Alia.*

    Intelligo autem semper, quod non tantum aliæ instantiæ investigandæ
10 sint (istas enim paucas solummodo exempli loco adduximus) sed etiam, ut novi Topici articuli, prout rerum natura fert, adjiciantur.

1–2 Lux . . . aquarum] *om* in *Op* (*loc. cit.*) / *SEH* (*loc. cit.*) notes the difference but follows *Op*, which begins the next sentence with Ultimo, quod which is *om* in *Sc*   2 generatur] generetur *Op* (*loc. cit.*) / *SEH* (*loc. cit.*) notes the difference and follows *Op*
10 solummodo exempli loco] exempli loco solummodo *Op* (L6ʳ)

transparent and is blocked off on all sides. Light, as in the depths of the waters, gets further down than sound. All sound is produced in motion and by the manifest elision of bodies; the same is not true of light.

But for the adversaries of light (unless you want to take ¹ privations for adversaries) none spring to mind; but it is very easy to believe that the sluggishness of bodies in their parts is light's main enemy. For practically nothing gives light unless it is either extremely mobile in its very nature, or stimulated by heat or motion or vital spirit. *Other examples.*

Now my intention is always that not only are other instances to be investigated (for I have adduced these few only by way of example), but also that new topics of inquiry should be added, according as nature brings them up.

PRODROMI SIVE ANTICIPATIONES
PHILOSOPHIÆ SECVNDÆ

¹ PRODROMI *Sive* ANTICIPATIONES
PHILOSOPHIÆ SECVNDÆ.

PRÆFATIO.

Existimamvs eum & animantis civis & viri prudentis personam bene
5 simul sustinuisse, qui interrogatus an optimas leges suis civibus dedisset,
optimas certe dixit *ex iis, quas illi accepturi fuissent.* Atque certe quibus
non tantum bene cogitasse satis est (quod non multo secus est ac bene
somniasse) nisi obtineant quoque & rem ad effectum perducant, iis non
optima utique, sed ex iis, quæ probari verisimile est, potissima
10 quandoque eligenda sunt. Nobis vero, licet Humanam Rempubli|cam,
Patriam communem, summo prosequamur amore, tamen legislatoria
illa ratione, & delectu uti liberum non est. Neque enim leges Intellectui
aut rebus damus ad arbitrium nostrum, sed tanquam scribæ fideles ab
ipsius Naturæ voce latas & prolatas excipimus & describimus. Itaque
15 sive illæ placeant, sive per opinionum suffragia antiquentur, fides nostra
omnino exsolvenda est. Neque tamen spem abjecimus, quin sint atque
exoriantur apud posteros nonnulli, qui optima quæque capere &
concoquere possint, & quibus ea perficere & colere curæ erit. Itaque ad
illa ipsa tendere, atque fontes rerum & utilitatum aperire, & viarum
20 indicia undique conquirere (invocata Numinis ope) nunquam dum in
vivis erimus desistemus. Iidem nos de eo, quod ad omnes pertinere, &
in commune prodesse possit, solliciti, dum ad majora contendimus,
minora non aspernamur (cum illa remota, hæc parata esse soleant). Nec
potiora (ut arbitramur) afferentes, idcirco Veteribus ac receptis,
25 quominus illa apud plurimos valeant, intercedimus; quinetiam ea ipsa &
aucta & emendata, & in honore esse cupimus. Neque enim homines aut
omnes aut omnino, aut statim ¹ à receptis & creditis abducere conamur.
Sed quemadmodum sagitta aut missile fertur certe in processu, sed
tamen interim conversiones suas perpetuo expedit progrediendo &
30 nihilominus rotando; ita & nos dum ad ulteriora rapimur, in receptis &

---

6 *optimas . . . fuissent*] / editorial italics   10 vero,] ~ᴧ   23 soleant).] ~)ᴧ
Nec] lc

PRECURSORS *Or* ANTICIPATIONS OF THE
PHILOSOPHY TO COME

PREFACE

I believe that he well kept up the character at once of an active citizen
and of a wise man who, when asked whether he had given his citizens
the best laws, replied, *the best to be sure that they would have been willing
to entertain.* Those to whom it is not sufficient to think well about these
laws (which is little different from dreaming about them) without assert-
ing their ideas and putting them into effect, such people should sometimes choose, not at any rate the best, but the most effective course of
action which is likely to secure approval. But although I serve the
Republic of Mankind, ¹ our common homeland, with the greatest devo-
tion, I am not free to exercise the reasoning and choice of that legislator.
For I do not give laws to the intellect or to things at my own good pleasure but, as a faithful scribe, I take down and copy out ones dictated and
proclaimed by the very voice of nature itself. Therefore, whether they
find favour or get dismissed by the collective voice of people with other
ideas, I should keep complete faith with nature. Nevertheless, I have not
given up hope that there may exist or spring up among my successors
some who can get a grip on every one of the best things and bring them
to maturity, and whose job it will be to cultivate and perfect them.
Therefore, having called on the power of the Almighty, I shall not for as
long as I live give up pressing on towards these very things, opening up
the fountains of affairs and their utility, and searching on every side for
signs of the way forward. I am also that same person, concerned about
what can belong to all and promote the common good, who while he
hastens on towards greater goods does not despise the lesser (since the
former usually lie a long way off and the latter close at hand). Nor bringing, as I think, more powerful ideas, do I set myself up against those that
are ancient and accepted to stop them from having power among the
majority of men. Indeed, I long to see them increased and improved and
held in high esteem. For I am not trying to wean people ¹ away altogether, unconditionally, or immediately from received and trusted doctrines. But just as an arrow or missile is surely carried on its way and yet
in the meantime invariably accomplishes its motions by simultaneously

cognitis volvimur & circumferimur. Quamobrem nos quoque Rationis ipsius communis & demonstrationum vulgarium (abdicato licet imperio earum) honesta opera utimur; atque ea quæ nobis secundum eas inventa & judicata sunt, quæque plurimum & veritatis & utilitatis
5 habere possint, pari cum cæteris jure proponemus. Sed tamen neque per hoc iis, quæ de Rationis nativæ & Demonstrationum Veterum incompetentia dicta sunt, derogatum quidquam intelligimus. Quin hæc potius adjunximus, ad tempus & in gratiam eorum, qui justa excusatione aut virium, aut occupationum retardati, Contemplationes
10 suas intra Veteres Scientiarum plagas & provincias, aut saltem earum confinia contermina, sistere volent; Eadem iis, qui veram Naturæ interpretationem secundum indicia nostra accedent, eamque molientur,
[R2ᵛ] loco diverticulorum, aut tabernaculorum in via præbitorum ad soˡlatium & levamentum esse queant, atque interim humanas fortunas aliqua
15 ex parte juvare, & Mentes cogitationibus, quæ paulo arctiorem cognationem habeant cum natura, perfundere. Id vero ex facultate aliqua nostra, aut ejus fiducia, minime ominamur. Verum nobis dubium non est, si quis mediocris licet ingenii, sed tamen animi maturus, Idola mentis suæ deponere, atque Inquisitionem de integro sibi decernere,
20 atque inter vera Historiæ Naturalis atque ejus calculos attente & diligenter, & libere versari velit, & possit; quin ille ipse, quisquis sit, longe altius in Naturam penetraturus sit ex sese, & propriis & genuinis Mentis viribus, denique ex meris Anticipationibus suis, quam per omnigenam Authorum lectionem, aut meditationem abstractam
25 infinitam, aut disputationes assiduas & repetitas; etsi machinas non admoverit, nec Interpretandi formam secutus fuerit. Quare & simile quippiam nobis usu venire posse non diffidimus; præsertim cum accedat Interpretandi experimentum & exercitatio, quam ipsum habitum Mentis corrigere & mutare probabile est. Neque tamen hæc in eam
[R3ʳ] 30 partem accipi volumus, [ac] si fidem, quam ˡ Antiquorum placitis denegavimus, nostris adhiberi postulemus. Quin contra testamur & profitemur, Nos ipsos istis, quæ jam proponemus, qualiacunque ea sint, teneri minime velle, ut omnia Philosophiæ nostræ secundæ & Inductivæ

---

30 [ac]] / silently emended thus in *SEH* (II, p. 691)

going forward and rotating on its axis, so, while I am being swept along towards goals further off, I am also being turned round and about on the axis of opinions received and known. And that is why I too avail myself of the honest service of conventional reason itself and of ordinary demonstrations (though I have repudiated their authority); and the works which I have discovered and evaluated in accordance with that reason and those demonstrations, and which may carry a good deal both of truth and utility, I shall set forth with the same impartial judgement that I give to the rest. But I still do not intend by this to retract anything I have said about the inadequacy of natural reason and the ancient demonstrations. Indeed, I have rather introduced these things for the time being and to please those who, held back by the fair excuse either of inadequate resources or pressure of business, wish to keep their reflections to the old familiar fields of the sciences or at least to the ones adjacent to them. But for those who, following my guidelines, shall resort to the true interpretation of nature and work to bring it about, these same things can act as resting places or wayside inns made available to give them comfort ¹ and good cheer, and meantime to help human fortunes to some degree and flood minds with thoughts which have a rather closer kinship with nature. But I do not forecast this on the basis of any ability of mine or of any faith in anything of that kind. But at the same time I do not doubt that if anyone, though of moderate gifts but ripe judgement, could and would set aside the Idols of his mind and resolve to undertake the inquiry afresh, and involve himself attentively, diligently and frankly with the truths of natural history and its accounts, he himself would in fact be able, whoever he is, to penetrate much further into nature by himself using his own innate mental powers and, in short, by his own naked anticipations than by reading all kinds of authors, no end of abstract meditation, or regular and repeated disputations—even if he had not deployed the right machines nor followed the proper form of interpreting. Therefore I do not despair that I can experience something of this sort, especially since experiment and practice in interpretation may be present, that practice which it is probable can correct and change the very habit of the mind. All the same I do not wish this to be interpreted as if my position were that I expect the faith which ¹ I have denied to the tenets of the ancients to be extended to my own. No, I affirm and declare on the contrary that I do not in any way wish to be obliged in my second and inductive philosophy to hang on to everything which I am now about to propound, whatever its worth may be. Indeed, I have decided to scatter the thoughts themselves and not connect them

tamquam integra serventur. Cogitata autem ipsa spargere, non Methodo revincire visum est. Hæc enim forma, pubescentibus tamquam à stirpe de integro Scientiis debetur; atque ejus est, qui non Artem constituere ex connexis, sed Inquisitionem liberam instituere in singulis, in 5 præsentia tantum velit.

by rhetorical method. For this form of delivery belongs to the sciences in the springtime of their youth, and it is the form preferred by one who only wishes for the moment to establish not an art from notions strung together but to set up a free inquiry into things taken one by one.

THE COMMENTARIES

COMMENTARY ON
HISTORIA DENSI & RARI

Note: this is a *combined* commentary on *HDR(M)* and *HDR*: each section of the commentary is preceded by *c-t* signature references drawn from *HDR*; where the passage in question also appears in *HDR(M)* this reference is followed by the corresponding folio reference drawn from the manuscript *c-t*.

A1ʳ, cf. fo. 7ʳ

Page 36, l. 2, cf. p. 2, l. 2: Coitionis & Expansionis—the use of the term coitio as an apparent synonym for contractio is just one of several senses in which Bacon used it. He also used it (like William Gilbert) to refer to magnetic attraction (*NO*, 2D1ʳ (*SEH*, I, p. 274)), and to denote the motion of each kind of homogeneous part in a heterogeneous body towards other parts of its own kind (*NO*, 2P2ʳ (*SEH*, I, p. 336)).

A1ʳ⁻ᵛ

Page 36, ll. 5–9: *Nil mirum*—Bacon's fondness for accounting and financial metaphors has not, I believe, been noticed. These occur in at least two contexts: (i) where (as here) he wished to draw attention to the quantitative aspects of a natural-philosophical problem (*HDR*, B4ʳ, C1ʳ, D5ʳ (p. 60, ll. 13–14, p. 72, ll. 30–3, p. 102, ll. 32–3 above)) and (ii) where he spoke of the contents of Part V of *IM*; see, for example, *DO*, C3ʳ (*SEH*, I, pp. 143–4): 'At quinta pars ad tempus tantùm, donec reliqua perficiantur, adhibetur; & tanquàm fœnus redditur, vsque dum sors haberi possit.'

A1ᵛ–A2ʳ

Page 36, ll. 9–20: *Illud recte receptum*—for the fundamental proposition that the sum of matter neither increases nor decreases see *PhU*, O10ᵛ–O11ʳ (*OFB*, VI, p. 10, ll. 7–25); *NO*, 2K4ʳ⁻ᵛ (*SEH*, I, pp. 311–12); also cf. *CDNR*, R11ʳ–S1ᵛ (*SEH*, III, pp. 22–5). Telesio (*DRN*, I, pp. 60–4) also insisted that the quantity of matter was invariable; cf. *DPAO*, M6ʳ (*OFB*, VI, p. 258, ll. 21–2); also see *HDR*, p. 162, ll. 20–1; *HDR(M)*, p. 32, ll. 16–17 above.

l. 12: *absque Vacuo*—for the interspersed vacuum and Bacon's views on it see *OFB*, VI, p. 392. According to Bacon an interspersed vacuum is unnecessary because a fold or plica exists which allows matter to expand and contract. For this mysterious plica (the word does not occur in classical Latin) see *cmts* (p. 302 below) on *HDR*, p. 162, ll. 28–9, and *HDR(M)*, p. 32, l. 23. Also see Benedino Gemelli, *Aspetti dell'atomismo classico nella filosofia di Francis Bacon e nel seicento*, Leo S. Olschki: Florence, 1996, pp. 176–7 nn. 177–9, p. 178 n. 183.

ll. 14–19: *Auctorem suum secuti*—the criticisms in this passage echo the words of *NO* (H2ᵛ (*SEH*, I, pp. 173–4)): 'Primi generis [sophistical philosophers] exemplum in *Aristotele* maximè conspicuum est, qui Philosophiam Naturalem Dialecticâ suâ corrupit; quùm Mundum ex Categorijs effecerit; . . . negotium *densi & rari*, per quod corpora subeunt maiores & minores dimensiones siue spatia, per frigidam distinctionem Actus & Potentiæ transegerit . . .'. For late scholastic discussions of act and potency, and of condensation and rarefaction see Dennis Des Chene, *Physiologia: natural philosophy in late Aristotelian and Cartesian thought*, Cornell University Press: Ithaca and London, 1996, pp. 17–52, 106–8. For the Aristotelian categories see *CHSCP*, I, pp. 111–12, 178. Also see *DAS*, Q1^{r-v} (*SEH*, I, p. 523): 'Qui verò Materiam omninò Spoliatam, & Informem, & ad Formas Indifferentem introduxerunt, (vt *Plato & Aristoteles*) multò etiam propiùs & propensiùs ad Parabolæ [of Pan] figuram accesserunt. Posuerunt enim *Materiam* tanquam *publicam Meretricem*; *Formas* verò tanquam *Procos*. Adeò vt omnes de Rerum Principijs Opiniones hùc redeant, & ad illam distributionem reducantur, vt Mundus sit, vel à *Mercurio*; vel à *Penelope & Procis* omnibus.' For Aristotle on dense and rare see *Physica*, IV. 9 (216^b–217^b); and Richard Sorabji, *Matter, space and motion: theories in antiquity and their sequel*, Duckworth: London, 1988, pp. 80–1, 101–2. Also see *cmt* on *DPAO*, K3^v (*OFB*, VI, p. 420). Also see Ægidius Romanus, *Commentaria in octo libros phisicorum Aristotelis* [Venice, 1502], fo. 96^{r-v} for the ideas that Bacon was attacking, especially the theory of decuple proportions (on which see *cmts* (p. 227 below) on *HDR*, B8^r (p. 70, ll. 19–23 above).

ll. 20–1: *Naturalis Philosophiæ veluti Basis*—Bacon also insists on the fundamental importance of the study of dense and rare in *ANN*, where it appears as the first item on a list of eighty proposed investigations for it is the most universal and simple distinction in nature (see p. 174, ll. 3–15 above and *cmts* thereon, p. 307 below). The distinction is given the same priority in *TC* (G6^r (*OFB*, VI, p. 172, ll. 16–19)).

A2^r–A4^r

Page 36, l. 22–p. 38, l. 31: *Primo igitur*—cf. *NO* (2K4^{r-v} (*SEH*, I, pp. 311–12)). For the Creator's powers in relation to matter see *DPAO*, M2^r–M3^v and *cmt* thereon (*OFB*, VI, pp. 250–2, p. 432). For the conversion of air into water and vice versa see *CDNR*, R11^r–S1^v (*SEH*, III, pp. 22–5). When Bacon suggests that one barrel of water can be turned into a hundred rather than the ten of conventional opinion, he is looking forward to his attack on the decuple conversion theory of the Aristotelians (*q.v. HDR*, B8^r (p. 70, ll. 19–23 above and *cmt* thereon p. 227 below), and to experiments tending to show that the conversion of water into air produces an increase in volume of greater than 100 and to the rule (*ibid.*, G4^v (p. 164, ll. 1–2 above)) which asserts that pneumatic matter in general is more than one hundred times rarer than tangible. For experiments on the rarity of air in relation to water see *PhU*, Q3^r–Q4^v and *cmts* thereon (*OFB*, VI, p. 48, l. 2–p. 50, l. 13, p. 372).

A4ᵛ–A5ᵛ, cf. fo. 7ʳ

Page 40, l. 1–p. 44, l. 9, cf. p. 2, l. 4–p. 3, l. 30: Tabula Coitionis—this table also appears in *PhU* (*OFB*, VI, pp. 14–19), where the first 64 items are numbered, the rest not. The wording of the titles of three versions of the table differs in the following respects: *HDR(M)* reverses the Coitionis and Expansionis of *HDR* and *PhU*; after Tangibilibus *HDR* and *HDR(M)* have a parenthetical remark absent from *PhU*; and where *PhU* and *HDR* have rationum, *HDR(M)* has rerum. In the phrase Idem spatium . . . *PhU* and *HDR* have sive where *HDR(M)* has seu. The versions of the table differ as follows: (i) *Plumbi cinericei*: *HDR* and *HDR(M)* give *Den.* 10. *Gra.* 12. whereas *PhU* has *Den.* 10. *Gran.* 13.; (ii) *Marmoris*: *HDR(M)* has den. 2. gr. 22-d. but *PhU* and *HDR* give *Den.* 2. *Gra.* 22. *d.qu.*; (iii) *Cineris communis*: *PhU* and *HDR* have the same result whereas *HDR(M)* gives it an extra half-grain; (iv) after *Balsami Indi HDR* and *HDR(M)* have two items not mentioned in *PhU*; (v) after *Cepæ recentis HDR* and *HDR(M)* have an extra item; (vi) after *Caphuræ PhU* has *Radicis Caricæ*, an item unique to it, instead of which the other two versions have three extra items, viz. *Succi menthæ expressi, Succi boraginis expressi* and *Cervisiæ lupulatæ fortis*; (vii) from the point of view of weight *Succini lucidi* is out of order in *PhU*; it appears two items later in *HDR* and *HDR(M)*; (viii) also out of order by weight are the *Aquæ communis* and *Vrinæ* of *PhU*; they appear in the correct order in *HDR* and *HDR(M)*; (ix) the *Beniovis* and *Myrrhæ* of *PhU* appear in reverse order in the other versions.

Page 40, l. 11, cf. p. 2, l. 13: *Plumbi cinericei*—bismuth.

l. 13, cf. p. 2, l. 15: *Aurichalci*—aurichalcite, a mineral containing copper and zinc which, when reduced, yields brass.

Page 40, l. 19, cf. p. 2, l. 25: *Lapidis Lydii*—basanite, a black variety of quartz, used as a touchstone for precious metals.

l. 25, cf. p. 3, l. 1: *Salis gemmæ*—probably natural rock-salt, see *OED*, Sal-gem.

l. 27, cf. p. 3, l. 4: *Luti albi*—china clay?

l. 33, cf. p. 3, l. 12: *Vitroli albi*—natural zinc sulphate; alternatively, green vitriol (iron sulphate) dehydrated and powdered.

Page 42, l. 3, cf. p. 3, l. 15: *Olei vitrioli*—concentrated sulphuric acid.

l. 6, cf. p. 3, l. 20: *Olei sulphuris*—sulphuric acid, see *OED*, Sulphur, *sb.* 1. d.

l. 10, cf. p. 3, l. 25: *Aquæ fortis*—nitric acid (HNO_2).

l. 27, cf. p. 2, l. 27: *Succini lucidi*—not clear amber (the translation given in *SEH*, V, p. 341) but clear souse, a liquid used for pickling (see *cmt* on this, *OFB*, VI, p. 367).

l. 36, cf. p. 3, l. 7: *Aceti distillati*—for more on this see *cmt* (p. 292 below) on *HDR*, p. 114, ll. 21–9.

l. 40, cf. p. 3, l. 12: *Benjovin*—benzoin or benjamin, a resinous substance obtained, apparently, from the Indonesian tree *styrax benzoin* (*OED*, Benzoin, 1).

A5ᵛ–A6ʳ, cf. fo. 7ᵛ

Page 44, l. 11–p. 46, l. 4, cf. p. 3, l. 27–p. 4, l. 21: Intelligantur *Pondera*—this sentence appears almost verbatim in *PhU*. *PhU* says more than *HDR* and *HDR(M)* about the reasons for choosing gold as a standard (see *OFB*, VI, pp. 18–20). The weights are Troy weights (24 grains = 1 pennyweight = 1.56 grams. 20 dwt = 1 oz. 12 oz. = 1 lb.), see *OFB*, VI, p. 367. On the methods of doing the experiment, and on the weights and measures there is little difference between *HDR* and *HDR(M)*.

A6ʳ–A7ʳ, cf. fo. 8ʳ

Page 46, l. 6–p. 48, l. 5, cf. p. 4, l. 23–p. 5, l. 3: Parvitas vasis—the notes of advice are much more thorough than those given in *HDR(M)* but follow quite closely those given in *PhU* (P2ʳ⁻ᵛ (*OFB*, VI, p. 20, l. 29–p. 22, l. 21 and *cmt* thereon, p. 368). The remark that pneumatic bodies are weightless (p. 46, ll. 26–7) indicates that Bacon's conception of dense and rare is remote from the idea of specific gravity: weight or mass is not an intrinsic property of matter but an attribute which can be taken up or lost altogether, and pneumatic matter can convert tangible matter, which has weight, into itself and so cause matter to shed that attribute. I cannot make sense of the statement (p. 46, ll. 28–33) that tenuous bodies perhaps have more matter in the same bulk than the calculations allow. As for Bacon's remark that he compiled the table many years ago, the table did (as we know) appear in *PhU* (*OFB*, VI, pp. 14–18), a work written *c.*1611.

A7ʳ, cf. fo. 8ʳ

Page 48, ll. 7–16, cf. p. 5, ll. 5–6: Licet, atque adeo juvat—this paragraph is quite different from the corresponding materials in *PhU* (P3ʳ (*OFB*, VI, p. 22, ll. 23–5)), where the standard of comparison is 21 parts (obtained by dividing the weight of gold by that of spirit of wine), a standard identical to that given in *NO* (2K4ᵛ–2L1ʳ (*SEH*, I, p. 312)), viz. 21 (although 22 would be a better approximation). Bacon excludes from consideration the pure, super-dense tangible matter in the depths of the Earth; on this subject see *cmts* immediately below.

A7ʳ⁻ᵛ, cf. fo. 8ʳ

Page 48, l. 17–p. 50, l. 2, cf. p. 5, ll. 9–20: Opinio de *compositione*—this is the opening shot in Bacon's running battle against Aristotelian-scholastic element theory. Here he attacks mixtion theory: how can substances much lighter than gold combine to produce it? Clearly they cannot unless additional hypotheses are introduced. But the usual hypotheses are poor: (i) that when the Aristotelians speak of earth they mean not common but an elementary earth much heavier than any mixed body or (ii) that the lighter elements surrounding the heavier compress the denser to a greater density. As for (i), Aristotle himself made it plain that his elements were not to be regarded as ordinary earth, water, air and fire. Elementary earth, for example, was not natural earth but 'such-as-natural-earth'—any sample of natural earth always being a mixture of all four elements, see *De generatione et corruptione*, II. 3 (330ᵇ–331ᵃ). As for hypothesis (ii), I have found no source for it, but Bacon's knowledge of Aristotle's six-teenth-century commentators needs far more study than I have been able to give it. For the notion that the lighter 'elements' do not compress except by accident, see *HDR*, E7ᵛ (p. 130, ll. 8–17 above). This passage is not in *HDR(M)*. Bacon disposes of the second *ad hoc* hypothesis by arguing that super-dense earth would be situated in a place where no mixtion could readily take place. Fundamental here is Bacon's notion that the Earth's entrails consisted of super-dense and immutable tangible matter, a notion touched on in the mandata which follow on from this passage (see *cmt* on A8ʳ⁻ᵛ below).

A7ᵛ–A8ʳ
Page 50, ll. 3–13: Diligenter notanda est—cf. *PhU*, P3ᵛ (*OFB*, VI, p. 24, ll. 5–15).

A8ʳ⁻ᵛ
Page 50, ll. 15–30: Cvm *Fons Densitatis*—that the entrails of the Earth consisted of super-dense, immutable tangible matter is a theory that Bacon seems to have developed from ideas derived from Bernardino Telesio (1509–88) and William Gilbert (1540–1603). The theory is crucial to various aspects of the speculative philosphy—including the notion that the Earth was immobile; see *OFB*, VI, pp. lii–liii, 395, 425. For the natural occurrence of pure gold, the position of mineral veins, and on the generation of fossils and metals see *PhU*, P4ᵛ (*OFB*, VI, p. 26, ll. 3–16 and *cmt* thereon, *ibid.*, p. 368).

B1ʳ⁻ᵛ, cf. fo. 8ᵛ
Page 52, l. 29–p. 54, l. 3, cf. p. 6, ll. 1–5: Mistura omnis—this would not have evoked Archimedes' cry (not mentioned in *HDR(M)*): the Greek's insight was that a lighter substance would displace a larger amount of water than the same weight of a heavier. Cf. *DAS*, 2I2ᵛ (*SEH*, I, p. 631). The Archimedes story is told in at least one source known to Bacon, viz. G. B. della Porta, *Magiæ natvralis libri viginti . . . Francofvrti apud Andreæ Wecheli heredes . . .* 1591, pp. 629–32.

B1ᵛ–B2ʳ
Page 54, l. 4–p. 56, l. 6: Confectio *Auri—NO*, T1ʳ⁻ᵛ (*SEH*, I, pp. 230–1): 'At Præceptum siue Axioma de transformatione Corporum, duplicis est generis. Primum intuetur Corpus, vt turmam siue coniugationem Naturarum simpli-cium: vt in Auro hæc conueniunt; quòd sit flauum; quòd sit ponderosum, ad pondus tale; quòd sit malleabile, aut ductile, ad extensionem talem; quòd non fiat volatile, nec deperdat de quanto suo per ignem; quòd fluat fluore tali; quòd separetur & soluatur modis talibus; & similitèr de cæteris Naturis, quæ in Auro concurrunt. Itaque huiusmodi Axioma rem deducit ex Formis Naturarum sim-plicium. Nam qui Formas & Modos nouit superinducendi, flaui, ponderis, duc-tilis, fixi, fluoris, solutionum, & sic de reliquis, & eorum graduationes & modos; videbit & curabit, vt ista coniungi possint in aliquo corpore, vndè sequatur transformatio in aurum.' For Bacon's last words on the methods of making gold see *SS*, M2ᵛ–M3ᵛ (*SEH*, II, pp. 448–50): 'the *Worke* it selfe I iudge

to be possible; But the *Meanes* (hitherto propounded) to effect it, are, in the Practice, full of Errour and Imposture; And in the Theory, full of vnsound Imaginations.' Then follows an attack on the theories and superstitions of the alchemists which prepares for a statement of six principles that might produce gold by maturation of metals: 'These Principles', says Bacon, 'are most certaine, and true' and from them practical suggestions can be adduced. '*Gold* hath these *Natures: Greatnesse of Weight; Closenesse of Parts; Fixation; Pliantnesse,* or *Softnesse; Immunity from Rust; Colour* or *Tincture of Yellow.* Therefore the Sure Way, (though most about,) to make *Gold,* is to know the *Causes* of the Seuerall *Natures* before rehearsed, and the *Axiomes* concerning the same. For if a Man can make a *Metall,* that hath all these *Properties,* Let Men dispute, whether it be *Gold,* or no?' For the alchemical theories attacked here see *cmts* on this passage in *OFB,* XIV.

B2ʳ

Page 54, l. 25–p. 56, l. 6: Plumbum *tamen . . . plenius*—c-t has italics where no doubt large type was intended (see *tns,* p. 54 above). In this period underlining was generally used to indicate italics in printer's copy, but it was also used (along with other marks) for other purposes *including* other kinds of fount change; for example see J. K. Moore, *Primary materials relating to copy and print in English books of the sixteenth and seventeenth centuries* (Oxford Bibliographical Society Occasional Publication no. 24), Oxford, 1992, plates 20–1. *SS* (2D2ᵛ (*SEH,* II, p. 599)): 'This is certaine, and knowne of Old; That *Lead* will multiply, and Increase; As hath beene seene in *Old Statua's* of *Stone,* which haue beene put in *Cellars;* The *Feet* of them being bound with *Leaden Bands;* Where (after a time,) there appeared, that the *Lead* did swell; Insomuch as it hanged vpon the *Stone* like *Warts.*'

B2ᵛ, cf. fos. 8ᵛ–9ʳ

Page 56, ll. 7–29, cf. p. 6, ll. 6–28: *Tabula Exporrectionis*—the figures given are the same as those in *PhU* (P6ʳ–P7ʳ (*OFB,* VI, p. 28, l. 25–p. 30, l. 1, ll. 18–23)) except that (i) *PhU* makes powdered crystal 1 dwt. lighter; (ii) as in *HDR(M),* sandalwood is half a grain heavier (in the introductory table in *PhU, HDR(M)* and *HDR* the extra half-grain is absent); (iii) compared with *PhU* and *HDR(M),* *HDR* gives vinegar an extra grain. Here, but not in the introductory table, *HDR(M)* gives distilled vinegar one grain more than *PhU* and *HDR.* This may suggest that here Bacon was following *PhU* when he produced *HDR(M)* but by the time the work reached its *HDR* form, the figures had been checked for consistency.

Page 56, l. 17: *In* pulvere *præ-parato*—*Pharmacopœa Londinensis, in qva medicamenta . . . describuntur. Opera Medicorum Collegij Londinensis . . . Londini, excudebat Edwardus Griffin . . .1618,* Y1ᵛ:

CHALYBS PRÆPARATVS PER INSOLATIONEM.

℞ Chalybem per magnetem à sordibus repurgatur, humectetur toties aceto vini albi acerrimo & siccetur ad solem, donec possit in porphyrite teri in puluerem impalpabilem, affusa pauca aqua Cynamomi. Sufficiet autem duodecies irrorare, & siccare, mox in mortario ferreo terere, tandem læuigare, & seruetur ad vsum.

CHALYBS PRÆPARATVS PER VSTIONEM.

℞ Chalybem vt supra mundatum extinguatur candens duodecies in aceto albo acerrimo, & toties in vino Canarino aut Maluatico generosissimo, siccetur & vt supra, tritus in porphyrite cum aqua Cynamomi læuigatur, & seruetur ad vsum.

B3ʳ⁻ᵛ

Page 58, l. 2–p. 60, l. 11: *Modus* versionis—*HDR(M)* has none of these remarks on the tables. It passes straight from the tables themselves to discussion of pneumatic bodies (fo. 9ʳ, p. 6, l. 27).

ll. 10–18: Indigentissimæ—in line with the spirit of *HDR*, Bacon here proposes a further and very extensive programme of quantitative investigation.

B4ʳ, cf. fo. 9ʳ

Page 60, ll. 13–14: Atque *Tangibilia* per *Familias*—Bacon uses the language of the financial administrator or civil servant; see *cmt* on *HDR*, A1ʳ⁻ᵛ (p. 269 above). Classis is used in a metaphorical sense of social class when it refers to pneumatic bodies here. This idea is probably carried down to the word interprete which may here suggest an expositor or interpreter of law or agent of government. None of this can quite be rendered in English so as to capture the connotations Bacon had in mind; also see *cmt* (p. 279 below) on C1ʳ (p. 72 above).

ll. 14–17, cf. p. 6, ll. 27–8: Ea vero pondere—lack of weight in pneumatic bodies is one of their prime attributes, see *cmts* (p. 272 above) on A6ʳ–A7ʳ, p. 46, l. 6–p. 48, l. 5 above.

ll. 19–20: Quemadmodum in *Tangibilibus*—also see p. 136, ll. 23–6 above. Bacon did not take tangible bodies in the depths of the Earth into consideration because he said they were unknown to us, though he happened to believe they were super-dense, cold and immobile (see *cmts* (p. 273 above) on *HDR*, A8ʳ⁻ᵛ, p. 50, ll. 15–30). His reasons for not speaking about celestial substances are much the same: while adopting a formal position of ignorance regarding their nature he in fact believed they were pneumatic, i.e. celestial flame and ether; see *OFB*, VI, pp. xlii–xlvii.

B4ʳ, cf. fo. 9ʳ

Page 60, l. 21, cf. p. 7, p. 1: Sunt *Pneumatica*—this is the beginning of the most extensive and systematic classification of pneumatic substances that Bacon ever attempted.

l. 22–p. 62, l. 8, cf. p. 7, ll. 1–16: *Inchoata* sunt *Fumi*—the classification of fumes is much more precise than Bacon attempted elsewhere. In other works the terms are used a little less strictly, see, for example, *NO*, 2B1ᵛ (*SEH*, I, pp. 262–3): '*Prima* igitur *Differentia* ea est; quòd Calor sit Motus Expansiuus, per quem corpus nititur ad dilatationem sui, & recipiendi se in maiorem sphæram siue dimensionem, quàm priùs occupauerat. Hæc autem *Differentia* maximè ostenditur in flammâ; vbi fumus siue halitus pinguis manifestò dilatatur & aperit se in flammam.' *Ibid.*, 2L1ᵛ (*SEH*, I, p. 313): 'At paulò pòst Vapor siue Aura Spiritûs vini per calorem dilatati & in Pneumaticum versi, Vesicam paulatìm sufflauit . . .'. *Ibid.*, 2L4ʳ–2M1ʳ (*SEH*, I, p. 318): 'Flammæ enim multiplicant se super halitus Olei, Aer super vapores Aquæ.' *Ibid.*, 2P4ʳ⁻ᵛ (*SEH*, I, p. 339): 'Corpora similaria vertunt Corpora alia affinia, aut saltem benè disposita & præparata, in Substantiam & Naturam suam; vt Flamma, quæ super halitus & oleosa multiplicat se, & generat nouam Flammam; Aër, qui super Aquam & Aquea multiplicat se, & generat nouum Aerem . . .'. Also see *cmt* on *DPAO*, L9ᵛ–L10ʳ (*OFB*, VI, pp. 428–9).

B4ᵛ, cf. fo. 9ʳ

Page 62, ll. 9–18, cf. p. 7, ll. 17–25: At *Pneumatica Devincta*—these ideas are central to the terrestrial aspects of Bacon's speculative philosophy (see *OFB*, VI, pp. liii–lxv). Indeed, the distinction between animate and inanimate spirits enclosed in tangible bodies, and the idea that they have an airy-fiery nature are almost commonplaces in his thought; cf. *ANN*, fo. 24ᵛ, fos. 27ᵛ–28ʳ (p. 176, ll. 1–12, p. 186, l. 23–p. 188, l. 6 and *cmts* thereon (pp. 308, 312) below); *HIDA*, fos. 3ʳ–5ᵛ (pp. 228–34 above).

B4ᵛ–B5ʳ, cf. fo. 9ʳ

Page 62, ll. 18–20, cf. p. 7, ll. 26–7: At *Pneumatica Pura*—these are in fact only two—the terrestrial ones—of four such pure pneumatic substances. The other two, celestial flame and ether have already been excluded from discussion in *HDR*, see p. 60, ll. 19–20 above and *cmt* thereon, p. 275 above. For the pivotal function of air and flame in Bacon's speculative philosophy see *OFB*, VI, pp. xlii–xliii and liv–lvii.

B5ᵛ, cf. fo. 9ʳ

Page 64, ll. 9–10, cf. p. 8, l. 18–19: Appetitus petendi superiora—Bacon is thinking of the Aristotelian-scholastic 'natural' motion of air, see *cmts* (p. 314 below) on *ANN*, fos. 29ᵛ–30ʳ (p. 194, ll. 17–36 above).

B5ᵛ–B6ʳ, cf. fo. 10ʳ

Page 64, l. 31–p. 66, l. 2, cf. p. 9, ll. 5–13: *Spiritus crudos*—on the face of it, this is a surprising assertion as elsewhere Bacon argues that crude or inanimate spirits combine the qualities of air and flame and (since flame is rarer than air) crude or inanimate spirits should be less dense than air. He describes these spirits as crude in order to differentiate them from fat or flamy substances and draw attention to the fact that in them the airy component is dominant; see *HVM*, 2D6ᵛ–2D8ʳ (*SEH*, II, p. 216); *OFB*, VI, pp. liv–lvi.

B6ʳ, cf. fo. 10ʳ

Page 66, ll. 3–12, cf. p. 9, ll. 14–23: At *Spiritus vivos*—for animate or living spirit see *cmts* above (this page) on *HDR*, B4ᵛ (p. 62, ll. 9–18 above).

B6ʳ⁻ᵛ, cf. fo. 10ʳ⁻ᵛ

Page 66, ll. 13–19, cf. p. 9, ll. 24–30: Supremo Ordine—for the relations between water and air, and oil and flame see *OFB*, VI, pp. xlii–xliii and liv–lvi.

B6ᵛ–B7ʳ

Page 66, l. 20–p. 68, l. 29: Historia—this entire historia and the monitum following it are absent from *HDR(M)*, but the substance of them appears in *PhU*, Q8ʳ⁻ᵛ (*OFB*, VI, pp. 56–8). In *PhU* the experiment is used as a basis for calculating the relative densities of air and flame. The same experiment also appears in *NO* (2L1ʳ⁻ᵛ (*SEH*, I, pp. 312–13)), but with a two-pint bladder, and the experiment only yielded a hundredfold increase in volume. As for the units of measurement, the ounce is presumably the Troy ounce, see *cmt* (p. 272 above) on *HDR*, A5ᵛ–A6ʳ (p. 44, l. 11–p. 46, l. 4 above). The pint is the vintner's or wine pint (approx. 0.473 litres), see R. E. Zupko, *A dictionary of English weights and measures from Anglo-Saxon times to the nineteenth century*, University of Wisconsin Press: Madison, Milwaukee, and London, 1968, p. 127; also see *NO*, 2N1ᵛ (*SEH*, I, p. 324).

B8ʳ, cf. fo. 10ᵛ

Page 70, ll. 19–23, cf. p. 10, ll. 14–17: Commentum illud *Peripateticorum*—another aspect of the running critique of Aristotelian-scholastic element theory. Here he repudiates the theory that a given quantity of earth could be turned into ten times as much water, water into ten times as much air, and air into ten times as much fire. All that has led up to this observation (and especially the experiment considered in the previous *cmt*) demonstrates Bacon's readiness to use quantitative data derived from highly artificial theory-testing experiments to destroy rival doctrines in the realm of matter theory. Bacon also attacked the theory in *PhU* (Q3ʳ–Q4ᵛ, Q5ʳ⁻ᵛ (*OFB*, VI, pp. 48–50, 50–2)) and *NO* (F4ʳ⁻ᵛ (*SEH*, I, p. 165)). The theory of decuple proportions originated in a misunderstanding by his commentators of remarks by Aristotle, see *De generatione et corruptione*, II. 6 (333ᵃ). Also see Michel-Pierre Lerner, 'Le "parménidisme" de Telesio: origine et limites d'une hypothèse', in *Bernardino Telesio e la cultura napoletana*, ed. Raffaele Sirri and Maurizio Torrini, Guida Editore: Naples, 1992, pp. 79–105, p. 100 n. 54. Telesio criticized it (*DRN*, I, pp. 482–8, 512), as did William Gilbert, see *De mundo nostro sublunari philosophia nova*, Amsterdam, 1651, fac. repr. Menno Hertzberger: Amsterdam, 1965; pp. 43–5. Also see *OFB*, VI, p. 372.

B8ʳ, cf. fo. 10ᵛ

Page 70, l. 25–p. 72, l. 3, cf. p. 10, ll. 18–19: Non est, cur ista *Inquisitio*—only the point about qualities appears in *HDR(M)*. Cf. *SS*, E3ʳ⁻ᵛ (*SEH*, II, pp. 380–1): 'The Knowledge of man (hitherto) hath beene determined by the View, or Sight; So that whatsoeuer is Inuisible, either in respect of the *Finenesse of the Body* itselfe; Or the *Smallnesse of the Parts*; Or of the *Subtilty of the Motion*; is little inquired. And yet these be the Things that Gouerne Nature principally; and without which, you cannot make any true *Analysis* and Indication of the Proceedings of Nature. The *Spirits* or *Pneumaticals*, that are in all *Tangible Bodies*, are scarce knowne. Sometimes they take them for *Vacuum*; wheras they are the most Actiue of Bodies . . . And sometimes they will haue them to be the *Vertues* and *Qualities* of the *Tangible Parts*, which they see; whereas they are Things by themselues. And then, when they come to Plants and liuing Creatures, they call them *Soules* . . . Neither is this a Question of Words, but infinitely materiall in *Nature*. For *Spirits* are nothing else but a *Naturall Body*, rarified to a Proportion, & included in the *Tangible Parts* of *Bodies*, as in an Integument . . . And from them, and their *Motions*, principally proceed *Arefaction, Colliquation, Concoction, Maturation, Putrefaction, Viuification*, and most of the Effects of *Nature* . . . And the *Physitians* are content to acknowledge, that *Herbs*, and *Drugs* haue diuers Parts . . . But this whole *Inquisition* is weakly and Negligently handled. And for the more subtill differences of the *Minute Parts*, and the Posture of them in the Body, (which also hath great Effects) they are not at all touched: As for the *Motions* of the *Minute Parts of Bodies*, which doe so great Effects, they haue not beene obserued at all; because they are Inuisible, and incurre not to the Eye; but yet they are to be deprehended by Experience . . . Againe, as to the *Motions Corporall*, within the Enclosures of Bodies, wherby the effects (which were mentioned before) pass betweene the *Spirits*, and the *Tangible Parts*: (which are, *Arefaction, Colliquation, Concoction, Maturation*, &c.) they are not at all handled. But they are put off by the Names of *Vertues*, and *Natures*, and *Actions*, and *Passions*, and such other *Logicall* Words.'

B8ᵛ

Page 72, ll. 23–5: Quod si *Methodo*—Bacon generally used the term method in connection *not* with the generation of new knowledge but with the transmission of existing knowledge. Method means *rhetorical* method, and on the whole Bacon thought that strict rhetorical methods were inappropriate for the transmission of natural-philosophical knowledge. For a particularly biting attack on (Ramist) method see *DAS*, 2O2ᵛ–2O3ʳ (*SEH*, II, p. 663): 'Itaque *Methodi* genera (cùm varia sint) enumerabimus potiùs, quam partiemur. Atque de vnica *Methodo*, & Dichotomijs perpetuis, nil attinet dicere: Fuit enim Nubecula quædam Doctrinæ, quæ citò transijt: Res certè simul & leuis, & Scientijs damnosissima. Etenìm huiusmodi Homines, cum *Methodi* suæ Legibus res torqueant; &, quæcunque in Dichotomias illas non aptè cadunt, aut omittant, aut præter Naturam inflectant, hoc efficiunt, vt quasi Nuclei & Grana Scientiarum exiliant, ipsi aridas tantùm & desertas Siliquas stringant. Itaque inania Compendia parit hoc genus *Methodi*, Solida Scientiarum destruit.' Also note use of the word methodus in *NO*, A2ᵛ, M2ʳ, M4ʳ, O2ʳ (*SEH*, I, pp. 126–7, 193–4, 196, 203); *PAH*, a4ᵛ (*SEH*, I, p. 395); *PA*, R3ʳ (p. 264, ll. 1–2 above).

C1^r

Page 72, ll. 28–30: Satis sit si de Scripto—Bacon appears to be stating the obvious, but he is reminding readers of the scale of his natural-historical enterprise. He warns elsewhere that writing not memory should be used to record natural-historical instances, e.g. *NO*, O2^{r-v}; *DAS*, L24^v (*SEH*, I, pp. 203–4 and 647).

ll. 31–3: *Stipem* tantummodo—see *cmt* (p. 269 above) on *HDR*, A1^{r-v} (p. 36, ll. 5–9 above).

C1^r, cf. fo. 11^r

Page 74, ll. 4–6: *Dilatationes*—titles of this sort do not appear in *HDR(M)* but the transition to this subject does (see p. 10, ll. 20–1 above).

C1^v, cf. fo. 11^r

Page 74, ll. 20–2, cf. p. 10, l. 24: Extruunt pueri—cf. *NO*, 2C4^v (*SEH*, I, p. 273). For other natural-historical references to children's games see, for instance, *OFB*, VI, pp. 36, 38, 54.

Page 74, l. 27–p. 76, l. 4, cf. p. 10, ll. 24–5: At contra—for other remarks on the action of gunpowder see *NO*, 2I1^r–2I2^r (*SEH*, I, pp. 302–3). Also see *HDR*, E3^v (p. 120, ll. 15–20 above).

C2^r

Page 76, ll. 7–8: *Contiguum* differt—for the continuum/contiguum distinction and its sources see *OFB*, VI, p. 392.

l. 9: Tabula secunda & tertia—i.e. the tables on B2^v (p. 56 above).

C2^r, cf. fo. 11^r

Page 76, l. 11, cf. p. 10, ll. 26–7: *Hydrope, Tympanite*—these two examples do not appear in *HDR(M)*. Dropsy: watery or oedematous swelling, often of the limbs. Tympanites: a windy distension of uterus or abdomen. For hydroptical conditions see *HVM*, Z5^r, 2A7^r (*SEH*, II, pp. 200, 204). For Jean Fernel on these conditions see *Io. Fernelii . . . Vniversa medicina . . . Francofvrti M D LXXXI*, p. 590: 'Hydrops tympanias abdominis est distensio ex multo flatu in illius capacitate concluso. Moles quàm in ascite minor & minus grauis, parum fluctuans, sed rugitu obmurmurans: summus venter vngue percussus vt tympanum tinnit, multáque falsatus indicia existunt. Huius ergo materia flatus est ex imbecilla concoctione & cruditate genitus: qui cùm multus in ventriculo aut intestinis, velut in colico dolore coërcetur, nec exitum naturalem reperit, impetu viam sibi muniens, per cæcos tenuesúue ductus inter abdominis membranas magnis cruciatibus sese infert, ac demum variè impulsus in ipsum abdominis spatium penetrat aut deuoluitur.'

C2^r

Page 76, ll. 19–20: *Glans virgæ* in Masculis—*om* in *SEH* (V, p. 356) translation, so disturbing the numbering of the items in this history.

ll. 29–30: *Auriculam Iudæi*—cf. *SS*, T2^r (*SEH*, II, pp. 513–14). Also see *OED*, Jew's-ear: 'An edible cup-shaped fungus (*Hirneola* or *Exidia Auricula Judæ*) growing on the roots and trunks of trees, chiefly the elder, and formerly in repute as a medicine . . .'; also see John Gerard, *The herball or generall historie of plants*, London, 1597, p. 1233: 'There groweth oftentimes vpon the bodies of those olde trees or shrubs [*sci.* elders] a certaine excrescence called *Auricula Iudæ*, or Iewes eare, which is soft, blackish, couered with a skin, somewhat like now and then to a mans eare, which being plucked off and dried, shrinketh togither and becommeth hard.'

C2ᵛ–C3ʳ
Page 78, ll. 13–17: Audivi, *Mustum*—cf. *SS*, E1ᵛ (*SEH*, II, p. 377).

C3ʳ, cf. fo. 11ʳ
Page 78, ll. 22–5, cf. p. 11, ll. 6–10: Etiam *Gemmæ*—on the generation of gems see *DVM*, fo. 10ʳ (*OFB*, VI, p. 296, ll. 8–13); *NO*, 2D4ᵛ–2E1ʳ (*SEH*, I, p. 279).

ll. 26–7, cf. p. 11, ll. 10–11: in *Spermate*—for Bacon on vivification see *NO*, 2K2ᵛ–2K4ʳ (*SEH*, I, pp. 310–11); *SS*, Z3ᵛ (*SEH*, II, p. 559): 'Now the great *Axiome* of *Viuification* is, that there must be *Heat* to dilate the *Spirit* of the *Body*; An *Actiue Spirit* to be dilated; *Matter Viscous* or *Tenacious*, to hold in the *Spirit*; And that *Matter* to be *put forth*, and *Figured*.' Also see *cmt* (p. 281 below) on *HDR*, C4ʳ, p. 80, ll. 32–6; *cmt* (p. 309) on *ANN*, fo. 25ᵛ, p. 178, ll. 13–19 above. Vivification is a major topic of *HIDA*, see pp. 228–34 above.

l. 28, cf. p. 11, l. 11: *Vitriolum . . . arborescit*—it is not clear what Bacon has in mind here but perhaps he is thinking of a metal sulphate. Maybe a sulphate is being thrown down by precipitation and is crystallizing. Also possible but less likely is that he means gold or silver 'trees' produced when mercurous nitrate is added to either silver or gold nitrate. The former was known to alchemists as the arbor Diana, and vitriol may have been used to prepare aqua regia (a mixture of nitric and hydrochloric acids) and thence the nitrate. Bacon was familiar with metal trees, which he called 'sproutings'; see J. R. Partington, *A history of chemistry*, 4 vols., Macmillan: London, 1961–70, II, p. 402. However, the evidence of *BTT* (I5ʳ (*SEH*, III, p. 814)) seems to suggest that a crystalline precipitate formed by the action of sulphuric acid on a metal may be in question: 'For *Sprouting or Branching*, though it be a thing but transitory, and a kind or Toy or Pleasure, yet there is a more serious use of it; for that it discovereth the Delicate Motions of Spirits, when they put forth and cannot get forth, like unto that which is in Vegetables.' Bacon was here seeking information from Dr Meverel, whose answer (*ibid.*, I8ᵛ (*SEH*, III, p. 816)) was, '*Sprouting*. This is an accident of dissolution. For if the *Menstruum* be overcharged, then within short time the Metals will shoot into certain Crystals.' Also see *SS*, V3ᵛ–V4ʳ (*SEH*, II, p. 529): 'There be very few *Creatures*, that participate of the *Nature of Plants*, and *Metalls* both; *Coral* is one of the Nearest of both *Kindes*: another is *Vitrioll*, for that is aptest to sprout with *Moisture*.'

Page 78, l. 29–p. 80, l. 2, cf. p. 11, ll. 12–13: Lapides tempore—see *cmts* (p. 300 below) on *HDR*, F7ᵛ. Also see *SS*, N3ʳ, Q2ʳ (*SEH*, II, pp. 459–60, 485).

C3^{r-v}, cf. fo. 11^r

Page 80, ll. 3–9, cf. p. 11, ll. 14–19: *Sudores*—on the connection of vital spirits with sweat, pulse and voluntary motion see *DAS*, 2F2^{r-v} (*SEH*, I, pp. 609–10); *SS*, 2A3^{r-v} (*SEH*, II, pp. 565–7); *OFB*, VI, pp. lvii–lix; The more perfect animals mentioned here are those not bred from putrefaction, see *SS*, 2H3^r (*SEH*, II, pp. 638–9): 'Therefore all *Sperme*, all *Menstruous Substance*, all *Matter* whereof *Creatures* are produced by *Putrefaction*, haue euermore a *Closenesse, Lentour*, and *Sequacity*. It seemeth therefore, that the *Generation* by *Sperme onely*, and by *Putrefaction*, haue two Different *Causes*. The First is, for that *Creatures*, which haue a *Definite* and *Exact Shape*, (as those haue which are Procreated by *Copulation*,) cannot be produced by a *Weake*, and *Casuall Heat*; Nor out of *Matter* which is not *exactly Prepared*, according to the *Species*.' Also see *cmts* immediately below.

C4^r, cf. fo. 11^r

Page 80, ll. 32–6, cf. p. 11, ll. 20–4: In omne *Carie*—on the action of inanimate spirits in putrefaction see *SS*, M3^v–M4^r (*SEH*, II, p. 451): 'The *Enducing* and *Accelerating* of *Putrefaction*, is a Subiect of a very Vniuersall Enquiry: For *Corruption* is a Reciprocall to *Generation*: And they Two, are as *Natures* two *Termes* or *Bundaries*; And the *Guides* to *Life* and *Death*. *Putrefaction* is the Worke of the *Spirits* of *Bodies*, which euer are Vnquiet to *Get forth*, and *Congregate* with the *Aire*, and to enioy the *Sunbeames* . . . If the *Spirits* be detained within the Body . . . but Protrude a little, and that Motion be Confused, and Inordinate, there followeth *Putrefaction*; Which euer dissolueth the Consistence of the Body into much Inequality; As in *Flesh, Rotten Fruits, Shining Wood*, &c. And also in the *Rust* of *Metalls*. But if that Motion be in a certaine Order, there followeth *Viuification*, and *Figuration*; As both in *Liuing Creatures* bred of *Putrefaction*, and in *Liuing Creatures Perfect*.' Also see *NO*, 2K3^v–2K4^r (*SEH*, I, pp. 310–11); *ANN*, fo. 27^v (p. 186, ll. 14–22 above), fo. 32^v (p. 204, ll. 18–25 above) and *cmts* thereon (pp. 311–12, 319 below).

C4^r, cf. fo. 11^v

Page 80, ll. 37–p. 82, l. 7, cf. p. 11, ll. 25–7: Neque *spiritus*—on plants bred from putrefaction and another account of the lemon mould see *SS*, M4^v, V3^v–V4^r (*SEH*, II, pp. 453, 529). The *HDR(M)* allusion to this mould is one of a number of aides-mémoires waiting to be developed in *HDR*, and perhaps developed as a marginalium to the *Urtext* of *HDR(M)*?

Page 82, ll. 8–9 cf. p. 11, ll. 28–30: Similiter, *Rubigines*—cf. *NO*, 2K3^r (*SEH*, I, p. 310); *SS*, L1^v (*SEH*, II, p. 438): '*Heat* causeth the Spirits to search some Issue out of the Body; As in the *Volatility* of *Metalls*; And so doth *Time*; As in the *Rust* of *Metalls*.'

C4^v, cf. fo. 11^v

Page 82, ll. 17–26, cf. p. 12, ll. 1–4: At subito—*HDR(M)* has none of these materials except for the material on the Hereford landslide. Bacon seems to think that earthquakes were caused by air compressed beyond the point it would tolerate (see p. 154, ll. 24–6 above), a view not much different from the Aristotelian tradition that earthquakes were produced by dry exhalations trapped within the Earth. For Telesio on earthquakes see *Varii de naturalibus rebus libelli*, ed. Luigi De Franco, La Nuova Italia Editrice: Florence, 1981, pp. 57–8. For medieval, Renaissance and early modern vulcanology see Rienk Vermij, 'Subterranean fire. Changing theories of the earth during the Renaissance', *Early science and medicine*, 3, Nov. 1998, pp. 322–47.

C4^v–C5^r

Page 82, l. 27–p. 84, l. 3: Utrum *moles Aquarum*—Bacon discusses tide theories in *NO* (2G4^r–2H2^r (*SEH*, pp. 294–7)) and, above all, in *DFRM*, where the possibilities mentioned here are considered in some detail; Bacon's own theory was that tidal motion was part of the cosmic diurnal motion, see *OFB*, VI, pp. 68–76, and *cmts* thereon pp. 377–9. For a recent account of aspects of the intellectual context of Bacon's theories see Federico Bonelli and Lucio Russo, 'The origin of modern astronomical theories of tides: Chrisogono, de Dominis and their sources', *BJHS*, **29**, Dec. 1996, pp. 385–401. On water rising and falling in wells and fountains see *DFRM*, H8^v–H9^r and *cmts* thereon (*OFB*, VI, p. 70, ll. 9–11, pp. 377–8). The idea that waters erupt from the ground in very dry years is repeated on p. 134, ll. 1–3 above. Cf. *HV*, H3^r (*SEH*, II, p. 40): 'Etiam vbique notatum est, nonnihil attolli, & tumescere Aquas, ante tempestates.'

C5^v, cf. fo. 11^v

Page 84, ll. 25–6, cf. p. 12, ll. 12–13: Recepta est opinio—see *SS*, 2H2^{r-v} (*SEH*, II, pp. 636–7): 'For the *Increase* of *Moisture*, the Opinion Receiued is; That *Seeds* will grow soonest; and *Haire*, and *Nailes*, and *Hedges*, and *Herbs*, Cut, &c. will grow soonest; if they be Set or Cut, in the *Increase* of the *Moone*. Also that *Braines* in *Rabits*, *Wood-cocks*, *Calues*, &c. are fullest in the *Full* of the *Moone*: And so of *Marrow* in the *Bones*; And so of *Oysters*, and *Cockles*, which of all the rest are the easiest tried, if you haue them in *Pits* . . . It is like, that the *Braine* of *Man* waxeth *Moister*, and *Fuller*, vpon the *Full* of the *Moone*; And therefore it were good for those that haue *Moist Braines*, and are great *Drinkers*, to take *Fume* of *Lignum Aloës*, *Rose-Mary*, *Frankincense*, etc. about the full of the *Moone*. It is like also, that the *Humours* in *Mens Bodies*, Increase, and Decrease as the *Moone* doth . . . It may be, that *Children*, and *Young Cattell* that are *Brought forth* in the *Full* of the *Moone*, are stronger, & larger, than those that are brought forth in the *Wane*. And those also which are *Begotten* in the *Full* of the *Moone* . . . *Quare* also, whether great *Thunders*, and *Earth-Quakes*, be not most in the *Full* of the *Moone* ?' Also see *DAS*, X1^{r-v} (*SEH*, I, p. 555): '*Operatio Cælestium in Corpora omnigena non valet, sed tantùm in teneriora*, qualia sunt Humores, Aer, & Spiritus: Atque hic tamen excipimus Operationes Caloris, Solis & Cœlestium, qui & ad Metalla, & ad plurima Subterranea proculdubiò penetrat.'

Page 84, l. 32–p. 86, l. 2: De *Tumoribus*—for swellings of the air as causes of winds see *HV*, H7ʳ–I1ᵛ (*SEH*, II, pp. 42–3).

C6ʳ

Page 86, ll. 15–17: spectant ad *Titulos*—cf. p. 96, ll. 24–6 above. For the meaning of these titles see *ANN*, p. 174, ll. 23–8, p. 194, ll. 1–16, p. 202, l. 26–p. 204, l. 3, p. 208, ll. 23–9 above.

C6ᵛ, cf. fo. 12ʳ

Page 86, ll. 22–8, cf. p. 12, ll. 25–8: In *Ventosis*—for motus nexus see *ANN*, p. 190, l. 30–p. 192, l. 6 and *cmts* thereon, p. 313 below. On cupping glasses see *PhU*, Q9ʳ (*OFB*, VI, p. 58, ll. 27–33); *NO*, 2R4ᵛ–2S1ʳ (*SEH*, I, pp. 351–2); *SS*, 2H1ᵛ (*SEH*, II, p. 635).

C6ᵛ

Page 86, l. 29–p. 88, l. 7: Accipe *vitrum*—apart from evidence of Bacon's awareness of the need to design artificial experiments for specific purposes, the real point of this paragraph is contained in the last lines (ll. 6–7): he wishes to give credence to a cherished belief, namely that celestial ether (the substance that fills interplanetary space) is a rarer, more refined version of other members (mercury, water, and air) of its family of qualitatively related substances, a family elsewhere called the mercury quaternion; see *OFB*, VI, pp. xlii–xliv.

Page 88, ll. 8–14: In *Vitro*—for other references to the calendar glass see *HDR*, D6ʳ⁻ᵛ (p. 106, ll. 19–21, above), F6ᵛ–F7ʳ (p. 148, ll. 21–32 above), G6ʳ (p. 166, l. 25, above). The glass is not mentioned at all in *PhU* which suggests that the instrument was unknown to Bacon before *c.*1612. For other references see *HV*, I8ᵛ (*SEH*, II, p. 47) and *NO*, Z3ʳ⁻ᵛ (*SEH*, I, pp. 254–5), where the instrument is described in some detail. For its history and its place in the philosophy of Robert Fludd see Allen G. Debus, *Chemistry, alchemy and the new philosophy, 1500–1700*, Variorum Reprints: London, 1987, ch. XIII. This piece reproduces many of Fludd's illustrations of the instrument. Unfortunately no proper study, with appropriate contemporary illustrations and descriptions, of Bacon's knowledge and use of scientific instruments exists. For Drebbel's perpetual motion machine (a variant of the weather glass) alleged to imitate the tides see *cmt* (p. 304 below) on *HDR*, G6ʳ (p. 166, ll. 26–7 above).

C7ʳ, cf. fo. 12ʳ

Page 88, ll. 15–24, cf. p. 12, l. 29–p. 13, l. 7: *Hero* describit—for this device and its inventor see *PhU*, Q9ᵛ–Q10ʳ and *cmts* thereon (*OFB*, VI, p. 60. ll. 5–10, p. 374, p. 392).

C7ʳ, cf. fo. 12ʳ

Page 88, ll. 25–32, cf. p. 13, ll. 8–10: Inventum fuit *Fracastorii*—Girolamo Fracastoro, *c.*1478–1553, was taught at Padua by, among others, Pomponazzi. Published *Syphilis sive morbus gallicus* (1530); *Homocentrica* (1538); and *De causis* (1538). But see *Hieronymi Fracastorii Veronensis opera omnia, in vnum proxime* *post illius mortem collecta . . . Venetiis, apvd Ivntas, M. D. LXXIIII,* †5ʳ⁻ᵛ: 'Ferunt Hieronymum, dum langueret, cognito fatali morbo, post multas amicas sibi herbas in olfactum balbutiente lingua efflagitatas, amisso penitus sermonis vsu, manu sæpius in verticem exporrecta, ijs, qui aderant, innuere voluisse, vt celeriter cucurbitula affecto & laboranti cerebro, quo ille peroportuno remedio se Deo dicatam Veronæ virginem curasse adhuc meminerat, subuenirent: sed, re nequaquam intellecta, quum alij alia adhibenda tum esse remedia prædicarent, frustra expectato remedio, leniter sub noctem expirasse.' For other references to the sartago see *HVM*, 2B7ᵛ–2B8ʳ (*SEH*, II, p. 209); *NO*, 2G1ᵛ (*SEH*, I, p. 291): 'Inuentum illud celebre *Fracastorij* de Sartagine acritèr calefactâ, quâ circundant Medici capita Apoplecticorum desperatorum, expandit manifestè spiritus animales, ab humoribus & obstructionibus Cerebri compressos & quasi extinctos; illosque ad motum excitat, non aliter quàm Ignis operatur in Aquam aut Aërem; & tamen per consequens viuificat.' For other references to the revival of butterflies see *NO, loc. cit.*; *SS*, Z3ʳ, 2B4ʳ (*SEH*, II, pp. 559, 580). For the reviving qualities of hot and strong drinks, and of external frictions see *HVM*, O7ʳ, 2B7ᵛ–2B8ʳ (*SEH*, II, pp. 162, 209).

C7ʳ–C8ʳ, cf. fo. 12ʳ

Page 88, l. 33–p. 90, l. 33, cf. p. 13, ll. 11–22: *Apertura Aquæ*—the opening or openings up of liquids and other substances looks like one of Bacon's own lines of experimental inquiry (see *NO*, 2L4ʳ (*SEH*, I, pp. 316–17)). In *PhU* (Q2ᵛ–Q7ᵛ (*OFB*, VI, pp. 46–56)) the openings of water, oil, spirits of wine, vinegar etc. are dealt with in the same order as in *HDR*, but with other material intervening. Apertura is taken for a synonym of expansio in Francis Bacon, *Novum organum with other parts of the Great Instauration*, trans. and ed. Peter Urbach and John Gibson, Open Court: Chicago and La Salle, 1994, p. 236. However, apertura denotes effects—such, for instance, as chemical reactions—in addition to mere expansion, see *cmts* (pp. 291–2 below) on *HDR*, D7ᵛ–D8ʳ (p. 110, l. 3–p. 112, l. 25).

C8ᵛ, cf. fo. 12ᵛ

Page 92, ll. 13–24, cf. p. 13, l. 32–p. 14, l. 10: At ista omnia—for the volatility of quicksilver see *SS*, 2I3ʳ (*SEH*, II, p. 647): 'those that deale much in *Refining*, or other Workes, about *Metals*, and *Minerals*, haue their *Braines* Hurt and Stupefied by the *Metalline Vapours*. Amongst which, it is noted, that the *Spirits* of *Quick-Siluer*, euer fly to the *Skull*, *Teeth*, or *Bones*; In so much as *Gilders* vse to haue a Peece of *Gold* in their *Mouth*, to draw the *Spirits* of the *Quick-Siluer*; Which *Gold* afterwards they finde to be Whitened.' On the volatility of gold see *ibid.*, 2D3ʳ (*SEH*, II, p. 600): '*Gold* is the onely *Substance*, which hath nothing in it *Volatile*, and yet melteth without much difficulty. The *Melting* sheweth that it is not Ieiune, or Scarce in *Spirit*. So that the *Fixing* of it, is not *Want* of *Spirit* to fly out, but the *Equall Spreading* of the *Tangible Parts*, and the *Close Coaceruation* of them.' For potable gold see *HVM*, M8ᵛ–N1ʳ (*SEH*, II, pp.

155–6): '*Aurum* triplici Formâ exhibetur; Aut in *Auro* (quod appellant) *Potabili*; aut in *Vino Extinctionis Auri*; aut in *Auro in Substantiâ*; qualia sunt, *Aurum Foliatum*, & *Limatura Auri*. Quod ad *Aurum Potabile* attinet, cœpit dari in Morbis desperatis, aut grauioribus, pro egregio Cordiali, atque successu non contemnendo. Verùm existimamus *Spiritus Salis*, per quos fit Dissolutio, Virtutem illam, quæ reperitur, largiri potiùs, quàm ipsum *Aurum*; Quod tamen sedulò celatur; Quòd si aperiri possit *Aurum* absque Aquis Corrosiuis, aut per Corrosiuas, (modò absit Qualitas Venenata) benè posteà ablutas, Rem non inutilem fore arbitramus.' Bacon's remarks are judicious; his contemporary, Francis Anthony (1550–1623), attracted the hostility of the Royal College of Physicians for promoting potable gold as a cure-all in his *Medicinæ chymiæ* (Cambridge, 1610), a work that began a debate on the medicine's merits with such luminaries as Matthew Gwinne (1558?–1627) and John Cotta (1575?–1650?). For a summary of the debate see Allen G. Debus, *The English Paracelsians*, Oldbourne: London, 1965, pp. 142–5. Bacon seems to have agreed with Anthony's critics that potable gold could only be prepared with strong waters; Anthony himself seems to have believed that finely divided gold with vinegar would do the trick. For the medicinal properties of gold also see G. B. della Porta, *Magiæ natvralis*, pp. 430–3.

C8ᵛ, cf. fo. 12ᵛ

Page 92, ll. 25–7, cf. p. 14, ll. 11–13: Inquiratur . . . de *Vitro*—cf. *NO*, 2P4ʳ (*SEH*, I, p. 338): 'Certè Argentum viuum, quod aliàs se reuniret in Corpus integrum, prohibetur per saliuam hominis, aut Axungiam porci, aut Terebinthinam, & huiusmodi, ne partes eius coëant; propter malum Consensum quem habent cum huiusmodi Corporibus; à quibus vndique circumfusis se retrahunt; adeò vt fortior sit earum *Fuga* ab istis interiacentibus, quàm desiderium vniendi se cum partibus sui similibus; id quod vocant *Mortificationem* Argenti viui.' Also see *BTT*, I8ʳ⁻ᵛ (*SEH*, III, p. 817).

D1ʳ, cf. fo. 13ʳ

Page 94, ll. 3–7, cf. p. 14, ll. 22–5: Videntur *Ferrum*—cf. *DVM*, fos. 9ᵛ–10ʳ (*OFB*, VI, pp. 294–6); *NO*, 2B1ᵛ, 2K3ᵛ (*SEH*, I, pp. 263, 310–11).

D1ᵛ, cf. fo. 13ᵛ

Page 94, ll. 28–36, cf. p. 15, ll. 9–17: In *Corporibus*—cf. *DVM*, fo. 13ᵛ (*OFB*, VI, p. 310, ll. 7–12). For gunpowder see *HDR*, C1ᵛ (p. 74, l. 27–p. 76, l. 4) and *cmts* thereon, p. 279 above.

D2ʳ

Page 96, ll. 16–18: At in *Aridis*—on volcanoes and pumice see *NO*, Y1ᵛ (*SEH*, I, p. 248); *HV*, H4ᵛ (*SEH*, II, p. 41); *SS*, N4ʳ (*SEH*, II, p. 461). Bacon's knowledge of volcanoes was probably derived directly or indirectly from Pliny, *Historia naturalis*, II. 106. Also see *cmts* (pp. 281–2 above) on *HDR*, p. 82, ll. 17–26.

D2^{r-v}

Page 96, ll. 24–6: *Titulos* de *Calido*—this same set of titles also occurs above, see *HDR*, p. 86, ll. 15–17, and *cmts* thereon (p. 283 above).

D2^v–D5^r, cf. fos. 13^v–15^r

Page 96, l. 29–p. 104, l. 4, cf. p. 15, l. 18–p. 18, l. 2: Duplex est *Dilatatio*—this is Bacon's longest discussion of distillation; and much of it is fairly conventional, i.e. to be found in readily accessible sources such, for instance, as G. B. della Porta, *Magiæ natvralis*, pp. 397–446. For the definition of distillation and for the preparation of rose water see *ibid.*, pp. 398, 400–1.

D3^r

Page 98, 13–25: In *Distillationibus*—none of this is in *HDR(M)*; it is in effect a synopsis of *NO*, 2S4^r–2T1^r (*SEH*, I, pp. 356–7): 'Calorem verò quod attinet; Copia & Potestas nimirum homini abundè adest; Obseruatio autem & Inquisitio deficit in nonnullis, ijsque maximè necessarijs; vtcunque Spagyrici se venditent. Etenim Caloris Intensioris Opificia Exquiruntur & Conspiciuntur; Remissioris verò, quæ maximè in vias Naturæ incidunt, non tentantur, ideoque latent. Itaque videmus per Vulcanos istos qui in pretio sunt, Spiritus Corporum magnopere exaltari, vt in Aquis fortibus, & nonnullis alijs Oleis Chymicis, partes tangibiles indurari, & emisso Volatili, aliquando figi; partes homogeneas se¦parari; etiam Corpora heterogenea grosso modo incorporari & commisceri; Maximè autem Compages Corporum Compositorum, & subtiliores Schematismos destrui & confundi. Debuerant autem Opificia Caloris lenioris tentari & exquiri; vnde subtiliores Misturæ & Schematismi ordinati gigni possint, & educi, ad Exemplum Naturæ, & Imitationem Operum Solis; quemadmodùm in Aphorismo de Instantijs Fœderis quædam adumbrauimus. Opificia enim Naturæ transiguntur per longè minores portiones, & posituras magis exquisitas & varias, quàm Opificia Ignis, prout nunc adhibetur. Tum verò videatur Homo reuerà auctus Potestate, si per Calores & Potentias artificiales, Opera Naturæ possint Specie repræsentari, Virtute perfici, copiâ variari; Quibus addere oportet Accelerationem Temporis . . . Interim (quod nunc agitur) Omnes diuersitates Caloris cum Effectibus suis respectiuè diligenter & industriè vndique sunt colligendæ & exquirendæ: Cœlestium, per radios suos directos, reflexos, refractos & vnitos in speculis Comburentibus; Fulguris, Flammæ, Ignis Carbonum; Ignis ex diuersis Materijs; Ignis aperti, conclusi, angustiati & inundantis, denique per diuersas fabricas Fornacium qualificati; Ignis flatu exciti, quieti & non exciti; Ignis ad Maiorem aut minorem Distantiam remoti; Ignis per varia Media permeantis; Calorum humidorum, vt Balnei Mariæ, Fimi, Caloris Animalium per exteriùs, Caloris Animalium per interiùs, Fœni conclusi; Calorum aridorum, Cineris, Calcis, Arenæ tepidæ . . . Præcipuè verò tentanda est Inquisitio & Inuentio Effectuum & Opificiorum Caloris Accedentis & Recedentis graduatim, & ordinatim, & periodicè, & per debita spatia & Moras. Ista enim Inæqualitas ordinata reuerâ Filia Cœli est, &

Generationis Mater; Neque à Calore aut vehementi, aut præcipiti, aut subsultorio, aliquid magni expectandum est. Etenim & in vegetabilibus hoc manifestissimum est; Atque etiam in Vteris Animalium magna est Caloris Inæqualitas, ex Motu, Somno, Alimentationibus & Passionibus Fœmellarum quæ vterum gestant; Denique in ipsis Matricibus Terræ, ijs nimirum in quibus Metalla & Fossilia efformantur, locum habet & viget ista Inæqualitas. Quo magis notanda est Inscitia aliquorum Alchymistarum ex Reformatis, qui per Calores æquabiles Lampadum & huiusmodi, perpetuò vno tenore ardentium, se voti compotes fore existimarunt.'. Also see G. B. della Porta, *Magiæ natvralis*, pp. 404–7; and *SS*, Y4ᵛ–Z1ʳ (*SEH*, II, p. 552).

D3ʳ⁻ᵛ, cf. fos. 13ᵛ–14ʳ

Page 98, l. 26–p. 100, l. 3, cf. p. 15, l. 32–p. 16, l. 8: Distillationes & Dilatationes—see *NO*, 2T1ᵛ–2T2ʳ (*SEH*, I, p. 358). Also see *SS*, E3ᵛ–E4ʳ (*SEH*, II, pp. 382–3).

D3ᵛ–D4ᵛ, cf. fo. 14ʳ⁻ᵛ

Page 100, l. 5–p. 102, l. 15, cf. p. 16, l. 9–p. 17, l. 11: Utcunque tamen *Distillationes*—for the Vulcan of Paracelsian chemistry see Paracelsus, *Selected writings*, ed. J. Jacobi, trans. N. Guterman, Pantheon Books: New York, 1951, p. 218. The rationale for and results of the experiment with wood are given thus in *SS*, E3ᵛ (*SEH*, II, pp. 382–3): 'But if *Bodies* may be altered by *Heat*, and yet no such Reciprocation of *Rarefaction*, and of *Condensation*, and of *Separation*, admitted; then it is like that this *Proteus of Matter*, being held by the Sleeues, will turne and change into many *Metamorphoses* . . . I conceiue that since all *Inflammation*, and *Euaporation* are vtterly prohibited, and the *Body* still turned vpon it Selfe, that one of these two Effects will follow: Either that the *Body* of the *Wood* will be turned into a kinde of *Amalagma*, (as the *Chymists* call it;) Or that the Finer Part will bee turned into *Aire*, and the Grosser sticke as it were baked, and incrustate vpon the Sides of the *Vessell*; being become of a Denser Matter, than the Wood it selfe, Crude.' Cf. *DAS*, 2I3ʳ (*SEH*, I, p. 632): 'At *Destillationem Clausam*, (ita enim eam vocare possumus) nemo mortalium adhùc tentauit: Verisimile autem videtur vim Caloris, si intra claustra Corporis, sua in alterando edat facinora, cùm nec iactura fiat Corporis, nec etiam liberatio; tùm demùm hunc Materiæ Proteum, veluti Manicis detentum, ad complures transformationes adacturam; si modò Calor ita temperetur & alternetur, vt non fiat Vasorum Confractio. Est enim hæc res Matrici similis Naturali, vbi Calor operatur, nihil Corporis aut emittitur, aut separatur; Nisi quod in Matrice conjungatur Alimentatio; Verùm, quatenùs ad Versionem eadem res videtur.' *SS* also details the experiment with water (E3ᵛ–E4ʳ (*SEH*, II, p. 383)) with the idea that something more oily will be produced from the water, the implicit hope being that water–oil conversion will make something with nutritional value (see *HDR*, D4ᵛ–D5ʳ (p. 102, ll. 27–31 above). For the importance of water–oil conversions, also see *SS*, N3ʳ⁻ᵛ (*SEH*, II, pp. 459–60): 'it is one of the greatest *Magnalia Naturæ*, to turne *Water*, or *Watry Iuyce*, into *Oile* or *Oily* Iuyce: Greater in Nature, than to turne *Siluer*, or *Quick-siluer*, into *Gold*.

The Instances we haue, wherein *Crude* and *Watry* Substance turneth into *Fat* and *Oily*, are of foure kindes. First in the *Mixture* of *Earth* and *Water*, which mingled by the helpe of the Sunne, gather a Nitrous Fatnesse . . . The Second is in the *Assimilation* of *Nourishment*; made in the *Bodies* of *Plants*, and *Liuing Creatures*; Whereof *Plants* turne the Iuyce of meere *Water* and *Earth*, into a great deale of *Oily Matter*. *Liuing Creatures*, though much of their *Fat*, and *Flesh*, are out of *Oily Aliments*, (as *Meat*, and *Bread*,) yet they Assimilate also in a Measure their *Drinke* of *Water* . . . The third is the *Inception* of *Putrefaction*; As in *Water Corrupted*; And the *Mothers* of *Waters Distilled*; Both which haue a kinde of *Fatnesse*, or *Oyle*.

The Fourth is in the *Dulcoration* of some *Metalls* . . . The Intention of *Version* of *Water* into a more *Oily Substance*, is by *Digestion*; For *Oile* is almost Nothing else but *Water digested* . . . *Digestion* also is strongly effected by direct *Assimilation*, of *Bodies Crude* into *Bodies Digested*; As in *Plants*, and *Liuing Creatures*, whose Nourishment is far more Crude than their Bodies: But this *Digestion* is by a great Compasse, as hath beene said.' For the term schematism see *cmt* immdiately below. For magnalia naturæ see *cmt* (pp. 293–4 below) on *HDR*, E2ᵛ (p. 116, l. 23–p. 118, l. 9).

D4ᵛ

Page 102, l. 20: Metaschematismos—this should be interpreted in conjunction with schematismus (see *cmt* (p. 308 below) on *ANN*, fo. 25ʳ (p. 176, ll. 21–3 above)). Also cf. *NO*, G2ʳ (*SEH*, I, p. 168): 'Omnis etiam subtilior meta-schematismus in partibus rerum crassiorum (quam vulgò alterationem vocant, cùm sit reuerà latio per minima) latet similitèr: & tamen nisi duo ista, quæ diximus, explorata fuerint & in lucem producta, nihil magni fieri potest in Naturâ quoad opera.' *Ibid.*, G2ᵛ (*SEH*, I, pp. 168–9): 'Materia potiùs considerari debet, & ejus Schematismi, & Meta-schematismi, atque Actus purus, & lex Actûs, siue Motûs; Formæ enim Commenta animi humani sunt, nisi libeat leges illas Actûs Formas appellare.' Also see *ANN*, fo. 33ᵛ (p. 208, ll. 12–21 above). For brief details of the history of the term see Gemelli, *Aspetti dell'atomismo . . . di Francis Bacon*, pp. 182–5.

D4ᵛ, cf. fo. 14ᵛ

Page 102, l. 26, cf. p. 17, l. 16: *Pygmæum Paracelsi*—see *HIDA*, p. 232, ll. 23–4 above and *SS*, E4ʳ (*SEH*, II, p. 383): 'But of the Admirable Effects of this *Distillation in Close*, (for so we will call it), which is like the *Wombes* and *Matrices* of liuing creatures, where nothing Expireth, nor Separateth; We will speake fully, in the due place; Not that we Aime at the making of *Paracelsus Pygmey's*; Or any such Prodigious Follies; But that we know the Effects of *Heat* will be such, as will scarce fall vnder the Conceit of Man; If the force of it be altogether kept in.' Bacon seems to be confusing his pygmies with his homunculi, see Theophrastus Paracelsus, *Werke*, 5 vols., Schwabe & Co.: Basle, 1965–8, III, pp. 427–38, 462–98. Is Bacon misremembering a passage quoted in the savage anti-Paracelsian diatribe of Thomas Erastus? viz. *Dispvtationvm de nova Philippi Paracelsi medicina pars tertia* [Petrus Perna: Basle], 1572, pp. 224–5: ' "Sciendum hîc obiter est, inquit, homines hoc pacto absque matre patreq́*ue* parentibus generari . . . Non enim nihil est . . . Dampra in cucurbita conclusa vel lutata in equino ve*n*tre per dies quinquaginta putrefactione summa putre-fiat, dum moueatur: quod facilè est cernere . . . Hanc si deinceps humano quotidie sanguine prudenter cibes seu alas, & in æquabili ventris equini calore conserues ac foueas, membris omnibus ornate instar infantis ex muliere nati apparebit: minor tamen quantitate. Hanc nos rem homunculum appellamus: qui postmodum tanquam verus puer seu infans accurata solicitudine ac diligentia educari debet, dum adoleuit. Hoc ex summis miraculis vnum est, adeoq́*ue* arcanorum omnium secretum maximum: quod tame*n* Pygmǽis & Gigantibus iam olim cognitum fuit: vt qui originem hinc suam acceperint. Nam ex illiusmodi homunculis, vbi ad virilem ætatem peruenerint, Pygmæi, Gigantes, aliaq́*ue* huiusce farinæ monstra pronascuntur.' Also see G. Pörksen, 'Die Bewohner der Elemente nach Paracelsus' Liber de Nymphis', *Nova Acta Paracelsica*, NS 6, 1991–2, pp. 29–50.

D4ᵛ–D5ʳ, cf. fo. 14ᵛ

Page 102, ll. 27–31, cf. p. 17, ll. 17–21: non efficiet—see *cmt* (pp. 287–8 above) on *HDR*, D4ʳ⁻ᵛ (p. 100, l. 5–p. 102, l. 15) above. The *Tensili* that Bacon has in mind are wombs, see *cmt* immediately above.

D5ʳ, cf. fos. 14ᵛ–15ʳ

Page 102, l. 32–p. 104, l. 4, cf. p. 17, l. 22–p. 18, l. 2: Bonum esset—for other such financial metaphors see *cmt* (p. 269 above) on *HDR*, A1ʳ–A1ᵛ (p. 36, ll. 5–9 above).

D6ʳ, cf. fo. 15ʳ

Page 106, ll. 4–17, cf. p. 18, ll. 3–12: De *Caloribus potentialibus*—I have not found a work with *tables* of medicaments displaying various of the secondary qualities, but see Jean Fernel, *Therapevtices vniversalis sev medendi rationis libri septem . . . Lvgdvni. Ex officina Lud. Cloquemin . . . 1574*, pp. 166–96. This gives one a good idea of what medicinal secondary qualities are but it's not in tabular form. On secondary qualities also see *HDR*, D7ʳ (p. 108, ll. 8–18 above). According to Bacon the specific inanimate spirits and the particular complex (*complexionem*)—here used in a quasi-Galenic sense—of the qualities of their tangible matter act on the body and, in particular, its extremely sensitive vital spirits (see *cmt* (p. 290 below) on *HDR*, D6ʳ⁻ᵛ (p. 106, l. 21–p. 108, l. 7 above)).

l. 7: *Confortantia*—also see *NO*, 2S3ʳ (*SEH*, I, pp. 354–5): 'At Opiata & eorum Affinia, Spiritus planè fugant, ex qualitate suâ malignâ & inimicâ. Itaque si applicentur parti exteriori, statim aufugiunt Spiritus ab illâ parte, nec amplius libentèr influunt: sin sumantur interiùs; Vapores eorum ascendentes ad Caput,

Spiritus in Ventriculis Cerebri contentos, vndequaque fugant; Cùmque se retra-
hant Spiritus, neque in aliam partem effugere possint, per Consequens coëunt,
& condensantur; & quandoque planè extinguuntur & suffocantur; licèt rursùs
eadem Opiata moderatè sumpta, per accidens secundarium, (videlicèt
Condensationem illam quæ à Coitione succedit) confortent Spiritus, eósque
reddant magis robustos, & retundant eorum inutiles & incensiuos Motus, ex
quo ad Curas Morborum, & vitæ Prolongationem haud parùm conferant.'

l. 8: *Abstergentia*—cleansing agents, see *OED*, abstergent. Also see *SS*, D2^{r-v}
(*SEH*, II, p. 368): 'For the Hurt, that they may doe after *Purging*; It is caused by
the *Lodging* of some *Humours* in *ill Places*: For it is certaine, that there be
Humours, which somewhere placed in the Body, are quiet, and doe little hurt;
In other Places, (especially Passages,) doe much mischiefe. Therefore it is good,
after *Purging*, to vse *Apozumes*, and *Broths*, not so much *Opening* as those vsed
before *Purging*, but *Abstersiue* and *Mundifying Clisters* also are good to conclude
with, to draw away the Reliques of the Humours, that may haue descended to
the *Lower Region* of the *Body*.' Also see *HVM*, S8^{r-v} (*SEH*, II, p. 181):
'Adducantur in Vsum, idque maximè in *Iuuentute, Clysteria* nihil omninò
Purgantia, aut *Abstergentia*; sed solummodò *Refrigerantia*, et nonnihil
Aperientia; Probata sunt quæ fiunt ex Succis *Lactucæ, Portulacæ, Hepaticæ*, etiam
Sedi maioris, & *Mucilaginis Seminis Psillij*, cum *Decoctione* aliquâ temperatâ
Aperiente, admisto aliquanto *Caphoræ*: Verùm *vergente Ætate*, omittatur *Sedum
maius*, & *Portulaca*, & substituantur *Succi Boraginis*, & *Endiuiæ*, aut similium;
Atque retineantur *Clysteria* huiusmodi, quantùm fieri potest, ad Horam scilicet,
autampliùs.' Also see *SS*, 2B1^v, 2E4^r, 2F4^r (*SEH*, II, pp. 573, 609, 620).

l. 9: *Aperientia* quoad orificia—laxatives, see *OED*, aperient. Also see *BTT*,
M3^{v-v} (*SEH*, III, p. 831–2).

l. 10: *Aperientia* quoad poros—*SS*, 2K4^v (*SEH*, II, p. 662): 'For *Opening*, I
Commend *Beads*, or *Peeces* of the *Roots* of *Carduus Benedictus*: Also of the *Roots*
of *Piony* the *Male*; And of *Orris*; And of *Calamus Aromaticus*; And of *Rew*.'

l. 11: *Digerentia* cum maturatione—agents promoting digestion, see *OED*,
digerent.

l. 12: *Digerentia* cum discussione—agents promoting suppuration perhaps,
see *OED*, digerent.

l. 13: *Caustica*—substances that burn or destroy living tissues, see *OED*, caus-
tic, **B**. *sb.*

D6^v

Page 106, l. 22–p. 108, l. 7: perceptio Spiritus Animalibus—perception here
means the automatic reaction of air or vital spirit to heat and cold; for more on
perception see *ANN*, fo. 35^r (p. 212, l. 27–p. 214, l. 15 above) and *cmt* thereon
(p. 322 below). For vital spirit see *ibid.*, fo. 28^r (p. 188, l. 8 above) and *cmt*
thereon (p. 312 below). For calendar glasses see *HDR*, C6^v (p. 88, ll. 8–14) and
cmt thereon (p. 283 above).

D7ʳ, cf. fo 15ʳ
Page 108, ll. 8–18, cf. p. 18, ll. 13–23: Possit esse res—on secondary medical qualities see *cmt* (pp. 289–90 above) on *HDR* D6ʳ (p. 106, ll. 4–17 above). The kind of thinking exhibited here is what Bacon called experientia literata (see *DAS*, 2H2ʳ–2I3ᵛ (*SEH*, I, p. 623–33)).

D7ʳ⁻ᵛ, cf. fo 15ʳ⁻ᵛ
Page 108, ll. 20–9, cf. p. 28, ll. 23–28: Transeundum ad *Dilatationes*—the inanimate spirits' predatory urge to break out of their tangible prisons is one of the fundamental impulses that Bacon attributed to them, and an impulse which he used to explain an extraordinary range of effects in the terrestrial world (see *OFB*, VI, pp. lvi–lxv). For the fact that the spirits in metals need the help of heat or strong waters to escape see *NO*, 2B1ᵛ (*SEH*, I, p. 263): 'Ostenditur [the expansive motion of heat] etiam in colliquatione Metallorum; quæ (cùm sint corporis compactissimi) non facilè intumescunt & se dilatant; sed tamen Spiritus eorum, postquàm fuerit in se dilatatus, & maiorem adeò dilatationem concupierit, trudit planè & agit partes crassiores in Liquidum. Quòd si etiam Calor fortiùs intendatur, soluit & vertit multum ex ijs in volatile.' *SS*, M4ᵛ (*SEH*, II, pp. 452–3): 'The Eight [method of accelerating putrefaction] is, by the *Releasing of the Spirits*; which before were close kept by the Solidnesse of their Couerture, and thereby their Appetite of Issuing checked; As in the *Artificiall Rusts* induced by strong Waters, in *Iron, Lead,* &c. And therefore *Wetting* hasteneth *Rust*, or *Putrefaction* of any thing, because it softeneth the Crust, for the *Spirits* to come forth.'

D7ᵛ, cf. fo 15ᵛ
Page 110, ll. 3–16, cf. p. 19, ll. 2–14: Accipe pondus *Auri*—without knowing the concentration of the acid it is difficult to know how accurate Bacon's claims are, but see *BTT*, K6ᵛ (*SEH*, III, p. 822), where he gives the same 12 : 1 ratio of acid to metal.

D7ᵛ–D8ʳ, cf. fo. 15ᵛ
Page 110, ll. 17–21, cf. p. 19, ll. 15–19: Accipe *Argenti vivi*—cf. *SS*, 2D1ᵛ (*SEH*, II, p. 596): 'Take of *Aqua-Fortis* two *Ounces*, of *Quick-siluer* two *Drachmes*; (For that Charge the *Aqua-Fortis* will beare;) The *Dissolution* will not beare a *Flint*, as big as a *Nutmeg* . . .'. It is not clear what these *Drachmes* are. The drachm or dram is a unit in the apothecary and avoirdupois systems. In the former it contains 3 scruples of 20 grains each, and 8 drams to an ounce (a dram equals 3.888 grams). The avoirdupois dram contains 27.344 troy grains (1.1772 grams) and equals one-sixteenth of an avoirdupois ounce. See Zupko, *A dictionary of English weights*, pp. 50–1.

ll. 22–5, cf. p. 19, ll. 20–3: Accipe *Plumbum*—see *BTT*, I7ʳ (*SEH*, III, p. 816).

D8ʳ, cf. fos. 15ᵛ–16ʳ
Page 110, l. 26–p. 112, l. 5, cf. p. 19, l. 24–p. 20, l. 2: Accipe *Argenti*—again it is difficult to know what to make of this without knowing how strong the aqua fortis was.

D8^{r-v}, cf. fo. 16^r

Page 112, ll. 6–16, cf. p. 20, ll. 3–13: Accipe *Cuprum*—cf. *NO*, X3^v (*SEH*, I, p. 246). (vi) Copper 1 : 6 incorporation.

D8^v

Page 112, ll. 17–20 Accipe *Stannum*—cf. *NO*, X3^v (*SEH*, I, p. 246). The cream or curd-like result is metastannic acid, see Partington, *History*, II, p. 411.

D8^v, cf. 16^r

Page 112, ll. 21–5, cf. p. 20, ll. 14–19: Accipe *Ferri*—cf. *NO*, V2^r (*SEH*, I, p. 237). Here as elsewhere in this section of *HDR* Bacon brings the chemical and the quantitative together as no other work of his does.

E1^r

Page 112, l. 31–p. 114, l. 8: Qualis sit ista *Dilatatio*—this quantitative experiment, absent from *HDR(M)*, presumably does not rely on the silver vessels used in the experiments whose results are reported in the large table at the beginning of *HDR* (A6^r (p. 44, ll. 17–21 above)) for silver is attacked by aqua fortis. As to whether the solution would support stones or tin, *SS* (2D1^v (*SEH*, II, p. 596)) reports that this '*Dissolution* will not beare a *Flint*, as big as a *Nutmeg* . . .'.

E1^v, cf. fo. 16^v

Page 114, ll. 21–9, cf. p. 20, l. 25–p. 21, l. 2: Tumultus intra partes—the gravel was presumably a limestone gravel, which, if very small and placed in a flat dish, would be moved around by the carbon dioxide produced by its reaction with the vinegar. Cf. G. B. della Porta, *Magiæ natvralis*, pp. 651–2: 'Proditur ab antiquis trochitem lapidem, & astroitem supra alium lapidem planum ex se ipsis moueri, addito aceto . . . Sit infra porphyreticum marmor planum, extrema superficie perpolitum, suprà imponantur trochites, aut astroites, etiam extrema superficie leuigati, inde addito aliquantisper aceti, vel limonis succi, statim ex se ipsis tàm trochites, quàm astroites, nullo impellente ad decliuiorem superficiem amulabunt, mira quadam iucunditate . . .' [Cardan says a vapour given off by the stone moves it. Porta disagrees, saying that air is driven from the veins in the stone by the vinegar]. Dr Peter Morris (personal communication) suggests that the vinegar used by Bacon was much stronger than the probable 15% (± 2%) undistilled vinegar mentioned in the main table of *HDR* (see p. 42, l. 25 above) and perhaps as strong as the distilled vinegar mentioned in the tables at the start of *HDR* (see p. 42, l. 36, p. 56, l. 29 above). Andreas Libavius in his *Alchemia* (1597) describes the production of 'radical vinegar' by distillation. On vinegar and acetic acid see Partington, *History*, II, pp. 266, 297, 685. As for the type of stone or fossil that behaves in vinegar like the pea gravel, Bacon was probably thinking of another form of limestone; for Bacon 'fossil' generally means a refractory stone (see *OFB*, VI, pp. 8, 24, 216, 365).

E2ʳ, cf. fo. 16ᵛ

Page 116, l. 11, cf. p. 21, l. 4: *Tragacanthum*—i.e. gum tragacanth, the sap, only partially soluble in water, produced by several species of *Astragulus* and used as a vehicle for drugs. Cf. *HVM*, V4ᵛ–V5ʳ (*SEH*, II, p. 187): '*Pillulas ex Aloe, & Mastice, & Croco*, præsertìm Temporibus Hyemalibus, ante Prandium sumptas, probamus; ita tamen, vt *Aloe* non tantum Succo *Rosarum* multis vicibus abluta sit, sed etiam in Aceto, (in quo dissolutum fuerit *Tragaganthum*) & posteà in *Oleo Amydalino* Dulci, & Recenti, ad aliquot horas macerata sit, antequàm formetur in *Pillulas*.' Tragacanth was known in the ancient world, see Pliny, *Historia naturalis*, XIII. 21.

E2ʳ

Page 116, ll. 17–21: *Gaudia subita*—these effects, not mentioned in *HDR(M)*, are elsewhere explained in terms of the action of the vital spirits: *SS*, 2A4ʳ (*SEH*, II, pp. 568–9): '*Ioy* causeth a *Chearfulnesse*, and *Vigour* in the *Eyes; Singing; Leaping; Dancing;* And sometimes *Teares.* All these are the *Effects* of the *Dilatation*, and *Comming* forth of the *Spirits* into the *Outward Parts;* Which maketh them more *Liuely*, and *Stirring.* We know it hath beene seene, that *Excessive Sudden Ioy*, hath caused *Present Death*, while the *Spirits* did spread so much, as they could not retire againe. As for *Teares*, they are the Effects of *Compression* of the *Moisture* of the *Braine*, vpon *Dilatation* of the *Spirits.* For *Compression* of the *Spirits* worketh an *Expression* of the *Moisture* of the *Braine*, by *Consent*, as hath beene said in *Griefe.* But then in *Ioy*, it worketh it diuersly; *viz.* by *Propulsion* of the *Moisture*, when the *Spirits* dilate, and occupy more Roome.' Also see *ibid.*, Z2ʳ (*SEH*, II, p. 556): 'The *Pleasure* in the *Act* of *Venus* is the greatest of the *Pleasures* of the *Senses:* The Matching of it with *Itch* is vnproper; though that also be Pleasing to the touch. But the *Causes* are Profound. First, all the *Organs* of the *Senses* qualifie the *Motions* of the *Spirits;* And make so many Seuerall *Species* of Motions, and *Pleasures* or *Displeasures* thereupon, as there be *Diuersities* of *Organs* . . . For *Smells*, wee see their great and sudden Effect in fetching *Men* againe, when they swoune: For *Drinke*, it is certaine, that the *Pleasure* of *Drunkennesse*, is next the *Pleasure* of *Venus:* And *Great Ioys* (likewise) make the *Spirits* moue, and touch themselues: And the *Pleasure* of *Venus* is somewhat of the same Kinde.'

E2ᵛ, cf. fo. 16ᵛ

Page 116, l. 23–p. 118, l. 9, cf. p. 21, ll. 8–14: Cogitandum de inveniendis—Bacon here has in mind a practical proposal advanced in *HVM* (2F1ᵛ–2F2ʳ (*SEH*, II, p. 331)): '*Videmus omnia, quæ per* Nutritionem *peraguntur, fieri per longas Ambages; quæ verò per* Amplexus similiu*m* (*vt fit in* Infusionibus) *non longam requirere Moram: Itaque vtilissima foret* Alimentatio *per Exterius, atq*ue *eò magis, quod deciduæ sint* Facultates Concoctionum *sub* Senectute, *Quamobrèm si possint esse* Nutritiones *aliæ Auxiliares, per* Balneationes, Vnctiones, *aut etiam per* Clysteria, Coniuncta *possint proficere, quæ* Singula *minùs valeant*.' The radical

humours which are to be reinvigorated are those which writers in the Arabo-Latin medical tradition took to be the keys to longevity—which is not to say that Bacon accepted the traditional theory (see *OFB*, VI, pp. lxv–lxix). As for magnalia naturæ see *NO*, 2E2ᵛ (*SEH*, I, pp. 281–2): 'Neque enim desistendum ab Inquisitione [viz. *Instantiarum Monodicarum*], donec proprietates & qualitates, quæ inueniuntur in huiusmodi rebus quæ possunt censeri pro Miraculis Naturæ, reducantur & comprehendantur sub aliquâ Formâ siue Lege certâ; vt Irregularitas siue Singularitas omnis reperiatur pendere ab aliquâ Formâ Communi; Miraculum verò illud, sit tandem solummodò in Differentijs accuratis, & gradu, & concursu raro, & non in ipsâ Specie: vbi nunc Contemplationes hominum non procedant vltrà, quàm vt ponant huiusmodi res pro Secretis & Magnalibus Naturæ, & tanquàm Incausabilibus, & pro Exceptionibus Regularum Generalium.' *NO*, 2F1ʳ (*SEH*, I, p. 285): 'Exempla autem huiusmodi Instantiarum [i.e. *Potestatis*] particularia nihil opus est adducere, propter copiam eorundem. Nam hoc omninò agendum; vt visitentur & penitùs introspiciantur omnes Artes Mechanicæ, atque Liberales etiam (quatenùs ad Opera) atque inde facienda est Congeries siue Historia Particularis, tanquam Magnalium, & Operum Magistralium, & maximè perfectorum in vnaquâque ipsarum, vnà cum Modis effectionis siue operationis.' Examples are given in *SS* (B4ʳ, D3ᵛ, L4ʳ, N3ʳ, S3ᵛ, 2B4ʳ (*SEH*, II, pp. 350, 372, 442, 459, 507, 580)). A list of magnalia is appended to *NA* (g3ʳ⁻ᵛ (*SEH*, III, pp. 167–8)).

E3ʳ, cf. fos. 16ᵛ–17ʳ
Page 118, ll. 14–27, cf. p. 21, ll. 23–5: Processus *Desiccationis*—these are basic principles of Bacon's theory of matter in so far as it applies to inanimate spirits. These spirits are air–flame compounds with the airy component dominant; the spirit therefore conspires with air to break out of its tangible prisons; in circumstances where the spirits cannot escape immediately they convert tangible matter into more spirit and then escape into the air, and that causes weight loss in the tangible bodies affected. The activities of inanimate spirit can be curbed by putting a barrier between them and the air (paint and other oily substances) or by keeping the bodies moist and soft. Other references to these principles and their ramifications permeate Bacon's philosophical writings; see, for example, *NO*, 2K2ᵛ–2K3ᵛ (*SEH*, I, pp. 309–11); *HVM*, D8ᵛ–E6ʳ (*SEH*, II, pp. 119–21); *SS*, 2F3ʳ (*SEH*, II, pp. 616–17). Also see *HDR*, p. 132, l. 24–p. 134, l. 3 (above) and *cmts* thereon (p. 296 below); *HDR(M)*, p. 24, ll. 27–30 (above). The relations between these ideas and Bacon's matter theory as a whole are discussed in *OFB*, VI, pp. liv–lxv.

E3ᵛ
Page 120, ll. 15–20: At quod potentissimum—see p. 74, l. 27–p. 76, l. 4 above and *cmts* thereon (p. 279 above).

E3ᵛ–E4ʳ

Page 120, ll. 21–3: Notant autem *Chymistæ*—cf. *NO*, 2I2ʳ, 2P4ʳ (*SEH*, I, pp. 303, 338–9); *SS*, B4ᵛ (*SEH*, II, p. 351). Fulminating gold is described by Oswald Croll and Basil Valentine, whose writings were known to Bacon. Valentine says that it was prepared by dissolving gold leaf in a mixture of sal ammoniac and aqua fortis and precipitating with salt of tartar (potassium carbonate); see Partington, *History of chemistry*, II, pp. 176, 197. For mercury fulminate see *ibid.*, II, p. 377.

E4ʳ

Page 120, ll. 29–30: *Titulum* de *Motu Libertatis*—for this motion see *ANN*, p. 192, ll. 7–19 above, and *cmt* thereon (pp. 313–14 below).

E4ᵛ, cf. fo. 17ʳ

Page 122, ll. 17–30, cf. p. 22, ll. 22–6: Qualem *Rarefactionem*—cf. *PhU*, Q1ʳ⁻ᵛ (*OFB*, VI, p. 44); instead of a tenth part *PhU* says an eighth. Also cf. *NO*, 2N1ʳ, 2S1ᵛ (*SEH*, I, pp. 323–4, 352–3).

E5ʳ

Page, 124, ll. 5–16: Suspicor etiam—for motus nexus see *ANN*, fo. 29ʳ (p. 190, l. 30–p. 192, l. 6 above) and *cmt* thereon (p. 313 below). Also see *PhU*, Q2ʳ (*OFB*, VI, p. 46, ll. 1–5).

E6ᵛ

Page 128, ll. 3–5: Consule *Instantias*—see *HDR*, C1ʳ–C2ʳ (pp. 74–6 above).

E6ᵛ–E7ʳ, cf. fo. 17ᵛ

Page, 128, ll. 6–20, cf. p. 23, ll. 16–19: *Metalla* pura—for the image *potestas Clavium* (at start of E7ʳ) cf. *DAS*, 2D1ᵛ (*SEH*, I, p. 596): 'Equidem memini Medicum quendam apud nos in Angliâ, Practicâ celebrem, Religione propè Iudæum, Librorum lectionè tanquam Arabem, solitum dicere, *Medici vestri Europæi sunt quidem viri docti; sed non norunt particulares curationes morborum.* Quinetiam idem ludere solebat, parum decorè, dicendo, *Medicos nostros similes esse Episcopis; ligandi & soluendi claues habere, & nihil ampliùs.*'

E7ʳ⁻ᵛ; cf. fo. 17ᵛ

Page 128, l. 28–p. 130, l. 6, cf. p. 23, ll. 16–19: *Modi Mortificationem*—see *cmt* (p. 285) on C8ᵛ, p. 92, ll. 25–7 above.

E7ᵛ–E8ᵛ; cf. fos. 17ᵛ–18ʳ

Page 130, l. 8–p. 132, l. 22, cf. p. 23, l. 24–p. 24, l. 26: *Dilatationibus* per *spiritum*—this is a rehearsal of fundamental doctrines of the pneumatic theory of matter with particular reference to the effects of the actions of inanimate spirits; cf. *ANN*, fo. 24ᵛ (p. 176, ll. 1–11 above); *NO*, 2K3ʳ–2K4ʳ (*SEH*, I, pp. 310–11; *HVM*, E3ʳ–E5ᵛ (*SEH*, II, pp. 120–1); *SS*, L1ᵛ (*SEH*, II, pp. 438–9). Also see *cmt* (p. 291 above) on *HDR*, D7ʳ⁻ᵛ (p. 108, ll. 20–9 above). For the implications of *HDR*, p. 130, l. 8–p. 132, l. 17, see *cmt* on A7ʳ⁻ᵛ (pp. 272–3 above). For dissolution through time see *DVM*, fo. 4ᵛ (*OFB*, VI, p. 278, ll. 22–9).

Commentary *on* Historia densi & rari, *pp. 132–8*

E8ᵛ–F1ʳ, cf. fo. 18ʳ

Page 132, l. 26–p. 134, l. 3, cf. p. 24, ll. 27–30: In senectute *Cutes*—cf. *DVM*, fo. 4ʳ (*OFB*, VI, p. 276, l. 32–p. 278, l. 11); *HVM*, E3ᵛ (*SEH*, II, p. 120). Also see *HDR*, p. 118, ll. 14–17 and *cmts* thereon (p. 294 above).

F1ʳ⁻ᵛ

Page 134, l. 11–p. 136, l. 3: *Lutum* per Fornaces—this section of history (nos. 1–10) is not in *HDR(M)*. For the action of heat on materials such as these, see *DVM*, fos. 10ᵛ–11ʳ (*OFB*, VI, p. 300, ll. 6–19); *SS*, E1ʳ⁻ᵛ (*SEH*, II, pp. 376–7).

F1ᵛ–F2ʳ, cf. fo. 18ᵛ

Page 136, ll. 5–13, cf. p. 25, ll. 4–14: Quamdiu . . . *spiritus* in corpore—cf. *DVM*, fo. 12ʳ (*OFB*, VI, p. 306, ll. 2–15); *NO*, 2K3ᵛ (*SEH*, I, pp. 310–11).

F2ʳ, cf. fo. 18ᵛ

Page 136, ll. 24–6, cf. p. 25, ll. 17–19: Maxime potens—once again Bacon alludes to his doctrine that the interior of the Earth was the abode of super-dense and extremely cold tangible matter (cf. *HDR*, (p. 60, ll. 19–20 above, and *cmts* thereon (p. 275, above)). Also see *NO*, 2S2ʳ⁻ᵛ (*SEH*, I, pp. 353–4): 'claudicat planè Potentia humana, tanquàm ex vno pede. Habemus enim Calorem Ignis, qui Caloribus Solis (prout ad Nos deferentur) & Caloribus Animalium, quasi infinitis partibus potentior est & intensior. At deest Frigus, nisi quale per tempestates hyemales, aut per Cauernas, aut per Circundationes Niuis & Glaciei, haberi potest: quod in Comparatione æquari potest cum Calore fortassè Solis Meridiano in Regione aliquâ ex Torridis, aucto insuper per reuerberationes Montium & Parietum . . . Nihili autem sunt ferè præ Calore Fornacis ardentis, aut alicuius Frigoris quod huic gradui respondeat. Itaque omnia hîc apud nos vergunt ad Rarefactionem, & Desiccationem, & Consumptionem: nihil ferè ad Condensationem & Intenerationem, nisi per Misturas & Modos quasi spurios. Quare Instantiæ Frigoris omni diligentiâ sunt conquirendæ; quales videntur inueniri in Expositione Corporum super Turres quando gelat acritèr; in Cauernis subterraneis; circundationibus Niuis & Glaciei in locis profundioribus, & ad hoc excauatis . . . & huiusmodi. Quinetiam quæ interueniunt in Naturâ Condensationes, factæ per Frigora, similitèr sunt inuestigandæ; vt Causis eorum cognitis, transferri possint in Artes. Quales cernuntur in exudatione Marmoris & Lapidum; in Rorationibus super Vitra per interius Fenestrarum, sub Auroram, post gelu Noctis; in Originibus & Collectionibus Vaporum in Aquas sub Terrâ , vndè sæpè scaturiunt Fontes; & quæcunque sunt huius generis.'

F2ᵛ–F3ʳ, cf. fo. 18ᵛ

Page 138, ll. 3–20, cf. p. 25, l. 23: Aer in *vitro*—*HDR(M)* has material equivalent only to first sentence of *HDR*. For calendar glasses see *cmt* (p. 283 above) on *HDR*, C6ᵛ (p. 88, ll. 8–14 above).

F3ʳ, cf. fos. 18ᵛ–19ʳ

Page 138, ll. 21–4, cf. p. 25, ll. 24–7: *Stellæ* tempori hyemali—cf. *DGI*, F1ᵛ, F10ᵛ
(*OFB*, VI, p. 156, ll. 6–8) and *cmt* thereon (*ibid.*, p. 402).

F3ʳ⁻ᵛ, cf. fo. 19ʳ

Page 138, l. 25–p. 140, l. 14, cf. p. 25, l. 28–p. 26, l. 16: *Rores matutini*—they are
vapours, and imperfectly mixed (on imperfect mixture see *ANN*, p. 184, ll. 1–6
and *cmt* thereon (pp. 310–11 below)).

F3ᵛ, cf. fo. 19ʳ⁻ᵛ

Page 140, ll. 15–22, cf. p. 26, ll. 17–24: *Argentum vivum*—Agricola gives five
methods of purifying mercury; the third seems to come closest to what Bacon
describes, see *Georgii Agricolae de re metallica libri xii . . . Froben Basileae M D
LXI*, F4ʳ–G1ʳ.

F3ᵛ, cf. fo. 19ᵛ

Page 140, ll. 27–9, cf. p. 26, ll. 29–31: Solebant antiquitus—Pliny, *Historia naturalis*, XXXI. 6: 'Quia sæpe navigantes defectu aquæ dulcis laborant, hæc
quoque subsidia demonstrabimus: expansa circa navim vellera madescunt
accepto halitu maris, quibus humor dulcis exprimitur: item demissæ reticulis: in
mare concavæ è cera pilæ, vel vasa inania obturata, dulcem intra se colligunt
humorem: nam in terra, marina aqua argilla percolata dulcescit.' Also cf. *SS*, D3ᵛ
(*SEH*, II, p. 372).

F4ʳ, cf. fo. 19ᵛ

Page 140, ll. 30–6, cf. p. 26, ll. 32–4: Etiam expertus sum—in *SS* (D3ᵛ (*SEH*, II,
p. 372)), Bacon reports that the wool 'increased in weight, (as I now remember)
to a fifth Part'.

F4ʳ

Page 142, l. 5: Anglice *Rynes*—i.e. rimes or hoar-frosts.

F4ʳ, cf. fo. 19ᵛ

Page 142, ll. 8–11, cf. p. 27, ll. 1–2: *Anhelitus*—cf. *NO*, 2N4ᵛ–2O1ʳ; *HVM*, D2ʳ⁻ᵛ;
SS, E2ʳ (*SEH*, I, p. 329; II, pp. 116, 378).

F4ᵛ, cf. fo. 19ᵛ

Page 142, ll. 19–22, cf. p. 27, ll. 5–8: *Nebulæ*—clouds are imperfectly mixed bodies. For other uses of the notion of imperfect mixture see *OFB*, VI, pp. 396–7, 406.
Also see *HDR*, p. 138, l. 2–p. 140, l. 14 above, and *ANN*, p. 184, ll. 1–6 and *cmt*
thereon (pp. 310–11) below. For Gilbert on cloud formation see *De mundo*, 2I2ᵛ.

ll. 24–32, cf. p. 27, ll. 9–13: Quia versio *Aeris*—cf. *SS*, D4ʳ (*SEH*, II, p. 373):
'There is also a *Version of Aire into water*, seene in the *Sweating* of *Marbles*, and
other *Stones*; And of *Wainscot* before and in moist weather: This must be, either
by some *Moisture* the Body yeeldeth; Or else by the Moist Aire thickned against
the hard body. But it is plaine, that it is the latter; For that we see *Wood painted
with Oyle Colour*, will sooner gather drops in a moist Night, than *Wood* alone:

which is caused by the Smoothnesse and Closenesse; which letteth in no part of the Vapour, and so turneth it backe, and thickeneth it into Dew.' It is notable that between here and p. 152 there is much material which also appears in *SS* at D4ʳ–E1ᵛ, M4ʳ, N4ʳ⁻ᵛ (*SEH*, II, pp. 373–6, 452, 462).

F5ᵛ

Page 144, l. 25: *Æraque dissiliunt*—Virgil, *Georgics*, III. 363; the quotation is accurate.

ll. 27–8: Etiam *Clavi*—cf. *NO*, 2B2ʳ (*SEH*, I, p. 263): 'Frigus enim corpus omne contrahit & cogit in angustius; adeò vt per intensa Frigora claui excidant ex parietibus, æra dissiliant, vitrum etiam calefactum & subitò positum in Frigido dissiliat & frangatur.'

F5ᵛ, cf. fo. 20ʳ

Page 146, ll. 1–9, cf. p. 27, l. 29–p. 28, l. 2: *Condensantur* manifesto—cf. *SS*, N4ʳ (*SEH*, II, p. 462): 'It is a Report of some good credit, that in *Deepe Caues*, there are *Pensile Crystall*, and *Degrees* of *Crystall* that drop from aboue; And in some other, (though more rarely) that rise from below. Which though it be chiefly the Worke of Cold, yet it may be, that Water, that passeth thorow the Earth, gathereth a Nature more clammy, and fitter to Congeale, and become Solide, than Water of it self.' Also cf. *NO*, 2O3ᵛ (*SEH*, I, p. 332): 'At si interueniat Frigus intensum & continuatum, mutat se sponte sua & libentèr in condensationem Glaciei; atque si planè continuetur Frigus, nec à teporibus interrumpatur (vt fit in Speluncis & Cauernis paulò profundioribus) vertitur in Crystallum, aut materiam similem, nec vnquam restituitur.'

F5ᵛ

Page 146, ll. 10–14: *Lutum* manifesto—the hardening of the clay in the material is given as an example of motion of assimilation in *NO*, 2Q1ʳ (*SEH*, I, p. 340); also see *SS*, E1ᵛ (*SEH*, II, p. 377) and *Op*, L1ᵛ. For motion of assimilation see *ANN*, fo. 30ᵛ (p. 196, l. 27–p. 198, l. 3 above) and *cmt* thereon (p. 316 below).

F6ʳ, cf. fo. 20ʳ

Page 146, ll. 15–19, cf. p. 28, ll. 3–5: Sunt quædam *Aquæ*—cf. *SS*, E1ʳ (*SEH*, II, p. 375): 'It is already found, that there are some *Naturall Spring-waters*, that will Inlapidate *Wood*; So as you shall see one peece of *Wood*, whereof the Part aboue the *Water* shall continue *Wood*; And the Part vnder the *Water* shall be turned into a kinde of *Grauelly Stone*. It is likely those *Waters* are of some *Metalline Mixture*; But there would be more particular Inquiry made of them.' For William Gilbert on petrification of wood see *De mundo*, 2M3ʳ, 2R2ʳ⁻ᵛ.

ll. 21–6, cf. p. 28, ll. 6–7: Probabile est *Aquas Metallicas*—cf. *SS*, E1ʳ (*SEH*, II, p. 375): 'Another Triall is by *Metalline waters*, which haue virtuall *Cold* in them. Put therefore *Wood*, or *Clay*, into *Smiths water*, or other *Metalline water*; And try whether it will not harden in some reasonable time. But I vnderstand it, of

Metalline waters, that come by Washing, or Quenching, And not of *Strong Waters* that come by dissolution; for they are too Corrosiue to consolidate.'

F6ʳ

Page 146, ll. 28–32: In *China*—cf. *NO*, 2S2ʳ⁻ᵛ (*SEH*, I, pp. 353–4): 'Instantiæ Frigoris omni diligentiâ sunt conquirendæ; quales videntur inueniri in . . . Defossione Corporum in Terrâ (qualis fertur apud Chinenses esse Confectio Porcellanæ, vbi Massæ ad hoc factæ dicuntur manere intra terram per quadraginta aut quinquaginta Annos, & transmitti ad hæredes, tanquàm Mineræ quædam artificiales) . . .'. Also see *SS*, E1ʳ (*SEH*, II, pp. 375–6). Bacon's source may be J. C. Scaliger, *Exotericarvm exercitationvm liber qvintvs decimvs, de svbtilitate, ad Hieronymvm Cardanvm . . . Lvtetiæ, . . . M. D. LVII.* fo. 134ʳ: 'Centesimo anno pro perfecto [the Chinese] effodiunt, ac uenale opus habent. Quod eorum uitæ superest, hæredi testamento transcribunt . . . Alij putant: non uasa, sed materiæ condi massam. Qua extracta confiant uasa.'

F6ʳ⁻ᵛ

Page 148, ll. 1–4: Accepi rem—cf. *SS*, E1ʳ (*SEH*, II, p. 375): 'It is certaine, that an *Egge* was found, hauing lien many yeeres in the bottome of a Moate, where the Earth had somewhat ouergrowen it; And this Egge was comen to the Hardnesse of a *Stone*; And had the Colours of the white and yolke perfect: And the Shell shining in small graines like Sugar, or Alabaster.'

  ll. 16–18: Sequitur *Actio*—see *HDR*, D6ʳ–D7ʳ (pp. 106–8 above).

F6ᵛ–F7ʳ, cf. fo. 20ʳ⁻ᵛ

Page 148, ll. 21–32, cf. p. 28, ll. 10–20: Quemadmodum consulendæ—for medicinal tables of secondary qualities which produce potential cold see *cmt* (p. 289 above) on *HDR*, p. 106, ll. 4–17 above). For narcotic condensation of vital spirits see *NO*, 2S3ʳ (*SEH*, I, pp. 354–5) quoted on pp. 289–90 above. For narcotics and trying them out as meat preservatives or to counter gangrene, cf. *SS*, M4ʳ (*SEH*, II, 452): 'The Fifth [method of accelerating putrefaction] is, either by the *Exhaling*, or by the *Driuing back* of the *Principall Spirits*, which preserue the Consistence of the *Body*; So that when their Gouernment is Dissolued, euery *Part* returneth to his Nature, or Homogeny. And this appeareth in *Vrine*, and *Bloud*, when they coole, and thereby breake; It appeareth also in the *Gangrene*, or *Mortification* of *Flesh*, either by *Opiates* or by *Intense Colds*.' For calendar glasses see *HDR*, C6ᵛ (p. 86, l. 29–p. 88, l. 14 above and *cmts* thereon, p. 283 above).

F7ʳ, cf. fo. 20ᵛ

Page 150, ll. 1–9, cf. p. 28, ll. 21–7: Apud *Indias*—for the water-bearing canes with joints see Samuel Purchas, *Pvrchas his pilgrimage. Or relations of the world . . .*, William Stansby: London, 1614, p. 877: '*Aluarados* Armie, which he brought into Peru had perished, as *Cieza* relateth, with drought, but for certain Canes as bigge as a mans legge, which between the knots contained a pottle of

water, extracted from the dewes; for there fell no raine in those parts.' For the
dripping trees see *NO*, 2S4ʳ (*SEH*, I, pp. 355–6). Also see Richard Hakluyt, *The
principall navigations, voiages and discoveries of the English nation, made by sea or
ouer land, to the most remote and farthest distant quarters of the earth at any time
within the campasse of these 1500. yeeres: deuided into three seuerall parts, according
to the positions of the regions wherunto they were directed*, London, 1589, p. 524:
'In one of these Islands, called "*de Fierro*, there is by the reportes of the inhabitants, a certaine tree that raineth continually, by the dropping whereof, the
inhabitants and catell are satisfied with water, for other water haue they non in
all the Island. And it raineth in such abundance, that it were incredible vnto
man to beleeue such a vertue to be in a tree, but it is knowen to be a diuine matter, and a thing ordained by God, at whose power therein, we ought not to
maruell, seeing he did by his prouidence, as we read in the Scriptures, when the
children of Israell were going into the land of promise, feede them with *Manna*
from heauen, for the space of 40. yeeres. Of the trees aforesaid, we sawe in
Guinie many, being of great heigth, dropping continually, but not so abundantly as the other, because the leaues are narrower, and are like the leaues of a
peare tree . . .' [Voyage of John Hawkins to the coast of Guinea, 1564].

F7ʳ⁻ᵛ
Page 150, ll. 10–14: Invenitur super *Folia*—cf. *NO*, 2S4ʳ (*SEH*, I, pp. 355–6):
'*Paracelsus* autem ait, Herbam vocatam *Rorem Solis* Meridie & feruente Sole
Rore impleri, cùm aliæ Herbæ vndique sint siccæ. At nos vtramque narrationem
fabulosam esse existimamus. Omninò autem illæ Instantiæ nobilissimi forent
vsûs, & introspectione dignissimæ, si essent veræ. Etiam Rores illos Mellitos, &
instar Mannæ, qui super folijs Quercûs inueniuntur Mense Maio, non existimamus fieri & densari à Consensu aliquo, siue à Proprietate Folij Quercûs; sed
cùm super alijs Folijs pariter cadant, contineri scilicèt & durare in Folijs
Quercûs quia sunt benê vnita, nec spongiosa, vt plurima ex alijs.' Also see *SS*,
R3ʳ, 2C4ᵛ (*SEH*, II, pp. 497–8, 593).

F7ᵛ, cf. fo. 20ᵛ
Page 150, ll. 15–28, cf. p. 28, l. 28–p. 29, l. 6: Vix invenitur corpus—on the espe-
cial potential cold of nitre see *SS*, E1ʳ (*SEH*, II, p. 375); also see *HVM*, P5ᵛ–P6ʳ
(*SEH*, II, p. 166): '*Nitrum* est tanquam *Arôma* Frigidum; Idque indicat Sensus
ipse. Mordet enim, & tentat Linguam, & Palatum Frigore, vt *Aromata* Calore;
Atque inter ea quæ nouimus, vnicum est, & solum, quod hoc præstet.' The
same experiments of the bladder submerged in nitre and in quicksilver are mentioned in *SS*, D3ᵛ–D4ʳ (*SEH*, II, p. 372). For medicinal uses of nitre's cold quality see *SS*, N2ᵛ–N3ʳ (*SEH*, II, p. 459). Also see *cmts* (p. 280 above) on *HDR*, p.
78, l. 29–p. 80, l. 2 above.

F8ʳ, cf. fos. 20ᵛ–21ʳ
Page 152, ll. 9–13, cf. p. 29, ll. 13–17: *Calor ignis* per *Antiperistasin*—cf. *NO*, X3ᵛ,
2E2ʳ, 2P3ᵛ (*SEH*, I, pp. 245–6, 281, 338). Antiperistasis is a violent reaction of one

nature against a surrounding and contrary one. Bacon also applied the idea to celestial phenomena; see *TC*, G7ʳ (*OFB*, VI, p. 174, ll. 20–4). Aristotle used it to explain certain meteorological phenomena, see S. K. Henninger, Jr., *A handbook of Renaissance meteorology*, Duke University Press: Durham, NC, 1960, pp. 39 f.

F8ʳ⁻ᵛ, cf. fo. 21ʳ
Page 152, ll. 19–23 cf. p. 27, ll. 18–23: Merito dubitari—see *cmt* (p. 299 above) on *HDR*, F6ᵛ–F7ʳ (p. 148, ll. 21–32 above).

F8ᵛ
Page 154, l. 5: Supra notavimus—see p. 146, ll. 10–14 above and *cmt* thereon (p. 298 above).

G1ʳ⁻ᵛ, cf. fo. 21ᵛ
Page 154, l. 27–p. 156, l. 21, cf. p. 30, ll. 16–18: Accipe *catinum*—the instances of the inverted bowl and the diving bell appear with different wording in *PhU* (see *OFB*, VI, p. 40, ll. 9–34 and *cmts* thereon (*ibid.*, pp. 370–1)). For Cornelis Drebbel (1572–1633), the inventor of the diving bell, see *OFB*, VI, pp. xxvii–xxviii. For other Drebbel inventions see *HDR(M)*, fo. 23ᵛ (p. 34, ll. 11–13 above) and *HDR*, G5ʳ (p. 166, ll. 25–7 above and *cmts* thereon, pp. 303–4 below).

G2ʳ, cf. fo. 21ᵛ
Page 156, ll. 25–33, cf. p. 30, ll. 19–21: *Globum* fieri fecimus—cf. *PhU*, P12ᵛ (*OFB*, VI, p. 42, ll. 14–21). *HDR(M)* on this last experiment cites 'lib. ii. in organo nouo, vbi & loquimur de quanto condensationis aquæ', which seems to indicate that this part of *HDR(M)* was written after 1620. *NO*, 2N1ᵛ (*SEH*, I, p. 324) details this experiment though the wording differs from that of *HDR*. In addition *NO* tells us that the capacity of the lead globe was two wine pints (see *cmt* (p. 277 above) on *HDR*, B6ᵛ–B7ʳ (pp. 66–8 above)) and that Bacon calculated how far the globe's volume was reduced; none of the works give a result for the experiment. *SEH* (I, p. 324 n. 3) notes that this experiment was conducted by the Accademia del Cimento almost half a century later with a silver container and was thereafter known as the Florentine experiment.

G2ʳ, cf. fo. 21ᵛ
Page 156, l. 34–p. 158, l. 5, cf. p. 30, ll. 22–7: At omnis *Motus*—on violent motion see *cmt* (pp. 313–14 below) on *ANN*, fo. 29ʳ (p. 192, ll. 7–19 above).

G2ʳ, cf. fo. 21ᵛ
Page 158, ll. 9–11, cf. p. 31, ll. 1–3: *Flamma* simpliciter compressa—cf. *NO*, V1ᵛ, Z1ʳ⁻ᵛ (*SEH*, I, pp. 237, 252).

G4ʳ, cf. fo. 22ʳ
Page 162, ll. 10–11, cf. p. 32, ll. 8–9: *Limus*—Virgil, *Eclogues*, VIII. 80; this quotation (also used in *DAS*, V2ᵛ (*SEH*, I, p. 550) to the same effect) is accurate.

G4ᵛ–G6ʳ, cf. fos. 22ᵛ–23ʳ

Page 162, l. 19–p. 166, l. 10, cf. p. 32, l. 15–p. 34, l. 1: *Canones Mobiles*—each of the following twenty-nine canones would presumably have been followed by an explicatio (explanation) had *HDR* been finished; for such explicationes see *HVM*, 2C7ʳ–2F8ᵛ (*SEH*, II, pp. 212–26). It is worth noting that all these canones appear in *HDR(M)*, i.e. they were formulated *before* all the material that turned *HDR(M)* into *HDR* was added to the text.

G4ᵛ, cf. fo. 22ᵛ

Page 162, ll. 20–1, cf. p. 32, ll. 16–17: Summa *Materiæ*—for the principle that the sum of matter neither increases or diminishes see *cmt* (p. 269 above) on *HDR*, A1ᵛ–A2ʳ (p. 36, ll. 9–20 above).

ll. 26–7, cf. p. 32, ll. 21–2: Est *Terminus*—the limits of density and rarity were no doubt to be found in two places beyond direct human experience: the Earth's entrails (see *cmt* (p. 273) above on *HDR*, A8ʳ⁻ᵛ (p. 50, ll. 15–30 above)) and the heavens (see *DGI*, E6ᵛ (*OFB*, VI, p. 126, ll. 5–9)).

l. 28–9, cf. p. 32, l. 23: Non est *Vacuum*—Bacon's most forthright denial of a vacuum either collected or interspersed (for this distinction see *DGI*, E6ᵛ–7ʳ (*OFB*, VI, p. 126, ll. 10–31); *NO*, 2R1ᵛ (*SEH*, I, p. 347)); the denial suggests that Bacon made a list of canones before he wrote *HDR* or *HDR(M)* for the collected vacuum is nowhere discussed in either version of the text, and the interspersed vacuum is mentioned only once in *HDR* (see *cmts* (p. 269 above) on *HDR*, A1ᵛ–A2ʳ, p. 36, l. 12 above) and not at all in *HDR(M)* with its *identical* list of canones mobiles.

ll. 30–1, cf. p. 32, ll. 24–5: Inter *Terminos*—like the collected vacuum, the mysterious plica materiæ is not actually discussed in the text at all. This plica or fold would apparently allow expansion and contraction to be explained without resorting to the vacuum hypothesis, see *NO*, 2R1ᵛ (*SEH*, I, p. 347); *cmt* (p. 269 above) on *HDR*, p. 36, l. 12, and *cmt* (*OFB*, VI, p. 392) on *DGI*, E6ᵛ–E7ʳ.

ll. 32–3, cf. p. 32, ll. 26–7: *Differentiæ Densi*—see *HDR*, A7ᵛ–A8ʳ (p. 50, ll. 3–13 above).

Page 164, ll. 1–2, cf. p. 32, ll. 28–9: *Differentia à rarissimo*—see *HDR*, B6ᵛ–B7ʳ, B8ʳ (p. 66, l. 21–p. 68, l. 29, p. 70, ll. 19–23 above).

Page 164, l. 3, cf. p. 33, l. 1: *Flamma* est *Aere*—see *HDR*, B6ʳ⁻ᵛ (p. 66, ll. 13–19 above).

G5ʳ, cf. fo. 22ᵛ

Page 164, ll. 4–12, cf. p. 33, ll. 2–10: *Flamma* non est *Aer*—canones 9–13 set out basic principles of the pneumatic theory of matter. These principles are sketched out in *HDR*, B4ᵛ–B5ʳ (p. 62, ll. 9–20 above).

G5ʳ, cf. fos. 22ᵛ–23ʳ

Page, 164, ll. 13–23, cf. p. 33, ll. 11–18: *Densum* & *Rarum*—cf. *DPAO* (*OFB*, VI, p. 224, l. 35–p. 226, l. 6).

G5ʳ, cf. fos. 22ᵛ–23ʳ

Page 164, ll. 17–19, cf. p. 33, ll. 13–14: Calor in Tangibili—cf. *DVM* (*OFB*, VI, p. 306, ll. 10–12, pp. 442–3).

G5ʳ, cf. fo. 23ʳ

Page 164, ll. 20–1, cf. p. 33, ll. 15–16: *Norma*—this is a canon in *DVM*, see *OFB*, VI, p. 304, l. 29–p. 306, l. 1, p. 437; also see HVM, R7ʳ⁻ᵛ (*SEH*, II, p. 175).

G5ᵛ, cf. fo. 23ʳ

Page 164, ll. 24–5, cf. p. 33, ll. 19–20: Post *Calorem*—see *NO*, 2S3ᵛ–2S4ʳ (*SEH*, I, p. 355).

ll. 26–7, cf. p. 33, l. 21: *Restitutio*—see, for example, *HDR*, p. 122, l. 5–p. 124, l. 3 above.

ll. 28–9, cf. p. 33, ll. 22–3: *Assimilatio*—see *HDR*, p. 118, l. 2–p. 120, l. 23, p. 152, l. 25–p. 154, l. 21 above.

Page 164, ll. 36–7, cf. p. 31, ll. 29–31: Potentissima—see *HDR*, p. 120, ll. 15–20 above.

Page 166, ll. 3–4, cf. p. 33, l. 32: *Densum*—see *HDR*, p. 52, ll. 20–7 above.

ll. 5–6, cf. p. 33. ll. 33–4: Parce suppeditatur—cf. *NO*, 2S2ʳ⁻ᵛ (*SEH*, I, pp. 353–4).

G5ᵛ–G6ʳ, cf. fo. 23ʳ

Page 166, ll. 7–10, cf. p. 33, l. 35–p. 34, l. 1: *Ætas*—see *HDR*, p. 130, l. 19–p. 132, l. 22 above.

G6ʳ, cf. fo. 23ʳ

Page 166, l. 12, cf. p. 34, l. 2: *Optativa cum Proximis*—see *HNE*, C5ᵛ–C6ʳ (*SEH*, II, p. 18): 'Opera, *& * Res impossibiles, *aut saltem adhuc non inuentas, quæ sub singulis* Titulis *cadunt, proponimus; atque unà ea, quæ iam inuenta sunt, & in* Hominum potestate, atque Impossibilibus *illis, & non Inuentis, sunt* Proxima, *& maximè cognata, subiungimus; ut simul & Industria humana excitetur, atque animi addantur.*'

ll. 12–14, cf. p. 34, ll. 3–4: Versio Aeris in Aquam—see *HDR*, p. 138, l. 29–p. 140, l. 29, p. 142, l. 24–p. 106, l. 12.

ll. 15–17, cf. p. 34, ll. 4–5: Augmentum Ponderis—see *HDR*, p. 52, l. 29–p. 56, l. 6 above and *cmts* thereon (pp. 273–4 above).

G6ʳ, cf. fo. 23ʳ⁻ᵛ

Page 166, ll. 18–22, cf. p. 34, ll. 6–8: Insaxatio Terræ—see *HDR*, p. 146, ll. 1–26, p. 154, ll. 8–10 above.

G6ʳ, cf. fo. 23ᵛ

Page 166, ll. 23–7, cf. p. 34, ll. 10–13: *Varii usus*—for the calendar glass see *HDR*, C6ᵛ (p. 86, l. 29–p. 88, l. 14 above and *cmt* thereon, p. 283 above); *Altare Heronis*—see *cmt* (p. 283 above) on *HDR*, p. 88, ll. 15–24 above; see *cmt* on *PhU*, Q9ᵛ (*OFB*, VI, p. 374); *Organum musicum* splendentibus radiis solis—another of Cornelis Drebbel's inventions, see *cmt* (p. 301 above) on *HDR*, G1$^{r–v}$ (p. 154, l. 27–p. 156, l. 21 above); also see *PhU*, Q9^v (*OFB*, p. 60, ll. 10–15).

ll. 26–7, cf. p. 31, ll. 12–13: *Impostura de Imitatione Fluxus*—this perpetual motion device which appeared to imitate the motion of the tides is another Drebbel device, see H. Michel, 'Le mouvement perpétuel de Drebbel', *Physis*, fasc. 3, a. 13, 1971, pp. 289–94. The machine is also briefly described in Rosalie L. Colie, 'Cornelis Drebbel and Saloman de Caus: Two Jacobean models for Salomon's House', *HLQ*, 18, 1955, pp. 245–60, pp. 258–9. A sketch of the machine was reproduced in Thomas Tymme's *A dialogve philosophicall . . . Together with the wittie inuention of an artificiall perpetuall motion*, London, 1612, I3^r. This invention is not mentioned in *PhU*. I do not know why Bacon thought this was an imposture. For a detailed account of this device (essentially a torus-like form of the calendar glass), together with illustrations from seventeenth-century sources see Jennifer Drake-Brockman, 'The *perpetuum mobile* of Cornelis Drebbel', in *Learning, language and invention: essays presented to Francis Maddison*, ed. W. D. Hackmann and A. J. Turner, Variorum and the Société Internationale de l'Astrolabe: Aldershot and Paris, 1994, pp. 124–47. I am indebted to Dr J. B. Sokol for drawing my attention to these sources.

G6$^{r–v}$

Page 166, ll. 28–33: *Inteneratio Membrorum*—these lines are not to be found in *HDR(M)*, but see *HDR*, p. 92, l. 28–p. 30, l. 9; also see p. 116, l. 23–p. 118, l. 2 above and *cmts* thereon (pp. 293–4 above). The title referred to here is no doubt *HVM*. Since Bacon had meant to publish *HDR* before *HVM* (see *HNE*, A4^r (*SEH*, II, p. 11)) but did not do so, the future tense (videbimus) suggests that this paragraph may have been drafted before the publication of *HVM*.

G6^v

Page 168, ll. 1–4: *Monitum*—these lines are not to be found in *HDR(M)*.

COMMENTARY ON
ABECEDARIUM NOUUM NATURÆ

fo. 24ʳ

Page 172, l. 1: Abecedarium nouum naturæ—not an alphabet of nature (as in the *SEH* translation (V, p. 208) but a new ABC. There is an alphabet of nature and also its abecedarium. The alphabet consists of the letters of the book of nature. An abecedarium is not an alphabet (Bacon used the word 'alphabetum' only once in *ANN* (p. 190, l. 18 above)) but an alphabet book, child's primer, or absey book, see *LF*, col. 6; *OED*, **ABC** *sb*; also see *DAS*, F2ᵛ (*SEH*, I, pp. 460–1): 'Respuunt enim quasi Abecedarium Naturæ, Primumque in Operibus diuinis tyrocinium, quod si non facerent, potuissent fortassè gradatìm & sensim, post Literas simplices, & deinceps Syllabas, ad Textum & volumen ipsum Creaturarum expeditè legendum ascendere. At illi contrà, iugi mentis agitatione, vrgent & tanquam inuocant suos Genios, vt vaticinentur eis, edantque Oracula, quibus meritò & suauitèr decipiuntur.' For Bacon a *secondary* meaning of abecedarium naturæ might be 'an A to Z of nature', i.e. a summary survey of all nature's basic elements. The analogy between letters and the elements of nature was not new, see for instance Lucretius, *De rerum natura*, II. 688–94: 'Quin etiam passim nostris in versibus ipsis | multa elementa vides multis communia verbis, | cum tamen inter se versus ac verba necesse est | confiteare alia ex aliis constare elementis; | non quo multa parum communis littera currat | aut nulla inter se duo sint ex omnibus isdem, | sed quia non volgo paria omnibus omnia constant.' For ABC books see *STC* 17.7–22.5. Also see *cmt* (p. 306 below) on *ANN*, p. 172, l. 13. Bacon was not the first philosopher of his age to use the abecedarium metaphor, see for instance John Case, *ABCedarium moralis philosophiae*, 1596.

l. 4: *Amice, verba tua*—never one to let a good line go to waste, Bacon used the same remark to the same effect at the very end of *DAS* (3R1ʳ (*SEH*, I, p. 837)): 'Interìm, in Mentem mihi venit Responsum illud Themistoclis, qui, cùm ex Oppido paruo Legatus quidam, magna nonnulla perorasset, Hominem perstrinxit; *Amice, verba tua Ciuitatem desiderant.*' Here, as in his 1624 collection of apophthegms (*SEH*, VII, p. 144), he misattributed the remark to Themistocles. The words are Lysander's, see Plutarch, *Lives* (Loeb Classical Library) London and Cambridge, Mass., vol. IV, 1916, repr. 1986, pp. 292–3: 'He was harsh of speech also, and terrifying to his opponents . . . And when a Megarian, in some conference with him, grew bold in speech, he said: "Thy words, Stranger, lack a city." ("Οἱ λόγοι σου," εἶπεν, "ὦξένε, πόλεως δέονται.")'

l. 4: *Equidem verissime*—cf. *DAS* (3R1ʳ (*SEH*, I, p. 837)): 'Certè obijci mihi rectissimè posse existimo, quod Verba mea *Seculum* desiderent. *Seculum* fortè *integrum,* ad Probandum; *Complura* autem *Secula,* ad Perficiendum. Attamen, quoniàm etiàm Res quæque maximæ Initijs suis debentur, mihi satis fuerit seuisse *Posteris,* & *Deo Immortali.*'

l. 5: quoad opus Instaurationis—here it is more likely that Bacon means the work of renewal rather than the six-part sequence of works that was designed to bring it about.

ll. 6–7: spem magnam non habeo—for the thinking associated with this see Michèle Le Dœuff, 'Hope in science', *FBLT,* pp. 9–24.

ll. 8–9: vt ait ex politicis nescio quis—I have not been able to identify this source.

l. 11: opus in æuum spargo—cf. *NO,* P4ᵛ (*SEH,* I, p. 212) where, admitting that he will not complete Part VI of *IM,* he adds 'interìm semina veritatis sincerioris in posteros spargamus, atque initijs rerum magnarum non desimus'. Also see *ANN,* p. 222, l. 22 above; and Bacon's letter of June 1621 to Gondomar, *LL,* VII, p. 285: 'Me verò jam vocat et ætas, et fortuna, atque etiam Genius meus, cui adhuc satis morosé satisfeci, ut excedens è theatro rerum civilium literis me dedam, et ipsos actores instruam, et posteritati serviam.' Cf. Bacon's letter to Fulgenzio, *ibid.,* VII, pp. 531–2 and *Op,* L6ᵛ–L7ᵛ.

l. 13: imitationem quandam tanquam puerilem—Ronald Latham (personal communication) tentatively suggested that a child's copybook was meant here and I have adopted the suggestion. This takes up the imagery mentioned in the *cmts* (p. 305) above on *ANN,* p. 172, l. 1.

ll. 15–16: nisi sub persona infantis—Mark 10: 15. Also see *NO,* I2ʳ⁻ᵛ (*SEH,* I, p. 179): 'Atque de *Idolorum* singulis generibus, eorùmque apparatu iàm diximus; quæ omnia constanti & solenni decreto sunt abneganda, & renuncianda, & Intellectus ab ijs omninò liberandus est, & expurgandus; vt non alius ferè sit aditus ad Regnum Hominis, quod fundatur in Scientijs, quàm ad Regnum Cœlorum, *in quod, nisi sub personâ infantis, intrare non datur.*' *VT,* pp. 16–17 (*SEH,* III, p. 224): 'it is a point fitt and necessary in the fronte and begininge of this worke without hesitacíon or reservacíon to be professed, that it is noe lesse true in this humane kingdome of knowledge, then in gods kingdome of heauen that noe man shall enter into it *Except he become first as a little childe.*' Also see *PhU,* O9ʳ (*OFB,* VI, p. 6, l. 1–p. 8, l. 4).

l. 17: Pertinet autem Abecedarium ad Instaurationis partem quartam—see Introduction, pp. xxi–xxii above.

ll. 20–1: Vtilius autem—cf. *HNE,* B6ʳ⁻ᵛ (*SEH,* II, p. 15): 'Etsi enim haud pauca, eáque ex præcipuis, supersint in *Organo* nostro absoluenda, tamen consilium est, vniuersum Opus *Instaurationis,* potius promouere in multis quàm perficere in paucis . . .'.

ll. 21–2: ne sim id quod sacerdotibus quispiam objicit—this densely allusive remark refers to Matthew 23: the 'someone' is Christ, and the priests are the scribes and Pharisees who, in response to Christ's charge that they neglected the weighty matters of the law to deal in quibbles (23: 23), claimed that had they been living in the days of their fathers they 'would not have been partakers with them in the blood of the prophets' (23: 30–1). Christ turns this on his critics (23: 32–4): 'Fill ye up then the measure of your fathers . . . I send unto you prophets, and wise men, and scribes: and some of them ye shall kill and crucify; and some of them shall ye scourge in your synagogues, and persecute them from city to city . . .'. Bacon therefore puts himself on the side of Christ as one destined to map out the groundwork of a great project rather than to lose himself in details; he also seems to be suggesting that if others took up his project they would (at any rate initially) be swimming against the tide. For another allusion to this chapter see *DAS*, 3K1ʳ (*SEH*, I, pp. 788). The parallel to the Matthew passage is Luke 11: 42 but Luke does not allude to the scribes' attempt to dissociate themselves from their fathers.

Page 174, l. 2: Exporrectiones—a term is here used (uniquely) to cover the first five titles of *ANN*, titles separated off and treated as aspects of dense and rare. The first five are called schematisms everywhere else. The *c-t* reading—Exporrectrices—is extremely doubtful (cf. p. 188, ll. 18–22). The term is not found in any thesaurus or lexicon known to me, and a search of *Patrologia latina* on CD-ROM by Dr James Binns failed to discover it.

fo. 24ʳ⁻ᵛ

Page 174, ll. 3–15: Cum omnis omnium corporum diuersitas—see *NO*, 2K4ʳ (*SEH*, I, p. 311): 'At differentia Schematismorum maximè radicalis & primaria sumitur ex copiâ vel paucitate Materiæ, quæ subit idem spatium siue dimensum. Reliqui enim Schematismi (qui referuntur ad dissimilaritates partium, quæ in eodem corpore continentur, & collocationes ac posituras earundem) præ illo altero sunt secundarij.' Also see *cmts* on *HDR*, A1ᵛ–A2ʳ (p. 269 above). The three kinds of motion distinguished here (p. 174, ll. 7–10), are the motions of expansion and contraction (spherical), the circular motion of the heavenly bodies (cf. *ANN*, fo. 31ᵛ (p. 200, ll. 16–25 above)), and rectilinear motion or 'motus congregationis majoris' as it is called elsewhere in *ANN* (fos. 29ᵛ–30ʳ (p. 194, ll. 17–36 above)). For other uses of sphæricus and its cognates for expansion and contraction see *OFB*, VI, pp. 12, 34, 44, 60; also see *NO*, 2B1ʳ⁻ᵛ, 2M4ᵛ, 2O3ʳ (*SEH*, I, pp. 262, 323, 332); curiously enough this usage never occurs in *HDR(M)* or *HDR*. For coitio and its meanings see *cmt* on *HDR*, A1ʳ (p. 269 above).

fo. 24ᵛ

Page 174, ll. 16–22: Cum natura grauis—cf. the contemptuous remark in *NO*, 2G2ʳ (*SEH*, I, p. 291): 'At corpora cætera (Grauia quæ vocant, & Leuia, extrà loca scilicèt connaturalitatis suæ sita) feruntur rectâ ad Massas siue congregationes similium; Leuia sursùm, versùs ambitum Cœli; Grauia deorsùm, versùs Terram. Atque ista pulchra dictu sunt.' Also see *ANN*, fos. 29ᵛ–30ʳ (p. 194, ll. 17–36 above). Bacon intended to produce an *Historia grauis & leuis*, see *HNE*, R8ᵛ–S2ʳ (*SEH*, II, p. 80); *OFB*, VI, p. lxxxiv.

ll. 23–8: Cum densum—cf. *HDR*, G5ʳ (p. 164, ll. 13–14 above). Also see *DPAO*, M8ᵛ–M9ʳ (*OFB*, VI, pp. 262–4); *ANN*, fo. 29ᵛ (p. 192, l. 28–p. 194, l. 16 above).

fos. 24ᵛ–25ʳ

Page 176, ll. 1–12: At termini magni—the distinction developed here is a primary one in Bacon's theory of matter, a theory which rests on the antithesis between tangible and pneumatic. For this distinction see *OFB*, VI, pp. xlii and l. The pneumatics which are visible because they are bright are terrestrial and celestial fire (*ibid.*, pp. xlii–xliii). Bacon also used the family metaphor (l. 11) in connection with another primary feature of his matter theory, namely the sulphur and mercury quaternions, see *cmts* (p. 312 below) on p. 188, l. 17–p. 190, l. 6 above.

fo. 25ʳ

Page 176, ll. 13–18: Rursus quia inueniuntur—for the bodies which are volatile in this sense see *HDR*, B4ʳ–B5ʳ (p. 60, l. 21–p. 64, l. 2 above). For bodies which resist becoming volatile see *ibid.*, C8ᵛ (p. 92 above).

ll. 21–3: Transeundum est . . . ad schematismos—schematism, a key term in Bacon's philosophy, is used in three ways. In the first place, it refers to the contrasted pairs of simple natures which make up inquiries 6–19 of *ANN*—pairs which in *DAS* (X4ʳ–ᵛ (*SEH*, I, p. 560)) *also* include the first five inquiries of *ANN*. In the second, it refers to the fine structure or latent schematisms of bodies, i.e. the schematisms 'particulares & accuratos' denied a place in *ANN* but which appear in *NO* (T3ʳ–T4ʳ (*SEH*, I, pp. 233–4)). In *ANN* (fo. 36ᵛ (p. 220, ll. 1–11 above)) the term is used in its third sense, viz. to refer to the structure of the universe (cf. *DPAO*, K4ᵛ (*OFB*, VI, p. 212, ll. 3–5)). This last, with latent schematisms, and schematisms of matter correspond respectively and rather neatly to three of the branches of physics distinguished in the *De augmentis*: 'de Mundo sive de *Fabrica Rerum*', concrete physics and abstract physics (see pp. xxxviii–xxxix above). Also see *cmts* on *DGI*, D8ᵛ–D9ʳ and D9ʳ–ᵛ (*OFB*, VI, pp. 385–6); Rees, 'Bacon's philosophy: some new sources', *FBTF*, pp. 238–40. For the term tela see *DPAO*, K12ʳ (*OFB*, VI, p. 224, l. 34–p. 226, l. 4), where it seems to be a synonym of textura. For a recent and valuable account of these terms and their history see Gemelli, *Aspetti dell'atomismo . . . di Francis Bacon*, pp. 182–8, esp. the discussion (pp. 184–5) of ancient and Renaissance uses of σχηματισμός (schematismus) by Libavius, Jungius, Diogenes Laertius on Epicurus etc. Also see *CHRP*, p. 299.

l. 25–p. 178, l. 3: Sunt quædam corpora—on determinate and fluid see *CDNR*, S1ᵛ–S4ᵛ (*SEH*, III, pp. 25–8). For the meanings of the term primordia and its cognates see *OFB*, VI, pp. 365, 406.

fo. 25ʳ–ᵛ

Page 178, ll. 4–12: Inquisitio de potentiali ad fluorem—by a pneumatic fluid Bacon means a vaporous or (if an anachronism be allowed) a gaseous substance, as distinct from a liquid.

fo. 25ᵛ

Page 178, ll. 13–19: Inueniuntur corpora quæ sunt mediæ cuiusdam naturæ—for Bacon and intermediate states see *OFB*, VI, pp. liii, liv–lv, 396–7. His interest in glutinous substances springs in the main from his theory of vivification, see *HIDA* (pp. 228–35 above) and *cmts* thereon (pp. 327–9 below). Note that consistente is not an –i ablative, and so must be taken as a noun not an adjective. Accordingly, the title of the inquiry is (unusually) not an axiological anithesis. I am indebted to Dr James Binns for close discussion of this point.

ll. 20–9: Rursus inueniuntur corpora–for criticism of the primary qualities of moist and dry in the received philosophy see *NO*, G4ᵛ–H1ʳ (*SEH*, I, pp. 171–2). Also see Keith Hutchinson, 'Dormitive virtues, scholastic qualities, and the new philosophies', *History of Science*, **29**, 1991, pp. 245–78.

fos. 25ᵛ–26ʳ

Page 180, ll. 1–10: Atque naturæ colliquabilis—for pneumatic fluids see *cmt* (p. 308 above) on *ANN*, p. 178, ll. 4–12 above. For motion of percussion see *NO*, 2O2ᵛ (*SEH*, I, pp. 331–2): 'At longè magis necessarium est (quia multa secum trahit) vt intimetur hominibus, Motum Violentum (quem nos *Mechanicum*; *Democritus*, qui in Motibus suis primis expediendis etiam infrà Mediocres Philosophos ponendus est, Motum *Plagæ* vocauit) nil aliud esse quàm Motum Libertatis, scilicèt à Compressione ad Relaxationem.'

fo. 26ʳ

Page 180, ll. 11–19: Alter natura est fragile—in relation to the distinction between fragile and tensile, *NO* (2F1ᵛ–2F2ʳ (*SEH*, I, pp. 285–6)) has this to say: 'Instantia *Monodica* Artis, est Papyrus; res admodùm vulgata. At si diligentèr animum aduertas, Materiæ Artificiales aut planè Textiles sunt per fila directa & transuersa; qualia sunt, Pannus Sericus, aut Laneus, aut Linteus, & huiusmodi; aut coagmentantur ex succis concretis; qualia sunt Later, aut Argilla figularis, aut Vitrum, aut Esmalta, aut Porcellana, & similia; quæ si bene vniantur, splendent; sin minùs, indurantur certè, sed non splendent. Attamen omnia talia [i.e. ceramics, glass, etc.], quæ fiunt ex succis concretis, sunt fragilia, nec vllo modo hærentia, & tenacia. At contrà, Papyrus est corpus tenax, quod scindi & lacerari possit; ita vt imitetur & ferè æmuletur Pellem siue Membranam alicuius Animalis, aut Folium alicuius Vegetabilis, & huiusmodi opificia Naturæ. Nam neque fragilis est, vt Vitrum; neque textilis, vt Pannus; sed habet fibras certè, non fila distincta, omninò ad modum Materiarum Naturalium: vt inter Artificiales Materias vix inueniatur simile aliquod, sed sit planè *Monodicum*. Atque præferenda sanè sunt in Artificialibus ea quæ maximè accedunt ad imitationem Naturæ; aut è contrario eam potentèr regunt & inuertunt.'

Page 180, l. 20–p. 182, l. 4: Cum vero certissimum—for the Earth's interior see *cmt* (p. 273 above) on *HDR*, A8ʳ (p. 50, ll. 15–30). The qualities (l. 27–8) mentioned here are attacked in *NO*, H4ʳ⁻ᵛ (*SEH*, I, p. 176): 'Atque prima cogitatio qualitates primas elementares, secunda proprietates occultas, & virtutes specificas, nobis peperit; quarum vtraque pertinet ad inania contemplationum compendia, in quibus acquiescit animus, & à solidioribus auertitur . . . atque nisi ex illis duobus . . . compendijs (qualitatibus scilicet elementaribus, & virtutibus specificis) illa altera (quæ rectè notata sunt) corrumperent, reducendo illa ad primas qualitates, earumq̀*ue* mixturas subtiles & incommensurabiles; aut ea non producendo cum maiore & diligentiore obseruatione ad qualitates tertias & quartas, sed contemplationem intempestiuè abrumpendo; illi multò meliùs profecissent.' Cf. e.g. Jean Fernel, *Vniversa medicina . . . Francofvrti M D LXXXI*, p. 105: secondary qualities arise from the four primary qualities (hot, cold, moist and dry)—'Ex harum [viz. qualitates] autem genere aliæ sunt principes, aliæ ex his ortæ: principes, calor, frigus, humor, siccitas; ex his ortæ, quæ in moli, duro, crasso, tenui, læui, aspero sunt corpore, quæ variæ dicuntur & multiformes.' The distinction between intrinsic and adventitious spirit is developed in *DVM* (fo. 8ᵛ (*OFB*, VI, pp. 290–2)).

fo. 26ᵛ

Page 182, ll. 5–12: Rursus accidit corporibus—cf. *NO*, T4ʳ (*SEH*, I, p. 234). For examples see *SS*, N1ᵛ, 2D3ʳ (*SEH*, II, pp. 445, 600).

Page 182, ll. 13–20: Rursus inueniuntur corpora—cf. *DVM*, fo. 28ʳ (*OFB*, VI, p. 344).

fo. 26ᵛ

Page 182, ll. 21–31: Atque videtur hic locus—Bacon is here preparing the way for the inquiry outlined on fos. 27ᵛ–28ʳ (p. 186, l. 23–p. 188, l. 7).

fos. 26ᵛ–27ʳ

Page 184, ll. 1–6: Prima itaque diuisio—the contrast between absolute and imperfect mixtures is ultimately Aristotelian. According to the early *CDSH*, fo. 226ᵛ (*SEH*, III, p. 190), the History of Meteors dealt with bodies 'ex imperfecté mistis', a category which included comets. For meteorological imperfect mixtures see *HDR*, p. 138, l. 25–p. 140, l. 10, p. 142, ll. 19–22, above. For other absolute and imperfect mixtures see *NO*, 2M1ʳ (*SEH*, I, p. 318): 'Oleum & Aqua inter se compositionem aut agitationem imperfectè admodùm miscentur; eadem in Herbis, & Sanguine, & Partibus Animalium, accuratè & delicatè miscentur. Itaque simile quiddam fieri possit circa Misturam Flammei & Aerei generis in Spiritalibus; quæ per Confusionem simplicem non benè sustinent Misturam, eadem tamen in Spiritibus Plantarum & Animalium misceri videntur . . . si non de Perfectioribus Misturis Spiritalium, sed de Compositione tantùm inquiratur; nempè, vtrùm facilè inter se incorporentur, an potiùs (exempli gratiâ) sint aliqui Venti & Exhalationes, aut alia Corpora Spiritalia, quæ non miscentur cum Aëre communi; sed tantùm hærent & natant in eo, in globulis & guttis, & potiùs franguntur ac comminuuntur ab Aere, quàm in ipsum recipiuntur & incorporantur; hoc in Aere Communi & alijs Spiritalibus, ob subtilitatem corporum, percipi ad Sensum non potest; attamen imago quædam huius rei, quatenùs fiat, concipi possit in Liquoribus

Argenti viui, Olei, Aquæ; atque etiam in Aere, & fractione eius, quando dissipatur & ascendit in paruis portiunculis per Aquam; atque etiam in Fumis crassioribus; denique in Puluere excitato & hærente in Aere; in quibus omnibus non fit Incorporatio.'

Page 184, ll. 7–14: Cum vero inueniantur corpora—for the distinction between bodies with heterogeneous and ones with homogeneous parts see *DVM*, fo. 15ʳ (*OFB*, VI, p. 314); *NO*, 2P1ᵛ–2P2ʳ (*SEH*, I, pp. 334–5).

Page 184, ll. 15–20: corpora quæ habent inæqualitatem—cf. *NO*, T4ʳ (*SEH*, I, p. 234): 'Essentia tangibilis (quæ non pauciores recipit differentias, quàm spiritus) atque eius villi, & fibræ, & omnimoda textura; rursùs autem collocatio Spiritûs per copoream molem, eiusque pori, meatus, venæ, & cellulæ, & rudimenta, siue tentamenta Corporis organici, sub eandem Inquisitionem [i.e. into latent schematism] cadunt.'

ll. 21–33: Atque paulo altius—as in the previous inquiry Bacon is here concerned with investigating an aspect of what he calls latent schematism, see *NO*, T3ʳ⁻ᵛ (*SEH*, I, p. 223): 'Atque in Anatomiâ Corporum Organicorum (qualia sunt hominis, & animalium) opera sanè rectè & vtilitèr insumitur, & videtur res subtilis, & scrutinium Naturæ bonum. At hoc genus Anatomiæ spectabile est, & sensui subiectum, & in corporibus tantùm organicis locum habet. Verùm hoc ipsum obuium quiddam est, & in promptu situm, præ Anatomiâ verâ *Schematismi latentis* in corporibus, quæ habentur pro similaribus; præsertìm in rebus specificatis, & earum partibus, vt ferri, lapidis; & partibus similaribus, plantæ, animalis, velutì radicis, folij, floris, carnis, sanguinis, ossis, &c.' Also see *DVM*, fo. 18ᵛ (*OFB*, VI, p. 324, l. 33–p. 326, l. 6). For latent schematism see *cmt* (p. 308 above) on *ANN*, fo. 25ʳ (p. 176, ll. 13–18 above).

fo. 27ᵛ

Page 186, ll. 1–7: Sequitur Inquisitio—cf. *NO*, 2P4ʳ (*SEH*, I, p. 339); *SS*, Z3ᵛ (*SEH*, II, pp. 559–60).

ll. 8–15: Inquisitio de specificato—cf. *NO*, T3ᵛ (*SEH*, I, p. 233).

ll. 16–22: corpora quæ sunt rudimenta—Bacon used the term rudimentum to denote a state of arrested development or something on its way to being perfect but not quite making it, i.e. it is a synonym for tentamentum (see e.g. *NO*, T4ʳ (*SEH*, I, p. 234)), an essay at or imperfect realization of something; alternatively, it meant something 'in infimâ virtute' (*ibid.*, 2C4ʳ (*SEH*, I, pp. 272–3)). Also see *HIDA*, fo. 4ʳ (p. 230, l. 13 above). The actual objects Bacon has in mind here are beings bred spontaneously from putrefaction and decay, beings such as worms, mosses, flies and other 'imperfect' creatures, see *HDR*, C4ʳ (pp. 80–2 above); *SS*, Z2ᵛ f. (*SEH*, II, pp. 557 f.). Also see *NO*, Y2ᵛ, 2K3ʳ–2K4ʳ, 2P2ʳ⁻ᵛ (*SEH*, I, pp. 249, 310–11, 336). These are distinguished from biform creatures or beings of mixed species, which are not spontaneous generations or necessarily interspecific hybrids but forms which occupy 'in-between' situations in the chain of being—such, for instance, as flying fish (transitional between fish and birds), bats (between birds and quadrupeds) and apes (between quadrupeds and humans), see *DAS*, Q2ᵛ–Q3ʳ, T2ᵛ, 2E2ᵛ–2E4ᵛ (*SEH*, I, pp. 525–6, 543–4, 604–7); *NO*, 2E4ʳ (*SEH*, I, p. 283).

fos. 27ᵛ–28ʳ

Page 186, l. 23–p. 188, l. 7: Cum vero ventum est—a summary of fundamental theories expressed in many places elsewhere. For an account of these theories and their historical context see *OFB*, VI, pp. xxxvii, lii–lxv; also see *HIDA*, p. 234, ll. 8–15 above.

fo. 28ʳ

Page 188, ll. 8–16: Atque hoc genus—advancing from the previous title, Bacon distinguishes between the two kinds of animate or vital spirit: (i) that organized in channels in vegetable bodies and (ii) the warmer kind in which the channels are connected to a congregation of spirit in the cerebral ventricles. This concentration of spirit is the key to the higher functions that animals possess but plants do not. For this aspect of the vital spirit see *OFB*, VI, pp. lvii–lxi. For other instances of the figurative language that Bacon attached to the ventricular concentrations of spirit see *DVM*, fos. 17ʳ, 27ᵛ (*OFB*, VI, p. 318, ll. 21, 30, p. 342, l. 28).

fo. 28ʳ⁻ᵛ

Page 188, l. 17–p. 190, l. 6: Superest natura—the sulphur–mercury distinction is central to Bacon's thinking about the nature of matter and the structure of the cosmos, a fact accentuated by its special placing in the alphabetical sequence. If not quite the alpha (there are distinctions—the first five presented in *ANN*—which are more general), the distinction is certainly the omega. It is 'primordial' or fundamental to the nature of things (for primordial distinctions see *OFB*, VI, pp. 365, 406). To spell out the meaning of the distinction and its relationship to salt and to the various names (vocabulis) by which it is known would require a note of disproportionate length. Suffice it to say that a summary account of the place of sulphur, salt and mercury in Bacon's philosophy can be found elsewhere in *OFB* (VI, pp. xlii–li, liv–lv), and that the importance of these entities is underlined in many works, for instance, *TC* G6ʳ⁻ᵛ (*OFB*, VI, pp. 172–3); *DVM*, fo. 18ʳ⁻ᵛ (*OFB*, VI, pp. 324–5); *SS*, N3ʳ (*SEH*, II, p. 459); *HNE*, S5ʳ–S8ʳ (*SEH*, II, pp. 82–3); *LL*, III, p. 94; and *NO*, 2T2ᵛ (*SEH*, I, p. 359): 'Nam non malè notatum est à Chymicis, in principiorum suorum Triade, Sulphur & Mercurium, quasi per Vniuersitatem rerum permeare. (Nam de Sale inepta ratio est, sed introducta, vt possit comprehendere Corpora terrea, sicca, & fixa). At certè in illis duobus videtur Consensus quidam Naturæ ex maximè Catholicis conspici. Etenim Consentiunt Sulphur, Oleum, & Exhalatio pinguis, Flamma; & fortassè Corpus Stellæ. Ex alterà parte Consentiunt Mercurius, Aqua & Vapores Aquei, Aer, & fortassè Æther purus & interstellaris. Attamen istæ Quaterniones geminæ, siue Magnæ rerum Tribus, (vtraque intra Ordines suos) Copiâ Materiæ atque Densitate immensùm differunt, sed Schematismo valdè conueniunt: vt in plurimis se produnt.' Also see *cmt* immediately below.

fo. 28ᵛ

Page 190, ll. 7–18: Atque Inquisitiones—for forms of the first class cf. *DAS*, Y3ᵛ
(*SEH*, I, p. 566): '*Formam* inquirendo *Leonis, Quercûs, Auri*; imò etiam *Aquæ*,
aut *Aeris*, Operam quis luserit: *Formam* verò inquirere *Densi, Rari; Calidi,
Frigidi; Grauis, Leuis; Tangibilis, Pneumatici; Volatilis, Fixi*; & similium, tam
Schematismorum, quam *Motuum*, quos in *Physicâ* tractandâ, magnâ ex parte,
enumerauimus (& *Formas Primæ Classis* appellare consueuimus) quique (veluti
Literæ Alphabeti) numero haud ita multi sunt, & tamen *Essentias* & *Formas*
omnium substantiarum conficiunt & sustinent; hoc est, inquam, illud ipsum,
quod conamur; quódque eam partem *Metaphysicæ*, de quâ nunc inquirimus,
constituit & diffinit.' Also cf. *HSMS*, S5ᵛ–S6ʳ (*SEH*, II, p. 82): '*Illud tamen non
malè cum illorum Opinione conuenit, quod duo ex illis,* Sulphurem *scilicet,* &
Mercurium (*sensu nostro accepta*) *censemus esse Naturas admodùm primordiales,
& penitissimos* Materiæ Schematismos; *& inter* Formas primæ classis *ferè præ-
cipuas.*' As for the catholicity of *ANN*, cf. p. 176, ll. 21–3, p. 214, ll. 4–5 above.

Page 190, l. 19: Motus Simplices—Bacon now turns to the simple motions,
which are also considered in great detail in *NO* (2O1ᵛ–2R1ʳ (*SEH*, I, pp.
330–46)) and summarily in *DAS* (X4ᵛ–Y1ʳ (*SEH*, I, pp. 560–1)). For the structure of this and of inquiries 25–60 see Introduction, pp. xliii–xliv above.

ll. 20–1: Quantum Naturæ—for this fundamental proposition see *cmt* on
HDR, A1ᵛ–A2ʳ (p. 269 above); also see *PhU*, O10ᵛ (*OFB*, VI, p. 10).

fos. 28ᵛ–29ʳ

Page 190, ll. 21–9: Inest siquidem—this is also the first of the simple motions to
be dealt with in *NO* (2O1ʳ (*SEH*, I, p. 330)) and *DAS* (X4ᵛ (*SEH*, I, p. 560)).
NO gives no examples of this motion as it subsists in all bodies. *NO* notes that
the schoolmen refer to this motion in the axiom that two bodies cannot be in
the same place, and that they call it the motion that prevents penetration of
dimensions. This 'axiom' is vigorously supported by Aristotle in *Physica*, IV. 1
(209ᵃ), IV. 6 (213ᵇ); *De caelo*, III. 6 (305ᵃ); *De anima*, I. 5 (409ᵇ), II. 7 (418ᵇ). For
the ancient debate on interpenetration of bodies see Sorabji, *Matter, space and
motion*, pp. 60–122.

fo. 29ʳ

Page 190, l. 30–p. 192, l. 6: Corpora mutuo nexu—motion of connection also
comes second in *NO* (2O1ᵛ (*SEH*, p. 330)) and *DAS* (X4ᵛ (*SEH*, I, p. 560)).
According to *NO*, this is the motion which the schoolmen call '*Ne detur vacuum*', and a motion exemplified by the drawing up of water by suction, the
action of cupping glasses, '& innumera id genus'. For Bacon and the vacuum
hypothesis see *OFB*, VI, pp. 126–8, 214, 260–2, 434–5. Also see *HDR*, p. 162,
ll. 28–9 and *cmts* thereon (p. 302 above).

Page 192, ll. 7–19: Corpora naturalia suam exporrectionem—motion of liberty also comes third in *NO* (2O2ʳ–2O3ʳ (*SEH*, pp. 330–2)) and *DAS* (X4ᵛ
(*SEH*, I, pp. 560–1)). In *NO* the motion of water in swimming and rowing, the

action of clock springs and of popguns are given as instances of liberation from pressure; liberation from tension is exemplified by the contraction of air in partially evacuated glass eggs when the hole is unstopped, and by anything that springs back when stretched. Like *ANN*, *NO* identifies this motion with 'violent motion', i.e. what the Aristotelians called projectile motion and other motions of bodies away from their natural places in the sublunary realm. For a powerful study of natural and violent motion and their theoretical contexts from antiquity to the early modern period see Sorabji, *Matter, space and motion*, *passim*. Also see *CHSCP*, I, pp. 442–4. In *NO* it is clear that Bacon's theory of violent motion is quite different from the received one; it has a wider scope than the scholastic theory. On violent motion see *HDR*, G2^r (p. 156, l. 34–p. 158, l. 5 above). Also cf. *NO*, 2H4^v–2I1^r (*SEH*, I, pp. 301–2). For 'natural' motion, the antithesis of violent, see *cmts* (pp. 314–15 below) on *ANN*, p. 194, ll. 17–36.

fo. 29$^{r–v}$

Page 192, ll. 20–7: Etiam illibenter ferunt corpora—in *NO* (2O3$^{r–v}$ (*SEH*, pp. 332–3)) and *DAS* (X4^v (*SEH*, I, p. 561)) motion of continuity and motion of hyle are taken in reverse order. *DAS*, like *ANN*, positions motus continuationis as a special form of motus nexus. According to *NO*, this motion shows itself particularly in the fact that there is a limit to the smallness of cracks that water will flow through, i.e. a limit to water's willingness to be finely divided. The same is true of air, and even solids resist being ground down into very small particles.

ll. 28–33: Itaque muniuntur—*NO* and *DAS* do not explicitly identify the first four motions of *ANN* as motions of self-preservation; *ANN* is tidier in this respect than *NO* and *DAS*.

fo. 29^v

Page 194, ll. 1–16: Primo itaque certum est corpora—motion of hyle in *NO* (2O3$^{r–v}$ (*SEH*, I, p. 332)) and *DAS* (X4^v (*SEH*, I, p. 561)) is the fourth not the fifth motion (their fifth is motion of continuity). In *ANN* motion of hyle is the first of four motions by which bodies seek to improve their situation. In *NO* this motion is seen as a kind of converse ('Motus Antistrophus') of motion of liberty; for example, that air stretched by suction will not try to spring back when heated, and that water subjected to cold will condense and, in caves, even become crystalline and not wish to return to its original state. Also see *HDR*, C6^r, p. 86, ll. 14–18 above; *PhU*, O11$^{r–v}$ (*OFB*, VI, p. 12, ll. 4–10).

fos. 29^v–30^r

Page 194, ll. 17–36: Corpora appetunt coniungi cum globis—motion of the major congregation also comes sixth in *DAS* (X4^v (*SEH*, I, p. 561)) but seventh in *NO* (2O4^v (*SEH*, p. 334)). Not only does *NO* have an extra motion (of gain or want) in sixth place (*ibid.*, 2O4$^{r–v}$ (*SEH*, pp. 333–4)), but it establishes the magnetic motion (conflated with motion of the major congregation in *ANN*) as a motion (the ninth) in its own right as a kind of intermediate and imperfect congregative motion ('Media & imperfecta') between the major and the minor congregations (*ibid.*, 2P3ʳ (*SEH*, p. 337)). For magnetic motions see *cmt* (this page) on *ANN*, p. 194, ll. 27–34 above. For Bacon and the scholastic view of natural motion see *NO*, II ʳ (*SEH*, I, p. 177). On 'natural' rectilinear motion (motion towards connatural bodies) as an intermediate state between circular motion and stasis see *DGI*, FI ʳ (*OFB*, VI, p. 138); *NO*, 2GI ᵛ–2G2ʳ, 2Q3 ᵛ–2Q4ʳ (*SEH*, I, pp. 291, 344–5).

fo. 30ʳ

Page 194, l. 20: Orbis virtutis—for William Gilbert's idea of the orb of virtue see *De mundo*, pp. 47–8, 56–7, 61. Bacon liked the idea; see *DGI*, FII ʳ (*OFB*, VI, p. 156, ll. 20–9); *DAS*, Q3ʳ, 2K2ᵛ (*SEH*, pp. 526, 637–8); *NO*, 2G2ᵛ–2G3ʳ, 2H3 ʳ⁻ᵛ (*SEH*, I, pp. 292–3, 298–9).

l. 21: exules repatriari gaudent—cf. *DGI*, E2ᵛ (*OFB*, VI, p. 118, ll. 26–9).

ll. 27–34: motum magneticum magnum—in *NO* this is a separate species of motion (see *cmt* (this page) on *ANN*, p. 194, ll. 17–36 above). Magnetic motions are elsewhere numbered amongst those *TC* calls mutual motions ('motus ad invicem'), see *OFB*, VI, pp. 184 ff., 411–13. Bacon's wording suggests what was in fact the case, i.e. that he did not himself believe that the Moon's influence was a cause of most tidal motions (in particular, the sexhorary), though he was convinced that the magnetic motion held Mercury close to the Sun. For these phenomena and their causes see *OFB*, *loc. cit.*); also see *NO*, 2M3ᵛ (*SEH*, I, pp. 321–2). It should be noted that these motions do *not* seem to comprise phenomena associated with the loadstone (see *cmts* on fo. 30ᵛ below).

Page 196, ll. 1–13: At particulares & proprias corporum amicitias—motion of the minor congregation is also seventh in order in *DAS* (X4ᵛ (*SEH*, I, p. 561)). In *NO* (2PI ʳ–2P3ʳ (*SEH*, I, pp. 334–7)) it is the eighth. According to *NO*, it takes place within bodies when like parts of a composite body desert their mixture and come together, as when the parts of blood and urine separate out on cooling; the motion also takes place *between* bodies as when iron is drawn to the loadstone, and quicksilver to gold. Bacon varies his terminology: he appropriates the Empedoclean language of strife and friendship, and the natural-magical language of sympathy and antipathy. For the former see *NO*, H2ᵛ (*SEH*, I, p. 174); *DPAO*, LI2 ʳ⁻ᵛ and *cmt* thereon (*OFB*, VI, p. 248, ll. 4–8, p. 430). For the latter, and Bacon's extreme distrust of much talk about sympathies and antipathies see *NO*, 2EI ᵛ (*SEH*, I, p. 280): 'Verùm in his omninò est adhibenda Cautio grauis, & seuera; vt accipiantur pro *Instantijs Conformibus & Proportionatis*, illæ quæ denotant Similitudines (vt ab initio diximus) Physicas; id est, reales & substantiales, & immersus in Naturâ; non fortuitas & ad speciem; multò minùs superstitiosas aut curiosas, quales Naturalis Magiæ scriptores (homines leuissimi, & in rebus tam serijs, quales nunc agimus, vix nominandi) vbique ostentant; magnâ cum vanitate & desipientiâ, inanes Similitudines & Sympathias rerum describentes, atque etiam quandoque affingentes.' Also see *NO*, 2T3ᵛ (*SEH*, I, p. 361): 'At Interiores Corporum Consensus & Fugæ, siue Amicitiæ & Lites (tædet enim nos fere vocabulorum Sympathiæ

& Antipathiæ, propter Superstitiones & inania) aut falsò Ascriptæ, aut Fabulis conspersæ, aut per neglectum Raræ admodùm sunt.' The strictures entered in the preface to the projected *Historia sympathiæ, & antipathiæ rerum* (S2ᵛ–S4ᵛ (*SEH*, II, p. 81)) are just as severe.

fo. 30ᵛ

Page 196, ll. 14–21: Videtur autem inesse—motion of disposition also stands eighth in *DAS*. In *NO* it stands in fourteenth place and is called motus configurationis. In *NO* (2Q2ᵛ–2Q3ʳ (*SEH*, I, pp. 342–3)) the position of the poles of the heavens is referred to this motion; the reason why the poles are positioned as they are is unknown but Bacon thinks their position arises 'ex quadam Harmonia & Consensu Mundi', a certain harmony or consent of the world, which deserves investigation; also referred to this motion are 'Verticitas, & Directio, & Declinatio Magnetis', i.e. the motions other than the attractive motion (which is an instance of motion of the minor congregation).

ll. 22–6: Neque vero dotauit—here Bacon opens his account of the third of the four groups of simple motions, the group comprising those by which bodies impose themselves on others.

Page 196, l. 27–p. 198, l. 3: Inuenitur in corporibus—motion of assimilation, the eleventh in *NO* (2P4ʳ–2Q1ʳ (*SEH*, I, pp. 339–40)), comprises not just the generation of organs from food in plant and animal bodies but also the conversion of oil into flame and water into air, and the generation of inanimate spirit through its conversion of tangible matter into itself.

fos. 30ᵛ–31ʳ

Page 198, ll. 4–13: Neque vero assimilant—motion of excitation is also the tenth in order in *DAS* (X4ᵛ (*SEH*, I, p. 561)). In *NO* (2Q1ʳ⁻ᵛ (*SEH*, I, pp. 340–1)) is the twelfth and, we are told, it differs from motion of assimilation in that it transmits or increases virtues (virtutes) not substances, e.g. in the communication of heat from one body to another, or of magnetism from loadstone to iron where the iron's gain is not the loadstone's loss.

fo. 31ʳ

Page 198, ll. 14–23: At in motu—motion of impression is also eleventh in order in *DAS* (X4ᵛ (*SEH*, I, p. 561)). It is thirteenth in *NO* (2Q1ᵛ–2Q2ᵛ (*SEH*, I, pp. 341–2)), where Bacon also differentiates this from motions of assimilation and excitation. The latter pair are motions of Jove because something remains once the motion ceases; but motion of impression is a motion of Saturn for it is swallowed up at birth, i.e. once the cause is removed nothing remains.

ll. 24–30: Admoniti autem contemplatione—media of motions do not figure on the *DAS* list (X4ᵛ (*SEH*, I, p. 561)), but according to *NO* (2Q3ʳ (*SEH*, I, p. 343)), 'Sit Motus decimus quintus, *Motus Pertransitionis*, siue *Motus secundùm Meatus*; per quem Virtutes Corporum magis aut minùs impediuntur, aut prouehuntur à Medijs ipsorum, pro Naturâ Corporum & Virtutum Operantium,

atque etiam Medij. Aliud enim Medium Luci conuenit, aliud Sono, aliud Calori
& Frigori, aliud Virtutibus Magneticis, necnon alijs nonnullis respectiuè.'

Page 200, ll. 1–6: Atque de corporum appetitu—prefatory remarks to the last
of the four groups of four simple motions, motions manifested by bodies enjoy-
ing their own nature.

fo. 31^{r-v}

Page 200, ll. 6–15: Atque primo, cum corpora—royal motion is twelfth on
DAS list (X4^v–Y1^r (*SEH*, I, p. 561)) and thirteenth in *ANN*. In *NO* (2Q3^{r-v}
(*SEH*, I, p. 344)) this motion, the sixteenth, is especially apparent in 'Spiritibus
Animalium, qui Motus omnes partium reliquarum . . . contemperat', and in
spirits when they prevent the parts of blood separating out. In bodies without
a powerful spirit it is the grosser parts which exercise royal motion and so resist
transformation of the bodies in question. Also see *DVM*, fos. 9^v and 14^r (*OFB*,
VI, p. 294, ll. 16–27, p. 312, ll. 5–15). On fo. 14^r Bacon actually uses the language of the later works: in certain bodies the spirits hold 'dominatum quasí
regium'.

fo. 31^v

Page 200, ll. 16–25: Corpora vero—motion of spontaneous rotation is the thirteenth on the *DAS* list (Y1^r (*SEH*, I, p. 561)) and seventeenth in *NO*. In *NO*
(2Q3^v–2Q4^r (*SEH*, I, p. 344–5)) this is the motion of the heavenly bodies,
though Bacon adds that it may also descend to the air and waters, by which of
course he means the wind and tidal motions which he habitually regarded as
participating in the great cosmic motion. For a full account of this see *OFB*, VI,
pp. xxxvii–liii.

ll. 26–31: Huic subiungitur inquisitio—motion of repose is the fifteenth on
DAS list (Y1^r (*SEH*, I, p. 561)). In *NO* (2Q4^v–2R1^r (*SEH*, I, p. 346)) it is the nineteenth and last motion to be discussed. There Bacon states (albeit obliquely)
that this motion (or lack of it) prevails in the absolute stasis of the bowels of the
Earth. For the Earth's innards see *cmts* (p. 273 above) on *HDR*, A8^{r-v} (p. 50,
ll. 15–30 above).

fos. 31^v–32^r

Page 202, ll. 1–7: Inter hos duos motus—motion of trepidation is the fourteenth
on the *DAS* list (Y1^r (*SEH*, I, p. 561)), and eighteenth in *NO*. This motion is that
of heart and pulse and not, as *NO* (2Q4^v (*SEH*, I, p. 345–6)) points out, the
astronomical motion of the same name, by which Bacon meant (whether he
knew it or not) the one which some medieval astronomers, following Thābit ibn
Qurra (836–901), had attributed to the eighth sphere of the Aristotelian universe. According to this hypothesis, the equinoxes did not precess but oscillated
about an average position. See B. R. Goldstein, 'On the theory of trepidation',
Centaurus, 10, 1964, pp. 232–47.

fo. 32ʳ

Page 202, ll. 9–12: Ii autem coniuncti—cf. *DAS*, Y1ʳ (*SEH*, I, p. 561): 'Huiusmodi sunt *Motus Simplices*, qui ex Penetralibus Naturæ verè prodeunt; quíque Complicati, Continuati, Alternati, Frænati, Repetiti, & multis modis aggregati, *Motus* illos *Compositos*, siue *Summas Motuum*, quæ receptæ sunt, aut illis similes constituunt. *Summæ Motuum*, sunt decantati illi Motus, *Generatio*; *Corruptio*; *Augmentatio*; *Diminutio*; *Alteratio*, & *Latio*; Etiàm *Mixtio*, *Separatio*; *Versio.*'

ll. 13–19: Transeundum itaque—see *NO*, H4ᵛ–I1ʳ (*SEH*, I, p. 177): 'Sed multò adhuc maiore cum malo fit, quòd quiescentia rerum principia, *ex quibus*; & non mouentia, *per quæ*, res fiunt, contemplentur & inquirant. Illa enim ad sermones, ista ad opera spectant. Neq*ue* enim vulgares illæ differentiæ Motûs, quæ in Naturali Philosophiâ receptâ notantur, *Generationis, Corruptionis, Augmentationis, Diminutionis, Alterationis*, & *Lationis*, vllius sunt pretij. Quippè hoc sibi volunt; Si corpus, aliàs non mutatum, loco tamen moueatur, hoc *Lationem* esse; si manente & loco, & specie, qualitate mutetur, hoc *Alterationem* esse; si verò ex illâ mutatione moles ipsa, & quantitas corporis non eadem maneat, hoc Augmentationis & Diminutionis motum esse; si eatenùs mutentur, vt speciem ipsam & substantiam mutent, & in alia migrent, hoc Generationem & Corruptionem esse. At ista merè popularia sunt, & nullo modo in Naturam penetrant; suntque mensuræ & periodi tantùm, non species motûs. Innuunt enim illud, *Hucusque*, & non, *Quomodò*, vel *Ex quo fonte*. Neque enim de corporum appetitu, aut de partium eorum processu, aliquid significant; sed tantùm quùm motus ille rem aliter ac priùs, crasso modo, sensui exhibeat, inde diuisionem suam auspicantur. Etiam quùm de causis motuum aliquid significare volunt, atque diuisionem ex illis instituere, differentiam motûs naturalis & violenti, maximâ cum socordiâ, introducunt; quæ & ipsa omninò ex notione vulgari est; cùm omnis motus violentus etiam naturalis reuerà sit, scilicet cùm externum efficiens naturam alio modo in opere ponet, quàm quo priùs.' In Aristotle's *Categoriae*, 12–14 (14ᵇ–15ᵇ) six species of motion are identified and listed (in Ioannes Argyropulos' Latin translation) thus: 'Motus species sunt sex: generatio, corruptio, accretio, decretio, alteratio & ea mutatio quæ loco accommodatur.' Aristotle makes a point of saying that alteratio (change of quality) is different from other motions in that it does not strictly speaking have a contrary. For a discussion of this topic in late scholasticism see Des Chene, *Physiologia*, pp. 25–7. Also see H. C. Castanæus (*Celebriorvm distinctionvm tvm philosophicarvm tvm theologicarvm synopsis*, London, 1617, K4ᵛ), who lists six kinds: generatio, corruptio, augmentatio, diminutio, alteratio ('quæ terminatur ad QVALITATEM') and latio or motus ('qui terminatur ad VBI'). *DAS* (Y1ʳ (*SEH*, p. 561)) lists these species of motion but adds one or two on Bacon's own account. Also see *CDNR*, R8ʳ–R9ʳ (*SEH*, III, pp. 19–21). In *De anima*, I. 3 (406ᵃ) Aristotle mentions only four species, generation and corruption being omitted.

ll. 21–5: Primo igitur inquiramus—what Bacon probably has in mind are aspects of other sums mentioned in *ANN* and perhaps, in particular, the phenomena of disintegration wrought by the action of inanimate spirit on tangible matter (see *cmts* immediately below).

l. 26–p. 204, l. 3: Separatio corporum—see *cmt* (p. 315–16 above) on *ANN*, fo. 30ʳ (p. 196, ll. 1–13). Also see *DVM*, fos. 13ᵛ–15ʳ (*OFB*, VI, p. 310, l. 30–p. 314, l. 26).

fo. 32ᵛ

Page 204, ll. 4–17: At compositio & mixtura—as well as mechanical mixtures Bacon seems (among other things) to have been thinking of the incorporation of metals etc. in strong waters, see *HDR*, D7ᵛ–E1ʳ (p. 108, l. 27–p. 114, l. 13 above). For other kinds of composition see *NO*, 2T4ʳ (*SEH*, I, p. 362).

Page 204, ll. 12–13: Mixtionem autem quatuor elementorum—Bacon was very critical of Aristotelian element theory but this is one of the few places in which he attacks this aspect of it, but see *NO*, H4ʳ (*SEH*, I, p. 176): 'Inficitur autem Intellectus humanus ex intuitu eorum, quæ in Artibus Mechanicis fiunt, in quibus corpora per compositiones aut separationes vt plurimùm alterantur; vt cogitet simile quiddam etiam in naturâ rerum vniuersali fieri. Vndè fluxit commentum illud Elementorum, atque illorum concursu, ad constituenda corpora naturalia.' Also see *CV*, fo. 257ʳ (*SEH*, III, p. 604): 'Aristotelis de quatuor elementis Commentum, cui ipse potius aucthoritatem quam principium dedit (quod avidé á Medicis acceptum quatuor complexionum, quatuor humorum, et quatuor primarum qualitatum conjugationes post se traxit), tanquàm malignum aliquod et infaustum sydus infinitam et Medicinæ, nec non compluribus Mechanicis rebus sterilitatem attulisse; dum homines per hujusmodj concinnitates, et compendiosas ineptias, sibj satisfierj patientes, nil ampliùs curant.' For a learned and comprehensive attack on scholastic element and mixtion theory—an attack almost certainly read by Bacon—see Tommaso Campanella, *Philosophia sensibus demonstrata*, ed. Luigi De Franco, Vivarium: Naples, 1992, pp. 597–628.

ll. 18–25: A disordinatione—for putrefaction as a rudiment of generation see *HDR*, p. 80, l. 32–p. 82–l. 6 and *cmts* thereon (p. 281 above); *ANN*, fo. 27ᵛ (p. 186, ll. 16–22) and *cmts* thereon (pp. 311–12 above); also see *HIDA*, fos. 3ᵛ–4ᵛ (p. 228, l. 22–p. 230, l. 30) and *cmts* thereon (pp. 327–9 below). For the superinduction of new forms see, for instance, *NO*, S3ʳ, S4ᵛ (*SEH*, I, pp. 227, 229).

fos. 32ᵛ–33ʳ

Page 204, ll. 26–33: Iam vero sequitur—for Bacon's theory of the generation of living beings see *ANN*, p. 186, l. 23–p. 188, l. 16 above and *cmts* thereon (p. 312 above); *HIDA*, pp. 228–30 above; also see *OFB*, VI, pp. liv ff.

fo. 33ʳ

Page 206, ll. 1–9: Huic summæ generationis—it is not clear how this sum differs from putrefaction except where it is extended to take in metals. For mortification of metals see *HDR*, E7^{r-v} (p. 128, l. 28–p. 130, l. 6 above). For Aristotle on corruption and how it differs from alteration see *De generatione et corruptione*, I. 1–2 (314^a–315^b).

fo. 33^{r-v}

Page 206, ll. 10–32: Inter terminos generationis—Bacon apologizes for including this here perhaps in part because conservation is not numbered among the motions recognized by Aristotle (see *cmt* (p. 318) on p. 202, ll. 13–19 above). Conservation of bodies, and in particular the prolongation of human life were among the chief aims of Bacon's philosophy (see *OFB*, VI, pp. lvi–lxix), and close examination of methods of alimentation (ll. 22–32) was an important aspect of his proposals for prolonging life (see, for instance, *HVM*, 2F1^v–2F2^v (*SEH*, II, p. 222)).

fo. 33^v

Page 208, ll. 1–10: Sequitur summa augmentationis—for various aspects of Bacon's thinking about augmentation see, for instance, *HDR*, C1^r–C5^r (pp. 72–84 above). The sort of diminution Bacon has in mind here is that resulting from the action of inanimate spirit, see *NO*, 2K3^r–2K4^r (*SEH*, I, pp. 310–11); *OFB*, VI, pp. lix–lxv.

ll. 12–21: Visum est autem hoc loco—for the term metaschematismus see *HDR*, D4^v, p. 102, l. 20 above and *cmts* thereon (p. 228 above). Note that here Bacon seems to be using the term to take in a kind of local motion distinguished later in *ANN* (see p. 208, l. 29–p. 210, l. 5 above).

fo. 34^r:

Page 208, ll. 22–9: Iam vero deuenit—alteration for Bacon is a catch-all; for Aristotle's more restricted definitions, see *De generatione et corruptione*, I. 1–2 (314^a–315^b); *Categoriae*, 12–14 (14^b–15^b).

l. 29–p. 210, l. 11: Superest summa—as *PAH* (b3^v–b4^r (*SEH*, I, p. 399)) points out, local motion is the key to the mechanical arts. For local motion within bodies see *cmt* (p. 320 above) on p. 208, ll. 12–21 above; and cf. *NO*, T2^v–T3^r (*SEH*, I, pp. 232–3): 'Neque hîc rursùs, hæc tantùm in generatione aut transformatione Corporum quærenda sunt; sed & in omnibus alijs alterationibus, & Motibus, similitèr inquirendum, quid antecedat, quid succedat; quid sit incitatius, quid remissius; quid Motum præbeat, quid regat; & huiusmodi. Ista verò omnia Scientijs (quæ nunc pinguissimâ Mineruâ, & prorsùs inhabili contexuntur) incognita sunt & intacta. Cùm enim omnis Actio naturalis per minima transigatur, aut saltèm per illa quæ sunt minora, quàm vt sensum feriant, nemo se Naturam regere aut vertere posse speret, nisi illa debito modo comprehenderit, & notauerit.'

Page 210, ll. 12–16: Postquam vero iam de motibus simplicibus—here begins the list of measures of motions, measures which, according to *DAS* (Y1^r (*SEH*, I, p. 561)), constitute the fourth and final part of abstract physics and an appendix to the other three, i.e. those concerned with schematisms, simple motions and

sums of motions. The fact that these measures are seen as an appendix is consistent with the positioning of mathematics in general in *DAS* (2A1^{r-v} (*SEH*, I,
pp. 576–7)) as an appendix to physics and metaphysics and their operative coun-
terparts, mechanics and magic. *ANN* lists six titles concerned with measures,
and so does *DAS* (Y1^r (*SEH*, I, p. 561)), though it omits mensura vinculi and
divides the mensura temporis of *ANN* in two thus: 'Quid possint *Incitatio* &
Tarditas? Quid breuis aut longa *Mora?*' In *NO* (2M2^v–2O1^v (*SEH*, I, pp.
320–9)), four of the measures mentioned in *ANN*—quantity, distance, time and
strength—are examined in detail in consecutive aphorisms; these four form a
special group among the *Instantias Practicas*, a group called *Instantias
Mathematicas* or *Instantias Mensuræ*. For the connection between mathematics
and practice see next *cmt*.

fo. 34^{r-v}
Page 210, ll. 16–19: accedendum propius ad mathematica—for Bacon's view of
the relationship between mathematics and natural philosophy and on mathematics as a bridge between theory and practice see Graham Rees, 'Quantitative
reasoning in Francis Bacon's natural philosophy', *Nouvelles de la république des
lettres*, 1985, pp. 27–48; *idem*, 'Mathematics and Francis Bacon's natural philosophy', *Revue internationale de philosophie*, **159**, fasc. 4, 1986, pp. 399–426. For
Bacon's last extended remarks on mathematics—written in the same period as
ANN—see *DAS*, 2A1^r–2A2^r (*SEH*, I, pp. 576–8).

Fo. 34^v
Page 210, ll. 19–23: de mensura quanti—in *NO* (2N4^v–2O1^r (*SEH*, I, p. 329))
Bacon holds that the virtues of bodies vary as the quantity of the bodies varies:
water in the oceans ebbs and flows but virtually no such effect is observable in
rivers; wine and beer mature more quickly in small rather than large containers;
a fragment of a loadstone will not draw as much iron as a whole one, etc. Where
possible measurement is to be made definite, e.g. common sense suggests that
two ounces of lead fall twice as fast as one ounce but that is not the case, and
accurate measurements will have to be made to determine what actually happens.

    ll. 24–9: Quoniam vero quantitas—it is not at all clear what Bacon means by
measure of bonding, and it may be that it is a make-weight introduced to bring
the number of inquiries listed by the end of the treatment of measures of motion
up to sixty; after all *DAS* does not mention this measure (Y1^r (*SEH*, I, p. 561)).
All the same, this measure may have something to do with a state of affairs mentioned in *DVM* (fo. 14^v (*OFB*, VI, p. 313)): 'In consistent bodies things are different, for the bond which keeps unlike particles together consists in the very
structure, strong and close as it is, of the grosser parts which 'so' dread motion
'that', though joined with dissimilar bodies, they are more content to stay as they
are than to set themselves in motion so as to enjoy the company of similar
bodies.'

Page 210, l. 30–p. 212, l. 5: de mensura spatij—in *NO* (2M3ʳ–2N2ʳ (*SEH*, I, pp. 321–23)) these are called *Instantias Virgæ* and are concerned with the distances over which virtues operate—from no distance at all (where a virtue is communicated by contact alone) to the measurement of the sphere of influence of amber and loadstone (short-distance effects) and to cosmic magnetic effects (long-distance effects). For cosmic magnetic effects see *cmt* (p. 315 above) on *ANN*, fo. 30ʳ, p. 194, ll. 27–34.

Page 212, ll. 6–11: de mensura temporis—in *NO* (2N2ʳ–2N4ʳ (*SEH*, I, pp. 325–9)) Bacon gives a range of examples, from the timing of the motions of the heavens to the minimum time needed for the eye to register motion.

fos. 34ᵛ–35ʳ
Page 212, ll. 12–19: de mensura fortitudinis—in *NO* (2O1ʳ–2R2ᵛ (*SEH*, I, pp. 330–49)) discussion of this measure consists of a treatment of the simple motions which prepares the way for an account (2R1ʳ–2R2ᵛ) of what Bacon calls '*Prædominantias* Virtutum' or '*Instantias Luctæ*'. This account gives us instances in which various of the simple motions predominate over others.

fo. 35ʳ
Page 212, ll. 20–6: Quoniam vero fortitudo—Stimulus Peristaseos is the last of the measures mentioned in *DAS* (Y1ʳ (*SEH*, I, p. 561)). A principal concern here is no doubt with the effect of ambient bodies on the operations of the internal, inanimate spirits trapped in all tangible bodies. For these operations see, for example, *DVM*, fos. 7ᵛ–8ᵛ, 19ʳ⁻ᵛ (*OFB*, VI, pp. 286–90, 326–30).

Page 212, l. 27–p. 214, l. 15: Atque inquisitiones—for the broad signification Bacon gave to perception and how he differentiated it from sensation see *DAS*, F2ᵛ–F3ʳ (*SEH*, I, pp. 610–11). Here the term perception is used in (for Bacon) a restricted sense to denote the involuntary reactions of vital spirit which conduct impressions to the brain and its faculties. Reductive experiments are presumably those 'Instantias Deductorias' which belong among the Evoking Instances which 'deducunt Non-Sensibile ad Sensibile' (*NO*, 2K2ʳ, 2K4ʳ (*SEH*, I, pp. 309, 310)). Bacon wrote very little about the individual senses, but for vision and hearing see *HSA*, G8ʳ–K1ʳ (*SEH*, III, pp. 658–80); *SS*, K1ᵛ–K3ᵛ (*SEH*, II, pp. 428–33). Bacon saw taste as an interior sense of smell coupled with a kind of refined sense of touch (*NO*, 2D3ʳ (*SEH*, I, pp. 276–7)). Also see *SS*, F2ᵛ (*SEH*, II, p. 389)): 'the *Sense of Hearing* striketh the *Spirits* more immediatly, than the other *Senses*; And more incorporeally than the *Smelling*. For the *Sight, Taste*, and *Feeling*, haue their Organs, not of so present and immediate Accesse to the *Spirits*, as the *Hearing* hath. And as for the *Smelling*, (which indeed worketh also immediatly vpon the *Spirits*, and is forcible while the Obiect remaineth,) it is with a Communication of the Breath, or Vapour of the *Obiect Odorate*: but *Harmony* entring easily, and Mingling not at all, and Comming with a manifest Motion; doth by Custome of often Affecting the *Spirits*, and Putting them into one kinde of Posture, alter not a little the Nature of the *Spirits*, euen when the

Obiect is remoued.' Histories of the particular senses and their objects are listed in the same order in the catalogue of histories appended to *PAH* (d4ᵛ (*SEH*, I, pp. 408–9)).

fo. 35ᵛ

Page 214, l. 16–p. 216, l. 6: Massæ majores–these are not abstract natures of the kind dealt with elsewhere in *ANN* but actual bodies of matter. The six inquiries listed here cover matters dealt with in three of the five departments of History of Generations in *DGI* and *PAH*. According to *DGI* (D8ᵛ–D9ʳ (*OFB*, VI, p. 109)): 'I establish five parts of the History of *Generations* or *Nature uncon-strained*: these are the History of the *Ether*, the History of *Meteors* and what are known as the *Regions of the Air* . . . In the third place comes the History of the *Earth and Sea*, which together form a single globe. Now up to this point I have distributed the nature of things according to places and objects set in their places; but the last two parts distinguish the substances of things, or rather their masses. For connatural bodies are grouped together into greater and lesser masses, which I usually call Greater and Lesser *Colleges of Things* and, in the polity of the world, they are related to each other as tribes and families. Thus I place the History of Elements or of the greater *Colleges* fourth in order, and fifth and last the History of *Species* or of the lesser *Colleges*. For I mean the elements to be understood not as the beginnings of things, but only as the greater masses of connatural bodies. Now that greatness comes from the texture of their mat-ter being easy, simple, obvious and prepared; whereas species are supplied spar-ingly by nature because their texture is dissimilar and very often organic.' *PAH* (b2ᵛ (*SEH*, I, pp. 397–8)) follows *DGI* closely, for instance, 'Quarta, Elementorum (quæ vocant) Flammæ, siue Ignis, Aëris, Aquæ, & Terræ. Elementa autem eo sensu accipi volumus, vt intelligantur non pro Primordijs Rerum, sed pro Corporum Naturalium Massis Maioribus. Ita enim Natura Rerum distribuitur, vt sit quorundam Corporum Quantitas siue Massa in Vniuerso perquàm Magna; quia scilicèt ad Schematismum eorum requiritur Textura Materiæ facilis & obuia; qualia sunt ea quatuor (quæ diximus) Corpora'. As he intimates here, Bacon did not of course accept Aristotelian element theory, see *cmts* (pp. 272, 277 above) on *HDR*, p. 48, l. 17–p. 50, l. 2; p. 70, ll. 19–23 above.

Page 216, ll. 7–11: Conditiones Entium—according to *AL* (2E4ᵛ–2F1ʳ, 2G1ᵛ (*OFB*, IV, pp. 76–8, 82)) and *DAS* (T1ʳ, T2ʳ–T3ʳ (*SEH*, I, pp. 540, 543–4)), the study of these constitutes one of two branches of philosophia prima, the other branch being concerned with axioms belonging to more than one science. Philosophia prima is not first philosophy in the Aristotelian or late scholastic sense (i.e. metaphysics). Nor do the transcendental properties of reality form part of the subject-matter of the first philosophy as they did for the Iberian scholastics, see Charles H. Lohr, 'The Aristotelian division of the speculative sci-ences', in *The shapes of knowledge from the Renaissance to the Enlightenment*, ed. D. R. Kelley and R. H. Popkin (Archives Internationales d'Histoire des Idées

124), Kluwer Academic Publishers: Dordrecht, Boston, and London, 1991, pp. 49–58, pp. 53–5; also see *CHRP*, p. 607 and *passim*). According to *AL* and *DAS* (see references above), the conditions of beings (being, non-being; much, little; like, unlike; possible, impossible) should be handled in a new way. For if people 'had considered *Quantitie, Similitude, Diuersitie,* and the rest of those *Externe Characters* of things, as *Philosophers*, and in Nature: their inquiries must of force haue beene of a farre other kinde then they are. For doth anie of them, in handeling Quantitie, speake of the force of vnion, how, and how farre it multiplieth vertue? Doth any giue the reason, why some things in Nature are so common and in so great Masse, and others so rare, and in so small quantitie? Doth anie in handling Similitude and Diuersitie, assigne the cause why Iron should not mooue to Iron, which is more like, but mooue to the Loadestone, which is lesse like? why in all Diuersities of things there should bee certain Participles in Nature, which are almost ambiguous, to which kind they should bee referred? But there is a meere and deepe silence, touching the Nature and operation of those *Common adiuncts* of things, as in Nature; and onely a resuming and repeating of the force and vse of them in speeche or argument.' In short (*DAS*, T2ᵛ (*SEH*, I, p. 544)), 'Quamobrem horum *Transcendentium,* siue *Conditionum Entium aduentitiarum* Inquisitionem veram, & solidam, secundum Naturæ non Sermonis leges, *Philosophiam Primam* recipere volumus.'

Page 216, ll. 11–20: Primo igitur cum optime obseruatum fuerit a Democrito—Gemelli notes no source for Democritus' remark, but believes that indiuiduorum may be atoms or types of atom, see *Aspetti dell'atomismo . . . di Francis Bacon*, pp. 146–7 n. 25. As for being and non-being, Bacon discusses this matter in *NO* (2F3ᵛ–2F4ʳ (*SEH*, I, p. 288)) where, speaking of 'fixed' or 'universal' propositions, he advises that if no universal affirmative or negative exists, that lack should be recorded as a Non-Ens—as, for instance, in the case of heat there is no body which lacks it or, in the case of incorruptibility, there is no body in our neck of the woods which has it. He adds that universal propositions should be subjoined to any concrete body that seems to come nearest to non-being—as in the case of heat, the softest and gentlest flames and, in the case of incorruptibility, gold, which comes closest to it. Such things mark out the boundaries of Nature 'inter Ens & Non-Ens', and help circumscribe forms by stopping them straying beyond 'the conditions of matter (conditiones Materiæ)'.

fo. 36ʳ

Page 216, ll. 21–4: At possibile—see *DPAO*, M7ʳ (*OFB*, VI, p. 260, ll. 6–12). Also see *NO*, 2E3ᵛ–2E4ʳ (*SEH*, I, p. 283).

Page 218, ll. 3–7: Multum, paucum—cf. *NO*, 2O1ʳ (*SEH*, I, p. 329): 'Denique in omni Inquisitione Naturæ *Quantum* Corporis requiratur ad aliquod Effectum, tanquàm Dosis, notandum; & Cautiones de *Nimis* & *Parùm* aspergendæ.'

ll. 8–12: Durabile & transitorium—see *HVM*, B7ᵛ–C7ᵛ (*SEH*, II, pp. 110–14).

ll. 13–17: Naturale & monstrosum—for this distinction see *PAH*, a4ᵛ (*SEH*, I, p. 395), and *DAS*, L4ʳ⁻ᵛ (*SEH*, I, p. 496).

ll. 18–23: Naturale . . . artificiali—for this distinction see *DGI*, D5ʳ⁻ᵛ (*OFB*, VI, p. 102, ll. 4–24, and p. 384).

fo. 36ᵛ

Page 220, ll. 1–11: Supersunt inquisitiones—here schematismus is used in one of its three senses, viz. to refer to the structure of the universe (cf. *DPAO*, K4ᵛ, K7ᵛ (*OFB*, VI, pp. 212, 216)). For the other two senses see *cmts* (p. 308 above) on *ANN*, fo. 25ʳ (p. 176, ll. 21–3 above). The distinction between substantive and relative natures might, for instance, place spontaneous rotation (see *ANN*, fo. 31ᵛ (p. 200, ll. 16–25 above)) amongst the latter since it takes place only in the heavens.

ll. 12–14: de vicissitudine rerum—see *DPAO*, I11ʳ (*OFB*, VI, p. 100, ll. 19–21). Also see *DAS*, B3ʳ (*SEH*, I, p. 434): '*Omnia Deus condidit, vt vnumquodque pulchrum sit in tempore suo: Mundum quoque ipsum indidit cordi eorum: inuenire tamen Homo non potest opus, quod operatus est Deus, ab initio vsque ad finem. Quibus verbis haud obscurè innuit, Deum fabricatum esse Animum humanum instar speculi, totius Mundi capacem, Eiusque non minùs sitientem, quam oculum Luminis: neque gestientem solùm conspicere varietates, vicissitudinesque Temporum, verùm etiàm perscrutandi, explorandique immotas, atque inuiolabiles Naturæ Leges, & Decreta, ambitiosam.*' Also see the *Ess*, 2V1ʳ–2X2ᵛ (*OFB*, XV, pp. 172–6) for the kinds of events that count as vicissitudes. On Bacon and vicissitude see B. H. G. Wormald, *Francis Bacon: history, politics and science, 1561–1626*, Cambridge University Press: Cambridge, 1993, pp. 68–9, 345–8.

ll. 23 ff.: Norma abecedarij—these are very closely modelled on the norma of *HNE*, see *cmts* below.

fos. 36ᵛ–37ʳ

Page 220, l. 24–p. 222, l. 5: Historiæ & experimenta—the wording at points is almost identical to that in *HNE* (C3ᵛ–C4ᵛ (*SEH*, II, pp. 17–18)). For experiments of light see *HIDA*, fo. 3ʳ (p. 228, ll. 2–3 above); *OFB*, VI, pp. 363–4. For crucial instances see *NO*, 2G3ᵛ–2I3ʳ (*SEH*, I, pp. 294–304). For the meaning of mandata and historia designata see *OFB*, VI, pp. xxiv–xxv.

fo. 37ʳ

Page 222, ll. 6–16: Modum experimenti—the wording here is a shorter form of that found in *HNE* (C4ᵛ–C5ᵛ (*SEH*, II, p. 18)).

ll. 17–22: Denique tentamenta—this has no parallel in *HNE*, and suggests that Bacon was going to go much further into the realms of theory in Part IV of *IM* than in Parts II or III. The modesty formula is typical of most of his general statements about his essays at theoretical speculation, as is the acuteness with which he felt (as the years slipped away) the lack of a reliable stock of natural-historical data.

l. 18: licet prorsus humi—perhaps an echo of Horace, *Epistulae* II. 1. 250–1: 'nec sermones ego mallem | repentis ad humum quam res componere gestas'.

l. 22: initijs rerum non desimus—cf. *NO*, P4ᵛ (*SEH*, I, p. 212): 'Quin nec spem habemus vitæ producendæ, ad sextam *Instaurationis* partem (quæ Philosophiæ, per legitimam Naturæ interpretationem, inuentæ, destinata est) absoluendam; sed satis habemus, si in Medijs sobriè & vtilitèr nos geramus; atque interìm semina veritatis sincerioris in posteros spargamus, atque initijs rerum magnarum non desimus.'

ll. 26–9: Ad vsum—cf. *HNE*, C5ᵛ–C6ʳ (*SEH*, II, p. 18).

fo. 37ᵛ

Page 224, ll. 1–5: Deus vniuersi conditor—this prayer appears in the same words at the end of the general preface to *HNE* (B8ᵛ–C1ʳ (*SEH*, II, p. 16)).

COMMENTARY ON
HISTORIA & INQUISITIO DE ANIMATO
& INANIMATO

fo. 3ʳ

Page 228, l. 1: Historia & Inquisitio—cf. the description of the same inquiry in *ANN* (fos. 27ᵛ–28ʳ, p. 186, l. 23–p. 188, l. 7 above). This is both an historia and an inquisitio; in the norma of *ANN* Bacon explains that in Part IV inquiries 'Historiæ & experimenta' will come in first place (*ibid.*, fo. 36ᵛ, p. 220, ll. 24–7 above).

ll. 2–3: Experimenta Vulgaria absque luciferorum—cf. *ANN*, fo. 37ʳ (p. 222, ll. 1–11 above). Also see *NO*, I3ʳ⁻ᵛ (*SEH*, I, p. 180); *PhU*, O7ʳ⁻ᵛ (*OFB*, VI, p. 4, ll. 14–18).

ll. 8–16: fluido siue liquido—this list is not unlike what Bacon elsewhere called a '*Tabulam declinationis*, siue *Absentiæ in proximo*' (*NO*, V3ʳ (*SEH*, I, p. 239)), i.e. an enumeration of substances or states which lack the nature under investigation but which have a close affinity with it. However, Bacon may have thought of the list here as an exhaustive synopsis of conditions in which by themselves life could never inhere; consequently the notion of 'absence in proximity' would not arise at this point. The qualification (l. 13 f.) to 'Humido merè aqueo' reflects Bacon's belief that all living things embodied oil–water mixtures—hence the non-literal translation of 'sed'.

fo. 3ᵛ

Page 228, ll. 17–20: Quoniam . . . Grandissimis &c.—the slug, oyster and whale are instances corresponding (in order) to the first three items in the preceding list (see *cmt* above), and are instances of what might be called presence in proximity, i.e. of instances exhibiting the nature under investigation (in this case, life) which come closest to natures which cannot support life. Cf. the discussion in *NO*, 2F4ʳ (*SEH*, I, pp. 288–9) of instances of ultimity or limit ('*Vltimitatis* siue *Termini*'); these point out the real divisions of nature and the transitional points between one nature and something else—for instance, gold surpasses everything in weight, the whale exceeds all animals in size, while worms in skin are far smaller than other living things. Also see *SS*, 2G1ʳ (*SEH*, II, p. 622).

ll. 22–3: Videndum . . . de menstruis—see *SS*, 2H2ᵛ–2H3ʳ (*SEH*, II, pp. 638–9): 'Some *Liuing Creatures* are Procreated by *Copulation* betweene *Male*, and *Female*. Some by *Putrefaction* . . . For the *Cause* of both *Generations*: First, it is most certaine, that the *Cause* of all *Viuification*, is a *Gentle* and *Proportionable Heat*, working vpon a *Glutinous* and *Yeelding Substance*: For the *Heat* doth bring forth *Spirit* in that *Substance*: And the *Substance*, being

Glutinous, produceth Two *Effects:* The One, that the *Spirit* is *Detained,* and cannot *Breake forth:* The Other, that the *Matter* being *Gentle,* and *Yeelding,* is driuen forwards by the *Motion* of the *Spirits,* after some *Swelling* into *Shape,* and *Members.* Therefore all *Sperme,* all *Menstruous Substance,* all *Matter,* whereof *Creatures* are produced by *Putrefaction,* haue euermore a *Closenesse, Lentour,* and *Sequacity.* It seemeth therefore, that the *Generation* by *Sperme* onely, and by *Putrefaction,* haue two Different *Causes.* The First is, for that *Creatures,* which haue a *Definite* and *Exact Shape,* (as those haue which are Procreated by *Copulation,*) cannot be produced by a *Weake,* and *Casuall Heat;* Nor out of *Matter,* which is not *exactly Prepared,* according to the *Species.* The Second is, for that there is a greater *Time* required, for *Maturation* of *Perfect Creatures;* For if the *Time* required in *Viuification* be of any length, then the *Spirit* will Exhale, before the *Creature* be *Mature:* Except it be Enclosed in a *Place* where it may haue *Continuance* of the *Heat, Accesse* of some *Nourishment* to maintaine it, and *Closenesse* that may keepe it from *Exhaling.* And such *Places* are the *Wombes,* and *Matrices,* of the *Females.* And therefore all *Creatures,* made of *Putrefaction,* are of more *Vncertaine Shape;* And are made in *Shorter Time;* And need not so Perfect an *Enclosure,* though some *Closenesse* be commonly required.' On the spontaneous generation of worms and other 'imperfect' creatures, see *HDR,* C4^r (p. 80, l. 32–p. 82, l. 7); *SS,* Z2^v f., (*SEH,* II, pp. 557 f.). Also see *NO,* Y2^v, 2K3^r–2K4^r, 2P2^{r-v} (*SEH,* I, pp. 249, 310–11, 336); Rees, 'Francis Bacon's biological ideas', in *Occult and scientific mentalities in the Renaissance,* ed. Brian Vickers, Cambridge University Press: Cambridge and London, 1984, pp. 297–314, pp. 305–7.

fos. 3^v–4^r
Page 230, ll. 3–8: miscendo in vna olla—see *SS,* V2^{r-v} (*SEH,* II, pp. 524–5); also *NO,* 2T3^r (*SEH,* I, p. 360).

fo. 4^r
Page 230, ll. 12–14: Videndum etiam de diuersis generibus muscj—see *cmt* (p. 311 above) on *ANN,* fo. 27^v (p. 186, ll. 16–22 above).

fo. 4^{r-v}
Page 230, ll. 17–28: Loquimur de animalibus—some of the remarks here and their very phrasing are recapitulated in *SS,* Z2^v ff. (*SEH,* II, pp. 557 ff.).

ll. 24–30: Obseruatio autem—*SS,* 2H2^r (*SEH,* II, p. 636): 'For the *Inducing* of *Putrefaction* . . . Try it also with *Holland-Cheese,* hauing *Wine* put into it, whether [it] will breed *Mites* sooner, or greater?'

fo. 4^v
Page 230, ll. 27–8: motus pilorum ex cauda equina—a classic instance of the difficulty of translating a passage if you do not know beforehand, independently of English rendering, what the Latin is driving at. I had no clear idea what 'pilorum' meant (threads? hairy creatures?), save that it referred to animalcules gen-

erated spontaneously. And as for 'cauda', did it mean 'tail', 'penis' or the more general 'rear'? A sampling of Renaissance works on horse medicine yielded no satifactory result. My final translation and this note, both inserted at proof stage, are based on Dr. Maria Wakely's discovery that Bacon is talking about horsehair worms. These cream, brown or black nematomorphoric worms are as thin as pencil leads and up to two feet long. They are also known as gordian worms because they group together in elaborate knots as they wriggle in pools and other freshwater habitats. They were once common in troughs and other places where horses drank, and many believed (Bacon too, apparently) that they were horsehairs, shed from mane or tail, which had taken on a life of their own. I thank Maria for her persistence, but regret that I had no more time to search the Renaissance literature for a possible source or sources. In the meantime, these worms have websites.

fo. 5^r

Page 232, ll. 23–4: Nam pygmeus Paracelsi—see *HDR(M)*, p. 17, l. 16 and *HDR*, p. 102, l. 26 and *cmt* thereon (pp. 288–9 above).

fo. 5^v

Page 232, l. 30–p. 234, l. 2: Videndum similiter in ouis—for materials on the embryology of birds and mammals, materials which Bacon may have had in mind, see *Aldrovandi on chickens: the ornithology of Ulisse Aldrovandi (1600) Volume II, Book XIV*, trans. from the Latin with introduction, contents and notes by L. R. Lind, University of Oklahoma Press: Oklahoma, 1963, pp. 66–124. According to Joseph Needham, Aldrovandi (1522–1605), 'was the first biologist since Aristotle to open the eggs of hens regularly during their incubation period, and to describe in detail the appearances which he found there', see *A history of embryology*, 2nd edn. rev., Cambridge University Press: Cambridge, 1959, p. 100. But more important still was the work of Fabricius ab Aquapendente (*c.*1533–1619), see *The embryological treatises of Hieronymus Fabricius of Aquapendente. The formation of the egg and of the chick [De formatione ovi et pulli]. The formed foetus [De formato foetu], A facsimile edition with an introduction, a translation and a commentary*, ed. H. B. Adelmann, 2 vols., Cornell University Press: Ithaca, 1942; for mammalian (including human foetal development see II, p. 455. *De formatione ovi et pulli* has the first printed illustrations of the development of the chick.

COMMENTARY ON
INQUISITIO DE MAGNETE

K7ᵛ

Page 238, ll. 2–7: *Magnes* trahit pulverem—Bacon was actually working on these experiments towards the end of his life, see *SSWN*, fo. 29ʳ and Graham Rees, 'An unpublished manuscript by Francis Bacon: *Sylva sylvarum* drafts and other working notes', *Annals of Science*, **38**, 1981, pp. 377–412, esp. p. 394. For the making of prepared steel (used, says Gibert, in treatment of spleen and liver disorders) and of crocus martis (essentially prepared steel heat-treated in a reverberatory furnace) see *DM*, C5ʳ–C6ʳ. Also see *cmt* (pp. 274–5 above) on *HDR*, p. 56, ll. 17–19 above. According to *DM* (H4ʳ), crocus martis is not attracted at all by loadstones. As to whether or not dissolved iron can be attracted by a loadstone, this issue is put as a question in *DAS* (2H4ʳ (*SEH*, I, pp. 626–7)): 'Item *Magnes Ferrum integrum* trahit: Nùm etiàm Frustum Magnetis, in Dissolutione Ferri immersum, Ferrum ad se alliciet, & se Ferro obducet?' The issue is not addressed in *DM*. Also see *DAS*, 2I2ʳ (*SEH*, I, p. 630): 'Exemplum *Compulsionis* tale est. *Magnes Ferrum trahit*: Vrge ergò Ferrum, aut vrge Magnetem, vt ampliùs non fiat Attractio: Veluti, nùm fortè si Magnes vstus fuerit, aut in Aquis Fortibus maceratus, virtutem suam deponet, aut saltem remittet? Contrà, si Chalybs, aut Ferrum in Crocum Martis redigantur, vel in Chalybem quem vocant Præparatum, vel etiam in Aquâ Forti soluantur, nùm adhùc ea alliciat Magnes?' Also see *cmt* (this page) on *IDM*, p. 238, ll. 24–5 above.

ll. 8–10: *Magnes* Scobem suum—see *DM*, H3ᵛ–H4ʳ.

ll. 11–13: Pone *Magnetem*—presumably Bacon means that the loadstone should be capped and not that the cap should be placed anywhere in between the iron and the stone; cf. *NO*, 2M2ʳ⁻ᵛ (*SEH*, I, pp. 319–20). Also see *DM*, H1ᵛ–H2ʳ, H5ᵛ–H6ʳ, I4ʳ⁻ᵛ.

ll. 14–15: *Magnes* immissus—according to *DM* (D1ʳ, H5ʳ), aqua fortis (i.e. nitric acid) *reduces* the strength of loadstones, as does oil of vitriol (i.e. strong sulphuric acid).

K8ʳ

Page 238, ll. 16–17: *Magnes* Fricatione—for the amber effect see *DM*, D5ᵛ–E3ʳ.

ll. 18–23: *Magnes* alius alio—*DM*, I4ᵛ: Gilbert tests the strength of a stone with a versorium not by touching with knives. Also see *DM*, H4ᵛ–H5ᵛ.

ll. 24–5: *Magnes* ad æque distans—cf. *DAS*, 2I2ʳ (*SEH*, I, p. 630): 'Exemplum *Compulsionis* tale est . . . *Magnes Ferrum trahit per Vniuersa*, quæ nouimus, *Media*: Nempe si interponatur Aurum, Argentum, Vitrum: Vrge igitur aliquod Medium, si fieri possit, quod Virtutem intercipiat; Probetur Argentum Viuum;

Probentur Oleum, Gummi, Carbo ignitus, & alia, quæ adhùc probata non sunt.' Also see *NO*, 2I4ʳ, 2L4ᵛ (*SEH*, I, pp. 306, 317).

ll. 26–8: *Magnete*, aut pulvere ejus—another experiment that Bacon seems actually to have performed towards the end of his life, see *SSWN*, fo. 29ᵛ and Rees, '*Sylva sylvarum* drafts and other working notes', p. 395. For the consubstantiality of the loadstone and iron see *DM*, C6ᵛ–D2ʳ.

ll. 29–32 *Pulvis Magnetis*—iron touched is iron that has been stroked by a loadstone.

K8ʳ⁻ᵛ

Page 238, l. 33–p. 240, l. 6: *Acus* super planum—it is not clear what Bacon has in mind here. For the legend that adamant (i.e. diamond) restricts the action of a loadstone see *PAH*, cIᵛ (*SEH*, I, p. 401) and Gilbert's attack on the notion in *DM* (AIʳ⁻ᵛ, A3ᵛ–A4ʳ).

K8ᵛ–LIʳ

Page 240, ll. 18–29: *Magnes* combustus—for the effects of fire on loadstones see *DM*, lib. 2, cap. iv, and lib. 3, cap. 3.

ll. 30–3: *Experimentum* factum est—Bacon may well have been to the top of old St Paul's Cathedral (see *SS*, H4ᵛ (*SEH*, II, p. 415)) but I do not know who carried out this experiment.

COMMENTARY ON *TOPICA*
INQVISITIONIS DE LVCE ET LVMINE

X3^{r-v}

Page 244, ll. 5–16: Videndum primò—for these examples see also *NO*, X1^{r-v} (*SEH*, I, pp. 242–3); *DAS*, 2F3^v–2F4^r (*SEH*, I, pp. 612–13): 'Ferrum, Metalla, Lapides, Vitrum, Ligna, Oleum, Seuum, ab Igne, vel Flammam vibrant, vel saltèm rubescunt: At Aqua, Aer, acerrimo & tanquàm furenti Calore feruefacta, nihil tamen *Lucis* adipiscuntur, nec splendent. Quod si quis hoc eò fieri putet, quod proprium sit Ignis *lucere*, Aqua autem & Aer Igni omninò inimica sint; Is sanè nunquàm per Obscura Noctis, in Aquâ salsâ, tempestate calidâ, remigauit; cùm guttulas Aquæ, ex Remorum Concussione subsilientes, micare & lucescere videre potuisset. Quod etiàm fit in Spumâ Maris feruentiore, quam *Pulmonem Marinum* vocant. Quid denique habent commune cum Flammâ & Ignitis, Cicendulæ & Luciolæ; & Musca Indica, quæ Cameram totam illustrat; Et Oculi quorundam Animalium in Tenebris; & Saccharum inter radendum aut frangendum; & Sudor Equi nocte æstuosâ festinantis; & Alia nonnulla? . . . Attamen quando Aer Calore non ignescat, & Lucem manifestò concipiat, quomodò tandem fit, vt Noctuæ, & Feles, & alia nonnulla Animalia, noctù cernant? Adeò vt ipsi Aeri . . . necesse est inesse *Lucem* aliquam Natiuam & genuinam, quamvis tenuem admodùm & infirmam, quæ tamen sit Radijs Visiuis huiusmodi Animalium proportionata, ijsque ad videndum sufficiat.'

X3^v

Page 244, ll. 17–23: ventrale cujusdam fœminæ—on alum and sugar cf. *NO*, X1^r (*SEH*, I, p. 242): 'certissimum est, circa Equum in itinere sudantem, noctù & sudâ tempestate apparuisse quandoque Coruscationem quandam absque manifesto calore. Atque paucis abhinc annis, notissimum est, & pro miraculo quasi habitum, Gremiale cuiusdam Puellæ paulò motum aut fricatum coruscâsse: quod fortassè factum est ob alumen aut sales, quibus gremiale tinctum erat, paulò crassiùs hærentia & incrustata, & ex fricatione fracta. Atque certissimum est, Saccharum omne, siue Conditum (vt vocant) siue simplex, modò sit durius, in tenebris fractum aut cultello scalptum coruscare.' I have not been able to find the source of this story but see Menna Prestwich, *Cranfield: politics and profits under the early Stuarts*, Clarendon Press: Oxford, 1966, pp. 163–4; and A. F. Upton, *Sir Arthur Ingram c.1565–1642: a study of the origins of an English landed family*, Oxford University Press: Oxford, 1961, pp. 106–47. The primary sources for these passages on the scandalous alum monopoly may shed some light on the matter.

Page 246, l. 1: *Tabula absentiæ*—for the function of this class of instance and examples see *NO*, V3^r–X4^v (*SEH*, I, pp. 239–248). Also see *cmt* (p. 327 above) on *HIDA*, p. 228, ll. 8–16 above.

X3ᵛ–X4ʳ

Page 246, ll. 2–11: Videndum etiam—for 'instantibus migrantibus' (p. 246, ll. 7–8) see *NO*, 2C1ᵛ–2C3ʳ (*SEH*, I, pp. 269–71). Bacon here seems to take it for granted that the reader is already acquainted with the terminology of *NO*. For other uses of the examples given here see *NO*, X1ᵛ, Z2ʳ, 2M2ʳ (*SEH*, I, pp. 243, 253, 320).

X4ʳ

Page 246, ll. 12–15: *Tabula graduum*—in *NO* too the tabula graduum comes immediately after the tabula absentiæ; for the function of the former see *NO*, Y1ʳ (*SEH*, I, p. 248). For the examples used here cf. *NO*, X1ʳ, Y4ᵛ, Z1ʳ (*SEH*, I, pp. 242, 251–2).

X4ʳ⁻ᵛ

Page 246, ll. 16–24: *Colores Lucis*—cf. *NO*, 2C1ʳ⁻ᵛ, 2G3ᵛ (*SEH*, I, pp. 269, 293–4): 'Videtur omninò esse diuisio vera & certa, Lucis, quæ est Visibile originale, & primam copiam facit visui; & Coloris, qui est Visibile secundarium, & sine luce non cernitur, ita vt videatur nil aliud esse quàm imago aut modificatio Lucis. Attamen ex vtrâque parte circa hoc videntur esse *Instantiæ Fœderis*; scilicèt, Nix in magnâ quantitate, & Flamma sulphuris; in quarum alterâ videtur esse Color primulùm lucens, in alterâ Lux vergens ad colorem.' On colour also see 2C2ᵛ (*SEH*, I, p. 269). For Telesio on colour see *DRN*, III, pp. 126–38. Telesio's reflections on light in general help us understand Bacon's views. For Telesio on light see Luigi De Franco, 'La teoria della luce di Bernardino Telesio', in *Bernardino Telesio e la cultura napoletana*, ed. Raffaele Sirri and Maurizio Torrini, Guida Editore: Naples, 1992, pp. 53–77.

X4ᵛ

Page 248, ll. 1–8: *Reflexiones Lucis*—Bacon had a particular interest in the possibility that light could be reflected from a lucid body: he believed that the Moon was not a solid, opaque body but a flamy, pneumatic one, but one which could none the less reflect the Sun's light. If solid bodies alone could reflect light then Bacon's whole theory of the heavens would be compromised. On this issue see *NO*, 2H4ʳ⁻ᵛ (*SEH*, I, pp. 300–1) and *OFB*, VI, pp. 400–1 and *cmt* (p. 335 below) on *TDL*, p. 248. ll. 15–17 above.

The reading lucis (l. 7) is from *Sc*; the reading in *Op* (L3ᵛ) is *luminis*. Title apart, *TDL* mentions 'lumen' only once (p. 254, l. 1 below). The lux–lumen distinction has a long history for which see David C. Lindberg, 'The genesis of Kepler's theory of light: light metaphysics from Plotinus to Kepler', *Osiris*, 2nd ser., 2, 1986, pp. 5–42: the distinction was used by Cardan, Scaliger, Patrizi and Gilbert. F. Patrizi writes (*Nova de vniversis philosophia*, Venice, 1593 (the section that attracted Bacon's attention was entitled *Pancosmia*), fos. 73ᵛ–75ʳ)) thus on lux and lumen: 'Quid autem facilius fundi potuit per spacium, quam lumen . . . Lux autem è se lumen emittere, non potest. Neque lumen aliunde, potest emicare, quam a luce. A prima igitur luce, est lumen primum. Et lumen primum est a luce prima, sicuti a secundis lucibus sunt secunda lumina . . . Emicuit ergo a Dei luce, lumen primigeniu*m* . . . Ab vna luce, lumen vnum . . . Gilbert more prosaically but more clearly puts it thus (*De mundo*, p. 214): 'Lvmen ingreditur omne corpus vel opacissimum aliquantulum, quo ingressu fœdatur.

Lux est eadem quæ flamma. vide ignem.

Lumen est lucis effusio, rarefacientis naturæ seu rarescentis humidi extensio seu diffusio, quod rursus recollectum à crasso idipsum attenuat, urit, & in flammam aliquando agit. Non lucent corpora sine flamma.

Quæ in flammis lucent animalcula aut corpora, non lumen habent in summis tenebris, sed tantum splendent in crepusculis, cum lumen in äere evanidum colligunt. Lumen est ens. Lux est actus assurgens ab humore attenuante. Lumen est actus procedens à lucido. Lumen est ens immateriale, effusum à luce, à corpore exceptum. Lumen transit ætherem, nec in eo manit, aut est, à denso & opaco sistitur. Tenebræ sunt luminis privatio. Lux est forma. Lumen est actus procedens a luce.' Cf. Scaliger, *Exotericarvm exercitationvm liber*, pp. 108^r–109^r: 'Nunc aute*m* cu*m* lumen à luce distinximus, ut lux sit qualitas corporis lucidi, lumen sit actus diaphani: uidendu*m* porrò esset, utru*m* lume*n* hoc, sit ipsa lux eade*m* numero, quæ in corpore, & quæ à corpore in diaphano. Quæ lux sese propagat in pellucidu*m*, sicut & color. Id quod appellant recentiores ens reale. An uerò lumen sit illius lucis species, quam recentiores iidem dicunt speciem intentionalem. Quæ non sit eadem numero cum luce, sed à luce, generata: sicuti generata coloris species in pariete uiridis à uiriditate, quæ est in uitro per solariu*m* radiorum transmissionem. Quæ difficultas cùm sit à maximis uiris uentilata, non est hîc argumentorum recitationibus repetenda. Sed dicendum: Lumen esse speciem, id est lucis repræpresentationem. Qualis est uiriditas illa, ab illa uiriditate. Alioquin esset accidens extra subiectum suum. Quippe extra lucidum corpus, in aere. Præterea res cælestis, ac planè diuina identidem generaretur, & corrumperetur. Intercepta nanque obiice quopiam, puta fenestræ clausione, haud amplius apparet. At proecto haud scio, an rerum cælestium ulla sit excellentior ipsa luce. Vt mihi religio sit arbitrari, eam interire posse. Quid uerò sit ea species, & an eadem cum illa, quam repræsentat: suo loco dictum est, ubi agimus de intellectione . . . Qvod uerò scribis [Cardan], lume*n* minus à maiore tegi: de hoc quid sentiamus, & iam diximus aliquid, & hic nonnihil admonendum es. Nihil pati lumen minus à minore. Sed quemadmodum declarabamus, utriusque produci speciem. Nulla enim ratio est quare non producatur. Educitur ergo lumen minus: & recipitur quidem in medium, quan quam à maiore iam illustratum: sed nihil fit noui . . . Non igitur quicquam patitur lumen minus: sed perfectioris perficitur accessione. Sic candelæ lumen non extinguitur à Solis lumine, sed necessitudinis similitudine, atque communione augetur.' For a brief but important discussion of light and lumen and the context in which investigation of the topic should take place see *DAS*, 2F3^r –2F4^r (*SEH*, I, pp. 612–13).

Commentary *on* Topica inquisitionis, *pp. 248-52*

X4ᵛ–X5ʳ

Page 248, ll. 9–13: *Multiplicationes Lucis*—see *SS*, K2ʳ (*SEH*, II, p. 430), and on microscopes and telescopes see *NO*, 2K1ʳ–2K2ʳ (*SEH*, I, pp. 307–8).

X5ʳ

Page 248, ll. 15–17: qua de causa Luna—see *OFB*, VI, pp. 152–4, 176, 254, 408; also see *cmt* (p. 333 above) on *TDL*, p. 248, ll. 1–8 above.

l. 18–p. 250, l. 2: utrum aggregatio corporum—see *NO*, 2C2ᵛ (*SEH*, I, p. 270). Page 250, ll. 3–7: *Modi obruendi*—cf. *NO*, 2H4ᵛ (*SEH*, I, p. 301): 'Sanè radij aperti Solis incidentes in Flammas obscuriores, videntur eas quasi mortificare, vt conspiciantur magis instar Fumi albi, quàm Flammæ . . . Sed notandum semper est, Reflexionem à Flammâ non esse expectandam, nisi à Flammâ alicuius profunditatis; nam alitèr vergit ad Diaphanum. Hoc autem pro certo ponendum, Lucem semper in Corpore æquali, aut excipi & transmitti, aut resilire.'

X5ᵛ

Page 250, ll. 8–10: *effectus lucis*—*SS*, 2G3ᵛ–2G4ʳ (*SEH*, II, p. 630) 'The *Obiects* of the *Sight*, may cause a great *Pleasure* and *Delight* in the *Spirits* . . . The *Glimpses* and *Beames* of *Diamonds* that strike the *Eye*; *Indian Feathers*, that haue glorious Colours; The *Comming* into a *Faire Garden*; The *Comming* into a *Faire Roome* richly furnished; A *Beautifull* Person; And the like; doe delight and exhilarate the *Spirits* much. The *Reason*, why it holdeth not in the *Offence*, is, for that the *Sight* is the most *Spirituall* of the *Senses*; whereby it hath no *Obiect* Grosse enough to offend it. But the *Cause* (chiefly) is, for that there be no *Actiue Obiects* to offend the *Eye*.' For colour as a broken 'imago' of light see *cmt* (p. 333 above) on *TDL*, X4ʳ⁻ᵛ (p. 246, ll. 16–24). Ellis (*SEH*, I, p. 269 n. 1) thought that Bacon used the term imago as an equivalent of the Telesian term species.

Page 2250, ll. 15–20: *Mora Lucis*—see *NO*, 2H4ᵛ (*SEH*, I, p. 300).

X5ᵛ–X6ʳ

Page 250, l. 21–p. 252, l. 6: *Viæ & processus Lucis*—cf. *SS*, K3ʳ (*SEH*, II, pp. 432–3): 'the *Impression* of *Colour* is so weake, as it worketh not but by a Cone of Direct *Beames*, or Right Lines . . . For the *Beames* passe, and giue little Tincture to that Aire, which is Adiacent; which if they did, we should see *Colours* out of a Right line. But as this is in *Colours*, so otherwise it is in the *Body* of *Light*. For when there is a Skreene between the Candle and the Eye, yet the *Light* passeth to the Paper wheron One writeth; So that the *Light* is seene, where the Body of the *Flame* is not seene; And where any *Colour* (if it were placed where the Body of the *Flame* is) would not be seene.' Also see *SS*, I2ᵛ (*SEH*, II, pp. 420–1).

X6ʳ

Page 252, ll. 6–13: Lux, corpora fibrosa & inæqualis posituræ—cf. *NO*, 2C1ᵛ (*SEH*, I, p. 269): 'Album enim & Nigrum Marmoris, & maculæ Albi & Purpurei in floribus Garyophylli, conueniunt ferè in omnibus præter ipsum colorem. Vnde facilè colligitur, Colorem non multum rei habere cum Naturis

335

alicuius corporis intrinsecis, sed tantùm situm esse in Positurâ partium crassiori
& quasi Mechanicâ.' Also see *SS*, F4ᵛ (*SEH*, II, p. 394).

X6ʳ⁻ᵛ

Page 252, ll. 14–21: *Diaphaneitas Lucidorum*—see *NO*, 2C2ʳ⁻ᵛ, 2C4ᵛ, 2H4ᵛ
(*SEH*, I, pp. 270–1, 273, 301).

X6ᵛ–X7ʳ

Page 252, l. 24–p. 254, l. 7: Cognationem maxime—in essence this is an attack
on Telesian theory, cf. the treatment of intances of divorce in *NO* (2I3ᵛ (*SEH*,
I, p. 305)): 'Exempli gratia: sint Naturæ Inquisitæ, quatuor Naturæ illæ, quas
Contubernales vult esse *Telesius*, & tanquàm ex eâdem Camerâ: viz. Calidum,
Lucidum, Tenue, Mobile siue promptum ad Motum. At plurimæ inueniuntur
Instantiæ Diuortij inter ipsas. Aër enim Tenuis est & habilis ad Motum, non
Calidus aut Lucidus: Luna Lucida, absque Calore; Aqua feruens, Calida absque
Lumine; Motus Acûs ferreæ super Versorium, pernix & agilis, & tamen in
Corpore Frigido, Denso, Opaco; & complura id genus.' For the Telesian notion
of the inseparability of these four natures see *DPAO*, K12ᵛ–L1ʳ (*OFB*, VI, pp.
226–8 and (*cmts*) pp. 423–4).

X7ʳ⁻ᵛ

Page 254, l. 10–p. 256, l. 11: In his conveniunt lux—cf. *SS*, H4ʳ, I2ᵛ and esp.
K1ᵛ–K3ᵛ (*SEH*, II, pp. 414, 420–1, 428–33).

COMMENTARY ON *PRODROMI SIVE ANTICIPATIONES PHILOSOPHIÆ SECVNDÆ*

R1ʳ

Page 260, ll. 4–6: Existimamvs eum—cf. *DAS*, D2ʳ (*SEH*, I, pp. 445–6): 'De quo tamen abundè è propriis Fontibus admoneri possunt. Solon enim interrogatus, an optimas Ciuibus suis dedisset Leges? *Optimas*, inquit, *ex illis, quas ipsi voluissent accipere*. Ita Plato, videns corruptiores suorum Ciuium mores, quam vt ipse ferre posset, ab omni publico munere abstinuit, dicens; *Sic cum patriâ agendum esse, vt cum parentibus; hoc est, suasu, non violentiâ; obtestando, non contestando.*' Solon (according to Plutarch) spoke at a time of acute social division between rich and poor in Athens, see *Lives* (Loeb Classical Library) Cambridge, Mass., and London, vol. I, 1914, repr. 1998, pp. 442–3.

R1ᵛ

Page 260, ll. 12–16: Neque enim leges—cf. *PAH*, c3ʳ (*SEH*, I, p. 403).

R2ʳ

Page 260, l. 28–p. 262, l. 1: Sed quemadmodum sagitta—the effect of this analogy stems from the fact that Bacon thought that missiles spun on their axes as they passed through the air; cf. *NO*, 2B2ʳ (*SEH*, I, p. 264): 'sagitta aut spiculum simul & progrediendo rotat, & rotando progreditur.' Also cf. *ibid.*, 2O3ʳ (*SEH*, I, p. 332).

R2ʳ⁻ᵛ

Page 262, ll. 13–14: loco diverticulorum—cf. *DO*, C3ʳ (*SEH*, I, p. 144), where, speaking of the contents of Part V of *IM*, Bacon remarks, 'Etenim cùm, ex perpetuâ nostrâ cum Natura consuetudine, maiora de Meditationibus nostris, quàm pro ingenii viribus, speramus; tùm poterunt ista veluti tabernaculorum in viâ positorum vice fungi, vt mens ad certiora contendens in iis paulispèr acquiescat.'

R3ʳ

Page 262, l. 32–p. 264, l. 1: Nos ipsos istis—cf. *DO*, C3ʳ (*SEH*, I, p. 144): 'Attamen testamur interìm, nos illis ipsis, quòd ex verâ interpretandi formâ non sint inuenta, aut probata, teneri minimè velle.'

Page 264, ll. 1–2: non Methodo revincire—cf. *NO*, M2ʳ (*SEH*, I, p. 193); on method also see *cmt* (p. 278 above) on *HDR*, B8ᵛ p. 72, ll. 23–5.

APPENDIX I

The *Opuscula varia posthuma* and *Scripta*: Bibliographical Description and Technical Notes

(*a*) The *Opuscula*: Bibliographical Description and Technical Notes

[*printed title*: cancellandum: Wing 314; Gibson, no. 230 (p. 203) also see Plate V below, and pp. lxxxvii–lxxxviii above]
OPUSCULA | Varia Pofthuma, | PHILOSOPHICA, | CIVILIA, | Et | THEOLOGICA, | Francisci Baconi, | Baronis de *Verulamio*, Vice-| Comitis *Sancti Albani,* | *Nunc primum Edita.* | Cura & Fide Guilielmi Rawley, | Sacræ Theologiæ Doctoris, primo Do-| minationi fuæ, poftea Sereniffimæ | Majeftati Regiæ, à Sacris. | *Vna cum Nobiliſſimi Auctoris Vita.* | [Rule] | *LONDINI,* | Ex Officina R. Danielis, 1658.

[*printed title*: cancellans: Wing 315; Gibson(S), no. 230b (p. 4) also see Plate VI below pp. lxxxvii–lxxxviii]
OPUSCULA | Varia Pofthuma, | PHILOSOPHICA, | CIVILIA, | Et | THEOLOGICA, | Francisci Baconi, | Baronis de *Verulamio*, Vice-| Comitis *Sancti Albani,* | *Nunc primum Edita.* | Cura & Fide Guilielmi Rawley, | Sacræ Theologiæ Doctoris, primo Do-| minationi fuæ, poftea Sereniffimæ | Majeftati Regiæ, à Sacris. | *Vna cum Nobiliſſimi Auctoris Vita.* | [Rule] | *LONDINI,* | Excudebat R. Daniel, Impenfis | Octaviani Pulleyn ad infigne Rofæ | in Cœmiterio Paulino, 1658.

Coll: 8°: *⁸ (±*1) (*1ᵛ blank) 2*⁸ 3*² A–K⁸ (±K5, K6) L–N⁸ O⁴ (G7ᵛ L8ᵛ N7ᵛ blank) [$4 (−*1, O3, O4) signed] 126 leaves present, pp. [*36*] 1–108 *109–110* 111–174 *175–176* 177–204 *205–206* 207–216.

Contents: *1ʳ: printed title. *1ᵛ: blank. *2ʳ: 'LECTORI | S.' ending (*2ᵛ) 'GUIL. RAWLEY.' *3ʳ: '*Nobiliſſimi Auctoris* | VITA.' ending (2*7ᵛ) 'GUIL. RAWLEY.' 2*8ʳ: commendatory verses: 'In Auctorem Inftaurationis.' ending (2*8ᵛ) 'GEORGIUS HERBERTUS, | Orator Publicus Academiæ | Cantabrigiensis.' 3*1ʳ: commendatory verse: '*Viro omni laude majori,* | FRANCISCO BACONO, | *Patrono mihi unice observando.*' ending (3*2ʳ) '*Nomini tuo deditiimus,* | IOHANNES BURRHUS, | *poftea Eques Auratus, & principalis* | *Heraldus, Garterius dictus.*' 3*2ᵛ: 'Index *Tractatuum* in hoc *Volumine* | contentorum.' A1ʳ: 'Hiftoria Denfi & Rari; nec- | non Coitionis & Expanfionis | Materiæ per Spatia.' G7ʳ: title: 'OPUSCULA | sex | PHILOSOPHICA | fiimul collecta. | . . . [nine lines of contents etc.] . . .| FRANCISCO BACONO, | Barone de Verulamio, Vice-| comite Sancti Albani. | [rule] | Anno Domini 1658.' G7ᵛ: blank. G8ʳ: 'Historia *&* Inquisitio prima

OPUSCULA

Varia Pofthuma,

PHILOSOPHICA,

CIVILIA,

ET

THEOLOGICA,

FRANCISCI BACONI,

Baronis de *Verulamio*, Vice-
Comitis *Sancti Albani*,

Nunc primum Edita.

Cura & Fide GUILIELMI RAWLEY,
Sacræ Theologiæ Doctoris, primo Do-
minationi fuæ, poftea Sereniffimæ
Majeftati Regiæ, à Sacris.

Vna cum Nobiliſsimi Auctoris Vita.

LONDINI,
Ex Officina R. DANIELIS, 1658.

V *Opuscula*: Printed title—cancellandum—(approx. actual size),
Trinity College Cambridge NQ 10. 88

OPUSCULA

Varia Pofthuma,

PHILOSOPHICA,

CIVILIA,

Et

THEOLOGICA,

FRANCISCI BACONI,
Baronis de *Verulamio* , Vice-
Comitis *Sancti Albani*,

Nunc primum Edita.

Cura & Fide GUILIELMI RAWLEY,
Sacræ Theologiæ Doctoris, primo Do-
minationi fuæ, poftea Sereniffimæ
Majeftati Regiæ, à Sacris.

Vna cum Nobilißimi Auctoris Vita.

LONDINI,
Excudebat R. DANIEL, Impenfis
OCTAVIANI PULLEYN ad infigne Rofæ
in Cœmiterio Paulino, 1648.

VI *Opuscula*: Printed title—cancellans—(approx. actual size)
Trinity College Cambridge T. 30. 1

| de fono & auditu, & *de* Forma | foni, & latente proceffu foni. *Sive,* | Sylva foni & auditus.' K1ᵛ: 'Articuli Quæftionum circa | *Mineralia.*' K7ᵛ: '*Inquifitio* de *Magnete.*' L1ᵛ: '*Inquifitio* de *Verfionibus, Tranf-* | *mutationibus, Multiplica-* | *tionibus,* & *Effectionibus Corporum.*' L2ᵛ: '*Topica Inquifitionis* de *Luce* & *Lumine.*' L6ᵛ: '*Epiftola* ad *Fulgentium.*' L8ʳ: title: 'OPUS ILLUSTRE | *In Felicem Memoriam* | ELIZABETHÆ | Angliæ Reginæ, | . . . [9 lines of contents etc.] . . . | [rule] | Anno Domini 1658.' L8ᵛ: blank. M1ʳ: 'In felicem memoriam | ELIZABETHÆ | *Angliæ Reginæ.*' N2ʳ: 'Imago Civilis *Iulii Cæfaris.*' N6ʳ: 'Imago Civilis *Augufti Cæfaris.*' N7ʳ: title: 'CONFESSIO | FIDEI, | ANGLICANO | Sermone confripta | Per | FRANCISCUM BACONUM, | . . . [4 lines (Bacon's titles etc.)] . . . | [rule] | Anno Domini 1658.' N7ᵛ: blank. N8ʳ: 'Confeffio Fidei.' ending (O4ᵛ) 'FINIS.'

RT] *3ᵛ–2*7ᵛ: Auctoris Vita. (with a period) | Auctoris Vita. (with a period). Hiftoria Vita. (with a period) (2*7ʳ).

A1ᵛ–G6ᵛ: Hiftoria Denfi | & Rari, &c. (with a period).

G8ᵛ: Hiftoria Soni. (with a period). | H1ʳ (blank).

H1ᵛ–K1ʳ: Hiftoria & Inquifitio | de Sono & Auditu. (with a period).

K1ᵛ: (blank). | K2ʳ Articuli Quæftionum, &c. (with a period).

K2ᵛ–K7ʳ: Articuli Quæftionum | circa Mineralia. (with a period).

K8ʳ–L1ʳ: Inquifitio de Magnete. (with a period). | Inquifitio de Magnete. (with a period).

L1ᵛ–L2ʳ: (blank) | Inquifitionibus de Verfionib. &c. (with a period).

L2ᵛ–L3ʳ: (blank) | Topica Inquifitionis, &c. (with a period).

L3ᵛ–L6ʳ: Topica Inquifitionis | de Luce, & Lumine. (with a period).

L6ᵛ–L7ʳ: (blank) | Epiftola ad *Fulgentium.* (with a period).

L7ᵛ: Epiftola ad Fulgentium. (with a period).

M1ʳ–N1ᵛ: In felicem memoriam | *Elizabethæ* Angliæ Reginæ. (with a period). *Elizabethæ* (M7ʳ, M8ʳ). In felicem memoriam, &c. (with a period) (N1ᵛ).

N2ᵛ–N5ᵛ: Imago Civilis | Iulii Cæfaris. (with a period). N5ᵛ: Imago Civilis Iulii Cæfaris. (with a period) (N5ᵛ).

N6ᵛ: Imago Civilis Augufti Cæfaris. (with a period).

N8ᵛ–O4ᵛ: Confeffio Fidei. (with a period) | Confeffio Fidei. (with a period).

Signatures: invariant in all copies examined.

CW] [no cw on *1ʳ, *1ᵛ] *2 (*de-*)*figna-*[*fignatum*] *6ᵛ Circa [Circa] *8ʳ (commemo-)rando [rando] 2*4ʳ (il-)li [li] 2*4ᵛ Quorum: [Quorum] C2ᵛ (vexatio-)nes [nes] C3ᵛ (*plu-*)*mas* : [*mas*:] C5ᵛ At- [ATque] E3ᵛ quan- [quandoque] F3ᵛ 9. Etiam [9. Etiam] F8ᵛ 4. Omnia [4. Omnia] G1ʳ (la-)bra. [bra:] [no cw on G6ᵛ, G7ʳ, G7ᵛ] I6ʳ (inquir-)rendum [rendum.] I7ʳ (nonnul-)la, [la] K5ʳ (cancellandum) De [penitus] K5ʳ (cancellans) De [De] K5ᵛ (cancellandum) De [De] K5ᵛ (cancellans) *cor-* [*corporis*] L1ᵛ *Aqua* [*Aqua,*] L4ʳ *Lucis,* [*Lucis,*] [no cw on L7ᵛ, L8ʳ, L8ᵛ] M7ᵛ (hu-)juf- [jufmodi] N2ᵛ (composi-)to, [to] [no cw on N7ʳ, N7ᵛ]

Typography: [Auctoris Vita]: 28 ll. (*4) 132(143) × 76mm, roman (with some italic) 47mm for 10 roman ll. [commendatory verse]: 32 ll. (3*1^v) 132(136) × 62mm, roman 41mm for 10 roman ll. [Index]: 20 ll. (3*2^v) 126(136) × 76mm, italic (with some roman) 55mm for 10 italic ll (+ 4 ll. of interlinear leads). [*Historia Densi* (Aditus)]: 18 ll. (A1^v) 129(143) × 76mm, italic (with some roman) 72mm for 10 italic ll. [*Historia Densi* (Tabula)]: 40 ll. (A5^r) 132(143) × 76mm, italic (with some roman) 33mm for 10 italic ll. [*Historia Densi* (Monita)]: 32 ll. (A6^v) 132(143) × 76mm, roman (with some italic) 41mm for 10 roman ll. [*Historia Densi* (Canones)]: 28 ll. (G5^r) 132(143) × 76mm, roman (with some italic) 47mm for 10 roman ll. [*Historia & inquisitio de sono*]: 32 ll. (H2^r) 132(143) × 76mm, roman (with some italic) 41mm for 10 roman ll. [*Inquisitio de magnete*]: 28 ll (K8^r) 132(143) × 76mm roman (with some italic) 47mm for 10 roman ll. [*Confessio fidei*]: 32 ll. (O1^r) 132(143) × 76mm, roman (with some italic) 41mm for 10 roman ll.

Paper and Watermarks: the tranchefiles and the watermarks indicate common octavo format. On leaves where the evidence has not been trimmed away, the tranchefiles are situated parallel and adjacent to the fore-edges of leaves 1, 2, 3 and 4. Tranchefiles are *not* found in that position on leaves 5, 6, 7 and 8— a circumstance which would indicate 'inverted' octavo format. The water-mark of each sheet is situated exactly where it should be in an octavo edition, i.e. divided into four parts with each part located in the angle between head- and spine-edge of either leaves 2, 3, 6, and 7 or leaves 1, 4, 5 and 8. An excep-tion is sheet O (octavo half-sheet imposition) where the four parts occur either on leaves 1, 2, 3 and 4 or not at all. Watermarks are not easy to make out because all are impaired by cutting and trimming. Two watermarks occur frequently in the edition. One is a crowned spread eagle which, when recon-structed, measures approximately 95 × 80mm and sits astride chainlines set at 24mm intervals. For a published facsimile of a similar watermark see Heawood, no. 1268. The other watermark is a bunch of grapes which is rela-tively small and so parts of it always occur on only *two* leaves of any gather-ing, most often on 2 and 3 or 1 and 4. This situation is complicated by the presence of an elaborate countermark, parts of which occur on leaves 1 and 4 when the watermark appears on 2 and 3, and on 2 and 3 when the watermark appears on 1 and 4. This can deceive one into thinking that the marks on all four leaves are parts of a single *water*mark (resembling Piccard, no. 462 or Heawood, no. 2336) but they are no such thing.

Copies collated (shelfmarks in round brackets; Wing nos. in square):
Beinecke Library, Yale (Ih B132 c658) [B314]
Bibliothèque de l'Arsenal (8° Sc. A. 860 (1)) [B314]
Bibliothèque municipale de Lyon (338704) [B314]
Biblioteca Nazionale Braidense, Milan (B. IX. 4,950) [B314]
BL (535. a. 15) [B314]
Bodl. (8° A 82 Linc.) [B315]

The Scripta

Cambridge University Library (LE. 7. 84) [B314]; (LE. 19. 56) [B314]
Carlisle Cathedral Library (8A4.8) [B315]
Christ Church Oxford (a. 3. 259) [B315]
Christ's College Cambridge (E. 1. 11) [B314]
Copy owned by G. Rees (control copy; owner's signature on fly leaf) [B315]
Corpus Christi College Cambridge (Y. 6. 21) [B314]
Corpus Christi College Oxford (VI. 31) [B315]
Emmanuel College Cambridge (512. 6 (2)) [B314]
Folger Library (B314) [B314]
Heythrop College Library (B 1180 OP) [B314]
Houghton Library, Harvard (Phil 1850. 76) [B314]
King's College Cambridge (Keynes A.7.2) [B314]
Library of Congress (B1155 1658) [314]
Philosophy Library, Oxford (B. 4. 10) [B314]
Preussische Staats-Bibliothek, Berlin (AK 5477) [B315]
Queen's College Oxford (HS.c.15) [B314]
Royal College of Surgeons, London (CQ B128) [B314]
Royal Irish Academy, Dublin (MR/43/U/25) [B314]
Trinity College Cambridge (NQ 10. 88) [B314] (Newton's copy); (T. 30. 1.) [B315]
Trinity College Dublin (HH.ll.30) [B315]
Universitätsbibliothek, Ludwig-Maximilians-Universität, Munich (8 Misc. 1569) [B315]
University of London Library ([D-L. L.] (XVII) Bc [Bacon—Two or more Works]) [B315]
University of Toronto (bac B33 O68 1658a) [B315]
Vatican Library (RG. FILOSOFIA V. 541) [B315]

(*b*) The *Scripta*: Bibliographical Description—Some Corrections

A bibliographical description of the *Scripta* is given in *OFB*, VI, pp. 451–9. However, there are four errors in the description and I put them right here. The first occurs in the description of the printed title (p. 451): for the date 'cI I LIII.' read 'cIↃ I Ↄ c LIII.' Secondly, for 'CIↃ IↃ LIII.' (*4ᵛ) read 'CIↃ IↃC LIII.' (these dates were correct on my computer disc but that is no excuse for missing the errors at proof stage). The other two occur in the description of the contents (p. 451): for the absurd 'LECTORIS.' (*5ʳ) read 'LECTORI S.' and (A1ʳ) after 'INTERPRETATIONE' insert a lineation mark (i.e. |). I owe the corrections to the lynx-eyed Robin Robbins whose judicious review[1] of vol. VI made me completely recheck the bibliographical description of the *Scripta*.

[1] *British journal for the history of philosophy*, 6, part I, 1998, pp. 127–31.

343

APPENDIX II

Signature and Folio References in this Edition with corresponding Page Numbers in *SEH*

(*a*) *Historia densi & rari*

This Edition (Dupuy text)	This Edition (Rawley text)	*SEH*, vol. II	*SEH* trans., vol. V
—	A1^r	243	339
—	A1^v	243	339
—	A2^r	243	339–40
—	A2^v	243–4	340
—	A3^r	244	340
—	A3^v	244	340
—	A4^r	244	340
fo. 7^r	A4^v	245	341
fo. 7^r	A5^r	245	341
fo. 7^{r-v}	A5^v	245–6	341–2
fo. 7^v	A6^r	246–7	342–3
fo. 8^r	A6^v	247	343–4
fo. 8^r	A7^r	247–8	344
fo. 8^r	A7^v	248–9	344–5
—	A8^r	249	345
fo. 8^v	A8^v	249–50	345–6
fo. 8^v	B1^r	250	346
fo. 8^v	B1^v	250–1	346–7
—	B2^r	251	347
fo. 8^v	B2^v	252	347–8
—	B3^r	252–3	348
—	B3^v	253	348–9
fo. 9^r	B4^r	254	349
fo. 9^r	B4^v	254–5	349–50
fo. 9^{r-v}	B5^r	255	350
fos. 9^v–10^r	B5^v	255–6	350–1
fo. 10^{r-v}	B6^r	256	351–2
—	B6^v	256–7	352–3
—	B7^r	257–8	353
fo. 10^v	B7^v	258	353–4
fo. 10^v	B8^r	259	354
—	B8^v	259–60	354–5

This Edition (Dupuy text)	This Edition (Rawley text)	*SEH*, vol. II	*SEH* trans., vol. V
fo. 11^r	C1^r	260	355–6
—	C1^v	260–1	356
fo. 11^r	C2^r	261–2	356–7
—	C2^v	262	357
fo. 11^r	C3^r	262–3	357–8
fo. 11^r	C3^v	263–4	358–9
fo. 11$^{r–v}$	C4^r	264	359
fo. 11^v	C4^v	264–5	359–60
—	C5^r	265	360
fo. 11^v	C5^v	265–6	360–1
fo. 12^r	C6^r	266–7	361
—	C6^v	267	361–2
fo. 12^r	C7^r	267–8	362–3
—	C7^v	268–9	363
fo. 12$^{r–v}$	C8^r	269	363–4
fos. 12^v–13^r	C8^v	269–70	364–5
fo. 13^r	D1^r	270	365
fo. 13$^{r–v}$	D1^v	270–1	365–6
—	D2^r	271–2	366
fo. 13^v	D2^v	272	366–7
fo. 13^v	D3^r	272–3	367
fos. 13^v–14^r	D3^v	273	367–8
fo. 14$^{r–v}$	D4^r	273–4	368
fo. 14^v	D4^v	274–5	368–9
fos. 14^v–15^r	D5^r	275	369–70
—	D5^v	275–6	370
fo. 15^r	D6^r	276	370–1
—	D6^v	276–7	371–2
fo. 15^r	D7^r	277	372
fo. 15$^{r–v}$	D7^v	277–8	372–3
fos. 15^v–16^r	D8^r	278–9	373
fo. 16^r	D8^v	279	373–4
fo. 16$^{r–v}$	E1^r	279–80	374–5
fo. 16^v	E1^v	280	375
fo. 16^v	E2^r	280–1	375–6
fo. 16^v	E2^v	281	376
fos. 16^v–17^r	E3^r	281–2	376–7
fo. 17^r	E3^v	282	377–8
fo. 17^r	E4^r	282–3	378
fo. 17^r	E4^v	283–4	378–9
—	E5^r	284	379–80

This Edition (Dupuy text)	This Edition (Rawley text)	*SEH*, vol. II	*SEH* trans., vol. V
—	E5ᵛ	284–5	380
fo. 17ᵛ	E6ʳ	285	380–1
fo. 17ᵛ	E6ᵛ	285–6	381
fo. 17ᵛ	E7ʳ	286–7	381–2
fo. 17ᵛ	E7ᵛ	287	382
fos. 17ᵛ–18ʳ	E8ʳ	287–8	382–3
fo. 18ʳ	E8ᵛ	288	383
fo. 18ᵛ	F1ʳ	288–9	384
fo. 18ᵛ	F1ᵛ	289	384–5
fo. 18ᵛ	F2ʳ	289–90	385
fo. 18ᵛ	F2ᵛ	290–1	385–6
fos. 18ᵛ–19ʳ	F3ʳ	291	386
fo. 19ʳ⁻ᵛ	F3ᵛ	291–2	386–7
fo. 19ᵛ	F4ʳ	292–3	387–8
fo. 19ᵛ	F4ᵛ	293	388
fos. 19ᵛ–20ʳ	F5ʳ	293–4	388–9
fo. 20ʳ	F5ᵛ	294–5	389–90
fo. 20ʳ	F6ʳ	295	390
fo. 20ʳ	F6ᵛ	295–6	390–1
fo. 20ʳ⁻ᵛ	F7ʳ	296–7	391
fo. 20ᵛ	F7ᵛ	297	392
fos. 20ᵛ–21ʳ	F8ʳ	297–8	392–3
fo. 21ʳ	F8ᵛ	298	393
fo. 21ʳ⁻ᵛ	G1ʳ	298–9	393–4
fo. 21ᵛ	G1ᵛ	299	394–5
fo. 21ᵛ	G2ʳ	299–300	395
fo. 21ᵛ	G2ᵛ	300–1	395–6
fo. 21ᵛ	G3ʳ	301	396
fos. 21ᵛ–22ʳ	G3ᵛ	301–2	396–7
fo. 22ʳ	G4ʳ	302	397
fo. 22ʳ⁻ᵛ	G4ᵛ	302–3	398
fos. 22ᵛ–23ʳ	G5ʳ	303	398–9
fo. 23ʳ	G5ᵛ	303–4	399
fo. 23ʳ⁻ᵛ	G6ʳ	304	399–400
—	G6ᵛ	304–5	400

(*b*) *Abecedarium nouum naturæ*

This Edition	*SEH*, vol. II	*SEH* trans., vol. V
fos. 24ʳ–35ʳ	Not given in *SEH*	Not given in *SEH*
fo. 35ᵛ	85–6	208–9
fo. 36ʳ	86–7	209–10
fo. 36ᵛ	87	210

This Edition References and SEH *Pages*

This Edition	*SEH*, vol. II	*SEH* trans., vol. V
fo. 37ʳ	87–8	210–11
fo. 37ᵛ	88	211

(*c*) *Inquisitio de magnete*

This Edition	*SEH*, vol. II	*SEH* trans., vol. V
K7ᵛ	311	403
K8ʳ	311–12	403–4
K8ᵛ	312	404
L1ʳ	312	404–5

(*d*) *Topica inquisitionis de luce et lumine*

This Edition	*SEH*, vol. II	*SEH* trans., vol. V
X3ʳ	317	409
X3ᵛ	317–18	409–10
X4ʳ	318	410
X4ᵛ	318–19	410–11
X5ʳ	319	411
X5ᵛ	319–20	411–12
X6ʳ	320	412
X6ᵛ	320–1	412–13
X7ʳ	321	413
X7ᵛ	321–2	413–14
X8ʳ	322	414

(*e*) *Prodromi sive anticipationes philosophiæ secundæ*

This Edition	*SEH*, vol. II	*SEH* offers no trans.
R1ʳ	690	
R1ᵛ	690–1	
R2ʳ	691	
R2ᵛ	691	
R3ʳ	691–2	

SELECT BIBLIOGRAPHY

The bibliography has two parts. The first is given over to Bacon's works and records the principal texts used in the preparation of this edition; manuscript and printed works are listed separately. The former are accompanied, where applicable, by the alphanumerics assigned to them in Beal's *IELM*. The latter begin with *opera omnia* and descend via collections to single works and, where applicable, they are accompanied by their Gibson numbers. The second part of the bibliography lists a selection of other works cited or used in the preparation of this volume. These have been ordered alphabetically by author, but where a single author has more than one item listed, the items appear in chronological order. This bibliography supplements those found in other volumes of *OFB* and, in this case particularly, the bibliography of volume VI.

PART 1

MANUSCRIPTS

Abecedarium nouum naturæ (*ANN*): BN coll. Dupuy no. 5, fos. 24^r–37^v. There is also a copy in BN fonds français 4745, fos. 39–62 (BcF 286).

Calor et frigus (*CF*): BL Harley MS 6855, vol. I, fos. 52^r–60^v.

Cogitata et visa (*CV*): The Queen's College Oxford, MS 280, fos. 205^r–233^v (BcF 289).

Cogitationes de scientia humana (*CDSH*): BL Add. MS 4258, fos. 214–27 (BcF 290).

Commentarius solutus (*CS*): BL Add. MS 27278 (BcF 153).

De vijs mortis (*DVM*): MS Hardwick 72A (Chatsworth House) (BcF 294 and BcF 287).

Historia densi & rari (manuscript version) (*HDR(M)*): BN coll. Dupuy no. 5, fos. 7^r–23^v. There is also a copy in BN fonds français 4745, fos. 9^r–38^v (BcF 295).

Historia & inquisitio de animato & inanimato (*HIDA*): BN coll. Dupuy no. 5, fos. 3^r–5^v (BcF 296).

Redargutio philosophiarum (*RPh*): BL Harley MS 6855, vol. I, fos. 4^r–31^v (BcF 306).

Sylva sylvarum (working notes) (*SSWN*): BL Add. MS 38693, fos. 30^r–48^v (BcF 283).

PRINTED BOOKS

The works of Francis Bacon, Baron of Verulam, Viscount St. Albans, and Lord High Chancellor of England, ed. Thomas Birch, 5 vols., London, 1765.

The works of Francis Bacon, Lord Chancellor of England, ed. Basil Montagu, 16 vols., William Pickering: London, 1825–36.

Œuvres philosophiques de Bacon, publiées d'après les textes originaux, avec notice, sommaires et éclaircissemens [*sic*], ed. M. N. Bouillet, 3 vols., Paris, 1834.

JAMES SPEDDING, *The letters and life of Francis Bacon*, 7 vols., London, 1861–74.

The works of Francis Bacon, ed. James Spedding, Robert Leslie Ellis, and Douglas Denon Heath, 7 vols., London, 1859–64.

Scripta in natvrali et vniversali philosophia, Amsterdam, 1653 (Gibson, no. 223).

Resuscitatio, London, 1657 (Gibson, no. 226).

Opuscula varia posthuma, 1658 (for bibliographical details see Appendix I above).

Baconiana. Or certain genuine remaines of S^r. *Francis Bacon, Baron of Verulam, and Viscount of St. Albans*, ed. Thomas Tenison, London, 1679 (Gibson, no. 237a).

GRAHAM REES (assisted by CHRISTOPHER UPTON), *Francis Bacon's natural philosophy: a new source. A transcription of manuscript Hardwick 72A with translation and commentary*, British Society for the History of Science Monographs 5, 1984.

SIR FRANCIS BACON, *The essayes or counsels, civill and morall*, ed. Michael Kiernan, Clarendon Press: Oxford, 1985. This volume was reissued in 2000 as volume XV of *The Oxford Francis Bacon*.

Francesco Bacone: dai naturalisti Greci a Telesio, ed. Enrico De Mas, Laboratorio Edizioni: Cosenza, 1988 (mainly an edition of *DPAO* with facing-page Italian translation).

FRANCIS BACON, *Novum organum with other parts of the Great Instauration*, trans. and ed. Peter Urbach and John Gibson, Open Court: Chicago and La Salle, 1994.

The history of the reign of King Henry VII, ed. Brian Vickers, Cambridge University Press: Cambridge, 1998.

PART 2

AB AQUAPENDENTE, FABRICIUS, *The embryological treatises of Hieronymus Fabricius of Aquapendente. The formation of the egg and of the chick* [*De formatione ovi et pulli*]. *The formed foetus* [*De formato foetu*], *A facsimile edition with an introduction, a translation and a commentary*, ed. H. B. Adelmann, 2 vols., Cornell University Press: Ithaca, 1942.

AGRICOLA, GEORGIUS, *De re metallica libri xii . . . Froben Basileae M D LXI*.

ÅKERMAN, S., 'The forms of Queen Christina's academies', in *The shapes of knowledge from the Renaissance to the Enlightenment*, ed. D. R. Kelley and R. H. Popkin (Archives Internationales d'Histoire des Idées 124), Kluwer Academic Publishers: Dordrecht, Boston, and London, 1991, pp. 165–88.

ALDIS, H. G., *A dictionary of printers and booksellers in England, Scotland and Ireland, and of foreign printers of English books, 1557–1640*, Bibliographical Society: London, 1910.

ALDROVANDI, ULISSE, *De animalibvs insectis libri septem . . . Bonon: apud Ioan. Bapt: Bellagambam*, 1602.

Select Bibliography

ALDROVANDI, ULISSE, *Aldrovandi on chickens: the ornithology of Ulisse Aldrovandi (1600) Volume II, Book XIV*, trans. from the Latin with introduction, contents and notes by L. R. Lind, University of Oklahoma Press: Oklahoma, 1963.

BALAYÉ, SIMONE, *La Bibliothèque Nationale des origines à 1800*, Librairie Droz: Geneva, 1988.

BEAL, PETER, *Index of English literary manuscripts 1450–1625*, I, parts 1 and 2, London, 1980.

—— *In praise of scribes: manuscripts and their makers in seventeenth-century England*, Clarendon Press: Oxford, 1998.

BELL, MAUREEN, 'Entrance in the Stationers' Register', *The Library*, 6th ser., 16, no. 1, 1994, pp. 50–4.

BLOMEFIELD, FRANCIS, *An essay towards a topographical history of the County of Norfolk*, 5 vols., Fersfield, 1739.

BONELLI, FEDERICO, and RUSSO, LUCIO, 'The origin of modern astronomical theories of tides: Chrisogono, de Dominis and their sources', *BJHS*, 29, Dec. 1996, pp. 385–401.

BRIQUET, C. M., *Les filigranes: dictionnaire historique des marques du papier*, 4 vols., repr. New York, 1966.

CAMPANELLA, TOMMASO, *Philosophia sensibus demonstrata*, ed. Luigi De Franco, Vivarium: Naples, 1992, pp. 597–628.

CÉARD, PAUL, 'Encyclopédie et encyclopédisme à la Renaissance', in *L'Encyclopédisme: actes du colloque de Caen 12–16 janvier 1987*, ed. Annie Becq, Éditions Klincksieck: Paris, 1991, pp. 57–67.

CHARTIER, ROGER, *Forms and meanings: texts, performances, and audiences from codex to computer*, trans. Lydia G. Cochrane *et al.*, University of Pennsylvania Press: Philadelphia, 1995.

CLAY, WILLIAM KEATINGE, *A history of the parish of Landbeach in the County of Cambridge*, Cambridge Antiquarian Society. Octavo Publications, no. VI, Deighton, Bell & Co: London, 1861.

COLERIDGE, K. A., 'The printing and publishing of Clement Walker's *History of Independency* 1647–1661', *Bulletin of the Bibliographical Society of Australia and New Zealand*, 8, 1984, pp. 22–61.

COLIE, ROSALIE L., 'Cornelis Drebbel and Saloman de Caus: Two Jacobean models for Salomon's House', *HLQ*, 18, 1955, pp. 245–60.

DEBUS, ALLEN G., *Chemistry, alchemy and the new philosophy, 1500–1700*, Variorum Reprints: London, 1987.

DE FRANCO, LUIGI, 'La teoria della luce di Bernardino Telesio', in *Bernardino Telesio e la cultura napoletana*, ed. Raffaele Sirri and Maurizio Torrini, Guida Editore: Naples, 1992, pp. 53–77.

DELLA PORTA, G. B., *Magiæ natvralis libri viginti . . . Francofvrti apud Andreæ Wecheli heredes . . .* 1591.

DES CHENE, DENNIS, *Physiologia: natural philosophy in late Aristotelian and Cartesian thought*, Cornell University Press: Ithaca and London, 1996.

DRAKE-BROCKMAN, JENNIFER, 'The *perpetuum mobile* of Cornelis Drebbel', in *Learning, language and invention: essays presented to Francis Maddison*, ed. W. D. Hackmann and A. J. Turner, Variorum and the Société Internationale de l'Astrolabe: Aldershot and Paris, 1994.

ERASTUS, THOMAS, *Dispvtationvm de nova Philippi Paracelsi medicina pars tertia* [Petrus Perna: Basle], 1572.

EYRE, G. E. BRISCOE and RIVINGTON, C. R. (eds.), *A transcript of the registers of the worshipful Company of Stationers; from 1640–1708 A. D.*, 3 vols., privately printed for the Roxburghe Club: London, 1913–14.

FATTORI, MARTA (ed.), *Francis Bacon: terminologia e fortuna nel XVII secolo*, Edizioni dell'Ateneo: Rome, 1984.

—— 'Fortin de la Hoguette entre Francis Bacon et Marin Mersenne: critique du syllogisme et théologie: autour de l'édition française de 1624 du *De augmentis scientiarum*', in Marta Fattori, *Linguaggio e filosofia nel seicento*, Olschki: Florence (forthcoming).

FERNEL, JEAN, *Therapevtices vniversalis sev medendi rationis libri septem . . . Lvgdvni. Ex officina Lud. Cloquemin . . . 1574.*

—— *Io. Fernelii . . . Vniversa medicina. . . Francofvrti M D LXXXI.*

FERRETTI, GIULIANO, *Un 'soldat philosophe': Philippe Fortin de la Hoguette (1585–1668?)*, ECIG: Genoa, 1988.

—— (ed.), *Fortin de la Hoguette ou le vertige de la politique: lettres aux frères Dupuy et à leur entourage (1623–1661)*, unpub. diss., Université de Lausanne, 1995.

—— (ed.), Philippe Fortin de la Hoguette, *Lettres aux frères Dupuy et à leur entourage (1623–1662)*, 2 vols., Leo S. Olschki: Florence, 1997.

FRACASTORIUS, HIERONYMUS, *Opera omnia, in vnum proxime post illius mortem collecta . . . Venetiis, apvd Ivntas, M. D. LXXIIII.*

GARBER, DANIEL, and AYRES, MICHAEL (eds.), *The Cambridge History of Seventeenth-Century Philosophy*, 2 vols., Cambridge University Press: Cambridge, 1998.

GAUDRIAULT, RAYMOND, *Filigranes et autres caractéristiques des papiers fabriqués en France aux XVIIe et XVIIIe siècles*, CNRS Éditions: Paris, 1995.

GEMELLI, BENEDINO, *Aspetti dell'atomismo classico nella filosofia di Francis Bacon e nel seicento*, Leo S. Olschki: Florence, 1996.

GERARD, JOHN, *The herball or generall historie of plants*, London, 1597.

GIBSON, R. W., *Francis Bacon: a bibliography of his works and of Baconiana to the year 1750*, Scrivener Press: Oxford, 1950.

—— *Francis Bacon: a bibliography of his works and of Baconiana to the year 1750: Supplement*, privately issued: Oxford, 1959.

GILBERT, WILLIAM, *De magnete, magneticisqve corporibvs, et de magno magnete tellure; physiologia noua . . .* Londoni excvdebat Petrvs Short anno MDC.

—— *De mundo nostro sublunari philosophia nova*, Amsterdam, 1651, fac. repr. Menno Hertzberger: Amsterdam, 1965.

GOLDSTEIN, B. R., 'On the theory of trepidation', *Centaurus*, 10, 1964, pp. 232–47.

GREG, W. W., *A Companion to Arber: being a calendar of documents in Edward Arber's* Transcript of the Registers of the Company of Stationers of London 1554–1640, Clarendon Press: Oxford, 1967.

HAKLUYT, RICHARD, *The principall navigations, voiages and discoveries of the English nation, made by sea or ouer land, to the most remote and farthest distant quarters of the earth at any time within the campasse of these 1500. yeeres: deuided into three seuerall parts, according to the positions of the regions wherunto they were directed*, London, 1589.

HEAWOOD, E., *Watermarks mainly of the 17th and 18th centuries*, Hilversum, 1950.

HENNINGER, Jr., S. K., *A handbook of Renaissance meteorology*, Duke University Press: Durham, NC, 1960.

HUTCHINSON, KEITH, 'Dormitive virtues, scholastic qualities, and the new philosophies', *History of Science*, 29, 1991, pp. 245–78.

JARDINE, LISA, *Francis Bacon: discovery and the art of discourse*, Cambridge University Press: Cambridge, 1974.

KEISER, G. R., 'Medicines for horses: the continuity from script to print', *Yale University Library gazette*, 69, April, 1995, pp. 111–28.

KYNASTON-SNELL, H. F., *Jean Baudoin et les Essais de Bacon en France jusqu'au XVIIIᵉ siècle*, Jouve: Paris, 1939.

LA HOGUETTE, PHILIPPE FORTIN DE, *Testament . . . d'un bon père à ses enfans*, Antoine Vitré: Paris, 1648.

—— *Lettres inédites*, ed. Philippe Tamizey de Larroque, N. Textier: La Rochelle, 1888.

LE DŒUFF, M., 'Bacon chez les grands au siècle de Louis XIII', *FBTF*, pp. 155–78.

—— 'Hope in science', *FBLT*, pp. 9–24.

LERNER, MICHEL-PIERRE, 'Le "parménidisme" de Telesio: origine et limites d'une hypothèse', in *Bernardino Telesio e la cultura napoletana*, ed. Raffaele Sirri and Maurizio Torrini, Guida Editore: Naples, 1992, pp. 79–105.

LINDBERG, DAVID C., 'The genesis of Kepler's theory of light: light metaphysics from Plotinus to Kepler', *Osiris*, 2nd ser., 2, 1986, pp. 5–42.

LOHR, CHARLES H., 'The Aristotelian division of the speculative sciences', in *The shapes of knowledge from the Renaissance to the Enlightenment*, ed. D. R. Kelley and R. H. Popkin (Archives Internationales d'Histoire des Idées 124), Kluwer Academic Publishers: Dordrecht, Boston, and London, 1991, pp. 49–58.

MCKITTERICK, DAVID, *A history of Cambridge University Press*, vol. I, Cambridge University Press: Cambridge, 1992.

MALCOLM, NOEL, *De Dominis (1560–1624): Venetian, Anglican, ecumenist and relapsed heretic*, Strickland & Scott Academic Publications: London, 1984.

Select Bibliography

Masters, Robert, *The History of the College of Corpus Christi and the B. Virgin Mary (Commonly called Bene't) in the University of Cambridge, from its foundation to the present time*, J. Bentham for the author: Cambridge, 1753.

Michel, H., 'Le mouvement perpétuel de Drebbel', *Physis*, fasc. 3, a. 13, 1971, pp. 289–94.

Moore, J. K., *Primary materials relating to copy and print in English books of the sixteenth and seventeenth centuries* (Oxford Bibliographical Society Occasional Publication no. 24), Oxford, 1992.

Needham, Joseph, *A history of embryology*, 2nd edn. rev., Cambridge University Press: Cambridge, 1959.

Paracelsus, *Selected writings*, ed. J. Jacobi, trans. N. Guterman, Pantheon Books: New York, 1951.

—— *Werke*, 5 vols., Schwabe & Co.: Basle, 1965–8.

Partington, J. R., *A history of chemistry*, 4 vols., Macmillan: London, 1961–70.

Patrizi, F., *Nova de vniversis philosophia*, Venice, 1593.

Peiresc, Nicolas-Claude Fabri de, *Lettres de Peiresc aux frères Dupuy*, ed. Philippe Tamizey de Larroque, 7 vols., Imprimerie Nationale: Paris, 1888–98.

—— *Lettres à Cassiano dal Pozzo (1626–1637)*, ed. Jean-François Lhote and Danielle Joyal, Adosa: Clermont-Ferrand, 1989.

Pharmacopœa Londinensis, in qva medicamenta . . . describuntur. Opera Medicorum Collegij Londinensis . . . Londini, excudebat Edwardus Griffin . . . 1618.

Piccard, G., *Wasserzeichen*, Verlag W. Kohlhammer: Stuttgart, 1983.

Plomer, H. R., *A dictionary of the booksellers and printers who were at work in England, Scotland and Ireland from 1641–1667*, Bibliographical Society: London, 1907.

Plutarch, *Lives* (Loeb Classical Library) Cambridge, Mass., and London, vol. I, 1914, repr. 1998.

—— *Lives* (Loeb Classical Library) London and Cambridge, Mass., vol. IV, 1916, repr. 1986.

Pörksen, G., 'Die Bewohner der Elemente nach Paracelsus' Liber de Nymphis', *Nova Acta Paracelsica*, NS 6, 1991–2, pp. 29–50.

Prestwich, Menna, *Cranfield: politics and profits under the early Stuarts*, Clarendon Press: Oxford, 1966.

Purchas, Samuel, *Pvrchas his pilgrimage. Or relations of the world . . .*, William Stansby: London, 1614.

Ravensdale, J. R., 'Landbeach in 1549: Ket's rebellion in miniature', *East Anglian Studies*, 1968, pp. 94–116.

—— *Liable to floods: village landscape on the edge of the fens AD 450–1850*, Cambridge University Press: Cambridge, 1974.

Rawley, William, *A sermon of meekenesse, preached at the Spittle vpon Easter Tuesday, M. D. C. XXIII*, John Haviland: London, 1623.

—— (ed.), *Memoriæ . . . Francisci, baronis de Verulamio, sacrum*, John Haviland: London, 1626.

REÉ, JONATHAN, 'Being foreign is different: can we find equivalents for philosophical terms?', *Times literary supplement*, 6 Sept. 1996, pp. 12–13.

REES, GRAHAM, 'An unpublished manuscript by Francis Bacon: *Sylva sylvarum* drafts and other working notes', *Annals of science*, **38**, 1981, pp. 377–412.

—— 'Francis Bacon's biological ideas', in *Occult and scientific mentalities in the Renaissance*, ed. Brian Vickers, Cambridge University Press: Cambridge and London, 1984, pp. 297–314.

—— 'Quantitative reasoning in Francis Bacon's natural philosophy', *Nouvelles de la république des lettres*, 1985, pp. 27–48.

—— 'Mathematics and Francis Bacon's natural philosophy', *Revue internationale de philosophie*, **159**, fasc. 4, 1986, pp. 399–426.

RICHARDSON, BRIAN, *Print culture in Renaissance Italy: the editor and the vernacular text, 1470–1600*, Cambridge University Press: Cambridge, 1994.

ROMANI, ANNA RITA, 'Francis Bacon e il carteggio puteano', in *Cassiano dal Pozzo: atti del seminario internazionale di studi*, ed. Francesco Solinas, De Lucca: Rome, 1989, pp. 31–5.

ROMANUS, ÆGIDIUS, *Commentaria in octo libros phisicorum Aristotelis* [Venice, 1502].

SCALIGER, J. C., *Exotericarvm exercitationvm liber qvintvs decimvs, de svbtilitate, ad Hieronymvm Cardanvm . . . Lvtetiæ, . . . M. D. LVII.*

SCHMITT, CHARLES B., SKINNER, QUENTIN, and KESSLER, ECKHARD (eds.), *The Cambridge History of Renaissance Philosophy*, Cambridge University Press: Cambridge, 1988.

SESSIONS, WILLIAM A. (ed.), *Francis Bacon's Legacy of Texts*, AMS Press: New York, 1990.

A short-title catalogue of books printed in England, Scotland, & Ireland and of English books printed abroad 1475–1640, ed. A. W. Pollard and G. R. Redgrave, 2 vols., 2nd edn. revised and enlarged by W. A. Jackson, F. S. Ferguson and Katharine F. Pantzer, London, 1976–86. Vol. III, *Indexes*, compiled by K. Pantzer and P. R. Ridler, London, 1991.

Short-title catalogue of books printed in England, Scotland, Ireland, Wales, and British America and of English books printed in other countries 1641–1700, ed. Donald Wing, 2nd edn., revised and enlarged, 4 vols., Modern Language Association of America: New York, 1988–98.

SORABJI, RICHARD, *Matter, space and motion: theories in antiquity and their sequel*, Duckworth: London, 1988.

TELESIO, BERNARDINO, *De rerum natura*, ed. Luigi De Franco, vol. I, Casa del Libro: Cosenza, 1965; vol. II, Casa del Libro: Cosenza, 1971; vol. III, La Nuova Italia: Florence, 1976.

—— *Varii de naturalibus rebus libelli*, ed. Luigi De Franco, La Nuova Italia Editrice: Florence, 1981.

TOPSELL, EDWARD, *The historie of fovre-footed beastes . . . Collected out of all the volumes of Conradvs Gesner. . .*, W. Jaggard: London, 1607.

TYMME, THOMAS, *A dialogve philosophicall . . . Together with the wittie inuention of an artificiall perpertuall motion,* London, 1612.

UPTON, A. F., *Sir Arthur Ingram c.1565–1642: a study of the origins of an English landed family,* Oxford University Press: Oxford, 1961.

VERMIJ, RIENK, 'Subterranean fire. Changing theories of the earth during the Renaissance', *Early science and medicine,* 3, Nov. 1998, pp. 322–47.

WORMALD, B. H. G., *Francis Bacon: history, politics and science, 1561–1626,* Cambridge University Press: Cambridge, 1993.

WRIGHT, A. P. M., and LEWIS, C. P. (eds.), *A history of the County of Cambridge and the Isle of Ely,* vol. IX (Victoria History of the Counties of England), Oxford University Press for the Institute of Historical Research: Oxford, 1989.

ZUPKO, R. E., *A dictionary of English weights and measures from Anglo-Saxon times to the nineteenth century,* University of Wisconsin Press: Madison, Milwaukee, and London, 1968.

GENERAL INDEX

Note: numbers given in **bold** refer to pages in the edited Latin texts; all other numbers, whether arabic or roman, refer to editorial introductory or end matter.

General Index

experience: learned xxxvi, 291
ether, *see* spirits
experiment(s): with acids and metals
19–20, 110–12, 114; with bladder 277; on
closed distillation 16–17, 100–2; on
condensation of air 154–6; crucial
instances 222, 325; for establishing
densities, 3–5, 44–8, 66–8, 272; the
Florentine experiment 301; on generation
of plants 228–30; with glass egg 22; 122;
of light (as opposed to fruit) 222, 228,
325; need for 283; with nitre 150, 300;
quantitative xli, 17, 66–8, 277, 292; on
rarefaction of air 86–8; ones unique to
Historia densi xxxv; on swelling of water
84; on water to air conversions 34, 66–8,
270; *see also* calendar glasses; quantitative
researches

Fattori, Marta viii, lix
Ferretti, Giuliano: editorial methods of liii n.
on La Hoguette and Diodati lii;
researches on La Hoguette xlix, lix, lx
flame 276; extinguished 148; and its fuel
120; a pure spirit 7, 8, 9, 68–70; rarer
than air 33, 66; relations with oil 277; *see
also* spirits
forms: Aristotle and Plato on 270; in Bacon
xxxix, 313
fossils (i.e. refractory stones): Bacon on 50,
134, 273, 287, 292
Fracastoro, Girolamo: his life, and last
illness 283–4; cure for apoplexy 13, 88,
frost 142

games: children's 74, 279
gems: generation of 27–8, 78, 279
generation, spontaneous, *see* vivfication
Gilbert, William: and coition and Earth's
entrails 273; and element theory 277; and
orb of virtue 315; and prepared steel 330
glass 92
God: and matter 36, 270
gold: aqua fortis does not dissolve it 118;
and aqua regia 19, 110; densest substance
2, 40, 44, 272, 273; fulminating 120, 295;
leaf 23, 122–4, 126; manufacture of 34,
54–6, 273–4; nature of 284; opening of 14,
92, 110; potable, 14, 92, 285; where found
50
Granier, *see* Mauléon, Auger Granier de
Gruter, Isaac: correspondence with Rawley
lxxvii; inherits manuscripts from William

Boswell lxxiii; publishes the *Scripta* 1653
xix; and the *Prodromi* lxxxiii; and the
Topica inquisitionis lxxiii, lxxxi–lxxxii
gunpowder 10, 70; action of 31, 74–6, 94,
120, 279
Gwinne, Matthew 285

Haviland, John: printer of *Historia ventorum*
and *Historia vitæ* xxx, xxxi
heat: and age 24, 33, 130–2; 166; potential
289
heavenly bodies: physical nature of 275, 283;
see also spirits
heavy and light: allied to dense and rare xli,
33, 52, 166, 174; and natural motion 174,
194, 307; see also *Historia grauis & leuis*;
motion, Aristotelian natural
Herbert of Cherbury lii
Hero of Alexandria: his self-extinguishing
altar 12–13, 34, 88, 166, 283
history, natural: anyone can help with it 72;
factual accumulative norms of xxxvi;
place in Bacon's philosophy xxxvi–xxxvii;
role of 220; and simple natures xxxvii;
weakness of existing history 222, *see also*
induction
Horace 325
hot and cold: and motion of hyle 194;
produce dense and rare 174
hybrids, interspecific 311

intermediates: and glutinous matter 178,
309; and motion 315; between plants and
metals 280
induction: perfects natural history 72; new
philosophy to rest on 262
iron: and aqua fortis 20, 112, 244; density of
2, 40

jew's ear fungus 76, 279–80

Laertius, Diogenes 308
La Hoguette, Philippe Fortin de: and
Bacon's manuscripts liv–lv, lv–lix; his
Bacon manuscripts ultimate source of
coll. Dupuy no. 5 copies lxx–lxxi; his
descriptions of his Bacon manuscripts lxx
& n. meets Bacon lii–liii; and Bacon's
portrait liv; career of xlix; courage of liv n.
and Diodati lii; and the Dupuy *cabinet*
xlix–l; and the Granier de Mauléon fracas
lv–lviii; handwriting of lxvi–lxviii; letters
of liii n. translation of *Meditationes sacræ*

360

natural: distinguished from artificial and
monstrous xlviii, **218**

natures, simple: also called cardinal virtues
xxxvii–xxxviii, xl–xli; a principal topic of
Abecedarium xxxix, **174–90**

night vision 332

nitre **2**, 28–9, **40**, 78–80, **150**, 300

openings: experiments on **13–14**, 90–2; of
glass, gold, iron **14**, **92**; of metals with
strong waters **19–20**; of oil **90**; by
pulverisation **56–8**; of water 88

Paracelsus: his pygmies **17**, **102**, **232**, 288–9;
on *ros solis* 300

Peiresc, N.-C. Fabri de: admirer of Bacon l,
li n. contacts with England li; and the *De
augmentis* liv; and La Hoguette l; and La
Hoguette's Bacon manuscripts lv, lvi–lvii,
lvii–lviii; and the translations of 'Of
Religion' and 'Of Superstition' lxix–lxx;
see also Dupuy, Jacques and Pierre; La
Hoguette

perception: and sensation xliv, **214**, 322–3;
and vital spirits **106**, 290

petrification **28**, **34**, **146**, **166**

philosophia prima: branches of xlvi, 323–4;
see also conditions of beings

physics: abstract xxxviii, 320; branches of
xxxvi–xxxvii, xxxviii, xlv, 308

Plato: and forms 270

pneumatic matter, *see* spirits

porcelain: Chinese make artificial mines of it
146, 299; nature of 309

Porta, G. B. della 286; on vinegar's reaction
with limestone 292

powders **58–60**; *see also* openings

primordia **176**, 308, 312

printers: marking up manuscript copy 274

prolongation of life xlii–xliii, **21**, **116–18**,
293–4, 320; *see also* moisture, radical

Pulleyn, Octavian: career and publication of
Opuscula lxxxiii–lxxxiv

pulse **80**

putrefaction **11**, **80**, **204**, 299, **311**, 319,
319–20; *see also* spirits; vivification

qualities: philosophers have ascribed to
them what they should have ascribed to
spirits 70–2, **180**, **186**; primary **10**, **178**,
309, 309–10; secondary **18**, **28**, **106**, **108**,
148, 289, 291, 299

quantitative researches 2–3, **17–18**, **19–20**,
38, **40–6**, **52–4**, **102–4**, **110–12**, **144**,

210–14, 277, 292

quaternions: central to Bacon's speculative
philosophy **188–90**, 312

quicksilver, *see* mercury

rare, *see* dense and rare

rain: cause of **26**, **138–40**, **152**

Rawley, William: Bacon's protégé lxxiv; and
Bene't (Corpus Christi) College
Cambridge lxxiii–lxxiv, lxxv; complaints
against lxxv; and Diodati lxxvi; as editor
lxxviii–lxxxiii; and Isaac Gruter lxxvi,
lxxvii; and the Landbeach living
lxxiv–lxxv, lxxvi, his list of Bacon's late
works xxv–xxvii; his preface to *De
augmentis* lxxvi–lxxvii; publishes *Certaine
miscellany works* lxxvii; publishes
Operum…tomus lxvii; publishes *Opuscula*,
xix, lxxviii; and the *Sylva* lxxvii;
translation of *Historia vitæ* lxxvii; reasons
for delaying publication of Bacon
manuscripts lxxviii; and the *Resuscitatio*
lxxviii

reason: 'natural' or 'conventional' **262**

Redmayne, John lxxxiii, lxxxiv

Rigault, Nicolas: career of lxii–liv;
handwriting of lxiii; and the Dupuy
brothers l; produces copies of
Abecedarium and *Historia densi* lxii,
lxiv–lxv, lxviii

rhetoric: and method **264**, 278

Royal College of Physicians 285

rudiment: and generation **11**, 80–2, **186**,
204, **234**, 319; meaning of 311; of plants
230

rusting **11**, **82**, 281, 291

salt: not a principle **188–90**

Scaliger, J. C. 334

schematism(s): and metaschematism (*q.v.*)
288; methods of changing **17**; most
fundamental difference of **176**, 307; as
structure of universe xlviii, **188–90**, **220**,
325; three meanings of 308, 310; varieties
of xxi, xlii–lxiii

scholasticism, *see* Aristotelianism

Séguier, Pierre li, lix & n.

sensation, *see* perception

sex **116**, 293

silver: and aqua fortis **19**, **110–12**; density of
2, **40**; dissolution of **110–12**, 291, 292;
sheets **23**, **126**

'similar' and 'dissimilar' bodies xliii n, **184–6**